I0519129

Perspectives from *Historical Archaeology*

Investigations of Craft and Industrial Enterprise

Compiled with an introduction by
Christopher C. Fennell

No. 9

SOCIETY *for* HISTORICAL ARCHAEOLOGY

A Society for Historical Archaeology Publication

© 2016 Society for Historical Archaeology
Library of Congress Control Number: 2016957473

13017 Wisteria Drive #395
Germantown, MD 20874, U.S.A.

Compiled with an introduction by:
Christopher C. Fennell
Department of Anthropology
University of Illinois at Urbana-Champaign
109 Davenport Hall, MC-148
607 S. Mathews Ave., Urbana, IL 61801

Cover: Allom, Thomas, 1831. Dolcoath Copper Mine in Camborne, Cornwall, steel engraving. In Cornwall Illustrated, in a Series of Views of Castles, Seats of the Nobility,
Mines, Picturesque Scenery, Towns, Public Buildings, Churches, Antiquities, original
drawings by Thomas Allom, engraved on steel by J. Thomas, Le Petit, et al., with historical and descriptive accounts by J. Britton and E. W. Brayley. Fisher and Company,
London.

www.sha.org

Perspectives from Historical Archaeology is a reader series providing collected articles from the journal of the Society for Historical Archaeology (SHA). Published since 1967, <u>Historical Archaeology</u> is the oldest North American scholarly publication on the archaeology of sites and materials from the historic past, and one of the world's premier publications on this subject. Each volume in the *Perspectives* series is developed on either a subject or regional basis by a compiler, who selects the articles for inclusion and their order. The compilers also provide an introduction that presents an overview of the substantive work on that topic. *Perspectives* volumes offer non-archaeologists a convenient source for important publications on a subject or a region; an excellent resource for students interested in developing a specialization in a specific topic or area; as well as a convenient reference for archaeologists with an interest in the material.

The *Perspectives* series is managed by the SHA's Co-Publications Editor and is published through the SHA's Print-On-Demand Press. Individuals interested in compiling a volume for publication through this series are encouraged to contact the Series Editors:

Annalies Corbin, PhD
Co-Publications Editor, SHA
The PAST Foundation
1003 Kinnear Road
Columbus, OH 43212
annalies@pastfoundation.org

J. W. Joseph, PhD, RPA
Perspectives Series Co-Editor, SHA
New South Associates, Inc.
6150 East Ponce de Leon Avenue
Stone Mountain, GA 30083
jwjoseph@newsouthassoc.com

Formed in 1967, the SHA is the largest scholarly group concerned with the archaeology of the modern world (A.D. 1400-present). The main focus of the society is the era since the beginning of European exploration. SHA promotes scholarly research and the dissemination of knowledge concerning historical archaeology. The society is specifically concerned with the identification, excavation, interpretation, and conservation of sites and materials on land and underwater. Geographically the society emphasizes the New World, but also includes European exploration and settlement in Africa, Asia, and Oceania.

To learn more about the SHA and historical archaeology, visit www.sha.org.

Part V. Transport Enterprises

Part VI. Kilns and Metallurgy

Part I: Introduction

Christopher C. Fennell

Manufacturing Relationships in Industry, Craft, and Heritage

Abstract

This introduction to *Perspectives from Historical Archaeology: Investigations of Craft and Industrial Enterprise* provides a summary of trends in the archaeology of craft and industrial enterprises over the past several decades, outlines ongoing development of theories, research questions, and interpretative frameworks, and provides an overview of the selected readings included in this volume. Industrial archaeology projects provide highly valuable contributions to scientific knowledge and heritage initiatives.

Introduction

What are cyclones called
when they stand still?
— *Pablo Neruda (1974:68)*

Archaeologists investigating sites of craft or industrial enterprise often puzzle over Neruda's question. Locations of remarkable energy, tumult, and creativity now stand silent. The subfield of industrial archaeology within the field of historical archaeology first developed in Britain with a focus on description and conservation of existing structures and ruins. This domain of studies focuses on the industrial revolution of the 18th and 19th centuries, which started in Britain and then spread to Europe and the Americas (see, e.g., Jones 2006; Scarlett and Sweitz 2012; Trinder 1992). The label of industrial archaeology for such investigations became more popular after Michael Rix (1955) employed the term in publications focused on avocational researchers and local community projects for mapping, describing, and preserving industrial ruins in England (Buchanan 2000; Palmer 2000; Palmer and Orange 2016). Soon after, Kenneth Hudson (1966, 1979) and J. P. Pannell (1966) also published guidebooks that provided accessible discussions of studies in Britain for avocational researchers and communities seeking to record sites and advocate for preservation of surviving structures.

John Cotter (1968:422) observed a dilemma in these churning developments of ongoing industrialization and the intersecting themes of preservation and research in England: "The real paradox of the situation arose from the fact that whereas British industry has been challenged, nay, ordered, to modernize its plants and equipment, it is meanwhile implored to conserve its heritage of early sites and machines." Historians of the industrial revolution often highlight this tendency of manufacturers' constant efforts to replace old systems with new, more efficient machinery and production processes. While businesses often sought to destroy the old to make way for the new, others in Britain worked to preserve the past machinery and sites of industry (Edensor 2005). A resulting focus on efforts of preservation in Britain often displaced concerns for developing long-term research designs for analyzing the historical processes of industrialization (Bracegirdle 1973; Palmer and Neaverson 1998:3; Symonds and Casella 2006:146).

Cotter and Paul Hudson (1957) had engaged in archaeological investigations of small-scale manufacturing at the Jamestown settlement, including pottery, glass, brick, lime, and iron production. Those Jamestown enterprises were on a scale of craft production, rather than high-volume industries (cf. Monroe and Mallios 2004). Yet, one can understand Cotter's (1968) concern for a disjunction between an early British focus on preservation and recording and his own interests in exploring theories and research designs for investigating sites of industry. Those diverse perspectives among researchers across the Atlantic basin led to three lines of focus within industrial archaeology that at times proceeded independently and at times intersected. One focus emphasized detailed description and recording of particular sites without investing in theory-driven questions. A second, related focus, placed primacy on present-day heritage claims concerning specific locations. A third area of research applied particular theories and interpretative frameworks to understand how processes of industrialization played out at different sites (see, e.g., Walker et al. 2003; Casella and Symonds 2005; Martin 2009). This circumstance of intersecting perspectives was not unique to industrial archaeology; one can describe a similar diversity of project designs within the broader fields of historical and post-medieval archaeology.

Organizations and initiatives for professionals and avocationalists also provided resources for preserving and studying industrial history. In 1958, the Council for British Archaeology formed an Industrial Archaeology Research Committee (Buchanan 2000:20). The Society for Historical Archaeology formed in 1967, with many members in the United States focusing more on the

Christopher C. Fennell

impacts of industry than on the machinery and built environment of factories and mines. In 1969, a new initiative, called the Historic American Engineering Record (HAER), was launched by the United States National Park Service (NPS) as an adjunct to the older Historic American Buildings Survey (HABS). HAER recognized the growing interest in industrial and engineering heritage, and focused on the documentation of American industrial sites, a focus similar to the conservation projects in Britain. HAER projects were dominated by historians, architects, and engineers, with little involvement of archaeologists, but generated expanding interest in industrial sites across disciplines (Martin 2009:287–288; Shackel 2004:45). The Society for Industrial Archeology was formed in 1971, followed by the Association for Industrial Archaeology in 1973. A comparative, global perspective was emphasized in the formation of The International Committee for the Conservation of the Industrial Heritage (TICCIH). In turn, TICCIH took on the role of a Scientific Committee for the International Council on Monuments and Sites (ICOMOS) in 2000 (ICOMOS 2011; Martin 2009:288–289).

Researchers in the United States also focused on the built environment and machinery of industrial sites over time. Early studies included Edward Hartley's (1957) research of the 17th-century Saugus iron works in Massachusetts and Arthur Bining's (1938) investigations of 18th-century iron production at sites in Pennsylvania. Farther south, Jeffrey Brown started archaeological investigations in 1976 of the remains of Bluff Furnace on the banks of the Tennessee River near Chattanooga. This facility was built in 1854 as a blast furnace for iron production and met its demise in the Civil War. This research advanced in the 1980s, culminating in a detailed archaeological study of the Bluff Furnace operations by Bruce Council, Nicholas Honerkamp, and Elizabeth Will. Their investigations included the furnace structure, a charging deck, boiler area, casting shed, slag pile, and chemical analyses of coal, coke, and slag samples (Brown 1977; Council et al. 1992).

A similar focus on the built environment and material culture of manufacturing guided comparative and historical studies of industrial enterprises worldwide (Gordon and Malone 1994; McVarish 2008; Stratton and Trinder 2000; Weitzman 1980). The NPS has also focused on detailed historical research and conservation of a number of production and mining facilities, including: Harper's Ferry armory and mills in West Virginia (operated from 1790-1865); Hopewell iron furnace in Pennsylvania (1771-1883); Kennecott copper

mill in Alaska (1909-1938); Keweenaw copper works in Michigan (1840-1968); textiles mills of Lowell, Massachusetts (1820-1960); Saugus iron works in Massachusetts (1646-1670); and Tredegar iron works in Virginia (1837-1865) (Martin 2009:291; Griswold and Linebaugh 2010).

When examining a history of manufacturing activities, a frequent spectrum of scale and complexity is described as extending from "craft" to "industry." How do we define a line between craft production and industrial enterprise? Some might look to the scale of production. Craft activities sound like affairs of limited output. Yet, large-scale production can be seen millennia ago. For example, the pottery shops in the Susiana plain during the Uruk period (3,500-3,000 BCE) were centralized and utilized wheel-thrown methods and molds to mass produce simple earthenware bowls. Those goods were distributed in exchange networks extending across that broad region of Mesopotamia (Ekholm-Friedman 2000; Wright and Johnson 1975). Thousands of years later, Scots-Irish entrepreneurs and enslaved African-American laborers established a group of stoneware potteries in Edgefield, South Carolina, starting in 1815. They too used wheel-thrown methods and manufactured thousands of large storage vessels for sale to neighboring plantations. A recent archaeology project revealed that these South Carolina potters built massive kilns with barrel vaults over 100 feet long. To do so, they copied the enormous "dragon" kiln design that had been used in the factory towns of southeast China since the medieval period (Calfas 2013; see Chen 1986; Hsu 1995; Bradford 2004; Needham et al. 2004). Should we call these pottery enterprises in Mesopotamia and Edgefield industrial, or craft productions of remarkable scale?

Many researchers define the domain of industrial enterprise by focusing on the elements of the industrial revolution from the 18th century onward. Those developments entailed a notable increase in the division of labor tasks and in the standardization and specialization of machinery used to produce commodities, facilitate transportation, and extract natural resources. Rather than a revolution, we can view these developments as involving a notable acceleration and intensification of such changes in modes of production that had incremental antecedents in earlier periods. Artisans in craft production often handled multiple tasks to produce a finished good. In contrast, the industrial revolution assigned workers to tend machines that each performed a single, specific task in an assembly process. Workers in extractive and transport industries focused on similarly specialized

Perspectives from Historical Archaeology:

tasks (Palmer and Neaverson 1998; Symonds and Casella 2006; ICOMOS 2011). From this perspective, one could view the pottery producers of Mesopotamia and Edgefield as engaged in craft enterprises with an industrial scale of output, but lacking the extent of mechanization and labor specialization seen in the industrial revolution. Researchers interested in industrialization will often address these relationships between craft and industry (Walker et al. 2003). Some will observe changes from one scale to another at a particular production site over time. Others will see evidence of craft-scale support businesses, such as smaller mill or mining enterprises, which provided resource inputs to industrial-scale production facilities (see, e.g., Hudson 1979; Casella and Symonds 2005; Shackel and Palus 2010).

Philip Scranton (1997) offers a useful framework of different levels of output and mechanization for categorizing production enterprises. He parallels a continuum of "craft" to "industry" with a similar spectrum of "specialty" to "routinized" modes of production (Scranton 1997:11). He further punctuates that continuum from small-scale, craft undertakings to large-scale industries by describing levels of custom, batch, bulk, and mass production. Custom work entails artisans who each undertake multiple, successive steps to produce an individualized, finished result in answer to an idiosyncratic demand. Examples include an individual making a tailored suit of clothes or a custom piece of machinery. Batch manufacturing introduces the use of patterns and templates and manufacture of multiple, similar products. Yet, a batch approach can still employ artisans and involve relatively little specialization of labor (e.g., Griggs 2001). The large-scale potteries of Mesopotamia and Edgefield represented such batch enterprises. Bulk production represents the move to relying on standardization of parts and production steps, increased specialization of worker tasks, use of machines for each manufacturing step, and assignment of relatively unskilled workers to serve as the tenders of the machinery (e.g., Miller and Sullivan 1984). Mass production elevates bulk manufacturing to high volumes of output of finished goods. These categories are not mutually exclusive, and businesses of different scales of work often interact and provide services to one another. For example, custom and batch manufacturers often produce the parts, fasteners, and machine tools needed by bulk and mass production businesses (Scranton 1997; Rotman and Staicer 2002).

Material culture studies spanning this spectrum from craft enterprises to mass production industries yield some observable and middle-range hypotheses of likely artifact distributions. Craft production sites may contain the artifacts of personalized tool kits and remains of discretionary consumption of tobacco and liquor. In factory work sites, with workers shifted to less skilled and segmented roles, these artisan-related artifacts should be far less frequent. The home sites of artisans may also contain artifacts of their personal tool kits that they regularly transported with them between work and home domains. The home sites of less skilled factory workers will less likely contain such tool assemblages. Homes of factory workers in company-controlled, residential districts may also reflect the successes and failures of company attempts to control their lifestyles. A number of companies, such as the Boott textile mills, attempted to restrict liquor consumption in housing spaces. Residential artifacts have often reflected workers' defiance of those company initiatives (see, e.g., Mrozowski et al. 1996; Seibert 2015).

A variety of research themes have developed within industrial archaeology projects across the globe. Many researchers focus on details of the operations, architecture, and machinery of particular sites (e.g., Gordon 2000). Others focus on changes over time in innovations, inventions, and experimentation within particular technologies. Some examine the impacts of production sites and operations on the cognitive and sensorial experiences of the people who worked there (e.g., Trinder 1982). An increasing number of projects examine the relationships between facets of industrialization and elements of colonialism, capitalism, and imperialism. Researchers ask how industrial operations impacted social dynamics of gender, age, class, consumption, residential domains, and occupational status (e.g., Griggs 2001; Cranstone 2004; see Figure 1).

Many researchers in the United States have focused more on the impacts of industry and capitalism on workers' lives, cultural landscapes, social relationships, settlement patterns, and environments (e.g., Cowen 1976; Langhorne 1976; Landon 1999; Quivik 2000; Gillespie and Farrell 2002; Bailey et al. 2004; Cassell and Stachiw 2005). For example, Stephen Mrozowski, Grace Ziesing, and Mary C. Beaudry (1996) studied the lifeways of textile workers at the Boott Cotton Mills in Lowell, Massachusetts. They focused on the archaeological record of the tenements and boarding houses in which the workers and their families resided. Donald Hardesty (1998) examined the ways in which extractive industries shaped the cultural landscapes and environments in frontier zones of California, Idaho, and Nevada. David Gradwohl and Nancy Osborn (1984)

FIGURE 1. Research questions spanning social structures, technologies, and workers' experiences can be addressed to settings like this. Teenage and adult miners led a mule-drawn rail car up a Pennsylvania Coal Company mine shaft. Whitewash applied to some rock walls provided meager aid to illumination by headlamps. (Photograph by Lewis Hines, 1911, courtesy of Library of Congress.)

studied the dynamics of segregation, race relations, and consumer choices in the coal-mining town of Buxton, Iowa. As James Symonds and Eleanor Casella observe (2006:147): "Through historical archaeology, these scholars aimed not only to read the built environment of industrial landscapes as expressions of hierarchical power relations, but also to consider the many ways in which workers refuted, subverted and alleviated the grinding poverty of industrial capitalism."

For example, Paul Shackel (1996) and other analysts undertook expansive studies of the armory factory, workers' housing, merchant sites, and surrounding mills in Harper's Ferry. These studies showed the transition from a craft enterprise of skilled artisans who each undertook all steps in producing a complete gun to a regime in which the armory workers were reduced to the tenders of machines. The industrialized gun factory was also supported by craft-scale mills in the town, such as a sawmill that supplied raw materials for the production enterprise. Development of this factory town was also significantly impacted by the transport industries of canal construction and early railroads and transitions from water power to steam engines (Caplinger 1997; Gilbert 1999; Shackel 1996, 2004; Shackel and Palus 2010).

A number of theoretical frameworks have been employed in industrial archaeology. For example, the insights of critical theory and neo-Marxian analysis illuminate the class struggles and the effects of changing modes of production. Particular studies of technologies and occupational contexts can contribute to an understanding of the varied spread of capitalism and industrialization across space and time (see, e.g., Wolf 1982; Paynter 1988; Johnson 1996). Theories concerning social dominance and related efforts of surveillance and disciplining of worker classes have direct applicability (e.g., Mrozowski 1991; Orser 1996). The operations of a manufacturing facility can also be addressed by the frameworks of chaîne opératoire and practice theory. The technologies and performance of productive activities can be analyzed as elements of habitus and doxa with changes through incremental innovations (e.g., Calfas 2013; Lawrence and Davies 2015; Lemonnier 1993).

The studies presented in Parts II through VI of this book are drawn from the pages of *Historical Archaeology*, the journal of the Society for Historical Archaeology. These analyses illustrate the incredible diversity of questions and sites examined within archaeologies of craft and industrial enterprises. Part II focuses on investigations of the impacts of industrialization on laborers and landscapes. Part III turns to studies of the sites of extractive technologies, such as oil, coal, copper, asbestos, and lumber. Part IV addresses the broad field of commodity production, with goods as diverse as saddletrees, dynamite, oysters, kelp, cheese, beer, and pottery. Developments in transportation infrastructure are addressed in the studies in Part V, with a focus on the construction of canals and railways. Lastly, a sampling of studies on the expansive topic of kilns, metal and mineral ores, and metallurgy is presented in Part VI.

Labor and Landscapes

The articles in Part II address the ways in which industrialization impacted workers and the social, occupational, and residential landscapes in which they lived. Paul Shackel (2004) opens this discussion in Chapter 2 with an examination of trends in such research themes. He points out that a research focus on the experiences of laborers can make industrial archaeology subjects more engaging to broader communities today. Past studies tended to focus primarily on technologies and manufacturing processes implemented over time, and thus engaged a smaller number of interested parties. An expanding focus on labor leads to examination of workers' experiences at industrial sites and related contexts of economic and residential life. Related themes can include ethnic and racial histories, worker mobility, labor communities, gender and age variables, political movements and unionization, and environment and health impacts (Shackel 2004). The NPS has worked to develop such thematic programs for examining labor histories in relation to industrial sites and national historic landmarks in the United States (e.g., Seibert 2015).

The subject of planned residential communities to support an industrial enterprise is the focus of Chapter 3. Matthew Tomaso and his colleagues (2006) examine Feltville, New Jersey, a small community operating a papermaking, printing, and bookbinding business from 1845 to 1860. Entrepreneur David Felt employed approximately 140 individuals, including young, unmarried women and married males with families. He avoided employment of married women and children. The main manufacturing edifice was a four-story high mill and production facility. He devised a planned community to surround the business, with a school, church, store, post office, and houses for himself, business managers, and employees. The store utilized company currency. Felt's house was of comparable scale to the others. Yet, the village was configured to separate areas for families of higher socioeconomic status from lower status workers and to separate school children from the business activities. The result represented "a compromise between radical utopian vision, mainstream American development, and reactionary Jeffersonian communalism" (Tomaso et al. 2006:33).

Archaeology projects at the Boott Cotton Mills in Lowell, Massachusetts and the Pullman District in Chicago found other versions of planned residential districts and spatial divisions. Unlike David Felt's modest house, the homes of agents and managers in Lowell resembled urban brownstones and houses for workers were spare and utilitarian in style (Mrowzowski 1991). In Pullman, the houses for managers and workers were different in scale and comfort and segregated in a spatial hierarchy (Baxter 2012).

Mark Pittaway (2005) turns to a dramatically different setting in Chapter 4. The city of Sztálinváros developed in the 1950s on the bank of the Danube River in Hungary, with a population of several thousand workers and their families. This metropolis was developed to support the rapid growth of the adjacent steel works facility to serve the needs of the socialist and communist regimes of the Soviet Union and Hungary during the Cold War. Military demand for steel, machinery, and armaments fueled rapid increases in mechanization and output at the Stalin Steel Works. An earlier landscape with a mix of residential, farming, and manufacturing spaces was transformed by a centrally planned concentration of large-scale factories. Provisioning grounds for families gave way to a community of workers in housing and apartment complexes, obtaining food almost entirely from stores. Natural landscapes were limited to recreational park spaces. A modernist design sought to

Christopher C. Fennell

relate the factory complex, residential city, and natural landscape. The city was buffered from direct exposure to the factory complex by an intervening belt of woodlands one kilometer long and one-half kilometer wide. A main boulevard, called Stalin Street, extended from the factory complex entrance, through the woods, and into a central square in the city surrounded by governmental offices. The socialist political design omitted spaces for religious worship within Sztálinváros. The division of labor at this broad scale relied upon villages 20 kilometers away as sources for new workers and food supplies (Pittaway 2005).

Chapter 5 returns to the terrain of Harpers Ferry along the Shenandoah and Potomac Rivers, and to impacts of industry that lie between the scales of Feltville and Sztálinváros. Paul Shackel and Matthew Palus (2010) outline the history of the federally funded armaments factory in a town that would host other, supporting enterprises. Notably in American history, the drive for interchangeability of parts was first motivated at the turn of 19th century by military preferences and not the cost efficiencies of manufacturers. The United States Army officials sought rifles with interchangeable parts so that one gun could be repaired in the field with parts from another gun. Standardization and interchangeability of parts would be developed as more of a manufacturing efficiency at the turn of the 20th century, particularly in the automobile industry.

Harpers Ferry grew with a central manufacturing enterprise supported by other businesses that operated at a scale of craft production and artisan services. Lewis Wernwag was a talented entrepreneur, inventor, and engineer who operated in both the fields of artisans and industries. He designed and built large-scale bridges for the railways connecting this factory town to regional market centers. Yet, Wernwag also developed Virginius Island in the 1820s and 1830s along the edge of Harpers Ferry to host houses, a rail extension, water mills and raceways, a sawmill, machine shop, and other craft businesses including carpenters, masons, and blacksmiths. He ran the saw mill and enjoyed a near monopoly in providing wood supplies to the armaments factory. These interactions represented some of the frequent types of interactions of craft and industrial enterprises that played out in the industrial revolution (Scranton 1997). Unlike the planned, segregated spaces of Feltville, Sztálinváros, and the factory district of Harpers Ferry, the residential, recreation, and occupation spaces on Virginius Island were all intermixed (Shackel and Palus 2010).

Extractive Industries

Many research projects have focused on the energy and evolving methods invested in extracting oil, coal, iron, lumber, and other metals and minerals from the earth (e.g., O'Dell and George 2014). Yet, the number of archaeological investigations of underground mining sites has been constrained by the hazardous character of those spaces. In the United States alone, there exist over 200,000 abandoned mines (White 2016:163). Archaeological investigations of such sites can encounter a wide variety of remains. For example, mines included surface structures and equipment in addition to subsurface shafts, tunnels, and extraction assemblies. The grounds surrounding the surface structures often included varied activity areas in which ore was broken down and processed through successive steps (Figure 2). These past actions often created an archaeological record of considerable complexity. The extractive industries also entailed numerous conflicts between managers and employees. Part III of this book presents a sample of these dynamics.

Scott Baxter's (2002) study of oil fields opens this sampling of research projects in Chapter 6. He examined the terrain of oil production and related workers' dwellings in the Squaw Flats area during the late 19th century. That location traversed a rugged topography in the Piru Mountains of southern California, with potential oil deposits in fissures and fault lines. As a general matter, in such exploratory oil well operations laborers typically "lived surrounded by oil derricks piercing the sky, oil burning boilers, the pounding of cable tool rigs, the continuous clank of machinery, and the crack of the blacksmith's hammer" (Baxter 2002:21). Oil fields were thus generally known for intermixing residential and work spaces. Laborers at Squaw Flats, in contrast, attempted some buffering of those spaces. They leased parcels on which to construct dwellings, often with company subsidies. Archaeological surveys identified the locations of past oil wells, a bunkhouse, a boarding house, storage tanks, and trash dumps. In the rolling ridge and valley terrain, some residential structures were positioned so that a ridge partly obscured the noise, smell, and visibility of nearby wells and boilers. The trash dump areas for residential and work activities were also separated from one another, perhaps as an additional way of making some differentiation of dwelling and work environments (Baxter 2002:24).

The coal fields of Ludlow, Colorado are examined by Randall McGuire and Paul Reckner's (2002) study

FIGURE 2. An example of the wide array of structures, equipment, and activity areas in a mine operation, illustrated by the Dolcoath Copper Mine in Camborne, Cornwall, United Kingdom. (Allom 1831.)

presented in Chapter 7. These analysts argued persuasively that such extractive industries in the western states should not be perceived as the activities of simplistic frontier regions. Instead, these enterprises are better conceptualized as part of periphery zones of natural resource production operating within world economic systems that included semi-peripheries and industrialized, core zones. The Ludlow example highlights an additional factor: extractive industries such as coal mining were very hazardous, with accident rates up to three times higher than national averages (McGuire and Reckner 2002:47–50).

Archaeological investigations at Ludlow revealed the material culture of the tent dwellings of strikers and their families as they existed in April 1914. The United Mine Workers union had provided tents, stoves, food rations, and other supplies to support the workers in their strike against the Ludlow mining company. Striking workers were forced out of the company-provided housing and they relocated to a nearby tent colony of approximately 150 dwellings and 1,200 residents. The archaeologists employed a technique of projecting 1914 photographic images of the tent settlement onto the current landscape with a method developed by Eugene Prince in his work

with James Deetz. Exploring those mapped locations, the archaeologists at Ludlow found that many families had dug cellar spaces under their tents for storage and possible refuge from violent reprisals (McGuire and Reckner 2002).

Such violence exploded on April 20, 1914, in the infamous Ludlow massacre. John Rockefeller's coal mining company solicited the assistance of National Guard troops to confront the strikers and their families in the tent colony. When gunfire erupted and many tents were set on fire, most striking families fled from the combat zone. However, 20 people died in the violence, including 2 women and 11 children who sought refuge in one of the cellar spaces, but met a dread fate when the tent above them burned. Progressive politicians later focused on this incident to vilify Rockefeller and his business policies (McGuire and Reckner 2002; Walker 2003). The Ludlow archaeology project was notable for the collaboration of members of the current labor movement in the research and commemoration initiatives (Seibert 2015:11). McGuire and Reckner (2002:44) contend that the Ludlow massacre and later reactions to the event marked "a pivotal point in U.S. history, when labor relations began to move from class warfare to policies of negotiation, co-option, and regulated strikes." The Ludlow tent colony and massacre site has accordingly been designated as a National Historic Landmark (Siebert 2015:32). Similar studies of conflict related to extractive industries have focused on sites such as the 1897 Lattimer massacre in Pennsylvania and the 1921 battle at Blair Mountain, West Virginia (Roller 2013; Seibert 2015; Brown 2016; Shackel and Westmont 2016).

We move from coal and oil to early 20th-century mining of copper and asbestos on the island of Cyprus, as examined by Michael Given (2005) in Chapter 8. He observes the ways in which mining companies applied strategies similar to colonial administration. Companies first imposed their own names onto the landscape and then implemented surveillance methods. The mining landscape included "hut settlements, overseers' houses, workshops, mines, and railway" (Given 2005:52). The British-controlled colonial administration built police stations at the approach to each village with elevated second floors that aided visual surveillance. The mining company overseers' houses were positioned on prominent ridges for similar purposes (Given 2005:53).

These mining companies on Cyprus also imported food supplies for the workforce and their families, displacing traditional and local culinary practices. This approach brought potential profits for company retail stores. These policies connected Cyprus to international commodity chains in which agricultural exports flowed out of regions in Britain, the United States, and Australia. Company initiatives also included construction of houses for workers' families with designs viewed as modern and affordable by management officials. In contrast, indigenous workers found that the designs thwarted their vernacular uses of domestic spaces and social gathering spaces (Given 2005).

In Chapter 9, Janet Brashler's (1991) study explores the expansion of extractive industries in some regions following the installation of rail and roadway infrastructure across the terrain. The lumber industry in West Virginia expanded along such arteries. Virgin forest covered two thirds of the state in 1880 and only five percent by 1930. Expansion of coal operations followed a similar trajectory in that region. Brashler also observed more complex gender dynamics in the logging enterprises than had been expected. Women and children worked in logging camps in some cutting tasks, foraging, and handling supply wagons and teams hauling logs. She also found a notable portability of the logging infrastructure. Narrow gauge railways could be pulled up and moved to new locations to access fresh cutting zones. Company-provided shanty cars served as workers' dwellings and were equally mobile (Brashler 1991). John Franzen (1992) examined similar 19th-century, logging enterprises in northern Michigan, with a focus on ethnic groups, cultural practices, and work-place adaptations.

Commodity Production

Part IV of this book presents studies of the many businesses that manufactured, harvested, or processed natural and human-made commodities. Deborah Rotman and John Staicer's (2002) study in Chapter 10 examines the built environment of a craft enterprise, or "specialty firm." From 1878 to 1972, the Schroeder factory in Madison, Indiana, made wooden frames, called saddletrees, on which saddles could be manufactured by other businesses. This was a craft process employing only several employees, who nonetheless produced high volumes of saddletrees each year. Rotman and Staicer (2002) provide a systematic framework for analyzing the intersecting operations of businesses that range across scales from craft to mass production operations.

Joanna Behrens' (2005) study shifts our focus to South Africa and the manufacture of dynamite in Chapter 11. This commodity production occurred in the context of developments in gold-mining techniques. Early methods of surface mining were succeeded with inclined shafts and deep-level blasting to extract gold ore. By 1895 the largest dynamite manufacturing facility in the world was established at Modderfontein near Johannesburg. The workforce of several hundred included experienced workers from Europe and Russia and a remarkable degree of national and ethnic diversity: "Italian, German, Russian, Austrian, Dutch, Transvaal Burgher, English, Swiss, French, Danish, Cape Colonial, Swedish, Spanish, Turkish, Belgian, and Orange Free State Burgher" (Behrens 2005:66). The factory owners attempted to structure the facility and related housing through planned, clustered spaces divided roughly along ethnic group lines.

A clash of methods in natural commodity harvesting is examined by Bradford Botwick and Debra McClanes' (2005) study in Chapter 12. The commodity of oysters in the Chesapeake Bay were typically harvested by small-scale teams using manual techniques of long-handled tongs to collect the oysters from beds in the Bay. This was demanding work undertaken by workers with "skilled or artisan-like qualities," including knowledge of when and where oyster beds should be targeted for harvesting

(Botwick and McClane 2005:95). Newer, mechanized dredging methods presented a jarring departure from that traditional approach. Workers on dredges operated more as the tenders of devices. Competing approaches played out in varied conflicts across the fishing range of the Bay and in related residential villages (Botwick and McClane 2005). An interesting, comparative study focuses on abalone fishing off the Channel Islands of northern California in the 19th century. Successful fishing enterprises by Chinese immigrants were targeted for restriction by local legislation due to racial tensions and discrimination (Braje et al. 2007). Other studies have focused on the contingencies of cod fishing in Maine (Faulkner 1985) and whale and shark fishing off the Donegal coast of Ireland (McNeary 2007).

Chapter 13 draws our attention across the Atlantic basin once again. Thomas McErlean (2007) studied the production of processed sea weed as a soda, alkali, and iodine sources for the glassmaking and textile industries. The market for iodine started as a bleaching agent for linen manufacturing, and later extended to uses as ingredients in the production of dyes, medicines, and photographic processing supplies. McErlean examined the remains of coastal facilities in Northern Ireland for burning a variety of sea weeds into a processed form referred to as "kelp." A workforce of 300 labored in these tasks in that landscape in the 18th and early 19th centuries. They created and utilized kilns, in the form of "open, stone-lined" pits, and storage houses to change tons of sea weed into the ingredients for other commodities (McErlean 2007:86).

In Chapter 14, James Gibb, David Bernstein, and Daniel Cassedy (1990) explore changes from a craft to factory scale of production of cheeses in 19th-century New York. Gibb and his colleagues (2009) examined broader changes in a variety of agricultural enterprises in that region in a later study. Earlier house and kitchen production of cheese was displaced in the New York region in the 1860s by specialized factory spaces. While the dairy inputs remained local within these factory approaches, the resulting commodity distribution markets included North America, Europe, and Australia. The Columbus Center Cheese factory, for example, dated from the 1860s through 1900. That facility included a spatial layout and equipment array for specialized tasks by laborers in the successive steps of producing cheese packages. Workers could also be specialized on a narrow range of tasks, such as weighing and containing raw milk, collecting curd, separating the whey, pressing the

curd, and curing the raw cheese in separate spaces in a dedicated, multi-level factory (Gibb et al. 1990).

Deborah Hull-Walski and Frank Walski (1994) examine bottling and brewing businesses in Harpers Ferry, West Virginia, in the late 19th and early 20th centuries in Chapter 15. Increasing mechanization in both brewery and bottling was accompanied by long working hours, injuries involving equipment, and exposure to vapors such as carbonic and sulfuric acids (Hull-Walski and Walski 1994). The rate of workplace accidents was notably high in breweries due to the high speed of the machinery (Shackel 2004:49). Possible expressions of displeasure and opposition by workers were uncovered in trash deposits of their local residences. For example, local beer bottles were designed to be returnable to keep resource costs lower. Managers of the brewery and bottling facilities also promoted temperance among the workforce members. Yet, a boarding house privy yielded numerous local beer bottles that were discarded there, rather than being returned to the nearby bottling plant. This pattern of discard may have resulted due to workers illicitly appropriating the beer products from the business premises for their own consumption at home (Hull-Walski and Walski 1994). This interpretation is supported by similar finds of numerous beer bottles discarded covertly in hidden wall spaces and an elevator shaft at the brewery (Shackel 2000).

As was seen in studies of extractive industries, commodity production industries were also impacted by expansions in transportation infrastructure. New canals and railways lowered the costs for transporting resources to manufacturing facilities. The same transport arteries expanded avenues of commodity distribution and intensified competition among the manufacturers within various wholesale and retail markets. Sophia Kelly's (2013) study in chapter 16 examines the shift from earthenware manufacturing to stoneware production in the northeastern United States in the early 1800s. Potteries making earthenware goods could utilize lower-quality, local clay deposits and kiln designs that did not have to withstand notably high temperatures (e.g., Kelso and Chappell 1974; Steen 1999). Shifting to stoneware production presented a number of challenges. The kiln design had to be improved to withstand the high temperatures that would harden the clay to the stone-like quality of a non-porous vessel. A pottery would need access to higher-quality clay supplies that produced such non-porous paste without fracturing in the kiln's firing. The expansion of canals and railways in the northeastern United States in the 1820s dramatically lowered the cost of transporting such clay supplies from the more limited locations in which such higher-quality clays were found (Kelly 2013).

Pottery operations that produced earthenware goods were often conducted in craft style, with all employees performing the full spectrum of relevant tasks. With the shift to stoneware production, manufacturers often shifted to greater differentiation and specialization of their workers. Different workers handled the steps of clay preparation, throwing and shaping vessels, maintaining and firing the kiln, and applying decorations to vessels. Increased mechanization could also be introduced, employing devices that sped and standardized the shaping of vessels. Manufacturers who benefitted from these developments could in turn out-compete smaller operators in the wholesale and retail markets due to decreased distribution costs via canals and railways. For small businesses such as Elijah Cornell's pottery in Ithaca, New York, transport improvements benefitted his production capabilities, but greatly burdened his retail sales due to increased market competition (Kelly 2013; cf. Scarlett et al. 2006).

Transport Enterprises

Part V of this volume turns to studies of transport industries. Richard Dent's (1986) analysis of the 18th-century development of the Patowmack Canal along the Potomac River between Maryland and Virginia opens this part in Chapter 17. Merchants, investors, and government representative interested in developing the flow of trade in the Potomac River valley concentrated their efforts on readily available river routes. Development of the Potomac and Shenandoah Rivers was initiated by the Patowmack Company, chartered in 1786, to improve transport on those rivers by building locks and by-pass canals to overcome falls and poorly navigable spots. With construction of five by-pass canals along the length of the Potomac River by 1802, the Company succeeded in improving the movement of goods along a 218-mile length of the river and its 2,000 foot drop in elevation from west to east (Dent 1986).

Transports used on the river were often called sharpers, bateaux, or gondolas, and measured 50-75 feet in length and 5-10 feet in width. These vessels were capable of hauling 70-120 barrels of flour, as well as other products such whiskey, grain, lumber, and iron ore (Caldwell 1951; Gilbert 1999). Development of the steam engine for use in boats by 1800 led to expanded use of such transports in river traffic, making upstream travel easier.

The Patowmack Company also developed infrastructure along the Shenandoah River near Harpers Ferry, but its plans were ultimately thwarted by insufficient capital investment and the disruptions of events such as the War of 1812 (Dent 1986; Johnson 1995; Caplinger 1997). The locks and canal segments of the Patowmack Company entailed relatively simple designs. Later periods of construction of canals and dams could at times employ a bewildering array of equipment and support structures (Figure 3). In addition to understanding developments in the waterways and port facilities, other researchers have focused on technologies of ship-building and the evolution of steam-powered, maritime vessels (e.g., Pastron and Delgado 1991; Garrison 1995).

The expansion of railroads fueled an interdependent expansion in iron and steel production (Figure 4). Construction of new rail lines entailed successive steps of surveying a route, grading the planned corridor, building up the road bed, erecting culverts and bridges, and installing the wood ties and iron rails. Such building projects can be examined in detail through archaeology, landscape and spatial analysis, and close study of engineering records and other archival materials (e.g., Fennell 2010).

Lucy Taksa's (2005) study of locomotive and rail car manufacturing facilities in Sydney, Australia is presented in Chapter 18. She emphasizes the interdependence of railroad enterprises in expanding transport infrastructures for other businesses, increasing demands for iron ore extraction and steel production, and creating manufacturing centers for railroad equipment. The New South Wales railway workshops studied by Taksa employed 2,500 people by the 1890s to assemble and repair railroad cars and locomotives. She found that workers who specialized in particular tasks, such as carriage or locomotive assembly, developed occupational group identities reminiscent of craft guilds, but in a factory setting. Yet, these segregated occupational groups were later united in collective, union-based opposition to management initiatives such as new time accounting protocols (Taksa 2005).

The remarkable growth of the railroads enabled an entrepreneur like George Pullman to create a factory town for production of rail cars. He developed this complex starting in 1880 on the south side of Chicago. The community was built on a 4,000 acre tract and eventually included 1,300 buildings, with company retail stores, theatre, schools, common areas, library, hotel, train station, the Palace Car factory complex, and houses for managers and employees. Much of the architecture

FIGURE 3. Example of intensive equipment and support material in a dam construction project at the head of the Pawtucket Falls in Lowell, Massachusetts, September 20, 1875. (Image courtesy of the Library of Congress.)

FIGURE 4. An example of the way in which the steel and railroad industries worked interdependently, at Irondale Iron and Steel Plant site in Washington state, established 1881. (Image courtesy of the Library of Congress.)

was constructed in similar styles and facades of red brick to provide a uniformity of design. This was a planned town of Pullman's design, rather than an intentional community shaped by the residents, which included approximately 5,500 employees. The landscape was shaped as a grid of streets, blocks, and open vistas that facilitated surveillance and visibility of all activities. Archaeological investigations of the yards of workers' houses and of common areas in the town yielded very few artifacts, possibly the result of workers purposefully avoiding those areas of surveillance (Scranton 1997:166–170; Baxter 2012).

In 1894 Pullman cut his employees' wages, but did not reduce the rents charged for housing or prices in the retail stores. When workers responded with a strike that slowed regional rail traffic, he persuaded the federal government to send troops to impose order. The resulting violence and destruction of property created enduring animosity between the strikers and Pullman. The strike failed and ended later in 1894, but Pullman's planned factory town also came to an end within a couple of years. He died of a heart attack in 1897, and was buried in Graceland Cemetery on the north side of Chicago. His tomb was designed with an industrial flair. The

structure below ground consisted of a bunker of railroad ties, asphalt, and concrete to prevent disgruntled former workers from desecrating his coffin (Scranton 1997:166–170; Baxter 2012). Much of the Pullman town buildings were reused by later owners and were well preserved. The town, now a neighborhood within Chicago, was recently declared a National Monument.

Construction of railroads in the western states relied heavily on thousands of immigrant laborers from the Guangdong region of China. Other workers were from diverse backgrounds, including African Americans, Native Americans, English, Irish, and Germans. Such projects included the transcontinental railroad from California to Nebraska, where it linked to more eastern lines. Undertaken from 1865 to completion in 1869, this project created a transcontinental connection that reduced coast-to-coast travel time for the United States mail from six weeks to six days. Michael Polk's (2015) study in Chapter 19 explores the camps of ethnic Chinese workers who built in earth, stone, timbers, and iron near Promontory Summit in Utah. Laborers in these large-scale projects largely segregated themselves in residential camps along ethnic lines. Camps of Chinese workers included dugout and tent structures and imported material culture (Polk 2015).

Ryan Harrod and John Crandall (2015) examine the remains of 13 Chinese males from a 19th-century cemetery in Nevada in Chapter 20. These men had worked on building the transcontinental railroad, and their graves were inadvertently disturbed in a 20th-century construction project. This study provides a relatively rare forensic analysis of workers' health and well-being in a context of industrial archaeology. Harrod and Crandall (2015) found that these individuals endured significant physiological strains, maladies, and injuries related to their manual labor and living conditions.

Kilns and Metallurgy

Part VI of this book presents a sample of studies concerning the broad subjects of kilns, production of metal and mineral ores, and metallurgy. Early forms of smelting furnaces for processing metals possessed structural elements similar to kilns used for firing minerals and ceramics (e.g., Heite 1974; Scarlett et al. 2006). Later, more advanced designs of blast furnaces for metals incorporated larger-scale structural elements. The ruins of such facilities often include masonry-lined pits that once housed large fly wheels that provided power distribution within the facility (Figure 5). The industrial town of Fayette, Michigan, for example, operated a blast furnace for producing iron for the Jackson Iron Company from 1867 to 1891 (Cowie 2011). The built environment included the remains of the production facility and residential quarters. The housing for managers, supervisors, and laborers was segregated in space within the company town and ranged from high quality homes for managers to log house construction for laborers' dwellings (Cowie 2011). A diversity of research projects across these subjects of kiln and furnace operations also include microscopic, metallurgical, and

FIGURE 5. Industrial archaeology sites often present the foundation pits for fly wheels, such as the one shown here from the Irondale Iron and Steel Plant site in Washington state, established 1881. (Image courtesy of the Library of Congress.)

chemical analysis of iron, coke, and slag (e.g., Brown 1977; Council et al. 1992; Gordon and Killick 1992).

Chapter 21 opens part VI with a detailed study of Spanish colonial kilns in Peru by Prudence Rice and Sara Van Beck (1993). Intensive mining operations for silver ore were started in Potosí in the highlands of Peru in the 16th century and are still productive today. An ancillary economy grew during the same period in the nearby Moquegua valley to produce wine for the large population of mine workers and other residents in the region. The wineries (called bodegas in Spanish) included a variety of kilns to fire ceramic storage vessels and to process calcium minerals, such as limestone and gypsum, for mortar, plaster, or fertilizer ingredients. Kiln designs in colonial Spain exhibited an extraordinary diversity of influences, including Iberian, Moorish, and Roman technology traditions. The 26 kilns of the Moquegua valley bodegas were typically made of adobe brick, with some fired tiles as flooring, in a roughly circular, updraft design. Over half of these kilns were built into hill-sides or slopes to provide support and insulation to the walls and to take advantage of air currents across the topography. Rice and Van Beck (1993) provide a valuable over-view of various European kiln designs as a background to their analysis of these structures in Peru.

Steven DeVore's (1990) study of blacksmith operations in 19th-century North Dakota examines the multiple scales of such work sites in Chapter 22. Blacksmiths at times operated as a principal provider of metal-working for a broad clientele, delivering services to consumers ranging from nail manufacturing to repair of wagons and tools. Blacksmiths were not displaced by growing mass-production industries so much as incorporated as specialized labors (Hayman 2005). By the late 19th century, many of the metal products once produced in blacksmith shops, such as nails, fasteners, and hardware, were manufactured instead by industrial-scale operations that retained blacksmiths to repair their machinery. The spatial layout of blacksmith operations and the spectrum of equipment they employed have been examined in detail in studies such as those by DeVore (1990) and John Light (2007).

The impacts of intensive silver and zinc mining at Porco, Bolivia, spanning Inka, colonial, and modern periods, are examined by Mary Van Buren and Brendan Weaver's (2012) study in Chapter 23. The Inka period of several centuries ago saw the highland resources marked by targeted silver mining, construction of a shrine space, and access paths across the landscape to transport the silver to the ruling class in Cuzco. Colonial and modern periods intensified the silver extraction and added facilities for zinc and tin mining. Colonial-period operations in the area introduced sites for grinding and smelting silver ore and stamping mills powered by overshot water wheels. On the landscape today one sees these mountain locations reshaped with office facilities, tin and zinc concentration plants, tailings ponds, residential districts laid out in grids, and expanded roadway networks. Unlike the vast mining operations at nearby Potosí, the economy of Porco developed with a diversification of time investments by a local workforce. Many resident employees of the mines at Porco also invested in agricultural production at other times of the year, providing food supplies and an economic buffer to sole reliance on wages from the mines (Van Buren and Weaver 2012; cf. Svensson et al. 2009).

Shifting our attention back to North America, Ann Ramenofsky, David Vaughan, and Michael Spilde (2008) explore 17th-century mining and metal processing in New Mexico in Chapter 24. Archaeological investigations proved highly valuable in uncovering this history, as surviving archival sources spoke little of mining in that region and time period. Mining and ore smelting activities in that early period were mostly performed by indigenous residents of area pueblos. Smelting furnaces were circular in form, built of adobe brick, and often only one meter wide at the base. Archaeologists uncovered evidence of those metallurgical activity areas, implements, and debris, and derived dates on such remains through radiocarbon and luminescence methods. Researchers also analyzed smelting by-products using scanning electron microscopy to identify mineral contents and primarily found the presence of lead and copper. The same ore deposits of this area later became the focus of large-scale, extraction enterprises targeting copper, silver, zinc, and lead in the early 1900s (Ramenofsky et al. 2008).

Industrial Heritage Initiatives

The small city of Jingdezhen in southeast China grew as a pottery production center over several centuries. Henry Wadsworth Longfellow wrote about that factory town in the 1870s, when it hosted hundreds of dragon kilns producing a stream of thousands of ceramic vessels for international markets. He imagined himself flying over the city and gazing down:

> And bird-like poise on balanced wing
> Above the town of King-te-tchin
> A burning town, or seeming so—

Three thousand furnaces that glow
Incessantly, and fill the air
With smoke uprising, gyre on gyre
And painted by the lurid glare,
Of jets and flashes of red fire
(Longfellow 1878).

Today, Jingdezhen is recognized by UNESCO in its "Creative Cities Network" that promotes heritage and cultural tourism. Once a clamoring, smoke-filled terrain, the city now attracts a lucrative flow of visitors to see exhibits of its industrial past (UNESCO 2016).

Industrial archaeology in Britain had roots in local heritage initiatives to record, map, and commemorate the ruins of mills and factories. Abandoned industrial sites continue to attract attention not just as research subjects, but as potential heritage and memorial projects (see, e.g., Cleere 2000). Hilary Orange (2008:85) observes: "During the second half of the 20th century the cultural meaning of industrial structures began to change. A transformation occurred which turned industrial remains from derelict functional structures to icons of an innovative industrial past." Local, community-based initiatives to commemorate, repurpose, and reanimate these structures have increased over time (Orange 2015). Donald Hardesty (2000:46) suggests that archaeologists' research designs encompass the dynamics of such heritage investments: "the immediacy of many industrial sites to living people increases their value as signs or symbols that intentionally communicate messages or associations with recent historical events or that evoke responses tied to 'deep cultural memories.'"

The preservation and reuse of defunct industrial structures can yield notable benefits. The High Line elevated park in New York City provides an excellent example. The High Line was an elevated freight railway constructed by the New York Central Railroad Company from 1929 to 1934 across the west side of lower Manhattan. This elevated freight line avoided street-level crossings and provided deliveries of production supplies, finished

FIGURE 6. The rails of the defunct freight line along a northern part of the High Line Park still under development in Manhattan, with a view across the lower Hudson River. (Photograph by the author, 2014.)

goods, and food products to the warehouses and factories in that part of Manhattan through the 1960s. The line fell into disuse as manufacturing facilities moved out of Manhattan and was largely abandoned by the 1990s. Eyed for demolition, the High Line was saved by a grass-roots preservation movement that formed the Friends of the High Line. In collaboration with the city government, this non-profit conservancy commissioned architects to transform the elevated tracks into a linear, raised park extending for a mile and half across this urban space. The results were so popular that the High Line corridor became a magnet for new, residential

FIGURE 7. The rails of the past train line extend through the surrounding High Line Park's elevated and landscaped spaces, surrounded by new residential developments in Manhattan's west side neighborhood. (Photograph by the author, 2014.)

Perspectives from Historical Archaeology:

development (Figures 6, 7). The aesthetic attraction of the new park is estimated to have motivated over $2 billion in private development projects along its length and 12,000 new jobs (Douet 2012; Okada 2012:149).

Conclusion

Research projects focused on craft and industrial enterprise span a remarkable spectrum of diverse perspectives. Some limit their efforts to recording, mapping, and studying the mechanics of a site. Others examine comparative questions of changes of technologies over time and space. Many analysts look away from the buildings and equipment of the workplace and focus instead on the workers, their families, residences, lifeways, and health experiences. With many sites presenting standing ruins, historians and archaeologists often encounter local stakeholder groups who wish to promote heritage themes and tourism potentials. All of these perspectives can be pursued with significant advances in research and curation methods. Investigations often range from microscopic analysis of product constituents to large-scale, three-dimensional recording of locations and features with high-resolution, laser technologies. Past debates concerning a primacy of heritage recording or archaeological research questions has evolved into frequent collaborations across interest groups. Decades of research projects have shown us that there is no clear dividing line between craft and industry, and rather a complex and contingent interdependence of enterprises across multiple scales of investment and output.

References

ALLOM, THOMAS
1831   Dolcoath Copper Mine in Camborne, Cornwall, steel engraving. In *Cornwall Illustrated, in a Series of Views of Castles, Seats of the Nobility, Mines, Picturesque Scenery, Towns, Public Buildings, Churches, Antiquities,* original drawings by Thomas Allom, engraved on steel by J. Thomas, Le Petit, et al., with historical and descriptive accounts by J. Britton and E. W. Brayley. Fisher and Company, London.

BAILEY, DANIEL N., JOHN W. LAWRENCE, AND PAUL W. SCHOPP
2004   The Rise of the Industrial Rural Tenant Laborers and the Rise of the Industrial Economy: Historical Ethnography of the Heminitz Property, Site 36LH267, Upper Macungie Township, Lehigh County, Pennsylvania. *Northeast Historical Archaeology* 33(1):91–110.

BAXTER, JANE E.
2012   The Paradox of a Capitalist Utopia: Visionary Ideals and Lived Experience in the Pullman Community, 1880-1900. *International Journal of Historical Archaeology* 16(4):651–665.

BAXTER, R. SCOTT
2002   Industrial and Domestic Landscapes of a California Oil Field. *Historical Archaeology* 36(3):18–27.

BEHRENS, JOANNA
2005   The Dynamite Factory: An Industrial Landscape in Late-Nineteenth-Century South Africa. *Historical Archaeology* 39(3):61–74.

BINING, ARTHUR C.
1938   *Pennsylvania Iron Manufacture in the Eighteenth Century.* Pennsylvania Historical and Museum Commission, Harrisburg.

BOTWICK, BRADFORD, AND DEBRA A. MCCLANE
2005   Landscapes of Resistance: A View of the Nineteenth-Century Chesapeake Bay Oyster Fishery. *Historical Archaeology* 39(3):94–112.

BRACEGIRDLE, BRIAN, EDITOR
1973   *The Archaeology of the Industrial Revolution.* Heinemann, London.

BRADFORD, KELVIN
2004   Introduction of the Original Anagama in Fifth Century; Comparison between Ogama and Anagama, *Ceramics Monthly* 52(6):126–128.

BRAJE, TODD J., JON M. ERLANDSON, AND TORBEN C. RICK
2007   An Historic Chinese Abalone Fishery on California's Northern Channel Islands. *Historical Archaeology* 41(4):117–128.

BRASHLER, JANET G.
1991   When Daddy Was a Shanty Boy: The Role of Gender in the Organization of the Logging West Virginia. *Historical Archaeology* 25(4):54–68.

BROWN, JEFFREY L.
1977   Exploratory Archaeological Excavations at the Bluff Furnace Site. Miscellaneous Paper I. Institute of Archaeology, University of Tennessee, Chattanooga.

BROWN, RICHELLE C.
2016   Power Line: Memory and the March on Blair Mountain. In *Excavating Memory: Sites of Remembering and Forgetting,* Maria T. Starzmann and John R. Roby, editors, pp. 86–107. University Press of Florida, Gainesville.

BUCHANAN, R. ANGUS
2000   The Origins of Industrial Archaeology. In *Perspectives on Industrial Archaeology*, Neil Cossons, editor, pp. 18–38. Science Museum, London.

CALDWELL, JOHN E.
1951   *A Tour through Part of Virginia in the Summer of 1808*. Dietz Press, Richmond, VA; facsimile reprint of 1809 edition published by the author in New York.

CALFAS, GEORGE W.
2013   Nineteenth Century Stoneware Manufacturing at Pottersville, South Carolina: The Discovery of a Dragon Kiln and the Reinterpretation of a Southern Pottery Tradition, Ph.D. Diss., Department of Anthropology, University of Illinois.

CAPLINGER, MICHAEL W.
1997   *Bridges Over Time: A Technological Context for the Baltimore and Ohio Railroad Main Stem at Harpers Ferry, West Virginia*. Morgantown: West Virginia University Institute for the History of Technology and Industrial Archaeology.

CASELLA, ELEANOR C., AND JAMES SYMONDS, EDITORS
2005   *Industrial Archaeology: Future Directions*. Springer, New York.

CASSELL, MARK S., AND MYRON O. STACHIW
2005   Perspectives on Landscapes of Industrial Labor. *Historical Archaeology* 39(3):1–7.

CHEN, LIQIONG
1986   The Qionglai Kilns. In *Scientific and Technological Insights on Ancient Chinese Pottery and Porcelain*, pp. 321–324. Shanghai Institute of Ceramics and Science Press, Peking.

CLEERE, HENRY
2000   The World Heritage Convention as a Medium for Promoting the Industrial Heritage. *IA: Journal of the Society for Industrial Archaeology* 26(2):31–42.

COTTER, JOHN L.
1968   Review of "Industrial Archaeology: An Introduction," by Kenneth Hudson. *American Anthropologist* 70:422.

COTTER, JOHN L., AND PAUL J. HUDSON
1957   *New Discoveries at Jamestown, Site of the First Successful English Settlement in America*. National Park Service, Washington, DC.

COUNCIL, R. BRUCE, NICHOLAS HONERKAMP, AND M. ELIZABETH WILL
1992   *Industry and Technology in Antebellum Tennessee: The Archaeology of Bluff Furnace*. University of Tennessee Press, Knoxville.

COWEN, RUTH S.
1976   The "Industrial Revolution" in the Home: Household Technology and Social Change in the Twentieth Century. *Technology and Culture* 17(1):1–23.

COWIE, SARAH E.
2011   *The Plurality of Power: An Archaeology of Industrial Capitalism*. Springer, New York.

CRANSTONE, DAVID
2004   The Archaeology of Industrialization—New Directions. In *The Archaeology of Industrialization*, David Barker and David Cranstone, editors pp. 313–320. Maney Publishing, Leeds, UK.

DENT, RICHARD J.
1986   On The Archaeology of Early Canals: Research on the Patowmack Canal in Great Falls, Virginia. *Historical Archaeology* 20(1):50–62.

DEVORE, STEVEN L.
1990   Fur Trade Era Blacksmith Shops at Fort Union Trading Post National Historic Site, North Dakota. *Historical Archaeology* 24(3):1–23.

DOUET, JAMES
2012   Introduction. In *Industrial Heritage Re-tooled: The TICCIH Guide to Industrial Heritage Conservation*, James Douet, editor, pp. 1–4. The International Committee for the Conservation of the Industrial Heritage, Lancaster, UK.

EDENSOR, TIM
2005   *Industrial Ruins: Spaces, Aesthetics and Materiality*. Berg, Oxford, UK.

EKHOLM-FRIEDMAN, KAJSA
2000   On the Evolution of Global Systems, Part I: The Mesopotamian Heartland. In *World System History: The Social Science of Long-term Trade*, Robert A. Denmark, Jonathan Friedman, Barry K. Gills, and George Modelski, editors, pp. 153–168. Routledge, London.

FAULKNER, ALARIC
1985   Archaeology of the Cod Fishery: Damariscove. *Historical Archaeology* 19(2):57–86.

FENNELL, CHRISTOPHER C.
2010   Damaging Detours: Routes, Racism and New Philadelphia. *Historical Archaeology* 44(1):138–154.

FRANZEN, JOHN G.
1992   Northern Michigan Logging Camps: Material Culture and Worker Adaptation on the Industrial Frontier. *Historical Archaeology* 26(2):74–98.

GARRISON, ERVAN G.
1995   Three Ironclad Warships—The Archaeology of Industrial Process and Historical Myth. *Historical Archaeology* 29(4):26–38.

GIBB, JAMES G., DAVID J. BERNSTEIN, AND DANIEL F. CASSEDY
1990   Making Cheese: Archaeology of a 19th Century Rural Industry. *Historical Archaeology* 24(1):18–33.

GIBB, JAMES G., DAVID J. BERNSTEIN, AND STEPHEN ZIPP
2009   Farm and Factory: Agricultural Production Strategies and the Cheese and Butter Industry. *Historical Archaeology* 43(2):83–107.

GILBERT, DAVID T.
1999   *Waterpower: Mills, Factories, Machines and Floods at Harpers Ferry, West Virginia, 1762-1991.* Harpers Ferry Historical association, Harpers Ferry, WV.

GILLESPIE, WILLIAM B., AND MARY M. FARRELL
2002   Work Camp Settlement Patterns: Landscape-Scale Comparisons of Two Mining Camps in Southeastern Arizona. *Historical Archaeology* 36(3):59–68.

GIVEN, MICHAEL
2005   Mining Landscapes and Colonial Rule in Early-Twentieth-Century Cyprus. *Historical Archaeology* 39(3):49–60.

GORDON, ROBERT B.
2000   Analysis and Interpretation of Artifacts in Industrial Archaeology. *IA: Journal of the Society for Industrial Archaeology* 26(1):103–111.

GORDON, ROBERT B., AND DAVID J. KILLICK
1992   The Metallurgy of the American Bloomery Process. *Archaeomaterials* 6:141–167.

GORDON, ROBERT B., AND PATRICK M. MALONE
1994   *The Texture of Industry: An Archaeological View of the Industrialization of North America.* Oxford University Press, New York.

GRADWOHL, DAVID M., AND NANCY M. OSBORN
1984   *Exploring Buried Buxton: Archaeology of an Abandoned Iowa Coal Mining Town with a Large Black Population.* Iowa State University Press, Ames.

GRIGGS, HEATHER J.
2001   "By Virtue of Reason and Nature": Competition and Economic Strategy in the Needletrades at New York's Five Points, 1855-1880. *Historical Archaeology* 35(3):76–88.

GRISWOLD, WILLIAM A., AND DONALD W. LINEBAUGH, EDITORS
2010   *Saugus Iron Works: The Roland W. Robbins Excavations, 1948-1953.* National Park Service, Washington, D.C.

HARDESTY, DONALD L.
1998   *The Archaeology of Mining and Miners.* Society for Historical Archaeology Special Publication Series, No. 6. Society for Historical Archaeology, Pleasant Hill, CA.

2000   Speaking in Tongues: The Multiple Voices of Fieldwork in Industrial Archaeology. *IA: Journal of the Society for Industrial Archaeology* 26(2):43–47.

HARROD, RYAN P., AND JOHN J. CRANDALL
2015   Rails Built of the Ancestors' Bones: The Bioarchaeology of the Overseas Chinese Experience. *Historical Archaeology* 49(1):148–161.

HARTLEY, EDWARD N.
1957   *Ironworks of the Saugus: The Lynn and Braintree Ventures of the Company of Undertakers of the Ironworks in New England.* University of Oklahoma Press, Norman.

HAYMAN, RICHARD
2005   *Ironmaking: The History and Archaeology of the Iron Industry.* Tempus, Stroud, UK.

HEITE, EDWARD F.
1974   The Delmarva Bog Iron Industry. *Northeast Historical Archaeology* 3(3):18–34.

HSU, YOUZHI
1995   Building and Firing Technique of Jingdezhen Ancient Wood Kiln. In *Science and Technology of Ancient Ceramics 3: Proceedings of the International Symposium,* Guo Jinkun, editor, pp. 286–290. Shanghai Research Society of Science and Technology of Ancient Ceramics, Shanghai.

HUDSON, KENNETH
1966   *Industrial Archaeology: An Introduction.* Humanities Press, New York.

1979   *World Industrial Archaeology.* Cambridge University Press, Cambridge, UK.

HULL-WALSKI, DEBORAH A., AND FRANK L. WALSKI
1994   There's Trouble a-Brewin': The Brewing and Bottling Industries at Harpers Ferry, West Virginia. *Historical Archaeology* 28(4):106–121.

INTERNATIONAL COUNCIL ON MONUMENTS AND SITES (ICOMOS)
2011   Joint ICOMOS-TICCIH Principles for the Conservation of Industrial Heritage Sites, Structures, Areas, and Landscapes. Adopted by the 17th ICOMOS General Assembly, November 28.

JOHNSON, MARY
1995   A Nineteenth-Century Mill Village: Virginius Island, 1800-60. *West Virginia History* 54: 1–27.

JOHNSON, MATTHEW
1996   *An Archaeology of Capitalism.* Wiley-Blackwell, New York.

JONES, WILLIAM
2006   *Dictionary of Industrial Archaeology.* 2d ed. Sutton Publishing, Stroud, UK.

KELLY, SOPHIA E.
2013   The Role of Technological Transitions in the Development of American Ceramic Industries: Elijah Cornell and the Shift from Redware to Stoneware Production. *Historical Archaeology* 47(4):45–70.

KELSO, WILLIAM M., AND EDWARD A. CHAPPELL
1974   Excavation of a Seventeenth Century Pottery Kiln at Glebe Harbor, Westmoreland County, Virginia. *Historical Archaeology* 8:53–63.

LANDON, DAVID B.
1999   Interpreting Social Organization at Industrial Sites: An Example from the Ohio Trap Rock Mine. *Northeast Historical Archaeology* 28(1):89–103.

LANGHORNE, WILLIAM T., JR.
1976   Mill Based Settlement Patterns in Schoharie County, New York: A Regional study. *Historical Archaeology* 10:73–92.

LAWRENCE, SUSAN, AND PETER DAVIES
2015   Innovation, Adaptation and Technology as *Habitus*: The Origins of Alluvial Gold Mining Methods in Australia. *Archaeology in Oceania* 50(Supp.):20–29.

LEMONNIER, PIERRE
1993   Introduction. In *Technological Choices: Transformations in Material Cultures since the Neolithic,* Pierre Lemonnier, editor, pp. 1–35. Routledge, London.

LIGHT, JOHN D.
2007   A Dictionary of Blacksmithing Terms. *Historical Archaeology* 41(2):84–157.

LONGFELLOW, HENRY WADSWORTH
1878   King-te-tching. In *Poems of Places, Vol. 23, Asia: Persia, India, Chinese Empire, Japan,* edited by Henry Wadsworth Longfellow, p. 212. Houghton, Osgood and Co., Boston.

MARTIN, PATRICK E.
2009   Industrial Archaeology. In *International Handbook of Historical Archaeology,* Teresita Majewski and David Gaimster, editors, pp. 285–297. Springer, New York.

MCERLEAN, THOMAS C.
2007   Archaeology of the Strangford Lough Kelp Industry in the Eighteenth- and Early-Nineteenth Centuries. *Historical Archaeology* 41(3):76–93.

MCGUIRE, RANDALL H., AND PAUL RECKNER
2002   The Unromantic West: Labor, Capital, and Struggle. *Historical Archaeology* 36(3):44–58.

MCNEARY, RORY W. A.
2007   "Guns, Harpoons, Lances, Casks and Every [Necessary] Article"; An Account of the History and Archaeology of an Eighteenth-Century Shore-Based Whaling and Basking Shark Fishery in Donegal Bay. *Historical Archaeology* 41(3):115–124.

MCVARISH, DOUGLAS C.
2008   *American Industrial Archaeology.* Left Coast Press, Walnut Creek, CA.

MILLER, GEORGE L., AND CATHERINE SULLIVAN
1984   Machine-Made Glass Containers and the End of Production for Mouth-Blown Bottles. *Historical Archaeology* 18:83–96.

MONROE, J. CAMERON, AND SETH MALLIOS
2004   A Seventeenth-Century Colonial Cottage Industry: New Evidence and a Dating Formula for Colono Tobacco Pipes in the Chesapeake. *Historical Archaeology* 38(2):68–82.

MROZOWSKI, STEPHEN A.
1991   Landscapes of Inequality. In *The Archaeology of Inequality,* Randall H. Mcguire and Robert Paynter, editors, pp. 79–101. Basil Blackwell, Oxford, UK.

MROZOWSKI, STEPHEN A., GRACE H. ZIESING, AND MARY C. BEAUDRY
1996   *Living on the Boott: Historical Archaeology at the Boott Mills Boardinghouses of Lowell, Massachusetts.* University of Massachusetts Press, Amherst, MA.

NEEDHAM, JOSEPH, HO PING-YU, LU GWEI-DJEN, AND WANG LING
2004   *Chemistry and Chemical Technology, Part 12: Ceramic Technology. Vol V: Science and Civilization in China.* Cambridge University Press, Cambridge, UK.

NERUDA, PABLO
1974   *The Book of Questions.* Translated by William O'Daly. Copper Canyon Press, Port Townsend, Washington.

O'DELL, GARY A., AND ANGELO I. GEORGE
2014   Rock-Shelter Saltpeter Mines of Eastern Kentucky. *Historical Archaeology* 48(2):91–121.

OKADA, MASAAKI
2012   Industrial Ruins. In *Industrial Heritage Re-tooled: The TICCIH Guide to Industrial Heritage Conservation,* James Douet, editor, pp. 149–154. The International Committee for the Conservation of the Industrial Heritage, Lancaster, UK.

ORANGE, HILARY
2008   Industrial Archaeology: Its Place within the Academic Discipline, the Public Realm and the Heritage Industry. *Industrial Archaeology Review* 30(2):83–95.

2015   Introduction. In *Reanimating Industrial Spaces: Conducting Memory Work in Post-Industrial Societies,* Hilary Orange, editor, pp. 13–27. Left Coast Press, Walnut Creek, CA.

ORSER, CHARLES E., JR.
1996   *A Historical Archaeology of the Modern World.* Plenum Press, New York.

PALMER, MARILYN
2000   Archaeology or Heritage Management: The Conflict of Objectives in the Training of Industrial Archaeologists. *IA: Journal of the Society for Industrial Archaeology* 26(2):49–54.

PALMER, MARILYN, AND PETER NEAVERSON
1998   *Industrial Archaeology: Principles and Practice.* Routledge, London.

PALMER, MARILYN, AND HILARY ORANGE
2016   The Archaeology of Industry: People and Places. *Post-Medieval Archaeology* 50(1):73–91.

PANNELL, J. P. M.
1966   *The Techniques of Industrial Archaeology.* David and Charles, Ltd., Newton Abbot, UK.

PASTRON, ALLEN G., AND JAMES P. DELGADO
1991   Archaeological Investigations of a Mid-19th-Century Shipbreaking Yard, San Francisco, California. *Historical Archaeology* 25(3):61–77.

PAYNTER, ROBERT
1988   Steps to an Archaeology of Capitalism: Material Change and Class Analysis. In *The Recovery of Meaning: Historical Archaeology in the Eastern United States,* Mark P. Leone and Parker B. Potter, Jr., editors, pp. 407–434. Smithsonian Institution Press, Washington, D.C.

PITTAWAY, MARK
2005   Creating and Domesticating Hungary's Socialist Industrial Landscape: From Dunapentele to Sztálinváros, 1950-1958. *Historical Archaeology* 39(3):75–93.

POLK, MICHAEL R.
2015   Interpreting Chinese Worker Camps on the Transcontinental Railroad at Promontory Summit, Utah. *Historical Archaeology* 49(1):59–70.

QUIVIK, FREDRIC L.
2000   Landscapes as Industrial Artifacts: Lessons from Environmental History. *IA: Journal of the Society for Industrial Archaeology* 26(2):55–64.

RAMENOFSKY, ANN F., C. DAVID VAUGHAN, AND MICHAEL N. SPILDE
2008   Seventeenth-Century Metal Production at San Marcos Pueblo, North-Central New Mexico. *Historical Archaeology* 42(4):105–131.

RICE, PRUDENCE M., AND SARA L. VAN BECK
1993   The Spanish Colonial Kiln Tradition of Moquegua, Peru. *Historical Archaeology* 27(4):65–81.

RIX, MICHAEL
1955   Industrial Archaeology. *Amateur Historian* 2(8):225–229.

ROLLER, MICHAEL
2013   Rewriting Narratives of Labor Violence: A Transnational Perspective of the Lattimer Massacre. *Historical Archaeology* 47(2):109–123.

ROTMAN, DEBORAH L., AND JOHN M. STAICER
2002   Curiosities and Conundrums: Deciphering Social Relations and the Material World at the Ben Schroeder Saddletree Factory and Residence in Madison, Indiana. *Historical Archaeology* 36(2):92–110.

SCARLETT, TIMOTHY J., JEREMY RAHN, AND DANIEL SCOTT
2006   Bricks and an Evolving Industrial Landscape: The West Point Foundry and New York's Hudson River Valley. *Northeast Historical Archaeology* 35(1): 29–46.

SCARLETT, TIMOTHY J., AND SAM R. SWEITZ
2012   Constructing New Knowledge in Industrial Archaeology. In *Global Perspectives on Archaeological Field Schools: Constructions of Knowledge and Experience,* Harold Mytum, editor, pp. 119–143. Springer, New York.

SCRANTON, PHILIP
1997   *Endless Novelty: Specialty Production and American Industrialization, 1865-1925.* Princeton University Press, Princeton, NJ.

SEIBERT, ERIKA M., EDITOR
2015   *Labor Archeology of the Industrial Era: Identifying and Evaluating Nationally Significant Archeological Sites of Labor in the Industrial Era in the United States.* National Park Service, Washington, D.C.

SHACKEL, PAUL A.
1996   *Culture Change and the New Technology: An Archaeology of the Early American Industrial Era.* Plenum Press, New York.

Christopher C. Fennell

2000 Craft to Wage Labor: Agency and Resistance in American Historical Archaeology. In *Agency Theory in Archaeology*, John Robb and Marcia-Anne Dobres, editors, pp. 232–246. Routledge Press, London.

2004 Labor's Heritage: Remembering the American Industrial Landscape. *Historical Archaeology* 38(4):44–58.

SHACKEL, PAUL A., AND MATTHEW PALUS
2010 Industry, Entrepreneurship, and Patronage: Lewis Wernwag and the Development of Virginius Island. *Historical Archaeology* 44(2):97–112.

SHACKEL, PAUL A., AND V. CAMILLE WESTMONT
2016 When the Mine Closed: Heritage Building in Northeastern Pennsylvania. *Bulletin of the General Anthropology Division* 23(1):1, 7–10.

STEEN, CARL
1999 Pottery, Intercolonial Trade, and Revolution: Domestic Earthenwares and the Development of an American Social Identity. *Historical Archaeology* 33(3):62–72.

STRATTON, MICHAEL, AND BARRIE TRINDER
2000 *Twentieth Century Industrial Archaeology.* Taylor and Francis Group, New York.

SVENSSON, EVA, SARA BODIN, HANS HULLING, AND SUSANNE PETTERSSON
2009 The Crofter and the Iron Works: The Material Culture of Structural Crisis, Identity and Making a Living on the Edge. *International Journal of Historical Archaeology* 13(2):183–205.

SYMONDS, JAMES, AND ELEANOR C. CASELLA
2006 Historical Archaeology and Industrialization. In *The Cambridge Companion to Historical Archaeology*, Dan Hicks and Mary C. Beaudry, editors, pp. 143–167. Cambridge University Press, Cambridge, UK.

TAKSA, LUCY
2005 The Material Culture of an Industrial Artifact: Interpreting Control, Defiance, and Everyday Resistance at the New South Wales Eveleigh Railway Workshops. *Historical Archaeology* 39(3):8–27.

TOMASO, MATTHEW S., RICHARD F. VEIT, CARISSA A. DEROOY, AND STANLEY L. WALLING
2006 Social Status and Landscape in a Nineteenth-Century Planned Industrial Alternative Community: Archaeology and Geography of Feltville, New Jersey. *Historical Archaeology* 40(1):20–36.

TRINDER, BARRIE S.
1982 *The Making of the Industrial Landscape.* J. M. Dent and Sons, London.

TRINDER, BARRIE S., EDITOR
1992 *The Blackwell Encyclopedia of Industrial Archaeology.* Blackwell, Oxford, UK.

UNITED NATIONS EDUCATIONAL, SCIENTIFIC, AND CULTURAL ORGANIZATION (UNESCO)
2016 Creative Cities Network: Jingdezhen, http://en.unesco.org/creative-cities/jingdezhen

VAN BUREN, MARY, AND BRENDAN J. M. WEAVER
2012 Contours of Labor and History: A Diachronic Perspective on Andean Mineral Production and the Making of Landscapes in Porco, Bolivia. *Historical Archaeology* 46(3):79–101.

WALKER, JOHN, MICHAEL NEVELL, AND ELEANOR CASELLA
2003 Introduction: Models, Methodology and Industrial Archaeology. In "From Farmer to Factory Owner: Models, Methodology and Industrialization," Michael Nevell, editor, special issue. *Archaeology North West* 6(16):11–16.

WALKER, MARK
2003 The Ludlow Massacre: Class, Warfare, and Historical Memory in Southern Colorado. *Historical Archaeology* 37(3):66–80.

WEITZMAN, DAVID
1980 *Traces of the Past: A Field Guide to Industrial Archaeology.* Charles Scribner's Sons, New York.

WHITE, PAUL J.
2016 The Archaeology of Underground Mining Landscapes. *Historical Archaeology* 50(1):154–168.

WOLF, ERIC R.
1982 *Europe and the People without History.* University of California Press, Berkeley.

WRIGHT, HENRY T., AND GREGORY A. JOHNSON
1975 Population, Exchange and Early State Formation in Southwestern Iran. *American Anthropologist* 77(2):267–289.

CHRISTOPHER C. FENNELL
DEPARTMENT OF ANTHROPOLOGY
UNIVERSITY OF ILLINOIS AT URBANA-CHAMPAIGN
109 DAVENPORT HALL, MC-148
607 S. MATHEWS AVE., URBANA, IL 61801

Part II:
Labor and Landscapes

Paul A. Shackel

Labor's Heritage: Remembering the American Industrial Landscape

ABSTRACT

Archaeology at industrial sites provides some of the greatest opportunities to tell the story of the impact of industrialization on workers and their communities. Archaeologists working on industrial sites have a long tradition of interpreting technology and industrial landscapes while issues related to labor are overlooked or glossed over. Other historical archaeologists have laid the groundwork for understanding labor relations and daily life in industrial contexts. An overview of the current state of industrial archaeology is provided, and a renewed call for addressing an archaeology of labor is issued. Work performed at industrial sites needs to address issues related to labor. The draft National Historic Landmark study by the National Park Service on labor archaeology serves as a good framework to deal with these ideas. Additional avenues of inquiry are also explored.

Introduction

Where history, archaeology, and memory meet at industrial sites is where we find the excitement of labor archaeology as well as some of the troubling aspects of how nations and communities use their past. Industrial archaeologists have a long tradition of documenting the engineering feats of the industrial age. Understanding what is studied, remembered, and interpreted at these industrial sites can show us who we are as a community and a nation. There are often inconsistencies between the official and unofficial memories of labor and capital. The memory of industry and its representation on the American landscape is like the memory of all significant events in history. There are winners and losers. In a time when American and international corporations continue to undermine the American workforce by weakening unions and extending the average workweek, we as a society need to think about labor issues and remember the long, arduous struggle of workers to secure a 40-hour workweek and other conces-sions from capital that many take for granted today. Understanding labor as a component of industrial archaeology provides us the tool necessary to revisit the history of industrial sites, and it gives us a mechanism to think about labor in the past, present, and future. In the following, I provide a review and a plan for how archaeologists working in industrial contexts can create a more inclusive interpreta-tion of the past by addressing issues related to laborers and their families.

Labor's Heritage

While many federally funded museums in the United States extol the glories of economic and social progress as a result of industry, some working class members view the preservation of old buildings and ruins as an attempt to save a degrading phase of human history. Robert Vogel once noted, "The dirt, noise, bad smell, hard labor and other forms of exploitation associated with these kinds of places make preservation [of industrial sites] ludicrous. 'Preserve a steel mill?' people say, 'It killed my father. Who wants to preserve that?'" (quoted in Lowenthal 1985:403). While I am not advocating the destruction or the neglect of industrial buildings, it is important to recognize individual dissenting views on the true effects of industrialization. T. E. Leary (1979: 182) suggested more than two decades ago that the restoration of 19th-century factories could be useful for interpreting and understanding work conditions that people faced several generations ago. Telling the story of labor's struggle can make the preservation of industrial complexes more acceptable to a greater portion of the working class community. Industrial archaeol-ogy has the potential to be an educational tool that provides "a sort of Rosetta Stone to decipher the language peculiar to industrial tombs" (Leary 1979:182).

Industrial archaeology can lead to a better understanding of life and work in an industrial capitalist system. While industrial archaeologists have made strides to tell the story of labor and the impact on daily life, the discipline still has a long way to go to meet Leary's expectations.

Since 1987 the America's Industrial Heritage Project, now called the Southwestern Pennsylvania Heritage Preservation Commission, began a long-term project inventorying surviving historic engineering works and industrial resources in the region. The Historic American Buildings Survey (HABS) and the Historic American Engineering Record (HAER), both part of the National Park Service, helped to record significant industrial sites in southwest Pennsylvania. The emphasis has been the recording of industrial engineering feats, the mission of HAER, while creating several important social histories. However, many of these engineering studies do not go beyond particularistic and functional inquiries, a state of the field that Leary (1979) and later George Teague (1987) cautioned us about.

There are some noteworthy museums that do describe the daily lives of workers, such as the Eckley Miners Village in Pennsylvania. The village is located near Hazleton, once the center of 19th-century anthracite mining. In 1971, a group of businessmen organized the Anthracite Historical Site Museum, Inc., and purchased the village of Eckley, with 200 residents still in the village. They deeded the land over to the state in order to create the country's only mining town museum. Today, fewer than 20 people reside in Eckley. The town has been preserved, and the museum interprets the daily living experience of mining families. Exhibits discuss the hardships of life in a mining community, such as impoverishment, illness, accidents, death, and labor discontent (Wesolowsky 1996). However, these frank discussions in public museums that highlight the workers' experiences do not dominate many of the discussions of industrial heritage on the American landscape.

There are few communities that celebrate labor while muting the voice of capital. Another community that does is the postindustrial city of Lawrence, Massachusetts. The official memory of Lawrence is presented in the Lawrence Heritage State Park, situated in the midst of the city's decaying industrial core. The museum is located in a restored boardinghouse with two floors of exhibit space devoted almost entirely to labor issues and the Bread and Roses Strike of 1912. The strike, led by young women and followed by immigrants of 30 different nationalities, closed most of the Northeast region's mills in an attempt to acquire better wages and improved work conditions. Even though the strike stimulated broader appeals for better working conditions by labor throughout the Northeast, the strike failed. Workers went back to their jobs without acquiring any concessions. Today, there are mixed reactions to remembering this strike. Some citizens believe the story should be told, while others want to forget the days of exploitation (Green 2000:57–60). "How beautiful it is to sweetly forget the clubbings of 1912, the jailings of 1919, and the clubbings again of 1931," noted one former factory worker (quoted in Green 2000:60). The city remembers this labor tradition through a museum that provides a memory of labor strife. Lawrence suffered like many other northeastern industrial cities as textile mills fled the region during the 1920s in search of cheaper, unorganized labor in the southern United States. These former textile centers lost significant capital. It was not until the 1970s that some northern industrial cities were able to retool and begin revitalization. Lawrence remains one of the poorest cities in Massachusetts, suffering from the loss of its major economic base. While the official history of the United States has a long tradition of emphasizing and glorifying industry and capitalism, Lawrence is an example of a place that remembers the struggle of labor.

The city of Lowell, Massachusetts, embraces its industrial past. Statues have been placed around the town to celebrate the efforts of industrial workers. At Lowell National Historical Park many of the exhibits present a history that includes the story of both labor and capital. One exhibit extols the material benefits of industry, but the exhibit also explains labor strife. Visitors are invited to walk through the mill with earplugs while more than 100 machines operate simultaneously. The experience is enough to make one realize the strain on the mill girls and later immigrants as they labored 10 hours per day.

The above are examples of how some stories of industry and labor are represented on the American landscape and have been made part of the national public memory. While labor and capital compete for the official memory of the past, a large proportion of the industrial archaeology performed in the United States and Great Britain has been about understanding the industrial process, often at the expense of labor.

The Story of Labor's Heritage

There are many who have gone to great lengths to document and popularize the technological side of industrial archaeology (Hudson 1971, 1978, 1979; Weitzman 1980). Other works in the United States have charted new ways to understand the development of industrial technologies (Kumar 1992; Caplinger 1997; Harshberger 2002; Miller 2003) and industrial archaeology techniques (Gordon and Malone 1994; Kemp 1996; Palmer and Neaverson 1998). A major part of industrial archaeology has explained phenomena related to technological development, the economy of industry, and the industrial revolution (Trinder 1983; Stratton and Trinder 2000; Gordon 2001). Some industrial archaeologists believe that the study of industry's physical remains and landscapes is what distinguishes industrial archaeology from other disciplines (Minchinton 1983; Clark 1987). In many of these cases, either labor is not mentioned, or it serves as a secondary thought when discussing industrial technology and landscapes at these sites (Heite 1993; Pletka 1993; Howe 1994; Butler 1999). One prominent British industrial archaeologist wrote:

> ... patterns of government, religious allegiance, domestic and foreign policy, patterns of trade (although perhaps not of consumer spending)—are better arrived at by other means. Familiarity with, or even interest in, all aspects of working life in the industrial period is not essential for the industrial archaeologist so long as he [sic] recognizes their existence and is prepared to ask for advice from other specialists whose interest they are (Palmer 1990:282).

This tradition is also prominent in the United States and is reflected in *IA: The Journal of the Society for Industrial Archeology*. The articles in it are more about industry and technology than issues related to labor (Gordon 1988; Malone 1988; Holley 2001). Some of the more recent articles do acknowledge the important role workers once played at these sites, although the authors do not explore labor issues in detail (Landon et al. 2001; Wermiel 2001). Many of the studies mentioned above are good examples of industrial archaeology that focus on machines, machine products, physical layout, and power systems, but in most cases they do not address labor issues in any significant way.

I believe archaeologists working in industrial contexts need to make labor a significant part of their studies, as many historians and anthropologists have done (Gutman 1976; Wallace 1978; Brody 1979, 1980, 1993; Montgomery 1979). Historical and anthropological perspectives on labor help to define issues related to the impact of changing technology on workers and their families. These transformations in industry not only affected work, but they also impacted domestic life and health conditions. Labor historian David Brody (1989) has also encouraged scholars to look more closely at issues related to politics and power. At the recent plenary session for the annual meeting of The Society for Historical Archaeology, there was a call for archaeologists to include social history (Martin 2003) and labor (Shackel 2003b) when examining industrial sites. Others have also made the inclusion of labor and daily life a part of their archaeology (Beaudry and Mrozowski 1989; Brashler 1991; Wegars 1991; Workman et al. 1994; Shackel 1996, 2000b; Costello 1998; Trinder and Cox 2000; Van Bueren 2002).

A. Bernard Knapp (1998:2) writes about the importance of recognizing that technology in an industrial context must also consider labor and try to understand how people could negotiate social, political, and economic relationships. Acknowledging this type of relationship allows for few generalities. Each community and region has its own distinct history, and archaeology can play a powerful role in exploring these differences while also celebrating a common labor history. An important document that provides a good starting point for understanding labor's heritage is the *Labor Archaeology National Historic Landmark Theme Study*, a draft report being developed by National Park Service (Solury 1999). This document provides a brief overview of work cultures in the United States from the colonial period until recent times. The study examines the experiences of workers and addresses issues like ethnic histories, labor mobility, community studies, worker experiences, women and minority studies, and political behavior. The study provides archaeological case studies of sites that are on the National Register of Historic Places and explores issues of labor archaeology at industrial sites. Once completed, the study will help elevate the importance of labor archaeology on the national level.

Housing and Communities

The rise of American industry during the late-18th and early-19th centuries was one of the most significant issues that faced the United States as a new nation. Capitalists intentionally located factories in nonurban areas because they thought they could avoid the ills of European industrial cities that were plagued with diseases, pollution, and unemployment (Marx 1964; Kasson 1979; Prude 1983:31–41; Shelton 1986:28ff). For this reason, many companies provided housing for their workers, a tradition that began in England with Arkwright's new industrial establishments at Cromford in 1771 (Burnett 1978:12; Lowe 1982). Many industrialists believed that the control of space was as important as the control of time. Therefore, while factory owners controlled workers for 10 to 12 or more hours a day in the factory or the mines, they also controlled portions of workers' domestic lives by creating regulations in town plans and housing.

Archaeological work at Lowell, Massachusetts, best summarized by Stephen Mrozowski, Grace Ziesing, and Mary Beaudry (1996), showed the effects of changing boardinghouse policies established by industrialists for a new workforce of mill girls in the first half of the 19th century. At Lowell and at other northeastern industrial cotton mill sites, women from the countryside were brought into the labor force because they were perceived as cheap and idle hands (Dublin 1979). These industrial communities contained rows of boardinghouses with standardized facades that mimicked factory architecture. The boardinghouses were always in close proximity to the factory. The interior of the boardinghouses created an atmosphere of egalitarianism as all of the rooms were of the same size. This was but one component of a strategy by corporations to exert their control to create a compliant workforce (Dublin 1979; Hareven 1982). Archaeology shows that by the end of the 19th century, the paternal philosophy for operating the boardinghouses, whereby owners influenced and to some extent controlled the domestic lives of the mill girls, had disappeared. Poor sanitation and health conditions and the degradation of the surrounding environment became the norm for northeastern industrial towns, including Lowell (Mrozowski et al. 1996).

Not all industries operated in this fashion (Shackel and Winter 1994). In the case of the United States Armory at Harpers Ferry, the federal government did not initiate any form of corporate paternalism in the early-19th century, and this lack of paternalism eventually came to haunt those who tried to manage labor in the gun factory (Smith 1977). For instance, in the early-19th century, workers built their own houses, almost anywhere in town, as long as it was outside of the industrial complex. One worker built his house in the middle of a little traveled street. Generally, workers and their families could express their own personal identity within the confines of their own homes. Each domestic site excavated shows very different house floor plans, and armory workers used a variety of construction materials. The domestic landscape of Harpers Ferry appeared eclectic, unlike the standardized boardinghouses found in the Northeast. Each armory worker family had very different ceramic forms and types (Lucas 1994; Lucas and Shackel 1994; Shackel 2000b).

The armory workers defied any attempt to unify them as a workforce and resisted the industrial process much longer than their counterparts in Springfield, Massachusetts. Supervisors made it difficult for northerners who tried to introduce new mechanized processes. The armory superintendent gave very little support to John Hall, a gun maker from Maine working in Harpers Ferry, as he perfected the process of interchangeable parts. The archaeological record shows that armorers practiced their craft in a piecework system at home until about 1841 when the military took over control of the facility and made all workers abide by a standard work discipline found in industries throughout the country. After 1841 armory work was no longer performed in a domestic context (Shackel 1996, 1999a, 1999b).

By the end of the 1840s, the Ordnance Department took control of the management of the facility's operations. Engineers imposed a grid pattern over the town, dismantling those houses that were inconveniently placed and did not follow the new plan, like the house built in a roadway. The federal government also supported a major rebuilding of the factories. The early armory managers built factory buildings on an as-needed basis, thus creating an inefficient production line. The Ordnance Department replaced the old buildings with new structures that closely followed an orderly line of production, while skilled workers became wage laborers. Both work and home spaces were reorganized in order to create a more efficient and compliant workforce (Shackel 1996).

While the federal government at Harpers Ferry chose not to implement any form of paternalist control such as was commonly found at other industrial complexes in the northeast in the first half of the 19th century, other private industrialists in the Harpers Ferry area did recognize the value of controlling workers' space and time at work and at home. An archaeological example can be found at Virginius Island, a small industrial community adjacent to Harpers Ferry. The community began as a small industrial complex with more than a dozen small crafts and industries owned by various individuals. Entrepreneurs placed their small industrial complexes at strategic points on the landscape to access waterpower, and they did not follow a development plan. One local newspaper called it a "little Pittsburgh" (Palus 2000).

By the 1850s Abraham Herr owned most of the island. Unlike the previous owners, he subscribed to the model of paternalistic oversight. Controlling workers' living space by standardizing the built environment appears to have been part of Herr's ideal for an industrial community. Herr constructed a row house for his workers that consisted of a standardized façade, much like the row houses found in northeastern industrial communities. Archaeology shows that each house had a standardized floor plan on at least the first floor. Herr built his family's dwelling on the other side of the railroad tracks from his mill and the workers' housing, keeping both places within close eyesight of the owner (Palus 2000).

Other archaeologists have examined the relationship between the built environment, town plans, and paternalistic oversight. In the American Southwest, many of the company mining towns and large labor encampments from the late-19th century usually followed a grid pattern that reflected order and rationality, while the smaller towns formed in linear strips along roadways. Such strategies allowed owners to easily account for their workforce. Donald Hardesty's work in the American West provides

considerable attention to the composition of settlements and households. He shows that hierarchy and power are explicit in town layouts (Hardesty 1988:13–14,88; 1998).

Working Conditions at Labor Sites

Factory owners often characterized unproductive workers as unreliable, careless, or lazy. Many interpret this behavior as a deliberate attempt to resist the dominance of a machine-based system of production that left operatives with little room for personal autonomy or craft pride (Prude 1983; Scott 1990). While craftsmen often owned their own means of production and were likely to treat them with care, factory workers had little loyalty to the machines that someone else owned. "Some workers abused their machinery to show that they had little traditional pride in or attachment to their machines or to the products they made" (Zonderman 1992: 48). Workers broke machinery through various acts of sabotage in an effort to reassert the primacy of human beings over machines (Paynter 1989; Paynter and McGuire 1991).

Goods were sometimes stolen even though operatives knew that they could be fired if caught. Yet pilfering was seen by operatives as a way to "even the score" and compensate for low wages. "If they were denied what they saw as the full value of their labor, they would find a way to get what they thought was due them" (Zonderman 1992:196). Operatives were also rumored to have taken revenge by setting fires to factories. While they might have lost their jobs, they could have easily found another one at another factory in a neighboring town. In one instance, suspicious fires occurred at the Springfield Armory in 1842, when the armory management was shifted from civilian to military control. Neither the armorers nor the surrounding community helped to extinguish the fires (Zonderman 1992:196).

Factory workers' search for freedom and their expression of grievances against entrepreneurs were expressed from the outset of industrialization by quitting and moving to other jobs, rather than staying and fighting for change to alleviate the boredom, tedium, and low wages of factory labor. In some ways, the workers' transient state undermined their stability and strength as they lacked the cohesiveness for social and labor change. This does not mean that protests were nonexistent. They did occur, but often they were less collective and less overt than strikes. The earliest organized strike occurred in the early 1820s. By the 1830s and 1840s, regional labor organizations became more powerful in the Northeast. The number of strikes increased dramatically thereafter (Dublin 1977, 1979; Foner 1977; Vogel 1977; Prude 1983; Stansell 1986; Zonderman 1992:197–203). The shift from craft to industry continued into the early-20th century (Fonse-Wolf 1996). When workers were not powerful enough to organize a strike, they protested by work slowdowns, working on their own projects in the factory, and theft (Scott 1990; Bruno 1998:5,11–19).

Finding labor discontent in the archaeological record often means providing a thorough contextual analysis of the labor conditions. One example is the archaeological excavation performed by Michael Nassaney and Marjorie Abel (1993) at the John Russell Cutlery Company in the Connecticut River Valley. Their study shows how discontented workers challenged the existing power structure found in the workplace. Archaeologists found a large quantity of artifacts related to interchangeable manufacturing along the riverbank near the former cutting room and trip hammer shop. These objects tended to be inferior or imperfectly manufactured parts. While it would be easy to conclude that these artifacts form a typical industrial waste pile, the archaeologists looked at the larger context of 19th-century industrial labor relations in which discontented workers often broke machinery, tools, or products. Nassaney and Abel proposed that the abundance of imperfectly manufactured parts might represent a form of defiance against the implementation of the new industrial work system. Their work shows that by understanding context, knowing that discontent existed when manufacturing shifted to the new industrial system that alienated the work process, new interpretations can be developed related to labor and working conditions at industrial sites.

The study of labor protest camps such as the Ludlow Tent Colony Site in Colorado serves as another good example of how archaeologists may explore issues related to labor concerns and living conditions for workers and their families. The Colorado coal strike ignited a yearlong cycle of violence beginning in 1913 and culminated when the militia charged the tent colony and set fire to the tents, killing 2 women and 11 children. A guerilla-style war ensued for 10 days, and the miners attacked militia encampments, mine guards, and coalmines. The United Mine Workers of America (UMWA) ran out of funds to support the workers, and the strike was soon over. The workers received few concessions for their struggle. Through the archaeology of the tent colony, the Ludlow cooperative is exploring questions about the formation of temporary communities, protest labor movements, and government and military intervention. More important, the archaeology at Ludlow, which is supported by the UMWA, raises the visibility of this bloody episode in labor relations. It is helping make this incident part of the broader public memory (Walker 2000; Ludlow Collective 2001; McGuire and Reckner 2002; Wood 2002).

Another study related to labor unrest focuses on the bottling works associated with the Harpers Ferry brewery. While monitoring some of the stabilization and rehabilitation of the building, archaeologists found more than 100 empty beer bottles stashed behind the wall lathing in the former bottling room. They also discovered more than 1,000 beer bottles in the basement of the bottling works' elevator shaft, most of them broken after falling more than two stories (Shackel 2000a:104–113). In the 19th century, the typical brewery worker labored about 14 hours a day, 6 days per week, and on Sunday for about half this time. By 1910 brewery unions had successfully fought for a 10-hour workday. Workers were exposed to radical temperature shifts and breathed air contaminated with carbonic acid and sulfuric acid. Diseases like tuberculosis were common. Brewery-related accidents were almost 30% higher than in other industrial trades because of the higher speeds of machinery (Hull-Walksi and Walski 1994). The archaeological evidence suggests that workers drank the owners' profits and concealed their subversive behavior by disposing of the otherwise reusable bottles in walls and by dropping others down the elevator shaft. Fires at the brewery in 1897, 1906, and 1909 coincided with times of labor unrest in the brewery industry, highlighting the link between labor strife and acts of sabotage. Brewing unions eventually made major strides to improve the conditions of the workers (Shackel 2000a:104–113).

In another case study, Jed Levin (1985) compared the archaeological remains of the Telco Block and Supply Company site in New York City and the Supply Mill site in Billerica, Massachusetts (from Schuyler and Mills 1976). He noted that while entrepreneurs increasingly enforced an industrial discipline in the late-19th and early-20th centuries, there was a clear pattern of alcohol use by workers on the job site. Skilled workers often resisted the transition to industrial worker. The use of alcohol at these sites may have been a form of resisting work discipline.

Other Directions for a Labor Archaeology

Race

The questions related to labor archaeology are numerous, and they need to be made part of the national public memory. I have mentioned only a few case studies, but there are many issues that a labor archaeology can and should also address. For instance, the relationship between race and industry presents a unique opportunity for those interested in labor archaeology (Dew 1994; Shackel and Larsen 2000; Shackel 2001). Industrial slave labor is understudied and this topic has the potential to reveal not only the inequalities found between labor and capital, but it can also highlight the injustices found in race relations in an industrial context.

Ann Denkler's (2001:31–32) research on race in the Shenandoah Valley shows the importance of the iron industry in relationship to an agricultural community. In particular, the Catherine Furnace and the Shenandoah Iron Works, both dating to 1836, employed enslaved and freed blacks in the furnaces along with whites. Today, the tourist literature remembers the furnaces as important because they supported the Confederacy. Iron was shipped to Richmond and Harpers Ferry. No sources in the historical society mention the laborers at the site, nor do they recognize that African Americans, freed or enslaved, participated in the industry.

Race and labor relations also become an interesting part of the post-emancipation era story. After the Civil War, northern industrialists had a chance to hire and train a newly freed workforce.

Instead, industrialists turned to a new generation of European immigrants, thus shutting out African Americans in many northern industries and keeping many tied to tenant farming in the South (Horton 2000).

From the 1890s, northern industries began their large-scale flight to the South in search of cheaper unorganized labor (Carlton 1982). But before this transition could happen, a shift in the official memory of the Civil War was necessary. Until the 1890s the struggle for emancipation served as one of the official memories of the Civil War. But after the death of Frederick Douglass and the beginning of the Jim Crow era, the emancipationist view of the war lost out to a reconciliationists' memory. Reconciliation developed between white northerners and white southerners, making African Americans and the issues of slavery and the rights of full citizenship for blacks no longer part of the Civil War story (Shackel 2003a).

Many white southerners experienced a difficult transition into industrial capitalism. They found themselves in an increasingly individualistic and competitive society, and they suffered through the economic recessions of the 1880s and the depression of the 1890s. The move to revitalize a Confederate heritage helped southerners cope with defeat and the imposition of the new industrial order in the South (McConnell 1992:213). Whites worked in the new southern industries and African Americans remained disenfranchised. An industrial archaeology in the postbellum South as well as the North needs to understand the local and regional contexts for labor, and it must look at the issue of race.

The archaeology of Buxton, Iowa, performed in the early 1980s, examines the material remains of a predominantly black coal-mining town. The place thrived as an interracial town that was mainly inhabited by African Americans in the first quarter of the 20th century. The minority of the population consisted of European-derived nationalities. One newspaper called it "the Negro Athens of the north" (quoted in Gradwohl and Osborn 1984: 192). Archaeologists demonstrated through the material remains that the residents were part of the regional, national, and international trade networks. The spatial layout is a reflection of power and separations. The superintendents' residences stood on an isolated scenic hilltop across a valley and overlooking the main part of town (Gradwohl and Osborn 1984:192).

While African Americans were disenfranchised from industrial labor in the South, other ethnic groups had to fight prejudices too. For instance, while there was a large migration of Chinese workers to America during the California Gold Rush in the 1850s, they became unwelcome competition for employment by the early 1870s. Embracing Social Darwinism, many Anglos considered the Chinese to be less than human; anthropologists placed them on the lower end of the evolutionary scale. Chinese immigrants had few legal rights and could be legally discriminated against. By 1882, the United States legally barred people of Chinese descent from migrating to the United States (Chan 1991; Choy 1995; Salyer 1995).

The National Register nomination, Chinese Mining Camp Archaeological Site – Idaho (Elliott 1994), provides evidence of Chinese workers keeping strong material and cultural ties to their heritage at the work site and on the domestic front while they faced severe discrimination. The government prohibited Chinese workers in the Warren Mining District until 1869, and only after 1870 were they allowed to lease mining operations, although they could not purchase any land. Between 1870 and 1910, five separate Chinese companies mined in the Warren District. Archaeologists found the remains of canvas and repair tools, indicating that workers constructed impermanent homes in a distinctive Chinese style. Their assemblage contained imported Asian goods such as kitchen utensils and opium bottles, and the workers built Chinese-style garden terraces. Their mining techniques and tools were also different from those of the European Americans. The archaeological record shows that the workers at this mining camp retained their strong Chinese heritage on the domestic front (Striker and Sprague 1993).

Environment, Health, and Industry

Labor archaeology should examine the health conditions at industrial sites and towns. For instance, many mining sites endangered the health and life of workers. Work sites were often unstable, machinery often malfunctioned, pollution and harmful fumes contaminated the air, and workers often put in exhaustive work hours. These are all variables that led to accidents, chronic illnesses, and deaths. Industrialists were known for their efforts to accelerate machinery; the result was increased fatigue and an increased rate of injuries for workers (Schivelbusch 1986). Until about the mid-20th century, industrialists paid little attention to the impact that factories had on the surrounding environment until workers, scientists, and environmentalists brought these issues to the forefront of the American conscience.

One well-known example of the impact of environmental stress and pollution on the health of a working community comes from Donora, a town along the Monongahela River in Pennsylvania. Incorporated in 1901, the town contained coke ovens, coal stoves, zinc furnaces, metal works, and steel mills. The shrieking mill whistles guided the daily routines of its citizens (Davis 2002b:6). Fumes from the town's industrial plants became part of the everyday environment. The landscape stood mostly barren of vegetation because of these poisonous gasses (Davis 2002a:B9). Oral accounts attest to the extreme pollution as women reminisced about washing their curtains every week: by the time the women washed all of the windows in a house, the first one was dirty again. It was common to see elderly people in town with oxygen tanks. One person remarked, "Well, we used to say, 'That's not coal dust, that's gold dust.' As long as the mills were working, the town was in business. That's what kept your Zadde and your father employed. Nobody was going to ask if it made a few people ill. People had to eat" (Davis 2002b:8). Donora's death rate was significantly higher than that of the surrounding nonindustrial towns.

Donora became infamous on 26 October 1948 when massive blinding smog covered the town. A temperature inversion over the entire Monongahela Valley trapped the smoke and fumes of the steel mills and zinc furnace. The fumes became so thick that traffic stopped along its roads because drivers could not see in front of them. The noxious poisons killed 24 people in 24 hours. The steelworkers' union sponsored an investigative study into the sudden deaths of the workers and townspeople of Donora. Only partial and preliminary reports exist. The scanty information shows that those who died had 12 to 25 times the normal level of fluoride in their blood, a clear case of fluoride poisoning. While the investigative team never produced a final report, and the source of poison was never officially identified, the incident at Donora made the country more aware of the impact of air pollution on human health (Davis 2002b:15–25).

In a study of human osteological remains, comparing medieval urban and early industrial sites in England, Mary Lewis (2002) shows the devastating impact of industrialization on children. Children from industrial towns showed a higher rate of mortality, retarded growth, higher levels of stress, and a greater prevalence of metabolic and infectious diseases. Children from an industrial town were also more than an inch shorter than those from a contemporary urban trading town. While differences in urban and rural populations did exist in the past, Lewis (2002) argues that industrialization had the greatest impact on children's health.

Archaeology can be an important tool to examine working and living conditions at industrial towns. Archeologists have demonstrated the effectiveness of using soil samples from the area in and around factories and dwellings to search for toxins to examine general health conditions. Privy samples at workplaces may reveal the presence of parasites and other toxins, indications of poor health and resistance to paternalism (Reinhard et al. 1986; Beaudry et al. 1991; Reinhard 1994). Pollen and macrofloral samples may also supply some indication of the changing landscape and its relationship to changing ideals related to industrialization (Mrozowski et al. 1989; Cummings 1994; Rovner 1994). Exploring general sanitation landscape features (Ford 1994) and identifying the presence of medicinal and alcohol bottles may provide clues regarding workers' general health (Bond 1989; Larsen 1994). The impact of industrial pollution has had a devastating impact on human populations. It is important that these issues are made part of the story of industry and labor.

Conclusion

When we look at the historical American industrial landscape, we often see renovated buildings and stabilized ruins that tell the story of our early industrial prowess. These structures are often interpreted as a reminder of industry and stand mute when it comes to telling the story of labor practices. In 1878, Abraham J. Ryan wrote about a land of ruins in the postbellum South:

> A land without ruins is a land without memories, a land without memories is a land without liberty. A land that wears a laurel crown may be fair to see; but twine a few sad cypress leaves around the brow of any land, and, be that land barren, beautiless, and bleak, it becomes lovely in its consecrated cornet of sorrow, and it wins the sympathy of the heart and of history (quoted in Wilson 1980:59).

Industrial ruins may win the hearts of history, and they are a way to remember a prosperous economic past, but we also need to make sure that they are part of the memory of a labor archaeology.

Michael Shanks and Randall McGuire (1996) remind us that the act of archaeology is a form of commemoration. When we do archaeology, we create a memory of the past that is rooted in our present-day concerns. Therefore, labor archaeology can be a way to remember and unveil a history that has been buried all too long. The work at Lowell, Harpers Ferry, the Chinese Mining Camp, and mining sites in Nevada, the John Russell Cutlery factory, and Ludlow show that a labor archaeology may effectively address labor's heritage.

Politics will always impact the way we develop labor's history. For instance, during the Reagan and G. H.W. Bush administrations, Lynne Cheney, chair of the National Endowment for the Humanities, argued in her report to Congress that scholars were occupying themselves with issues related to gender, race, and class (Nash et al. 1998:103). She discouraged funding projects that encouraged a pluralistic view of the past. Cheney packed the Advisory Council with critics of multiculturalism and the committee rejected proposals if they questioned consensus history. NEH sharply curtailed any projects dealing with women, labor, racial groups, or any project that might conflict with the national collective memory (Nash at al. 1998:103). At about the same time columnist George Wills (1991:72) wrote that these scholars were "forces ... fighting against the conservation of the common culture that is the nation's social cement."

Recently, Secretary of the Interior Gail Norton rescinded the National Historic Landmark designation of the Fresno Sanitary Landfill because of the negative connotations associated with the site (Melosi 2002). The site was nominated for NHL status because it represents an important engineering innovation in the United States. The landfill developed because refuse could be buried and rendered inert and could not pose a health hazard or a nuisance. Landfills came into wide use after World War II because of the success of the Fresno Sanitary Landfill, and they became the primary disposal option for Americans for the second half of the 20th century. Unfortunately, the Fresno Sanitary Landfill did not have a liner, and hazardous substances were found in the adjacent groundwater. The site was closed in 1987, and it became a superfund site in 1989. The Fresno Sanitary Landfill operated for more than 50 years. Many historians consider it as the oldest "true" landfill in the United States (Melosi 2002:23–26). Unfortunately, the Bush administration, which has received increasing pressure from environmental groups (like the Sierra Club) for its environmental policies, does not want to be associated with a landfill or a landfill that is also known as a superfund site, despite its historical significance to American industrial technology.

There are always lessons and alternative views at many significant historic sites. They are places not only to celebrate our past but also to learn lessons about our history. If we look at industrial sites, there is always a counter memory to the importance of technological advancement. For instance, what about historic mills? Their history is about technological development and entrepreneurship, but it is also about exploitation of workers. And what about coal mining towns? Coal extraction was about technology and profit, but the process also destroyed landscapes and polluted water (Melosi 2002:34). These are all examples of the American past that we choose to remember and use to teach us about the past by making them part of our official history. I wonder, then, if a place that celebrates labor strife and workers' struggles for decent wages like Ludlow could receive NHL designation in today's political climate.

No matter the political climate, archaeologists should endeavor to make labor issues part of the official history of the United States. One way is to nominate these sites to the National Register of Historic Places and as National Historic Landmarks. We are all agents who have crucial moral and political choices to make. History is shaped by human intervention, and while tough choices and stances were made in the past, we need to confront what we study and how to remember our past. Designating industrial places as a prominent part of our past should also be about remembering people and their struggles. The question for all of us working at industrial sites is this: Will archaeologists working at industrial sites be courageous like the town of Lawrence, Massachusetts, and commemorate labor's heritage, or will we choose to celebrate capital and create an official history that glorifies technology at the expense of labor? That is the challenge, I believe, for any professional working in industrial contexts.

ACKNOWLEDGMENTS

A brief version of this article was presented at the plenary session at the 36th Annual Conference on Historical and Underwater Archaeology, Providence, Rhode Island. Several people were kind enough to share several sources, including Brett Burk, Bob Chidester, Terrance Martin, Randy McGuire, and Larry Zimmerman. Barbara Little and Matthew Palus provided valuable feedback on earlier drafts of this paper. I also appreciate the comments provided to me by the three journal reviewers: Thad Van Bueren, Adrian Praetzellis, and Karen Metheny.

REFERENCES

BEAUDRY, MARY C., LAUREN J. COOK, AND STEPHEN A. MROZOWSKI
1991 Artifacts as Active Voices: Material Culture as Social Discourse. In *The Archaeology of Inequality*, Randall H. McGuire and Robert Paynter, editors, pp. 150–191. Basil Blackwell, New York.

BEAUDRY, MARY C., AND STEPHEN A. MROZOWSKI
1989 The Archaeology of Work and Home Life in Lowell, Massachusetts: An Interdisciplinary Study of the Boott Cotton Mills Corporation. *IA, The Journal of the Society for Industrial Archeology*, 19(2):1–22.

BOND, K. H.
1989 The Medicine, Alcohol, and Soda Vessels from the Boott Mills. In Interdisciplinary Investigations of the Boott Mills, Lowell, Massachusetts, Vol. 3, The Boarding House System as a Way of Life, Mary C. Beaudry and Stephen A. Mrozowski, editors, pp. 121–140. *Cultural Resources Management Study*, No. 21. U.S. Department of the Interior, National Park Service. North Atlantic Regional Office, Boston, MA.

BRASHLER, JANET G.

1991 When Daddy Was a Shanty Boy: The Role of Gender in the Organization of the Logging Industry in Highland West Virginia. *Historical Archaeology,* 25(4):54–68.

BRODY, DAVID

1979 The Old Labor History and the New. *Labor History,* 20(1):111–21.

1980 Labor History in the 1980s: Toward a History of the American Worker. In *The Past before Us: Contemporary Historical Writing in the United States,* Michael Kammen, editor, pp. 252–69. Cornell University Press, Ithaca, NY.

1989 Labor History, Industrial Relations, and the Crisis of American Labor. *Industrial and Labor Relations Review,* 43(1):5–18.

1993 *In Labor's Cause: Main Themes on the History of the American Worker.* Oxford University Press, New York.

BRUNO, ROBERT

1998 Working, Playing, and Fighting for Control: Steelworkers and Shopfloor Identity. *Labor Studies Journal,* 28 (Spring):3–30.

BURNETT, JOHN

1978 *A Social History of Housing 1815–1970.* Davis and Charles, London, England.

BUTLER, WILLIAM B.

1999 The Grand Lake Lodge Sawmill, Rocky Mountain National Park, Grand County, Colorado. *Southwest Lore,* 65(1):9–42.

CAPLINGER, MICHAEL

1997 *Bridges over Time: A Technological Context for the Baltimore and Ohio Railroad Main Stem at Harpers Ferry, West Virginia.* Institute for the History of Technology and Industrial Archaeology, Morgantown, WV.

CARLTON, DAVID L.

1982 *Mill and Town in South Carolina, 1880–1920.* Louisiana State University Press, Baton Rouge.

CHAN, SUCHENG (EDITOR)

1991 *Entry Denied: Exclusion and the Chinese Community in America, 1882–1943.* Temple University Press, Philadelphia, PA.

CHOY, PHILIP P.

1995 *Coming Man: 19th-Century American Perceptions of the Chinese.* University of Washington Press, Seattle.

CLARK, C. M.

1987 Trouble at T'Mill: Industrial Archaeology in the 1980s. *Antiquity,* 61(232):169–179.

COSTELLO, JULIA G.

1998 Bread Fresh from the Oven: Memories of Italian Breadbaking in the California Mother Lode. *Historical Archaeology,* 32(1):66–73.

CUMMINGS, LINDA SCOTT

1994 Diet and Prehistoric Landscape during the Nineteenth- and Early-Twentieth Centuries at Harpers Ferry, West Virginia: A View from the Old Master Armorer's Complex. *Historical Archaeology,* 28(4):94–105.

DAVIS, DEVRA LEE

2002a The Heavy Air of Donora, Pa. *The Chronicle Review: The Chronicle of Higher Education,* Section 2:B7–B12.

2002b *When Smoke Ran Like Water: Tales of Environmental Deception and the Battle against Pollution.* Basic Books, New York.

DENKLER, ANN

2001 Sustaining Identity, Recapturing Heritage: Exploring Issues of Public History, Tourism, and Race in a Southern Rural Town. Doctoral dissertation, American Studies, University of Maryland.

DEW, CHARLES B.

1994 *Bonds of Iron: Master and Slave at Buffalo Forge.* W.W. Norton and Co., New York.

DUBLIN, THOMAS

1977 "Women, Work, and Protest in the Early Lowell Mills; 'The Oppressing Hand of Avarice Would Enslave Us.'" In *Class, Sex, and the Women Worker,* Milton Cantor and Bruce Ware, editors, pp. 43–63. Greenwood Press, Westport, CT.

1979 *Women at Work: The Transformation of Work and Community in Lowell, Massachusetts, 1826–1860.* Columbia University Press, New York.

ELLIOTT, JOHN H.

1994 Chinese Mining Camp Archaeological Site, Warren Mining District 01IH1961. National Register Nomination. U.S. Department of the Interior, National Park Service, Washington, DC.

FONER, PHILIP S. (EDITOR)

1977 *The Factory Girls.* University of Illinois Press, Urbana.

FONSE-WOLF, KEN

1996 From Craft to Industrial Unionism in the Window-Glass Industry: Clarksburg, West Virginia, 1900–1937. *Labor History,* 37(1):28–49.

FORD, BENJAMIN

1994 The Health and Sanitation of Postbellum Harpers Ferry. *Historical Archaeology,* 28(4):49–61.

GORDON, ROBERT B.

1988 Material Evidence of the Manufacturing Methods Used in "Armory Practice." *IA, The Journal of the Society for Industrial Archeology,* 14(1):23–36.

2001 *A Landscape Transformed: The Iron Making District of Salisbury, Connecticut.* Oxford University Press, New York.

GORDON, ROBERT B., AND PATRICK M. MALONE
    1994 *The Texture of Industry: An Archaeological View of the Industrialization of North America.* Oxford University Press, New York.

GRADWOHL, DAVID M., AND NANCY M. OSBORN
    1984 *Exploring Buried Buxton: Archaeology of an Abandoned Iowa Coal Mining Town with a Large Black Population.* The Iowa State University Press, Ames.

GREEN, JAMES
    2000 *Taking History to Heart: The Power of the Past in Building Social Movements.* University of Massachusetts Press, Amherst.

GUTMAN, HERBERT
    1976 *Work, Culture, and Society in Industrializing America: Essays in American Working Class and Social History.* Alfred Knopf, New York.

HARDESTY, DONALD
    1988 The Archaeology of Mining and Miners: A View from the Silver State. The Society for Historical Archaeology, *Special Publication Series,* No. 6. California, PA.
    1998 Power and the Industrial Mining Community in the American West. In *Social Approaches to an Industrial Past: The Archaeology and Anthropology of Mining,* A. Bernard Knapp, Vincent C. Pigott, and Eugenia W. Herbert, editors, pp. 81–96. Routledge, London.

HAREVEN, TAMARA T.
    1982 *Family Tie and Industrial Time: The Relationship between the Family and Work in a New England Industrial Community.* Cambridge University Press, New York.

HARSHBERGER, P.
    2002 Brooklyn: Review of the 31st Annual Conference. *Society for Industrial Archeology Newsletter,* 31(3–4): 1–2, 4–5, 7–10.

HEITE, EDWARD F.
    1993 Can Sizes and Waste at the Lebanon Cannery Site: Unscrewing the Inscrutable. *Archaeological Society of Delaware Bulletin,* 30:43–48.

HOLLEY, I. B., JR.
    2001 Steamrollers: Those Majestic Machines. *IA, The Journal of the Society for Industrial Archeology,* 27(2):37–48.

HORTON, JAMES
    2000 Freedom Fighters: African Americans, Slavery, and the Coming Age of the Civil War. Paper presented at the National Park Service Symposium on Strengthening Interpretation of the Civil War Era. Ford's Theater National Historic Site, Washington, DC, May 9.

HOWE, DENIS E.
    1994 Industrial Archaeology: A Survey of Research in New Hampshire. *New Hampshire Archeologist,* 33–34(1): 105–113.

HUDSON, KENNETH
    1971 *A Guide to the Industrial Archaeology of Europe.* Fairleigh Dickinson University Press, Madison, NJ.
    1978 *Food, Clothes, and Shelter: Twentieth-Century Industrial Archaeology.* J. Baker, London.
    1979 *World Industrial Archaeology.* Cambridge University Press, New York.

HULL-WALSKI, DEBORAH A., AND FRANK WALSKI
    1994 There's Trouble a- Brewin,: The Brewing and Bottling Industries at Harpers Ferry, West Virginia. *Historical Archaeology,* 28(4):106–121.

KASSON, JOHN F.
    1979 *Civilizing the Machine: Technology and Republican Values in America, 1776–1900.* Penguin Books, New York.

KEMP, EMORY L.
    1996 *Industrial Archaeology: Techniques.* Krieger Publishing Co., Malabar, FL.

KNAPP, A. BERNARD
    1998 Introduction. In *Social Approaches to an Industrial Past: The Archaeology and Anthropology of Mining,* A. Bernard Knapp, Vincent C. Pigott, and Eugenia W. Herbert, editors, pp. 1–23. Routledge, London.

KUMAR, PRADEEP
    1992 *A Structural Analysis of Patented Bollman Suspension Trusses.* Institute for the History of Technology and Industrial Archaeology, Morgantown, WV.

LANDON, DAVID, PATRICK MARTIN, ANDREW SEWELL, PAUL WHITE, TIMOTHY TUMBERG, AND JASON MENARD
    2001 "…A Monument to Misguided Enterprise": The Carp River Bloomery Iron Forge. *IA, The Journal of the Society for Industrial Archeology,* 27(2):5–22.

LARSEN, ERIC
    1994 A Boardinghouse Madonna: Beyond the Aesthetics of a Portrait Created through Medicine Bottles. *Historical Archaeology,* 28(4):68–79.

LEARY, T. E.
    1979 Industrial Archeology and Industrial Ecology. *Radical History Review,* 21:171–182.

LEWIS, MARY E.
    2002 Impact of Industrialization: Comparative Study of Child Health in Four Sites from Medieval and Postmedieval England (A.D. 850–1859). *American Journal of Physical Anthropology,* 119(3):211–223.

LEVIN, JED
    1985 Drinking on the Job: How Effective Was Capitalist Work Discipline? *American Archaeology,* 5(3):195–201.

LOWE, JEREMY
    1982 Housing as a Source for Industrial History: A Case Study of Blaenafon, A Welsh Ironworks Settlement, from 1788 to c.1845. *IA, The Journal of the Society for Industrial Archeology,* 8(1):13–36.

LOWENTHAL, DAVID
    1985   *The Past Is a Foreign Country.* Cambridge University Press, Cambridge, MA.

LUCAS, MICHAEL
    1994   An Armory Worker's Life: Glimpses of Industrial Life. In An Archeology of an Armory Worker's Household: Park Building 48, Harpers Ferry National Historical Park, Paul A. Shackel, editor, pp. 5.1–5.40. *Occasional Report*, No. 12, U.S. Department of the Interior, National Park Service, Washington, DC.

LUCAS, MICHAEL, AND PAUL A. SHACKEL
    1994   Changing Social and Material Routine in Nineteenth-Century Harpers Ferry. *Historical Archaeology*, 28(4): 27–36.

LUDLOW COLLECTIVE
    2001   Archaeology of the Colorado Coal Field War, 1913–1914. In *Archaeologies of the Contemporary Past*, V. Buchli and G. Lucas, editors, pp. 94–107. Routledge Press, London.

MALONE, PATRICK M.
    1988   Little Kinks and Devices at Springfield Armory, 1892–1918. *IA, The Journal of the Society for Industrial Archeology*, 14(1):59–76.

MARTIN, PATRICK E.
    2003   The Archaeology of Industrialization. Paper presented at the 36th Annual Conference on Historical and Underwater Archaeology, Providence, RI.

MARX, LEO
    1964   *The Machine in the Garden: Technology and the Pastoral Ideal in America.* Oxford University Press, New York.

McCONNELL, STUART
    1992   *Glorious Contentment: The Grand Army of the Republic, 1865–1900.* The University of North Carolina Press, Chapel Hill.

McGUIRE, RANDALL H., AND PAUL RECKNER
    2002   The Unromantic West: Labor, Capital, and Struggle. *Historical Archaeology*, 36(3):44–58.

MELOSI, MARTIN V.
    2002   National Historic Landmarks: Controversies and Definitions. The Fresno Sanitary Landfill in an American Cultural Context. *Public Historian*, 24(3): 17–35.

MILLER, CAROL POH
    2003   Study Tour Takes a Close-Up Look at Sweden's Industrial Heritage. *Society for Industrial Archeology Newsletter*, 31(1):1–8,17.

MINCHINTON, WALTER
    1983   World Industrial Archaeology: A Survey. *World Archaeology*, 15(2):125–136.

MONTGOMERY, DAVID
    1979   *Worker's Control in America: Studies in the History of Work, Technology, and Labor Struggle.* Cambridge University Press, New York.

MROZOWSKI, STEPHEN A., GRACE H. ZEISING, AND MARY C. BEAUDRY
    1996   *Living on the Boott: Historical Archaeology at the Boott Mills Boardinghouses, Lowell, Massachusetts.* University of Massachusetts Press, Amherst.

MROZOWSKI, S. A., E. L. BELL, M. C. BEAUDRY, D. B. LANDON, AND G. K. KELSO
    1989   Living on the Boott: Health and Well Being in a Boardinghouse Population. *World Archaeology*, 21(2):298–319.

NASH, GARY B., CHARLOTTE CRABTREE, AND ROSS E. DUNN
    1998   *History on Trial: Culture Wars and the Teaching of the Past.* Knopf, New York.

NASSANEY, MICHAEL S., AND MARJORIE R. ABEL
    1993   The Political and Social Contexts of Cutlery Production in the Connecticut Valley. *Dialectical Anthropology*, 18(3–4):247–289.

PALMER, MARILYN
    1990   Industrial Archaeology: A Thematic or a Period Discipline? *Antiquity*, 64(243):275–282.

PALMER, MARILYN, AND PETER NEAVERSON
    1998   *Industrial Archaeology: Principles and Practice.* Routledge, New York.

PALUS, MATTHEW
    2000   *"They Worked Regular": Archaeology of the Virginius Island Mill Community, Package 123 in Harpers Ferry National Historical Park, Harpers Ferry, West Virginia.* U.S. Department of the Interior, National Park Service, Harpers Ferry National Historical Park, Harpers Ferry, WV.

PAYNTER, ROBERT
    1989   The Archaeology of Equality and Inequality. *Annual Review of Anthropology*, 18:369–99.

PAYNTER, ROBERT, AND RANDALL H. McGUIRE
    1991   The Archaeology of Inequality: Material Culture, Domination, and Resistance. In *The Archaeology of Inequality*, McGuire and Paynter, editors, pp. 1–27. Basil Blackwell, Cambridge, MA.

PLETKA, KARYN L.
    1993   Industrial Archaeology at the Robinson-Herring Sawmill Site, Greenbush, Wisconsin. *Michigan Archaeologist*, 39(1):1–35.

PRUDE, JONATHAN
    1983   *The Coming of Industrial Order: Town and Factory Life in Rural Massachusetts, 1810–1860.* Cambridge University Press, New York.

REINHARD, K. J.
1994 Sanitation and Parasitism of Postbellum Harpers Ferry. *Historical Archaeology,* 28(4):63–67.

REINHARD, K. J., S. A. MROZOWSKI, AND K. A. ORLOSKI
1986 Privies, Pollen, Parasites, and Seeds: A Biological Nexus in Historical Archaeology. *MASCA Journal,* 4(1):31–36.

ROVNER, IRWIN
1994 Floral History by the Back Door: A Test of Phytolith Analysis in Residential Yards at Harpers Ferry. *Historical Archaeology,* 28(4):37–48.

SALYER, LUCY E.
1995 *Laws Harsh as Tigers: Chinese Immigrants and the Shaping of Modern Immigration Law.* University of North Carolina Press, Chapel Hill.

SCHIVELBUSCH, WOLFGANG
1986 *The Railway Journey: The Industrialization of Time and Space in the Nineteenth Century.* University of California Press, Berkeley.

SCHUYLER, ROBERT L., AND CHRISTOPHER MILLS
1976 The Supply Mill on Content Brook in Massachusetts. *Journal of Field Archaeology,* 3(1):61–95.

SCOTT, JAMES
1990 *Hidden Transcripts: Domination and the Arts of Resistance.* Yale University Press, New Haven, CT.

SHACKEL, PAUL A.
1996 *Culture Change and the New Technology: An Archaeology of the Early American Industrial Era.* Plenum Press, New York.
1999a Public Memory and the Rebuilding the Nineteenth-Century Industrial Landscape at Harpers Ferry. *Quarterly Bulletin: Archeological Society of Virginia,* 54(3):138–144.
1999b Town Planning and Nineteenth-Century Industrial Life in Harpers Ferry. In The Archaeology of 19th-Century Virginia, Theodore R. Reinhart and John H. Sprinkle, Jr., editors, pp. 341–364. Council of Virginia Archaeologists, *Special Publication,* No. 36 of the Archeological Society of Virginia.
2000a *Archaeology and Created Memory: Public History in a National Park.* Klewer Academic/Plenum Publishing Corp., New York.
2000b Craft to Wage Labor: Agency and Resistance in American Historical Archaeology. In *Agency Theory in Archaeology,* John Robb and Marcia-Anne Dobres, editors, pp. 232–246. Routledge Press, London.
2001 Public Memory and the Search for Power in American Historical Archaeology. *American Anthropologist,* 102(3):1–16.
2003a *Memory in Black and White: Race, Commemoration, and the Post-Bellum Landscape.* AltaMira Press, Walnut Creek, CA.
2003b Remembering the American Industrial Landscape. Paper presented at the 36th Annual Conference on Historical and Underwater Archaeology, Providence, RI.

SHACKEL, PAUL A., AND DAVID L. LARSEN
2000 Labor, Racism, and the Built Environment in Early Industrial Harpers Ferry. In *Lines That Divide: Historical Archaeologies of Race, Class, and Gender,* James Delle, Robert Paynter, and Stephen Mrozowski, editors, pp. 22–39. University of Tennessee Press, Knoxville.

SHACKEL, PAUL A., AND SUSAN E. WINTER (EDITORS)
1994 An Archaeology of Harpers Ferry's Commercial and Residential District. *Historical Archaeology,* 28(4).

SHANKS, MICHAEL, AND RANDALL H. MCGUIRE
1996 The Craft of Archaeology. *American Antiquity,* 61(1996):75–88.

SHELTON, CYNTHIA
1986 *The Mills of Manayunk: Industrialization and Social Conflict in the Philadelphia Region, 1787–1837.* The Johns Hopkins University Press, Baltimore, MD.

SMITH, MERRITT ROE
1977 *Harpers Ferry Armory and the New Technology: The Challenge of Change.* Cornell University Press, Ithaca, NY.

SOLURY, THERESA E.
1999 The Labor History Theme Study: Archaeology Component. Draft version manuscript. National Register of Historic Places, National Park Service, Washington, DC.

STANSELL, CHRISTINE
1986 *City of Women: Sex and Class in New York, 1789–1860.* Alfred A. Knopf, New York.

STRATTON, MICHAEL, AND BARRIE TRINDER
2000 *Twentieth-Century Industrial Archaeology.* E&FN Spon, London.

STRIKER, MICHAEL, AND RODERICK SPRAGUE
1993 Excavations at the Warren Chinese Mining Camp Site, 1989–1992. Report to the Forest Supervisor's Office, Payette National Forest, McCall, ID.

TEAGUE, GEORGE
1987 The Archaeology of Industry in North America. Doctoral dissertation, Department of Anthropology, University of Arizona.

TRINDER, BARRIE
1983 New Course in Industrial Archaeology. *World Archaeology,* 15(2):218–223.

TRINDER, B., AND N. COX (EDITORS)
2000 *Miners and Mariners of the Severn Gorge: Probate Inventories for Benthall, Broseley, Little Wenlock, and Madeley, 1660–1764.* Phillimore & Co., Ltd., Chichester, W. Sussex, England.

VAN BUEREN, THAD M. (EDITOR)
2002 Communities Defined by Work: Life in Western Work Camps. *Historical Archaeology,* 36(3).

VOGEL, LISE
1977   Hearts to Feel and Tongues to Speak: New England Mill Women in the Early-Nineteenth Century. In *Class, Sex, and the Woman Worker,* Milton Cantor and Bruce Ware, editors, pp. 64–82. Greenwood Press, Westport, CT.

WALKER, MARK
2000   Labor History at the Ground Level: Colorado Coalfield War Archaeology Project. *Labor's Heritage,* 11(1): 58–75.

WALLACE, ANTHONY F. C.
1978   *Rockdale: The Growth of an American Village in the Early Industrial Revolution.* Alfred Knopf, New York.

WEGARS, PRISCILLA
1991   Who's Been Workin' on the Railroad? An Examination of the Construction, Distribution, and Ethnic Origins of Domes Rock Ovens on Railroad Related Sites. *Historical Archaeology,* 25(2):37–60.

WEITZMAN, DAVID L.
1980   *Traces of the Past: A Field Guide to Industrial Archaeology.* Scribner, NY.

WERMIEL, SARA E.
2001   America's 19th-Century British-Style Fireproof Factories. *IA, Journal of the Society for Industrial Archeology,* 27(2): 23–36.

WESOLOWSKY, TONY
1996   A Jewel in the Crown of Old King Coal: Eckley Miners' Village. *Pennsylvania Heritage Magazine,* 22(1). <http://www.phmc.state.pa.us/ppet/eckley/> 17 July 2003.

WILLS, GEORGE F.
1991   The Politicization of Higher Education. *Newsweek,* 22 April:72.

WILSON, CHARLES REAGAN
1980   *Baptized by Blood: The Religion of the Lost Cause, 1865–1920.* University of Georgia Press, Athens.

WOOD, MARGARET
2002   Fighting for Our Homes: An Archaeology of Women's Domestic Labor and Social Change in a Working Class, Coal Mining Community, 1900–1930. Doctoral dissertation, Department of Anthropology, Syracuse University.

WORKMAN, MICHAEL E., PAUL SALSTROM, AND PHILIP W. ROSS
1994   *Northern West Virginia Coal Fields: Historical Context.* Institute for the History of Technology and Industrial Archaeology, Morgantown, WV.

ZONDERMAN, DAVID A.
1992   *Aspirations and Anxieties: New England Workers and the Mechanized Factory System, 1815–1850.* Oxford University Press, New York.

PAUL A. SHACKEL
DEPARTMENT OF ANTHROPOLOGY
UNIVERSITY OF MARYLAND
1111 WOODS HALL
UNIVERSITY OF MARYLAND
COLLEGE PARK, MD 20742

Matthew S. Tomaso
Richard F. Veit
Carissa A. DeRooy
Stanley L. Walling

Social Status and Landscape in a Nineteenth-Century Planned Industrial Alternative Community: Archaeology and Geography of Feltville, New Jersey

ABSTRACT

Feltville is located in Union County, New Jersey. This small-scale planned industrial village was designed and operated by David Felt, a liberal Unitarian printer and stationer, from 1845 to 1860. Archaeological and documentary materials recovered over the last six years paint a picture of conditions in Felt's rural industrial reformist alternative and provide a glimpse into the worldview of the community architect. Examination of Feltville and its historical context allows for the evaluation of the potential practical and theoretical contributions of historical archaeology in the study of utopian movements. Specifically, the diversity of sociopolitical ideals expressed prior to the advent of Marxian socialism calls into question the conflation of communalist and utopian social designs in some contemporary treatments.

Introduction: Questions of Utopia

Utopia, in real life and in text, has the dual sense of a society based on sociopolitical ideals and an escape from, or living critique of, that which is not ideal. Often, the authors of utopian and dystopian fact and fiction make their points by discussing the downfall of the ideal communities they imagine (Zamiatin 1952; Orwell 1961; Noyes 1966) or by providing purely theoretical idealizations of social forms that embed critiques of the sociohistorical contexts of the authors themselves (Bellamy 1967; More 1969). The most common tangible elements of past utopian societies are simply particular places and times—geographic boundaries, beginnings, and ends. Utopias, then, can be operationally defined as compromised realizations of political and/or social ideals, bounded in time and space.

As Friedrich Engels, Karl Marx, and many of their contemporaries remind us, the mid-19th century was, for the Western world, far from an ideal time and place for the common person. In the cities of the eastern United States of America, there was certainly plenty to escape from. The American industrial revolution, though still in its infancy, was reaching new heights of production and exploitation in 1845 when David Felt purchased a large tract of land in central New Jersey and built an industrial village that would later become known as Feltville (Figure 1).

Feltville, which operated as a papermaking and binding town from 1845 to 1860, has been characterized as a utopian community (Veit et al. 1999), but mention of its history is conspicuously absent in the numerous Fourierist, Owenist, and other tracts on social reform published during what has been called the "middle period" of American history (Holloway 1966; Nordhoff 1966; Noyes 1966; Guarneri 1991; Francis 1997). This characterization raises questions: If Feltville was, in fact, utopian, how so and to what extent? What was the vision behind its social engineering? Why was it "abandoned" in 1860 by Felt and, presumably, most of his laborers, and does this abandonment mark the end of its utopian phase? How can historical archaeologies of places like Feltville contribute ideas regarding social practice and theory to the social sciences and humanities? Finally, what happens to communities like Feltville as their utopian phases pass, and what can that history tell about the successes and failures of planned communities? These questions give rise to other, more challenging questions.

If *utopia* is to be defined as an ideal society, then it may be very difficult to discuss utopian communities in a general sense because ideals vary tremendously among political thinkers of any age. One aspect of utopianism is clear: it always presents an alternative to the dominant sociopolitical and economic order of the time and place. Perhaps the term *counter-hegemonic* is appropriate here. The Gramscian concept of hegemony does not rule out resistance to domination or existing power structures but, rather,

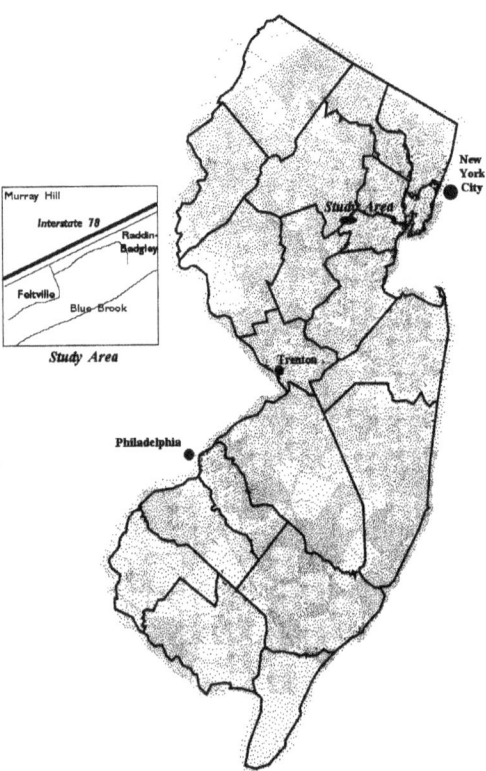

FIGURE 1. Location of the Feltville/Glenside Park study area in central New Jersey. (Drawing by Matthew S. Tomaso, 2002.)

points out the historical tendency of successful resistance to become encompassed within the ever-evolving hegemonic discourse. So, while resistance is certainly possible, hegemony, as a totalizing atemporal and ahistorical concept, cannot of itself be resisted. Eventually, hegemony moves also in the direction and flow of its own more successfully resistant elements (Gramsci 1971). One of the most powerful aspects of hegemony, it seems, is its ability to encompass a wide variety of political perspectives parsimoniously under the guise of "multivocality," or even freedom of speech.

What is not clear is how, and in what way, a community must be different in order to be called "utopian." Utopias of fiction are easier to digest than those of fact. Fictive utopias are often inhabited by people who are somewhat interchangeable with one another. In dystopian literature, utopias are usually doomed, and their ends are appropriately foreshadowed by a fatal flaw that always

seems to justify political-philosophical statements by the author or creator. More often than not, the message is something like "things really aren't all that bad right here and right now," or "while there are many things to criticize in the contemporary world, and many improvements which I have suggested, perfection is as unattainable in society as it is in human individuals, if not more so," or "don't sweat the small stuff." These facts concerning utopian fictions contrast strongly with utopian communities of reality. Utopian fiction is often used as critique, satire, and parody. Utopian reality is a lived experience, based on a compromise between social ideals and the real. The collapses of real utopias such as the North American Phalanx (Kirchmann 1980; Guarneri 1991) and several of the examples discussed in this volume and elsewhere (Reps 1965; Holloway 1966; Nordhoff 1966; Noyes 1966; Hayden 1976) occurred most commonly for economic reasons, sometimes coupled with natural disasters or corruption. Nevertheless, a definable beginning and end seem to be two of the unique aspects of utopian communities in fact and fiction. Most communities cannot be so precisely mapped in time or space. Perhaps it is ultimately the encompassing effect of hegemony that erases the temporal boundaries of more successful and long-lived utopian communities.

If a utopia were to survive or at least dissolve into mainstream society noncatastrophically, as Feltville apparently did, would we still call it utopian? Feltville, perceived as a utopia, is quite unusual if not unique. Its members do not appear to have suffered terribly from its eventual dissolution; it had only a few discernable communalistic aspects—a multidenominational church, Felt's factory, a school, and, possibly, a communal dining room. None of these was uncommon in factory towns of its time. Moreover, Feltville was presided over by a deeply but very liberally religious man who came to be known as King David. These and other elements of life and labor at Feltville distance it from both utopian movements and mainstream America of the antebellum period. Felt's ideal society does not appear to have been one founded on unifying political or religious beliefs.

It is not the intent of the authors to dismiss political economic thinking in this examination of the concept of utopia nor to stretch the concept of utopia beyond its usefulness. It is believed, however, that a holistic, contextual understanding of any utopian community, let alone entire diverse utopian movements such as those of 19th-century America, requires an open minded use of any and all aspects of information, interpretive thought, and source material. This is because utopias, on close inspection, seem to go to great lengths to differentiate themselves in as many respects as possible from that which has gone before. Perhaps this can be stated as a desire to be counter-hegemonic, even if the long-term goal is seldom, if ever, attained.

**Feltville Archaeology Project:
Theoretical and Historical Context**

The Feltville Archaeology Project (FAP) focuses on social issues, including the changing concepts of social identity, gender, class, and, perhaps, ethnicity, as they evolved at the local level and in conjunction with regional and national trends. Involved in this project are the analysis and comparison of the concrete conditions of everyday life at the village through techniques of historical geography and archaeology. The approach taken on the FAP could be described as contextual because all of the work is grounded in tangible archaeological and historical facts operating at multiple geographic and social scales (in the sense of Braudel 1980) and approached both hermeneutically and scientifically. The FAP is the longest-running academic historical archaeology project in New Jersey (Veit 2002).

With regard to Feltville's quasi-utopian phase, the FAP involves interpretation of the dynamics of social engineering at Feltville—Felt's ideological model for the village—approached both geographically and through documentary sources. Feltville includes an odd juxtaposition of Jeffersonian and romantic-period elements with the industrial optimism of the mainstream of Federalist society as well as the marriage of religious tolerance (at least a dozen different Christian sects attended Felt's church) and probably temperance. It is interesting to consider how all of this might have fed into the viability of the resort known as Glenside Park, which recycled Feltville's landscape and buildings in the late-19th century. These quasi-utopian notions also play a part in the contemporary development of the ideology of rustification, which is manifest

in several late-19th-century resorts and spas throughout the Adirondacks and the Mid-Atlantic and New England areas. The goal of the FAP is to contribute scholarship concerning local and alternative variations in the construction of class, gender, social identity, work discipline, and everyday life during the American industrial revolution.

**Feltville/Glenside Park: Context of
Mid-Nineteenth-Century Utopianism**

Feltville, located in central New Jersey, occupied a position between three important industrial centers—New York City, Philadelphia, and Paterson—in what had been at the time of its establishment the industrial hinterland of New Jersey (Fleming 1984). Paterson was a concentrated textile-producing industrial center, while New York and Philadelphia had a diversity of smaller industries (Licht 1995). Felt, who had made a successful career as a printer and publisher in Boston and New York City planned and built his mill village using what was, at the time, an urban model of village structure and construction. Felt was a devout Unitarian and has been described as religiously tolerant but stern. The publications of his Stationers' Hall Press included politically reformist moral and religious essays and sermons such as Orville Dewey's (1838) *Moral Views of Commerce, Society, and Politics in Twelve Discourses*. Unfortunately, few examples of his own writing and ideas are preserved, so the cultural landscape of Feltville, and the ideology that engineered it, must be discerned archaeologically and through the use of circumstantial documentary evidence such as census and tax records; oral histories recorded by previous researchers; old maps, photographs and drawings; newspaper articles; and personal documents, such as letters.

Many utopian ventures developed out of the milieu of a weak but increasingly centralized federal government during the rise of Federalism and the ideologies of industrial capitalism. Typically, these are described by contemporary historians, geographers, and sometimes archaeologists as anticapitalist, antimercantilist, or communalist. Feltville was none of these. It was built with regard to older Jeffersonian communal capitalist ideals and ethics, emphasizing profitable but dispersed agrarian and self-contained industrial community as a vision for American development in place of full commitment to industrialization.

The United States suffered an economic depression in the 1830s, but by 1845 a new spirit of optimism had risen along with a politically, if not economically and socially, strengthened federal government. The North was industrializing, consolidating its power, and rapidly outpacing the economic growth of the South. Seeds of tensions, which would erupt in open warfare later in the century, were palpable. The northern states had (on paper) abolished slavery, emphasized industry over agrarianism, and established enough mutual agreement to carry the federal government in many matters that southerners felt to be trespassing on state rights. Consequently, the mid-1840s were a time of uncertainty, but one when many possibilities existed. Older Jeffersonian political concepts were falling into disfavor among northern Federalists.

Locating David Felt

Felt, despite his success and importance as an entrepreneurial printer in New York City, is virtually unknown as an historical figure. A single direct quote has been attributed to Felt on the occasion of his sale of the community in 1860 to Amassa Foster: "King David is gone, and the village will go to hell" (Hawley 1964). Note the paternalism and the obscured sense of loss in this statement. Austin Craig, a nationally respected minister and theological scholar of the mid-19th century, received his first charge at the invitation of Felt in 1852. Craig's letters and a letter received by Craig from Feltville's management committee provide sparse but poignant and tantalizing evaluations of the religious and social life of Feltville (Harwood 1908). Craig, writing in a letter to Felt after his resignation, refers to the community of Feltville as "The Free Religious Society" and suggests that if Felt were to leave the village its future would likely be sacrificed (Harwood 1908:115). Moreover, Craig was at the forefront of a movement in mainstream American Christianity to reduce denominational conflict and sectarian interests, which paralleled and interacted with the diverse social, political, and economic experiments of Fourierists and other

utopian associations (Noyes 1966; Guarneri 1991). Unlike many of the later ventures, such as Oneida, early- and mid-19th-century American utopias were more often secular and irreligious or very liberal with respect to religion (Noyes 1966).

Utopian movements typically involved the physical relocation of a group of people from a variety of economic classes and backgrounds into less populated or less expensive lands (see Reps 1965; Noyes 1966), sometimes inadvertently helping to expand the infrastructure of the same society and government from which utopians felt alienated. These communities were often led by one ideologue, a religious visionary, or a committee of like-minded persons who felt varying degrees of discomfort with the industrializing, urbanizing, and/or power-centralizing reality of mainstream society. More often than not, these discomforts focused on the morality of mainstream America, not its economic or practical realities. Urbanization, coupled with industrialization, was perceived as a demoralizing and, for that matter, unhygienic future. Most utopian thinkers, far from being millenarian, took advantage of the rhetoric of the American constitution and defined their own manner of existence with practical economic groundwork before the inevitable march of economic expansion resulted in their co-optation, absorption, or, more simply, competitive extinction through the calling in of debts and the cashing in of stock (Noyes 1966).

In these areas, again, Feltville stands apart from both mainstreams. Feltville's utopian elements were attempts to solve practical problems experienced by laborers during the industrial revolution—such as poor housing, lack of access to community facilities, and an urban environment that was increasingly seen as unhealthy and demoralizing. New Jersey's North American Phalanx, a nearly successful Fourierist community in central New Jersey, is probably one of the best examples of an early socialist society of this time and certainly one of the longest lived. Notably, the phalanx was established in the same year as Feltville and met its demise because of a disastrous fire and resultant economic insolvency in 1855, five years before the end of Feltville's "utopian phase."

Feltville, like its cousin Smithville (Bolger 1980), if it is to be considered utopian, is the kind of utopia a political philosopher like Ayn Rand might have established. It was, in its balance of romantic naturalistic rusticity and industrial promise, an urban capitalist's reformist enclave in a largely agrarian region. Felt stressed education, rural life, some level of community, reformism, and industry in his geographic plan for the village (Figure 2). Although today, Feltville looks very much like an early model suburb, it was in no way an anachronistic foreshadowing of things to come to the New Jersey hinterland during the later apex of American industry. What then, is to be gained by assigning the label "utopia" to a mill village like Feltville?

If nothing else, Feltville was an early American experiment in social engineering and geographic planning. It is also likely to have been a subtle political and religious statement expressing Felt's promotion of the then reactionary Jeffersonian democratic ideal, seasoned with a few altruistic nods to acknowledge common complaints of the working class—such as the lack of public schools, the exploitation of women and children, long work hours, and poor wages. It is, at least, an alternative to the typical mill village or industrial town of its time. In any case, it dissolved peacefully as a corporate entity when Felt consolidated his business interests back in New York in 1860. Perhaps, most importantly, it seems to exemplify the percolation of utopian social ideals into mainstream society and social engineering.

Felt's abandonment of the village, like the demise of the North American Phalanx, had many causes. The death of his brother (long-term business partner), the development and the competitive spread of steam power (which he never adopted), and economic problems associated with the secession and his company's

FIGURE 2. Artist's reconstruction of Feltville as it may have looked ca. 1850. (Reprinted from Hawley 1964:16, with permission of the publisher.)

continued reliance on waterpower instead of steam are all likely reasons. By 1852, Felt had sold most of his holdings in New York to Collins, Bowne and Hall (*New York Daily Times* 1852), and by 1867 he had petitioned the State of New York for bankruptcy (Betts 1868). The nearly complete abandonment of the village from 1862 to 1880 not only supports Austin Craig's prophetic comment on Felt's importance to the village but also makes its complex and dramatic archaeological stratigraphy relatively easy to interpret.

Archaeology and Geography of Feltville/Glenside Park

The National Register District of Feltville/ Glenside Park (Figure 3) is the subject of the FAP, a field school and grant-based research program sponsored by Montclair State University, the Union County Division of Parks and Recreation, and the New Jersey Historical Commission. Since 1996, Montclair State University's archaeological field school has been

conducted at this National Register of Historic Places District in the Watchung Reservation of central New Jersey. This field school has been the centerpiece of the FAP since the project's inception in 1998. Previous archaeological and historical research within the district, conducted under National Historic Preservation Act Section 106 guidelines, focused on the development and implementation of a master plan for management and conservation and National Register listing (Kraft 1975; Detwiler 1977; Lane 1979; Kardas and Larrabee 1985; Oppenheimer and Vogelstein 1987; Watson and Henry Associates 1989; Burrow and Bower 1993; Pan-American Consultants 1997). Unfortunately, the documentary record of Feltville and its predecessor, Peter's Hill, is mediocre. Photographs, census records, letters, genealogies (Littell 1999), maps, and secondary syntheses compiled from oral histories (Johnson 1947; Hawley 1964) are the best archival sources available.

The FAP has examined the geographic and archaeological manifestations of the dramatic social and economic changes the village has

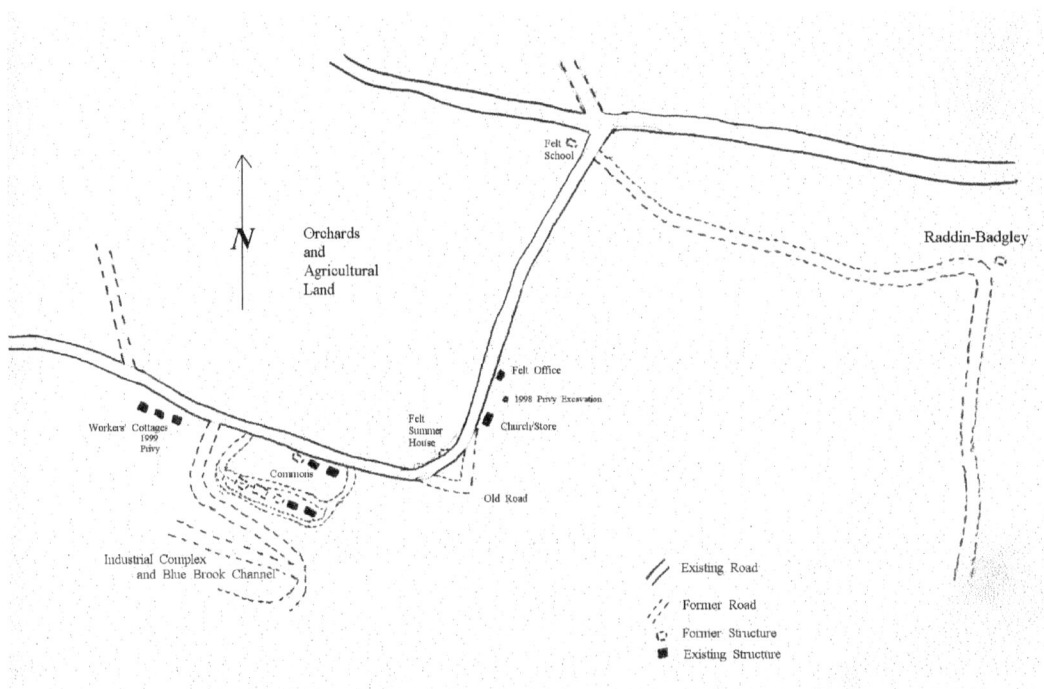

FIGURE 3. Major archaeological areas of Feltville/Glenside Park (28UN18). (Drawing by Matthew S. Tomaso.)

seen from its earliest history in the 18th century as a frontier farming community through the Felt era (1845–1860) to its near abandonment after Felt's exodus; its successful late-19th-century Adirondack-style resort phase as Glenside Park (1882–1916); to its second period of abandonment around 1916; and, finally, to its use as a housing-relief area during the Great Depression.

Originally, the goal was to see how well, if at all, archaeological deposits at Feltville would allow an in-depth examination of the daily lives of the people who inhabited the community as these changes took place. In 1999, the primary author began to sharpen the project's research orientation to focus on the effects of regional and national economic, ideological, and technological changes on Feltville's village structure, geography, and ways of life as they are reflected by its built environment and architectural and archaeological remains (Tomaso and Walling 1999; Veit et al. 1999; Tomaso 2000; Tomaso et al. 2001a, 2001b). Six seasons of field school research have led to the identification of intact and rich archaeological deposits and features that represent all of the major phases of the site's occupation, and many of these deposits have been sampled. Archaeological areas defined by the FAP and discussed below are presented in Figure 3.

Research conducted between 1998 and 2002 examined features and recovered assemblages representing each major period within the occupational span mentioned above, including the Felt era (Tomaso et al. 2001a; Tomaso and DeRooy 2003). From 1999 to the present, work focused on locating and intensively sampling stratified features from the Felt era in the backyard of two of the workers' cottages, commons, and Raddin-Badgeley House. Reconnaissance and testing was performed in the areas of Felt's summer residence as well as for the entire length of New Providence Road, one of the village's first major conduits.

Since the end of the 2002 field season, the FAP has been making a transition into a lab-based analytical phase. Most of the artifacts resulting from this project have been subjected only to preliminary analysis at this time, but several observations can nevertheless be made from both field data and geography. Essentially, there are four known subsurface contexts that represent the Felt era. These contexts consist of buried artifact-bearing *A* horizons located beneath mid-19th-century gravel walkways between cottages in the workers' cottages and commons areas, the lowest stratum of night soil in the workers' cottages privy, and the Raddin-Badgeley House cellar fill. The authors are confident in regard to the chronological assignments for these components, which are based on field and preliminary analyses.

Hermeneutics of the Feltville Archaeology Project

Bookbinding, papermaking, and printing—all of which were practiced in Feltville's factory—had been mechanized in New England and in Europe to the extent that only a few workers were needed to operate the machines. The details of Felt's manufacturing process are unknown, but his village did house and employ about 140 people from 1850 to 1860. Many of the employed residents worked in the factory, and almost all of them worked directly or indirectly for Felt (Table 1).

Felt seems to have gone out of his way to provide employment for single young women and married men with families in his factory. The 1850 census suggests the existence of boarding houses or dormitories for both unmarried men and women. Although these are also briefly mentioned in a few secondary sources, no evidence of separate housing for unmarried workers has been located in primary or archaeological records, despite intensive subsurface testing, ground-penetrating-radar surveys, and pedestrian reconnaissance of the areas where these dormitories were supposedly located. Notably, neither these dormitories nor the Felt "mansion" appear in the single verifiable eyewitness account of the village thus far obtained. Instead, Felt is said to have had a "Summer residence" in the village (*The Home Journal* 1847). Using this source, we were able to locate Felt's summerhouse during the 2003 field season. A comparative artifact sample will be obtained in 2004 from this location. It seems very likely, based on the census records and the lack of structural evidence for the location specified in Figure 2, that Feltville's boarding houses were located on either side of one of the duplex cottages, not in separate structures. Also challenging secondary sources (including Figure

TABLE 1

OCCUPATION AND SEX DATA COMBINING 1850 AND 1860 FEDERAL CENSUS DATA FOR FELTVILLE

Sex	Occupation	Married	0–4 yrs	5–14 yrs	15–24 yrs	25–34 yrs	35–44 yrs	45–54 yrs	55–64 yrs	65+ yrs	Totals
Female	factory labor	0	0	2	22	4	3	0	0	0	31
	service	0	0	0	3	1	2	1	0	0	7
	student	0	1	15	2	0	0	0	0	0	18
	teacher	0	0	0	1	0	0	0	0	0	1
	unspecified[a]	44	21	15	19	15	18	4	3	1	96
Male	clergy	0	0	0	0	1	0	0	0	0	1
	factory labor	7	0	0	7	8	2	0	1	0	18
	factory management	3	0	0	1	0	2	0	1	1	5
	factory specialist	3	0	0	7	1	4	0	0	0	12
	farmer	11	0	0	2	9	2	2	0	0	15
	merchant	0	0	0	1	0	0	0	0	0	1
	service	4	0	0	1	0	3	0	1	0	5
	skilled trade	9	0	0	0	4	3	2	0	0	9
	student	0	0	9	0	0	0	0	0	0	9
	unemployed	1	0	0	0	0	1	0	0	0	1
	unspecified	2	19	9	6	2	0	0	1	1	38
	unspecified labor	6	0	0	1	3	3	1	0	0	8
Total		90	41	50	73	48	43	10	7	3	275

[a]The category "unspecified" includes presumed housewives.

2) and based on 2003 surface inspection and limited testing, Felt's summerhouse was apparently no more grand than any other cottage in the village. Although a complete measurement of the cellar hole will not be obtained until late 2005, investigations of the Felt house cellar hole carried out in 2003 and 2004 suggest a house that was not substantially larger than other houses in the village, even though its ground plan differed substantially. A more detailed investigation of the house will be completed in the near future.

Unlike contemporary Paterson, Passaic, and Lowell, Felt did not, apparently, permit married women or children to work in the factory. Geographically, the village appears to have been structured with respect to the daily segregation of social identities and socioeconomic classes. The school was the northernmost structure in the community, and the mill was the southernmost (Figure 2). Between child (school house) and adult male/unmarried female (industrial complex) daytime domains, was the domestic area, predominately populated by married women (commons and workers' cottages). To the east of the residential core were Felt's office, a combined church and store, and Felt's summer residence (*The Home Journal* 1847). To the west of the workers' cottages, livestock was kept. Life at the village, then, would have allowed middle- and upper-class professionals as well as the clergy to minimize interaction with workers except, perhaps, on Sunday or when provisions were needed. This pattern is also generally reflected in the occupational data recorded in 1850 and 1860 census documents (Table 2). Notably, managers, skilled tradespersons, clergy, and merchants are clustered to the west, farthest from the workers' cottages area, and the nearby commons area houses the highest number of specialists employed in Felt's operation. Similarly, children were educated in a geographically distinct environment, separated from the village by about half a mile of cultivated fields and orchards.

Taking a closer look at the details of Feltville's construction efforts and considering its historical context more carefully, some telling patterns emerge. Felt built a quaint, one-room school and located it near the northern boundary of the village, as far from his four-story mill as possible. Apparently, this school was not only attended by the children of his employees (Table 1) but also by children from neighboring towns (Hawley 1964). We interpret this

location as serving a dual purpose, segregating children from both the adult female and male domains and allowing local school-age children from the surrounding community easy access. Significantly, 1850 and 1860 census records identify only men as workers in Felt's factory, and many of the minors are identified as school children (Table 1). The sturdy structure stood until 1964, changing function along with the rest of the community.

Along with the school, Felt, a devout Unitarian, built a multidenominational church into the top floor of his company store and even a post office. His employees had many of the benefits of urban life but were able to avoid the notorious pitfalls of a rapidly industrializing urban environment. They had fresh air, a quiet neighborhood, house gardens, and relatively clean water because of the well-built and carefully placed wells and privies. In addition, though they may seem cramped by modern standards, Felt's workers' cottages were

TABLE 2
NUMBER OF PERSONS IN VARIOUS OCCUPATIONS AT FELTVILLE IN 1850 AND 1860,
BY ARCHAEOLOGICAL AREA

Census Year	Occupation	Boarding Houses (2)	Commons (8)	Felt House Area (3)	New Providence Road (3)	Workers' Cottages (3)	Total
1850	clergy			1			1
	factory labor	30	2		2	2	36
	factory management		1	2			3
	factory specialist	4	7			1	12
	farmer		4		1	1	6
	merchant			1			1
	service	2	4	2			8
	skilled trade		2	1		1	4
	student		6	5	1	2	14
	teacher			1			1
	unemployed			1			1
	unspecified	4	34	6	19	21	84
	unspecified labor	2	1	1	3	1	8
1860	factory labor	7	3			3	13
	factory management		1	1			2
	farmer	1			1	1	9
	service		1	1		2	4
	skilled trade		1		4		5
	student	1	4		1	4	13
	unspecified	3	13	2	7	15	50
Total		54	84	24	39	54	274

probably substantially more appealing than most of the farmsteads in the local area and are certainly more attractive than the tenements and row houses of the typical industrial city of the time. These structures, as time has shown, were also built to last. Eight of Felt's buildings stand today, despite brief periods of abandonment and long periods of neglect. Felt was clearly trying to do something different in his little village, and even its planning and structure reflect a desire for permanence, religious tolerance, and possibly temperance.

It is often difficult for field school students to imagine Feltville as the realization of a utopian vision. While it is a carefully planned community (even the sugar maples along the edges of the roads were spaced 12 ft. apart), with uniform house and lot sizes, it is geographically a far cry from a commune or a classless village. As some students have expressed, "It may have been a utopia for David Felt, but certainly not for his workers." Some aspects of the village's living conditions also tend to offend today's sensibilities. In each laborer's cottage resided two extended families, typically with six to eight people in each. It is likely that each row of three houses—up to 48 people—shared a single two-seat privy.

Workers' Cottages Privy

One of these privies was excavated in 1999 (Tomaso et al. 2001a, 2001b). Comparison of the construction method of the privies excavated from behind Felt's office and behind the workers' cottages is most telling. All of the architecture of Felt's village can be described as "overbuilt." Felt built for longevity and invested a great deal of planning and, apparently, labor in the construction of cut-and-fitted sandstone foundations for all of the buildings, a four-story factory, and an elaborate and extremely lengthy covered race to power his manufacturing enterprise. This attention to detail and sparing of no expense is matched by the privy between his office and the church/store. This privy vault, exposed in 1998 (Veit et al. 1999) was built from cut, fitted, and mortared sandstone and had a floor composed of wooden planking, possibly to facilitate periodic cleaning. This "false bottom" must have also served as a primitive septic system, slowing the percolation of contaminants into the soil. The privy vault of the workers' cottages, excavated in 1999 and shared by as many as 40 people during the height of Feltville's occupation around 1850, was composed of loosely laid field stone, with no mortar or containment of any kind. Based on the artifact content of this very large and deep vault, it was rarely cleaned, and when it was, the cleaning was not very thorough. Discrete event stratigraphy (Figure 4) was discernable for all of the 19th-century phases of occupation at Feltville/Glenside Park (Tomaso et al. 2001a).

The workers' cottage privy revealed a rich and stratified assemblage of redware chamber pots, uniform and plentiful apothecary bottles, and faunal remains from the Felt era. Ceramics were typically inexpensive yellow-slipped redwares, with an occasional stoneware item. The approximately 50 apothecary vessels were all nearly identical and probably reflect purchases made at Felt's company store, using Felt's currency—which was the currency of the village during Felt's time. Field identification of the fauna suggests locally obtained game and fish, such as box turtle, opossum, raccoon, wild turkey, trout, bass, and deer. It is very interesting that none of the Felt-era deposits encountered so far contains alcohol bottles, unusual even in a community focused on temperance. Analysis of the thousands of artifacts recovered from this privy vault is currently incomplete, and though the statements made above are accurate, they are based on preliminary analyses.

Deposits below the Walkways

Census records of 1850 and 1860 show a few of the same surnames. At least a few of Felt's laborers apparently felt compelled to remain in the village despite the documented high mobility of skilled and unskilled labor at the time (Licht 1995; Gowaskie 1996). Archaeological data from the backyards of the workers' cottages and several associated features suggest that a few people continued to live in the area after Felt's abandonment of the community. From 1860 to 1882, the village developed the reputation that gives the area its contemporary moniker of "The Deserted Village." Seven different speculators and entrepreneurs owned and operated Feltville

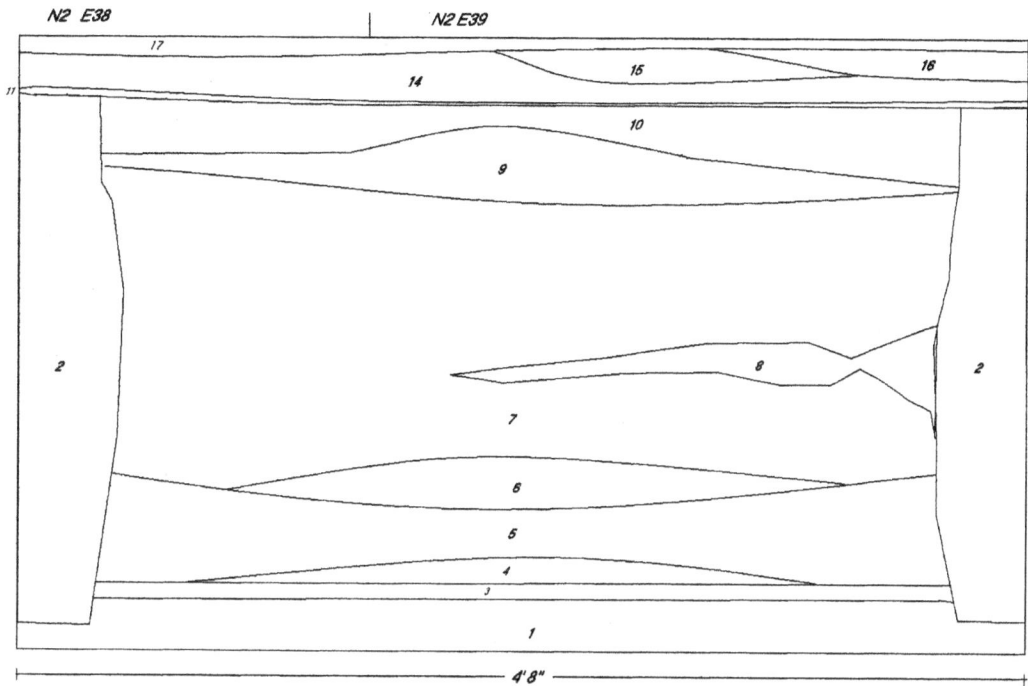

FIGURE 4. Representative stratigraphic section of the workers' cottages (1999) privy: (*1*) Pleistocene truncated *B* Horizon; (*2*) unconsolidated basalt privy vault walls; (*3*) night soil with concentrated Albany slip red earthenware; (*4*) pile of bricks; (*5*) mid-19th-century artifact bearing night soil with lime pockets; (*6*) concentrated basalt cobbles; (*7*) mid- to late-19th-century artifact bearing night soil with pockets of lime; (*8*) rodent burrow filled with redeposited 19th-century artifacts and night soil; (*9*) pile of lime; (*10*) artifact-bearing truncated *A* Horizon; (*11*) ash bed; (*14*) redeposited artifact-bearing fill with few artifacts; (*15*) concentrated trap rock gravels; (*16*) concentrated pebbles; (*17*) incipient *A* Horizon. (Drawing by Matthew S. Tomaso.)

in a variety of failed economic ventures from 1860 to 1882. Archaeology of the workers' cottages area suggests limited occupation during this period but does not reflect complete abandonment.

In 1999 and 2001, respectively, buried gravel walkways were discovered in the back and front yards of the workers' cottages and corresponding locations in the commons area (Tomaso 2002). Testing of the workers' cottages walkways was concluded in 2001, and testing in the commons area was completed in 2003. Artifacts suggest that the walkways fell out of use in the early-20th century or perhaps earlier. The dates of artifacts thus far encountered within these walkways and 19th-century descriptions of Feltville and Glenside Park suggest that the walkways were constructed and used after the Felt occupation (*The Home Journal* 1847; Johnson 1947; Tomaso and DeRooy 2003). Consequently, it

is believed that artifacts located below the walkways may have accumulated during Felt's occupation and/or slightly thereafter (Figure 5). Assemblages from walkway and below-walkway contexts located in the geographic middle of the village, the commons area, contrast with those of the workers' cottages. Whiteware and porcelain are seen in relative abundance in the commons area, while red earthenwares and yellowwares dominate the workers' cottages assemblages (DeVito et al. 2002; Tomaso and DeRooy 2003). A minor discrepancy in this overall pattern, the presence of relatively expensive, ca. 1815 English willow-pattern pearlwares below one of the workers' cottages walkways could be explained by presence of an English immigrant family in the associated cottage in 1850 (Tomaso and DeRooy 2003).

During later Glenside Park times, the workers' cottages were inhabited by laborers who likely included animal handlers, maids, and maintenance workers; whereas, the houses surrounding the commons were rented out to middle-class patrons—thus elaborating class

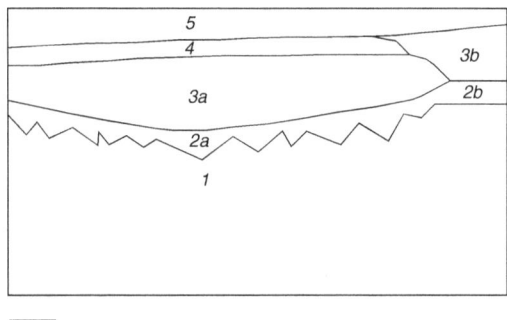

FIGURE 5. Representative stratigraphic section of the workers' cottages backyard walkway (Unit N15E25.5, west wall): (1) undifferentiated Holocene sediment; (2a) artifact-bearing, early- to mid-19th-century sediment; (2b) artifact-bearing early- to mid-19th-century sediment with lithologically distinct upper boundary; (3a) concentrated 3–7-cm gravels with mid-19th-century artifacts; (3b) artifact-bearing, mid- to late-19th-century sediment with lithologically distinct boundaries; (4) concentrated medium to fine (<3 cm) gravels with late-19th-century artifacts; (5) active a horizon with late-19th to mid-20th-century artifacts. (Drawing by Matthew S. Tomaso.)

divisions and segregation that may have been established during Felt's reign. This may be related to intensified class division and segregation on a regional and national scale during the American industrial revolution (Reps 1965; Licht 1995).

Raddin-Badgeley House

During Felt's time, the piedmont and highlands of central New Jersey were dominated by subsistence-level farmsteads. Felt purchased the 660 acres that became Feltville from one of the first farming families to settle the area, the Willcockses. The Willcocks family, along with the Raddins and Badgeleys, had established a diversified frontier farming economy with two mills, a smithy, and a quarrying operation in what had been called Peter's Hill (Littell 1999). These industries, already in place along with the

numerous house gardens and orchards present in the village (*The Home Journal* 1847), might have allowed the village a better foundation for self-sufficiency than many of the failed utopian experiments of the day.

A cellar hole dating to the Felt era and earlier was located by survey crews in the northeastern corner of the district in 1999. It has since been identified as the home of Hannah Raddin, mother of Jeremiah Raddin, Felt's coach driver. The widow Raddin remarried a Badgeley between 1850 and 1860 and left her house in Feltville for destinations unknown. By 1860, the Raddin-Badgeley house ceased to appear on maps, and her name no longer appears in local census records. From 2000 to 2003, a substantial sample of archaeological remains was obtained from this location. These remains represent abandonment materials from the apparently razed structure and also a significant number of casual discards strewn around the perimeter of the poorly preserved and buried foundation. Analysis of materials from the Raddin-Badgeley House area is also ongoing. A few preliminary observations can be made about these assemblages, but considerably more work is necessary before a complete presentation of data from this area is available.

In short, Mrs. Raddin could be said to have had a messy yard. The backyard and cellar hole assemblages are diverse, including everything from black or dark-green glass wine bottles to whiskey bottles to redware and a surprising number of buttons. Coins minted in 1786–1835 helped to date the assemblage. Artifacts throughout the cellar-fill assemblage all date from the mid-18th to mid-19th centuries and are believed to be chronologically discrete. A composite stratigraphic model reflects the depositional processes involved in the formation of this site and strongly suggests a very rapid succession of burning, collapse, and in-filling (Figure 6), perhaps occurring over a period of less than 10 years. Excavations suggest that the contents of the house were never salvaged and so represent a deposit with a *terminus post quem* no later than 1860.

The Raddin-Badgeley house and its surrounding yard provide a dramatic contrast with the clean, alcohol bottle free, and highly uniform assemblages from the backyards and privy of the workers' cottages and commons areas.

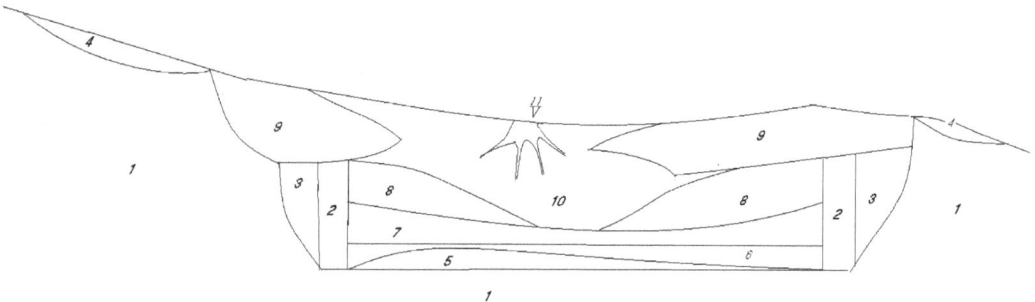

FIGURE 6. Model of formation processes resulting in major stratigraphic contexts of the Raddin-Badgeley cellar hole: (*1*) Pleistocene colluvium and slope wash; (*2*) badly damaged composite sandstone and basalt foundation; (*3*) construction-trench fill redeposited basalt and undifferentiated sediment; (*4*) occupational deposits outside of cellar hole; (*5*) ca. 1855 floor assemblage; (*6*) ponding facies with high concentration of ash and charcoal, including carbonized flooring; (*7*) foundation-collapse colluvium and ponding facies; (*8*) chimney- and foundation-collapse colluvium, grading into 10; (*9*) secondary colluvium and bedded slope wash; (*10*) second ponding facies, no artifacts; (*11*) tree-fall bioturbation (English walnut tree fell in 1998). (Drawing by Matthew S. Tomaso.)

While people in the surrounding countryside were living as they had for decades, Felt was apparently encouraging something different.

If life at Feltville was somewhat different from the developing norm, it would seem that Feltvillians might have had a difficult time adjusting to Felt's exodus after 1860. However, we suspect that despite Felt's ultimate abandonment of the community, some of his employees were able to either continue on under the new landowners or simply move back into mainstream society with little difficulty. Like many other alternative communities and utopias of the 19th century and like his successors, Feltville's founder eventually fell into economic ruin. Unlike many architects of utopia, however, Felt did not drag his followers down with him.

Conclusion: The Example of Feltville

With no direct way to access Felt's vision of a perfect society and no primary source to describe daily life in his village, archaeology and historical geography must be made to speak for them. The values that seem to have been built into Feltville, both literally and metaphorically, suggest a product of Felt's time—a secular but Christian, practical capitalist and classist community into whose very geography was encoded the class and gendered structure of an industrializing society. The pecking order, from livestock to laborers to capitalists and the clergy, was written into the village's landscape from west to east. From north to south, gender and social identity is spatially coded: with school children in the school to the north; married women in the residential area in the middle; and, finally, the factory, representative of the male domain but also including unmarried females, to the south. Nevertheless, quasi-utopian elements —answers to the common complaints of the labor class of the time—are easily discerned amidst the village infrastructure.

As understanding of the district grows, increasingly the focus can be sharpened on areas of interest in 19th-century American history. Among these are the persistent themes of class segregation and unequal means, the rise of utopianism and planned communities, and of course, the effect of national political and economic patterns on small communities. The economic history of Feltville reflects sensitivity to external conditions, as evidenced by the sweeping effects of the Civil War, the expansion of railroads, the rise of the ideological romanticization of rustication associated with the development of Adirondack resorts, the emergence of a strong middle class late in the industrial revolution, and, finally, the depression. Each of the village's major economic changes can be linked to contemporary large-scale changes in national economy and politics. The broad view of history available today, which allows us to link the history of this town to national economic and social patterns, contrasts sharply with the practical lessons and historical interpretations drawn by John Noyes in 1870 in *The History of American Socialisms*. While Noyes recognizes the importance of fiscal viability in the structure of utopia, he fails to correlate the failure of any of the communities he discusses with national social, economic, or political patterns and does little to suggest remedies for the practical concerns that ultimately destroyed so many utopian efforts. Notably, Feltville blended time-honored practical solutions with civic improvement and religious tolerance and can therefore be seen as a compromise between radical utopian vision, mainstream American development, and reactionary Jeffersonian communalism.

Felt's community is an example of social architecture from a time when many social thinkers were still very optimistic about the capitalist industrial system. As a pre-Marxian example of a practical model community, Feltville stands out. Even though it does not measure up to post-Marxian standards of egalitarianism and communalism, nor does it fit an Owenist, Fourierist, or even a joint-stock model, Felt's little village was probably a welcomed alternative for the workers who resided there.

Is it fair to say that Felt's vision of community life embedded some fatal flaw, like many of the utopias of fact and fiction? The authors argue that the answer is "no." It is important to consider the fact that despite Felt's personal evacuation of the village and the subsequent shifts in economy and social structure, the village never fell into complete disrepair and was probably never completely deserted.

The tendency to rigidly identify utopia with communal societies does an injustice to the changing and diverse perspectives that punctuate the history of political and social ideas, especially in the antebellum period. Because of the tendency to identify utopia with social, religious, and political extremes, not just ideals, there is also a tendency to expect failure. This village, however, survived because it was adaptable and was not an extreme example of a utopian community. It might even be fair to state that Felt left his workers and their children better prepared for life in mainstream society

than many of the other social experiments being conducted in his time. Through a comparative, contextual, and diachronic approach to the study of diversity in the history of social and political ideas and by paying attention to the historically shifting ranges of possibilities (as opposed to norms, modes, and means), historical archaeology can provide more satisfactory practical and theoretical lessons for the design and implementation of social practice in addition to an understanding of agentive social change. In this way, contemporary studies of the history of utopian societies may build upon the lofty goals and ideals of 19th-century utopians rather than adopting the more contemporary and jaded perspective with which such histories are often approached in academia.

The FAP is a small example of the potential significance of historical archaeology's contribution to our understanding of utopian ideas and literature. If Feltville can be seen as utopian, it stands as an example of the unique perspective on the commonplace structure of daily life within such societies offered by historical geography and archaeology. If it can only be seen as a planned mill village with many utopian elements, it stands, and perhaps more significantly, as an example of the percolation of utopian ideas into mainstream American life. The stuff of daily life, which is too often taken for granted and overlooked in historical treatments—artifacts, spatial patterns, transportation routes—may have an effect upon the social and political consciousness of individuals that supercedes that of text and theory. This is the stuff of historical archaeology.

Acknowledgments

Thanks to Montclair State University (MSU) Field School students, staff, and laboratory interns 1996–2003; Union County Parks and Recreation; New Jersey Historical Commission; Departments of classics and general humanities, anthropology, and earth and environmental studies, MSU; and the following individuals who have helped to make the FAP a reality: Daniel Bernier, David Goode, David Hall, and Priscilla Hayes. Special thanks to fellow contributors to this volume for excellent critical comments.

References

BELLAMY, EDWARD
1967 *Looking Backward.* Harvard University Press, Boston, MA.

BETTS, GEORGE F.
1868 Public notice. *The New York Times,* 30 January:[1].

BOLGER, WILLIAM C.
1980 The Smith System: Profile of a Machine-Age Community. In *Planned and Utopian Experiments: Four New Jersey Towns,* Paul Stellhorn, editor, pp. 77–108. New Jersey Historical Commission, Trenton.

BRAUDEL, FERNAND
1980 *On History.* University of Chicago Press, Chicago, IL.

BURROW, IAN, AND ERNEST BOWER
1993 An Archaeological Evaluation of the Church/Store (Building 2) at the Deserted Village of Feltville/Glenside Park Berkeley Heights Township Union County, New Jersey. Report to Union County Division of Parks and Recreation, Elizabeth, NJ, from Hunter Research, Inc., Trenton, NJ.

DETWILER, CHARLES H., JR.
1977 Report on Historic and Culturally Important Sites Affected, Environmental Impact Study for Route 78-Section 4N, 5, P and N. Manuscript, New Jersey Historic Preservation Office, Department of Environmental Protection, Trenton, NJ.

DEVITO, MELISSA, CARISSA DEROOY, AND MATTHEW S. TOMASO
2002 Interpretation of Archaeological Results. In *Archaeology and Geoarchaeology of the Feltville/Glenside Park (28 UN 18) Commons Area: Final Report of Test Excavations and Mapping for the 2001 Field Season,* Matthew S. Tomaso, editor, pp. 32–46. Manuscript, New Jersey Historic Preservation Office, Department of Environmental Protection, Trenton, NJ.

DEWEY, ORVILLE
1838 *Moral Views of Commerce, Society, and Politics in Twelve Discourses.* David Felt and Co. Stationers' Hall, New York, NY.

FLEMING, THOMAS
1984 *New Jersey: A History.* W. W. Norton and Co., New York, NY.

FRANCIS, RICHARD
1997 *Transcendental Utopias: Individual and Community at Brook Farm, Fruitlands, and Walden.* Cornell University Press, Ithaca, NY.

GOWASKIE, JOSEPH
1996 *Workers in New Jersey History.* New Jersey Historical Commission, Trenton.

GRAMSCI, ANTONIO
1971 *Selections from the Prison Notebooks.* International Publishers, New York, NY.

GUARNERI, CARL J.
1991 *The Utopian Alternative: Fourierism in Nineteenth-Century America.* Cornell University Press, Ithaca, NY.

HARWOOD, W. S. (EDITOR)
1908 *Life and Letters of Austin Craig.* Fleming H. Revell Co., New York, NY.

HAWLEY, JAMES B.
1964 *The Deserted Village and the Blue Brook Valley.* Trailside Museum Association, Mountainside, NJ.

HAYDEN, DOLORES
1976 *Seven American Utopias: The Architecture of Communitarian Socialism, 1790–1975.* Massachusetts Institute of Technology Press, Cambridge, MA.

HOLLOWAY, MARK
1966 *Utopian Communities in America, 1660–1880.* Dover Publications, New York, NY.

THE HOME JOURNAL
1847 A New and Beautiful Village. *The Home Journal* 36:[2]. New York, NY.

JOHNSON, ARTHUR
1947 *The Deserted Village.* Union County Park Commission, Union County, NJ.

KARDAS, SUSAN, AND EDWARD LARRABEE
1985 Archaeological Reconnaissance, Feltville, Watchung Reservation. Report to Oppenheimer and Vogelstein, AIA, New York, NY, from Historic Sites Research, Princeton, NJ. Manuscript, New Jersey Historic Preservation Office, Department of Environmental Protection, Trenton, NJ.

KIRCHMANN, GEORGE
1980 Why Did They Stay? Communal Life at the North American Phalanx. In *Planned and Utopian Experiments: Four New Jersey Towns,* Paul Stellhorn, editor, pp. 11–28. New Jersey Historical Commission, Trenton.

KRAFT, JOHN C.
1975 Route 78 E.I.S. Identification and Evaluation of Archaeological Sites. Manuscript, New Jersey Historic Preservation Office, Department of Environmental Protection, Trenton, NJ.

LANE, MICHAEL
1979 Feltville, the Deserted Village: Nomination to the State and National Register[s] of Historic Places. Manuscript, New Jersey Historic Preservation Office, Department of Environmental Protection, Trenton, NJ.

LICHT, WALTER
1995 *Industrializing America: The Nineteenth Century.* Johns Hopkins University Press, Baltimore, MD.

LITTELL, JOHN
1999 *Family Records, or Genealogies of the First Settlers of the Passaic valley (and Vicinity,) Above Chatham.* Willow Bend Books, Westminster, MD. Originally published 1852.

MORE, THOMAS
1969 *Utopia.* Yale University Press, New Haven, CT.

NEW YORK DAILY TIMES
1852 Miscellaneous. *New York Daily Times,* 12 January [1].

NORDHOFF, CHARLES
1966 *The Communistic Societies of the United States: From Personal Observations.* Dover Publications, New York, NY.

NOYES, JOHN H.
1966 *Strange Cults and Utopias of 19th-Century America.* Dover Publications, New York, NY. Original title (1870) *A History of American Socialisms.*

OPPENHEIMER AND VOGELSTEIN, AIA
1987 Master Plan for the Deserted Village of Feltville, New Jersey. Report to Union County Division of Parks and Recreation, Elizabeth, NJ, from Oppenheimer and Vogelstein, AIA, New York, NY. Manuscript, New Jersey Historic Preservation Office, Department of Environmental Protection, Trenton, NJ.

ORWELL, GEORGE
1961 *1984.* New American Library, New York, NY.

PAN-AMERICAN CONSULTANTS
1997 Phase I Cultural Resource Survey for the Green Brook Flood Control Project Upper Basin Project Area Union and Somerset Counties, New Jersey. Report to U.S. Army Corps of Engineers, New York District, New York, NY, from Pan-American Consultants, Depew, NY. Manuscript, New Jersey Historic Preservation Office, Department of Environmental Protection, Trenton, NJ.

REPS, JOHN W.
1965 *The Making of Urban America: A History of City Planning in the United States.* Princeton University Press, Princeton, NJ.

TOMASO, MATTHEW S.
2000 Utopia, New Jersey? The Village of Feltville in the Mid-Nineteenth Century. Paper presented in the Dreaming of a Better World: Visions of Utopia and Fantasy Conference, 7 December, Montclair State University Institute for the Humanities, Upper Montclair, NJ.

2002 Sediments, Soils, and Contexts of the Lower Road/Commons Area. In Archaeology and Geoarchaeology of the Feltville/Glenside Park (28 UN 18) Commons Area: Final Report of Test Excavations and Mapping for the 2001 Field Season, Matthew S. Tomaso, editor, pp. 23–32. Manuscript, New Jersey Historic Preservation Office, Department of Environmental Protection, Trenton, NJ.

TOMASO, MATTHEW S., AND CARISSA A. DEROOY
2003 Social Archaeology of the 19th Century: Evidence from the Walkways at Feltville/Glenside Park, NJ. Paper presented at the 68th Annual Meeting of the Society for American Archaeology, Milwaukee, WI.

TOMASO, MATTHEW S., RICHARD F. VEIT, AND STANLEY L. WALLING
2001a Class, Event Stratigraphy, and the Quotidian: Two Privies from Feltville/Glenside Park, Union County, New Jersey. Paper presented at the 66th Annual Meeting of the Society for American Archaeology, New Orleans, LA.

2001b Ideological and Economic Change in a Nineteenth-Century Industrial Utopia: The Archaeology of Feltville, New Jersey. Paper presented at the 34th Conference on Historical and Underwater Archaeology, Long Beach, CA.

TOMASO, MATTHEW S., AND STANLEY L. WALLING (EDITORS)
1999 Final Report of 1996 Archaeological Investigations at Feltville, Union County, New Jersey. Report to Union County Division of Parks and Recreation, Elizabeth, NJ, from Center for Archaeological Studies, Montclair State University, Upper Montclair, NJ. Manuscript, New Jersey Historic Preservation Office, Department of Environmental Protection, Trenton, NJ.

VEIT, RICHARD F.
2002 *Digging New Jersey's Past: Historical Archaeology in the Garden State.* Rutgers University Press, New Brunswick, NJ.

VEIT, RICHARD F., MATTHEW S. TOMASO, AND STANLEY L. WALLING
1999 King David is Dead and the Village Will Go to Hell: Archaeology of a Nineteenth-Century Planned Industrial Community. Paper presented at a meeting of the Northern New Jersey Chapter of the Archaeological Institute of America, Montclair State University, Upper Montclair, NJ.

WATSON AND HENRY ASSOCIATES
1989 Historic Structures Report for the Deserted Village of Feltville/Glenside Park; Watchung Reservation, Union County, New Jersey. Report to Union County Division of Parks and Recreation, Office of New Jersey Heritage NJDEP, and the National Park Service, from Watson and Henry Associates, New York, NY. Manuscript, New Jersey Historic Preservation Office, Department of Environmental Protection, Trenton, NJ.

ZAMIATIN, YEVGENY
    1952 *We.* E. P. Dutton, New York, NY.

MATTHEW S. TOMASO
CENTER FOR ARCHAEOLOGICAL STUDIES, AND
DEPARTMENTS OF EARTH AND ENVIRONMENTAL
STUDIES AND ANTHROPOLOGY
MONTCLAIR STATE UNIVERSITY
104 DICKSON BUILDING
UPPER MONTCLAIR, NJ 07059

RICHARD F. VEIT
DEPARTMENT OF HISTORY AND ANTHROPOLOGY
MONMOUTH UNIVERSITY
WEST LONG BRANCH, NJ 07764-1898

CARISSA A. DEROOY
U.S. ARMY CORPS OF ENGINEERS, NEW YORK
DISTRICT
26 FEDERAL PLAZA, ROOM 2142
NEW YORK, NY 10278-0900

STANLEY L. WALLING
CENTER FOR ARCHAEOLOGICAL STUDIES, AND
DEPARTMENTS OF CLASSICS AND GENERAL
HUMANITIES AND ANTHROPOLOGY
MONTCLAIR STATE UNIVERSITY
104 DICKSON BUILDING
UPPER MONTCLAIR, NJ 07059

Mark Pittaway

Creating and Domesticating Hungary's Socialist Industrial Landscape: From Dunapentele to Sztálinváros, 1950–1958

ABSTRACT

Eastern Europe's socialist new cities have been seen as embodying "politicized landscapes"; in other words, landscapes created by socialist dictatorships according to their own ideological purposes. The region's socialist new cities were indeed identified as distinctively socialist landscapes, but the processes by which they came to be understood as such by the citizens of socialist states were far more complex than top-down accounts allow. The reactions of both builders and residents of the Hungarian new city of Sztálinváros (Stalin City) to the urban form are examined in order to show how the city came to be seen as a distinctively socialist industrial landscape. Employing an approach based on a dialogue between the methods of historical archaeology and social history is employed, demonstrating that an examination of popular responses to material culture can reveal much about state socialism in Eastern Europe and its nature.

Introduction

Above the main factory gate of the Danube Steel Works there is a mural entitled "The Worker and Peasant Alliance." It depicts a ceremony held in green fields in which peasants give food to those who worked in the steel works. The picture's message is not hard to decipher. It was intended to depict the social relationship on which the ideology of Hungary's postwar socialist order was founded—between the working class and the cooperative peasantry. The Danube Steel Works stands on the southern side of the city of Dunaújváros, which had around 60,000 inhabitants by the mid-1990s. The city was built in the early 1950s near to the village of Dunapentele, which lies some 70 kilometres south of Budapest on the west bank of the Danube (Figure 1). The core of the city was built in the early 1950s—a core now surrounded by prefabricated high-rise housing estates erected during the 1960s and 1970s to solve the housing crises in the town generated by earlier socialist industrialization (Miskolczi 1980; Erdős 2000).

The city of Dunaújváros is probably one of the most striking examples of an industrial landscape that embodies the legacy of the socialist state that ruled the country between 1948 and 1989. As World War II drew to a close and Hungary became the site of battle between the insurgent forces of the Red Army and the retreating forces of Nazi Germany, all that stood on the site of contemporary Dunaújváros was the village of Dunapentele and the fields that surrounded it. In interwar Hungary, Dunapentele, like much of the county of Fejér in which it is located, was dominated by agriculture with a population made up predominantly of poor rural smallholders, fishermen, and manorial laborers (Farkas 1975; Schlitterné Nyuli 1994; Lukács 2000). The village was at the center of fighting for two months at the beginning of 1945. Those months brought not only death and destruction but also the social revolution of land reform as the estates were expropriated and their land distributed to the landless and poorer smallholders. Throughout the three years that followed the end of the war, when Hungary was ruled by an antifascist popular-front coalition government, the institutions of democracy and a smallholder-based society were consolidated locally (Imréné Szőnyegi, 2000).

With the onset of the Cold War, the Soviet Union and Hungary's own Communists tightened their grip on power from the summer of 1947, destroying the institutions of the country's postwar democracy and laying the foundations of dictatorship. Determined to pursue a program of "building socialism," the state initiated drives to collectivize agriculture in 1948 and began to make preparations for a five-year plan designed to transform Hungary into "a country of iron, steel, and machines." Although it seemed at first that "the construction of socialism" would only impact on Dunapentele through the collectivization of agriculture, in fact the village came to play a central role in the program of socialist

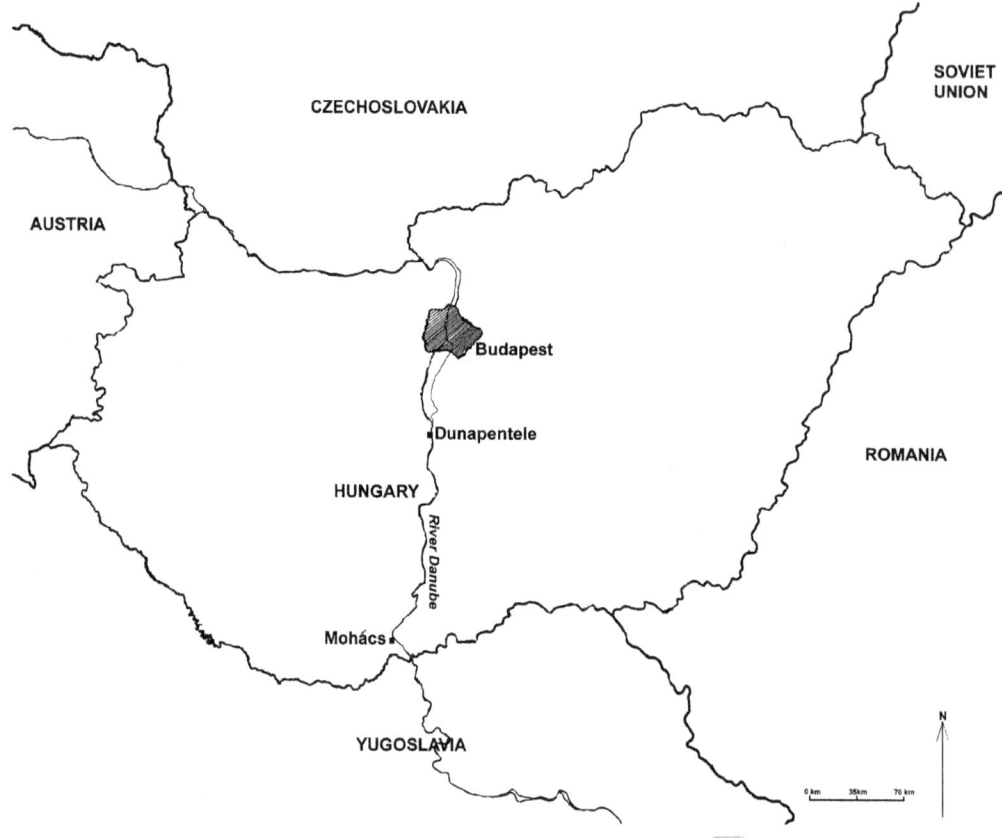

FIGURE 1. Map of Hungary ca. 1949 showing the locations of Dunapentele and Mohács.

industrialization. Socialist industrialization in the country was designed to meet the needs of the Soviet military that believed a third world war was imminent. To feed their demand for armaments, machine manufacture was to be radically expanded. Hungary, however, lacked the capacity to produce the steel needed to supply a machine industry of the size envisaged, and planners sought to construct, consequently, a new, large steel plant to meet the expected demand. Initially they planned on building the steel plant at Mohács in the south of the country, next to the Yugoslav border, but deteriorating relations between the two countries in the wake of Tito's split with Stalin rendered this location impractical. The planned steel plant was moved north along the Danube to rural Dunapentele. Construction of both the steel plant and a new city—Hungary's "first socialist new city"—were begun in May 1950. Named

Sztálinváros from November 1951 until November 1961, or Stalin City, it has been seen as a distinctive socialist landscape (Weiner 1959; Miskolczi and Rózsa 1969; Birta 1970; Erdős 2000; Horváth et al. 2000).

During the 1950s Sztálinváros was a showpiece of socialist planning; it was one of the most obvious material manifestations of the socialist dictatorship's desire to reshape society. From 1948 the Hungarian state sought to integrate all social groups into a new society organized around the performance of collective labor in socialized enterprises in both industry and agriculture. Small-scale peasant agriculture was to be eliminated through punitive taxation and several collectivization campaigns throughout the decade that would replace smallholdings with agricultural units organized along industrial lines. During the early 1950s particularly, the country's industrial sector was expanded with the state giving priority to heavy industry. Private businesses, both in manufacturing and commerce, were all but eliminated (Lampland 1995; Róna-Tas 1997; Pittaway 1998a; Valuch 2001; Varga 2001). This program of social transformation was not, however, restricted to Hungary. With the onset of the Cold War, socialist regimes were established across East-Central Europe. Inspired by the Stalinist model pioneered in the Soviet Union two decades before, states sought to effect similar socialist transformations across the region during the 1950s (Kideckel 1993; Kenney 1997; Kopstein 1997; Bokovoy 1998; Creed 1998). Because of the material manifestations of this transformation and its nature, the socialist experience in Eastern Europe presents boundless opportunities for those examining the material cultures of labor. Agrarian landscapes were completely transformed by collectivization; cities and towns were shaped out of agglomerations of villages as well as from nothing. The nature of production was transformed as mixed residential-industrial neighborhoods were swept away by the nationalization of small businesses, and production was concentrated in large factories.

The analysis of the material culture of socialism in East-Central Europe is still in its infancy, however. It has been widely noticed by analysts of material culture that everyday material objects associated with the socialist period have played a central role in shaping popular memories of the socialist dictatorships right across the region (Betts 2000; Pittaway 2003). This has fed an interest in the everyday material objects generated by socialist economies in the region and consumed by East European citizens. Concern has focused on socialist consumerism in particular in order to consider the question of whether a distinctive material culture generated by socialist consumerism existed and, if so, whether it shaped distinctive East European identities (Vörös, 1995; Pittaway 1998b; Merkel 1999; Reid and Crowley 2000; Pence 2000). This concentration on issues of consumerism has restricted our understanding of state socialist material culture in two senses. First, much work on consumerism tends to divide the socialist period into two distinct subperiods. The first one, of Stalinism lasting between 1948 and 1956, was characterized by considerable poverty. The second subperiod was, according to much

of this work, the one in which a distinctive socialist material culture evolved. Such a distinction tends to ignore the everyday material culture of the period in which socialist transformation was pursued most single-mindedly by the state. Second, very little attention has been given to the popular experience of place and space in the region. Some work has been done on the social history of the private sphere and the built environments associated with it (Buchli 1998; Pittaway 2000); there has, however, been little work on either the public sphere or the landscapes of socialist transformation.

Socialist urbanization and in particular showpiece socialist new towns form a partial exception to this rule (French and Hamilton 1979; Musil 1980; Samson 1984). Very little of this work has sought to examine the socialist town or city as a distinctive cultural landscape—a distinctive socialist landscape or urban form. Where issues of socialist urban form as cultural landscape have been considered, socialist towns, suburbs, or cities have been seen as the ultimate politicized landscapes. That is to say they have been seen as the material realization of a revolutionary ideology that had broken with previous patterns of urban design. According to this view, settlements were built that embodied the will of a dominant state (Aman 1992). Such views of urban spaces as distinctive politicized landscapes have stemmed from a notion that has stressed the "totalitarian" nature of socialist societies. This notion has been subjected to relentless criticism by social historians. Many of these historians have worked on the societies of socialist new towns. They have uncovered a complex dynamic of conflict and consent, accommodation and opposition in the societies of these settlements (Kotkin 1995; Dowling 1999; Lebow 1999, 2001). This research has concentrated on the social history of the residents and has tended to underplay the material dimensions of new town life. Little consideration, if any, has been given to the residents' experiences of socialist new towns as cultural landscapes.

In 1951 the Communist journalist and Sztálinváros resident András Sándor wrote, "the city differs considerably in nature from the capitalist city" (Sándor 1951a:21). Sztálinváros's urban form embodied elements of the social vision of its creators. State socialism in its Stalinist variant envisaged a unity between politics and production, a unity based on a close link between performance in the socialized, industrialized workplace and loyalty to the single workers' party that ruled the state (Pittaway 1998a: 63–72). The socialist landscapes created during the Stalinist years were almost always landscapes of industrial labor development. Sztálinváros was no exception; the city was planned around the twin poles of political authority and socialist labor. At one end of the city, planned and built in the 1950s, lies the factory, which is separated from the city by a 1-kilometer stretch of woodland. From the major factory gate on its north side through the swathe of woodland into and through the city is its main street. Originally named Stalin Street (now Vasmű Út, or Steel Works Street), it was to end in what was conceived as the main square—although in the 1960s and 1970s it would be extended with the construction of new housing estates. Around the square were to be the major public buildings—the headquarters of the city party committee, the local council, and public administration.

Certain elements of this landscape bear a striking similarity to certain kinds of industrial capitalist landscapes, particularly the industrial company town. The central role played by the factory—the site of industrial production—within the urban form is one feature; another is the organic link between industrial production and public authority. There are other parallels in more mundane features of the city as it was conceived in the early 1950s; workers were to be housed in flats with no gardens that could be used for food production. Workers were to be producers of steel only and just consumers of food. Green space was purely recreational, taking the form of parks. Sztálinváros's landscape embodied ideologies of work and social reform that would be familiar in industrial capitalist contexts (Mrozowski 1991; Crawford 1995).

Despite these apparent similarities, the city's landscape has been identified in Hungarian popular consciousness as the most striking example of a socialist landscape in the country. This is particularly visible in the way in which the landscape of Sztálinváros has played a central role in shaping and articulating memories of the years of Stalinist dictatorship in Hungary. In the later years of state socialism during the 1970s, many living outside the city identified it with social upheaval, if not with outright criminality. This negative perception was met with a fierce local patriotism that emphasized the role the town played in giving work and a secure livelihood to the former rural poor and the industrial working class. These debates were as much about the painful memories of the violent process of state-directed social change in Hungary during the early 1950s as about the city itself, which had come to symbolize that transformation (Miskolczi 1980). The city's landscape has continued to carry, shape, and articulate Hungarian memories of socialism into the present. This has in part been a legacy of its representation in early socialist culture. Zoltán Tábori—who has written on the difficulties the city has faced during the harsh economic climate of the 1990s—described how he became fascinated with the city as boy, looking at its representation in the Hungarian postage stamps of the early 1950s (Tábori 1998:7).

Given the role that landscapes play in the shaping and articulation of popular memory (Schama 1995), the issue of how landscape comes to be defined is one of central importance. Work on landscapes has come to see them as part of a process of dynamic social interaction through which societies define their sense of place and, consequently, where social and cultural identities are forged. While landscapes are often created by the powerful and can serve to naturalize dominant ideologies, they are also constantly appropriated, contested, and reinterpreted by those who populate them. It is through these complex and conflicting processes that landscapes have come to be defined (Cosgrove 1984; Bender 1993; Mitchell 1994; Hirsch and O'Hanlon 1995). Sztálinváros's urban form served to define it as a distinctively socialist landscape, as did the political context in which it was created. If the roots of its definition as a distinctively socialist landscape are to be interrogated and the meaning of such a definition is to be uncovered, due attention needs to paid, however, to how the landscape was received, used, and interpreted by those who interacted with it.

To determine how Sztálinváros was defined as a distinctively socialist landscape, perspectives from historical archaeology and social history are used. In the latter, historians have increasingly sought to use artifacts as evidence at the same time as material culture itself has become the subject of historical study (Donald and Hurcombe 1998; Reid and Crowley 2000). This interest parallels the work of historical archaeology where historical approaches have been fruitfully used to aid interpretation of the archaeological record (Beaudry et al. 1991; Andrén 1998). The process by which Sztálinváros was defined stems from the twin processes of the city's creation as a socialist "new" town and its domestication. The first of these processes represented both the creation of the socialist new city as a distinctive urban space and the physical process of its construction. Its construction bought many people from different corners of the country into contact with the city; their reactions to its urban form played a central role in defining it as a socialist landscape. Yet its domestication, namely the process through which the city was populated by a body of permanent residents that followed its creation, produced a more positive view of the city, but one, nevertheless, which also identified it as a distinctively socialist place. Through these processes Sztálinváros's socialist industrial landscape came to symbolize the changes brought about by the socialist dictatorship's transformation of Hungarian society during the 1950s. The interaction between the social groups that, both temporarily and permanently, came to inhabit the city and its landscape embodied a range of deeper political and social conflicts that could only be indirectly articulated in the repressive climate that prevailed in Hungary after the suppression of the revolution of 1956.

The development of Sztálinváros's urban form, paying particular attention to how the policies and ideologies of the state influenced its development, are examined. How the developing urban form was experienced by the original residents of the village of Dunapentele and then by those who came to build the city is considered. Finally, the city's domestication is examined through the experiences of those who came to live in one of the city's earliest neighborhoods.

Sztálinváros as Urban Space

Writing in 1959, Tibor Weiner, who headed the team of architects and urban planners that shaped Sztálinváros during the 1950s, emphasized its novelty. In the 1940s during the immediate postwar period, "in terms of urban construction the first tasks of the reconstruction were simply the construction of small blocks of flats …. the whole concept of the socialist city in Hungary only emerged with the construction of the city alongside the Danube Steel Works. Dunapentele-Sztálinváros became the school for Hungarian urban construction" (Weiner 1959:19). Weiner's comment underlines the experimental nature of Sztálinváros's urban landscape; something to which inadequate attention has been paid hitherto. Because of the profusion of socialist new towns in Eastern Europe that were built during the 1950s, it has been tempting to see the new towns as simply the realizations of a blueprint exported from the Soviet Union to states like Hungary. This assumption understates the complexity of the processes by which Hungary's socialist industrial landscape was made. Soviet models were certainly important, but they interacted both with the material factors of Hungary's cold war industrialization drive and more local circumstances to produce Sztálinváros's urban form. Weiner's comment belies another cliché frequently used by Hungarian architectural historians, that Sztálinváros was a "planned" city designed for the demands of politics and ideology, rather than for its people (Szendrői 1972). Like Hungarian Stalinism as a whole, the city's urban form was a product of a combination of Stalinist ideology, cold war circumstance, and social tension.

The fundamental determinant of Sztálinváros as a landscape was the gigantic Stalin Steel Works; the largest single investment of Hungary's first five-year plan. The steel works would dominate the city both physically and economically. The city's origin was determined by a series of political decisions made about the works. The state's decision to invest in the works stemmed, according to the minister of heavy industry serving at the time the decision was taken, from "the climate of the cold war." Fear of imminent war pushed the state to expand machine manufacture, thus creating a shortage of steel production capacity in Hungary. A large steel works was the state's answer. Originally it was to be built at Mohács, close to the southern border, which would have provided the infrastructure to support the population employed by the new steel works.

Fear of war with Yugoslavia, whose northern border lay only 12 kilometers from the proposed site, forced the state to reconsider and to move the city northward to a site next to the Danube, 2 kilometers south of the village of Dunapentele. (Miskolczi and Rózsa 1969:26–49). The area was, however, completely rural with no major towns in the vicinity, while Dunapentele with a population of just over 4,000 was a small rural community, utterly incapable of accommodating the workforce of a large steel plant (Imréné Szőnyegi 2000: 238). According to the original plans at the outset of construction in 1950, the steel plant was to employ 6,535 people by 1954 of whom 5,000 would be workers. It was decided in 1949 that a new city would have to be built alongside the factory to accommodate the workforce, their families, and the services they would need. From November 1949 preparations were made to build the city on the 2 kilometers of land that lay between the factory and Dunapentele (Miskolczi and Rózsa 1969: 47–50).

The factory was to be constructed on a plateau that formed part of a range of hills ranging in height from 30 to 50 meters that flanked the western bank of the Danube. The plateau was agricultural land used by the smallholders of Dunapentele, whose village lay north of the plateau on the other side of the valley of a small tributary of the Danube. The northernmost 2 kilometers of the plateau between Dunapentele and the steel works were made available for the new city (Figure 2). The city was planned in such a way as to achieve unity between village, factory, city, and the natural landscape (Weiner 1959:42). The urban landscape, however, also reflected and embodied the ideologies that underpinned the social transformation that was then underway in Hungary. This ideology determined that the city was to be organized around the twin poles of politics and production; as the city's chief engineer put it when presenting his plan to his fellow architects in print in 1951, "the socialist city and the socialist industrial site are two poles of one unified unit. The city centre and the main gate of factory must lie in a direct line from one another" (Weiner 1951:589).

The monumental factory gate flanked by the offices of the management of the steel works formed the main northern entrance of the fac-

tory. Linking the factory gate to the city center was the main street, named the Stalin Street (Sztálin út) throughout the 1950s. A straight, broad street, it ran from south to north initially through a half-kilometer band of woodland designed to provide a recreational space for residents and, more importantly, to shield the city from the factory. It then was to drive northward through the city until it reached the center. The city center was marked by the main square (Figure 3). Just as the monumental factory gate was to act as a symbol of socialized production, the main square was to act as the site of political power, with the main street linking the two elements. According to its planner, "the main square is to be a large, stone-flagged, vegetation free square," which was "the consequence of its functional role as the end of point of demonstrations" (Weiner 1951:591). The square was to be the site of political power in the city, to be flanked on three sides. On one side the seat of the city council and thus local public administration was placed. Opposite the council house was to be built the smaller, neoclassical

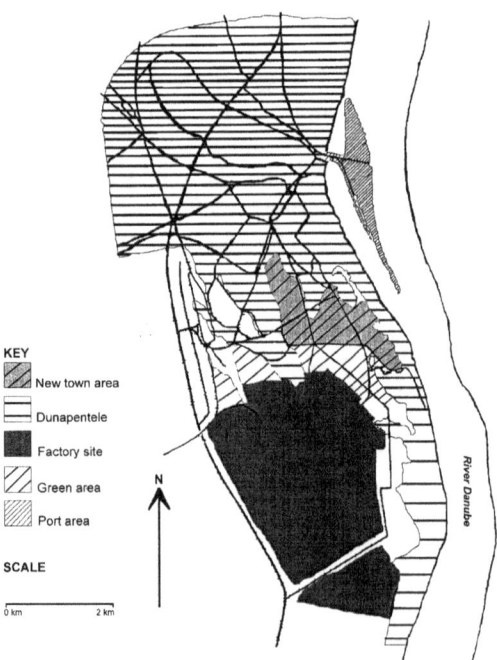

FIGURE 2. Map of Sztálinváros ca.1954 showing the city's component elements.

KEY
1-Council House
2-House of Culture
3-Party Headquarters
4-Main Square
5-Medical surgery
6-Hospital
7-Stalin street
8-Cinema
9-Red Star Hotel/Offices
10-Residential district shopping
11-lst May Street
12-Gyorgy Dozsa Street

0   500m

To
Steel Works

FIGURE 3. Map of the city center and the first residential district of Sztálinváros ca. 1953.

party headquarters (which today serves as the Dunaújváros city museum), the seat of the representative of national political authority (Gyárfás 1951:618–619; Weiner 1951:596).

In this central element of Sztálinváros's landscape lay the embodiment in bricks and mortar of an ideology of politicized production by which loyalty to the state was to be demonstrated through the performance of industrial labor and participation in public spectacle. In designing the main square as the end point of political demonstrations and other marches, Weiner was consciously designing urban space to act as a stage set for the performance by Sztálinváros citizens of their loyalty to Hungary's socialist state. South of the main square, along the side of Stalin Street, Weiner planned a series of mini-centers; these were groups of buildings that served particular community needs. The first of these lay 100 meters south of the main square on the western side of Stalin Street and was a cluster of building designed for purposes of relaxation. Facing onto the street stood the Red Star Hotel, with a patisserie (cukrászda) for city residents at ground level. South of the hotel set back from the

street was a small square where the planners built the city's cinema (Figure 4). Although the cinema was planned as a space for depoliticized leisure, at times the authorities would use it for propaganda purposes. In 1952 five "undisciplined" workers described in the local press as "scroungers" were convicted of unauthorized absenteeism before a court convened in the style of a show trial in the cinema, which had then only just opened (Sztálin Vasmű Építője 1952; Fejér Megyei Levéltár 1952a). As the decade continued, the cinema reverted to the role for which it had originally been built.

The planning of Stalin Street suggested that priority was given to collectively provided services rather than to private leisure or consumption. Directly opposite the cinema on the eastern side of Stalin Street were built the city's hospital and central medical surgery—both intended as symbols of the state's intention to provide comprehensive health insurance coverage to Hungary's industrial working class (Figure 5). The hospital would become the city's second largest employer after the steel works. András Ivánka's design for the city's central medical surgery was to make it a showpiece of Hungarian socialist realist architecture (Gyárfás 1951:611–612; Horváth et al. 2000:92). Although private consumption was given space on Sztálin út, it was incorporated into the design of the five-storied apartment blocks that flanked the street south of the city center (Hámor 1951).

Approximately 700 meters west of the Stalin Street, the planners placed another large street running from north to south, György Dózsa Street (Dózsa György út). On this arterial street a bus station was located and also, significantly, a market space where peasants from the surrounding area were permitted to sell goods they had produced that were left over after they had met compulsory deliveries. Private markets were legalized in 1951, and the Sztálinváros market was created in 1952. In theory the smallholders in the neighboring countryside were to come to sell goods to urban consumers—a sort of realization of the "worker-peasant alliance" as captured on the mural at the factory gate. It did not, however, quite work out like this, as the market was not as widely used as hoped by "working class" consumers. In reply to the question of who shopped on the "free

FIGURE 4. The Dózsa cinema.

market" an official replied, "in the morning it is the housewives who live locally, after work the workers come down to get necessary things. The real situation is that very few use it" (Fejér Megyei Levéltár 1952b:2).

The incursion of older "capitalist" elements into the landscape of the new socialist city was less worrying for the authorities during the 1950s than the incorporation of the village of Dunapentele into Sztálinváros. By the mid-1950s it was commonly referred to as "the old city" (óváros). The authorities regarded its smallholder population with profound suspicion because of their covert resistance to the state's collectivization campaigns, their cultural alienation from the socialist city itself and their stubborn support for the principal of the private ownership of land. The village's craftsmen and small businessmen were regarded similarly; during 1951 the local authority forcibly organized the village's craftsmen into an industrial cooperative and nationalized its two private bakeries (Fejér Megyei Levéltár 1954a). The influence of organized religion in the village also roused suspicion; some 75% of Dunapentele residents paid church tax to the Catholic Church in 1955. Furthermore, the village had the only church in the area. Concern was expressed that many "politically unreliable" elements in

the city attended church in Dunapentele (Fejér Megyei Levéltár 1955:1–6).

Constructing Sztálinváros as a Socialist Landscape

The planning of the city's urban form to achieve unity between village, factory, city and the natural landscape (Weiner 1959:42) had resulted in the creation of a settlement that did not entirely reflect the intentions of the Stalinist state. Instead, it incorporated several disparate elements. Hungary's socialist rulers were not especially happy with some of these elements. The city was not unproblematically a politicized, socialist landscape in the sense that it materialized state ideology, yet it came to be defined as a socialist landscape. The interaction between those who observed and populated the landscape and the urban form itself during its construction came to shape popular definitions of the city's landscape.

The state intended Sztálinváros to act as a showcase for the socialist society that it sought to create in postwar Hungary. The regime believed that it should materialize the promise of industrial transformation, thus serving as a space that would give industrial employment to the country's rural poor, thus transforming

FIGURE 5. View from the front of the cinema of the medical surgery and hospital, looking across Stalin Street.

them into full members of the country's working class and granting them full citizenship in the new Hungary. Villages like Nagykarácsony in the south of Fejér county, some 20 kilometers from the new city, were to be among those transformed by its creation. A former manorial estate village and then (after land reform in 1945) a settlement of poor peasants, Nagykarácsony was to act as a supplier of both labor and food to the city and the factory. Communist journalist Sándor wrote in 1951 about the way in which Sztálinváros was to serve as a beacon of the future for communities like Nagykarácsony: "At night the fires of Pentele's chimneys light the sky; their sparks like sparkling red stars breaking apart the darkness. Above the former prairie and the banks, the woods and the gardens they rise, lighting the tractors [that] stand in the fields" (Sándor 1951b:213).

If Sztálinváros's construction was intended to represent a beacon marking the route to a socialist industrial future for the villagers of Nagykarácsony, then for those of Dunapentele it represented an attack on their very way of life. With the creation of socialist dictatorship in 1948, compulsory deliveries of agricultural products by farmers and land taxation had been sharply increased while campaigns to collectivize agriculture in the village began. In a predominantly agrarian community, these were interpreted as an attack on the way of life of village residents. The farmsteads on the plateau where the new city and factory were to be built were nationalized. The state paid what was regarded as only negligible compensation (Lukács 2000:219–220). The state security services moved to expel those it regarded as "politically unreliable" from the village. Forty-four families were forcibly removed, including the families of 33 smallholders (Erdős 2000:251). It was into this hostile climate that construction workers first arrived in May 1950. In the first three months of construction there were less than 1,000 workers and only around 150 who were qualified skilled workers. The vast majority of the first construction workers took work on the site to escape poverty and unemployment in rural Hungary (*Sztálin Vasmű Építője* 1951; Miskolczi and Rózsa 1969:54). The new arrivals were deeply unpopular among the Dunapentele residents; many remembered that prior to the construction of the barracks to house workers new to the site, the construction workers were housed in their appropriated farmsteads. The construction of the new city for them became a symbol of their dispossession (Lukács 2000:220).

The construction site was transformed in 1951. That year was intended to be the decisive year for the construction of the new city. By Christmas 1950, the site had 5,860 workers; their numbers rose rapidly throughout 1951, reaching a total of 14,708 by January 1952 (Magyar Országos Levéltár 1950:120; Fejér Megyei Levéltár 1952c:1). The construction workers generally came from the former rural poor; according to those who collected their life histories, most had been members of the families of agricultural laborers prior to land reform. They had gained small amounts of land in 1945 that had been insufficient or only just sufficient to satisfy their need for food. Given the lack of opportunities to perform casual labor during the high unemployment of the late 1940s, many had experienced the immediate postwar years as ones of considerable poverty (Dobos 1958). Furthermore, their perception of the earliest years of socialist dictatorship was shaped by increases in taxation and compulsory deliveries that came with the beginnings of agricultural collectivization. These policies caused considerable hardship in rural Hungary and generated much opposition. Typically construction workers on the site were the young male sons of poor smallholders who took work to weather the hardships their families faced at home. One typical case was A. S. who lived on a small farm. As a result of the farm's inability to guarantee an income for the family, he had to go to work at Sztálinváros. He remembered, "twice a month he could go home for one and a half days and had to spend half a day of free time travelling. He gave his family 200 Forints of his monthly earnings and had to live from the rest" (Open Society Archives 1953a:5).

These experiences meant that large numbers of construction workers on the site were hostile to the socialist regime. This hostility and the social attitudes they took from the villages where they lived shaped the way they experienced Sztálinváros as it was constructed and defined its landscape. Given the chaos, low wages, despotic management and poor working conditions on the construction site the alienating experience of performing socialist labor affected their view of the new city profoundly. By early 1953 the city had largely taken shape. Most construction workers, however, did not feel part of it. For Gy. A., a laborer originally from the rural southwest of the country, the public spaces of the new city "were not used by anyone, because the "working masses" had no time for relaxation." The city's shops and restaurants were, as far as he was concerned, simply for the benefit of its "communist elite," largely because the prices were far more than a construction worker could afford (Open Society Archives 1953c:1). According to T. A., another construction worker, one of the restaurants "offered anything that the mouth would wish for .... It was just the prices that were terrible" (Open Society Archives 1953d:13).

For workers who came from villages where typically the church had formed the center of the community (Jávor 2000), the new city's obvious lack of a place of worship represented a further source of alienation. To Gy. A., for example, "only the most important bulding is lacking in Sztálinváros and that is a church. The opinion of the workers is that 'this town has not accepted the good Lord and it has no blessing from him.'" For many rural construction workers the lack of any presence of organized religion within the fabric of the city represented an offence against the natural order and their own notions of morality. According to Gy. A., "if someone wants to marry, they are forced to go out of the city to marry in one of the village churches, or they have to be content with the civil marriage that some party person conducts" (Open Society Archives 1953c:3). For many construction workers the lack of any presence for organized religion in the new city fed a perception that the state encouraged cohabitation and forms of behavior that were considered immoral; T. A. interpreted cohabitation in the city as a symptom of "free love," apparently encouraged by socialism and the lack of religious influence (Open Society Archives 1953d:16).

These local perceptions of Sztálinváros's landscape found an echo across Hungary during the first half of the 1950s. Sztálinváros played a central role in both early socialist culture and in the propaganda of the regime. At the same time, the state sought to recruit labor to industry, including to Sztálinváros, to stem the labor shortage that was undermining the industrialization drive by 1951. Labor recruiters entered villages where acute social tension generated by the effects of agricultural collectivization, political repression, and state-sponsored anticlericalism bubbled close to the surface (Pittaway 1998a:198–207). For many Hungarian villagers during the early 1950s, going to work in industry was seen as little better than surrender to a state that sought to destroy their way of life (Open Society Archives 1953e:3). These factors shaped an image of Sztálinváros in rural Hungary that was in many ways a direct inversion of that presented in party propaganda. In this image, the city came to symbolize all that anti-Communist Hungarians saw as wrong with the socialist state. According to one such account from 1953, "one only hears bad things about the making of Sztálinváros. A worker can only get out through weakness, illness or internment" (Open Society Archives 1953b:2).

For construction workers building the new city, as well as for those Hungarians who opposed the socialist regime, the political context of the city's creation served to define it as a socialist landscape. Certain features of its urban form, notably the lack of space for organized religion in the city, played a role in shaping this definition. This process had less to do with any specific material forms embedded in the city's fabric as it did with the symbolic significance Hungarians invested in it. Because of the alienation of construction workers, Sztálinváros's definition as a socialist landscape was a negative definition. Construction workers, however, would not make up the bulk of permanent residents of the new city. This can be demonstrated through an analysis of a sample of the successful applications for settlement permits (*letelepedési engedélyek*) that prospective residents of the new town had to acquire to live there between 1951 and 1954. Of those economically active who became residents during this period only 13.1% had been initially employed in the town on the construction site, compared with a figure of 58.1% whose first place of work in Sztálinváros was the steelworks (Fejér Megyei Levéltár 1951). The permanent residents of the town came to shape a more positive definition of Sztálinváros as socialist landscape.

Domesticating Sztálinváros

The public face of the city, its main streets, squares, and public buildings represented a socialist monumentalism that privileged both political power and collectively provided services. Only in the construction of a cinema was space given in the city center for depoliticized leisure, while private consumption was given only a marginal role on the main street. South of the public buildings of the city center, Stalin Street was flanked by five-storied buildings that contained flats for families with shops at street level (Figure 6). Most residential space was tucked back from the arterial roads in several neighborhoods in which flats would be organized around a central square, park, and local facilities, including shops and schools.

The "first residential area" was planned together with the city as a whole during the first half of 1950, located between the southeast side of György Dózsa Street and the southwest side of Stalin Street (Figure 3). It was designed to be populated by 7,000 people and also contained shops, a theater, and an elementary school. The residential area was undoubtedly experimental, and its planners aimed to learn from the experiences of the first area to subsequently plan the others after it was finished in 1951 (Weiner 1959:54).

The flats for the new residents were designed to be manifestly superior to much of the housing for industrial workers in Hungary. In a country in which inside bathrooms and toilets only became commonplace in the 1970s, all flats in the new city were to be equipped with a bathroom and flushing toilet—something that much propaganda pointed to (Sándor 1951c). The housing was also designed to be spacious, at a time when in much of the rest of the country there was a severe shortage of adequate working-class housing due to low investment (Pittaway 2000:54–57). The city's planners, many of whom had been employed on the design of relatively small-scale housing projects in Budapest prior to their move to Sztálinváros, took several of their designs for standardized mass housing in the capital and built them in the city (Szende 1951). Housing of this kind was built along the 1 May Street (Május 1 utca), the first residential street in the city to be completed (Figure 7).

FIGURE 6 Five-storied apartment blocks on the western side of Stalin Street.

On the west side of the street five houses were built, each containing three stories and 12 family flats. Each flat contained a hall and two large rooms; one was a bedroom and the other, a living room. In addition, each flat also contained a kitchen, small bathroom, and a separate toilet. Although the flats that flanked the east side of the street were externally different, given that the blocks were larger with four stories, each containing 80 family flats, their internal design was fundamentally the same. In each case and in contrast to much working-class housing across the country, where a family would typically live in one room, they were designed to provide space for a family to live. In each flat the planner designed the main room to accommodate two tables, including a main table that would have seats for four people. Furthermore, in contrast to much state rhetoric, which stressed the value of collective services, the existence of both the kitchen and the planning of the main room to accommodate a dining table, suggested the planners envisaged the home as being one for a privatized, nuclear family (Hámor 1951:621).

The designers of the flats embraced an ideal of "stalinist domesticity" (Pittaway 2000:52) that was founded on an ideal of the nuclear family as the basic unit of urban society. In some regards, this model, which informed the design and regulation of the new flats, challenged certain aspects of working-class culture. In much of industrial Hungary, the home, together with the garden and allotment, played a central role in the self-provisioning of foodstuffs (Paládi-Kovács 2000; Pittaway 2000). Sztálinváros's city council was determined that this would not become the case in the new city. No garden space was made available to the new residents within the city boundaries, while the keeping of animals within the flats or the buildings that housed them was explicitly forbidden. The regulations for the residents in the new housing were to be policed by a specially employed *concierge* whose responsibility, among others, was to safeguard "socialist morality" (Horváth 2000:30–31).

The state envisaged that the city's residents should solely be consumers of food. Despite the later opening of the "free market" a short

FIGURE 7. May 1st Street, looking south.

distance away, the authorities sought to encourage consumption through the state-run retail network. To this end it built and opened a shopping center (*üzletház*) for the residential district in 1951 (Figure 8). This center was in effect a two-story building. On the ground floor were located a grocers and clothing shop together with their associated offices, while the top floor was given over to a restaurant that proved to be too expensive for the city's residents (Gyárfás 1951:209–210). The expense of the restaurant was not the only problem reported with the shopping center; standards of service in its shops left much to be desired during the early 1950s. Many complained that staff regarded customers as an inconvenience to be tolerated (Politikatörténeti és Szakszervezeti Levéltár 1951:2). In 1952 frequent complaints were received about staff in the shops deliberately underweighing quantities of milk, cheese, and meat and then overcharging consumers. This was combined with arbitrary pricing. Shop staff were often accused of unofficially changing prices from hour to hour (Fejér Megyei Levéltár 1953:1–2).

The vast majority of the new residents were from very different social origins from the construction workers, and, consequently, their reactions to the new city would be profoundly different. They were largely young, skilled workers from other industrial areas in the country. They sought to escape low wages and especially poor housing conditions in industrial Hungary and went to Sztálinváros to take skilled work and set up families in newer and better housing. There was considerable tension between the residents with an urban, working-class origin and the construction workers during the early 1950s. Often this tension took the form of street fighting at weekends and in the evenings between the young, single male factory workers and some of the construction workers (L. A. 1995).

The new urban residents were distrustful of the socialist state for the first half of the 1950s, although the reasons for that distrust were different from that of the construction workers. Few had direct experience of state policies towards rural areas and many were deeply distrustful of smallholders and those who lived in

FIGURE 8. The first residential district's shopping center.

line" for a family of four at 1,900 Forints, meaning that a working class Sztálinváros family needed two incomes to guarantee a basic standard of living for themselves (Magyar Országos Levéltár 1956). Because of the lack of light industrial employment in the city, there was a shortage of work for working-class women, effectively meaning that many families lived below or close to the trade unions' poverty line, which was calculated to allow only for the most basic standard of living (Fejér Megyei Levéltár 1956a:4).

If in the early years Sztálinváros's residents had little money to become socialist consumers and lacked the hedge of self-provisioning, then their flats also fell short of expectations. The early flats suffered from poor standards of construction. One new resident of a flat on Stalin Street complained that "when we moved in, the floor was so uneven we were afraid we were going to break our legs." Another worker "was delighted" with his new flat. "In the old days only wealthy capitalists and factory owners had such flats. Everything is wonderful—only the door frames are badly finished and the plaster falls off around them. It needs very little foresight to realize that the doors will be useless pretty soon" (*Szabad Nép* 1952).

During the first half of the 1950s, frustration was also common in Hungarian industrial communities beyond Sztálinváros with the poor quality of state-provided housing and food, the shortages of goods, as well as the continuing poverty (Pittaway 2000:57–59). These frustrations helped ensure, however, that during the Revolution of 1956 Sztálinváros was a center of antiregime activity (Erdős 2000:267–280). After 1956 the restored regime of János Kádár sought to reconstruct the authority of the socialist system through an appeal principally directed to Hungary's urban working class. The ruling party rhetorically emphasized its identity as a "workers' party" while wage levels were increased and social benefits were expanded (Pittaway 2001). Working-class residents in Sztálinváros proved much more receptive to these shifts in policy than the population of Hungary as a whole. This was in part because of the working class origins of many residents and also because the state's national measures were dovetailed with measures locally to expand light industrial employment, thus creating more

the villages. They had experienced socialism in the factories along with other industrial workers, an experience characterized by high work intensity, despotic management, and low wages. Furthermore they had been affected by the food shortages that plagued industrial areas during the early years of socialist industrialization. Although conditions were generally better in Sztálinváros than in the country as a whole, they were not fantastically so. Workers still experienced poverty and shortages of goods (Pittaway 1998a).

Average monthly wages for the largely male workforce of the steel workers stood at 1,283 Forints in January 1956, which was the average wage for workers in heavy industrial plants (Fejér Megyei Levéltár 1956b:2). At this time, the official trade unions calculated the "poverty jobs for women workers (Csatári 2000). New residents had already bought into the ideal of "stalinist domesticity" by moving to the city in the 1950s. With the improvements in living standards, the repair of their flats, and the realization of surrogate socialist consumerism in the late 1950s and early 1960s, they could believe that a reality underpinned this ideal (Pittaway 1998b). The more positive view of socialism among working-class Hungarians that these changes engendered brought about a positive definition of Sztálinváros as a "new socialist city." Life history interviews suggest that in the late 1950s a positive view of Sztálinváros emerged as a place that gave jobs and secure homes to its working-class residents. While this view ignored some of the shortcomings of socialist transformation as experienced by Sztálinváros residents, it is nevertheless the dominant one among residents who came to the city during the 1950s and continues to inform a fierce local patriotism (B. P.-né 1995; L. A. 1995; T. J.-né 1996).

Conclusion

Sztálinváros, now Dunaújváros, has been universally defined as a socialist industrial landscape. This stems from its creation, when it served as the flagship of a state-led policy of industrial transformation during the early 1950s and as a laboratory for socialist urban design in Hungary. The way in which the landscape created by the planners was received and appropriated at a popular level reveals much about the responses of social groups to socialist transformation and thus the regime that governed the country for 41 years. Both the rural construction workers who built the city and those who came to live there developed alternative definitions of Sztálinváros as a socialist landscape. The construction workers and, by extension, Hungary's rural majority interpreted the landscape as deeply alien to its culture. Another view, forged by the residents of the city who were largely of urban, industrial working-class origin was more positive, stressing the role of the city in providing secure jobs and superior homes.

The way in which the socialist landscape of Sztálinváros was given meaning parallels the way in which Hungarian society itself responded to socialist transformation. Throughout the post-war period Hungary had been marked by a deep political and cultural division between supporters of the right and left, even though in a single-party political system, such divisions could not be openly expressed within the public sphere. These broadly corresponded to class divisions between the working class on the one hand and agrarian and middle class social groups on the other. During Hungary's Stalinist years, when dictatorship in the country was at its harshest, both groups were discontented with the state even though their social and cultural values profoundly differed. After the 1956 revolution as the state sought to buy support by accommodating the working-class Hungarian society came to be divided into those with broadly positive and negative views of socialist transformation. Sztálinváros's very definition as a socialist landscape ensured that views of it would reflect these deep-seated political divisions.

Sztálinváros was not the only Hungarian or even East European landscape that became "politicized" from above and below during the socialist years. These landscapes and popular reactions to them have the potential to reveal much about the formation of political identities across the region—identities that were largely hidden from view by state repression. In the postsocialist era, the role that material culture has played, including landscapes, in articulating popular memories of socialism suggests that the discovery of the processes by which material culture was originally defined are of importance for interrogating contemporary social and political phenomena. This article suggests a need for work on a variety of "socialist" landscapes that interrogates not only their material reality but also their reception at the moment of their creation.

ACKNOWLEDGMENTS

I would like to thank the ESRC (Economic and Social Research Council) and the Research Committee of the Faculty of Arts at the Open University for financial support that made the research on which this article is based possible. I would like to thank the staff of the Intercisa Museum in Dunaújváros, the staff of the Factory History Collection of Dunaferr Rt., and the Pensioners' Club of the Dunaújváros branch of the Metalworkers' Trade Union for their assistance. In addition particular thanks are due to Mark Cassell but also to David Crowley, Padraic Kenney, Katherine Lebow, Nigel Swain, and Zsuzsanna Varga for discussions that have helped shape many of the arguments developed in this article.

REFERENCES

AMAN, ANDERS
1992 *Architecture and Ideology in Eastern Europe during the Stalin Era. An Aspect of Cold War History.* Architectural History Foundation, New York, NY.

ANDRÉN, ANDERS
1998 *Between Artifacts and Texts. Historical Archaeology in Global Perspective.* Trans. by Alan Crozier. Plenum Press, New York, NY.

BEAUDRY, MARY C., LAUREN J. COOK, AND STEPHEN A. MROZOWSKI
1991 Artifacts and Active Voices: Material Culture as Social Discourse. In *The Archaeology of Inequality*, Randall McGuire and Robert Paynter, editors, pp. 150–191, Blackwell Publishers: Oxford, England.

BENDER, BARBARA (EDITOR)
1993 *Landscape: Politics and Perspectives.* Berg, Oxford, England.

BETTS, PAUL
2000 The Twilight of the Idols: East German Memory and Material Culture. *The Journal of Modern History,* 72(3):731–765.

BIRTA, ISTVÁN
1970 A szocialista iparosítási politika néhány kérdése az első ötéves terv időszakában. *Párttörténeti Közlemények,* 16(3):113–151.

BOKOVOY, MELISSA
1998 *Peasants and Communists: Politics and Ideology in the Yugoslav Countryside, 1941–1953.* University of Pittsburgh Press, Pittsburgh, PA.

B. P.-NÉ
1995 Personal confidential interview with author, Dunaújváros, Hungary, 6 February.

BUCHLI, VICTOR
1998 *An Archaeology of Socialism.* Materializing Cultures, Berg, Oxford, England.

COSGROVE, DENIS E.
1984 *Social Formation and Symbolic Landscape.* Croom Helm, London, England.

CRAWFORD, MARGARET
1995 *Building the Workingman's Paradise: The Design of American Company Towns.* Verso, London, England.

CREED, GERALD W.
1998 *Domesticating Revolution: From Socialist Reform to Ambivalent Transition in a Bulgarian Village.* Pennsylvania State University Press, University Park, PA.

CSATÁRI, BENCE
2000 A forradalom leverésétől a rendszerváltásig. In *Dunaújváros Története,* Ferenc Erdős and Zsuzsánna Pongrácz, editors, pp. 281–298. Dunaújváros Megyei Jogú Város Önkormányzata, Dunaújváros, Hungary.

DOBOS, ILONA S.
1958 *Szegény Ember Vízzel Főz. Életrajzi Vállomások ("Igaz Történetek").* Magvető Könyvkiadó, Budapest, Hungary.

DONALD, MOIRA, AND LINDA HURCOMBE (EDITORS)
1998 *Gender and Material Culture in Historical Perspective.* Macmillan, Basingstoke, England.

DOWLING, TIMOTHY C.
1999 Building Socialism: Stalinstadt/Eisenhüttenstadt: A Model for (Socialist) Life in the German Democratic Republic. Doctoral dissertation, Modern European History, Tulane University, New Orleans, LA.

ERDŐS, FERENC
2000 Dunapentelétől Sztálinvárosig. In *Dunaújváros Története,* Ferenc Erdős and Zsuzsánna Pongrácz, editors, pp. 243–279. Dunaújváros Megyei Jogú Város Önkormányzata, Dunaújváros, Hungary.

FARKAS, GÁBOR
1975 Dunapentele története a kapitalizmus korában 1850–1950. *Fejér Megyei Történeti Évkönyv,* 9:163–216.

FEJÉR MEGYEI LEVÉLTÁR
1951 Letelepedési engedélyek gyűjteménye, 1951–1954. XXII fond, 506 csoport, 1–14 doboz.
1952a Hírdetmény az adonyi járásbiróság itéletei a gépgyári munkafegyelmet megsértő munkavállalók ügyében, XXIX fond, 17 csoport, 1 doboz.
1952b Jegyzőkönyv felvétetett 1952. Junius 3.-án megtartott pártbizottsági ülésen, a P.B. tanácstermében. Magyar Szocialista Munkáspárt Fejér Megyei Bizottság Archivium iratai 17f.1/24 ö.e.
1952c Jelentés a Sztálinvárosi Pártbizottság agitációs munkájáról. Magyar Szocialista Munkáspárt Fejér Megyei Bizottság Archivium iratai 17f.2/22 ö.e.
1953 A Sztálinvárosi Tanács végrehajtó Bizottságba ..... Magyar Szocialista Munkáspárt Fejér Megyei Bizottság Archivium iratai 9f. 2/PTO/48 ö.e.
1954a Feljegyzés a Sztálinvárosi Vegyesipari Vállalat elődvállalatainak szervezéséről, XXIII fond, 507 csoport, 2 doboz.
1955 Jegyzőkönyv felvéve 1955. Szeptember 24-én. A Sztálinvárosi Pártbizottság ülésen. Magyar Szocialista Munkáspárt Fejér Megyei Bizottság Archivium iratai 17f.1/19 ö.e.

1956a Jegyzőkönyv felvétetett 1956. Augusztus 4-én a Sztálinvárosi Pártbizottság és a Sztálin Vasmű Pártbizottság együttes ülésen. Magyar Szocialista Munkáspárt Fejér Megyei Bizottság Archivium iratai 17f.1/20 ö.e.

1956b Sztálin Vasmű bérezési problémai. Magyar Szocialista Párt Fejér Megyei Bizottság Archivium iratai 17f.1/37 ö.e.

FRENCH, R. A., AND F. E. IAN HAMILTON (EDITORS)
1979 *The Socialist City: Spatial Structure and Urban Policy.* John Wiley & Sons, New York, NY.

GYÁRFÁS, IVÁN
1951 A középületek tervezésének fejlődése a Sztálin Vasmű városépítésének tükrében. *Építés—Építészet,* 2(3): 605–619.

HÁMOR ISTVÁN
1951 Lakóháztípusok fejlődése a Sztálin Vasmű tükrében. *Építés –Építészet,* 2(3):620–628.

HIRSCH, ERICH, AND MICHAEL O'HANLON (EDITORS)
1995 *Anthropology of Landscape. Perspectives on Place and Space.* Oxford University Press, New York, NY.

HORVÁTH, ISTVÁN, FERENC SZABÓ, AND SÁNDOR CZINKÓCZI (EDITORS)
2000 *Dunaferr-Dunai Vasmű Kronika,* Dunaferr Rt., Dunaújváros, Hungary.

HORVÁTH, SÁNDOR
2000 A parasztság életmódváltozása Sztálinvárosban. *Mozgó Vílág,* 26(6):30–40.

IMRÉNÉ SZŐNYEGI, HAJNALKA
2000 A II. világháborútól a beruházások megkezdéséig. In *Dunaújváros Története,* Ferenc Erdős and Zsuzsánna Pongrácz, editors, pp. 221–243. Dunaújváros Megyei Jogú Város Önkormányzata, Dunaújváros, Hungary.

JÁVOR, KATA
2000 Egyház és a Vallásosság Helye és Szerepe a Paraszti Társadalomban. In *Magyar Néprajz VIII: Társadalom,* Attila Paládi-Kovács, editor, pp. 791–818. Akadémiai Kiadó, Budapest, Hungary.

KENNEY, PADRAIC
1997 *Rebuilding Poland: Workers and Communists 1945–1950.* Cornell University Press, Ithaca, NY.

KIDECKEL, DAVID A.
1993 *The Solitude of Collectivism: Romanian Villagers to the Revolution and Beyond.* Cornell University Press, Ithaca, NY.

KOPSTEIN, JEFFREY
1997 *The Politics of Economic Decline in East Germany, 1945–1989.* The University of North Carolina Press, Chapel Hill.

KOTKIN, STEVEN
1995 *Magnetic Mountain: Stalinism as a Civilization.* University of California Press, Berkeley, CA.

L. A.
1995 Personal confidential interview by author. Dunaújváros, Hungary. 10 July.

LAMPLAND, MARTHA
1995 *The Object of Labor: Commodification in Socialist Hungary.* Chicago University Press, IL.

LEBOW, KATHERINE A.
1999 Revising the Politicized Landscape: Nowa Huta, 1949–1957. *City and Society,* 11(1–2):165–187.
2001 Public Works, Private Lives: Youth Brigades in Nowa Huta in the 1950s. *Contemporary European History,* 10(2):199–219.

LUKÁCS, LÁSZLÓ
2000 Dunapentele gazdasági Néprajza. In *Dunaújváros Története,* Ferenc Erdős and Zsuzsánna Pongrácz, editors, pp. 197–220. Dunaújváros Megyei Jogú Város Önkormányzata, Dunaújváros, Hungary.

MAGYAR ORSZÁGOS LEVÉLTÁR
1950 Jelentés a Titkárság részére a Dunai Vasmű Párt- és Tömegszervezeteinek helyzetéről. M-szekció, 276 fond, 88 csoport, 306 ö.e.
1956 Tájékoztató a munkások és alkalmazottak létminimumának alakulásáról. M- szekció, 276 fond, 66 csoport, 36 ö.e.

MERKEL, INA
1999 *Utopie und Bedürfnis: Die Geschichte der Konsumkultur in der DDR.* Böhlau Verlag, Köln, Germany.

MISKOLCZI, MIKLÓS
1980 *Város lesz, csak azért is … …* Magyarország felfedezése, Szépirodalmi Könyvkiadó, Budapest, Hungary.

MISKOLCZI, MIKLÓS, AND ANDRÁS RÓZSA
1969 A Huszéves Dunai Vasmű. Manuscript, Dunaferr Gyártörténeti Gyűjtemény, Dunaújváros, Hungary.

MITCHELL, W. J. T. (EDITOR)
1994 *Landscape and Power.* University of Chicago Press, IL.

MROZOWSKI, STEPHEN A.
1991 Landscapes of Inequality. In *The Archaeology of Inequality,* Randall H. McGuire and Robert Paynter, editors, pp. 79–101. Blackwell, Cambridge, MA.

MUSIL, JIRI
1980 *Urbanisation in Socialist Countries.* M.E. Sharpe, White Plains, NY.

OPEN SOCIETY ARCHIVES
 1953a Transcript of interview, Item No. 06852/63, Open
       Society Archives, Radio Free Europe, Hungarian
       Research Department Collection, Central European
       University, Budapest, Hungary.
 1953b Transcript of interview, Item No. 059193/53, Open
       Society Archives, Radio Free Europe, Hungarian
       Research Department Collection, Central European
       University, Budapest, Hungary.
 1953c Transcript of interview, Item No. 04530/53, Open
       Society Archives, Radio Free Europe, Hungarian
       Research Department Collection, Central European
       University, Budapest, Hungary.
 1953d Transcript of interview, Item No. 04381/53, Open
       Society Archives, Radio Free Europe, Hungarian
       Research Department Collection, Central European
       University, Budapest, Hungary.
 1953e Transcript of interview, Item No. 12232/53, Open
       Society Archives, Radio Free Europe, Hungarian
       Research Department Collection, Central European
       University, Budapest, Hungary.

PALÁDI-KOVÁCS, ATTILA
 2000 Az Ipari Munkásság. In *Magyar Néprajz VIII.
      Társadalom.* Attila Paládi-Kovács, editor, pp. 239–308.
      Akadémiai Kiadó, Budapest, Hungary.

PENCE, KATHERINE
 2000 "You as a Woman Will Understand": Consumption,
      Gender, and the Relationship between State and
      Citizenry in the GDR's Crisis of 17 June 1953.
      German History, 19(2):218–252.

PITTAWAY, MARK
 1998a Industrial Workers, Socialist Industrialisation and
       the State in Hungary, 1948–1958. Doctoral thesis.
       Department of Economic and Social History,
       University of Liverpool, Liverpool, England.
 1998b Consumption, Political Stabilisation, and Social
       Identity: The Roots of Socialist Consumerism
       in Hungary, 1953–1960. Paper presented at the
       conference on Socialist Artefacts, Places, and
       Identities, Victoria and Albert Museum, London,
       England.
 2000 Stalinism, Working-Class Housing, and Individual
      Autonomy: The Encouragement of Private House
      Building in Hungary's Mining Areas, 1950–54. In
      *Style and Socialism: Modernity and Material Culture
      in Post-War Eastern Europe,* Susan E. Reid and David
      Crowley, editors, pp. 49–64. Berg, New York, NY.
 2001 Reconstructing Socialism in the Aftermath of
      Revolution: Industrial Labour and the Making of
      the Kádár regime in Hungary. Paper given at the
      Core Seminar in Modern European History: Social
      and Political Change in Europe, 1945–1975, Faculty
      of Modern History, University of Oxford, United
      Kingdom.
 2003 Dealing with Dictatorship: Socialism and the Sites of
      Memory in Contemporary Hungary. In *War, Culture,
      and Memory,* Clive Emsley, editor, pp. 269–308. The
      Open University, Milton Keynes, England.

POLITIKATÖRTÉNETI ÉS SZAKSZERVEZETI LEVÉLTÁR
 1951 Jelentés a munkásellátási munkáról, szállások és
      társadalmi ellenőrök munkájáról. Épitőipari Dolgozók
      Szakszevezete iratai, 939 dosszie.

REID, SUSAN E., AND DAVID CROWLEY (EDITORS)
 2000 *Style and Socialism: Modernity and Material Culture
      in Post-War Eastern Europe.* Berg, New York, NY.

RÓNA-TAS, ÁKOS
 1997 *The Great Surprise of the Small Transformation: The
      Demise of Communism and the Rise of the Private
      Sector in Hungary.* University of Michigan Press,
      Ann Arbor, MI.

SAMSON, STEVEN
 1984 *National Integration through Socialist Planning: An
      Anthropological Study of a Romanian New Town.*
      East European Monographs, Boulder, CO.

SÁNDOR, ANDRÁS
 1951a *Az Új Város.* A Népmûvelési Minisztérium Kiadása,
       Budapest, Hungary.
 1951b *Híradás a Pusztáról 1945–1950.* Széprirodalmi
       Könyvkiadó, Budapest, Hungary.
 1951c *Sztálinváros.* A Népmûvelési Minisztérium Kiadása,
       Budapest, Hungary.

SCHAMA, SIMON
 1995 *Landscape and Memory.* Harper Collins, London.
      England.

SCHLITTERNÉ NYULI, ANNA
 1994 *"Volt egyszer egy Dunapentele ....,"* 2 vols.,
      "Dunaújvárosért" Városszépítő és—védő Egyesület
      elnöksége, Dunaújváros, Hungary.

SZABAD NÉP
 1952 No title. *Szabad Nép,* 15 September 1952. Budapest,
      Hungary.

SZENDE, LÁSZLÓ
 1951 Az ötéves terv első évének lakástermelése. *Épités—
      Építészet,* 2(1):197–221.

SZENDRŐI JENŐ
 1972 *Magyar építészet 1945–70.* Corvina Kiadó, Budapest,
      Hungary.

SZTÁLIN VASMÛ ÉPÍTŐJE
 1951 No title. *Sztálin Vasmû Építője,* 31 December,
      Sztálinváros, Hungary.
 1952 No title. *Sztálin Vasmû Építője,* 11 January,
      Sztálinváros, Hungary.

TÁBORI, ZOLTÁN
 1998 *Vasmû.* Sík Kiadó, Budapest, Hungary.

T. J.-NÉ
 1996 Personal confidential interview by author, Dunaújváros,
      Hungary, 6 May.

VALUCH, TIBOR
2001 *Magyarország társadalomtörténete a XX. Század második felében.* Osiris Kiadó, Budapest, Hungary.

VARGA, ZSUZSANNA
2001 *Politika, paraszti érdekérvényesítés és szövetkezetek Magyarországon 1956–1967.* Politikatörténeti Füzetek, Napvílág Kiadó, Budapest, Hungary.

VÖRÖS, MIKLÓS
1997 Életmód, ideológia, háztartás. A fogyasztáskutatás politikuma az államszocializmus korszakában. *Replika,* 26:17–30.

WEINER, TIBOR
1951 Sztálinváros, szocialista város. A városépítés módszere. *Építés—Építészet,* 2(3):589–598.
1959 "Sztálinváros." In *Sztálinváros—Miskolc—Tatabánya. Városépítésünk Fejlődése,* Aladár Sós and Faragó Kálmán, editors, pp. 17–88. Műszaki Könyvkiadó, Budapest, Hungary.

MARK PITTAWAY
DEPARTMENT OF HISTORY, FACULTY OF ARTS
THE OPEN UNIVERSITY, WALTON HALL
MILTON KEYNES MK7 6AA
UNITED KINGDOM

Paul A. Shackel and Matthew Palus

Industry, Entrepreneurship, and Patronage: Lewis Wernwag and the Development of Virginius Island

ABSTRACT

In the 19th century, Virginius Island developed as a center for craft, industry, and service facilities that supported the United States Armory complex at Harpers Ferry, Virginia. The earliest phase of development in this community is represented at one tract of land that is associated with the family of engineer and entrepreneur Lewis Wernwag. Wernwag was an inventor, bridge builder, and machinist. A landscape and archaeological analysis shows the contradictions of living in a community transitioning to an industrial capitalist economy. While the landscape that Wernwag created reflects the traditional craft ethos—one that does not reinforce the separations of domestic and work life—the family's household assemblage shows that they did participate in modern consumerism and they reinforced separations around the table and between groups. An analysis of the Wernwags' property and assemblage shows how this family embraced emerging technological rationalities through material things.

Introduction

Virginius Island is situated adjacent to Lower Town Harpers Ferry, on the northern side of the Shenandoah River near the border between West Virginia and Maryland. During the 19th and early 20th centuries it was a manufacturing center that stood apart from Harpers Ferry. Even though it was firmly joined to its neighbor through social, political, and economic networks, it was excluded from the federal land reserve of the U.S. Armory. Many are aware of the nationally significant events that occurred in Harpers Ferry, such as the perfection of interchangeable gun parts by rifle manufacturer John Hall during the 1820s–1830s (Shackel 1996:34–37,41–42), which changed the nature of factory work throughout the armory at Harpers Ferry and foretold a nationwide shift towards mechanization and mass manufacturing. On the other hand, few people know of Virginius Island's place in the history of the American Industrial Revolution. Nothing remains of the community except for the ruined traces of workshops, factories, and waterways, as well as a few residual house foundations. Over the past two decades a major history and archaeology project undertaken by the National Park Service emphasized the social history of Virginius Island and highlighted its place in the industrial history of the United States (Johnson and Barker 1992; Palus 2000; Palus and Shackel 2006). To date, stabilization has concentrated only on the industrial ruins on the island, highlighting the past manufacturing prowess of this former community. The remains of the domestic structures continue to be impacted by the elements of nature and few are interpreted to the public (Figure 1).

The early history of Virginius Island is relevant to the development of Harpers Ferry and to cultural changes corresponding to the dramatic reorganization of work at the U.S. Armory during the early 19th century. In particular, the archaeological record associated with inventor and bridge builder Lewis Wernwag, whose career and accomplishments are well documented, offers some important insights into the ethos that promoted the mechanization of industry at Harpers Ferry and throughout the United States. Wernwag moved to Virginius Island with his family by 1824 and had manufacturing and building interests throughout Harpers Ferry, including the armory.

The evidence suggests that Wernwag was part of the generation that introduced technological rationality to American manufacturing, foreshadowing later transitions in industrial capitalism that were often detrimental to manufacturing rooted in a craft-based ethos. Wernwag himself was caught in this transition, and the Wernwag tract on Virginius Island yields contradictory messages about how the family participated in an emerging industrial capitalist society. The interplay of ideology and subjectivity is a complicated one, and in general, theories of subjection offer a tighter focus on the social lives of individuals and their (per)formative relationship to popular culture, society, authority, and law, and are integrated into most recent critical studies of racial, gender, and sexual identities. The ideology that would define the industrial subject-position is "technological rationality," a form of thought addressed

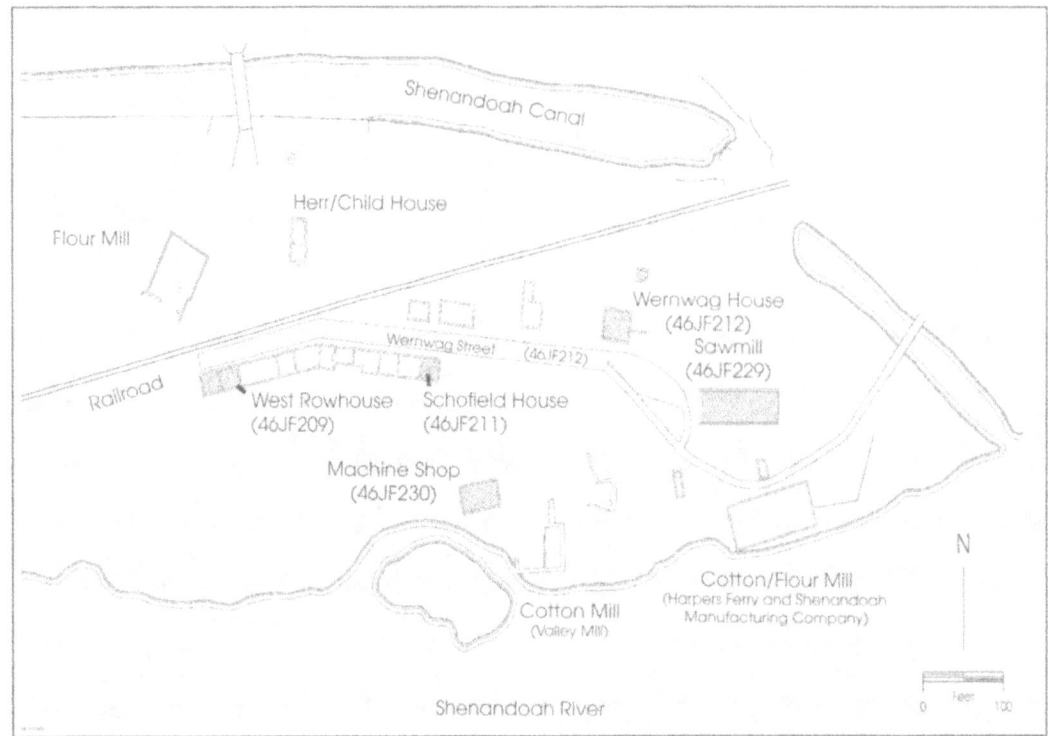

FIGURE 1. Overview of structures on Virginius Island, depicting the locations of Lewis Wernwag's house and sawmill. (Drawing by John Ravenhorst, 2000.)

by many of the Frankfurt School philosophers (Held 1980:263–267; Jay 1996; Horkheimer and Adorno 1998; Bottomore 2002) and defined by Herbert Marcuse (1982) as the fetishization of efficiency, which comes to govern many aspects of life under industrialized states or "technocracies" (de Certeau 1997).

The Wernwag family made significant contributions to the industrial and technological development of Virginius Island, while also connecting the town to regional markets through bridge building. The concern for efficiency that characterizes industrial capitalism (following Marcuse) is not reflected in Wernwag's landscape, however, where his house, two mills, raceways, and a railroad line do not appear to be placed in a rational manner. There are no boundaries or clear separations between domestic and craft enterprises. Conversely, the domestic archaeological assemblage provides evidence for the Wernwag family's consumption of the products of mass production in advance of much of the

town of Harpers Ferry (as it has been understood archaeologically).

Early Virginius Island

In 1794, the U.S. Congress decided to establish two armories for the manufacture and storage of arms, one in Springfield, Massachusetts, and the other in Harpers Ferry, Virginia (Smith 1977:147). Harpers Ferry developed as a small town with "a good tavern, several large stores for goods, a library, one physician, and a professor of the English language" (Noffsinger 1958:20). The development of new forms of transportation in the 1830s heightened Harpers Ferry's importance as a center between the Ohio and Shenandoah valleys and the East. In 1833 the Chesapeake and Ohio Canal reached the town, and the Baltimore and Ohio Railroad arrived one year later. The linking of Harpers Ferry to regional and national networks was instrumental to its continued economic growth (Bushong 1941:83–84; Everhart 1952:22).

While Virginius Island is situated adjacent to Harpers Ferry, very few of the area's earliest settlers took an interest in this property. Documentary research has uncovered little about the island in the first few years of the 19th century, but by 1820 several mills and a few dwellings existed on the island (Harpers Ferry Mill Co. v. Thos. H. Savery et al. 1887:35,42). Industry developed rapidly on the island in the 1830s. A newspaper article described the situation in Virginius Island in 1834: "Hands could be employed at the place very advantageously, without incurring the expense of erecting buildings for their residences. The families of the workmen in the Armory might find useful and constant employment in such Factories, *which might yield them a support independent of their parents* [emphasis added]" (*Virginia Free Press* [*VFP*] 1834). In other words, opportunities to labor on Virginius Island could turn dependents into individuals, fully formed industrial subjects. The island developed into a mixed residential and industrial community with dwellings often surrounding the various industrial clusters.

In the 1830s, enslaved African Americans comprised about 20% of the island's population. The 1830 and 1840 federal censuses indicate that most of the male heads of household on Virginius Island had some type of skilled or semiskilled occupation. These include three masons, a laborer, a tanner, a bricklayer, two carpenters, a master cooper and as many as four journeymen coopers, at least one master blacksmith and a journeyman blacksmith, two machinists, a founder, an armory employee, a druggist, one or two millwrights, and two merchants (Johnson and Barker 1992:15–17).

The Wernwag Family

The most intact archaeological context for the earliest occupation on Virginius Island is associated with the Wernwag household. Lewis Wernwag was one of the most prominent engineers to live in the Harpers Ferry region, if not *the* most prominent. Earlier in his career—in 1812—he constructed the Phoenix Nail Works in Chester County, Pennsylvania. There he managed the production of cut and wrought nails with 42 nail machines (Nelson 1990:59). Wernwag's reputation developed when bridge construction made tremendous strides in the United States at the turn of the 19th century, as builders began to

create bigger and more efficient bridges. In this historical perspective, Lewis Wernwag's Colossus (also known as the Fairmont Bridge), built in Philadelphia to span the Schuylkill River in 1812, was a 340 ft. clear-span wooden bridge, the longest in the world. As a technological feat it greatly surpassed contemporary design. It became world famous, and many considered it as one of the major engineering accomplishments of the early 19th century, not only because of its design, but also because of its span. "Even today, a 340 ft. clear span is considered a very daring concept" (Nelson 1990:40). In addition, between 1816 and 1819 Wernwag constructed bridges in New Hope, Delaware, and two spanning the Monongahela and Allegheny rivers in Pittsburgh, Pennsylvania (Johnson 1995:3).

The Wager family, which held a monopoly of all of the privately owned land in Harpers Ferry, convinced Wernwag to leave Philadelphia in order to construct a 750 ft. pedestrian bridge over the Potomac River at Harpers Ferry. After completing the bridge Wernwag decided to stay in Harpers Ferry, and he developed a machine and woodworking complex on a Virginius Island tract that he purchased from Armory Superintendent James Stubblefield. He operated a sawmill, and his ledger indicates he was cutting wood in 1822 and 1823 for the most politically prominent Harpers Ferry families, including the Wagers, Stubblefields, Stephensons, and Beckhams (Wernwag 1822–1826).

Lewis Wernwag profited from his close relationship with Armory Superintendent Stubblefield, as he received many contracts to perform milling work. Stubblefield also dismantled the armory's sawmill in the early 1820s soon after awarding contracts to his new friend Wernwag. Stubblefield was later accused of buying wood products from Wernwag at exorbitant prices in order to allow Wernwag to pay off his purchase of land from Stubblefield. Through his relationship with Stubblefield, Wernwag held a virtual monopoly over woodturning contracts to the U.S. Armory (Johnson and Barker 1992:240; Johnson 1995).

Wernwag, along with the other landowners of Virginius Island, petitioned the state assembly for the establishment of the town of Virginius, and by 8 January 1827 they successfully incorporated the island community (Joseph et al. 1993:3–18). Lewis Wernwag was named one of the original trustees of the community (Johnson 1995:5). A year later he advertised for a teacher for the growing village (*VFP* 1828).

The 1830 federal census lists 14 people in the Wernwag household. They included Lewis and his wife Elizabeth, who were both about 60 years old. The census also included three enslaved individuals, one male and one female between 24 and 36 years old, and one female between 10 and 24 years of age. Based on contemporary norms one can only assume that the male worked in Wernwag's industrial complex and the females served as domestic help. The remaining people in the census included family members and boarders (Jefferson County Deed Book [JCDB]1826:416–417). Wernwag's ledger indicates that he used his house as a boarding-house/tavern. Numerous entries indicate that visitors stayed from 1 to 15 days, and that his wife and/or domestics helped to serve them meals (Wernwag 1822–1826). The composition of the Wernwag household, including slaves, servants, and boarders, is especially important in interpreting artifact assemblages produced in part through the relations between these persons; artifacts associated with the household are not necessarily produced by the Wernwag family alone but from these intersubjective relationships.

In 1831, Wernwag patented, constructed, and sold "Self Regulating" railroad cars that were intended to "run around curves" (Nelson 1990:59). That same year he became involved in constructing a bridge over the Monocacy River, near Frederick, Maryland, for the Baltimore and Ohio Railroad. It was designed by B. H. Latrobe, Jr., and consisted of three 110 ft. arches (Nelson 1990:59).

In 1833, Wernwag constructed a lock for the Chesapeake and Ohio Canal (JCDB 1833:79). During the 1820s and 1830s Wernwag built dams on the Shenandoah and Potomac rivers for the U.S. Armory. He also built various structures for the gun factory (Johnson and Barker 1992:242). Wernwag advertised that he could turn all types of material including, "Wood, Brass, Iron, and Steel" (*VFP* 1833a, 1833b). He also constructed brick and frame dwellings on his property along Virginius Island's main (and only) street, named Wernwag Street (Johnson and Barker 1992:12–13).

In 1832 and 1833, Wernwag sold all of his rights to lands and industry that he had developed on the island. Perhaps after Stubblefield resigned from his position as superintendent of the armory in 1829 Wernwag was unable to keep his monopoly of woodworking contracts with the armory and he fell into some financial difficulty. Despite these sales, Wernwag remained on the island and leased the industrial shops (Johnson and Barker 1992:240; Johnson 1995).

While it appears that Wernwag was about to take a more limited role in his industrial activities, he entered into one last major enterprise. Prominent contemporary engineers were involved in the design and erection of the Baltimore and Ohio Railroad Bridge over the Potomac River at Harpers Ferry. The railroad let the contracts for construction of the bridge in two episodes. Charles Wilson performed the masonry work and Lewis Wernwag constructed the wooden superstructure, finishing the project by 1837 (Stinson 1970). The completion of the bridge revolutionized the economy of the town and the region, and goods and information could be imported from larger regional markets in a matter of hours. This and other connections to regional markets had the potential to revolutionize life in the town as well as its economy (Figure 2).

In 1840, Wernwag was still on Virginius Island, although his household had shrunk to five people, including Lewis and his wife Elizabeth. Two of the Wernwag sons had died by this year, and the whereabouts of some of the others is currently undetermined. No enslaved people were in the household, and it is documented that Elizabeth emancipated a slave named Matilda in 1838 (JCDB 1838:121).

While not owning any land on Virginius Island, Wernwag continued to be identified as a prominent person in the community. The *Virginia Free Press* (*VFP* 1839:3) wrote about his role in the Virginius Island Fourth of July celebration of 1839, suggesting that this use of the island was for him to give: "[A] very large and imposing Procession moved through the principal streets of the town, and halted in a pleasant grove on the island of Virginius, the use of which had been politely and kindly tendered to us for the occasion by our venerable and esteemed friend, Lewis Wernwag, Esq." Wernwag died in 1843, and in 1851 the community was incorporated into Harpers Ferry.

The Irony of an Emergent Rationality

Just as historical archaeologists struggle to identify and understand subaltern groups who were either left out of developing capitalism in

FIGURE 2. The Baltimore and Ohio Railroad Bridge spanning the Potomac River, ca. 1850s. Lewis Wernwag constructed the wooden superstructure of this bridge. (HF 255, Courtesy of Harpers Ferry National Historical Park.)

America or excluded themselves, here those who embraced and promoted it are described. With the Wernwags a self-conscious arrangement of the artifacts of 19th-century industrialism can be seen that can support a perspective on these developments from archaeological research at their home site. In part what this research reveals is a particular understanding of how the Wernwags identified themselves and what kinds of subjects they wanted to be, through evidence of consumer goods and the landscape that the Wernwags inhabited. The Wernwags were both industrialists and self-conscious consumers of the products of industrialism. Globally, archaeologists, anthropologists, and historians have explored the transition to industrial capitalist production, including local, frequently partial expressions of this transition. These transitions illustrate the ironies of emerging capitalist rationalities. Two examples illustrate the tenuous subject position we characterize as ironic, in that they span historical modes of production that imply very different economic and social relations without conforming well to prerational or rational industrialism.

Larkin (1986) chronicles the efforts of Ebenezer, George, and Dan Merriam to establish a newspaper in western Worcester County, Massachusetts at the end of the 18th century, and their subsequent efforts at book publishing during the early 19th century. Larkin takes the Merriams as his entrée into the economic and cultural life of rural New England during the early 19th century. He notes that after sending books by freight to booksellers in the cities,

> the Merriams did not receive cash in return or credits with other urban merchants and suppliers, since both were in short supply. Cash flowed primarily in one direction, up the hierarchy of community size, out of the hinterland and into the cities. ... The basic paradigm of the Merriams' interaction with the book trade was books for books, although occasionally books were traded for type or printing furniture. Debit and credit balances were totaled at irregular intervals ... and settled primarily in additional books or, sometimes, in printing work from the Merriams (Larkin 1986:47).

Larkin writes that in order to stay afloat, a rural printer required a secondary network in addition to the market directed towards the cities. This was to be developed in the surrounding countryside in the market for "utilitarian volumes" such as religious texts, schoolbooks, almanacs, and other commodities that the printers could exchange. Sometimes they would travel through or canvass a circuit of several towns in order to provision the household with basic necessities, or to accrue credit with merchants that could then be paid out in place of cash when this was necessary. In this manner "the printers balanced out accounts with books, the country merchants with goods" (Larkin 1986:48), and most of the real income from printing came from interaction with markets outside of the cities.

The tension and the irony here lay in the production of a quintessential modern commodity outside any rational system for abstracting the value of printed matter. The Merriams operated within a barter system under a bruising relationship to urban markets. Beginning in the 1820s however, Larkin detects in the Merriams's accounts the infiltration of cash and an incrementally greater use of cash in exchanges, rooted in a change in the terms of exchange with the Merriams's paper suppliers, who began to demand cash or negotiable notes redeemable for cash from the urban publishers who received the printed products of their work (Larkin 1986:55–56).

The shakeup resulting from this change in terms produced a suite of changes in the Merriams's business practices, with greater amounts of contract work completed in exchange for cash and generally greater engagement with urban-centered cash economies. Urban and rural economies, each now operating under a very different basis for the printer-publishers, eventually came into conflict. Early on, the manner of commodity exchange that characterized the book trade resembled the rural barter economy, creating conformity between the worlds spanned by the Merriams's business. Later on, the fit between these markets failed, and eventually the country publishing system failed as well (Larkin 1986:63).

In another similar study, Rotman and Staicer (2002:92) describe the material expressions of status and the irony of continuing craft production in the early 20th century, and the arrangements of labor under those circumstances of production. They describe the saddletree factory of John Schroeder in Madison, Indiana, a locus of specialty production from 1878 to 1972, and a handcraft industrial production site that required less-routinized work, with a workforce that was far more skilled than that required by mass production.

John Schroeder was positioned similarly to Wernwag (as well as the Merriams) in that he operated as part of a countercurrent to the advancing mechanization of manufacturing. Rotman and Staicer (2002:99) write,

> For the Schroeders, family and business were very closely associated. Understanding this intimate relationship was critical to interpreting the past at this site. ... The 'mixing' of industrial and domestic spaces was more than a function of the limited area available. ... It illustrated that a clear separation between the home and factory did not exist.

The archaeological record at this site bears out the strategies employed by the Schroeder family in surviving three national-scale economic depressions, with telltale disturbances to stratigraphy that mark recycling of construction materials, and reuse, repair, or repurposing of other products, characterized by the authors as a pattern of frugality, and sometimes even "curation" (Rotman and Staicer 2002:101). Also, the Schroeders practiced a paternalistic management style, if not a familial one, in which loyalty between owners and employees was prized. The authors suggest that manufacturing at the Schroeder saddletree factory was kin ordered (Rotman and Staicer 2002:103), with multiple generations of the same family apprenticed into the operation over the hundred-some years of its existence, and diversification of product lines to prevent job loss among workers when economic slowdowns threatened to close the factory.

Overt status displays at the site were few, and the authors mark only one architectural feature: a brick addition to the Schroeder home with fancy-cut wooden gables on three faces. They note that the ceramics assemblage generally consists of mismatched plates. The material—both aboveground and in subsurface deposits—does not show signs of the Schroeder's social position in the community. This allows the authors to conclude that "Status for them appeared to have been largely performance-based," displayed through their business practices and the success of their business itself. (Rotman and Staicer 2002:105).

The work by Larkin (1986) and Rotman and Staicer (2002) provides an important context for understanding the archaeological signatures of craft households as they negotiated their place in an industrial capitalist society. In the present case, Wernwag was known as a craftsman and a bridge builder. He was a central figure in Harpers Ferry's industrialization who helped connect the town and its surroundings to the East Coast markets. The development of mass markets is a complicated project of manufacturers and industrialists, insuring their continued prosperity while also impacting their own positions as individuals. In building these literal and figurative bridges to the industrializing East, Wernwag helped to bring new commodities and arguably new rationalities to Harpers Ferry and Virginius Island, building inroads for a different set of routines and relationships that in some ways conflicted with the existing, craft-based mode of production that dominated the early 19th century. How the Wernwags negotiated both worlds, craft and industrial, is played out in the archeological record in very different ways.

An Archaeology of Entrepreneurship and the Early Industrial Revolution

The goal of our archaeological analysis is to show the self-conscious, and as with all consciousness, the *partial* application of industrial principles on an intimate basis: the everyday at-home life of Wernwag and his family. If Wernwag was a modernizer of his community, how was this attitude manifested in his household and the ongoing production of his and his family's material circumstances? Landscape and consumer choices are all interrelated to the development of an industrial capitalist society; the archaeology on Virginius Island enables us to show the domestication of industrialization through the arrangement of an entrepreneur's household.

A number of archaeological features are associated with Lewis Wernwag's enterprises on Virginius Island from 1824 to the early 1840s. It is unclear what buildings stood on the parcel at the time of his original purchase, but they may have included the home of Wernwag's family and his sawmill. Wernwag's sawmill was a one-and-a-half story structure measuring 100 × 36 ft., widening to approximately 55 ft. on its

western end to form an L-shaped structure. Wernwag constructed his machine shop on his tract of land on Virginius Island between 1830 and 1832. An item in the *Virginia Free Press* (*VFP* 1852:3; Snell 1973:215) described the structure as "a stone machine shop, 50 by 30 feet, 3 stories high, leased and occupied." Soon after its completion Lewis Wernwag sold his interest in the machine shop to his son John in 1833. John Wernwag operated the machine shop with business partners until 1847, and seems to have benefited from his father's reputation. Newspaper advertisements indicate that the machine shop produced household items such as window locks and hardware, saws, and a patented washing machine, and also a broad range of industrial materials, including very precise machine castings for the U.S. Armory (Parsons 1995). In 1846, the shop became part of the holdings of the Harpers Ferry and Shenandoah Manufacturing Company, in which John Wernwag was a partner (Snell 1958:114; Johnson 1995:12–17).

Archaeological excavation located Lewis Wernwag's sawmill (Borden 1995) and machine shop (Parsons 1995). This tract has similar traits to the preindustrial landscapes described by Larkin (1986) and Rotman and Staicer (2002). Even though Wernwag was at the center of the industrial movement in Harpers Ferry, he did not create clear distinctions between his industrial enterprises and domestic life as did many other industrialists. His landscape consisted of a mix of domestic and industrial spaces. Railroad tracks and raceways did not create clear zones that separated industrial and domestic space. The Wernwag house, Site 46JF212 (Figure 1), lies adjacent to the sawmill (Site 46JF229), and both were located north of a railroad spur that went to another mill. The machine shop (Site 46JF230) sat south of the railroad tracks and was connected to the sawmill via one of the island's many raceways.

The main block of the Wernwag house is nearly square, approximately 35 × 32 ft., and the foundations are visible on the ground's surface today. It faces south onto Wernwag Street, and was described in an 1844 brochure as a "frame house, brick filling, two stories," though the foundation for the house is actually stone (Halchin 2000:3.16). In photographs of the Wernwag site taken in the 1860s, a large garden appears to the west of the Wernwag house, nearly abutting the neighboring dwelling. A substantial stone-lined privy is situated to the north of the house (Joseph et al. 1993; Halchin 2000).

Significant evidence for the landscape treatment in different parts of the Virginius Island community comes through pollen sampled from archaeological deposits. There are no photographs of the Wernwag house taken during the period of Lewis Wernwag's occupation, and no documentary sources specifically address the cultivation of the landscape around the house. Analysis of archaeological pollen produced little evidence for intensive landscaping and horticulture by the Wernwags. This might be taken as an indication of the Wernwag family's priorities: development and industry over finding a place for nature within the spaces that they occupied and inhabited. This dichotomy is not necessarily in keeping with the principles that guided the development of industrial capitalism in the United States, however. As Leo Marx (1964) writes, pastoralism figured significantly as industry developed in America, and industrialization demanded a harmonious relationship between the urban/industrial and natural influences, idealized within the garden and pastoral landscapes (Bunce 1994; Nye 1994). Modernity entails an engagement with nature, because properly applied, industry is not in itself disharmonious with nature. Yet, at the Wernwag house, pollen from the grass family is almost nonexistent, and pollen from weedy plants is in high proportion, indicating that maintaining a groomed or ornamental landscape may not have been a priority around the house. Floral analysis did not reveal any evidence of a cultivated garden during the Wernwag occupation (Cummings and Puseman 2000), though later photographs indicate the presence of a large garden plot to the west of the Wernwag house after Lewis Wernwag's death.

Archaeology and Consumer Choice

Excavations in the vicinity of the Wernwag family home (Figure 3) uncovered artifacts that largely postdate Lewis Wernwag's occupation of Virginius Island, owing to the action of the high-energy flood that obliterated cultural deposits in many areas of the island in 1870. The stone-lined privy at the Wernwag house is an important exception, having preserved deposits dating from the 1830s and 1840s (Palus et al.

2000:4.89–4.94). The assemblage analyzed here is taken entirely from this privy context (Figure 4). The privy contained large numbers of ceramic fragments including several partial chamber pots, glass, and other artifacts, fragments of lime, and a very high density of seeds, particularly in the uppermost of these levels. A minimum of 75 individual ceramic vessels and 25 glass vessels are from privy levels associated with the Wernwags. These ceramics seem to have been discarded while the Wernwags occupied the property. The entire ceramic vessel assemblage associated with the Wernwag household, totaling 117 vessels, is described in Tables 1–5.

Comparing this assemblage to two other contemporary ceramic assemblages from Harpers Ferry, one from the household of Master Armorer Benjamin Moor, deposited between 1832 and 1850 (Lucas 1993), and another one from an armory worker's household from 1821 to 1841 (Lucas 1994b), reveals relevant patterns in the way each household acquired, and arguably used various ceramic vessels. The ceramics from the Moor household are particularly important in this regard, as Benjamin Moor was a strong proponent of mechanization at the U.S. Armory, and his family seems to have embraced romantic consumerism (Shackel 1996:68,174–175). A comparison of the proportions of tablewares, tea wares, and cooking or storage wares from minimum vessel counts for these three assemblages are presented in Table 6. There is clearly a preponderance of tablewares in the Wernwag assemblage, and the diversity of vessel forms is also quite high (Table 1). Plates in various sizes appear in all three assemblages, but plates comprise a greater proportion of the Wernwag assemblage at 41% (n=48) of the ceramic vessels overall. Plates comprise 24% (n=15) of the vessels associated with the Moor household, though it should be noted that most if not all of the tablewares identified for this assemblage were plates or flatwares, indicating a relatively low diversity in tableware forms. Only 22.5% (n=34) of the vessels from the armory worker's household were identified as plates.

Tablewares from the assemblage of the Wernwag household can be taken to represent an elaborate service at mealtime. Plates comprise a high proportion of the overall vessel assemblage, and tablewares occur with greater frequency than other functional categories. Even compared with

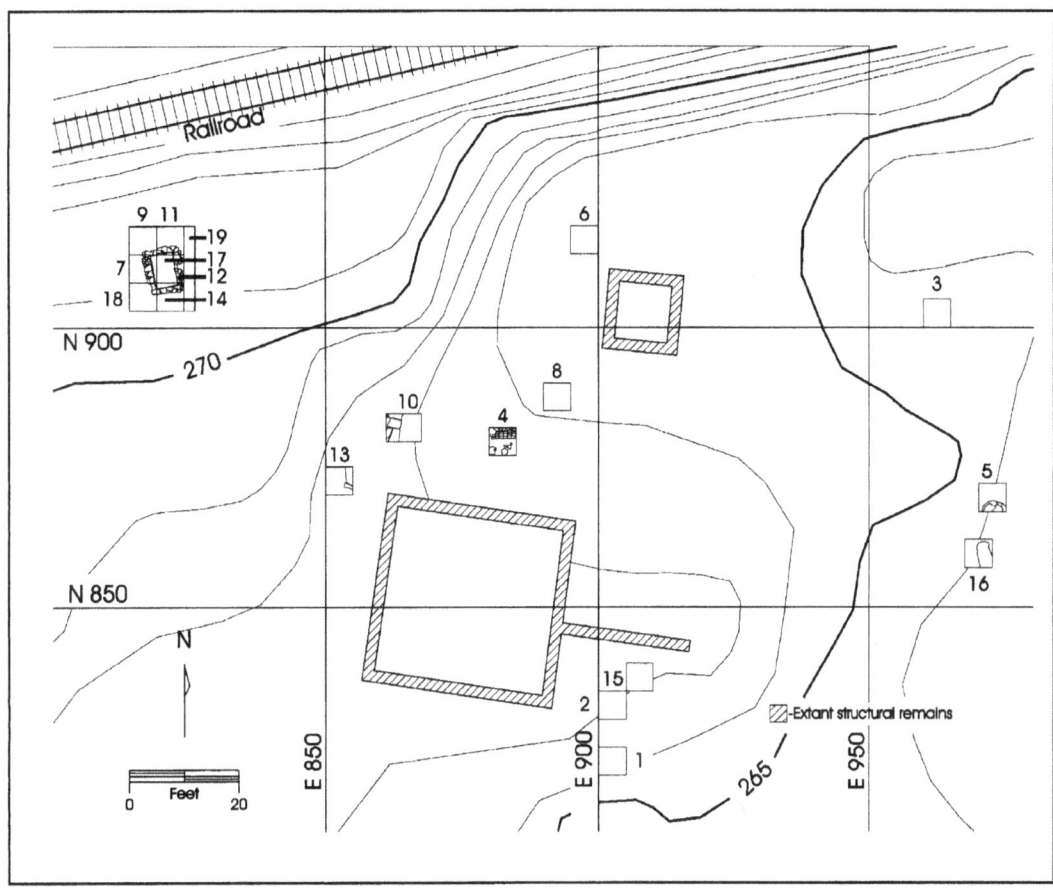

FIGURE 3. Plan of excavations and features at the Wernwag house on Virginius Island, depicting the location of the stone-lined privy, *upper left.* (Drawing by John Ravenhorst, 2000.)

other contemporary assemblages from Harpers Ferry, tablewares appear to comprise an unusually high proportion of the assemblage. Numerous platters, bowls, and tureens that would have been set on the table suggest an old English dining style (Lucas 1994a), in which all courses of a meal were present on the table and the need for servants in serving the meal was minimal. At the same time, the diversity of plate sizes suggests segmentation of the meal into numerous courses. In all, the assemblage may reflect flexibility between different styles of dining and the acquisition of sufficient vessels to serve meals in either style. The Wernwag vessel assemblage is weighted heavily with whitewares, and contains only a few examples of other ware types. Tablewares and tea wares are split between plain and decorated vessels. The majority of plates are either undecorated or have transfer-printed designs, while tea wares are split between plain, painted, and porcelain vessels.

Considering refined earthenwares separately from other wares, there is some patterning among these three assemblages. The proportions of transfer-printed vessels and undecorated vessels in the assemblage associated with Wernwag's family are 46.1% (n=54) and 29.1% (n=34), respectively. The occurrence of these wares in the Moor assemblage is very different, transfer-printed vessels comprising 41% (n=19) and undecorated vessels comprising only 4% (n=2) of the refined earthenwares. The armory worker's household assemblage includes a broader range of decorations, with 38.8% (n=47)

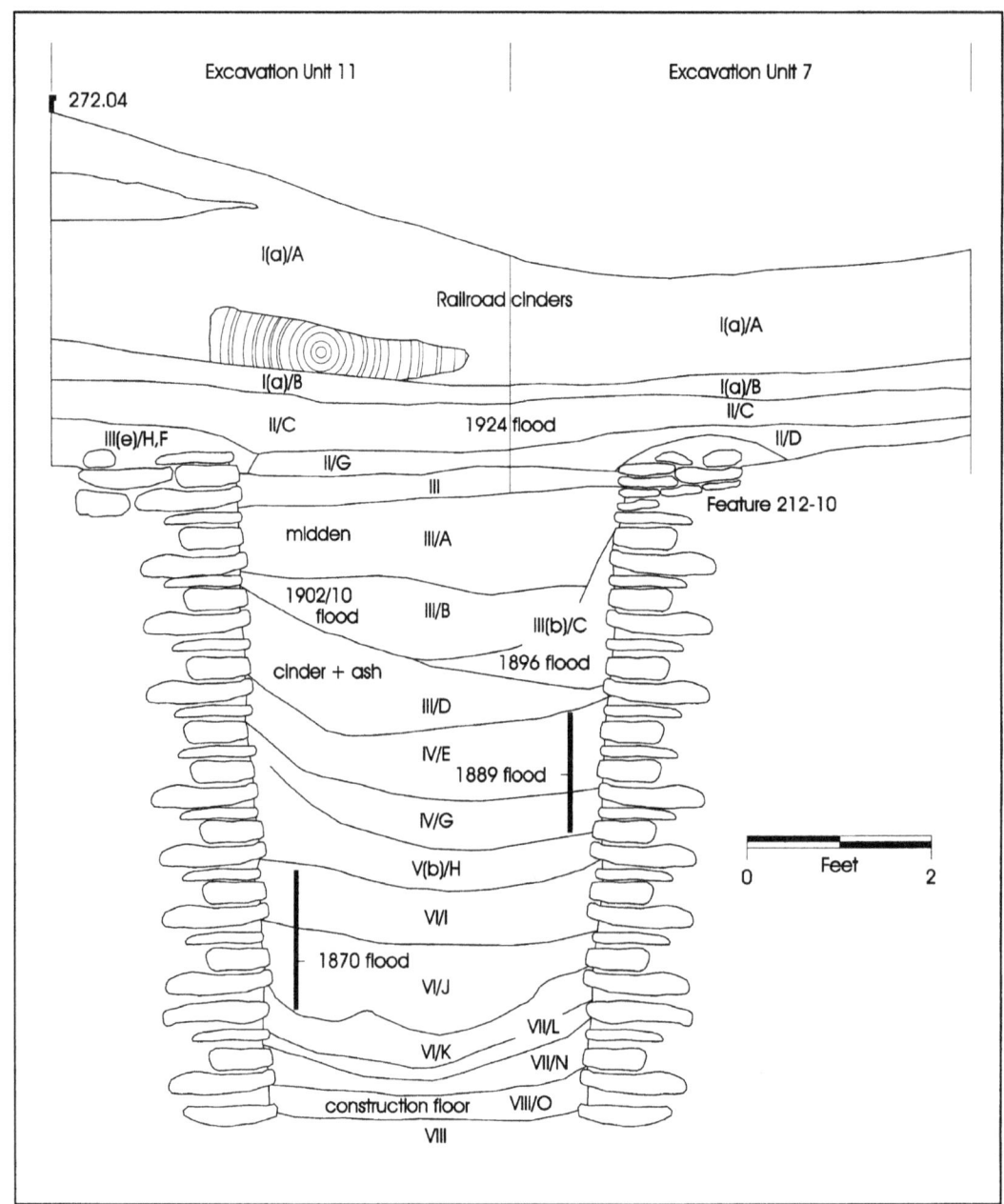

FIGURE 4. Stratigraphy of the stone-lined privy at the Wernwag house on Virginius Island. Deposits labeled *L, N,* and *O* correspond with stratigraphic layers associated with the Wernwag household. (Drawing by John Ravenhorst, 2000.)

of the refined earthenwares being decorated with transfer printing and only 5.8 % (*n*=7) of refined earthenwares being undecorated (Lucas 1993, 1994b; Palus 2000:5.6–5.8). From this information we conclude that the selection of tablewares by the Wernwag household was dissimilar to sets in use within the other two households used for this comparison, in that it included a greater proportion of plates to other vessels in the overall assemblage, and had a far greater proportion

TABLE 1
CERAMICS VESSELS FOUND AT THE WERNWAG SITE

Functional Category	Form	Number	Percentage of Functional Category	Percentage of Total Assemblage
Tableware	Plate, 10 in.	23	37.1	19.7
	Plate, 9 in.	4	6.5	3.4
	Plate, 8 in.	13	21	11.1
	Plate, 7 in.	5	8.1	4.3
	Plate (unid. diam.)	3	4.8	2.6
	Total plates	48	77.4	41
	Platter	8	12.9	6.8
	Flatware	4	6.5	3.4
	Tureen	0	0	0
	Pitcher	0	0	0
	Bowl, 6 in.	0	0	0
	Bowl, 5 in.	0	0	0
	Bowl, (unid. diam.)	2	3.2	1.7
	Total bowls	2	3.2	1.7
	Cup/mug	0	0	0
	Subtotal	62	100	53
Tea ware	Cup	7	50	6
	Saucer	7	50	6
	Teapot	0	0	0
	Creamer	0	0	0
	Subtotal	14	100	12
Storage/preparation	Crock	3	37.5	2.6
	Bowl	2	25	1.7
	Jug	0	0	0
	Bottle	0	0	0
	Baking dish	3	37.5	2.6
	Subtotal	8	100	6.8
	Flowerpot	0	0	0
	Hollowware	7	21.2	6
	Flatware	0	0	0
	Other	6	18.2	5.1
Other/unidentified	Chamber pot	15	45.5	12.8
	Lid	5	15.2	4.3
	Unidentified	0	0	0
	Subtotal	33	100	28.2
Total		*117*		*100*

of undecorated refined-earthenware vessels. The assemblages associated with the household of Benjamin Moor and a roughly contemporary armory worker included hardly any undecorated refined earthenwares at all.

Two explanations for the high proportion of undecorated refined earthenwares in the Wernwag assemblage present themselves. It is known from historic documents that the Wernwags had servants and slaves that may have dwelt in the Wernwag house, and that they took in boarders who would sometimes stay with the family for up to two weeks. The 1830 census enumerated 14 persons in the household, including 3 enslaved people and several nonfamily boarders. Artifacts recovered from the above-described privy could represent these groups. The vessels identified in the Wernwags' privy allow for dining with decorated or undecorated vessels, and this could indicate two sets of users, with the social

TABLE 2
CERAMIC VESSELS BY WARE TYPE
FROM THE WERNWAG SITE

Ware Type	Wernwag and Family Occupation, 1820s–1840s	
	n	Percentage
Porcelain	5	4.3
Whiteware	100	85.5
Pearlware	4	3.4
Creamware	1	0.9
Ironstone	2	1.7
Rockingham	0	0.0
Coarse earthenware	3	2.6
Yellow ware	1	0.9
Stoneware	1	0.9
Total	*117*	*100.0*

TABLE 3
TEA WARE DECORATION AT
THE WERNWAG SITE

Primary Type	n	Percentage
Painted	4	28.6
Transfer print	1	7.1
Porcelain	4	28.6
Lustre	0	0.0
Undecorated	5	35.7
Total	*14*	*100.0*

TABLE 4
PLATE DECORATION AT THE WERNWAG SITE

Primary Type	n	Percentage
Shell edge	11	22.9
Transfer print	30	62.5
Porcelain	0	0.0
Molded	0	0.0
Painted	0	0.0
Undecorated	7	14.6
Other	0	0.0
Total	*48*	*100.0*

TABLE 5
CERAMIC VESSELS BY DECORATION
FOR THE WERNWAG SITE

Decoration	n	Percentage
Shell edge	10	8.5
Transfer print	54	46.1
Painted	13	11.1
Enameled	0	0.0
Dipped	1	0.9
Sponge	0	0.0
Molded	4	3.4
Gilded	0	0.0
Decal	0	0.0
Mocha	1	0.9
Color glaze	0	0.0
Undecorated	34	29.1
Other/unid.	0	0.0
Total	*117*	*100.0*

TABLE 6

COMPARISON OF VESSEL FORMS FOR THE WERNWAG, MOOR, AND ARMORER HOUSEHOLDS[a]

	Wernwag Household		Moor Household[b]		Armorer Household[c]	
	n	Percentage[d]	n	Percentage[d]	n	Percentage[d]
Tablewares	62	63.9	22	36.0	46	30.5
Tea Wares	14	14.4	17	27.5	65	43.0
Cooking/Storage	21	21.6	17	27.5	19	12.6

[a]Numerical counts of ceramics are not exhaustive and do not represent complete assemblages for these contexts.
[b]Data from Lucas (1993).
[c]Data from Lucas (1994b).
[d]Percentages derived from counts of tablewares, tea wares, and cooking/storage vessels rather than complete assemblages of ceramic vessels from each site.

differentiation of the two sets being reaffirmed by material things. Alternately, differentiated low-quality and high-quality table and tea wares may reflect specific, exclusive practices in which one or another set of vessels was utilized (Wall 1991). Only the coherence of the assemblage argues for one alternative or another, and the relative likelihood that materials used in serving meals to enslaved people, servants, and boarders were mingled with those discarded by the Wernwag family itself.

Consumer Practices in a Preindustrial Landscape

When Lewis Wernwag and his family occupied Virginius it comprised some of the only land available for private ownership near Harpers Ferry with water power access (Joseph et al. 1993:3.16–3.23; Halchin 2000). Innovation in manufacturing, including the transition from the craft-based manufacture of arms in the U.S. Armory to an industrial plan, accelerated from the late 1820s. The armory developed surveillance techniques to control workers. For instance, the government constructed a wall around the armory to manage the movement of workers and supervisors built houses on higher ground. Workers were always under the threat of being observed. The dominant mode of production in Harpers Ferry became increasingly rationalized, and the armory rebuilt buildings so that the production of arms would proceed in a systematic manner and supervisors could easily observe workers. To the chagrin of armorers, they were transformed from craftsmen

to wage laborers working in a disciplined, mechanized factory (Shackel 1998:6–7). This transition was relevant to an ongoing struggle between competing political ideologies in the early 19th century. Classical republicanism supports the idea that government would look out for the workers' interests and many craftsmen adhered to this ideology. The newer liberal republicanism suggests that individuals are independent citizens, free to act in their own best interests, and also free to sell their labor (Shalhope 1990; Appleby 1992; Gilje 1996:172).

The different craft industries on Virginius Island may have offered a refuge from ongoing rationalization of manufacturing at the federal armory in Lower Town Harpers Ferry. Certainly, craftsmen would have continued to be necessary to cast and build the machines that armorers tended in the armory. A diverse base of craftsmen developed on Virginius and Wernwag was among them until the 1840s. By the 1850s many of the crafts disappeared from Virginius Island as a few industrialists developed large cotton and flour mills that relied on wage labor.

While living on Virginius Island, Lewis Wernwag made significant contributions to the development of industry and technology in the United States. As a craftsman and a famous bridge builder he stood at the forefront of the community's industrial development. He created a built landscape that did not follow the strict discipline found in other industrial communities, however, such as the growing trend in industrial America whereby industrialists separated work from domestic space. Wernwag was at the forefront of modernizing

Harpers Ferry, but he did not develop the separations in the landscape that were necessary for a rationalized and modernized industry.

The material remains of this household, however, show a different perspective on the natural habitat of the industrial island and the daily life of the entire family. While Larkin (1986) and Rotman and Staicer (2002) document individuals who were essentially in conflict with the changing industrial order, the archeological assemblage from the Wernwag household provides an interesting case. The Wernwag family chose to participate in a consumer society, and while living in a secluded industrial setting, nothing stopped the family from buying the most recent and up-to-date consumer goods. They also made choices about which types of goods they acquired, and the authors believe that the choices the Wernwags made allowed them to create social boundaries, potentially separations between themselves and others living in their household. The consumer patterns show that the Wernwags were entrenched in the life of the industrial era. Though the true "consumer revolution" was only beginning, the assemblage of ceramics associated with the household of Lewis Wernwag reflects self-conscious decisions regarding the purchase and use of these items. The Wernwags set an impressive table. In fact, this inventor, engineer, and community leader was at the forefront of the movement to modernize Harpers Ferry, and the Wernwag family could have used these mass-produced goods to represent their subscription to these values. This material culture would also reinforce these values among family members.

Archaeology helps to gauge how entrepreneurs who actively pursued modernization and industry within the Virginius Island community embraced a relatively new form of industrial capitalism, and it helps to describe a real shift that is grounded in material life. At a broader level, these changes to everyday procedures of living and working promoted a new kind of subject, in the Foucaultian sense of the word (Butler 1997), which might be termed an industrial subject. Importantly, archaeology at Harpers Ferry and other manufacturing sites (Nassaney and Abel 1993) reveals evidence for fugitive subjectivities that historical archaeologists have bracketed as "resistance," expressed as the refusal of this rationality. Yet what of the founding of technological rationality that

values efficiency so profoundly and eventually comes to institute efficiency as the order of things? What of those who paved the way for changes that took place at Harpers Ferry and founded the dominant industrial order across the United States (Praetzellis et al. 1988)? Wernwag occupies a very complicated position, as a quintessential subject of the old craft-based order of manufacturing and invention, which elevated efficiency to the point that craft work began to be eliminated altogether.

Acknowledgements

All excavations were performed with funding by the National Park Service, and we appreciate the support of Superintendent Donald Campbell and Regional Archaeologist Stephen Potter. John Eddins served as site supervisor for this project, while Paul Shackel served as supervisory archaeologist. Matthew Palus performed the synthesis of the archeological data and created the final edited report (Palus 2000) with financial support from Harpers Ferry National Historical Park and the University of Maryland. We appreciate any previous comments provided to us by Mia Parsons, Harpers Ferry Park archaeologist. We thank Christopher Fennell, Martha Zierden, and one anonymous reviewer, as well as associate editor Margaret Purser, for their consideration and suggestions.

References

APPLEBY, JOYCE
   1992   *Liberalism and Republicanism in the Historical Imagination.* Harvard University Press, Cambridge, MA.

BORDEN, ANNA C.
   1995   *Archeological Investigations of Lewis Wernwag's Sawmill, 46JF229, Virginius Island, Harpers Ferry, West Virginia.* Harpers Ferry National Historical Park, Harpers Ferry, WV.

BOTTOMORE, TOM
   2002   *The Frankfurt School and its Critics.* Routledge, London, UK.

BROWN, JOHN M.
   1844   Extract of April 1844 report. James Giddings, author, brochure, *Plan and Report with a Descriptive View of the Island of Virginious, at Harpers Ferry, Virginia.* Group 153, Military Reservation File, Box 44, Folder 7, National Archives, Washington, DC.

BUNCE, MICHAEL
1994   The Countryside Ideal: Anglo-American Images of Landscape. Routledge, London, UK.

BUSHONG, MILLARD K.
1941   A History of Jefferson County. Jefferson Publishing, Charles Town, WV.

BUTLER, JUDITH
1997   The Psychic Life of Power: Theories in Subjection. Stanford University Press, Stanford, CA.

CUMMINGS, LINDA SCOTT, AND KATHRYN PUSEMAN
2000   Pollen, Faunal and Parasites Analysis at Virginius Island. In They Worked Regular: Archeology of the Virginius Island Mill Community, Package 123 in Harpers Ferry National Historical Park, Harpers Ferry, West Virginia, Matthew Palus, editor, pp. 7.1-7.55. National Park Service, Regional Archeology Program, Washington, DC.

DE CERTEAU, MICHEL
1997   Culture in the Plural. University of Minnesota Press, Minneapolis.

EVERHART, WILLIAM C.
1952   A History of Harpers Ferry. Manuscript, Harpers Ferry National Historical Park, Harpers Ferry, WV.

GILJE, PAUL A.
1996   The Rise of Capitalism in the Early Republic. Journal of the Early Republic 16(2):159–181.

HALCHIN, JILL Y.
2000   Historic Documentation Relevant to Features and Stratigraphy at Three Sites on Virginius Island. In They Worked Regular: Archeology of the Virginius Island Mill Community, Package 123 in Harpers Ferry National Historical Park, Harpers Ferry, West Virginia, Matthew Palus, editor, pp. 3.1-3.21. National Park Service, Regional Archeology Program, Washington, DC.

HARPER'S FERRY MILL CO. V. THOS. H. SAVERY ET AL.
1887   Certificate of Evidence and Argument of Counsel, United States Circuit Court, District of West Virginia. Savery Collection, Savery Papers, Box III, Folder 1-A, Harpers Ferry National Historical Park, Harpers Ferry, WV.

HELD, DAVID
1980   Introduction to Critical Theory: Horkheimer to Habermas. University of California Press, Berkeley.

HORKHEIMER, MAX, AND THEODOR W. ADORNO
1998   Dialectic of Enlightenment. Continuum, New York, NY.

JAY, MARTIN
1996   The Dialectical Imagination: A History of the Frankfurt School and the Institute of Social Research, 1923–1950. University of California Press, Berkeley.

JEFFERSON COUNTY DEED BOOK (JCDB)
1826   Deed Book 14, 30 December. Jefferson County Courthouse, Charles Town, WV.
1833   Deed Book 18, 24 September. Jefferson County Courthouse, Charles Town, WV.
1838   Deed Book 23, 17 September. Jefferson County Courthouse, Charles Town, WV.

JOHNSON, MARY
1995   A Nineteenth-Century Mill Village: Virginius Island, 1800–60. West Virginia History 54:1–27.

JOHNSON, MARY, AND JOHN BARKER
1992   Virginius Island Community: Preliminary Social Analysis, 1800–1936. Report to Harpers Ferry National Historical Park, Harpers Ferry, WV.

JOSEPH, MAUREEN DELAY, PERRY CARPENTER WHEELOCK, DEBORAH WARSHAW, AND ANDREW KRIEMELMEYER
1993   Cultural Landscape Report: Virginius Island, Harpers Ferry National Historical Park. National Park Service, Washington, DC.

LARKIN, JACK
1986   The Merriams of Brookfield: Printing in the Economy and Culture of Rural Massachusetts in the Early Nineteenth Century. Proceedings of the American Antiquarian Society 96(1):39–73.

LUCAS, MICHAEL T.
1993   Ceramic Consumption in an Industrializing Community. In Interdisciplinary Investigations of Domestic Life in Government Block B: Perspectives on Harpers Ferry's Armory and Commercial District, Paul A. Shackel, editor, pp. 8.1–8.38. National Park Service, Occasional Report No. 6. Harpers Ferry National Historical Park, Harpers Ferry, WV.
1994a   A la Russe, à la Pell-Mell, or à la Practical: Ideology and Compromise at the Late Nineteenth-Century Dinner Table. Historical Archaeology 28(4):80–93.
1994b   An Armory Worker's Table: Glimpses of Industrial Life. In Domestic Responses to Nineteenth-Century Industrialization: An Archeology of Park Building 48, Harpers Ferry National Historical Park, Paul A. Shackel, editor, pp. 5.1–5.40. National Park Service, Occasional Report No. 12. Harpers Ferry National Historical Park, Harpers Ferry, WV.

MARCUSE, HERBERT
1982   Some Social Implications of Modern Technology. In The Essential Frankfurt School Reader, Andrew Arato and Eike Gebhardt, editors, pp. 138–162. Continuum, New York, NY.

MARX, LEO
1964   The Machine in the Garden: Technology and the Pastoral Ideal in America. Oxford University Press, Oxford, UK.

NASSANEY, MICHAEL S., AND MARJORIE R. ABEL
1993   The Political and Social Contexts of Cutlery Production in the Connecticut Valley. Dialectical Anthropology 18(3–4):247–289.

NELSON, LEE H.
1990   *The Collossus of 1812: An American Engineering Superlative.* American Society of Civil Engineering, New York, NY.

NOFFSINGER, JAMES P.
1958   Harpers Ferry, West Virginia: Contributions Towards a Physical History. Manuscript, Harpers Ferry National Historical Park, Harpers Ferry, WV.

NYE, DAVID
1994   *American Technological Sublime.* MIT Press, Cambridge, MA.

PALUS, MATTHEW M. (EDITOR)
2000   *They Worked Regular: Archeology of the Virginius Island Mill Community, Package 123 in Harpers Ferry National Historical Park, Harpers Ferry, West Virginia.* National Park Service, Washington, DC.

PALUS, MATTHEW M., JOHN T. EDDINS, AND ERIC L. LARSEN
2000   The Archeological Record; Stratigraphy, Features, and Material Culture. In *They Worked Regular: Archeology of the Virginius Island Mill Community, Package 123 in Harpers Ferry National Historical Park, Harpers Ferry, West Virginia*, Matthew Palus, editor, pp. 4.1-4.94. National Park Service, Washington, DC.

PALUS, MATTHEW M., AND PAUL A. SHACKEL
2006   *They Worked Regular: Craft, Labor, and Family in the Industrial Community of Virginius Island.* University of Tennessee Press, Knoxville.

PARSONS, MIA T.
1995   *Archeological Investigations at Wernwag's Machine Shop: Site 46JF230 on Virginius Island.* Harpers Ferry National Historical Park, Harpers Ferry, WV.

PRAETZELLIS, MARY, ADRIAN PRAETZELLIS, AND MARLY R. BROWN III
1988   What Happened to the Silent Majority?: Research Strategies for Studying Dominant Group Material Culture in Late Nineteenth-Century California. In *Documentary Archaeology in the New World*, Mary C. Beaudry, editor, pp. 192–202. Cambridge University Press, Cambridge, UK.

ROTMAN, DEBORAH L., AND JOHN M. STAICER
2002   Curiosities and Conundrums: Deciphering Social Relations and the Material World at the Ben Schroeder Saddletree Factory and Residence in Madison, Indiana. *Historical Archaeology* 36(2):92–110.

SHACKEL, PAUL A.
1996   *Culture Change and the New Technology: An Archaeology of the Early American Industrial Era.* Plenum Press, New York, NY.
1998   Classical and Liberal Republicanisms and the New Consumer Culture. *International Journal of Historical Archaeology* 2(1):1–20.

SHALHOPE, ROBERT E.
1990   *The Roots of Democracy: American Thought and Culture, 1760–1800.* Twayne, Boston, MA.

SMITH, MERRITT ROE
1977   *Harpers Ferry Armory and the New Technology: The Challenge of Change.* Cornell University Press, Ithaca, NY.

SNELL, CHARLES W.
1958   A History of Virginius Island, 1751–1870. Manuscript, Harpers Ferry National Historical Park, Harpers Ferry, WV.
1973   A Compendium of the Commercial and Industrial Advertisements of the Business and Manufacturing Establishments of Harpers Ferry and the Island of Virginius, 1824–1861, Virginia. Manuscript, Harpers Ferry National Historical Park, Harpers Ferry, WV.

STINSON, DWIGHT E.
1970   The First Railroad Bridge at Harpers Ferry. Manuscript, Harpers Ferry National Historical Park, Harpers Ferry, WV.

VIRGINIA FREE PRESS (*VFP*)
1828   No title. *Virginia Free Press* 3 December:4. Charles Town, WV.
1834   No title. *Virginia Free Press* 9 October:3. Charles Town, WV.
1833a   No title. *Virginia Free Press* 18 July:3. Charles Town, WV.
1833b   No title. *Virginia Free Press* 2 May:3. Charles Town, WV.
1839   No title. *Virginia Free Press* 13 July:3. Charles Town, WV.
1852   No title. *Virginia Free Press* 9 December:3. Charles Town, WV.

WALL, DIANA DI ZEREGA
1991   Sacred Dinners and Secular Teas: Constructing Domesticity in Mid-19th-Century New York. *Historical Archaeology* 25(4):69–81.

WERNWAG, LEWIS
1822–1826   Wernwag Ledger. Manuscript, HFD 283, Harpers Ferry National Historical Park, Harpers Ferry, WV.

PAUL A. SHACKEL
DEPARTMENT OF ANTHROPOLOGY
UNIVERSITY OF MARYLAND
COLLEGE PARK, MD 20742

MATTHEW PALUS
DEPARTMENT OF ANTHROPOLOGY
COLUMBIA UNIVERSITY
NEW YORK, NY 10027

Part III:
Extractive Industries

R. Scott Baxter

Industrial and Domestic Landscapes of a California Oil Field

ABSTRACT

By the turn of the 19th century, the United States was a heavily industrialized nation in the midst of the Victorian period. A series of intertwined values developed concerning the appropriate use of space both in and out of the work place and home. While the majority pursued these standards, individuals working in extractive industries were often on society's periphery. Squaw Flat is an isolated oil field in Ventura County, California, occupied from ca. 1912–1954. In a remote location with limited choices, workers at Squaw Flat were able to use the landscape to express societal values concerning professional, domestic, public, and private space.

Introduction

Archaeological and historical research was conducted on historic oil lease land known as Squaw Flat (Figure 1) in Ventura County, California. This location was chosen for study as it was historically and physically separated from other oil activities, providing a study area with relevant, discernible boundaries. Research consisted of historical research, oral history, and an intensive pedestrian survey (Figure 2). Historical research revealed a rich business history, but a paucity of documents related directly to the individuals working at Squaw Flat. Though no one who worked directly at Squaw Flat was located, persons who worked in the area gave valuable oral testimony concerning petroleum activities in the area. Pedestrian surveys focused on the claims, leases, and wells, limited in part by accessibility issues (poison oak and topography). While this work is considered preliminary, distinctive patterns have already emerged from the archaeological record.

Squaw Flat is located in a lucrative yet imposing location in a remote region of the Piru Mountains in the Transverse Ranges of Ventura County, California. Ample water and level ground for farming were counterbalanced by long distances from markets and a generally inhospitable environment. Despite those drawbacks,

FIGURE 1. Site location of Squaw Flat.

the A. A. Cohn (sometimes spelled Cohen) family was drawn here in the 1870s, reportedly constructing an adobe house and maintaining a peach orchard through the latter half of the 19th century (Friend 1997). Until the turn of the century, their homestead remained isolated. Historic developments would soon change and greatly advance exploitation of the area.

Petroleum and Squaw Flat

Most people today associate petroleum with automobiles, but the industry had a different origin. The market for illumination shaped the beginnings of the oil industry in the 19th century as a lighting fuel. In antebellum America, whale oil and camphene were the primary sources of lighting fuels. Whale oil was widely held as the best illuminating oil, but whale catches were dwindling, forcing the price of whale oil up to $2.50 per gallon. This prompted the search for an alternative. Chief among these was camphene. Produced primarily in the Carolinas, camphene supplies were cut off during the Civil War, forcing Unionists to find yet another alternative illuminating fuel. In 1859, Edwin Drake's famous Pennsylvania oil well proved the ready availability of petroleum. Refined petroleum produced kerosene. With some fits and starts, kerosene came to dominate the illuminating oil market (White 1968:2; Yergin 1991:22–23). Petroleum soon became a sought-

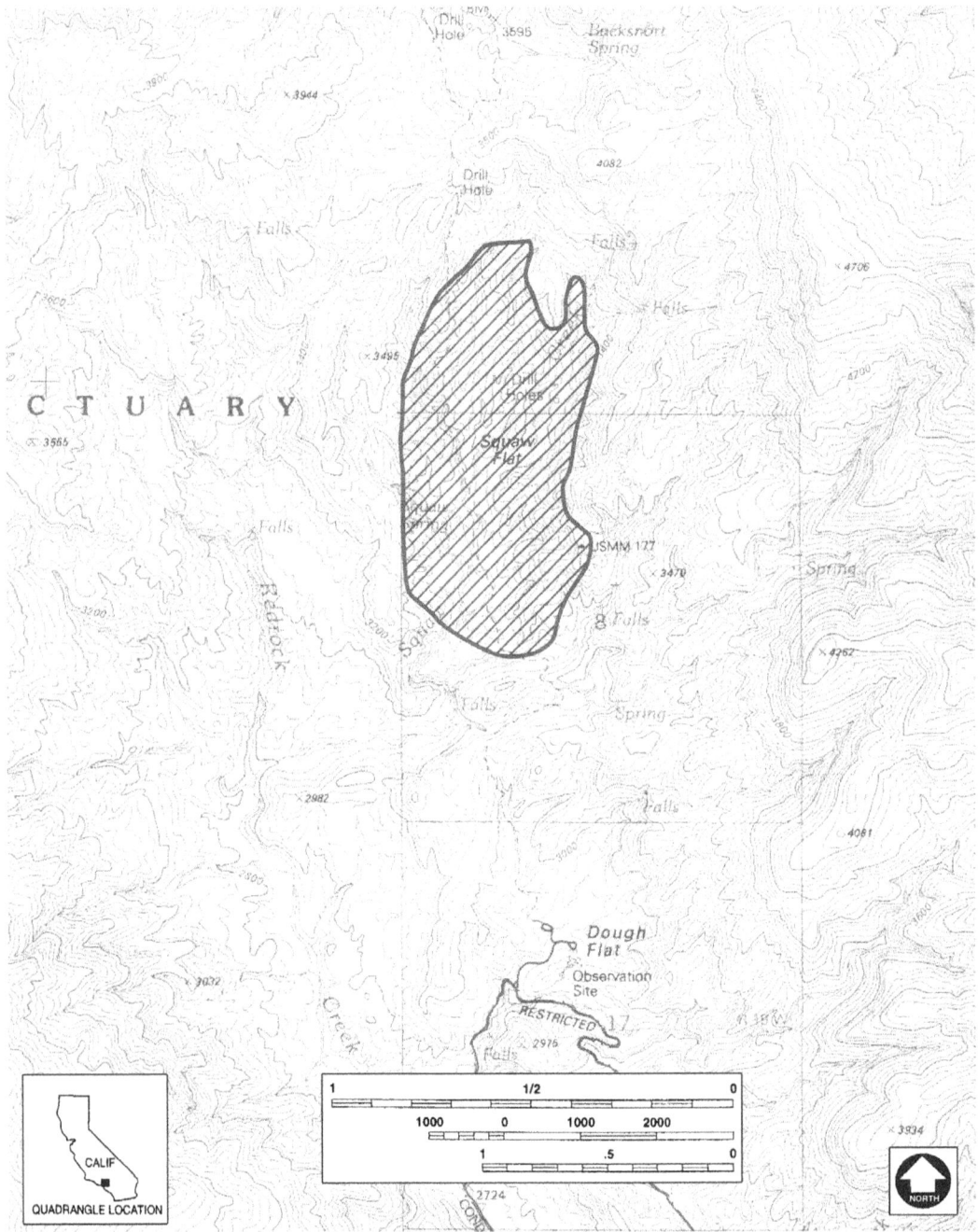

FIGURE 2. Squaw Flat survey area.

after commodity, and, with the constraints of the Civil War, California saw its first short-lived oil boom in 1860–61 (Caughey 1940:418; White 1962:4–9; Beck and Williams 1972:293).

With its many tar seeps, Ventura County in California was a hot spot for early oil exploration. While most oil fields provide pools of oil in contiguous, if ill-defined deposits, the fields of Ventura were different. Petroleum is deposited there in fissures and pockets in a fault-ridden strata of shale and sandstone. Drilling for oil remains a challenging activity, with dry holes drilled within feet of gushers. Drilling activity in the Ventura oil fields has been best defined as perpetual exploration rather than development (Daries 1997). A second key factor to the development of the area is its topography. Squaw Flat, part of the Sespe oil field, is located in one of the most rugged locations for an oil field in the continental U.S, the Piru Mountains. With few natural passes, the interior of this region remains extremely isolated. Roads snake along vertical slopes. At higher elevations, snow buries roads in winter. In the spring, snow melt and rain wash out roads at lower elevations. Still, petroleum resources in the area were lucrative enough to spur exploitation and development even in this most remote area.

Several companies explored the area for petroleum: Squaw Flat Oil Company (Pruztman 1913:101), New Moodey Gultch (Pruztman 1913:101), Big Chief (Pruztman 1913:101; Houston 1933a), Houston & Cohn (Department of Petroleum and Gas 1926, 1933; Houston and Cohn 1933, 1937; Patterson 1933; Bush 1934; Thomas 1934; Cohn, Amy 1937), Squaw Flat Placer (Friel 1920), Beesum (Harrell 1948; Kaplow 1950; Cohn 1952; Harrell 1952a, 1952b, 1970; Neese 1995), Stansburry Inc. (Pathfinder Petroleum 1933, 1953a, 1953b; Stansbury 1954a, 1954b; Neese 1995), and Border Oil Company No. 1 (Brothers 1926; MacDonald 1929; Houston 1933b, 1933c; Landers 1933; Houston and Cohn 1940). These companies worked in the area from some time before 1912 through 1954 (Figure 3). A. A. Cohn and C. W. Houston directed exploration, although the work was done under a variety of names. These two individuals entered into a series of contracts with a number of companies to carry out drilling and development. A placer claim filed in 1920 (Friel 1920) under the names A. A. Cohn and

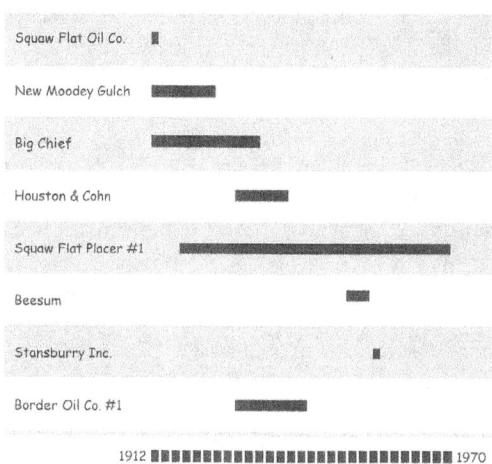

FIGURE 3. Time line of companies working in the area, 1912–1970.

S. Conner gives detailed descriptions of a highly developed claim, valued at $45,000. Assets listed in this claim include a boarding house, three bunkhouses, a water tank, a well, and a derrick. Conner drops from the record but Houston and Cohn are linked with continued work at Squaw Flat for the next three decades. This work included drilling at the following wells: Big Chief No. 1, Houston & Cohn, Beesum, and Border Oil Company No. 1. Workers contracted to work at these wells were housed in the bunk- and boarding houses listed in the 1920 placer claim. No quantities of oil were ever produced economically. Squaw Flat remained an exploratory location and drilling ended in 1954. The property was turned over to the U.S. Forest Service in the 1970s.

Oil Leases and Housing

California oil towns like MicKittrick, Taft, Maricopa, and Fillmore provided oil field workers with many of the luxuries of home: comfortable housing, hotels, saloons, restaurants, stores, and theaters (Rintoul 1978). Company towns like Fellows, California, were established to attract workers, although they served the dual purpose of maintaining a certain measure of control over the social life of their workers (Kaldenburg and Graham 1973). Even some smaller communities boasted comfortable accommodations. Rio Bravo, for example, was one of several communities established in 1908 by Standard Oil Company to maintain pump stations along its Central Valley pipeline. This small residential community boasted stylish, well designed, and well-constructed cottages, though it lacked the shops and businesses the larger communities maintained (Baxter 1995). The oil industry also spurred the development of what has become known as lease housing.

Historic oil leases, like any other mineral claim, provided the leaseholder with the right to extract petroleum or natural gas from the land, and "improve" the property as necessary, while the U.S. Government retained ownership of the land. Private landholders were also sometimes involved. Improvements might include oil wells, pipelines for transportation of oil, tanks for storage of oil and water, machine and/or blacksmith shops, roads, and residences or other such structures. Oil leases generally encompassed only the site of extraction where the oil was pumped from the ground. Oil was usually shipped elsewhere for refinement. Leases could be large- or small holdings of land in well-developed oil fields or small land tracts in peripheral but promising locations. Varied activities at lease sites included drilling new or exploratory wells, maintaining pumps at producing wells, and checking tank and pipelines. The majority of these activities were 24-hour per day jobs. Drilling was carried out around the clock in two 12-hour or three 8-hour shifts. At producing wells, machinery had to be lubricated at regular intervals, and boilers had to be checked and kept clean to avoid explosions.

Workers who drilled wells were generally not the men who operated them. Each process was a separate, specialized skill. On the whole, drillers were somewhat transient. Most were single men who only stayed in one location until the job was done, generally a matter of months. Well operators were usually tied to a production company and were generally more settled, facing a commitment of years rather than months. If accommodations were provided at a lease, their families frequently joined them.

Accommodations for the oil field's working men (and sometimes their families) were frequently located on lease lands. The more remote the lease location, the more likely that accommodations were provided. Such remoteness was not conducive to commuting from town,

and on-site housing ensured someone would be at the site 24 hours per day. Lease housing was widely variable in quality and quantity, depending primarily on the expected length of occupation. Often, housing on oil leases amounted to nothing more than a few tents, although accommodations were frequently made up of a mixture of wood-framed, bunk- and boarding houses. In 1889, at Torrey Canyon in Ventura County, California, accommodations were limited to a wood-framed bunkhouse and a cookhouse for the crew of men (Henderson n.d.:3). These sparse accommodations were probably due to the fact that these were only exploratory wells being drilled by Torrey Canyon Oil Company, a forerunner of Union Oil. It made little sense for the company to invest much capital in an, as yet, unproven area. Simple one-room bunkhouses were typical of exploratory locations and were usually inhabited only by oilmen and their support staff (the cook). By the 1910s, at their oil-producing leases at Tar Creek in Ventura County, Union Oil had built several permanent, single family, wood-framed structures and even a school house to accommodate the men and their families (Daries 1997). Generally the more established the operation at a particular location, the more elaborate the facilities constructed to house and provide for them. Places like Tar Creek were the culmination of this development, where oil workers were provided housing for themselves and their families as well as amenities such as schools or shops.

The purpose of lease housing was to locate the workers at the job site. They lived surrounded by oil derricks piercing the sky, oil burning boilers, the pounding of cable tool rigs, the continuous clank of machinery, and the crack of the blacksmith's hammer. The generally sparse accommodations constructed at exploratory oil leases like Squaw Flat restricted the separation of professional and domestic, and public and private space within their homes. Workers shared their rooms, dinner table, and (not infrequently) their shower and toiletry facilities with a host of other men.

Workers on oil-lease lands were highly dependent on the company, be it big or small, for their housing and supplies. Mary Alice Henderson (n.d.:3) and Gerald Lynch (1987) have noted that drillers and their crews had a pretty free hand in the construction and organization of the facilities, but their choices were limited by what the various companies could or would supply to the workers.

This scenario stands in contrast to the typical industrial period household. In many of America's industrial settings, workers enjoyed a separation of work and home. Societal guardians fostered a call for the physical separation of public and private space within the home as well (Crossick 1978:149; Daunton 1983:224; Davidoff and Hall 1987:359–361; Crow and Allan 1990:13). Smart business practice demanded the use of small, cheap, single room, bunk- and boarding houses at exploratory locations like Squaw Flat. Did the Squaw Flat laborers completely disregard society's practices of segregating and organizing space while living on these oil leases?

Separation of Professional and Domestic, Public and Private Space

With the rapid rise of American industry during the 19th century came radical changes in how society functioned in everyday life. Shifts in the organization and use of space were key among these changes, specifically the separation of the professional and domestic spheres and of public and private spheres within the home. As industrial production became more ingrained in American society, so too did this organization of space.

Industries found that by gathering increasingly specialized workers under one roof, they could produce goods more cheaply than by the traditional craft method. Where once a gunsmith built a complete firearm, now one person built the barrel, one person made ignition locks, another made the stock, and yet another put the firearm together. All the while, production was also becoming increasingly mechanized. More space and money were needed for such an operation. Production gradually shifted away from the home. In turn, this brought about the increased segregation of the workplace and the home. The focus of many laborers' lives shifted from work to the home (Kemp 1978:12; Clark 1988). As laborers replaced skilled craftsmen, people began to define themselves by class affiliation and values, rather than by association with a guild or trade (Davidhoff and Hall 1987:12).

The man was no longer a gunsmith, cobbler, or furniture maker. He and, in turn, his family were of the working class.

The home became an important tool in the maintenance of class values and relationships (Clark 1988). It also became a refuge from work for many urban and suburban dwellers (Fitts 1999:46; Crane 2000:25). ". . . [T]he central tenet of the new canon of domesticity . . . was the assertion that the household should be a refuge from the outside world, a fortress designed to protect, nurture and strengthen the individuals within it" (Clark 1986:29). The importance of home life is underscored by the fact that even as early as the colonial period, workers were living some distance from their jobs. They preferred to live in the appropriate neighborhood and be close to family rather than live close to their place of employment (Coontz 1988:165; Rothschild 1992:216–217). The home was primarily occupied during the day by housewives and their children, for by the mid-19th century, wage labor was increasingly a male-dominated pursuit (Ryan 1981:101; May 1987:111–113; Blumin 1989:184; Shackel 1996:2). This male-dominated wage labor further dichotomized work and home as men ventured into the professional realm of work, and women spent increasing amounts of time in the domestic space of the home (Roberts 1984:200–202; Shackel 1996:2). As Stephen Mrozowski (1991:80) has stated, "Where for centuries domestic space served as an area for work, now it performed more of an ornamental function."

James Deetz's (1977:92–117; 1996:125–164) discussion of 17th-century house plans illustrates the beginnings of the relation of floor plans, mindset, and the division of public and private space. This separation of public and private space peaked in the Victorian era. The parlor and other rooms devoted solely to public activities appeared in house plans with the specific goal of separating public activities from private ones (Clark 1988). Katherine Grier's (1992:51) recent analysis notes that, "One important characteristic of Victorian house architecture, including modest plan-book houses in the second half of the 19th century, was that public and private spaces were clearly defined and separated from one another as much as possible." This separation of public and private space was a key element of house plans throughout the Victorian period (Rotman and Nassaney 1997).

In short, with the rise of industrialism, the professional and domestic aspects of life were physically separated. Separation of public and private space within the home also became increasingly important. In looking at contemporary sources, it was generally espoused that this trend toward segmentation of space was beneficial to the family and something to which all aspects of society should aspire (Crossick 1978:149; Daunton 1983:224; Davidoff and Hall 1987:359–361; Crow and Allan 1990:13).

Spatial Patterning at Squaw Flat

The archaeological survey located 21 activity areas or loci. These included seven well locations, a bunkhouse, a boarding house, two unidentifiable structures, two separate tank locations, a claim marker, and seven dumps (Table 1). The author directly correlated many of these loci with features that appeared on historical maps (Figure 4). One such feature was a collapsed, wood framed, gable roofed, board-and-batten bunkhouse. This structure lacked partitions and appears to have been a simple one-room building. Survey also located the collapsed boarding house, a gable-roofed, board-

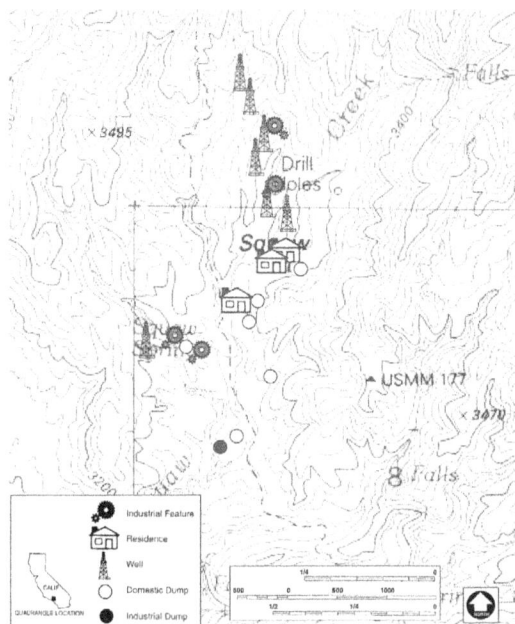

FIGURE 4. Feature map of Squaw Flat.

and-batten structure. This structure had piped-in and heated water, probably for shower facilities (an important "luxury" needed to remove the toxic grime of a day's work). Though listed

TABLE 1
LOCI AND HISTORIC AFFILIATION

Locus	Beesum	Houston &Cohn	Big Chief	Squaw Flat Placer	Border Oil	Stansbury Inc.	Unknown
A							dump
B							dump
C							dump
D				boarding house			
E				bunk house			
G							shed
H							dump
I							well?
J				tank			
K			well	well			
L							tanks
M	well						
N							dump
O							dump
P					well		
Q					shed?		
R				claim post			
S		well	well	well			
T						well	
U							dump
V			well	well			

as a boarding house (Friel 1920), no partitions were noted in the ruins to suggest segregated space. Several well and tank locations were correlated with historically recorded features as well. Two patterns were immediately apparent in these loci.

First, the residential units, both those listed in historical records and those located on the ground, are set apart from the industrial features (Figure 5). Residential units are scattered around the northern portion of Squaw Flat itself, while the wells and tanks are positioned on surrounding ridge tops and in the floors of surrounding canyons, effectively isolating one from the other.

Second, the dumps are segregated according to composition. Each of the seven dumps overwhelmingly contained either industrial or domestic refuse, with the dominant component generally composing 85–95% of the material (Table 2). In some cases, these dumps were located within a few feet of each other but were distinctly separated from one another by ridgelines and other landforms. Additionally, much of this material was hauled some distance to dump it where it is currently located, showing a fair amount of effort for no apparent reason.

Business Versus Culture

Houston and Cohn wished to produce oil with as little investment as possible. They were also faced with the challenge of drilling in an area that had yet to prove itself productive, making any investment tenuous. To provide labor at this remote location, the most economical option was to house the workers at the site. A practical solution was to provide small, cheap, one room, board-and-batten buildings that provided at least the appearance of protection from the elements.

A number of sources (Henderson n.d.:3; Lynch 1987) reported that these oil workers were provided needed building materials, but given a relatively free hand in setting up operations at these leases. This freedom was a concession on the part of the investors to mollify any bad feelings that may be generated by the less-than-desirable conditions faced by their employees.

Work and Home at Squaw Flat

The oilmen at Squaw Flat were placed in the middle of their place of work. Using the

freedom given them in constructing their camp, the oilmen did their best to separate their housing from the well sites. They used distance and landforms to block out the sight, sound, and smell of drilling from the atmosphere that immediately surrounded their temporary homes. This pattern could be explained through geologic needs (placing houses on areas that were not expected to produce oil), engineering requirements (putting houses on flat ground), or local logistical needs. Until recently, little science was behind deciding where to drill for oil in the Sespe Oil Field that encompasses Squaw Flat. Oil is deposited in these fields in discontinuous pockets and fissures. The area is well known for producing dry holes immediately adjacent to flowing wells. Oil drillers would, more or less randomly, stick holes in the ground until they hit oil, trying to drill where there was some indication or hope of oil (Daries 1997). Wells at Squaw Flat reflect this anarchic method of exploration with some located on ridge tops and others in canyon bottoms, not conforming to any stratigraphic or topographic details. Engineering was certainly an important factor in how the wells and machinery were constructed but seems to have had little impact on the location of the

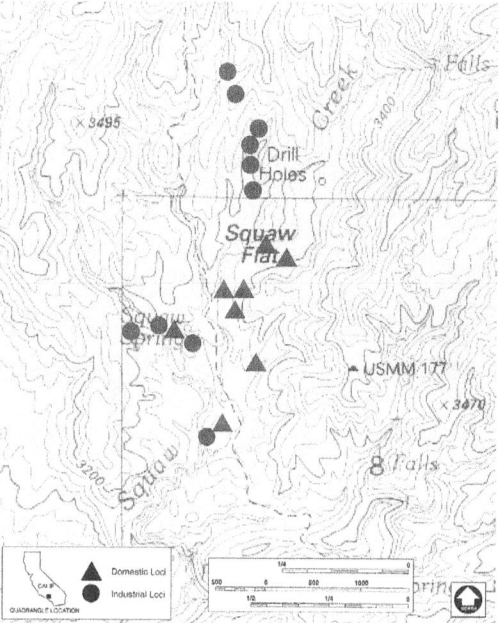

FIGURE 5. Residential and industrial loci of Squaw Flat.

TABLE 2
COMPOSITION OF REFUSE AT DUMPS

Locus	% Domestic Refuse	% Industrial Refuse	% Refuse of Unknown Origin
A	96	0	4
B	85	0	14
C	0	75	25
H	97	0	3
N	0	100	0
O	95	20	3
U	55	0	45

wells or residential structures. Though some naturally level ground was utilized, some was not, and some was created. Water and fuel oil were piped where needed. Aside from those two factors, there are few engineering constraints above ground on well location. Logistically it would have made some practical sense to provide housing at a location central to the wells, but some of the wells were drilled 30–40 years after the camp was constructed, and it is doubtful that Houston and Cohn had every possible well location delineated.

Aside from these more practical possibilities, an apparent desire is archaeologically evident to separate home from work, to distance the smells of the kitchen from smoke-belching boilers, and the strum of the guitar on the porch from the pounding of a drill. Following Victorian and post-Victorian working-class values, an appropriate home should be separated from the influences of that male domain, the workplace. Though surrounded by the evidence of active oil exploration, workers at Squaw Flat still managed to remove themselves from direct contact with these activities when not on duty. Though conveniently located at the job site, the oilmen did their best to separate themselves from their work.

Public and Private Space at Squaw Flat

These same men were also housed in simple one-room, bunk- and boarding houses, lacking in the separation of public and private space defined as so important to social well being during this time. As a result, they looked elsewhere for ways to separate their public and private lives. Their trash became a symbol of this separation. Workers and residents at Squaw Flat went well out of their way to separate their domestic refuse

from that generated by drilling. These dumps were used as more than simple repositories for useless items. They also represented the activities that generated them. In separating the slag, cable, broken machinery, and timbers of public work life from the ruined clothing, food cans, and broken personal items of the private home life, they were perhaps consciously separating these aspects of life.

In a broader sense, the landscape here was used as a mitigation device for mediating conflicting agendas between the developers and the drillers, the need of the employer to place them at their work place in simple structures, and the workers' desires to maintain important social parameters. Landforms and distance acted as fences separating the professional and domestic space, a pattern that has been noted elsewhere (Mrozowski 1991:94). Workers also used the landscape to help visually separate the public from the private.

ACKNOWLEDGMENTS

Thanks to Rebecca Allen, D. Jackson Scott, Gina Nichols, and Kimberly Wooten for their help and comments on this document, and Steven Horne and Los Padres National Forest for access to Squaw Flat.

REFERENCES

BAXTER, R. SCOTT
1995 *Life in a Twentieth Century Petroleum Work Camp.* Paper presented at the Annual Meeting of the Society for Industrial Archaeology, Baltimore, MD.

BECK, WARREN A., AND DAVID A. WILLIAMS
1972 *California: A History of the Golden State.* Doubleday and Company, Inc., Garden City, NJ.

BLUMIN, STUART
1989 *The Emergence of the Middle Class.* Cambridge University Press, London, England.

BROTHERS, C. R.
   1926   Form 105, 5 June. Division of Oil and Gas, Santa Paula, CA.

BUSH, R. D.
   1934   Letter to C. C. Thomas, 31 January. Division of Oil and Gas, Santa Paula, CA.

CAUGHEY, JOHN WALTON
   1940   *California*. Prentice-Hall, Inc., Englewood Cliffs, N.J.

CLARK, CLIFFORD E., JR.
   1986   *The American Family Home 1800–1960*. University of North Carolina Press, Chapel Hill.
   1988   Domestic Architecture as an Index to Social History: The Romantic Revival and the Cult of Domesticity in America, 1840–1870. In *Material Life in America 1600–1860*, Robert Blair St. George, editor. Northeastern University Press, Boston, MA.

COHN, A. A.
   1952   Form 102, 38353 11-36 9500. Division of Oil and Gas, Santa Paula, CA.

COHN, AMY
   1937   Letter to Beesum Oil Company, 16 May. Division of Oil and Gas, Santa Paula, CA.

COONTZ, STEPHANIE
   1988   *The Social Origins of Private Life: A History of American Families 1600–1900*. Verso, London, England.

CRANE, BRIAN D.
   2000   Filth, Garbage, and Rubbish: Refuse Disposal, Sanitary Reforms, and Nineteenth Century Yard Deposits in Washington, DC. *Historical Archaeology* 34(1):20–28.

CROSSICK, GEOFFREY
   1978   *An Artisan Elite in Victorian Society: Kentish London 1840–1880*. Croom Helm, London, England.

CROW, GRAHAM, AND GRAHAM ALLAN
   1990   Constructing the Domestic Sphere: The Emergence of the Modern Home in Post-War Britain. In *Politics of Everyday life: Continuity and Change in Work and the Family*, Helen Corr and Lynn Jamieson, editors, pp.11–36. St. Martin's Press, New York, NY.

DARIES, ROBERT
   1997   Personal Communication, 7 January.

DAUNTON, MARTIN J.
   1983   Public Place and Private Space: The Victorian City and the Working-Class Household. In *The Pursuit of Urban History*, D. Fraser and A. Suttcliffe, editors, pp. 75–85. Edward Arnold, London, England.

DAVIDOFF, LEONORE, AND CATHERINE HALL
   1987   *Family Fortunes: Men and Women of the English Middle Class, 1780–1850*. Hutchinson, London, England.

DEETZ, JAMES
   1977   *In Small Things Forgotten: An Archaeology of Early American Life*. Anchor Books, New York, NY.
   1996   *In Small Things Forgotten: An Archaeology of Early American Life*. Anchor Books, New York, NY.

DEPARTMENT OF PETROLEUM AND GAS
   1926   Form 111, 39803 7-25 10M. Division of Oil and Gas, Santa Paula, CA.
   1933   Letter, 27 February. Division of Oil and Gas, Santa Paula, CA.

FITTS, ROBERT K.
   1999   The Archaeology of Middle-Class Domesticity and Gentility in Victorian Brooklyn. *Historical Archaeology* 33(1):39–62.

FRIEL, LEGRAND
   1920   *MS 5504*. Microfiche, Bureau of Land Management, Sacramento, CA.

FRIEND, WILLIAM
   1997   Personal Communication.

GRIER, KATHERINE C.
   1992   The Decline of the Memory Place: The Parlor after 1890. In *American Home Life, 1880–1930: A Social History of Spaces and Services*, Jessica H. Foy and Thomas J. Schlereth, editors, pp. 49–74. University of Tennessee Press, Knoxville.

HARRELL, FORREST K.
   1948   Form 105. Division of Oil and Gas, Santa Paula, CA.
   1952a   Form 108, 24 June. Division of Oil and Gas, Santa Paula, CA.
   1952b   Form 159, 23 July. Division of Oil and Gas, Santa Paula, CA.
   1970   Form 176, 14 October. Division of Oil and Gas, Santa Paula, CA.

HENDERSON, MARY ALICE ORCUTT
   n.d.   *The Torrey Canon Oil Company*. Santa Paula Historical Society, CA.

HOUSTON, C. W.
   1933a   Letter and well log. California Division of Oil and Gas, Santa Paula, CA.
   1933b   Form 100, 28 February. Division of Oil and Gas, Santa Paula, CA.
   1933c   Form 9-331a, 9 August. Division of Oil and Gas, Santa Paula, CA.

HOUSTON C. W., AND A. A. COHN
   1933   Form 100, 73066 12-29 20M. Division of Oil and Gas, Santa Paula, CA.
   1937   Form 108, 34047 7-36 5M. Division of Oil and Gas, Santa Paula, CA.
   1940   Form 103, 6 March. Division of Oil and Gas, Santa Paula, CA.

KALDENBURG, RUSSELL L., AND KENNETH J. GRAHAM
1973 The Life Cycle of a Boom Town: A Case Study of Fellows, California, An Early Oil Field Community. Manuscript in possession of author.

KAPLOW, E. J.
1950 Letter to Beesum Oil Company, 3 May. Division of Oil and Gas, Santa Paula, CA.

KEMP, TOM
1978 *Historical Patterns of Industrialization*. Longman, Inc., New York, NY.

LANDERS, J. C.
1933 Form 107, 27 July. Division of Oil and Gas, Santa Paula, CA.

LYNCH, GERALD
1987 *Roughnecks, Drillers, and Tool Pushers: Thirty Years in the Oil Fields*. University of Texas Press, Austin.

MACDONALD, R. M.
1929 Form 107, 4 March. Division of Oil and Gas, Santa Paula, CA.

MAY, MARTHA
1987 The Historical Problem of the Family Wage: The Ford Motor Company and the Five Dollar Day. In *Families and Work*, Naomi Gerstel and Harriet Engel Gross, editors, pp. 111–131. Temple University Press, Philadelphia, PA.

MROZOWSKI, STEPHEN A.
1991 Landscape of Inequality. In *The Archaeology of Inequality*, Randall McGuire and Robert Paynter, editors, pp. 79–101. Basil Blackwell Ltd., Cambridge, England.

NEESE, FARIBA M.
1995 Letter to David J. Scott, 18 January. Los Padres National Forest, Frazier Park.

PATHFINDER PETROLEUM COMPANY
1933 Department of the Interior Form 9-331a. Division of Oil and Gas, Santa Paula, CA.
1953a Form 105, 21 May. Division of Oil and Gas, Santa Paula, CA.
1953b History of Oil or Gas Well, 5 November. Division of Oil and Gas, Santa Paula, CA.

PATTERSON, ROBERT C.
1933 Department of the Interior Form 9-331a. Division of Oil and Gas, Santa Paula, CA.

PRUTZMAN, PAUL W.
1913 *Petroleum in Southern California*. California State Mining Bureau, Bulletin No. 63.

RINTOUL, WILLIAM
1978 *Oildorado: Boom Times on the West Side*. Valley Publishers, Fresno, CA.

ROBERTS, ELIZABETH
1984 *A Women's Place: An Oral History of Working-Class Women 1890–1940*. Basil Blackwell, Oxford, England.

ROTMAN, DEBORAH L., AND MICHAEL S. NASSANEY
1997 Class, Gender, and the Built Environment: Deriving Social Relationships from Cultural Landscapes in Southwest Michigan. *Historical Archaeology* 31(2):42–62.

ROTHSCHILD, NAN A.
1992 Spatial and Social Proximity in Early New York City. *Journal of Anthropological Archaeology* 11(2):202–218.

RYAN, MARY
1981 *Cradle of the Middle Class: The Family in Oneida County New York, 1790–1865*. Cambridge University Press, London, England.

SHACKEL, PAUL A.
1996 *Culture Change and the New Technology: An Archaeology of the Early American Industrial Era*. Plenum Press, New York, NY.

STANSBURY, B. J.
1954a Form 107, 20 April. Division of Oil and Gas, Santa Paula, CA.
1954b History of Oil or Gas Well, 15 June. Division of Oil and Gas, Santa Paula, CA.

THOMAS, C. C.
1934 Letter to R. D. Bush, 26 January. California Division of Oil and Gas, Santa Paula, CA.

WHITE, GERALD T.
1962 *Formative Years in the Far West: A History of Standard Oil Company of California and Predecessors Through 1919*. Appleton-Century-Crofts, New York, NY.
1968 *Scientists in Conflict: The Beginnings of the Oil Industry in California*. The Huntington Library, San Marino, CA.

YERGIN, DANIEL
1991 *The Prize: The Epic Quest for Oil, Money, and Power*. Simon & Schuster, New York, NY.

R. SCOTT BAXTER
PAST FORWARD, INC.
PO BOX 201
10675 O'NEIL ALLEY
AMADOR CITY, CA 95601

Randall H. McGuire and Paul Reckner

The Unromantic West: Labor, Capital, and Struggle

ABSTRACT

A gang of historians has gunned down the "romantic West." They have dismissed the notion of the West as a frontier of opportunity for all comers. The American West has been redefined as an arena of struggle involving complex relations of class, gender, ethnicity, and race. Western work camps and company towns existed as extensions of a global economy centered on the eastern United States. From the mid-19th century through the first decades of the 20th century, capital and people flowed into the West from Europe, Asia, and Mexico. In this internal periphery of U.S. capitalism, workers experienced the same type of exploitation and engaged in the same struggles as their brethren in other parts of the United States. Perhaps nowhere is this more evident than in the coalfields of Colorado. The work camps and company towns that archaeologists excavate were loci of struggle, and historians cannot claim to understand them without considering these conflicts.

Introduction

On the morning of April 20, 1914, Colorado National Guard troops opened fire on a tent colony occupied by 1,200 striking coal miners and their families at Ludlow, Colorado. The shooting continued into the late afternoon, then the guardsmen swept through the camp looting it and setting it aflame. When the smoke cleared, 20 of the camp's inhabitants were dead, including 2 women and 11 children. For the next 10 days, the enraged and embittered miners struck back, attacking and destroying mines and mining towns. The Ludlow massacre stands as the most violent and best-known event of the 1913–1914 Colorado coal strike, but its significance goes far beyond an isolated struggle. The killing of women and children at Ludlow outraged the American public and helped turn popular opinion against violent confrontations with strikers. Such clashes were an all-too-common occurrence in late-19th- and early-20th-century labor conflicts. Ludlow marks a pivotal point in U.S. history, when labor relations began to move from class warfare to policies of negotiation, co-option, and regulated strikes. Historians have called the 1913–1914 strike the Colorado Coalfield War and declared it the "best" example of class warfare in the history of the United States (McGovern and Guttridge 1972).

The story of the Colorado Coalfield War is not a story of the romantic Wild West. The cast of characters is all wrong; nowhere are there cowboys and Indians, posses or rustlers. In fact, when travelers on Interstate Highway 25 follow road signs to the Ludlow massacre memorial just north of Trinidad, Colorado, they generally expect to be visiting the site of an Indian massacre (Walker 1999). What they encounter is a monument dedicated to the men, women, and children slain at Ludlow, with names like Pedragon, Valdez, Costa, and Tikas (Figure 1). The Colorado miners were primarily third-wave immigrants from southern and eastern Europe, with some Americans, Mexican Americans, Anglo-Americans, and a smattering of African Americans and Japanese. The staple conflicts of the romantic West, struggles over sheep and cattle, water, and land are also absent from the story. The miners struck for improved working conditions, for less company control of their lives, and for the right to join the United Mine Workers of America (UMW). They experienced the same type of exploitation and engaged in the same struggle as other workers in the rest of the United States.

Class and the Unromantic West

That one of the major events in U.S. labor history occurred in the West should not surprise us. A gang of historians has gunned down the "romantic West" (Smith 1950; Limerick 1987; Nash 1991; Cronon, Miles, and Gitlin 1998). They have dismissed the idea that the American West was a temporary stage in the march of national progress that ended at the beginning of the 20th century. They have argued instead for an unbroken continuum of western history intimately linked to social processes in the rest of the United States. They also dismissed the notion of the West as a frontier of opportunity for all comers. Scholars have redefined it as an arena of struggle involving complex relations of class, gender, ethnicity, and race (Limerick 1987;

Randall H. McGuire and Paul Reckner

FIGURE 1. The Ludlow Monument.

Malone and Etulain 1989; Hardesty 1991, 1998; Wylie 1993; Sheridan 1998; Purser 1999). Of these relations, the most inimical to the notion of the romantic West is class. In his famous frontier hypotheses, Frederick Jackson Turner (Smith 1950:3–4; Malone and Etulain 1989:1–2) argued that the frontier served as a social and economic release valve that shaped American identities in ways fundamentally different from those of continental Europe. The American characteristics generated by the frontier experience—individualism, democracy, and nationalism—denied the exploitative nature of capitalism and the impact of class conflict on Western social relations. Class was constructed as a distinctly Eastern (or European), urban, and industrial problem.

Given over a decade of active scholarship and heated debate, no one should be surprised to hear that the best example of class warfare in the history of the United States occurred in the West, but likely many people remain astonished by this fact. Revisionist histories of the West have not been accepted within some scholarly circles and have not permeated into popular perceptions of western history (McGuire 1995). Attempts at revisionism in movies such as

Dances with Wolves or the 1993 African-American Western *Posse* simply use the same stereotypes and change the color of the actors. In much popular history, it seems as if the revisionist critique has never happened. For an example, in the 1999 *World Book Multimedia Encyclopedia*:

> Western frontier life in America marks one of the most exciting chapters in American history. The settlement of the West represented the dreams of gold-hungry prospectors, and of homesteaders whose backbreaking labor transformed barren plains into fields of grain. It is the story of cowboys and the open range. It is the drama of Indians and outlaws, of the trains and stagecoaches they attacked, and of the citizens who brought order to the frontier. It is a living tradition that symbolizes to men and women everywhere the American achievement of taming a wild and beautiful land (Faulk 1998).

The mythic West remains difficult to escape in popular culture and historical narratives, and the conceptual legacy of the frontier has had a lasting impact on the discipline of historical archaeology. Despite significant recent changes in the focus of western historical archaeology—from pioneer homesteads and forts to urban and industrial sites, and from consensus approaches to conflictual frameworks—many, if not most, of the historical archaeologists who have recognized differentiation as a factor in western contexts focus on socioeconomic status rather than class. Status-based approaches transform the class concept from a tool for exploring struggle to an exercise in ranking. There has also been a tendency in archaeological studies of western communities to accentuate their uniqueness as western phenomena and to downplay their place in larger national processes of class conflict and labor struggle.

Socioeconomic Status versus Relational Class

Numerous historical archaeologists have looked at what Donald Hardesty (1991:2) has called the "counter classic West" by studying workers' camps, company towns, and mining towns. These studies have, by and large, equated class with social status (Toulouse 1970; Schulz and Gust 1983; Ewen 1986; O'Brien and Majewski 1989; Brock and Schwartz 1991; Schmitt and Zeier 1993; Spude et al. 1993; Staski and Reiter

1996). Thad Van Bueren's article in this volume is a notable exception as are Margaret Purser's (1991) study of gender and class, and Hardesty's (1998) study of power and class. A social-status approach likens class with occupation (for example, blue collar = working class or white collar = middle class) and/or with income. From this perspective, class is understandable in terms of standards of living, consumption, and material things. Also, the status approach tends to treat different status positions either as independent from each other or as points along a continuum. The archaeologist seeks to define status in terms of material culture as markers associated with a status position or attempts to fill in details as to what people of a particular status ate, what plates they used, or what kind of houses they lived in. This approach frequently downplays or ignores exploitation and class struggle. It is difficult, within a status-based framework, to truly understand how and why class warfare broke out in early-20th-century Colorado.

A relational or structural approach provides an alternative way to look at class in the West (Wurst 1999). In this approach, classes are defined by their relationship to the means of production and to each other. Thus, classes cannot exist independently from each other, and a relational approach emphasizes the different interests of class groups. Class groups pursue their interests on a terrain of unequal power relations so that the goals and desires of one or a few class groups dominate the interests of the others. The dominant class appropriates the labor or products of the primary producers and through this process reaps wealth. This is exploitation, the reason that class relations are virtually always loci of struggle.

The fundamental class relationship in capitalism is between the class of owners of the means of production and the working class (Marx 1906). Other class positions and class fractions also exist within this structure (Wurst 1999:10). Therefore, in a relational sense, a middle class of managers, administrators, and professionals exists between the owners and workers. An underclass, usually racially based in the United States, also exists of individuals who live on the margins of the economy and the society. Commonly, in the West, class fractions existed within the owners and the middle class, depending upon their sources of wealth. Members of these classes who derived their assets from local sources, such as farmers, shop owners, and self-employed tradesmen, would have had particular economic interests and relationships to the working class (Gutman 1987). These interests and relationships would have been different from those of the national bourgeois and their agents who extracted wealth from the region. By the same token, the working class of peripheral areas may have different interests than the working class in core industries. Among these complex relationships, the one most commonly ignored in studies of the West is the struggle between owners and workers (for example, the quote from Wegars 1991:100 cited in Wylie 1993:13).

The different perspectives on the West can be highlighted by considering how each would view the archetypical western figure, the cowboy. In the romantic West, the cowboy is young, heroic, self-reliant, Anglo-Saxon, and a free agent who is his own master because he can move from ranch to ranch and from region to region seeking work as he pleases. If the scholar sees the cowboy through the lens of social status, emphasis will be placed on how much money he made and what material goods, foods, and drinks this income allowed him. Historical archaeologists would look for the suite of material goods that would distinguish the cowboy from the miner or the Chinese cook. Adopting a relational class perspective, the cowboy is/was a wage worker laboring for employers engaged in capitalist—profit-driven—enterprises. The role of the cowboy existed because businesses such as ranches and trail drives needed workers to handle a commodity, in this case cattle, and these businesses continued to operate through the work of the cowboy/employee. Thus, the freedom of the cowboy was simply the freedom to choose his own master or to starve. Cowboys could take action to transform the economic relations that structured their employment, as was attempted in the little-known "cowboy strike" of 1883 that saw several hundred cowboys walk off their jobs at five major Texas ranches (Curtin 1991:56–59).

A relational view of class leads to two important realizations about the nature of the West.

The first of these is that the labor relations and class structures that defined class in the West extended far beyond the geographic extent of that region. The second is that class struggle has always been an important aspect of the history of the American West.

From Frontier to Periphery?

At no time since the establishment of a European presence in the West have the class relations that shaped the region operated outside of national and international economic structures. At all times, the West has been part and parcel of greater processes. Like the dismissal of the mythic West, many scholars of the American West generally acknowledge this fact. Even the traditional notion of the frontier recognizes the West as the edge of something bigger. Recently, many historical archaeologists have drawn on the terminology of world-systems theory and refer to the West as a *periphery* (Farnsworth 1989; Hardesty 1991; Crowell 1997).

Calling the West a periphery, as opposed to a frontier, should involve more than just a change in labels. Use of the periphery concept entails something very different from the idea of the West as a frontier. A frontier is defined as the leading edge of settled country, where the "wilds" begin or as the border of inhabited regions. The concept always implies a vacant or little-used land on the edge of civilization and the process of developing or civilizing this wilderness.

Periphery, on the other hand, signifies a position in a larger world system and in relations of power and domination (Wallerstein 1974). Core regions derive their wealth by exploiting peripheries. Thus, peripheries are not edges but, rather, are integral components of larger sets of economic, political, and cultural relations. Cores cannot exist without peripheries, and the underdeveloped nature of peripheries is a product of their domination by cores, not a result of their wilderness nature (Wallerstein 1974). In other words, cores do not simply encounter or discover underdeveloped wildernesses; they create and maintain peripheries (underdevelopment) through the extraction of natural resources and surplus labor value (Wallerstein 1991:80–103). In order to facilitate extraction, agents of core interests attempt to transform periphery production and social relations to conform to or articulate with systems present in the core. The foundation of the expansion of the capitalist world system was built on the subordination of labor (Arrighi et al. 1989:46–47). Wage labor was one such arrangement brought to the West through capitalist expansion. Localized historical circumstances influenced the process of class formation and something of the character of class relations once they were firmly established, but the centrality of class in the western periphery must be acknowledged.

The American West was, however, a rather special kind of periphery—an *internal* periphery. By the middle of the 19th century, the United States (or at least the northeastern United States) had established itself as a new core in the capitalist world economy. Also by this time, the United States had acquired through conquest, negotiation, and purchases the American West. As an internal periphery, the American West was more culturally, politically, and economically integrated with its core than were the overseas colonial holdings of European core states. This is especially true once the abolition of slavery made wage labor the normal and expected labor relationship throughout the entire country. Thus, labor flows, mechanisms to control labor, labor laws, and customary practices of work were intimately linked between the core and the periphery (Arrighi et al. 1989; Wallerstein 1991). Labor struggles also transcended the internal core and peripheries of the United States. The relationship of capital and labor in the western United States was a regional manifestation of larger class struggles in the United States as a whole (following Wallerstein 1991:58–59). We hold that any serious engagement with world-systems approaches necessitates a commitment to class analysis (Arrighi et al. 1989; Delâge 1993).

The global relationships of the world-system structured class relations in the West; however, people experienced these relations daily on the local level (Roseberry 1989). Thus, class struggle is realized and reproduced in the course of everyday life. When similar struggles take place throughout the structure, they may transform global relationships. The archaeological record of the historic West is largely the result of day-to-day lived experiences, and these experiences must have included class struggle (McGuire 1992:126).

Class and the Western American Periphery

Global processes and linkages to local economies and struggles are clearly illustrated in the development of the western coal-mining industry. In southern Colorado, industrialized coal production began in the late-19th century (Smith 1992). From the beginning, the organization of coal production in southern Colorado directly paralleled practices in the coal mines of the East and Midwest, particularly Pennsylvania and West Virginia, and this transfer even extended to methods for resolving labor strife (Corbin [1981] on West Virginia; Kenny [1998] on Pennsylvania). During the 1913–1914 strike in southern Colorado, both coal operators and the UMW drew resources directly from clashes in other coal regions of the U.S. The Baldwin-Felts detective agency, in the employ of the coal operators, brought agents and machine guns fresh from service in West Virginia, and the UMW provided the Ludlow strikers with tents from the same state (McGovern and Guttridge 1972:97, 105, 117). Those engaged in the coal industry, such as managers, engineers, mechanics, and miners, moved between the mines of the East and the West. Similar patterns of labor flow are seen across the country and internationally. In southern Colorado, the first miners were largely of Irish and Welsh origin, and they brought to the West their experiences of unionization and socialist politics amassed in the eastern mines and in the British Isles. In the first decade of this century, mine owners brought in third-wave immigrants, primarily eastern and southern Europeans, as strikebreakers. By the second decade of the century these workers had virtually replaced the Welsh and Irish in the pits. The British remained in the industry as managers and mechanics and in leadership positions within the United Mine Workers. This pattern of labor flow can be seen in almost all the coal mining regions of the United States (Long 1991).

Many might argue that this approach focuses too much on the modern "counter classic West" and not on the classical frontier West that Turner argued had ended when he gave his famous paper in 1893. Capitalist penetration, incorporation, and transformation of the American West as a periphery of the capitalist world economy was a long and dynamic process. It began well before 1893 and did not end until much more recently, perhaps as late as World War II. Capitalism did not simply come to the West riding the iron horse, as some historical archaeologists would seem to suggest (Schuyler 1991). It actually came to the West much earlier, conceivably on the backs of the American mountain men who built the fortunes of the Astors and Ashleys by trapping, processing, and transporting furs. The relative recency of the Ludlow massacre cannot be taken to account for its seemingly anomalous position in western history. We would suggest that what happened at Ludlow in 1914 was but one horrible incident in the long and still-unfolding history of class conflict in the American West.

The cattle and cowboys that loom large in popular images of the mythic West were put there as tools to accumulate profits for eastern and overseas capitalists. The large ranches of the West were the products of speculative investments by east coast, English, and especially Scottish entrepreneurs. These ranches were often organized as joint stock companies. Popular fiction has characterized the famous range wars of the late-19th century as conflicts between sheep and cattle. What is lost in this characterization is the ethnic and class character of these wars. Often the herders of sheep were small landholders, many of Mexican or Basque heritages, whose activities interfered with the bottom line of the large ranches. The centrality of class in these struggles is especially clear in cases like the 1892 Johnson County Cattle War in southern Wyoming, where Anglo cowboys and small holders faced off against a private army of "regulators" hired by the corporate ranches (Barber 1953). The similarity of these events to the 1892 strike at Homestead, Pennsylvania, where steel workers engaged in a pitched battle with a private army of Pinkerton agents, are rarely noted. Throughout the late-19th and early-20th centuries, labor struggles in the West paralleled strikes and conflicts in eastern industrial centers—meatpackers in Chicago, railroad and steelworkers in Pennsylvania, and textile workers in New Jersey and Massachusetts. The vast majority of Americans know of the shootout at the OK corral in 1881, but few have knowledge of the Texas cowboy strike of 1883 (Curtin 1991:56–59).

As the story of Ludlow demonstrates, many major episodes and struggles in American labor history occurred in the West. Among these was the development of the International Workers of the World (the IWW or the "Wobblies"), one of the most radical unions of this century. In 1893, hard-rock miners founded the Western Federation of Miners (WFM) in Butte, Montana. Following a series of violent strikes in the hard-rock mines of Colorado, the IWW was formed from the WFM in 1905 (Brissenden 1919; Phoner 1981). The IWW became a national union, but was always strongest in the West and especially so among miners and lumbermen. The IWW openly advocated socialism and the overthrow of the capitalist system. The U.S. government launched an all-out campaign against the IWW during World War I, and the union was no longer a major force after the 1920s.

Archaeology, Class, and the Ludlow Massacre

How does a commitment to class analysis and core-periphery relations inform archaeological practice? Archaeological data can simultaneously provide material evidence of large-scale interactions between core and periphery and, more importantly, of processes of class formation as they play out at the community level. Investigations of western communities have the potential to reveal, in intimate fashion, the nature and character of local conflicts and their relationships to broader national struggles. Integrating archival and material data, historical archaeology reveals in fine detail the day-to-day lives of historical agents. By focusing on class and core-periphery relations, it becomes possible to link the lived experiences of these agents to developments in core-periphery relations to examine (1) how their daily struggles were linked with broader movements, (2) how historical conditions influenced local processes of class formation, and (3) how the tensions inherent in class structures affected the material and social fabric of community life.

These three foci inform research currently being conducted on the 1913–1914 Colorado Coalfield War and the pivotal event of that

famous struggle, the Ludlow Massacre. The following sections provide an historical overview of the events of 1913–1914, and a review of the project's research agenda. The research is still underway and analyses are ongoing. The results of the first two seasons of excavation suggest that the data needed to address research goals are there.

War in the Coalfields: Historical Overview of the 1913–1914 Strike

In 1913, Colorado was the 8th largest coal-producing state in the United States (McGovern and Guttridge 1972). Most of this production centered on the bituminous coalfields in Huerfano and Las Animas counties north of Trinidad, Colorado (Figure 2). These mines primarily produced coking coal for the steel mills at Pueblo, Colorado. The Rockefeller-controlled Colorado Fuel and Iron Company (CF&I) was

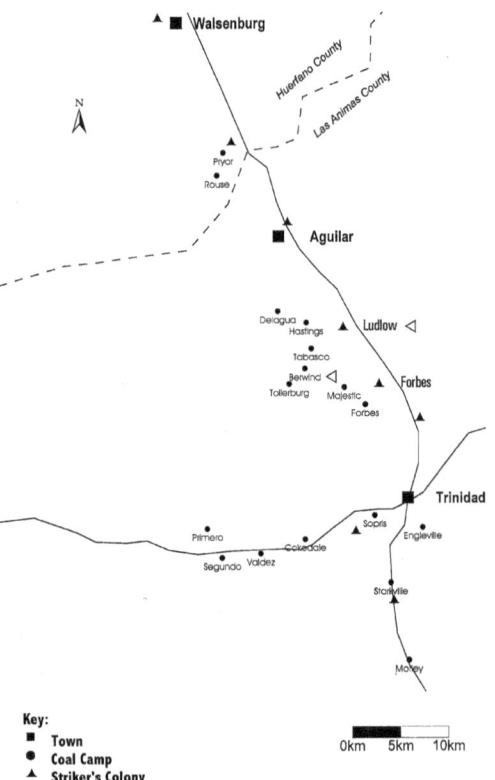

FIGURE 2. Map of the 1913–1914 coal strike zone.

the largest mining operation in the region, employing approximately 14,000 miners in 1913, 70% of whom were immigrants.

The conditions of the mines and of miners' lives were appalling (Beshoar 1957; McGovern and Guttridge 1972; Papanikolas 1982). In 1912 the accident rate for Colorado mines was triple the national average (Whiteside 1990). Colorado mining concerns operated in flagrant violation of several state laws that regulated safety and the fair compensation of miners. The miners lived in crude, isolated coal camps where companies controlled not only housing but mercantile establishments, medical facilities, saloons, and recreational facilities. Company guards acted as police and regulated who could enter or leave the communities. The companies also dominated the local political structure and used their power over employees to influence election results. Contemporary accounts described the situation as feudal (Seligman 1914).

The UMW began a massive organizing campaign in southern Colorado in 1913 and launched a strike in the fall of that year (Beshoar 1957; McGovern and Guttridge 1972; Papanikolas 1982). The strikers' demands included company recognition of the union, higher pay, and the enforcement of existing Colorado mining laws. In response, coal operators banded together under the leadership of CF&I management and brought in the Baldwin Feltz detective agency to violently suppress the strike. On 23 September 1913, more than 90% of the miners dropped their tools and joined the strike. Company agents promptly acted to eject families of union miners from their company-owned housing. Several thousand people moved into tent colonies set up by the UMW. The Ludlow colony, with approximately 150 tents and 1,200 residents, was the largest of these camps and also served as the UMW's Las Animas County headquarters. The residents of all 12 tent colonies represented a mix of nationalities, including Italians, Greeks, eastern Europeans, Mexicans, African Americans, and Welsh.

Violence between the strikers and coal operators broke out almost immediately after the strike was called, including physical assaults and murders (Beshoar 1957; McGovern and Guttridge 1972; Papanikolas 1982). In October, Colorado Governor Elias Ammons called up units of the National Guard to "restore order" to the region. Over the winter of 1913–1914, relations between the strikers and the guard deteriorated. The situation worsened when the governor recalled many of the regular troops in April. The mining companies replaced these troops with their own employees under the command of the remaining Colorado National Guard officers. In Ludlow the strikers dug cellars under their tents as refuges for women and children.

On 20 April 1914, the guard attacked the tent camp at Ludlow. That morning, the guard commander ordered Louis Tikas, the leader of the colony, to meet him at Ludlow Station. Fearing that this might be a pretext for an attack, armed strikers took up positions along a railroad cut overlooking the station. The National Guard had positioned a machine gun on a hill a mile to the south of the tent colony. Shots were fired by one of the parties (accounts vary), and the guardsmen began firing the machine gun into the tent camp. During the course of the attack, as many as 200 additional guardsmen joined the fray. They brought in a second, company owned, machine gun. After a few hours of firing, the tents were so full of holes that they looked like lace (Thomas 1971). In order to give their families time to escape the colony, the armed strikers engaged the guard and tried to draw their fire away from the camp.

Pandemonium reigned inside the Ludlow colony. Some residents sought refuge in a large walk-in well, while others huddled in the cellars under their tents. Camp leaders struggled throughout the day to move families away from the tents by way of a dry creek bed north of the camp. In the early afternoon, a 12-year-old boy named William Snyder came up out of a cellar and was shot and killed. As dusk gathered, a passing freight train pulled up in front of the machine guns, blocking their line of fire. During this brief respite, almost all of the remaining inhabitants left the colony, and the armed strikers withdrew. Guardsmen moved in and swept through the camp, looting and burning the tents. Unknown to the strikers, 4 women and 11 children in a cellar below tent 58 huddled in fear while the flames consumed the tent above them. The guardsmen seized Louis Tikas and two other camp leaders and summarily executed them. When dawn broke, the camp was a smoking ruin. Below tent 58, in the dark hole, 2 women and all 11 children were dead.

News of the deaths at Ludlow spread to the remaining tent colonies in the region, and in the wake of the attack, strikers throughout southern Colorado took up arms. Armed miners destroyed several company towns. Both company employees and strikers died. After 10 days of open revolt, President Wilson sent federal troops to Trinidad to restore order. The strike continued until December 1914 when a bankrupt UMW had to admit defeat.

The killing of women and children at Ludlow shocked the nation (Gitelman 1988). Prominent progressives such as Upton Sinclair and John Reed used the events to demonize John D. Rockefeller, Jr. The Commission on Industrial Relations (CIR) investigated the situation and issued a 1,200-page report. Rockefeller hired the first corporate public relations firm to deflect the unflattering national attention resulting from his involvement in the strike and the CIR investigation. CF&I also planned and instituted a series of reforms in their southern Colorado mining operations. What practical impacts these reforms had on the lives of miners and their families is unclear, but the district remained a center of worker activism throughout the 1920s. Union recognition in southern Colorado only came with the New Deal reforms of the 1930s (McGovern and Guttridge 1972).

Archaeology of the 1913–1914 Colorado Coalfield War

The work on the 1913–1914 Colorado Coalfield War integrated archaeological evidence with archival evidence to investigate how mundane experience shaped the course of a strike of national significance. Similarities in the day-to-day lives of miners' families crosscut ethnic and cultural differences within the community, and these shared experiences provided the basis for class consciousness and collective action. Strikes do not just involve male miners; women and children were major actors in the 1913–1914 strike. Their participation sprang from lived experiences as well, and their struggles helped redefine those experiences. Data are being obtained to test these propositions through excavations of domestic/residential deposits dating from the period immediately before the strike, during the strike, and in the decade after the strike. The results will have implications for understanding this important event in U.S. history, the process of labor struggle in the United States, and for current theoretical debates in archaeology over the forces of cultural change.

Several major historical works on the strike have mined the rich archival record of documents and photos related to the Colorado Coalfield War (Beshoar 1957; McGovern and Guttridge 1972; Papanikolas 1982; also Montgomery 1987). These studies primarily focus on the events of the conflict, strike leaders, and the organizational work of the UMW. A direct product of these historical concerns is an emphasis on male miners and the effect of a common work experience on miners' solidarity—a consciousness that united ethnically and racially diverse miners. These narratives imply, and sometimes assert, that the miners shared work-related experiences but returned to ethnically different home lives after their day's work was over. In this sense, they adopt a very traditional understanding of the basis of labor action that privileges the agency of men and casts women in the role of obstacles to class solidarity. This approach equates class and class struggle with active men in the workplace, and ethnicity and tradition with passive women in the home.

This research, along with work by other scholars, remains skeptical of that view (Long 1985, 1991; Beaudry and Mrozowski 1988; McGaw 1989; Cameron 1993; Shackel 1994, 1996; Mrozowski et al. 1996). Ethnic identities certainly crosscut class in southern Colorado and may have hindered the formation of class consciousness, but the equation of class = workplace = male, and ethnicity = home = female is questionable. Class and ethnicity crosscut workplace and home, men and women. Working-class men shared a common experience in the mines, and working-class women shared a common experience in the homes, both of which resulted from their class position. Furthermore, ethnic differences divided them in both contexts.

Existing analyses show that ethnic divisions existed in the workplace. In southern Colorado, the miners worked as independent contractors and formed their own work gangs. These work gangs were routinely ethnically based (Beshoar 1957; McGovern and Guttridge 1972; Papanikolas 1982; Long 1991). Historical and industrial archaeologists have also demonstrated in many other cases that 19th- and early-20th-century workplaces were ethnically structured (Hardesty 1988; Wegars 1991; Bassett 1994). In the traditional hypothesis, it is the commonality of the work experience that overcomes these ethnic divisions in the workplace and in an ethnically based home life to create a class consciousness.

The existence of a common experience derived from conditions of life in the home that also aided in the formation of class consciousness is difficult to support on the basis of historical analyses of the 1913–1914 strike. Narratives of the events generally agree that the day-to-day lives of miners' families were difficult and characterized by material privation, but little more than anecdotal evidence of these conditions is available. Historian Priscilla Long (1985), in an analysis that supports the alternative hypothesis, demonstrates that women in the Colorado coalfields shared a common experience of sexual exploitation (both by company goons and their husbands), but the research also lacks detailed data on the realities of day-to-day lived experience in the home.

The alternative hypothesis stresses the importance of the home in the creation of class consciousness, seeking to prove, on the basis of archaeological evidence, that the day-to-day material conditions of home life crosscut ethnic divisions, before, during, and after the strike. If this is the case, it will be argued that women and children were active agents with male miners in formulating a social consciousness to unify for the strike. If, on the other hand, the analyses shows that each ethnic group had distinctive day-to-day material conditions of home life, then the traditional notion will be accepted that families followed the lead of male miners who acquired a common class identity in the shafts.

The discipline of historical archaeology represents an ideal approach for research into the relationship between social consciousness, lived experience, and material conditions to processes of social transformation (Orser 1996; Shackel 1996). In historic periods in the U.S., the archaeologist is typically able to integrate primary documentary data with material culture to capture both the consciousness and material

conditions that form lived experience (Beaudry 1988; Leone and Potter 1988; Little 1992; Leone 1995; DeCunzo and Herman 1996). In documents, people speak about their consciousness, their interests, and their struggles, but not all peoples speak in the documents with the same force or presence. More importantly, they rarely speak in detail about their day-to-day lives. People, however, create the archaeological record from the accumulation of the small actions that make up their lived experience. The archaeological record consists primarily of the remains of people's mundane lives, and all people leave some traces in this record.

Archaeological research provides one means to gain a richer, more detailed, and more systematic understanding of the everyday reality of Colorado mining families than is available from documents of the 1913–1914 strike. Miners and their families unknowingly left a record of that reality in the ground. Archaeologists can recapture it in the burned remains of their tents, in the layout of camps, in the contents of their latrines, and by shifting through the garbage that they left behind. Linked with documentary and photographic sources, this evidence provides a useful basis for reconstructing that experience. By applying these methods to company towns occupied before the strike, the strikers' tent colonies, and to the company camps reoccupied after the strike, these propositions can be tested.

Excavations at the Ludlow Tent Colony and the Town of Berwind

Two years of fieldwork at the site of the Ludlow tent colony and in the company town of Berwind have been completed. The massacre site itself represents a near "perfect" archaeological context—a short-term occupation destroyed by fire (Figure 3). Subsequent uses of the site have had little impact on the archaeological remains. In Berwind, the streets, foundations, latrines, and trash pits remain visible on the surface. While collectors have visited these sites over the years, the scope of the sites and the shear volume of material present in both locations have made the overall impact of these activities negligible. Preliminary work

FIGURE 3. Excavations at Ludlow in summer 1997.

demonstrates that features and deposits can be located that can be sorted by time (before, during, and after the strike) and by ethnicity.

At Ludlow, features associated with the strikers' tent colony were located and the distribution and types of artifacts at the site were defined. Over most of the site, cultural deposits are quite thin, with features appearing at depths of 10 to 20 cm. Tent platforms and privies were excavated. Surface distributions of artifacts correlate closely with the plan of the colony as shown in period photographs.

Photographs have proven a great aid in the excavations and a rich source of information. Several hundred photographs exist of the strike, including dozens of the Ludlow tent colony. Tents were constructed by first digging a shallow basin, then laying wooden joists directly on the ground to support a wooden platform and frame. After the wood and canvas tents were erected over the platform, the strikers surrounded the base of each tent with an embankment of soil. In 1998, a suspected tent platform was excavated then defined based on shallow depressions (probably drip lines) and rows of nails that may have been associated with timber from frames or joists. A rich assortment of small objects were found in association with the tent area, including fragments of miners' lamps, buttons, ceramics, bottle glass, and fragments of shoes. A collection of religious medals suggests that the occupants of the tent were Roman Catholic.

One of the most important photos of the Ludlow colony was taken from nearby a railroad water tower only a few days before the massacre (Figure 4). A technique pioneered by Prince (1988) and Deetz (1993) was used to identify the position of tents and other structures in the colony. The location of the water tower was identified, and a mechanical lift was positioned accordingly. Using a transparency made from the photo and placed over the ground glass of a camera, researchers could look through the camera's viewfinder and see the photo image of the colony superimposed over the present-day landscape. Using this technique, more than a quarter of the tents in the colony were located with reasonable certainty. The map generated through this technique will guide future work at Ludlow and will be refined through excavation.

Berwind was a CF&I town located in Berwind canyon near Ludlow, occupied before and after the strike (Wood 2000). Many of the strikers at Ludlow originated from there. CF&I built the town in 1892 and abandoned it in 1931. In 1998 a detailed map of the community was made through which numerous discrete residential neighborhoods were defined. Test excavations revealed stratified deposits of up to 50 cm deep in the yards associated with houses. Several contexts dating to before, during, and after the strike were distinguished. The preliminary examination of artifacts from the tests, photos of the community at different points in time, and company records indicates that entire residential sections of Berwind date to before the strike, while others (one informant referred to them as

FIGURE 4. The Ludlow tent colony before the massacre. (Courtesy of Denver Public Library, Western History Department.)

"guilt houses") were constructed as part of the program of town improvements that followed the strike (Wood 2000). Former residents of Berwind and other communities in the area were contacted and oral history interviews are being conducted. In the most recent season, trash deposits and latrines dating to before and after the strike are being excavated.

Linking Theory and Practice: Interpretive Directions

The focus on class and conflict led to digs at Ludlow and the coal towns of southern Colorado and a look at localized, day-to-day life in terms of consciousness and identity. Local struggles must be understood as being embedded in larger structures of conflict, however. The 1913–1914 Coalfield War captured national attention and involved issues and interests reaching far beyond southern Colorado.

The UMW, a national labor organization, worked to organize and support the striking miners in 1913–1914. Material support took the shape of tents, stoves, rations and other goods that, in part, constituted the material record of the Ludlow colony. The physical structure of the tent colony itself was, in part, a product of conflicting relations between workers and coal operators but also a product of complex interactions between colony residents and representatives of the UMW.

The company towns occupied by coal miners and their families before and after the 1913–1914 strike were designed and constructed by agents of mining companies, such as the Rockefeller-owned CF&I, linked to national and global economic systems. The shape of these towns reflected and reasserted the class interests of company owners and managers—interests that clashed with those of the miners and their families. Coal camps became both sources of conflict and actual sites of struggle and were reshaped through class conflict.

The tent colonies and company towns of southern Colorado can be considered as problems of struggle and consciousness structured by complex local-global relationships. Focusing on the material conditions of day-to-day existence and integrating issues of class, gender, and ethnicity will allow us to approach these communities as both expressions and sources of local and global struggles. Excavations and analyses are producing the data necessary to address these issues.

Concluding Thoughts

The story of western communities defined by work is a story of struggle, and this struggle took its shape from class, gender, ethnic, and race relations operating within an expanding, capitalist world economy. In extreme cases, such as the Ludlow Massacre, class conflict erupted into open violence, but, assuredly, such tensions operated in all communities defined by work. Such communities were, in fact, produced through class struggles within the United States and embedded in larger patterns of the capitalist world system. Situated in the internal periphery that was the American West, these struggles acquired a distinct, regional character but could never be separated or qualitatively distinguished from broader national and international processes. A world-systems approach to western U.S. history—one that is truly divorced from Turner's frontier concept—must grapple with class conflict as a central theme.

Archaeological studies of western communities present researchers with the opportunity to examine, in a fine-grained manner, the relationship between local interactions and conflicts and larger economic and social structures. Evidence of the material conditions of life in western households and communities provides a basis for understanding local manifestations of class formation and struggle, while at the same time linking these processes and events to developments within the capitalist world system. Material culture in the form of spatial organization at the levels of household and community, house wares, food remains, tools, toys, and weapons was implicated in and can, therefore, inform us about these relationships. From an archaeological point of view, the site of the Ludlow tent colony is by no means unique. Just as in other communities, class and class struggle operated as structuring factors of social life and material conditions.

ACKNOWLEDGMENTS

The authors wish to thank Thad Van Bueren and Mary Maniery for inviting us to participate in the session

"Communities Defined by Work: Life in Western Work Camps and Towns" at the 1999 SHA meetings in Salt Lake City. Additional thanks go to Thad for grappling with the task of bringing this volume to print—no small accomplishment. We must also thank our colleagues from the Colorado Coalfield War Archaeology Project. The Ludlow Collective includes Donna Bryant, Phil Duke, Jason Lapham, Patrick Morgan, Dean Saitta, Mark Walker, and Margaret Wood. The material in the preceding article is as much theirs as ours. Excavations at Ludlow and Berwind would not have been possible without the help of students who worked in the field schools held at these sites over the past two seasons. Special thanks go to our volunteers and repeat offenders: Kara Weaver, Maureen Hoof, Dan Broockmann, Marco Aiello, Caroline Braker, and Tracy Schaffer. Kim Manecek developed materials for public education.

Permission to excavate at the site of the Ludlow Massacre was granted by the United Mine Workers of America (UMWA). The UMWA Women's Auxiliary local 9856 maintains the Ludlow monument and hosts the annual memorial services. Yolanda Romero and Carol Blatnick-Barros deserve special recognition for their assistance and commitment to the project. Michael Romero, president of local 9856, has also aided us in many ways. The families of the United Steel Workers of America LU 2102 welcomed us and shared their current struggle with us. We have received great help and support from several individuals at the Colorado Historical Society, including Paula Manini, Margaret Van Ness, and Susan Collins. Trinidad State Junior College has provided us with housing, lab space, and other essentials. Larry Conyers of the University of Denver performed several ground-penetrating radar surveys at both Ludlow and Berwind.

Project planning was made possible by through a faculty development grant from the State University of New York at Binghamton in summer 1996. The Colorado Historical Society funded our work in 1997, 1998, and 1999.

REFERENCES

ARRIGHI, GIOVANNI, TERENCE K. HOPKINS, AND IMMANUEL WALLERSTEIN
    1989 *Antisystemic Movements*. Verso, London, England.

BARBER, D. F.
    1953 *The Longest Rope: The Truth About the Johnson County Cattle War*. The Caxton Printers, Caldwell, ID.

BASSETT, EVERETT
    1994 "We Took Care of Each Other Like Families Were Meant To." Gender, Social Organization, and Wage Labor Among the Apache at Roosevelt. In *Those of Little Note: Gender, Race, and Class in Historical Archaeology*, Elizabeth Scott, editor, pp. 55–79. University of Arizona Press, Tucson.

BEAUDRY, MARY (EDITOR)
    1988 *Documentary Archaeology in the New World*. Cambridge University Press, Cambridge, England.

BEAUDRY, MARY C., AND STEPHEN MROZOWSKI
    1988 The Archaeology of Work and Home Life in Lowell, Massachusetts: An Interdisciplinary Study of the Boott Cotton Mills Corporation. *Industrial Archeology* 19:1–22.

BESHOAR, BARRON B.
    1957 *Out of the Depths: The Story of John R. Lawson, A Labor Leader*. Colorado Historical Commission & Denver Trades & Labor Assembly, Denver, CO.

BRISSENDEN, PAUL F.
    1919 *The I.W.W.: A Study of American Syndicalism*. Russell & Russell, New York, NY.

BROCK, JAMES, AND STEVEN J. SCHWARTZ
    1991 A Little Slice of Heaven: Investigations at Rincon Cemetery, Prado Basin, California. *Historical Archaeology* 25(3):78–90.

CAMERON, ARDIS
    1993 *Radicals of the Worst Sort: Laboring Women in Lawrence Massachusetts 1860–1912*. University of Illinois Press, Urbana.

CORBIN, DAVID A.
    1981 *Life, Work and Rebellion in the Coal Fields: The Southern West Virginia Miners, 1880–1922*. University of Illinois Press, Urbana.

CRONON, W., G. MILES, AND J. GITLIN (EDITORS)
    1998 *Under an Open Sky: Rethinking America's Western Past*. W.W. Norton and Co., New York, NY.

CROWELL, ARON L.
    1997 *Archaeology and the Capitalist World System: A Study from Russian America*. Plenum Press, New York, NY.

CURTIN, D. J.
    1991 Structuring History: Perceptions of American Cowboy Culture. Master's thesis, Binghamton University (SUNY), Binghamton, NY.

DE CUNZO, LU ANN, AND BERNARD L. HERMAN (EDITORS)
    1996 *Historical Archaeology and the Study of American Culture*. Henry Francis du Pont Winterthur Museum, Winterthur, DE.

DEETZ, JAMES
    1993 *Flowerdew Hundred: The Archaeology of a Virginia Plantation, 1619–1864*. University of Virginia Press, Charlottesville.

DELÂGE, DENYS
    1993 *Bitter Feast: Amerindians and Europeans in Northeastern North America, 1600–1664*. UBC Press, Vancouver, British Columbia, Canada.

EWEN, CHARLES R.
1986   Fur Trade Archaeology: A Study of Frontier Hierarchies. *Historical Archaeology* 20(1):15–28.

FARNSWORTH, PAUL
1989   Native American Acculturation in the Spanish Colonial Empire: The Franciscan Missions of Alta California. In *Center and Periphery: Comparative Studies in Archaeology*, T. C. Champion, editor, pp. 186–206. Unwin Hyman, London, England.

FAULK, O.
1998   Western Frontier Life in America. In *1999 World Book Multimedia Encyclopedia*. IVID Communications, Inc., San Diego, CA.

GITELMAN, HOWARD
1988   *Legacy of the Ludlow Massacre: A Chapter in American Industrial Relations*. University of Pennsylvania Press, Philadelphia.

GUTMAN, HERBERT
1987   The Workers' Search for Power. In *Power and Culture: Essays on the American Working Class*, Ira Berlin, editor. Pantheon Books, New York, NY.

HARDESTY, DONALD L.
1988   *The Archaeology of Mines and Mining: The View from the Silver State*. Society for Historical Archaeology, Pleasant Hill, CA.
1991   Historical Archaeology in the American West. *Historical Archaeology* 25(3):3–6.
1998   Power and the Industrial Mining Community in the American West. In *Social Approaches to an Industrial Past: The Archaeology and Anthropology of Mining*, A. Bernard Knapp, Vincent C. Pigott, and Eugenia W. Herbert, editors, pp. 81–98. Routledge, London, England.

KENNY, KEVIN
1998   *Making Sense of the Molly Maguires*. Oxford University Press, New York, NY.

LEONE, MARK B.
1995   A Historical Archaeology of Capitalism. *American Anthropologists* 97:251–268.

LEONE, MARK B., AND PARKER B. POTTER, JR.
1988   Introduction: Issues in Historical Archaeology. In *The Recovery of Meaning: Historical Archaeology in the Eastern United States*, Mark P. Leone and Parker B. Potter, Jr., editors, pp. 1–26. Smithsonian Institution Press, Washington, DC.

LIMERICK, P. N.
1987   *The Legacy of Conquest: The Unbroken History of the American West*. W.W. Norton and Co., New York, NY.

LITTLE, BARBARA (EDITOR)
1992   *Text-Aided Archaeology*. CRC Press, Boca Raton, FL.

LONG, PRISCILLA
1985   The Women of the CF&I Strike, 1913–1914. In *Women, Work, and Protest: A Century of U.S. Women's Labor History*, R. Milkman, editor. Routledge & Kegan Paul, London, England.
1991   *Where the Sun Never Shines: A History of America's Bloody Coal Industry*. Paragon Books, New York, NY.

MALONE, M. P., AND R. ETULAIN
1989   *The American West*. University of Nebraska Press, Lincoln.

MARX, KARL
1906   *Capital: A Critique of Political Economy*. The Modern Library, New York, NY.

McGAW, J. A.
1989   No Passive Victims, No Separate Spheres: A Feminist Perspective on Technology's History. In *In Context: History and the History of Technology*, S. H. Cutcliffe and R. Post, editors, pp. 172–191. Lehigh University Press, Bethlehem, PA.

McGOVERN, GEORGE S., AND LEONARD F. GUTTRIDGE
1972   *The Great Coalfield War*. Houghton Mifflin Company, Boston, MA.

McGUIRE, RANDALL H.
1992   *A Marxist Archaeology*. Academic Press, Orlando, FL.
1995   The Mythic West. In *Invisible America: Unearthing Our Hidden History*, Mark Leone and Neil Asher Silberman, editors, pp.254–255. Henry Holt and Company, New York, NY.

MONTGOMERY, DAVID
1987   *The Fall of the House of Labor*. Cambridge University Press, Cambridge, MA.

MROZOWSKI, STEPHEN, GRACE H. ZIESING, AND MARY C. BEAUDRY.
1996   *Living on the Boott: Historical Archaeology at the Boott Mills Boardinghouses, Lowell, Massachusetts*. University of Massachusetts Press, Amherst.

NASH, G. D.
1991   *Creating the West: Historical Interpretations, 1890–1990*. University of New Mexico Press, Albuquerque.

O'BRIEN, MICHAEL J., AND TERESITA MAJEWSKI
1989   Wealth and Status in the Upper South Socioeconomic System of Northeastern Missouri. *Historical Archaeology* 23(2):60–95.

ORSER, CHARLES
1996   *A Historical Archaeology of the Modern World*. Plenum Press, New York, NY.

PAPANIKOLAS, ZEESE
1982   *Buried Unsung: Louis Tikas and the Ludlow Massacre*. University of Utah Press, Salt Lake City.

PHONER, PHILIP S. (EDITOR)
1981 *Fellow Workers and Friends: I.W.W. Free-Speech Fights as Told by Participants.* Greenwood Press, Westport, CT.

PRINCE, GENE
1988 Photography for Discovery and Scale by Superimposing Old Photographs on the Present-Day Scene. *Antiquity* 62:12–116.

PURSER, MARGARET
1991 Several Paradise Ladies Are Visiting in Town: Gender Strategies in the Early Industrial West. *Historical Archaeology* 25(4):6–16.
1999 *Ex Occidente Lux?*: An Archaeology of Later Capitalism in the Nineteenth-Century West. In *Historical Archaeologies of Capitalism*, Mark P. Leone and Parker B. Potter, Jr., editors, pp. 114–142. Kluwer Academic/Plenum Press, New York, NY.

ROSEBERRY, WILLIAM
1989 *Anthropologies and Histories: Essays in Culture, History, and Political Economy.* Rutgers University Press, New Brunswick, NJ.

SCHMITT, DAVE, AND CHARLES ZEIER
1993 Not by Bones Alone: Exploring Household Composition and Socioeconomic Status in an Isolated Historic Mining Community. *Historical Archaeology* 27(4):20–38.

SCHULZ, PETER D., AND SHERRI M. GUST
1983 Faunal Remains and Social Status in 19th-Century Sacramento. *Historical Archaeology* 17(1):44–53.

SCHUYLER, R. L.
1991 Historical Archaeology in the American West: The View from Philadelphia. *Historical Archaeology* 25(3):7–17.

SELIGMAN, EDWIN R.
1914 The Crisis in Colorado. *The Annalist*, 4 May.

SHACKEL, PAUL
1994 A Material Culture of Armory Workers. In *Domestic Responses to Nineteenth-Century Industrialization: An Archaeology of Park Building 48, Harper's Ferry National Historical Park,* Paul Shackel, editor, pp. 10.1–10.7. U.S. Department of the Interior, National Park Service, National Capital Region, Regional Archaeology Program, Washington, DC.
1996 *Culture Change and the New Technology: An Archaeology of the Early American Industrial Era.* Plenum Press, New York, NY.

SHERIDAN, THOMAS F.
1998 Silver Shackles and Copper Collars: Race, Class, and Labor in the Arizona Mining Industry from the Eighteenth Century until World War II. In *Social Approaches to an Industrial Past*, A. B. Knapp, V. C. Pigott, and E. W. Herbert, editors, pp.174–188. Routledge, London, England.

SMITH, DUANE A.
1992 *Rocky Mountain West: Colorado, Wyoming, and Montana, 1859–1915.* University of New Mexico Press, Albuquerque.

SMITH, H. N.
1950 *Virgin Land: The American West as Symbol and Myth.* Vintage Books, New York, NY.

SPUDE, CATHERINE H., DOUGLAS D. SCOTT, AND FRANK NORRIS
1993 Father Turnell's Trash Pit, Klondike Gold Rush National Historical Park, Alaska. *Archaeological Investigations in Skagway, Alaska,* Volume 4. U.S. Department of the Interior, National Park Service, Denver Service Center.

STASKI, EDWARD, AND JOANNE REITER
1996 Status and Adobe Quality at Fort Fillmore, New Mexico: Old Questions, New Techniques. *Historical Archaeology* 30(3):1–19.

THOMAS, MARY
1971 *Those Damn Foreigners.* Minerva Books, Hollywood, CA.

TOULOUSE, JULIAN H.
1970 High on the Hawg, or, How the Western Miner Lived, As Told by the Bottles He Left Behind. *Historical Archaeology* 4:59–69.

WALKER, MARK
1999 Archaeology, Audiences and the Memory of Miners. Paper presented at the 1999 Meetings of the Society for Historical Archaeology, Salt Lake City, UT.

WALLERSTEIN, IMMANUEL
1974 *The Modern World System I: Capitalist Agriculture and the Origins of the European World-Economy in the Sixteenth Century.* Academic Press, New York, NY.
1991 *Unthinking Social Science: The Limits of Nineteenth-Century Paradigms.* Polity Press, Cambridge, England.

WEGARS, PRISCILLA
1991 Who's Been Workin' on the Railroad: An Examination of the Construction, Distribution, and Ethnic Origins of Domed Rock Ovens on Railroad-related Sites. *Historical Archaeology* 25:37–65.

WHITESIDE, JAMES
1990 *Regulating Danger: The Struggle for Mine Safety in the Rocky Mountain Coal Industry.* University of Nebraska Press, Lincoln.

WOOD, MARGARET
2000 Labor of Love: Women's Domestic Labor and the Struggle for Transformative Social Change. Paper presented at the 17th Annual Visiting Scholar Conference: The Dynamics of Power, Southern Illinois University, Carbondale.

WURST, LOUANN
   1999   Internalizing Class in Historical Archaeology.
          Historical Archaeology 33(1):7–21.

WYLIE, ALISON
   1993   Invented Lands/Discovered Pasts: The Westward
          Expansion of Myth and History. *Historical
          Archaeology* 27(4):1–19.

RANDALL H. MCGUIRE
DEPARTMENT OF ANTHROPOLOGY
BINGHAMTON UNIVERSITY (SUNY)
PO BOX 6000
BINGHAMTON, NY 13902-6000

PAUL RECKNER
DEPARTMENT OF ANTHROPOLOGY
BINGHAMTON UNIVERSITY (SUNY)
PO BOX 6000
BINGHAMTON, NY 13902-6000

Michael Given

Mining Landscapes and Colonial Rule in Early-Twentieth-Century Cyprus

ABSTRACT

In the early 20th century the large-scale copper and asbestos mines of Cyprus were intimately associated with colonial rule, both in their ideologies and in their actual operations. For the Cypriot miners, this represented a major disruption of long-standing values and required a new negotiation of their relationship with their British colonizers. Attempts to control mining landscapes and communities interplayed with a range of actions from submission to everyday resistance to strikes and riots. These dynamics are most clearly seen by examining the entire landscape. Particularly revealing aspects include the naming of mining landscapes, the surveillance of miners, the complex relationship between mining and agriculture, the actual and symbolic manipulation of artifacts, the expression of control and resistance in miners' housing, and shifting concepts of community.

Introduction

On 26 April 1929, a motor lorry driver for the Cyprus Asbestos Company stopped in the village of Kato Amiandos, on his way up to the mine. A woman gave him a bundle of cloth and requested him to take it to her husband, Stylli Hadji Ktori, who worked in the mine. He agreed and continued on his way up the mountain road. At the entrance to the territory controlled by the mining company, he was stopped by a mine official, distinguished by the cloth badge on his arm:

> He asked me if I had bread in my car. I said "no." He said that he would search my car. I said that he could search and when he searched he seized the bundle which was given to me by the wife of Stylli Hji Ktori saying that it contained 3 loaves of bread (Cyprus State Archives SA 1/909/1929, Red 14).

As Stylli Hadji Ktori knew very well, the Cyprus Asbestos Company refused to allow its employees to bring their own bread into the mine. Instead they had to buy the expensive bread made on the premises using flour imported from abroad. As this story shows, the Amiandos asbestos mine (Figure 1) and the other mines of early-20th-century Cyprus formed autonomous territories with their own border points, regulations, and economies. When the British colonial government heard about the bread incident, they were concerned that the mine was becoming an "*imperium in imperio*," and began a series of investigations (SA1/909/1929, Red 4).

"An empire within an empire" is precisely what the mines were. With their carefully regulated and orchestrated activities where each mine worker had a precisely defined role, with their paternalistic institutions such as benevolent societies and model workers' housing and clubhouses, and with their absolute control over a landscape dedicated to their own profit, the mining companies were modeled on colonial rule. They even became "models for" colonial rule, expressing the ideal of a perfectly regulated but paternalistic state. As with major state building projects, where the antlike activity of thousands of workers symbolizes the state's control of society (Paynter and McGuire 1991:9), so here does the mining landscape with its highly controlled processes and social organization reflect the ideal of colonial rule.

The investigation focused on the intimate relationship between the organization of mining landscapes and the mechanics of colonial rule. The open cast and underground copper and asbestos mines of the 1920s and 1930s in Cyprus provide a wealth of material, documentary, and oral information, and the political conditions of the time brought the imperialist organization of the mines into public debate—as Hadji Ktori succeeded in doing following the confiscation of his bread.

Methodology

The main historical sources in this paper consist of government correspondence preserved in the Cyprus State Archives in Nicosia and oral history data from informants in the former mining village of Mitsero and elsewhere.

FIGURE 1. Pano Amiandos Mine from the northeast.

Archaeological data come from the examination of mines and mining structures in Amiandos and Mitsero and from the Sydney Cyprus Survey Project, a multiperiod interdisciplinary archaeological survey project working in the copper ore zone in the Northern Troodos Mountains (Given and Knapp 2003).

The approach to this material is mostly based on historical archaeology and landscape archaeology. Historical archaeology, as practiced in North America and Australia, is a very recent discipline in the Mediterranean context. It undertakes both detailed examination of historical data and a fully contextual analysis of material culture. The history of mining in Cyprus has been discussed from perspectives that are technical (Bear 1963), descriptive (Lavender 1962), or political (Georghallides 1985:327–328). Historical archaeology adds a perspective that does not rely on the rhetoric of government reports or political pamphlets, or on the impersonal statistics of colonial bureaucracies. In particular, the examination of the role of artifacts, structures, and landscapes in social relations throws light on modes of domination and resistance not otherwise apparent (Paynter and McGuire 1991:13–19).

Landscape archaeology examines the organization of human activities in their full landscape context, rather than looking at particular activities or sites in isolation. An important refinement on this perspective is that different social groups have different perceptions of the landscape and different systems of organization within it. Particularly relevant for a study of 20th-century mining is the investigation not only of social and economic landscapes, such as settlement patterns and trade routes, but also of conceptual and ideational landscapes. This last includes communal or political associations that different groups may have with a landscape. With the mining landscapes of early-20th-century Cyprus, as has been recognized for prehistoric landscapes, it is impossible to separate the two categories (Knapp and Ashmore 1999:15). The social, economic, and ideational associations of the mining landscapes of early-20th-century Cyprus became so intense that they often verged on the ideological, carrying a much more explicit and unified set of associations (Knapp and Ashmore 1999:13).

Perspectives from Historical Archaeology:

Rather than describing and analyzing each mining operation one by one, the actual operation of control and resistance in a mining landscape is highlighted by discussing a series of mechanisms (here italicized). A mining landscape needed to be defined and *named* before it could operate as an entity. Once officially in existence, it had to be organized to allow proper *surveillance*. Because of the long rural tradition of Cyprus and the need to feed so many workers, there was a complex relationship with *agriculture*. Both domination and, more subtly, resistance were often expressed in the actual and symbolic manipulation of *artifacts*. The ideological imposition of control and order—and resistance to it—was often carried out by means of *architecture*. On a broader scale, this was done by means of shaping and manipulating the whole *community*.

Historical Background

Following the Congress of Berlin in 1878 the British took over the administration of Cyprus from the Ottoman Empire. Outright possession was not confirmed until 1914, when Britain formally annexed the island, and 1925, when it was declared a Crown Colony. Until 1927 this anomalous position included the payment of a heavy "tribute" to the Ottoman Empire raised from local taxes, which left very little to invest in the development of the island (Georghallides 1985:41–52). The economy of Cyprus during this period was very much based on agriculture. At the beginning of British rule six out of seven Cypriots were village dwellers, almost all of them smallholders relying on small-scale agriculture to feed their families, pay taxes (much of which went to the Ottoman "tribute"), and escape the twin evils of drought and debt (Katsiaounis 1996:99–109).

Because of historical records, the existence of copper ore was known from the beginning of British rule, and there were various half-hearted attempts at exploitation during the 1880s, particularly in the northwest of the island (Wood 1887:52; Lavender 1962:50). In 1912 the prospector Godfrey Gunther arrived on the island. Within a year he had bought land at the ancient copper mines of Skouriotissa (Figure 2) and was drilling systematically. The Cyprus Mines Corporation was launched in New York in 1916. After a series of financial difficulties, Gunther committed himself in 1920

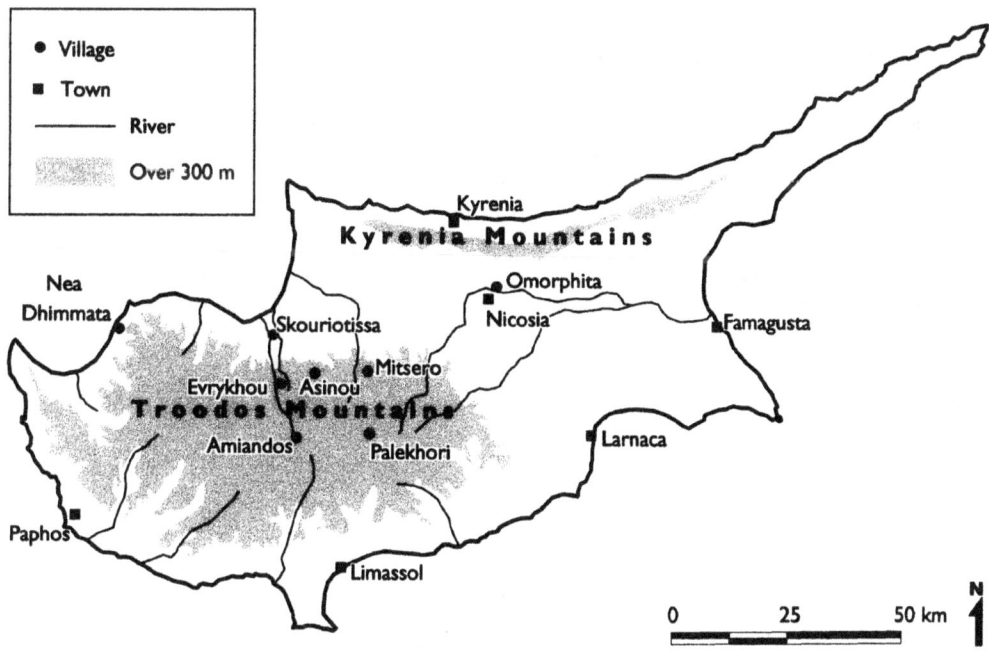

FIGURE 2. Map of Cyprus, with places mentioned in the text.

to producing 10,000 tons of pyrites in the first year of production (Lavender 1962:104,118). Other copper mines took longer to develop. At Mitsero and Agrokipia, for example, prospecting in 1936 was followed by the extraction of gold and silver, and after the foundation of the Hellenic Mining Company in 1948, large-scale pyrites extraction only took place in the 1950s (Bear 1963:30,67,70).

The development of asbestos mining began a little earlier than that of copper but followed essentially the same path. In 1904 a Limassol dentist-cum-entrepreneur named Cesar Trombetta extracted a sample from the deposits above the village of Amiandos, which itself means "asbestos" (SA1/3025/1904). In 1907 the government granted various concessions. In 1908 the Cyprus Mining Company founded an asbestos extraction, crushing, and cleaning establishment at Amiandos (SA1/1766/1907). Production and employment increased at a considerable rate, especially after World War I. In 1922 the company was bought up by the Cyprus Asbestos Company Ltd. By 1927 it owned eight separate crushing mills and 25 miles of light railway, with an aerial cable that took 2 hours 50 minutes to transfer the asbestos to the port at Limassol. The projected annual production for that year was 12,000 tons. In the winter 1,200 workers were employed and 6,000 in summer (SA1/1195/1927, Red 192).

The rise of the copper and asbestos mining industries in the 1910s, with their labor-intensive methods such as crushing ore by hand, coincided with the pressing need of poor or landless peasants to find alternative means of employment. Workforces increased dramatically during the 1920s, peaking in 1929, just before the industry was hit by the depression. This was also a period that saw a considerable increase in British attempts to control the population of Cyprus, using education and ideology as much as political or military means (Given 1997: 69–72; 1998:12–15). The mining landscapes of this critical period were just one component of the new ideological struggle for control over the Cypriot landscape and population.

Naming

By the 1920s Cypriot villages had a long historical tradition behind them. Even though some had been abandoned, particularly in the 17th century, the sites and names of the surviving ones generally went back at least to the 16th century and often before, as can be seen from historical village lists (Grivaud 1998: 445–472) and from the results of archaeological survey (Given and Gregory 2003:292–293). The needs of Ottoman and British administration divided up the entire landscape into districts, subdistricts, and village territories: every part of the landscape was defined and named.

The onset of large-scale mining in the 1910s and 1920s saw a new type of exploitation of the landscape with new divisions and settlements that did not coincide with the old village territories. As with the European colonies of 19th-century Africa, new entities were carved out with boundaries that had no respect for local organization or segmentation. A mining landscape, then, was a colonial creation with its boundaries, name, and identity imposed by the colonizers of the land. In this respect it was a model *of* the colony, as it followed the same system, and also a model *for* the colony because it illustrated the principle clearly in a limited and manageable area.

As Gunther's copper mining landscape developed, with its hut settlements, overseers' houses, workshops, mines, and railway, the colonial government realized that in administrative terms it was an anomaly. In particular, the area of the mining operations fell within the territories of three different villages and a monastery. In 1929, therefore, a characteristically drawn-out process was begun to provide this landscape with a named identity and an official existence. The Commissioner of Nicosia, Charles Hart-Davis, drew attention to policing problems and stressed that it was important to police the entire landscape, not just the settlement:

> The proposal to create a village here was intended primarily to meet police requirements. Disturbances, accidents, & incidents involving police action generally are far more likely to arise in the mines themselves and especially in the workshops than in the hutments. [Another reason was] to have one village authority, Moslem & Christian, responsible for the entire area so that there may be no uncertainty in what authority's area any disturbance, accident or other incident actually occurred (SA1/844/1929, Minute 35).

A further problem was the lack of a name, as Hart-Davis commented: "I am unable to suggest any name by which the area referred to ... was commonly known. I don't think it had any common name" (SA1/844/1929, Minute 35). The first suggestion was to call it Gunther's Village, on the grounds that it was "a name in common use among the villagers, perpetuating the memory of the discoverer of the mine and the founder of the village" (SA1/844/1929, Red 5). When the government realized that it had to provide a name for the whole of the mining landscape, rather than just the settlement as had originally been suggested, they chose Skouriotissa, the name of the local disused monastery that had become the headquarters of the mining operation.

A map was produced with a red line defining the new territory, land was taken from the surrounding villages to give to the new entity, and on 24 February 1931, a proclamation declared Skouriotissa a full village, with three village authorities (SA1/844/1929, Red 16). The mining landscape had been named, defined, and inscribed into the ledgers of imperial control.

Surveillance

One way of interpreting a landscape as experienced by people is as a complex web of lines of sight. When there are relationships between the people in that landscape, especially relationships of unequal power or status, these lines of sight become a medium for the playing out of those relationships. Surveillance is the key to control. Attention is particularly focused at important entrances into the mining landscape, such as the checkpoint where Stylli Hadji Ktori's bread was confiscated. The cloth badge to distinguish the mines official and the systematic searching of private possessions emphasize to all employees that they are very much under surveillance. Watchtowers, peepholes, and security cameras—the means of surveillance—can be as intimidating as the highest of walls.

Surveillance can also be carried out by means of the positioning of structures and activity areas across the landscape. In the coffee plantations of early-19th-century Jamaica, for example, the overseers' houses were carefully located to have views over the slave village and the coffee drying areas. The houses were equipped with verandas and balconies to maximize the field of view (Delle 1999:151–153). A

more extreme example can be seen in Michel Foucault's famous analysis of Bentham's *panoptikon*, where each inmate of an institution is isolated in a cell but overlooked by a watchtower in the center of the ring-shaped building (Foucault 1977:200–204).

This system, albeit not so elaborate, was certainly favored by the colonial government of Cyprus. In the 1910s and 1920s, the government built a series of village police stations according to a standard plan. This plan showed a building that was unusually high in proportion to its ground plan, with an upper story and a prominent balcony. Characteristically these police stations were situated a little outside the village, controlling the main approaches and with a view from their balconies over the surrounding countryside and communications routes. In 1912, for example, the police chief decided that the police station at Evrykhou, 6 kilometers south of Skouriotissa, should be moved to the hillside outside the village, so it would command the main road coming from Nicosia (SA1/1756/1910).

The organization of mining landscapes in 20th-century Cyprus shows this emphasis on surveillance, mostly expressed through the medium of policing. At Amiandos it was decided in 1916 to build a large police station, positioned beside the road coming into the mining concession from Nicosia (SA1/955/1916). During the government's inquiry into the bread confiscation case, it turned out that the company had been privately paying a bonus to policemen based at the mines since 1908, in return for support of their regime, without any authority from the colonial government (SA1/909/1929, Red 22).

The Mitsero-Agrokipia mining landscape of the 1950s, controlled by the Hellenic Mining Company, combines this emphasis on surveillance with a more subtle expression of class and status. The concession was divided across the middle by a high ridge, which formed a natural border between the two villages of Mitsero and Agrokipia (Figure 3). The company, however, had two mines on the Mitsero side and one on the Agrokipia side, regarding the whole area as one unit. To symbolize the new and, to the villagers, artificial unity and to demonstrate their surveillance of each side, the company built its overseers' and foremen's housing on top of the ridge, exactly straddling the boundary between

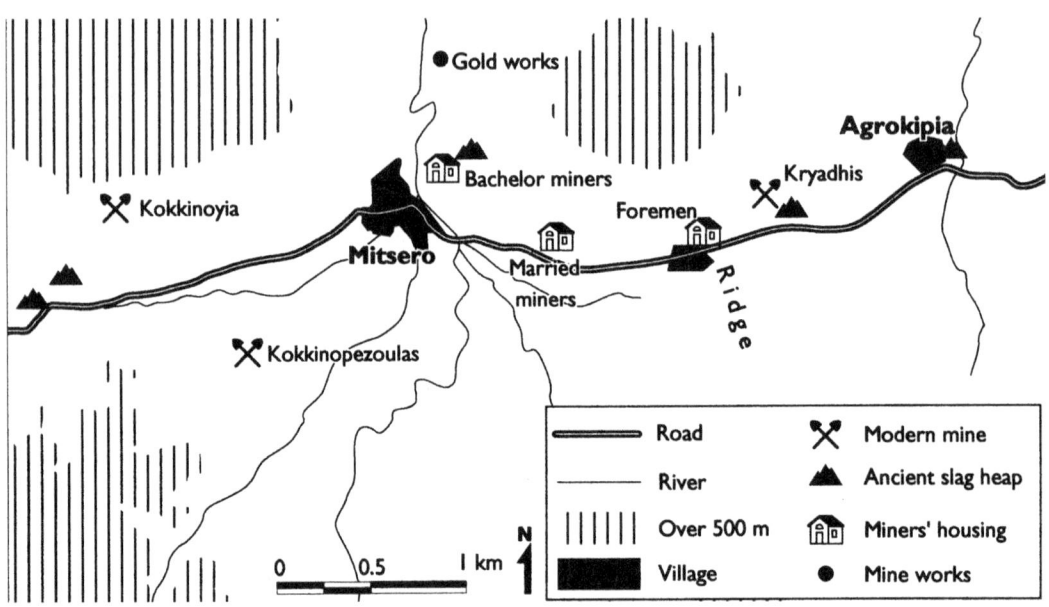

FIGURE 3. Map of the Mitsero-Agrokipia area.

the two village territories. Below them was a block of two-room housing for married miners, and at the bottom of the valley was Mitsero village itself with a large house with space for bachelor miners (Seretis and Diacopoulos 2003: 115–116).

A similar layout, with overseers' and staff houses topographically and symbolically above those of the workers, can be seen at Amiandos and Skouriotissa (Lavender 1962:229). These examples, however, hardly constitute a *panoptikon*. Even if the overseers had cared to venture out of their houses and look, they were too far to see precisely what individuals in the settlements were doing. The location of their houses was more to be seen than to see. They demonstrated visually that workers were part of a controlled and hierarchical mining landscape, rather than being members of different agricultural and kin-based village communities.

Agriculture

Full-time miners require others to produce a considerable agricultural surplus to maintain them. A system of "agricultural support settlements," for example, has been suggested for the copper miners and smelters of Late Bronze

Age Cyprus, based on archaeological survey (Knapp 1997:59). As William Douglass points out, however, there are many more possibilities than a simple increase in local agricultural production (Douglass 1998:105). In early-20th-century Cyprus, two specific factors complicate this relationship: the large number of poor agriculturalists requiring supplementary employment and the workings of colonial rule.

Because of successive droughts, insufficient investment in agriculture by the colonial government, and chronic rural indebtedness, there was a considerable body of poor or landless peasants who required some sort of extra employment for cash (Georghallides 1985:432; Katsiaounis 1996:34–35). The seasonal nature of most of the mining work, especially at the asbestos mine at Amiandos, was ideal. In 1927, for example, 6,000 workers were employed during the summer, of whom 4,800 were laid off for the winter (SA1/1195/1927). Even capital-intensive mining such as this can use seasonal and informal labor (Knapp 1998:4).

This balance between agricultural work and mining work is frequently commented on by elderly Cypriot villagers who once worked as miners—and farmers. In the village of Mitsero, Konstantinos Ttaouxis (interviewed 16

June 1998) described a typical summer day and night's work in the 1950s: he would walk in the evening with his donkey to his most distant fields 7 kilometers away, sleep a little, harvest all night on his own, then walk back to the pyrites washing plant, where he would leave his donkey and spend all day breaking up pyrites by hand with a hammer, return home in the afternoon, and in the evening walk back out to his fields. Other similar stories tell of men who married into the village and so owned no land and had to work at the mines. In the remote village of Asinou (now abandoned) the entire male population spent the summer at the asbestos mines of Amiandos, leaving the women and children to see to the crops and the goats.

Such stories and memories emphasize the part-time attitude towards mining, something never felt towards agriculture. Even while on the job, any spare time could be used for some useful task, even if there was no time to return to the fields. In the 1920s and 1930s, women were commonly employed at crushing ore, using hammers and flat stones as anvils, and on sieving, screening, and loading cars; "those not immediately engaged sat on the ground in sociable groups, feeding their babies and working on their beautiful Cypriot lace" (Lavender 1962:138,173).

In spite of such part-time arrangements, a workforce of 10,000 asbestos miners could not be expected to feed itself; a major system of food procurement was required. Rather than stimulating local production, however, which was desperately needed by many of the poorer mountain villages, the mining companies chose to import their food and sell it to their captive workforce. The Cyprus Asbestos Company set up a new company, Cyprus Hygienic Bakeries Limited, which was supposedly independent but in fact a subsidiary company, and forced its workers to buy their bread from it—hence the confiscation of the bread sent up to Hadji Ktori by his wife. Following Hadji Ktori's complaints, the government inquiry received the following justification from the bakery manager for his monopoly and high prices:

> We use for our bread the first quantity [sic] Australian and American flour, the English yeast, which we receive every fortnight from England. ... Presently it is impossible to reduce the price of our bread. According to the sliding Scale of Prices, the price of a 2-lbs. loaf in England is 4-1/2 d. [pence] or 135 Cyprus paras, but the cost of materials is higher here than in England: we pay £1.0.0 custom duty on each ton of flour and nearly double price for the fuel oil (SA1/909/1929, Red 6).

Adding to this a 9% markup on each loaf, the bakery made a handsome profit out of their workers (unless production was so low as to be uneconomical, which the manager claimed was often the case). It also supported farmers and wholesalers in Britain, America, and Australia—but not the poverty-stricken villagers just outside the mining concession.

Artifacts

Artifacts carry many more associations than the dates and functions generally attributed to them by archaeologists. In a colonial situation, thanks to historical archaeology, artifacts can convey important information about modes of domination and, more particularly, modes of resistance, including both implicit everyday resistance and open defiance (Paynter and McGuire 1991:12–13). This is often evident in conflicting traditions of foodways, which are archaeologically visible by means of the pottery used. Plantation slaves in 18th-century South Carolina, for example, used undifferentiated plain wares that emphasized local production and communal organization, in implicit opposition to the hierarchical and individualist ceramic styles used by their Euroamerican oppressors (Ferguson 1991:32).

One set of artifacts from the 20th-century asbestos mine of Amiandos clearly shows a similar conflict. Loaves of bread may not usually be archaeologically visible, but they are certainly artifacts and can take on considerable symbolic value. This particularly applied to the Greek Orthodox miners who were very much in the majority at the Amiandos mines. Each Sunday, loaves of village bread—the "bread of life"—were stamped with a cross and the letters "IΣ-NK" (Jesus Christ is victorious), and at the end of the Eucharist they were blessed and pieces were handed out to the congregation as they left.

This is why the Battle of the Bread at Amiandos became so significant. It was about more than economics or a personal preference for the taste of one's own village bread. The continual smuggling of a few loaves of bread for personal use or distribution to friends was a part of the ongoing resistance to the uniform and alien culture imposed by the foreign company and its servants. It was not uncommon for 45 loaves to be confiscated from a single lorry (SA1/909/1929, Red 12). Ending the bread monopoly became one of the rallying cries of strikers, along with shorter hours and more pay (SA1/1065/1929, Red 11), and was eventually discussed in the island's Legislative Council, though to no effect (Georghallides 1985:327–328).

Police reports reveal another form of ongoing resistance based on artifacts. At the Amiandos mines there was continual pilfering of sacks, rafters, and tools, so much so that whenever a worker was issued a sack, he was given a permit so he could prove it was not stolen (SA1/909/1929, Red 11). More important was the theft of wood, as F. Kukulas, the manager of the mine, told the government inquiry:

> During the course of a year we also expirernced [sic] hundreds of conversions of Company's property most of which are cases of destroying quarry equipment for the purpose of using the wood for burning and for making furniture (SA1/909/1929, Red 20).

In isolation, this seems like petty theft, caused by impoverished villagers making use of whatever resources were available. When viewed in the light of the forestry policy of the colonial government, it becomes more significant in ideological terms. Right from the beginning of colonial rule, the government had imposed restrictions on the collection of fuel and timber from the forests. During the 1920s the government progressively banned goatherds based in mountain villages from pasturing their goats in the forests, as it inhibited regeneration of the pine trees. This caused intense resentment from villagers, whose livelihood depended on pastoralism, producing a series of arson attacks on the forests (Georghallides 1985:449). Stealing wood from the mines provided the necessary fuel for cooking and heating and the material for making furniture, while simultaneously constituting another part of the ongoing resistance to the colonial regime. Similarly, stories are still told in Mitsero of smart operators who managed to outwit the authorities and extract gold from old

workings. The point of the stories is as much the outwitting as the financial profit.

On 25 July 1929 the Battle of the Bread came to a peak, with a major riot and a strike at the Amiandos mine. The police accounts stress a series of recurrent material indicators of the protest and the intimidation of other workers: wagons were upturned, sticks were brandished, stones were thrown, tools were taken away (SA1/1065/1929, Red 11). These were clearly intended as very visible indicators, as the agitators worked their way round the mine, demanding to be allowed to bring in their own bread. There was another material object in action on that day, which became a symbol of the riot to the colonial authorities. It so happened that Reginald Nicholson, the officer administering the government (i.e., the acting governor), was visiting Amiandos and arrived in the middle of the riot:

> The car came under fire & I stood up & signalled to the man on the terrace to stop. As I did so a stone *weighing half a pound came straight at my head from the terrace. I had no time to dodge & had to catch it, & got a cut & a nasty blow on the left hand. *weighed in Nicosia, & enclosed. RN (SA1/1065/1929, Red 8).

The miscreant stone, symbol of insurrection, was duly wrapped up and sent to the chief of police, along with Nicholson's account of what happened. This battle was fought with stones, loaves of bread, and conflicting perceptions of how the mining landscape should be organized.

Architecture

From the medieval period to the 1930s, Cypriot village houses had a very recognizable and familiar structure and layout. They were generally built in stone below and mud brick above, with a flat roof; all materials were local. An enclosed courtyard was entered from the street, and a variety of rooms round it were used for living, storage, and keeping animals (Ionas 1988:43–45). Each house formed a household for one nuclear family, according to the social structure of rural Cyprus and the system whereby parents gave a house as dowry for their daughter (Ionas 1988:11).

The mining companies needed to accommodate large numbers of men and women who were often separated from their families and only present for temporary periods of various lengths. They clearly required a very different solution. Initially these tended to be somewhat ad hoc. In the 1910s the workers' village at what was to be named Skouriotissa consisted of seven mud brick houses, plus a *khan* run by a man "said by local gossip to be a professional murderer" (Lavender 1962:100). A *khan* or *caravanserai* at this period in Cyprus was usually a large hollow square, lined with rooms facing inwards for travelers, merchants, and their animals. It was very much a symbol of impermanence. In 1922 Gunther built two barracks of mud brick tempered with seaweed, one for men and one for women. Additional space was provided by converting a large cave and an old sulphur and devil's mud store (Lavender 1962:168). All of this was not just a symbol of impermanence but was a negation of the strong kin-based values of rural Cypriot society.

The asbestos mines at Amiandos faced similar problems. One scheme of the early 1920s shows the beginnings of the paternalistic colonial desire to create a model settlement, based on their own perceptions of order and sanitation, rather than making it appropriate to the local social structure. The Pano Amiandos mineworkers' housing consists of separate blocks of housing, each block containing six two-room units with their own internal fireplace (Figure 4). They were stone built, with roofs of asbestos sheeting (appropriately enough for workers' housing at an asbestos mine). A small inner courtyard (10 x 6.5 m) contained two latrines, a large central fountain, and an open drain. To the eyes of the British architect who designed it and the mining companies who approved it, this was model housing: clean, visibly well organized, and cheap. To a Cypriot family, however, it provided no private courtyard, and no place to keep animals or engage in the small-scale agricultural activities that defined rural life.

Another attempt in the early 1950s to design modular family housing was a failure before it had even finished. The married workers' housing at Mitsero, halfway between the overseers' houses on the ridgeline and the village in the

FIGURE 4. Worker's housing block at Pano Amiandos.

valley (Figure 3), was designed along the lines of a *khan*, with four wings of two-room units forming a 65-m square. Once again, there was no organic structure appropriate to a kin-based society and none of the private courtyard space that an agricultural or rural outlook requires. With improvements in roads and motor transport in the 1950s, it was decided to abandon the structure when only its foundations had been laid (though one wing was later completed). Daily or weekly commuting by lorry meant that the characteristically part-time miners could still live in their own villages and cultivate their fields and vines as well as work in the mines. This rejection of planned housing is another aspect of the everyday resistance against the uniformity imposed by the mining company.

Community

A mining community is usually regarded as a temporary community—or not as a community at all. This especially applies to the "gold rush" type of mining camps in North America and Australia, which "flared and faded" as individuals shifted from one promising spot to another (Knapp 1998:5). Even this impermanence can allow some sense of community, when miners' shared aims and vocation bring them together in any number of different locations—not to mention friends and family coming out to join the pioneers (Douglass 1998:102,106). Excavation of 19th-century miners' housing at Dolly's Creek, west of Melbourne, shows that the material culture expresses this tension between the temporary and the permanent, the individual and the community. Tents were temporary and widely separated, but their arrangement in the landscape suggests a focused mining community, and the pipe-clayed fireplaces and a few finer possessions gave a sense of pride and belonging (Cheney 1992:39–40; cf. Behrens, this volume).

In the Cypriot context there was a major conflict between traditional perceptions of community and the regulations and organization imposed by the mining companies and the colonial government. The sense of community in a traditional rural village depended on more than the local materials, nuclear households, and agglomerated layout of its houses. Villages usually clustered round a central church

or mosque, with other institutions such as coffee houses, fountains, and annual fairs also playing an important role in community life (Ionas 1988:20–39; Given 2000:214–217). An agricultural lifestyle brought communal facilities such as olive presses and water mills as well as a seasonal cycle of labor shared by everyone in the community and a host of metaphors for the workings of everyday life. Conservatism in the architectural styles and icon painting of churches suggests a strong sense of continuity from the Byzantine and Medieval periods, which also appears in folk tales and songs.

The caves, barracks, and converted sulphur stores provided by Gunther at Skouriotissa could hardly be further from this ideal. In the mid 1920s he tried to improve conditions by providing communal facilities: a company hospital; communal bathhouses, with soap and wood for fuel available at cost price; and communal toilets and laundries (Lavender 1962:189). Yet such attempts, which were echoed at Amiandos, failed to address the actual workings of communal life in the rural villages of Cyprus. This failure was demonstrated graphically during the 1929 strike at Amiandos, which was led by miners from the mountain village of Palekhori. So important was this unit of identity that after the riot had been quelled, a rumor went round that the chief foreman would "dismiss all the Palechori people from the work because they were the cause of the trouble in the morning" (SA1/1065/1929, Red 11). Miners from a specific village retained that identity, despite all the company's attempts to foster a new sense of community.

The attempts of the mining companies to create new artificial communities foreshadowed the advent of town planning and model housing after the World War II, which saw a proliferation of such schemes in Cyprus. The colonial Public Works Department drew up designs for a "Subsidized Workers' Housing Scheme" at Omorphita in 1946, referred to disparagingly by its inhabitants as "The Standard" (Schaar et al. 1995:88–90). In the same year the Forestry Department decided to move the villagers of Dhimmata, who lived in houses of "the usual squalid type," to a new "model rural settlement," in order to make them an "example of social uplift in village life"—and incidentally to keep their goats out of the forest (SA1/970/1944/1,

Reds 39,32,44). Whether it was the Public Works Department, the Forestry Department, or a mining company attempting to impose artificial systems of social organization, Cypriot villagers firmly resisted, and continued to evolve their own sense of community.

Conclusions

Ktori was no innocent victim of the Cyprus Asbestos Company's injustice and tyranny. He had worked for two years collecting fees from traders in the company's market place, until it was discovered that he was creaming off some of the payments for himself (SA1/909/1929, Red 20). Even with the bread incident, he knew exactly what he was doing. Three weeks later, he tried to increase the stakes:

> On 14.5.29 I took 100 okes of bread to Amianto and sold to the laborers. I took purposely to see if any bread would be seized but nobody appeared, to remark to me. But Pte 4050 Hari [a policeman] was putting down the names of the laborers who were purchasing bread from me and I heard that all of the were taken before Mr. Kukulas who warned them if they buy again they would be sent away (SA1/909/1929, Red 13).

For all his determination, and in spite of the exhaustive government enquiry, no action was taken. The colonial secretary decided that "Government intervention would only be justified if evidence of harsh or unconscionable treatment were forthcoming," and the officer administering the government—the same one who had fielded the miner's stone—simply said, "I agree," and the matter was dropped (SA1/909/1929, Minutes 7,8).

The story of the confiscation of Ktori's bread, the ensuing strike, and his determined publicizing of the issue constitute much more than one single, aberrant episode. Because of the particular circumstances, including the persistence of one individual, it was investigated and recorded by the colonial government, and so is accessible to historians in the Cyprus State Archives. It was, however, just one critical point in the ongoing conflict between two differing interpretations of a mining landscape.

This conflict was played out using a variety of different weapons, both actual and symbolic. Surveillance, for example, could be countered by smuggling bread or pilfering firewood.

Often it was more a matter of maintaining an accustomed lifestyle, in the face of pressure to change. Throughout the whole period of large-scale mining in colonial Cyprus, there was a complex set of dynamics between mining company and colonial government, between overseer and miner, and between miners from different villages. These dynamics were negotiated not only by words but also by the manipulation of artifacts, structures, and landscapes.

ACKNOWLEDGMENTS

Most of the primary historical material for this paper comes from the Cyprus State Archives, and I am very grateful to the director, Effy Parparinou, and to all her staff for their constant help and support during my research there. The copyright of all material from the Cyprus State Archives remains with the Government of Cyprus. I am grateful to the many villagers in Mitsero and Amiandos who have told me about their mining history, especially Andreas Papanastasiou, Konstantinos Ttaouxis and Loïzos Xynaris. Thanks also to the members of the Sydney Cyprus Survey Project. The participants of the SHA 2000 "Landscapes of Industrial Labor" session gave many comments, suggestions, and ideas that were both helpful and stimulating. I would like to thank them and the session organizer Mark Cassell. All photographs and maps are by the author.

REFERENCES

BEAR, L. M.
1963 The Mineral Resources and Mining Industry of Cyprus. *Cyprus Geological Survey Department, Bulletin*, No. 1, Nicosia.

CHENEY, SUSAN L.
1992 Uncertain Migrants: The History and Archaeology of a Victorian Goldfield Community. *Australasian Historical Archaeology*, 10:36–42.

CYPRUS STATE ARCHIVES [SA]
1904–1944 Unpublished government correspondence. Cyprus State Archives, Nicosia. [*Red* refers to the page number of the correspondence in the back of the file; *minute* refers to the number of the minute in the front of the file. Copyright remains with the Republic of Cyprus.]

DELLE, JAMES A.
1999 The Landscapes of Class Negotiation on Coffee Plantations in the Blue Mountains of Jamaica: 1790–1850. *Historical Archaeology*, 33(1):136–158.

DOUGLASS, WILLIAM A.

1998 The Mining Camp as Community. In *Social Approaches to an Industrial Past: The Archaeology and Anthropology of Mining*, A. Bernard Knapp, Vincent C. Pigott, and Eugenia W. Herbert, editors, pp. 97–108. Routledge, London, England.

FERGUSON, LELAND

1991 Struggling with Pots in Colonial South Carolina. In *The Archaeology of Inequality*, Randall H. McGuire and Robert Paynter, editors, pp. 28–39. Blackwell, Oxford, England.

FOUCAULT, MICHEL

1977 *Discipline and Punish: The Birth of the Prison*, Alan Sheridan, translator. Penguin Books, Harmondsworth, England.

GEORGHALLIDES, G. S.

1985 Cyprus and the Governorship of Sir Ronald Storrs: The Causes of the 1931 Crisis. *Cyprus Research Centre, Texts, and Studies in the History of Cyprus*, No. 13. Nicosia, Cyprus.

GIVEN, MICHAEL

1997 Star of the Parthenon, Cypriot Mélange: Education and Representation in Colonial Cyprus. *Journal of Mediterranean Studies*, 7(1):59–82.

1998 Inventing the Eteocypriots: Imperialist Archaeology and the Manipulation of Ethnic Identity. *Journal of Mediterranean Archaeology*, 11(1):3–29.

2000 Agriculture, Settlement, and Landscape in Ottoman Cyprus. *Levant*, 32:215–236.

GIVEN, MICHAEL, AND TIMOTHY E. GREGORY

2003 Medieval to Modern Landscapes. In The Sydney Cyprus Survey Project: Social Approaches to Regional Archaeological Survey, Michael Given and A. Bernard Knapp, editors, pp. 284–294. *Monumenta Archaeologica*, No. 21. Cotsen Institute of Archaeology, University of California, Los Angeles.

GIVEN, MICHAEL, AND A. BERNARD KNAPP (EDITORS)

2003 The Sydney Cyprus Survey Project: Social Approaches to Regional Archaeological Survey. *Monumenta Archaeologica*, No. 21. Cotsen Institute of Archaeology, University of California, Los Angeles.

GRIVAUD, GILLES

1998 Villages Désertés à Chypre (Fin XIIe–Fin XIXe Siècle). *Archbishop Makarios III Foundation, Meletai kai Ipomnimata*, No. 3. Nicosia, Cyprus.

IONAS, IOANNIS

1988 *La Maison Rurale de Chypre (XVIIIe–XXe Siècle): Aspects et Techniques de Construction*. Cyprus Research Centre, Nicosia, Cyprus.

KATSIAOUNIS, ROLANDOS

1996 Labour, Society, and Politics in Cyprus during the Second Half of the Nineteenth Century. *Cyprus Research Centre, Texts, and Studies in the History of Cyprus*, No. 24. Nicosia, Cyprus.

KNAPP, A. BERNARD

1997 *The Archaeology of Late Bronze Age Cypriot Society: The Study of Settlement, Survey, and Landscape*. Department of Archaeology, University of Glasgow, Glasgow, Scotland.

1998 Social Approaches to the Archaeology and Anthropology of Mining. In *Social Approaches to an Industrial Past: The Archaeology and Anthropology of Mining*, A. Bernard Knapp, Vincent C. Pigott, and Eugenia W. Herbert, editors, pp. 1–23. Routledge, London, England.

KNAPP, A. BERNARD, AND WENDY ASHMORE

1999 Archaeological Landscapes: Constructed, Conceptualized, Ideational. In *Archaeologies of Landscape: Contemporary Perspectives*, Wendy Ashmore and A. Bernard Knapp, editors, pp. 1–30. Blackwell, Oxford, England.

LAVENDER, DAVID

1962 *The Story of the Cyprus Mines Corporation*. Huntington Library, San Marino, CA.

PAYNTER, ROBERT, AND RANDALL H. MCGUIRE

1991 The Archaeology of Inequality: Material Culture, Domination, and Resistance. In *The Archaeology of Inequality*, Randall H. McGuire and Robert Paynter, editors, pp. 1–27. Blackwell, Oxford, England.

SCHAAR, KENNETH W., MICHAEL GIVEN, AND GEORGE THEOCHAROUS

1995 *Under the Clock: Colonial Architecture and History in Cyprus, 1878–1960*. Bank of Cyprus, Nicosia, Cyprus.

SERETIS, KYLIE, AND LITA DIACOPOULOS

2003 SIA 5: Mitsero Village. In The Sydney Cyprus Survey Project: Social Approaches to Regional Archaeological Survey, Michael Given and A. Bernard Knapp, editors, pp. 109–118. *Monumenta Archaeologica*, No. 21. Cotsen Institute of Archaeology, University of California, Los Angeles.

WOOD, H. TRUEMAN (EDITOR)

1887 *Colonial and Indian Exhibition, London, 1886: Reports on the Colonial Sections of the Exhibition*. William Clowes and Sons, London, England.

MICHAEL GIVEN
DEPARTMENT OF ARCHAEOLOGY
UNIVERSITY OF GLASGOW
GLASGOW G12 8QQ
SCOTLAND

JANET G. BRASHLER

When Daddy Was a Shanty Boy: The Role of Gender in the Organization of the Logging Industry in Highland West Virginia

ABSTRACT

Literature and oral history of late 19th- and early 20th-century logging camps are replete with stories about lusty loggers who lived rigorous lives in the woods. Photo documentation in many of the logging histories supports the idea that logging was a single-gender, masculine activity. However, it is clear from recent work at the Monongahela National Forest and elsewhere in the East that women and children were present in some logging contexts. This article looks at the historic logging industry in West Virginia using gender as an organizing principle.

Introduction

This paper is an initial look at the extent to which gender can be used to understand the organization of the logging industry in a remote portion of Appalachia. The impetus to develop this research stems from interest in gender and family organization in addition to interest in understanding the archaeological record of the logging industry. The research described here focuses on the relationship between gender, family organization, and economic and subsistence strategies in the context of industrialization in rural West Virginia.

The late 19th- and early 20th-century history of logging the great forests of the eastern United States is dominated by discussions of big trees, logging technology, railroads, abusive clear cutting of the forest, and colorful stories revolving around the theme "when daddy was a shanty boy. . . ." Folk histories such as *Riders of the Flood* (Blackhurst 1954), *Sawdust in Your Eyes* (Blackhurst 1963), *Goin' Up Gandy* (Teter 1977),

and *Daylight in the Swamp* (Wells 1978) as well as more data-oriented works such as *Tumult on the Mountains* (Clarkson 1964) are full of stories and photographs about the logging life centering on the theme of the tough existence of a lumberjack in the woods and in that most masculine domain, the single-gender logging camp (Figure 1). References to women are contained in stories of weekend visits to the "hotels" in town where the lusty loggers could consort with "ladies of ill repute ready to separate the man from his hard earned money" (Clarkson 1964:79). Similarly, the only context in which women were mentioned during a recent oral history interview with a local historian was his familiarity with a site called "Whorehouse Hill" located adjacent to a large multi-structure logging camp of the early 20th century (Donald Rice 1989, pers. comm.). From the literature and at least some oral history, it appears that women were absent from the woods during the logging process.

The relatively recent addition of an archaeological and cultural resource management perspective to the study of the logging industry has resulted in the identification of thousands of archaeological logging camps and related sites on National Forest lands and in other forested lands in the East. Archaeological studies of the logging industry have understandably focused on the technology, subsistence, material culture, predictive models of logging camp location, and the troublesome question, "what is a significant [National Register eligible] logging camp?" (Franzen 1984; Dinsmore 1985; Karamanski 1985; Rohe 1985, 1986a, 1986b; Hulse 1989).

Only occasionally are women interviewed, much less mentioned in more recent historical studies and oral histories (e.g., Myer 1979; Karamanski 1982) and only rarely are recognized in the archaeological record of the logging industry. During a recent oral history interview, the son of an early 20th-century logger noted that his parents and brother had both lived in a series of logging camps, one of which was being evaluated for the National Register (Brashler 1987). In another interview, 91-year-old Edith Starkey (1987) described her childhood experience at a logging community known as Braucher. Recently discovered

FIGURE 1. Typical late 19th- to early 20th-century logging scene of men, horses, and logs (Photo by Finley Taylor; courtesy of Luther Baker and photo files, print # CBLC 80, Monogahela National Forest, Elkins, West Virginia.)

FIGURE 2. Men, women, and children at unknown Cherry River Boom and Lumber Company camp, ca. 1910–1930. (Photo by Finley Taylor; courtesy of Luther Baker and photo files, print # CBLC 82, Monongahela National Forest, Elkins, West Virginia.)

historic photos (including those illustrating this article) taken by Finley Taylor at the turn of the century show men, women, and children in a variety of logging contexts (Figure 2).

Thus, although it has become increasingly clear that women and children were present in logging communities, their exact roles have not been recognized or understood by the majority of people concerned with the history of the logging era. However, this paper is not limited to a facile description of women's and men's roles in the logging camps, communities, and towns. If that were so, the discussion would be no more interesting than the observation that women cooked, sewed, washed dishes and clothes, took care of kids, and did what most rural women of the late Victorian era did, while men went to the woods, cut big trees, and posed for all those fascinating photos. Rather, the focus of the article is to discuss the organization of logging in a portion of West Virginia from a gender-based perspective with the objective of accounting for observed patterns in the archaeological record which could be attributed to gender relationships.

Physical Environment

The approximately 300-sq.-mi. research area for this study is located in portions of Webster, Poca-

hontas, Greenbrier, and Nicholas counties in West Virginia (Figure 3). The area is characterized by rugged and isolated mountain terrain. Due to the higher altitudes and latitude, the area experiences cool, wet summers and moderate but snowy winters. Landform in this region of Appalachia is the result of successive weathering of uplifted Paleozoic sedimentary rocks leaving a system of high plateaus, ridges, and steep slopes dissected by narrow, shallow streams. In the research area, floodplains with Quaternary alluvium are non-existent, resulting in poor agricultural land. For the most part, the streams are not navigable, with the exception of short, unpredictable flash-flood periods in the spring during which snow melts and rains come.

The present vegetation of the area is a mixed hardwood forest of northern species such as beech, maple, birch, and poplar with central hardwood species such as oak and hickory. At elevations above 3,200 ft., conifers are dominant with single-component northern red spruce found on the high ridges and plateaus. During the pre-lumbering era, the forest was dominated by red spruce, hemlock, and other conifers found at elevations as low as 2,500 ft. (Core 1966).

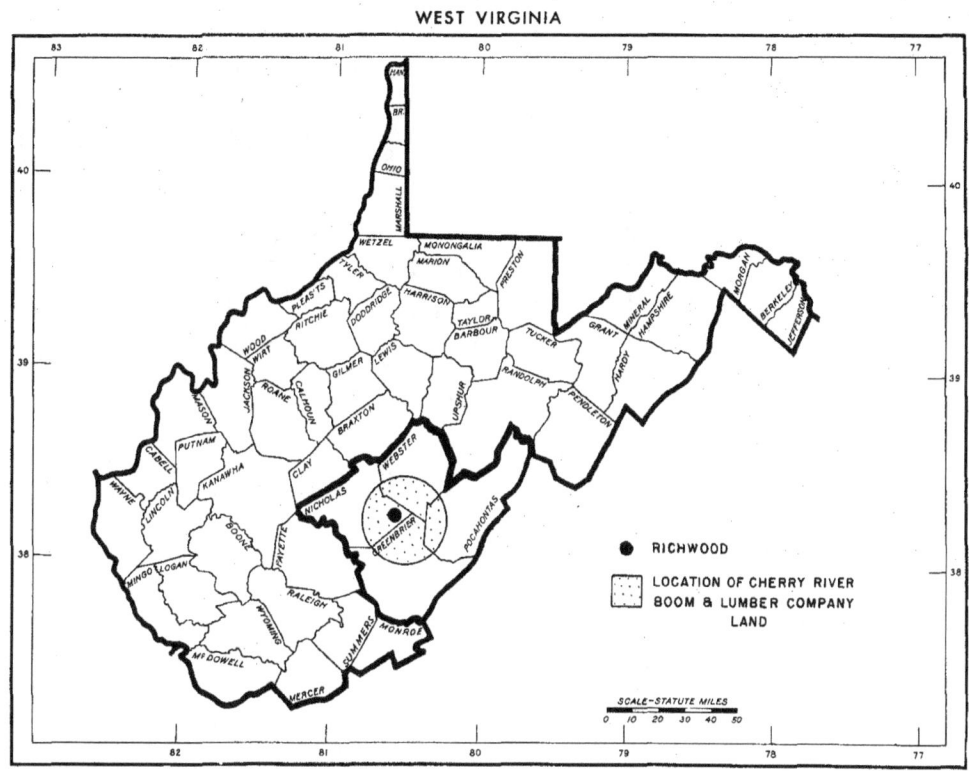

FIGURE 3. The study area in southeastern West Virginia.

Historical Context

Though only approximately 150 mi. from the Atlantic coast, historic settlement of this portion of West Virginia did not commence until the mid-18th century, although there were occasional forays by hunters and trappers. For 75 years, settlement was concentrated in the few larger stream valleys. The remote character of the study area and lack of adequate river transportation limited most settlement until after the Civil War. During the last half of the 19th century, numerous small subsistence farmsteads averaging approximately 80–100 acres were established by nuclear families in the gaps, hollows, coves, and on the ridge tops (Eller 1982). Women's work on the rural farm of preindustrial Appalachia focused on maintenance of family and kinship ties, subsistence farm activi-

ties, and household chores. Visits away from the farm involved church and other neighborhood social events. Women assumed male duties from time to time, but men seldom assumed women's roles. Men did the heavier farm work, and occasionally left to engage in the activities that linked the farm to the outside world, including hunting, trading, land and property transactions, and local politics (Eller 1982:31).

At the same time during the late 19th century, much of the rest of the East was caught up in the early stages of the industrial revolution. Appalachia, however, was cut off from these events by the mountains and lack of adequate transportation. Indeed, most of Appalachia was considered too remote for capital investment because it was far removed from, and inaccessible to, the centers of industry (Eller 1982). Until relatively late in the

19th century, the supply of timber and coal in the East was adequate to fuel the mills and factories there, and the demand for the resources abundant in Appalachia was met by states in the Northeast and Great Lake states of Michigan, Wisconsin, and Minnesota.

Between 1880 and 1900, land speculators and industrialists were drawn to the region by "local color" literature published in journals such as *Harper's*. This literature described the area as abundant in fish, game, pristine streams and forests, and mineral springs (Eller 1982:44). Recognizing the potential to attract business and development to the area, the state of West Virginia published and distributed thousands of copies of *The West Virginia Handbook and Immigrant's Guide* (Eller 1982:46). Once in the area, "Captains of Industry" such as Stephen Benton Elkins and Henry Gassaway Davis realized the potential of the vast timber and coal resources. In 1880 over two-thirds of the state (some 10–12 million acres) was in virgin forest (Clarkson 1964:38). By 1930, less than 5 percent remained. The industrialization of Appalachia began with the construction of a rail network by large corporations and railroad conglomerates to transport the natural resources out of the area.

During the last two decades of the 19th century, land ownership and utilization patterns changed dramatically. The small, privately owned farmsteads were replaced by large tracts of corporate land holdings accounting for over 50 percent of the land ownership. Much of the corporate land was acquired by railroads and related companies which, by 1882, had built lines across West Virginia connecting the eastern seaboard and the Midwest (Clarkson 1964; Eller 1982). The lumber boom in West Virginia occurred between 1880 and 1930. It was followed by a coal boom between 1900 and 1930. Both the coal and timber industries continue to be important in the economy of West Virginia today.

The Logging Industry in West Virginia

Harvesting trees in West Virginia began with the earliest settlement and was conducted mostly for

FIGURE 4. Men with peg and raker saws and axes from the early 20th century. (Photo by Finley Taylor; courtesy of Luther Baker and photo files, print # CBLC 143, Monongahela National Forest, Elkins, West Virginia.)

personal use, such as for homes, furniture, and fuel, until after the Civil War. Trees were felled and cut into logs and boards with axes or whip saws (Figure 4). A small amount of commercial logging supplemented the farm income with logs transported to mills by wagon or tram road.

Selective commercial logging began in earnest by 1880 along the larger rivers which were used to raft logs in arks to downstream mills and railheads. Arks consisted of logs bound together with structures on top to house the men transporting them (Figure 5). In Appalachia, transportation of the logs appears to have been accomplished by the seasonal labor of farmers (Eller 1982:87). These men maintained their family farms and supplemented family income, allowing the purchase of goods and participation in a cash economy. Outside timber companies appear to have had relatively little impact on the area until the 1890s, when companies bought much of their land. This reduced many former farm owners to tenants of absentee landlords.

Ultimately, the rural Appalachian landscape, dominated by its kinship-based society and nuclear-family subsistence farms, gave way to com-

FIGURE 5. Ark and crew of men on the Greenbrier River at Cass, Pocahontas County, West Virginia, 1898. (Courtesy of Monongahela National Forest, Elkins, West Virginia.)

pany land where families became increasingly dependent on wage income. Eller (1982:92) notes: ''As logging shifted from a family enterprise to a highly integrated industrial operation, mountain men spent more and more time away from the farm living in the timber camps and logging towns.'' At the same time, a few women and children began appearing in logging camp contexts as the family of the camp foreman or cook (Figure 6). Boys worked with their fathers occasionally in the logging enterprise. Older girls and women participated in the logging enterprise by foraging, driving supply wagons, and occasionally driving teams of horses skidding logs (Myer 1979) (Figures 7, 8).

Mill technology evolved from the sash to circular-saw and eventually to the extremely efficient band-saw mill, which could cut up to 140,000 bd.

ft. of timber in an 11-hour day (Clarkson 1964:30). Occasionally in areas adjacent to the study area, attempts were made to construct splash dams on smaller streams to float logs during high-water periods, but these attempts were generally unsuccessful. Most of the merchantable timber adjacent to the larger, navigable streams was cut by 1890. At about that time, land speculation and corporate acquisition became widespread. If the remaining timber in the hills away from the rivers was to be harvested economically and transported out of the region, it became imperative to adapt the Shay and Climax geared locomotives already in use in the Great Lake states to the mountains in Appalachia (Clarkson 1964). With construction by immigrant labor of thousands of miles of both standard- and narrow-gauge railroad, the previously isolated re-

FIGURE 6. Man and woman preparing food at unknown Cherry River Boom and Lumber Company camp, ca. 1910–1930. (Photo by Finley Taylor; courtesy of Luther Baker and photo files, print # CBLC 162, Monongahela National Forest, Elkins, West Virginia.)

FIGURE 7. Young woman with pail, perhaps berry picking. (Photo by Finley Taylor; courtesy of Luther Baker and photo files, print # CBLC 162, Monongahela National Forest, Elkins, West Virginia.)

gion of Appalachia was finally opened to the industrial harvest of timber (Figure 9).

From this historical summary, it appears that three distinct periods of development can be identified in the industrialization of Appalachia. The periods bear many similarities to stages of adaptation of the family to industrialization described by Tilly and Scott (1978) and Hareven (1982). Stage One, occurring before 1880, is characterized by rural, pre-industrial settlement where families are the primary production and consumption unit. Stage Two, occurring roughly between 1880 and 1900 in the study area, is characterized by transition between the kin-based subsistence economy and a wage-earning economy dominated by the

corporation. Families adapt to the presence of the industrial corporation by engaging in seasonal labor for wages while still maintaining the family farm. Stage Three, beginning around 1900 in this portion of Appalachia, is characterized by greater reliance on wage labor and includes the formation of company communities of families participating in a consumer economy to harvest timber and later to mine coal. The earlier stages of this transition have not been documented in the archaeological record. The process in the latest stage, however, can be illustrated by the development of the Cherry River Boom and Lumber Company (1905–1934), in highland West Virginia.

FIGURE 8. Man and woman on horse logging team at unknown Cherry River Boom and Lumber Company camp, ca. 1910–1930. (Photo by Finley Taylor; courtesy of Luther Baker and photo files, print # CBLC 39, Monongahela National Forest, Elkins, West Virginia.)

FIGURE 9. Immigrant laborers working on a Cherry River Boom and Lumber Company railroad, ca. 1910–1930. (Photo by Finley Taylor; courtesy of Luther Baker and photo files, print # CBLC 154, Monongahela National Forest, Elkins, West Virginia.)

The Cherry River Boom and Lumber Company

Between 1900 and 1901, the Baltimore and Ohio Railroad was extended to the juncture of the north and south forks of the Cherry River in Nicholas County, West Virginia. At this location, the Cherry River Boom and Lumber Company had built a small circular-saw mill to establish the center of a 200,000-acre logging operation located in Nicholas, Webster, Pocahontas, and Greenbrier counties (Figures 1, 10). A large band-saw mill was completed in July, and the town of Richwood was incorporated in November of 1901 (Clarkson 1964:93–94). Additional wood-products industries, including a clothespin factory, several broom and handle factories, a paper mill, and tannery, located in Richwood during the following 15 years.

In addition to the big mill at Richwood, the Cherry River Boom and Lumber Company operated at least three other band-saw mills at Holcomb (established 1909), Camden on Gauley (dates unknown), and Gauley Mills (1909–1932) (Figure 11). Numerous other lumber concerns operated mills throughout the four-county area until the late 1920s and early 1930s when the majority of the area was logged over (Clarkson 1964).

The Cherry River Boom and Lumber Company operated 75 mi. of its logging operation on standard-gauge railroad (Clarkson 1964:94). An unknown number of miles of narrow-gauge railroad appear to have been used also, since Cherry River Boom and Lumber operated 16 engines, at least one of which was a Shay locomotive. It was common for companies to operate a section of track until an area was cut out and then to pick up the rails and move them up or down stream to the next area to be harvested. Thus, the total number of miles of logging railroad constructed far exceeded the number of miles in operation at any one time (Clarkson 1964:60).

FIGURE 10. The mill at Richwood, ca. 1910–1930. (Photo by Finley Taylor; courtesy of Luther Baker and photo files, print # CBLC 179, Monongahela National Forest, Elkins, West Virginia.)

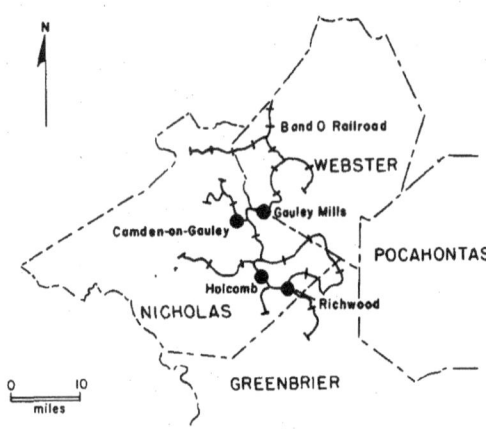

FIGURE 11. Cherry River sawmills and rail lines in the study area (after Clarkson 1964).

Evidence of Logging Sites

Maps of the Cherry River Boom and Lumber Company rail and logging operations—most of which are on file with the Monongahela National Forest, Elkins, West Virginia—show the main mill and rail yard at Richwood, in addition to numerous other lines and logging communities. The main rail lines are located along the forks of the Cherry, Cranberry, and Gauley rivers, with shorter, tem-

porary routes located up tributary streams. Rarely did lines cross the steep, high ridges. Logging sites are located predominantly at tributary stream junctures along the main rivers and rail lines, and usually at the headwaters of shorter tributaries. Longer tributaries appear to have several sites located along the stream and spur rail lines (Figure 11). All of the logging sites are identified either by number (e.g., Camp 34), by the name of the logger who was managing cutting in the drainage (e.g., Ferrell's Camp, Babar's Camp), or by a place name (e.g., Dogway). Not all known sites are on the Cherry River Boom and Lumber Company maps, and several maps are not in Monongahela National Forest files.

Within the last three years, field inventory has resulted in locating several logging sites along Dogway Fork of the Cranberry River (Figure 12), an area for which no archival or cartographic information is extant. Along this stream, 10 logging sites were located during surface surveys for Section 106 of the National Historic Preservation Act compliance inventory projects. Sites are located 1/4–3/4 mi. from each other along the rail line that paralleled Dogway Fork. With one exception, the sites today are small (usually less than 600 sq. ft.), are in open grassy areas, and contain evidence of one to four leveled shanty-car locations parallel to rail lines with associated artifacts, dispersed across the area and/or concentrated in dumps. Shanty cars were rectangular (approximately 12 × 25 ft.), one-story structures usually of board-and-batten construction which were brought to the site of a logging enterprise on flat-bed railroad cars and placed on leveled spots adjacent to the rails with a large crane (Figure 13). When an area was cut out, the company picked up the cars and moved the camp to the next area to be logged.

Nine of the sites in Dogway Fork appear to represent relatively small, temporary logging camps (Table 1). These sites are characterized by open areas with leveled locations for shanty cars, usually adjacent to a railroad grade. Today, shanty car locations are recognizable only by the leveled ground approximately 12 × 25 ft. in size. No foundations or other structural remains are visible on the surface.

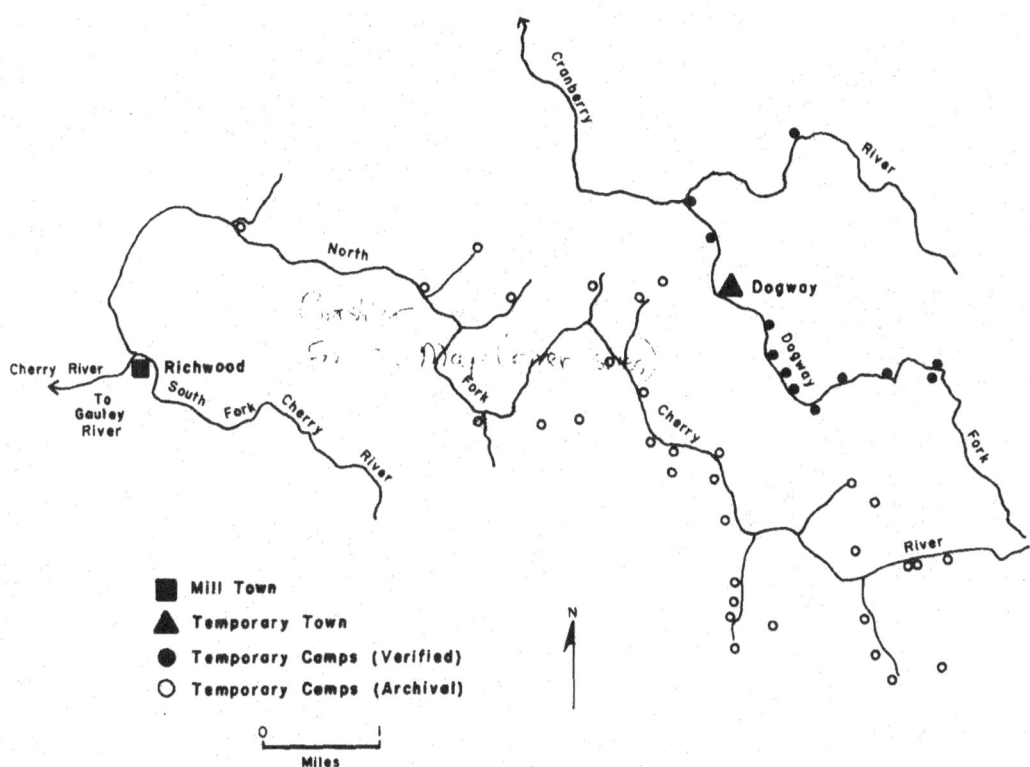

FIGURE 12. Cherry River Boom and Lumber Company logging sites in the study area along Dogway Fork.

The site of Dogway, located within 6 mi. of these nine sites, is remarkably different in terms of site size, artifact distribution, and features (Figure 14). Dogway is situated approximately 15 mi. northeast of Richwood and 2 mi. from the juncture of Dogway Fork and the main fork of the Cranberry River. The community was established by the Cherry River Boom and Lumber Company sometime between 1910 and 1915. The site was all but abandoned by 1927. At its peak, the community contained approximately 60 shanty-car houses scattered for a mile on either side of the railroad. A combined company store and hotel appears to have been the only structure constructed on the site.

Seven years after the tracks were pulled and operations at Dogway abandoned by the company, the cut-over lands were sold to the U.S. Forest Service. Today, the area is part of the Cranberry

FIGURE 13. Cherry River Boom and Lumber Company shanty cars located along a rail line at an unknown location. (Photo by Finley Taylor; courtesy of Luther Baker and photo files, print # CBLC 83, Monongahela National Forest, Elkins, West Virginia.)

Backcountry adjacent to the Cranberry Wilderness on the Monongahela National Forest.

TABLE 1

INVENTORY OF ARTIFACTS OBSERVED AT DOGWAY AND OTHER DOGWAY FORK LOGGING SITES

Site Number	Features Observed	Artifacts Observed
02–117 (Dogway)	Root cellar, brick chimney, railroad grades, sidings, leveled shanty-car locations, large area (1 × ¼ mi. along stream)	Tableware, transfer-print sherds, stove parts, barrel hoops, springs, tin cans, bottle fragments, etc.
02–218	Open area (100 × 650 ft.), railroad grade, cellar pit, collapsed smithy chimney	Spackle ware,[a] bottles, fire grates, steel track couplers
02–219	Open area (100 × 100 ft.), railroad grade, apple trees	Enameled tin ware, tin cans, logging boot fragments, cinder pile, barrel hoops, stove legs, mattock, etc.
02–220	Two shanty sites, open area, railroad grade roofing	Broken whiteware, bottle fragments, rotted asphalt
02–221	Three or four shanty locations, open area (75 × 200 ft.), railroad grade	Iron cookstove, iron pot spackle ware,[a] broken glass tableware, crockery, bottles, shoe, boot, and leather fragments
02–222	Railroad junction, open area (100 × 300 ft.), apple trees, cellar pits and/or privy	Spackle ware,[a] galvanized metal ware, cross-cut saws, ring rills
02–223	Railroad grade, open area (100 × 650 ft.)	Tar paper, bottles, stove parts, metal can dump
02–224	Open area (50 × 100 ft.), railroad grade	Spackle ware,[a] broken glass
02–225	Open area (50 × 100 ft.), railroad grade	Spackle ware,[a] zinc tubs, buckets, shovels, railroad steel, clams, barrel hoops, stove parts
02–226	Open area, railroad grade	Stove parts, bedsteads, zinc tubs, spackle ware[a]

[a] "Spackle ware" is a local term for enameled metal ware.

The Logging Community at Dogway

Shanty-car housing and the site plan of Dogway and related logging sites are unlike the majority of well-documented logging camps of the Great Lake states (Franzen 1986; Rohe 1986b). In the Great Lake states, most logging camps were constructed on site, typically containing a bunkhouse, cookhouse, barn, and camp operator's quarters located in an opening and in a block or clustered fashion. With the introduction of railroad logging in the Great Lake states, some camps reveal linear spatial arrangements, but the buildings still appear to be constructed on site (Rohe 1986a).

Shanties brought in for temporary housing at Dogway and in other logging as well as coal-mining communities (Brashler 1988) observed in the study area were oriented in a linear fashion along the railroad. Shanty locations are situated along the railroad for at least a half mile from the main community of Dogway. In larger communities, such as Dogway, the orientation of the con-structed store/hotel was still along the railroad, but apparently at a central location where several rail lines joined. Shanties provided loggers in this portion of Appalachia with portable housing in temporary logging communities reflecting the needs of the corporation to employ a mobile work force housed in both temporary and semi-permanent communities.

Dogway contains at least six rail lines and/or sidings which merge in the area of the hotel/store. One line ran east along Dogway Fork and northeast to join the line along the Cranberry River. A second line was laid north to Summit. The large number of rail lines, spurs, and shanty sites may be related to Dogway's function as both a railroad maintenance location and a logging community. There is no evidence of a mill at Dogway.

Few artifacts were collected during inventory at Dogway and other sites, but lists were made of observed items. Table 1 presents an inventory of items observed at the sites and a description of the features visible. A quick review of these data re-

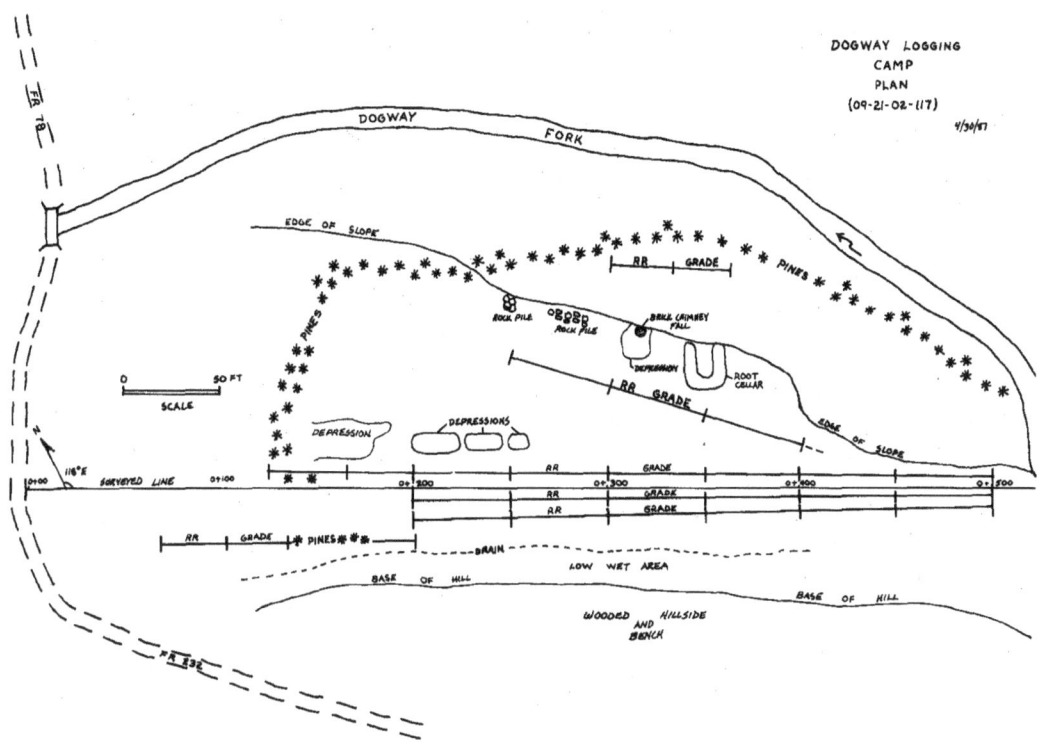

FIGURE 14. Site map of Dogway.

veals differences in the types of artifacts, site size, and features present at the sites examined.

Observed at shanty sites located near the large community along Dogway were a wide variety of artifacts, including fragile and decorative items as well as stove parts, barrel hoops, and miscellaneous metal fragments, cans, and bottles. The nine isolated shanty-car sites located upstream from Dogway produced only one decorative artifact, a thick transfer-printed porcelain serving bowl. Other artifacts observed at the smaller shanty sites include bottles, beer steins, enamelware, logging-boot fragments, iron pots and pans, tin cans, zinc tubs, logging equipment, barrel hoops, bed springs, and broken thick whiteware. Unfortunately, none of these sites has been tested, so it is not possible to do much more than describe the surface observations, and be cognizant of the problems of sampling bias at this time.

The surface data reveal variability in occupied space, artifact types, and organization of space in the camps. This variability can be accounted for in a number of ways. Site function, duration of occupation, gender composition, and socioeconomic status all could contribute to the observed variability. It seems likely that the main community at Dogway served as a more or less permanent community for a period of time, while the smaller sites seem to have functioned as temporary work camps. The presence of fragile glassware, pressed glass, decorative items such as vases, and other serving and display pieces at Dogway, when contrasted with their relative absence at the smaller sites, could reflect differential gender composition with the smaller sites occupied by all-male work groups. Contemporaneous nuclear family farmstead sites in the area exhibit similar kinds of artifacts as seen at Dogway. If it is true that smaller shanty sites represent single-gender logging residences and sites like Dogway represent communities with men, women, and children present, then these differences may reflect late Victorian perceptions of women as "more gentle" and "civilized" as well as differential consumption patterns of men and women of that era. Evidence that women and children were present at Dogway is presented below, but the gender composition of the smaller camps remains unknown.

Oral history of Dogway is based on an interview with Forest Service retiree Chester Carden in 1987. Mr. Carden stated that both of his parents, an older brother, and an uncle lived in the community. Mr. Carden had visited the site with his father as a boy and as an adult numerous times after it had been abandoned and was able to identify the location of his parents' shanty. The elder Mr. Carden and his brother worked for the Cherry River Boom and Lumber Company as loggers. They rode the train to the woods, felled and skidded trees to the railroad, and rode the cars with the logs back to camp at night to eat dinner with their wives and children. Clearly, Dogway was not a single-gender logging camp, nor was it a full-blown company town like the larger communities of Cass or Spruce, operated at the same time by West Virginia Pulp and Paper in nearby Pocahontas County. Hulse (1989) provides an excellent description of recent excavations at the town of Spruce in Pocahontas County, West Virginia.

Discussion

Based on the oral history, documents, photos, and observations at Dogway and the nine related sites, at least three types of logging communities can be hypothesized for the first years of the 20th century in this portion of Appalachia: mill town (Richwood), company family logging camp (Dogway), and shanty camp. Gender composition of temporary shanty camps could be all male, or it is conceivable that families may have lived in remote shanty-camp locations with men working cooperatively in logging a section of the forest. This typology represents a departure from the dichotomy used in most discussions of the logging era: logging camp and mill town or mill community. Materials from Dogway and other Cherry River Boom and Lumber Company sites—including photographs and oral history—clearly indicate the presence of men, women, and children living together as families in some logging communities. Artifact types and features at the nine smaller sites lack the more women-related serving and display pieces observed at Dogway. It is hypothesized that this artifact pattern represents the short-term occupation of small, all-male crews of loggers. Alternatively, a family could have occupied these more remote locales for a short period of time, with individuals from several families making up work parties. The artifact assemblage from such an occupation should produce a few women-related artifacts, but these would probably be more difficult to ascertain from surface survey observations alone. The settlement typology proposed here must certainly be tested with extensive excavation data to document the gender composition of these smaller sites.

It is not known whether these smaller shanty-car sites were contemporaneous with Dogway. It seems likely that they were, since the records of the Cherry River Boom and Lumber Company indicate that the area was logged during a relatively short period of time between 1910 and 1927.

Women and children were present in company camps in the Great Lake states such as Coalwood. Perhaps the nine shanty-car sites strung along Dogway Fork represent "bachelor quarters" for the single men who worked for the company out of Dogway. At sites like Coalwood, single men may have lived separately from families in boarding houses, though some families kept boarders (Swanberg 1986). In eastern Kentucky's Robinson Forest, a dispersed pattern of temporary shanty-car sites as well as larger sites have been observed based on surface survey and archival data. While many of these sites are badly disturbed, some appear to have been occupied by families (Kim A. McBride 1989, pers. comm.).

Summary and Conclusions

This initial examination of the logging industry using gender composition as a key variable has resulted in the identification of at least three major types of settlement (mill town, family company camp, and shanty camp); previously, only single-gender camps and mill towns were acknowledged. The presence of women in two and perhaps all three of these types of logging sites reveals that they remained a key part of the Appalachian household in the face of radical change from a rural subsistence economy to a rural industrial economy.

There is likely to be considerable functional and formal variability within each type which has not been addressed in this paper. So-called "traditional" logging camps have been described elsewhere (Franzen 1984; Rohe 1985) with respect to subsistence, chronology, and function. Mill towns such as Richwood and Camden on Gauley have not received much attention from historical archaeology with a few exceptions, such as recent work by Charles Hulse (1989) at the site of Spruce in Pocahontas County, West Virginia.

The pattern of shanty camp and family company camp is one that appears to have evolved as companies sought to employ laborers who moved from family farm to town as a result of industrialization of their region. Companies were understandably interested in reliable labor (Eller 1982; Swanberg 1986), and it seems likely that the mixed-gender family logging camp was a successful adaptation on the part of both the company and the family to the rural kin-based society of Appalachia. Families could stay together and the company had a reliable labor pool. Families (women and children) in company camps undoubtedly added stability as well as the early 20th-century woman's approach to the sometimes harsh existence of logging and later coal mining. In rural Appalachia, where kinship continues to be embedded in the social, political, and economic institutions of the region, the family company camp may well have been essential (Figure 15).

As in the case of all initial research, much remains to be done with this topic. Critical work needed includes the excavation of various types of logging communities proposed in this paper. Substantial work needs to be done on the consumption patterns of the early 20th century in rural Appala-

FIGURE 15. A family(?) group on the tracks next to a shanty car residence at an unknown Cherry River Boom and Lumber Company camp, ca. 1910–1930. (Photo by Finley Taylor; courtesy of Luther Baker and photo files, print # CBLC 90, Monongahela National Forest, Elkins, West Virginia.)

chia to document more clearly whether it is, in fact, possible to attribute certain artifact classes to one gender or another.

Fruitful future research should include refining the site settlement model (milltown, family company camp, single-gender camp, temporary family shanty camp). Do temporary family shanty camps exist in the area, or are all such sites single-gender camps? To what extent is the camp common in the area or is Dogway unique? At present, the number of family company camps is not known, though preliminary research suggests that they may be more numerous within the one-million-acre Monongahela National Forest than previously thought. Changes through time in the gender composition of camps can be incorporated into a more refined diachronic model of the logging industry, addressing settlement type and associated material culture.

Archaeologists need to define more clearly the artifact assemblages found in family camps, single-gender camps, family shanty camps, camps with red-light districts, and camps where one or two women might have been present as the wives

FIGURE 16. A family(?) group in front of shanty along the tracks at an unknown Cherry River Boom and Lumber Company camp, ca. 1910–1930. (Photo by Finley Taylor; courtesy of Luther Baker and photo files, print # CBLC 85, Monongahela National Forest, Elkins, West Virginia.)

FIGURE 17. Men and women near shanty car residence and an unknown Cherry River Boom and Lumber Company camp, ca. 1910–1930. (Photo by Finley Taylor; courtesy of Luther Baker and photo files, print # CBLC 185, Monongahela National Forest, Elkins, West Virginia.)

of the foreman or cook. An aggressive oral history project should be initiated to interview the few remaining women and men who lived and worked in the camps and to record their perceptions of how gender influenced the organization of the logging (and later coal) industries and how wage labor affected gender roles. Collections of logging-era photos should be located and their gender composition analyzed (Figures 16, 17).

Comparisons between the material culture of family logging camps and the coal camps which were established as the timber was being cut out of the region should be undertaken. Material remains, camp layout, and structures at one 1930s isolated coal camp (Camp Baldwin) are remarkably similar to the pattern observed at Dogway, though with fewer shanties. Comparisons between the development of the logging industry in Appalachia and elsewhere using a gender-based approach need to be made. Family company camps and temporary family shanty camps do exist in other areas, such as the Great Lake states (Swanberg 1986; John Franzen 1989, pers. comm.), but the development and historic context of these camps appears to be different from that seen in rural Appalachia.

As the final decade of the 20th century begins, it is fitting that historical archaeology starts to examine the earlier part of the century from a gender-based archaeological perspective. While there has been understandable reluctance among historical archaeologists to deal with the garbage of the 20th century (Hulse 1989), it is a particularly rich era to do gender-based archaeology because of the wealth of photographic records, oral history, and documentary data available. Gender-based historical archaeology clearly can be used with these historic and living resources better to understand oneself, a few short generations removed.

ACKNOWLEDGMENTS

This paper has been challenging for a feminist prehistorian to write. I am indebted to a number of people for their assistance. I am grateful to Donna Seifert for asking me to participate in this project. I am particularly indebted to Hunter Lesser for drafting the maps and commenting on a draft of the paper. Kim McBride provided especially insightful comments. Jeff Davis identified many of the historic artifacts. I am grateful to Chuck Hulse for already having struggled with the archaeology of a 20th-century logging site and providing some direction for this current endeavor. John Franzen, John Davis, and Rose Moore provided confirmation that women were present in Great Lake states logging communities. John Franzen was particularly helpful in discussing the paper in its early stages. However, I would never have undertaken this paper were it not for Chester Carden and Edith Starkey whose stories of the logging days in West Virginia piqued my curiosity and generated a desire to clarify the one-sided picture of early 20th-century logging.

REFERENCES

BLACKHURST, WARREN E.
1954 *Riders of the Flood*. Vantage Press, New York.
1963 *Sawdust in Your Eyes*. McClain, Parsons, West Virginia.

BRASHLER, JANET G.
1987 An Evaluation of Dogway. Forest Service File No. 09-21-02-17. Ms. on file, Monongahela National Forest, Elkins, West Virginia.
1988 Cultural Resources at the Baldwin Mine. Ms. on file, Monongahela National Forest, Elkins, West Virginia.

CHERRY RIVER BOOM AND LUMBER COMPANY
1905– Manuscripts, Land Abstracts, and Maps on file,
1934 U.S. Department of Agriculture Forest Service, Monongahela National Forest, Elkins, West Virginia.

CLARKSON, ROY B.
1964 *Tumult on the Mountains*. McClain, Parsons, West Virginia.

CORE, EARL
1966 *Vegetation of West Virginia*. McClain, Parsons, West Virginia.

DINSMORE, REBECCA E.
1985 Archaeological Perspectives of the Lumber Industry in Northern Lower Michigan. Unpublished M.A. thesis, Department of Anthropology, Western Michigan University, Kalamazoo.

ELLER, RONALD A.
1982 *Miners, Millhands, and Mountaineers: Industrialization of the Appalachian South, 1880–1930*. University of Tennessee Press, Knoxville, Tennessee.

FRANZEN, JOHN
1984 Intra-Site Settlement Pattern at 19th and 20th Century Logging Camps in Michigan's Upper Peninsula. Paper presented at the Annual Meeting of the Society for Historical Archaeology Conference on Historical and Underwater Archaeology, Williamsburg, Virginia.

HAREVEN, TAMARA K.
1982 *Family Time and Industrial Time: The Relationship Between the Family and Work in a New England Industrial Community*. Cambridge University Press, Cambridge.

HULSE, CHARLES
1989 Archaeological Investigations at Spruce, West Virginia: A Company-Owned Railroad and Mill Community of the Late Industrial Revolution Period. *Shepherd College Cultural Resource Management Series* No. 7. Shepherdstown, West Virginia.

KARAMANSKI, THEODORE
1982 Transcript of Taped Interview with Bertha Harding. Ms. on file, Mid-American Research Center, Loyola University, Chicago, Illinois.
1985 Logging, History and the National Forests: A Case Study of Cultural Resource Management. *The Public Historian* 7(2):26–40. University of California, Berkeley.

MYER, LINDA
1979 Lumberjills. *Wisconsin Trails* 20(4):31–33.

ROHE, RANDALL
1985 Settlement Patterns of Logging Camps in the Great Lakes Region. *Journal of Cultural Geography* 6(1):79–107.
1986a Archaeology—A Key to the Great Lakes Lumber Era. *Wisconsin Archaeologist* 66(4):359–384.
1986b The Evolution of the Great Lakes Logging Camp, 1830–1930. *Journal of Forest History* 30(1):17–28.

STARKEY, EDITH
1987 I Remember Braucher. *Goldenseal* 13(2):34–39. Charleston, West Virginia.

SWANBERG, FAYE
1986 The Cleveland–Cliffs Iron Company in Munising and Autrain Townships. In *Alger County: A Centennial History, 1885–1985*, pp. 184–194. Alger County Historical Society, Munising, Michigan.

TETER, DONALD
1977 *Goin' Up Gandy: A History of the Dry Fork Region of Randolph and Tucker Counties, West Virginia*. McClain, Parsons, West Virginia.

TILLEY, LOUISE A., AND JOAN W. SCOTT
1978 *Women, Work and Family*. Holt, Rinehart and Winston, New York.

WELLS, ROBERT W.
1978 *Daylight in the Swamp!* Doubleday, New York.

JANET G. BRASHLER
DEPARTMENT OF ANTHROPOLOGY AND SOCIOLOGY
GRAND VALLEY STATE UNIVERSITY
ALLENDALE, MICHIGAN 49401

Part IV:
Commodity Production

Deborah L. Rotman
John M. Staicer

Curiosities and Conundrums: Deciphering Social Relations and the Material World at the Ben Schroeder Saddletree Factory and Residence in Madison, Indiana

ABSTRACT

As a locus of hand-craft production during the late 19th and early 20th centuries, the Ben Schroeder Saddletree Factory and Residence began as a single structure and evolved into an eclectic arrangement of industrial and domestic buildings. At first glance, the site and its residents appear to be aberrations, "exceptions to the rule," perhaps even cautionary tales in historical archaeology. Upon closer inspection, however, it does not appear that this site is remarkably different from other loci of specialty production from this era. The Schroeder family, along with the documentary and material records that are their legacy, are a lens through which to view social relations at specialty production firms and the use of the material world by factory owners, particularly during times of major economic crisis.

Introduction

The Ben Schroeder Saddletree Factory and Residence in Madison, Indiana was a locus of specialty production from 1878 to 1972 (Figure 1). The data from this unusual site were comprised of complex archaeological deposits, an extensive archival collection, an assortment of industrial and domestic structures, and the tens of thousands of objects contained within them. This site provided a unique opportunity to explore the relations between owners and workers in specialty production firms and their interaction with the material world, particularly during national-scale economic crises.

Archaeological fieldwork at this site highlighted three important issues in historical archaeology. First, industrial and other sites from this time (1878–1972) have seldom been the focus of archaeological investigations, in part because they are perceived as being too recent. Second, research of production loci in the scholarly

FIGURE 1. The Ben Schroeder Saddletree Factory, looking south. Woodworking shop is at right. Blacksmith and Assembly shops are at the left and brick residence is at the rear. (Photo by J. Boucher; courtesy of Historic American Engineering Record, IN-26.)

literature has tended to focus upon large factories and corporate communities (Dawley 1976; Beaudry and Mrozowski 1987a, 1987b; Nassaney and Abel 1993; Shackel 1996) or on technical aspects of machinery and production (Cooper et al. 1982; Allen et al. 1990; Rolando 1992). Although these have been meritorious arenas of study, social relations at specialty production sites and their material expressions of class and status have remained poorly understood. Finally, national scale economic crises (the 1870s, 1890s, and 1930s) have rarely been recognized as powerful forces in shaping the worldview of these factory owners as well as their interactions with the built environment.

The first of these issues, the relative absence of late 19th and early 20th century hand-craft industries and other sites in the archaeological literature, will likely resolve itself in due course. Schuyler (1978:1) observed that historic remains will only be perceived as artifacts and potential archaeological sites with the passage of time and a recognition of cultural differentiation. Undoubtedly, with the dawn of the 21st century, the late 1800s and the first few decades of the 1900s will seem remote, even distant from our present experiences, and, therefore, worthy of scholarly attention. The other issues, social relations at specialty manufacturing sites and the impact of economic crises on human interactions with the material world, will require researchers to seek out these aspects of the past for further exploration and intellectual discussion.

This work is the result of one such investigation of these issues. This essay brings together archaeological, historical, and architectural lines of evidence from saddletree manufacturing in Madison and the Schroeder site to explore specialty manufacturing, particularly its relationship to and how it differs from other approaches to production that have been investigated in historical archaeology. The materiality of social relations between the owners and the workers of these firms is emphasized. Finally, we investigate the multiple, national-scale economic crises from the late 19th and early 20th centuries to understand their potential impact upon uses of the material world.

Understanding Specialty Production

Capitalism has principally been understood through the study of large factories and corporations (Wallace 1978; Beaudry 1989; Nash 1989; Gordon and Malone 1994). It has been depicted as a timeless struggle between owners and workers over profits and the accumulation of wealth (Marx and Engels 1967; Paynter 1988; Wood 1999). Researchers have recognized that capitalism developed unevenly across the globe (Amin 1974; Wolf 1982; Leone 1988; Wallerstein 1997), but the temporal dimension of uneven development has remained virtually unexplored in historical archaeology. Additionally, as Wolf (1982:297) observed, "the carrier industries of the capitalist mode dominated the [world economic] system, but these rested upon variable and shifting supports that were often embedded in different modes of production." Specialty production constituted a critical part of this support. Patterson (1993:363) further noted that carefully constructed comparisons of particular historical instances of capitalist development are needed to shed light not only on unique manifestations, but also to extend our understanding to underlying processes, class and state formation, and resistance. The Schroeder Saddletree Factory, begun in 1872, engaged in hand-craft production well into the third quarter of the 20th century and was, therefore, an ideal opportunity for exploring a particular aspect of capitalist development during this time.

Sectors of specialty production during the late 19th and early 20th centuries were organized in distinct ways and experienced some technological and organizational transformations not found in mass production. As such, specialty manufacturing was defined by the methods used in production and the social relations between employers and workers, rather than simply by the scale of the operation. Indeed, some specialty firms possessed extensive factory buildings and employed large numbers of workers.

Philip Scranton (1997) in his book, *Endless Novelty: Specialty Production and American Industrialization, 1865–1925,* has a particularly useful and interesting discussion of America's developing industrial economy. He (1997:10–12) describes four broad approaches to manufacturing—custom, batch, bulk, and mass production. Custom work consists of individually crafted items made to discrete specifications for a single purchaser (turbines, single-use foundry patterns, special-order cabinetry, and tailored clothing). Batch production entails making goods in lots of varied sizes, often according to advance orders (steam engines, stationery, household furniture, and ready-to-wear-styled garments). In bulk manufacturing, quick but relatively simple technology and lower-skilled workers are used to create staple goods in large quantities (mill hardware, wrapping paper, window glass, and cigars). Finally, mass production involves elaborate technology and significant capital outlays for producing standardized goods in huge volumes (standard steel rail, newsprint, household wiring, and canned foods).

Custom and batch operations were characterized as flexible or specialty manufacturing formats in which production had to be shifted constantly to meet fluctuating demands. Bulk and mass production approaches were routinized, where manufacturing was standardized and goods were made for a relatively stable market. Custom and batch sectors produced the hardware and raw materials that made mass production possible. Although often depicted as backward and unimaginative, these firms represented 80% to 90% of America's industrial capacity during the late 19th and early 20th centuries (Scranton 1997:7).

In routinized firms, workers were deskilled (that is, trained to perform a single task in the production process) and were as interchangeable as the parts used in manufacturing. Successful custom or batch operations, however, were dependent upon their ability to hire and retain skilled workers familiar with all aspects of fabricating and assembling their product. The vitality and reputation of specialty firms rested upon the ability of skilled craftsmen to produce a variety of high quality goods and/or meet complex specifications. The emphasis on worker retention fostered a management style that was more often personalistic and paternalistic rather than bureaucratic (Scranton 1997:17–18).

The social relations and spatial organization of specialty production firms and larger industrial enterprises were dramatically different. As one example, Mrozowski (1991:90–91) observed that the corporate paternalism at the Boott Cotton Mill in Lowell, Massachusetts was expressed through the organization of the built environment and strategic use of the material world, which emphasized class differences between workers and management. The homes of mill agents were constructed to resemble the stately brownstones of Boston, while the boarding houses for mill workers were stark, utilitarian dwellings. The placement of the agents' homes between the boarding houses and the manufacturing complex further accentuated the social hierarchy since workers had to pass by the homes of their employers every day to and from work. This, in turn, allowed mill agents to "police" their work force.

Corporate paternalism, however, existed in other forms as well. Henry Disston established a specialty sawmaking firm in Philadelphia in 1840 (Scranton 1997:49). By the 1870s, the business had grown significantly and, although his factory retained its specialty production format, it became a very extensive enterprise. Disston began the process of relocating his factory to a site adjacent to the Delaware River, erecting more than 500 homes for his workers to occupy. He even created a building and loan association to assist with financing for workers who wished to purchase rather than rent their homes. Disston's calculated paternalism allowed him to retain skilled workers necessary for production and "was widely acclaimed as evidence of [his] regard for his employees" (Scranton 1997:51).

Paternalism for specialty manufacturing has been described in this way:

The proprietor was the "Old Man" and workers related to him in a watchful fraternal way. This was not the stereotypical father-to-child paternalism (more common in masters' and skilled workers' relations with women, youths, and the unskilled) but instead represented the institutionalization of customary bonds between adult sons and their graying, often wise, and obviously experienced fathers (Scranton 1997:73).

If an overseer or foreman in a specialty firm asserted tyrannical authority, craftsmen would simply pack their tool kits to seek better employment conditions elsewhere or organize labor strikes. For specialty manufacturing, thus, corporate paternalism sought to strengthen relationships between owners and workers rather than emphasize divisions. Regardless of the specific form taken within a particular context, corporate paternalism was among the methods of social control used by factory owners to assure the company's prosperity and emphasized efficiency, time discipline, and moral behavior (Gutman 1977; Leone et al. 1987; Beaudry 1989; Wurst 1991; Shackel 1993; Leone 1999).

Specialty firms were usually operated by individuals or as partnerships. In marketing, they relied on their reputations for quality and not simply price as a consideration in sales. To meet their manufacturing needs, these firms invested primarily in general-purpose technologies that could be easily altered or adjusted to variations in the goods ordered (Scranton 1997:17).

Custom and batch manufacturers were susceptible to seasonal and business-cycle slumps that often could not be bridged by production for inventory (Scranton 1997:70–72). The last quarter of the 19th century was a particularly crucial time for specialty manufacturing in America. This era witnessed "an economy that repeatedly fell into recessions, the inconstancy of an electorate that twice favored a Democratic president who menaced the tariff, the surge of labor organizing that challenged proprietors' customary authority, and the growing complexity of technical change and national marketing" (Scranton 1997:82). These circumstances created challenges for business owners engaged in custom and batch production.

Specialty manufacturers rallied at two levels. First, within individual firms, proprietors managed market uncertainties by developing methods for shop management, cost figuring, sales, and worker payment—efforts toward systematization that were distinct from processes of standardization. Second, within business sectors and production regions, manufacturers formed organizations to address politics, labor relations, technical education, information flows, and marketing (Scranton 1997:82).

These strategies had spatial consequences. For specialty manufacturers that "sought to place accommodation notes, let contracts for patterns, parts, or services, and partake of an often-replenished pool of skilled labor, there was no better location than an urban industrial district filled with firms practicing comparable specialist strategies" (Scranton 1997:18). The contacts between individuals and firms fostered relationships of trust, reciprocity, and solidarity. These social relations have been recognized as "the special atmosphere of industrial districts, a spatially embedded sociocultural asset renewed through routines of interaction" (Scranton 1997:19).

There is no single model for specialty manufacturing in postbellum America. Nonetheless, specialty manufacturing connotes a range of variation of systematized production approaches and paternalistic social relations. At present, the material and spatial expressions of the relations between employers and workers in specialty firms remains virtually unexplored.

The Materiality of Social Relations

Material displays of class and status take various forms unique to the historical circumstances and social relations that shaped them. Architectural details (Glassie 1975; Johnson 1994; Pearson and Richards 1994), the spatial organization of dwellings (Spain 1992; Barber 1994), yards and gardens (Leone 1984; Mrozowski 1991; Jenkins 1994), refined earthenwares (Miller 1980; Spencer-Wood 1987; Yentsch 1991; Wall 1994), and other objects and landscape features have been implicated as indicators of class differences. Yet, since class relations are uniquely situated and not monolithic, so too are their material and spatial manifestations.

Exciting recent analyses in historical archaeology (Wurst and Fitts 1999) stretch our understanding of class and status by examining these social relations in new ways. Wurst (1999) eloquently summarizes a strategy for understanding class by using a dialectical theory of internal relations (Ollman 1993; Harvey 1996). With this approach, it is the relation that defines the entity, so that a factory owner and his employee are defined by that relation and do not exist apart from it. Wurst (1999:9) observes that relations among people vary according to particular context and, specifically, that class relations are historically constituted, fluid, and constantly changing. Using this dynamic model, a range of material and spatial expressions of class position can be envisioned.

Class differences are also not universally emphasized. In some contexts, expressing superior social position is either unwanted or unnecessary. In the case of the Burghardts, a family who owned a specialty firm in Upper Lisle, New York, "emphasizing social mobility was not relevant since the immigrant laborers [who comprised their work force] had very little hope of ever owning their own tannery" (Wurst 1999:13).

Additionally, class, as a relational concept, has been observed as being partially performance based. Mullins (1999:27) recognized that status for African-Americans in Annapolis, Maryland (1850–1930) was expressed through genteel social performance and espoused values such as self-control and rational morality. For turn-of-the-century farmers in North Carolina, character attributes such as being "crooked," slovenly, or lazy were more important than class, occupation, or racial category (Stine 1990:49). Consequently, marking class position in some contexts was achieved through social performance rather than through material objects.

The marking of class differences as well as not marking them varies through time and space. Additionally, these displays can occur through performance as well as through the possession of specific objects and differential use of the landscape. Historical archaeologists, therefore, can expect that the material and spatial manifestations of class differences at loci of production will be equally varied. Furthermore, periods of financial crisis influence the ways in which the material world was shaped and utilized.

National Economic Crises, Worldview, and the Archaeological Record

Unstable economic conditions during the late 19th and early 20th centuries undoubtedly had an impact upon human behavior, artifact deposition, and use of the built environment. There were multiple financial crises during the 1870s, 1890s, and 1930s (Terkel 1986; Sternsher and Sealander 1990; Watkins 1993). Wolf (1982:304–305) stressed that capitalist development varied through time. These phases of acceleration and deceleration resulted in differential uses of the material world.

Recessions and depressions, however, rarely figure prominently in discussions of archaeological sites as meaningful and powerful forces central to the lived experiences of site occupants (Klein 1973; Henry 1979; Rotman 1995; Rotman and Nassaney 1997; Purser 1999). Often, these circumstances are only mentioned as part of the historical background or invoked to explain anomalies in the material record (Kelly and Kelly 1977; Carlson 1990; Thiel 1998). In some instances, these financial cycles have not been recognized as part of a larger economic context and as having a potentially significant role in shaping archaeological deposits and research results. For example, reusing glass bottles in the eastern United States during this era may have been influenced by the lean economic times (Busch 1987). Local range disputes and increased cattle rustling for ranchers in Nevada during the late 19th century may have had roots in the uncertain and difficult financial circumstances of some individuals (Schoenwetter and Hohmann 1997). Additionally, African-Americans, as a marginal economic group, were likely to have been profoundly impacted by these crises, perhaps necessitating the use of worked glass rather than razor blades as cutting edges during this time (Wilkie 1996).

The purpose of this work is not to berate scientists for gaps in their scholarship but rather to illustrate how, as a discipline, we seem to be "missing the forest for the trees" in our research of the decades surrounding the turn of the 20th century. Many historical archaeologists undoubtedly have family stories about the Great Depression—grandmothers who hung tea bags on mini-clotheslines over the kitchen sink so they could be re-used or saved even the tiniest sliver of soap so as not to be "wasteful" (Linda Rotman, pers. comm. 1999). Yet because these economic crises are part of the lived experience of grandparents and great-grandparents rather than our own, they may appear to be both too recent and too distant to be in the intellectual foreground of our discipline. Their importance for understanding archaeological sites from this era, however, is profound.

The Great Depression, as an example, affected virtually all segments of the population. By the time President Roosevelt was inaugurated in 1933, there were approximately 40 million people who did not have a regular source of income and some states had extraordinary unemployment rates (39% in Arkansas; approaching 50% in Michigan) (Kerns 1977:52; Watkins 1993:115, 194). It was a time of soup kitchens and food vouchers, tent cities and homelessness, a time of extreme poverty for the majority of Americans. For most families, available resources and energies during the Great Depression and other economic crises were focused on aspects of daily survival.

Yet historical archaeologists often model people's interaction with the material world with little regard for whether or not times were good or bad. In times of financial instability, in some sectors of society, objects that would normally have been discarded (such as tea bags and slivers of soap) were curated, saved for future use. Likewise, repairs and maintenance to structures and equipment may have been made with whatever materials were readily available rather than done "properly." It is expected that status displays would also be modified or even suspended under these unique circumstances. A dialectical understanding of the materiality of economic crises, as with specialty production and expressions of status, allows for a variety of meaningful responses to these hardships that intersect with geographical, economic, and social contexts. Keeping in mind the variability in responses to difficult financial times as well as the variation in forms of capitalist enterprise in the late 19th and early 20th centuries is crucial for understanding the rather distinctive material assemblage of the Schroeder Saddletree Factory and Residence.

FIGURE 2. A Schroeder saddletree rests on a bench in front of a Madison-made specialty machine known as a cantle disher. (Photo by J. Boucher; courtesy of Historic American Engineering Record, IN-26.)

Saddletree Production and the Schroeder Factory

The specialty production of saddletrees (the wooden skeletons upon which saddles are assembled) began in Madison, Indiana as early as 1850 (Figure 2). Eight individuals were engaged as saddletree makers and three manufactories were in operation at mid-century (U.S. Bureau of the Census 1850). The industry remained virtually static over the next decade, with modest growth in the 1860s. By 1879 and the end of the depression of the preceding decade, 13 firms were in operation and employed 120 individuals (Haddock and Brown 1879). More than 156,000 saddletrees per annum were produced in Madison shops and sold to saddle makers throughout the United States as well as South America and Cuba (*Madison Weekly Courier* 1879a, 1879b). An examination of state gazetteers revealed that Madison was the center of this industry in Indiana (Ratio Architects 1995:20). On a national level, it was one of several centers of saddletree manufacturing across the country.

John Benedict "Ben" Schroeder entered the ranks of Madison's saddletree makers when the industry was nearly at its zenith. Born in Prussia in 1847, he emigrated to the United States in 1864 and was living in Madison by October 1871 (Jefferson County 1871:Miscellaneous Record Book 1:148–149; 1909:Death Record D7, 109). The city directory dating 1872–1873 showed that he worked as a saddletree maker

in the employ of John Schram (Hellrigle and Talcott 1872:92). Ben was an apprentice in the trade for at least five years before opening his own shop in 1878 (*Madison Weekly Courier* 1878).

The location of the Schroeder factory was unusual. It was situated on a narrow strip of land between a steep limestone bluff to the west and Crooked Creek to the east (Figure 3). Ben may have chosen this lot because it was affordable for a young man starting his own business or because of its close proximity to the German section of town and other saddletree

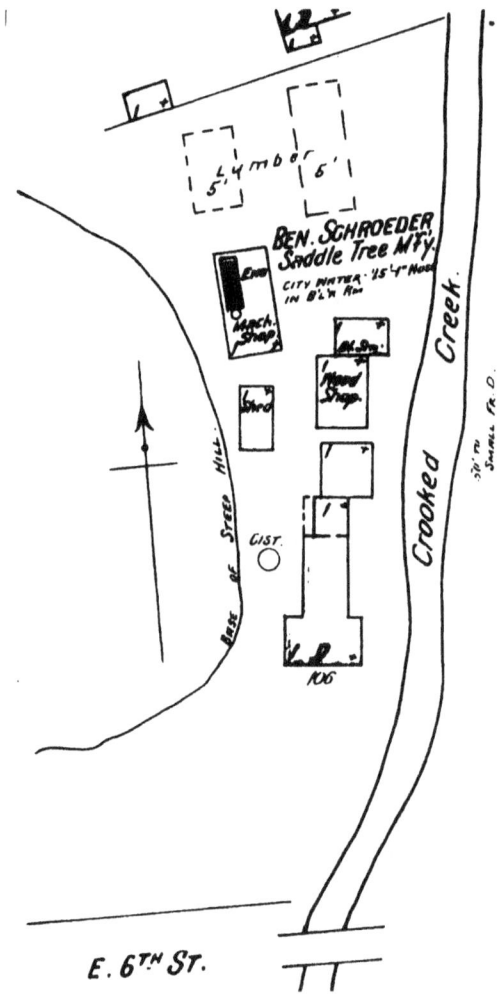

FIGURE 3. The Schroeder site in 1897. Note the location of the structures on the narrow lot between the steep limestone bluff and Crooked Creek. (1897 Sanborn Fire Insurance Map of Madison, Indiana)

makers. This rather curious decision may never be fully understood, but it had a profound impact on how he and his family used this site. Vertical expansion, for instance, was often required since horizontal space was extremely limited.

The property deed and earliest maps of Madison provided little information about the Schroeder site. The first factory structure, however, was described in an insurance policy as "one & a half story brick, shingle roof building, occupied as a saddle tree shop" (Fireman and Mechanic's Insurance 1880). There is no evidence that any other structures were present at the property in 1879.

By the following year, the Schroeder Saddletree Factory was one of only seven saddletree factories that remained in operation. The number of trees produced, their value, and the number of workers the family employed were compiled in Table 1. Despite the declining number of firms, the number of individuals employed in the trade remained constant (Ratio Architects 1995:13). The 119 people in saddletree manufacture at this time represented the single largest work force

TABLE 1

SCHROEDER SADDLETREE CO. PRODUCTION AND WORKER CENSUS, 1878–1972

Year	Trees Sold (n)	Value ($)[a]	Workers (n)	Profit/(Loss) ($)
1879/1880	9,200[b]	5,000[c]	10[d]	N/A[e]
1885	4,322	2,309	N/A	N/A
1890	10,699	4,027	N/A	N/A
1895	12,582	5,940	N/A	N/A
1900	7,322	3,638	N/A	N/A
1905	11,315[f]	5,562	5[g]	N/A
1910	11,304	9,932	5	198
1915	6,007	4,819	8	127
1920	8,697	15,400	8	(3,747)
1925	4,936	6,589	6	(330)
1930	1,798	2,763	7	(2,567)
1935	2,333	4,096	6	(1,654)
1940	1,096	2,243	7	(1,824)
1945	4,325	27,402	8	N/A
1950	9	63	0	N/A
1956[h]	632	4,096	3	N/A
1960[i]	540	2,339	3	N/A
Total	97,117	105,678		
Yearly Avg.	5,713	6,216	5.5	

[a]Dollar values rounded to the nearest whole dollar
[b]Estimated number of trees shipped by Ben Schroeder in the calendar year 1879. Estimate was compiled using numbers from Ben's account book, and shipping logs for rail and steamboat lines. The first railroad log entry is dated 12 March 1879 and the first steamboat entry is 12 January 1879.
[c]Value from the 1880 Census, Schedule 3, Manufacturers.
[d]Value from the 1880 Census, Schedule 3, Manufacturers. This is an average number of male employees older than 16 who during the census year 1 June 1879–31 May 1880. No females, children or youths were listed as being employed by Ben Schroeder or any other Madison tree makers.
[e]N/A means data were not available when the table was compiled.
[f]Production total for approximately a 10-month period as production figures for 1 January to 6 March 1905 do not exist.
[g]Worker numbers, from 1905 to 1960, represent average number of workers between January and March, inclusive, of each year. For the years 1920–1950, usually four Schroeder family members (Leo, Joe, Charlie, and Gertrude) are included in the worker figures. For the years 1950, 1956, and 1960, only Schroeder family members were listed in the payroll records. In 1950, zero were listed since there were virtually no saddletrees produced. Payroll records for 1950 have not been found.
[h]A boiler fire extensively damaged the woodworking shop on 1 July 1920.
[i]Dollar value of sales from 1920 to 1940 may include other products: cart trees, gig trees, packsaddle frames, stirrups, hames, lawn furniture, and/or clothespins. Gloves were also made from 1916 to 1919, but were tracked through a separate set of books.
[j]1955 data available for three months only, so 1956 sales data were substituted.
[k]No data were available after 1960.

among Madison's top industries (U.S. Bureau of the Census 1880). Saddletrees were identified as one of the city's six "principle exports," along with fruit, starch, flour, furniture, and lumber (*Indiana State Gazetteer* 1880:501).

Within a few years of starting his business, Ben expanded operations by constructing a frame vat house adjacent to the north elevation of the factory (Fireman and Mechanic's Insurance 1881). This structure housed large vats filled with lime solutions for storing animal hides. After being processed, the hides were tightly wrapped and hand-stitched around the finished saddletrees to bind the component parts together to create unity and add strength.

Changes to the site continued the following year when the brick factory was renovated into a residence. This alteration occurred presumably soon after Ben's marriage to Elizabeth Backus in July 1882 (Schroeder Collection n.d.; Jefferson County 1912:Marriage Applications 4(2), Mf 112). The couple had eight children over the next fifteen years (Schroeder Collection n.d.; St. Joseph's Cemetery 1962, 1965, 1972). Manufacturing activities were moved to a new structure, a "one story frame saddle tree shop about six feet north of the vat house" (Fireman and Mechanic's Insurance 1885). Choosing to renovate the factory into their home was a cost-effective, if peculiar, action that reflected the conservative manner in which the Schroeders conducted business and lived their lives.

The Schroeder factory was one of only four saddletree firms that continued to operate in Madison in 1890 (*Madison City Directory* 1890). The industry remained static during the depression that followed. By the turn of the century, only 28 saddletree craftsmen were working in the city, a decline of 76% from its zenith 20 years earlier (U.S. Bureau of the Census 1900). Despite this trend, the Schroeder factory continued its operations. Undoubtedly, the conservatism, frugality, and resourcefulness of the family enabled them to persist despite the financial crises of the previous decades. The 1897 Sanborn map shows how the property had evolved from a single factory structure to a complex of domestic and industrial buildings (Sanborn Map Company 1897:Plate 3) (Figure 3).

For the Schroeders, family and business were very closely associated. Understanding this intimate relationship was critical to interpreting the past at this site. Industrial spaces were interspersed with domestic activity areas. The family's vegetable garden was reportedly situated between the lumber piles and the blacksmith shop (Bruce Hackney, pers. comm. 1997). Wrapped saddletrees were hung in the first floor of the north addition to the house while they dried and finished product was warehoused in the residence until sold (Staicer 1994:32). The "mixing" of industrial and domestic spaces was more than a function of the limited area available on this narrow parcel of land. It illustrated that a clear separation between the home and factory did not exist.

Ben operated the saddletree factory as a sole proprietorship until his death in 1909, after which his widow and children ran the business (Jefferson County 1909:Death Records D7, 109). Leo, his oldest son, became the factory manager at age 21 (Staicer 1994:37).

Shortly after the death of their mother in 1919, the children incorporated the firm as the Ben Schroeder Saddle Tree Company (Staicer 1994:40). At that time, the family consisted of only six children—Pauline (Krumpelbeck), Leo, John, Gertrude, Joseph, and Charles. Two other sisters, Theresa and Rose, had died in 1897 and 1917, respectively.

The children comprised the Board of Directors, stockholders, and officers of the corporation. The factory and residence were deeded to the newly formed business and the children began paying the company room and board. Notes regarding the operation of the factory provided valuable insight into the family's work ethic and values:

Work hours—Start 7 o'clock, till 12 a.m. [sic] 1 o'clock to 5:30 pm. Quit work on Saturdays at 3 pm. No work, no pay. Paid extra for all overtime, regular amount. No intoxicating liquor allowed during work hours, or on premises. Anyone found intoxicated or under the influence of liquor during work hours consider himself fired. . . .

Vacation: One (1) week during busy time—a year. Paid on all Holidays Salaries same as usual. Board, lodging and washing $6.00 each per week. No bragging or boasting pretaining [sic] to business, outside of business.

Motto: Work hard when have it and work for each other and not against each other. When one is through with his work and others busy, help the others (Staicer 1994:40).

The guidelines established by the Schroeder children illustrated the communal nature of factory operation and home life. Although behavior was regulated both in and out of the shop, not all problems could be prevented. The newly formed corporation would face numerous difficulties in the years ahead.

Business was dismal during the 1920s and 1930s. Despite the prosperity of the "Roaring 20s," the automobile became increasingly affordable and widely used. Consequently, saddletree manufacturing and other horse-related industries were supplanted. This circumstance was exacerbated by the Great Depression. The Schroeders diversified their product line during the early decades of the 20th century to include canvas and leather work gloves (1916–1919), lawn furniture (late 1920s–early 1930s), stirrups and hames (1925–early 1940s), and clothespins (1935–1940) (Staicer 1994:40–51). General ledger notations indicated that there were times when the Schroeder children could not draw a salary for themselves (Schroeder Collection 1913). On 30 December 1932, Gertrude noted in the payroll ledger "There were 32 weeks of this year we received no pay" (Brady 1994:4). During this period, the family may have relied on other sources of revenue, such as the investments, rental properties, and savings accounts that they had acquired during more prosperous times.

In the midst of these economic difficulties, there was a dispute within the family. There was some disagreement regarding business operations and aspects of financial management. A mutual resolution of these matters could not be reached and ultimately John's "service [was] no more required by the Ben Schroeder Saddle Tree Co" (Schroeder Collection 1909). With John gone and Pauline living in Michigan with her husband, Gertrude, Joe, Leo, and Charlie were left to conduct factory business (Figure 4).

Sales improved briefly in the 1940s, but quickly slumped again. In 1949, only $60.58 worth of product left the factory (Schroeder Collection 1934:437–491). As business continued to

FIGURE 4. The Schroeder family, ca. 1946. From left, Gertrude, Joseph, Charles, and Leo. (Courtesy of the Schroeder Collection, Madison, IN.)

decline and the Schroeder children advanced in years, fewer alterations to the property occurred. After 1948, the home and factory entered a period of relative stasis (Sanborn Map Company 1948:Plate 10, paste over). Maintenance and repairs to existing buildings continued, but no additional construction projects were undertaken.

By the mid-1950s, Joe and Charlie were the only family members actively engaged in the business (*Madison Courier* 1955). Leo was ill and had stopped working in the factory. Gertrude took care of the bookkeeping and managed the household.

In June of 1956, Leo died of a heart attack (*Madison Courier* 1956). Joseph assumed leadership of the family and corporation (Staicer 1994:54). Gertrude died in 1962 (*Madison Courier* 1962) and Charlie followed in 1965 (*Madison Courier* 1965). Joe was left to carry on alone, until his own death in 1972 (*Madison Courier* 1972).

The Schroeder factory is not the first, nor the largest, nor the most sophisticated of saddletree manufactories. It is, however, extraordinary in that it outlasted all of its predecessors. It is the last known 19th-century saddletree factory complex in the United States and the only local manufactory to survive of an industry that was once so important to the vitality of Madison. Through the years, the Schroeder Saddle Tree Shop faced many difficulties; among them, the invention of the automobile, a devastating family dispute, and three national-scale depressions. Yet through determination, frugality, and resourcefulness, the family and business persevered.

Archaeological Investigations, Saddletree Production and the Schroeder Family

Archaeological investigation of the Schroeder site was undertaken during the 1997 and 1998 field seasons. The excavations served as field schools for students in the Department of Anthropology at Ball State University and were open to visitors from the general public. The purpose of these projects was to investigate archaeological deposits immediately threatened by preservation activities at the site and to interpret domestic and industrial utilization of the property.

Systematic shovel testing and hand-excavation were undertaken. Forty shovel tests at 5 m (16 ft.) intervals and a total of 36 m² (388 ft.²)in a combination of 1 x 1 m, 1 x 2 m, and 2 x 2 m units were excavated. Units were placed where cultural deposits were likely to be disturbed by restoration activities, including areas to be modified to improve drainage at the site or reinforce extant foundations. Areas investigated included those immediately adjacent to the house and factory buildings, the former location of a chicken coop and wood shed, and the center of the yard behind the blacksmith shop where many industrial and domestic activities took place (Figure 3). Excavation highlighted the high rate of curation of material objects by the Schroeder family (Rotman et al. 1998; Rotman 1999).

The Schroeder family interacted with the material world in an extremely conservative way, resulting in a number of curiosities and conundrums at the site. As an example, contractor bids clearly outlined that old materials were to be reused within new structures. This stipulation was adhered to for both major construction episodes as well as minor maintenance and repair activities at the site. The reuse of materials is clearly visible in the structures on the site. Many have the appearance of a patchwork quilt, with each episode of building, rebuilding, and repair represented by different colors and/or textures of wood, metal, or other materials.

Other occasions of "recycling" were also observed at the site. Saddletree patterns, for example, were made out of an assortment of cardboard products including boxes from Cap'n Crunch cereal and Blue Ribbon Malt Syrup. Parts from antiquated or obsolete machinery were scavenged for use in other factory equipment. Additionally, a damaged joint in a saw dust collection pipe in the woodworking factory was mended with a pair of men's cotton briefs.

The Schroeders apparently saved virtually everything that had potential for re-use in the home or factory. Hundreds of aluminum TV dinner trays were removed from the house. In the 1990s, during the dismantling of a badly deteriorated shed, it was discovered that the structure was literally held up by its contents. The extraordinary curation by the Schroeder family had implications for the archaeological record as well. For example, an undecorated pearlware sherd (1779–1840) (Lofstrom et al. 1982:5) was found during excavation to be in association with an amber-colored glass beer bottle fragment (with maker's mark from the Owens/Illinois Glass Company, 1956–1972) (Toulouse 1977:103). Consequently, material culture recovered via excavation could not be used for dating individual deposits. Information gleaned from the stratigraphy was, therefore, coupled with architectural and historical evidence in order to interpret the sequence and timing of cultural layers.

Archaeological investigations also revealed that flooding was a chronic problem that required constant attention. During the late 19th century, a large quantity of coal slag, ash, and clinkers was dumped around the buildings at the site,

FIGURE 5. Nearly one meter (88cm) of overburden along the east side of the bench shop, all of which was secondarily deposited material. (Photo by D. Rotman; courtesy of Archaeological Resources Management Service, Ball State University, Muncie, IN.)

particularly between structures and the adjacent creek. This activity may have helped to counteract erosion. Similarly, during the early and mid-20th century, the Schroeders piled rocks, debris, and other fill along the creek bank to stabilize the ground surface. Nearly a meter (88 cm [35 in.]) of secondarily deposited materials were excavated along the east elevation of the bench shop (Figure 5).

One of the most remarkable changes to the landscape occurred following a devastating flood in June 1903 (*The Sun* 1903). The central portion of the house was removed while the northern and southern additions remained in place. Approximately 32 inches of concrete was added to the top of the limestone foundation and the house was reassembled (Schroeder Collection 1903). The bid for this construction was one in which it specified that materials from the original house were to be re-used, if possible, in the new building. It is difficult to imagine the housekeeping nightmare that was created for Mrs. Schroeder as she contended with a house divided so literally.

Once the architectural construction was complete, the Schroeders reshaped the landscape around the house (Rotman et al. 1998; Rotman 1999). It was revealed archaeologically that three feet of dense clay and limestone was added around the foundation and sloped away from the structure to facilitate water drainage (Figure 6). This was likely no small undertaking when it was created since excavation of these deposits required the use of a mattock.

Even after the flood of 1903, overflow from Crooked Creek continued to present problems for the Schroeder family. In May 1911, a bid was secured for renovation of the bench (shown as the wood shop on the 1897 Sanborn map) and blacksmith shops (Schroeder Collection 1911). As with other projects at the property, the contractor was required to "recycle" as much of the old building material as possible. The two structures, as with the central portion of the house, were elevated 34 inches. Space was at a premium on this narrow lot and over the years, many of the renovations included vertical expansion (Sanborn Map Company 1927:Plate 10).

Multiple lines of evidence were utilized to decipher and interpret the past at the site. The archaeological data were woven together with

FIGURE 6. South profile of unit 1. The lowest layer of light colored soil contains numerous limestone inclusions and was lain down to facilitate water drainage away from the house. (Photo by D. Rotman; courtesy of Archaeological Resources Management Service, Ball State University, Muncie, IN.)

research into the primary documents (Staicer 1994) to create a narrative history of the Schroeder family and the saddletree factory as well as decipher the social relations at this site and their material expressions.

The Materiality of the Schroeder Factory

The Schroeder saddletree factory and residence provide a unique opportunity to explore a long-term domestic and industrial occupation that spans nearly a century. Historical and archaeological analyses at the site elucidate social relations at specialty manufactories from this era. Furthermore, the economic depressions experienced by the Schroeder family provide a glimpse into how these forces shaped the worldviews of factory owners, displays of class and status, and their interactions with the material world during these times of economic crises.

The Schroeder family engaged in the paternalistic social relations that characterized specialty production firms from the late 19th and early 20th centuries (Scranton 1997). Ben and his sons were actively involved in daily production at the site, along side a core of long-time employees, most of whom were also German immigrants. The management style of the Schroeders was indeed paternalistic, even familial, rather than bureaucratic. One employee was reported to have worked for the Schroeder family for 70 years (Madison Courier 1955). This kind of loyalty from their employees would have been unlikely had they been tyrants and demonstrated that the Schroeders were quite successful in retaining the skilled craftsmen so critical to specialty production.

In many ways, it was a kin-ordered mode of production—albeit, in some cases, fictive kin—rather than a capitalist mode of production that dominated social interaction and manufacturing at the saddletree factory (Wolf 1982). Peter J. Backus, Elizabeth Schroeder's brother, worked for the family between 1909 and 1915, and again in 1924 (Brady 1994:10). Additionally, the Schroeders employed multiple generations of the same families, although not always at the same time. These families included William Breidenbach and his son, Albert; Albert W. [Al] Dew and his sons, Albert F. [Bert] and Arthur J.; George Schnabel and his sons, William and Charles; and Frank J. Sheets and his son, Joseph; although not necessarily at the same time.

The role of women in production at this site is particularly interesting. In addition to his sons, Ben's daughters—Pauline, Rose, and Gertrude—also assisted with business operations by writing out documents for their father, taking care of the bookkeeping, and canvassing trees (binding the wooden components together with canvas covering) (Brady 1994:2–3). Another woman, Elizabeth "Lizzie" Koehler, began working for the Schroeders as a "coverer" in 1917 (at the age of 47). She continued to work intermittently for the family until 1947 (when she was 77 years old) and "was one of the last workers on the payroll when business declined in the late 1940s" (Brady 1994:20). Unfortunately, no comparative studies of women in specialty manufacturing firms could be identified. Therefore, the significance of the Schroeders' employment practices and the role of women at similar loci of production have remained poorly understood.

The Schroeder family further demonstrated their paternalistic management style through their commitment and loyalty to their employees. There were many years when payroll expenses exceeded company sales (Staicer 1994:40). Between 1920 and 1940, for instance, business records consistently indicated a net loss, yet the number of workers remained fairly constant (Table 1). The Schroeders may well have chosen to continue production and retain employees as long as it was feasible to do so. Diver-

sifying their product lines during the years when saddletree sales were slow may have been a strategy for keeping their long-time employees active on the payroll.

The success of the family's management style was indicated as much through the material culture of the site as it was by those objects not observed in the assemblage. For example, production failures (Nassaney and Abel 1993), which might have indicated resistance by workers to the Schroeders' corporate paternalism and defiance of company policies, were absent from the material record. It is possible, however, that production failures were not visible simply because saddletrees were made of wood and ruined components may have been burned in the boiler along with other scrap lumber.

Alcohol bottles, the presence of which have also been cited as evidence of worker resistance (Levin 1985), were another interesting phenomenon at the site. There were a number labels from beer bottles pasted on the wall around the glue pot on the north wall of the bench shop. The labels were primarily from Duesseldorfer Style Beer, although there was also one each of Hoosier Beer and Old English Ale. All of these were produced by the Indianapolis Brewing Company, which operated from 1889 to 1918 and 1933 to the 1940s (Bedenhamer and Barrows 1994:349). One additional label from Imperial Beer, a product of the John Hauck Brewing Co., was among them and also dated from about 1893 to 1920 (Wimberg 1989:53; Holian 2000).

Given the prominent display of these beer labels, it appeared that the Schroeders were aware that their employees were drinking during work hours, perhaps with their lunches. Allowing this practice may have been a way to retain skilled craftsmen on his payroll and may indicate another difference between management in specialty manufacturing settings and their counterparts in mass production.

Initially, this seemed to contradict the children's directive ca. 1919 against alcohol consumption during work hours. The change in policy, however, appeared to have been a matter of compliance with national prohibition (Bailey and Kennedy 1983:514) rather than the need for a new mechanism to control their work force.

Hand-craft production of saddletrees and other products continued at the site until the death of the last family member, Joe, in 1972. This persistence can likely be attributed to three factors. First, saddletrees are highly specialized objects with elaborately curved components and detailed specifications for each variety. Such a product was not conducive to standardization, a technique of mass production. Second, since the family and business were so closely related, the Schroeders may have perceived factory operations as more than merely a capitalist enterprise. Finally, by the time business began a consistent decline in the late 1920s with the widespread use of the automobile, the children remaining at the factory were in their late thirties and early forties. The limited production in the factory along with their investments, rental properties, and other financial reserves acquired during prosperous times may have been more than adequate to sustain the frugal and conservative lifestyle of the aging children.

Given the complexity of the Schroeder family and the material record at the site, understanding status displays was a point of particular interest. Ben was highly regarded in his community. He was known as "a gentleman of the highest type of honor and integrity" (*Madison Courier* 1909). His sons—particularly Leo, Joe, and Charlie—conducted their lives and business as their father had. Only one notable display of status was observed at the site. In May of 1897, Ben contracted John Forse to build an "addition to the Dwelling House" with "3 fancy gable pieces" (Schroeder Collection 1897) (Figures 7 and 8). The overall appearance of the new structure with its intricate carpenter's lace was one of prosperity. Passers-by on the street would no longer see a typical laborer's residence, but rather the well-proportioned, nicely trimmed brick dwelling of a successful business man (Staicer 1994:28).

Aside from the symbolic aspect of the residence façade, no other status displays were discerned. The ceramics recovered during excavation, for example, were an eclectic mix of mismatched wares, including undecorated and embossed ironstones, hand-painted whitewares, semi-porcelain decalcomania sherds, and annular-decorated yellowwares. No matched sets of dishes or expensive vessels were present in the assemblage. Additionally, no fragments of elaborate household furnishings such as chandelier shards or fancy furniture hardware were

FIGURE 7. South and west facades of the Schroeder residence (st.217.11). (Photo by John Staicer; courtesy of Historic Madison Foundation, Inc.)

observed. In sum, there was no evidence in the material culture from the site—both above ground and in subsurface deposits—which indicated that the Schroeders were asserting their social position through the objects they used.

FIGURE 8. Detail of gable screen on Schroeder Residence. (Photo by J. Boucher; courtesy of Historic American Engineering Record, IN-26.)

The Schroeders lived and worked within a tight-knit, predominantly German community. Status for them appeared to have been largely performance based. In addition to their visibility through the business, Ben and Leo served in public offices—the Madison City Council and the Madison Savings and Loan Association, respectively (Staicer 1994:34, 53). Significant investments in material displays of the family's social position were unnecessary. The Schroeders owned the means of production, were actively engaged in community affairs, and were known to be good, kind-hearted people. Their status was explicit and did not have to be asserted materially.

The three major economic crises that the Schroeders experienced during their occupation of the site may also have influenced material displays of class and status. There is clear evidence that the family curated and reused a variety of objects (saddletree patterns fashioned out of cereal boxes) and made repairs to structures and equipment in unusual ways (mended a damaged pipe with men's underwear). The extensive curation was also visible in the archaeological record at the site through the association of material objects from dramatically different time periods (pearlware and amber glass).

During lean economic times, financial and material resources would have been used conservatively and, in fact, such judicious uses may have been a status display in itself. Consequently, it would be expected that the Schroeders would not invest significantly in objects or the landscape to express their social position. Furthermore, such status displays during times of economic crises would likely have been deemed as decadent—both to the family and to the members of the community in which they lived.

The complexity of the material record at the Schroeder site made precise dating of individual strata difficult to determine. Specific periods of recession, for example, could not be identified. Cultural deposits at the site, however, consistently reflected conservative material behavior and high rates of curation. This phenomenon appeared to indicate that the family did not take improved financial times for granted and further supported our hypothesis that material displays of status were not a priority for them.

The Schroeders were not simply frugal and conservative; they were creative and resourceful. The family generated their own electricity on site to run their machinery. They developed a mechanized system whereby sawdust that collected around the bases of machines was vacuumed up and transported to a hopper near the boiler. Joe Schroeder experimented with a synthetic rawhide covering process, applying for a patent in 1946. The family even built their own specialty machines to meet production needs when existing equipment was inadequate. Clearly, business acumen, tenacity, and creativity played a significant role in the factory's longevity.

Summary

The Schroeder Saddletree Factory and Residence is an interesting case study. It offers an intriguing opportunity to explore specialty production and associated social interactions, the role of national economic crises in the formation of the archaeological record, and the intersection of these two in displays of class and status.

This investigation emphasized the need to conceptualize the relations of specialty production differently from large industrial complexes. Corporate paternalism was operationalized in both manufacturing settings to assure the company's prosperity. In specialty firms, however, paternalistic management sought to strengthen relationships between worker and employees rather than emphasize divisions. Consequently, evidence of worker resistance observed at mass production sites—such as production failures and illicit alcohol consumption—was not observed at the Schroeder factory.

Additionally, a kin-ordered mode of production appears to have operated within the capitalist mode of production at this site. All members of the family—with the exception of Mrs. Schroeder, who was busy raising eight children and running the household, and Theresa, who died as a young girl—participated in the business in some way. Uncle Peter Backus also worked for the firm, as did multiple members of the same families, many of whom were German immigrants. The Schroeders appeared to have been extremely loyal to their workers—employing them for extended periods of time (albeit occasionally intermittently), diversifying their product lines to keep craftsmen on the payroll, and occasionally paying employees before drawing salaries for themselves. Clearly, the management style of the Schroeders was indeed paternalistic, even familial, rather than bureaucratic.

The family was highly regarded for the relationships they fostered with their workers. Yet, the only material display of their high social status was the fancy woodwork on the gables of the residence. The Schroeders owned the means of production, were active members of the community, and had a reputation for being kind-hearted people. Their status was explicit and, therefore, was not asserted materially.

The three major economic crises that the Schroeders experienced during their occupation of the site may also have influenced material displays of class and status. The high rate of curation observed archaeologically and throughout the structures appeared to have been more than merely a penchant for saving things. Rather, the conservative uses of the material world—and resulting curiosities and conundrums at the site—may have been necessitated by the lean economic times and, in turn, were status displays in themselves.

The Schroeder saddletree factory and residence is a complex and fascinating place with an amazingly rich material and documentary record. It has provided intriguing glimpses into handcraft production during the late 19th and early 20th centuries, the social relations which guided human interactions, displays of class and status, and the potential impact of national scale economic crises upon uses of the material world. More research is needed, however, both at the Schroeder site and other specialty manufacturing firms in order to further understand these processes, the lived experiences of small factory owners from this era, and the workers they employed.

ACKNOWLEDGMENTS

The authors gratefully acknowledge the financial support of the Department of Interior Historic Preservation through the Indiana Department of Natural Resources, Division of Historic Preservation and Archaeology as well as Archaeological Resources Management Service (ARMS) at Ball State University and Historic Madison Inc./Historic Madison Foundation Inc. We are also indebted to a number of individuals without whom this project could not have been completed. John Galvin, President of Historic Madison Inc., and Kathleen Cooper, Administrative Assistant, provided valuable logistical and secretarial support. Troy Armstrong, David Benac, Rick Davies, Anita Downton, Julia Fabian, Rebecca Fabian, Steve Fabian, Cindy Hardesty, Rita Harlan, Jennifer Jacks, Wesley James, Brenda Jendraszkiewicz, Lilith Judd, Audrey Mancini, Jim Nicoson, Daniel Scarpino, Elizabeth M. Scott, Craig Seyboth, Adair Staicer, Shannon Staicer, Kisha Tandy, Bill Vest, and John Warner volunteered on the excavations. We are grateful to the students who participated in the archaeological field schools: Angela Bokori, Paul Butler, Karen Daubenspeck, Autumn Hazelbaker, Beth Herzog, Janet Holden, and Dolores Orich. Ken Pagel who volunteered his time to compile decades of sales figures for the factory. We appreciate his willingness and patience for undertaking this task. Employees with ARMS assisted with the laboratory processing and analysis of the materials from the projects: Mark Boatwright, Michelle Greenan, Christina Kirsch, and Ronnica Robbins. Jennifer Kirkmeyer, Rachel Mancini, Lisa McCarley, and Aaron Smith served as graduate assistants to the field schools. The professional staff at ARMS was a tremendous source of help throughout the projects. Our thanks to Don Cochran, Michael Angst, Karla Carmichael, Beth McCord, and Mitchell Zoll. A special thank you to Maureen Staicer for inviting field students and staff into her home and keeping us apprised of on-going cultural and social events in Madison. Robert Paynter, Don Cochran, Susan Goode-Null, and Tom Sproat served as intellectual support and editorial guidance. Finally, Thad Van Bueren and two additional, anonymous reviewers provided useful comments that greatly enhanced the final product.

REFERENCES

ALLEN, ROSS F., JAMES C. DAWSON, ROBERT B. GORDON, DAVID J. KILLICK, AND RICHARD W. WARD
1990 An Archaeological Survey of Bloomery Forges in the Adirondacks. *Industrial Archaeology*, 16(1):3–20.

AMIN, SAMIR
1974 *Accumulation on a World Scale: A Critique of the Theory of Underdevelopment.* Monthly Review Press, New York, NY.

BAILEY, THOMAS A., AND DAVID M. KENNEDY
1983 *The American Pageant: A History of the Republic.* D. C. Heath and Company, Lexington, MA.

BARBER, RUSSELL
1994 *Doing Historical Archaeology: Exercises Using Documentary, Oral, and Material Evidence.* Prentice Hall, Englewood Cliffs, NJ.

BEAUDRY, MARY C.
1989 The Lowell Boott Mills Complex and Its Housing: Material Expressions of Corporate Ideology. *Historical Archaeology*, 23(1):19–32.

BEAUDRY, MARY C., AND STEPHEN A. MROZOWSKI
1987a Interdisciplinary Investigations of the Boott Mills, Lowell, Massachusetts, Vol. I: Life at the Boarding Houses. North Atlantic Region, National Park Service, *Cultural Resource Management Study*, No. 18. Boston.
1987b Interdisciplinary Investigations of the Boott Mills, Lowell, Massachusetts, Vol. II: The Kirk Street Agent's House. North Atlantic Region, National Park Service, *Cultural Resource Management Study*, No. 19. Boston.

BEDENHAMER, DAVID J., AND ROBERT B. BARROWS (EDITORS)
1994 *The Encyclopedia of Indianapolis*. Indiana University Press, Bloomington.

BRADY, CAROLYN
1994 "Schroeder Saddletree Factory Workers." Ms., Schroeder Saddletree Factory, Historic Madison Inc./Historic Madison Foundation, Inc., Madison, IN.

BUSCH, JANE
1987 Second Time Around: A Look at Bottle Reuse. *Historical Archaeology*, 21(1):67–80.

CARLSON, SHAWN BONATH
1990 The Persistence of Traditional Lifeways in Central Texas. *Historical Archaeology*, 24(4):50–59.

COOPER, C. C., R. B. GORDON, AND H. V. MERRICK
1982 Archaeological Evidence of Metallurgical Innovation at the Eli Whitney Armory. *Industrial Archaeology*, 8(1):1–12.

DAWLEY, ALAN
1976 *Class and Community: The Industrial Revolution in Lynn*. Harvard University Press, Cambridge, MA.

FIREMAN AND MECHANIC'S INSURANCE COMPANY
1880 Policy No. 9807, 27 May. Fireman and Mechanic's Insurance Company, Madison, IN. Schroeder Collection.
1881 Policy No. 11298, 11 July. Fireman and Mechanic's Insurance Company, Madison, IN. Schroeder Collection.
1885 Policy No. 19420, 11 July. Fireman and Mechanic's Insurance Company, Madison, IN. Schroeder Collection.

GLASSIE, HENRY
1975 *Folk Housing in Middle Virginia*. University of Tennessee Press, Knoxville.

GORDON, ROBERT B., AND PATRICK M. MALONE
1994 *The Texture of Industry: An Archaeological View of the Industrialization of North America*. Oxford University Press, New York, NY.

GUTMAN, HERBERT G.
1977 *Work, Culture, and Society in Industrializing American*. Vintage Books, New York, NY.

HADDOCK AND BROWN
1879 *Haddock & Brown's General Business Directory of Madison, Columbus, Vevay, Ind. for 1879*. Haddock and Brown, Cincinnati, OH.

HARVEY, DAVID
1996 *Justice, Nature, and the Geography of Difference*. Blackwell Publishers, Malden MA.

HELLRIGLE AND TALCOTT
1872 *Hellrigle and Talcott's Madison Directory, 1872–1873*. Hellrigle and Talcott, Madison, IN.

HENRY, SUSAN L.
1979 Terra-Cotta Tobacco Pipes in 17th Century Maryland and Virginia: A Preliminary Study. *Historical Archaeology*, 13:14–37.

HOLIAN, TIM
2000 *Over the Barrel: The Brewing History and Beer Culture of Cincinnati, Vol. I, 1800–Prohibition*. Sudhaus Press, St. Joseph, MO.

INDIANA STATE GAZETTEER AND BUSINESS DIRECTORY
1880 *Indiana State Gazetteer and Business Directory, 1880–1881*, Vol. 1. R. L. Polk and Company, Indianapolis, IN.

JEFFERSON COUNTY
1871 Miscellaneous Records, Recorder's Office, Jefferson County, Madison, IN.
1909 Death Records, Recorder's Office, Jefferson County, Madison, IN.
1912 Marriage Records, Recorder's Office, Jefferson County, Madison, IN.

JENKINS, VIRGINIA SCOTT
1994 *The Lawn: A History of an American Obsession*. Smithsonian Institution Press, Washington DC.

JOHNSON, MATTHEW
1994 *Housing Culture: Traditional Architecture in an English Landscape*. Smithsonian Institution Press, Washington, DC.

KELLY, ROGER E., AND MARSHA C. S. KELLY
1977 Brick Bats for Archaeologists: Values of Pressed Brick Brands. *Historical Archaeology*, 11:84–90.

KERNS, JOHN
1977 *A Short History of Michigan*. Michigan History Division, Michigan Department of State, Lansing.

KLEIN, JOEL I.
1973 Models and Hypothesis Testing in Historical Archaeology. *Historical Archaeology*, 7:68–77.

LEONE, MARK
1984 Interpreting Ideology in Historical Archaeology: Using the Rules of Perspective in William Paca Garden in Annapolis, Maryland. In *Ideology, Power, and Prehistory*, D. Miller and C. Tilley, editors, pp. 25–35. Cambridge University Press, Cambridge, England.

1988   The Georgian Order as the Order of Merchant Capitalism in Annapolis, Maryland. In *The Recovery of Meaning: Historical Archaeology in the Eastern United States*, Mark P. Leone and Parker B. Potter, Jr., editors, pp. 235–262. Smithsonian Institution Press, Washington, DC.

1999   Ceramics from Annapolis, Maryland: A Measure of Time Routines and Work Discipline. In *Historical Archaeologies of Capitalism*, Mark P. Leone and Parker B. Potter, Jr., editors, pp. 195–216. Plenum Press, New York, NY.

LEONE, MARK P., PARKER B. POTTER, JR., AND PAUL A. SHACKEL

1987   Toward a Critical Archaeology. *Current Anthropology*, 28(3):283–302.

LEVIN, JED

1985   Drinking on the Job: How Effective was Capitalist Work Discipline? *American Archaeology*, 5(3):195–201.

LOFSTROM, TED, JEFFREY P. TORDOFF, AND DOUGLAS C. GEORGE

1982   A Seriation of Historic Earthenwares in the Midwest, 1780–1870. *Minnesota Archaeologist*, 41(1):3–29.

MADISON COURIER

1909   Mr. Benjamin Schroeder–The Sudden Ending of a Useful Life. *Madison Courier*, p. 4; 20 October. Madison, IN.

1955   Schroder Firm One of City's Oldest. *Madison Courier*, p. 1; 20 January. Madison, IN.

1956   Schroeder Mass Set for Tuesday at St. Mary's. *Madison Courier*, p. 8; 18 June. Madison, IN.

1962   Miss Schroeder Taken by Death at Home Here. *Madison Courier*, p. 16; 17 May. Madison, IN.

1965   C. Schroeder Dies Thursday at His Home. *Madison Courier*, p. 8; 3 April. Madison, IN.

1972   Obituary Listing. *Madison Courier*, p. 14; 27 January. Madison, IN.

MADISON CITY DIRECTORY

1890   *Madison City Directory, 1890–1891*. Matthews & Company, Madison, IN.

MADISON WEEKLY COURIER

1878   "City News" column. *Madison Weekly Courier*, p. 5; 26 June. Madison, IN.

1879a   "City News" column. *Madison Weekly Courier*, p. 5; 28 February. Madison, IN.

1879b   No title. *Madison Weekly Courier*, p. 4; 5 March. Madison, IN.

MARX, KARL, AND FRIEDRICH ENGELS

1967   *The Communist Manifesto*, reprint of 1872 edition. Penguin Books, London, England.

MILLER, GEORGE

1980   Classification and Economic Scaling of 19th Century Ceramics. *Historical Archaeology*, 14:1–40.

MROZOWSKI, STEVEN

1991   Landscapes of Inequality. In *The Archaeology of Inequality*, R. McGuire and Robert Paynter, editors, pp. 79–101. Basil Blackwell, Oxford, England.

MULLINS, PAUL

1999   Race and the Genteel Consumer: Class and African-American Consumption, 1850–1930. *Historical Archaeology*, 33(1):22–38.

NASH, JUNE

1989   *From Tank Town to High Tech: The Clash of Community and Industrial Cycles*. State University of New York Press, Albany, NY.

NASSANEY, MICHAEL, AND MARJORIE R. ABEL

1993   The Political and Social Contexts of Cutlery Production in the Connecticut Valley. *Dialectical Anthropology*, 18:247–289.

OLLMAN, BERTELL

1993   *Dialectical Investigations*. Routledge Press, New York, NY.

PATTERSON, THOMAS C.

1993   *Archaeology: The Historical Development of Civilizations*, 2nd edition. Prentice Hall, Englewood Cliffs, NJ.

PAYTNER, ROBERT

1988   Steps to an Archaeology of Capitalism. In *Recovery of Meaning: Historical Archaeology in the Eastern United States*, Mark P. Leone and Parker B. Potter, Jr., editors, pp. 407–433. Smithsonian Institution Press, Washington, DC.

PEARSON, MICHAEL PARKER, AND COLIN RICHARDS

1994   *Architecture and Order: Approaches to Social Space*. Routledge Publishing Company, London, England.

PURSER, MARGARET

1999   *Ex Occidente Lux?* An Archaeology of Later Capitalism in the 19th-Century West. In *Historical Archaeologies of Capitalism*, Mark P. Leone and Parker B. Potter, Jr., editors, pp. 115–141. Plenum Press, New York, NY.

RATIO ARCHITECTS

1995   The Ben Schroeder Saddletree Factory, Madison, Jefferson County, Indiana: Historic Structure Report. Ms., Historic Madison Foundation, Inc., Madison, IN.

ROLANDO, VICTOR R.

1992   Vermont's 18th- and 19th-Century Blast Furnace Remains. *Industrial Archaeology*, 18(1/2):61–78.

ROTMAN, DEBORAH L.

1995   Class and Gender in Southwestern Michigan: Interpreting Historical Landscapes. Master's thesis, Department of Anthropology, Western Michigan University, Kalamazoo.

1999 Continued Evaluation of Cultural Resources at the Ben Schroeder Saddletree Factory and Residence: Examining Additional Archaeological and Historical Evidence. Archaeological Resources Management Service, Ball State University, *Report of Investigations*, No. 52. Muncie, IN.

ROTMAN, DEBORAH L., RACHEL MANCINI, AND MARK BOATWRIGHT
1998 Archaeology and Preservation at the Ben Schroeder Saddletree Factory and Residence: Deciphering Nearly a Century of Domestic and Industrial Activity. Archaeological Resources Management Service, Ball State University, *Report of Investigations*, No. 49. Muncie, IN.

ROTMAN, DEBORAH L., AND MICHAEL S. NASSANEY
1997 Class, Gender, and the Built Environment: Deriving Social Relations from Cultural Landscapes in Southwest Michigan. *Historical Archaeology*, 31(2):42–62.

ST. JOSEPH'S CEMETERY
1962 Grave marker of Gertrude E. Schroeder, Madison, IN.
1965 Grave marker of Charles W. Schroeder, Madison, IN.
1972 Grave marker of Joseph A. Schroeder, Madison, IN.

SANBORN MAP COMPANY
1897 *Fire Insurance Map of Madison, Indiana.* Sanborn Map Company, New York, NY.
1927 *Fire Insurance Map of Madison, Indiana.* Sanborn Map Company, New York, NY.
1948 *Fire Insurance Map of Madison, Indiana.* Sanborn Map Company, New York, NY.

SCHOENWETTER, JAMES, AND JOHN W. HOHMANN
1997 Landuse Reconstruction at the Founding Settlement of Las Vegas, Nevada. *Historical Archaeology*, 31(4):41–58.

SCHROEDER COLLECTION
n.d. Jefferson County Birth Records, transcript. Schroeder Collection, Madison Bank and Trust, Madison, IN.
1897 Contract from John Forse, 17 May. Schroeder Collection, Madison, IN.
1903 Bid to Mr. Ben Schroeder from Peter Stephanus, 31 August. Schroeder Collection, Madison, IN.
1909 Account book, 1909–1929. Schroeder Collection, Madison, IN.
1911 Bids from Peter Stephanus, 8 May and 11 October. Schroeder Collection, Madison, IN.
1913 General Journal, March 1913–July 1920. Schroeder Collection, Madison, IN.
1934 General Journal, May 1934–December 1952. Schroeder Collection, Madison, IN.

SCHUYLER, ROBERT L.
1978 Emergence and Definition of a New Discipline. In *Historical Archaeology: A Guide to Substantive and Theoretical Contributions*, Robert L. Schuyler, editor, pp. 1–2. Baywood Publishing, Farmingdale, NY.

SCRANTON, PHILIP
1997 Endless Novelty: Specialty Production and American Industrialization, 1865–1925. Princeton University Press, Princeton, NJ.

SHACKEL, PAUL A.
1993 *Personal Discipline and Material Culture, An Archaeology of Annapolis, Maryland, 1695–1870.* University of Tennessee Press, Knoxville.
1996 *Culture Change and the New Technology: An Archaeology of the Early American Industrial Era.* Plenum Press, New York, NY.

SPAIN, DAPHNE
1992 *Gendered Spaces.* The University of North Carolina Press, Chapel Hill.

SPENCER-WOOD, SUZANNE M.
1987 *Consumer Choice in Historical Archaeology.* Plenum Publishing, New York, NY.

STAICER, JOHN
1994 A History of the Ben Schroeder Saddle Tree Company, Madison, Indiana, 1878–1972. Graduate research paper for the Cooperstown Graduate Program in History Museum Studies, State University of New York, College at Oneota, Oneota.

STERNSHER, BERNARD, AND JUDITH SEALANDER (EDITORS)
1990 *Women of Valor: The Struggle Against the Great Depression as Told in Their Own Life Stories.* Ivan R. Dee, Chicago, IL.

STINE, LINDA FRANCE
1990 Social Inequality and Turn-of-the-Century Farmsteads: Issues of Class, Status, Ethnicity, and Race. *Historical Archaeology*, 24(4):37–49.

THE SUN
1903 "Snapshots" column. *The Sun*, p. 4; 4 June. Brooksburg, IN.

TERKEL, STUDS
1986 *Hard Times: An Oral History of the Great Depression.* Pantheon Books, New York, NY.

THIEL, J. HOMER
1998 Phoenix's Hidden History: Archaeological Investigations at Blocks 72 and 73. Pueblo Grande Museum, *Anthropological Papers*, No. 26; *Center for Desert Archaeology; Anthropological Papers*, No. 7. Tucson, AZ.

TOULOUSE, JULIAN HARRISON
1977 *Fruit Jars: A Collector's Manual with Prices.* Everybody's Press, Hanover, PA.

UNITED STATES BUREAU OF THE CENSUS
1850 *Population Schedules of the Seventh Census of the United States, 1850.* United States Bureau of the Census, Washington, DC.
1880 *Products of Industry of the Tenth Census of the United States, 1880.* United States Bureau of the Census, Washington, DC.

1900 *Population Schedules of the Twelfth Census of the United States, 1900.* United States Bureau of the Census, Washington, DC.

WALL, DIANA DIZEREGA
1994 *The Archaeology of Gender: Separating the Spheres in Urban America.* Plenum Press, New York, NY.

WALLACE, ANTHONY F. C.
1978 *Rockdale: The Growth of an American Village in the Early Industrial Revolution.* Knopf Publishing, New York, NY.

WALLERSTEIN, IMMANUEL
1997 *The Capitalist World Economy: Essays by Immanuel Wallerstein.* Cambridge University Press, Cambridge, England.

WATKINS, T. H.
1993 *The Great Depression: America in the 1930s.* Little, Brown, and Company, Boston, MA.

WILKIE, LAURIE A.
1996 Glass-Knapping at a Louisiana Plantation: African-American Tools? *Historical Archaeology,* 30(4):37–49.

WIMBERG, ROBERT
1989 *Cincinnati Breweries.* Ohio Book Store, Cincinnati.

WOLF, ERIC
1982 *Europe and the People Without History.* University of California Press, Berkeley.

WOOD, ELLEN MEIKSINS
1999 *The Origins of Capitalism.* Monthly Review Press, New York, NY.

WURST, LOUANN
1991 "Employees Must Be of Moral and Temperate Habits": Rural and Urban Elite Ideologies. In *The Archaeology of Inequality,* R. McGuire and Robert Paynter, editors, pp. 125–149. Basil Blackwell, Oxford, England.
1999 Internalizing Class in Historical Archaeology. *Historical Archaeology,* 33(1):7–21.

WURST, LOUANN, AND ROBERT K. FITTS
1999 Confronting Class. *Historical Archaeology,* 33(1).

YENTSCH, ANNE
1991 The Symbolic Divisions of Pottery: Sex-Related Attributes of English and Anglo-American Pots. In *The Archaeology of Inequality,* R. McGuire and Robert Paynter, editors, pp. 192–230. Basil Blackwell, Oxford, England.

DEBORAH L. ROTMAN
CULTURAL RESOURCE ANALSTS, INC.
143 WALTON AVENUE
LEXINGTON, KY 40508

JOHN M. STAICER, DIRECTOR
SCHROEDER SADDLETREE FACTORY RESTORATION PROJECT
HISTORIC MADISON INC.
MADISON, IN 47250

Joanna Behrens

The Dynamite Factory: An Industrial Landscape in Late-Nineteenth-Century South Africa

ABSTRACT

The development of deep-level mining on the Witwatersrand, South Africa, in the mid-1880s and the concomitant increase in demands for blasting explosives led to the establishment, in 1895, of a dynamite factory at Modderfontein, northeast of Johannesburg. Staffed by laborers drawn from across the African subcontinent and professionals and artisans recruited from established European dynamite factories, the community was highly cosmopolitan in nature, a microcosm of burgeoning Johannesburg. At Modderfontein, however, corporate interpretation of this social diversity was particular. Perceptions of ethnic complexity and their appropriate jointing were seminal in the organizations and mediations of communities and are harnessed in a reading of the landscape. Although premised on European design theories, Modderfontein must be understood as a distinct colonial articulation, a specific late-19th-century interpretation of local and global historical trajectories.

Introduction

In March 1886 two gold prospectors, walking the land of a southern African farm, chanced upon an outcrop of the Main Reef Conglomerate, a banket of gold-bearing ore, arcing, virtually uninterrupted, for almost 100 miles. The world's greatest gold rush had been set in motion. Within months, the first settlement at Ferreira's Camp had burst across the high veld as thousands streamed towards this newest source of wealth. As canvas tents and reed huts gave way to corrugated iron shacks and bricked structures, the surface deposits of ore were rapidly exhausted. Diggers were forced underground, following the 30-degree tilt of the reef (Kallaway and Pearson 1986:7). Early incline-shaft technologies were replaced by pioneering deep-level techniques (Kallaway and Pearson 1986:2). By the early 1890s there was an unflagging demand for the local production of hard-rock blasting explosives. Accordingly, a manufacturing concession, or monopoly, was granted by Paul Kruger's Transvaal government to the Nobel Dynamite Trust, the directorate of a number of established factories in Europe and the Americas. The brief was simple: to produce 80,000 cases of dynamite each year (Cartwright 1964:3). A new factory *De Zuid Afrikaansche Fabrieken Voor Ontplofbare Stoffen Beperkt* (The South African Explosives Company) was floated, and in 1895 the world's largest dynamite factory was laid out at Modderfontein, 12 miles northeast of burgeoning Johannesburg (Figure 1). Continental alliances

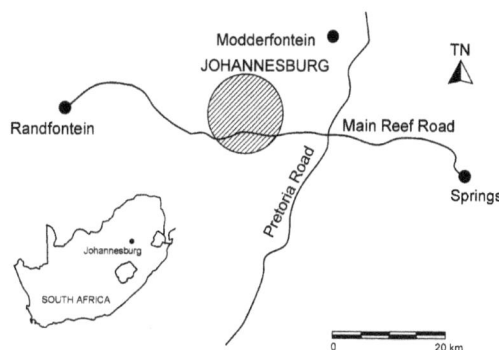

FIGURE 1. Location of Johannesburg and Modderfontein, South Africa.

coupled with a dearth of local skilled labor led to the recruitment of European artisans for the construction and operation of this enterprise. These migrants were reinforced by laborers drawn from across the African subcontinent, from as far afield as present-day Angola and Mozambique. The early Modderfontein community was thus highly cosmopolitan; its complex character was a microcosm of greater Johannesburg, where, by 1899, almost 90% of the whites were *uitlanders* or newcomers (Callinicos 1987:40). At Modderfontein, however, the interpretation and manipulation of this diversity was particular—perceptions of social complexity and their appropriate jointing were seminal in the organization of space and labor. Although premised on European design theories, the landscape must be understood as a distinct colonial articulation, a specific late-19th-century interpretation of local and global historical trajectories.

Industrial Landscapes

The late-19th century marked a period of general change in industrial landscapes (Trinder 1982:245). The acceleration of rational planning concepts (Preghill and Volkman 1993:280) was tied to a widespread perception that industry had "created slums and other sources of social unease" (Trinder 1982:247). The explicit belief that human behavior was directly influenced by the physical environment (Preghill and Volkman 1993:414) united practical, theoretical, and social rationalizations (Zukin 1991:8) as the new industries of the 1890s and 1900s sought "to be as little like those of the Industrial Revolution as possible" (Trinder 1982:249). Paternalistic concern with tempering moral degeneration and the economic wisdom of a stable, immobile workforce led philanthropists, legislators, and industrialists in a common pursuit of improved living conditions (Trinder 1982; Zukin 1991).

The provision of houses and basic amenities by employers was not a new idea with the origin of the company town or village stretching back to Arkwright's establishments at Cromford in 1771 (Marshall 1968:220; Burnett 1978:12). Throughout the 19th century, however, the efficiency and productivity of market culture was increasingly regarded as bound to the effects of place. New centralized factory towns became common as the needs of industrial capital were met by the attachment of laborers to places of employment (Zukin 1991:7). A new social regime was created in which "control of space [became as] important as the control of time in the imposition of work discipline" (Jackson 1989:82).

The rationalization of such control with ideals of moral responsibility spurred the imagination of factory and town planners encouraging local authorities, trusts, and model dwelling companies to initiate a new era in working-class housing: utopian visions of industrial endeavor set in quasi-rural environs with rustic timber-framed houses, curving streets, and gardens. Striking examples of this occurred not only in Britain (e.g., George Cadbury's Bourneville Village Trust and William Lever's Port Sunlight) but also on the continent and across the Atlantic (Preghill and Volkman 1993). As a total solution to the housing problems of an industrialized society, the approach, like the later Garden City Movement, was naive (Burnett 1978:178). Its contemporary persuasiveness, however, should not be underestimated (Gauldie 1974:194; Burnett 1978:178).

The Modderfontein Landscape

> The charming Gothic clocktower, the neat pointing of the brickwork, the elaborate wooden scrolls and eaves ... the houses ought to have had a background of snow and fir trees ... Instead they stood in the bare veld of the Transvaal (Cartwright 1964:65).

The creation of a "provincial German" village on the rolling high veld of South Africa late last century is the irony of Modderfontein. Projected as a rural idyll, in short, "the best place to live in the Transvaal" (*Rand Daily Mail* 1902), the landscape may be read from a number of different perspectives.

Like all settled landscapes, Modderfontein accommodates practical requirements and constraints. The European model of a "ruralesque" self-contained community complemented prudent safety concerns with a relative distance from population centers, and the factory areas were laid out in accordance with strict guidelines precedented at the Nobel factory at Ardeer in Scotland (Cartwright 1964:9). Managerial concerns, however, were not simply utilitarian. Extensive forestation of the area, for example, served the dual purpose of blast breaks and the explicitly stated intention to "turn the bare Transvaal into German countryside" (Köhler 1987:5). The cultural-symbolic associations of trees and their signification of social order (Davies 1988:33) were annexed. In an unfamiliar environment, trees were used as definition—to edge roads, parcel land into plots and ways, and detail lines of vision. As Philip Preghill and Nancy Volkman (1993:364) point out more generally, "the capture and management of plants and space was one way to assert control over an environment which was, at once, seen as both fruitful and hostile." Interestingly, the "political power of the picturesque" (Daniels 1988:73) was fading in England and Europe as it was appropriated in the "new worlds." There, nature was socialized, a process argued to "mask" and "naturalize" the growing inequalities of capitalism (Mrozowski 1991:95). As Stephen Mrozowski (1991:95) writes, "inequality was viewed as the outgrowth of natural processes that resulted in an ordered society; thus the ordered society of the city [or factory town], which included nature in the form of artificially maintained

green spaces was merely the product of nature itself." In pursuing this ideal "community in the countryside" (Daniels 1988:61), social boundaries could be expediently blurred.

This indulgence of lines of rank by the philosophies of corporate paternalism was, however, a delusion never seriously intended, for the Modderfontein landscape is, fundamentally, a design of control and social distinction, with boundaries of class and race fixing a feudal-like separation between laborers, artisans, and professionals. Adhering to contours, the grandiose general works manager's house was situated centrally, at a commanding point of the residential area (Figures 2, 3). Enclosed within circular approach routes were the houses of the assistant managers and in close proximity to the central factory area, the factory officials' dwellings lined High Street (Figure 2). In the low valleys, (Figure 3) artisan houses and villages situated "miles apart" (Beveridge 1919:3) stirred the rural imagination. Robert Beveridge, a young Scottish immigrant, wrote to his fiancé, "what strikes me most I think is the quietness of the place. One never sees anyone on the roads because the work peoples villages are quite far away ... in the evening ... one walks through the quiet lanes with woods on either side" (Beveridge 1919:3). Significantly, Beveridge (1919:3) notes, too, the physical circumscription of the majority of the Modderfontein labor force: "the natives are in the compound at night" (Figure 4).

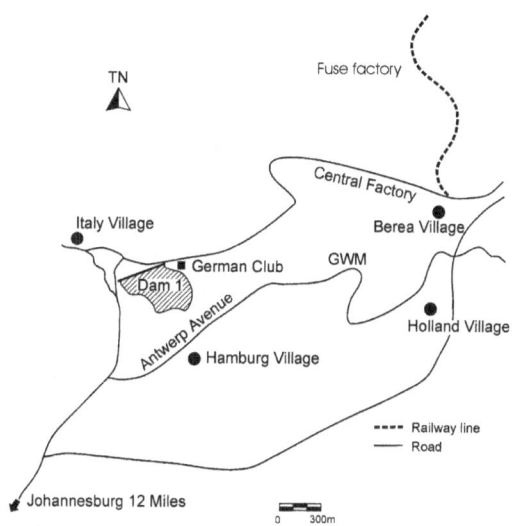

FIGURE 2. Modderfontein Factory; GWM indicates the location of the general works manager's house.

FIGURE 3. Looking out over Hamburg Village; the view from the general works manager's house, Modderfontein ca. 1897. (Courtesy of the Dynamite Company Museum Archive at Modderfontein, South Africa.)

FIGURE 4. Indian compound, Modderfontein ca. 1897. (Courtesy of the Dynamite Company Museum Archive at Modderfontein, South Africa.)

These territorial divisions were reinforced architecturally. In keeping with late-Victorian styles, the approach was eclectic, mixing neoclassicist formality and symmetry with picturesque Gothic vernacular (Sundelowitz 1987:8). The age's preoccupation with appearance is reflected in the "frontality" of gable fretwork applied to select buildings, including the houses of management and high-profile factory structures such as the laboratory (Sundelowitz 1987:5). By contrast, in the villages (Figure 3), utilitarian structures heeded the advisement recorded in company minute books that "unnecessary outlay should be avoided" (Modderfontein Company Minute Book 1899). The compounds (Figure 4) built for Native and Indian laborers were stark and inward looking, comparable to the compound architecture routine on Johannesburg gold mines, which, as Rob Turrell (1982:46) has argued, became "the most important site for the organisation and control of the labour force."

Such stratification and style, controlled paths of movement and lines of visual appropriation, are easily understood within the broad framework of industrial design and late-19th-century society. "In an age of social mobility, technological change, and uncertainty ... status had to be proclaimed and preserved" (Dennis 1984:44). In the fragile cradle of new Transvaal wealth, this was especially true.

More intriguing was the division of European artisans into apparently distinct ethnic villages: Italy, Hamburg (renamed Antwerp during World War I), Holland, and Berea (Figure 2). In fact, such divisions were not peculiar to Modderfontein and contemporary parallels in North America may be cited. For example, at Somersville, California, a coal-mining town that flourished between the 1870s and 1890s, Welsh, Irish, English, Chinese, and Mexican residents were segregated (Emerson 1987), and the Quincey Copper Mining Company in Hancock, Michigan, established a similar pattern (Day 1996). Nor were these divisions peculiarly colonial, for in English industrial cities the separation of the Irish was touted to ensure a labor force that "remained uncontaminated by incitement to revolution ... or the example of idleness" (Dennis 1984:286).

Such concerns with national exclusivity must, of course, be understood against an international backdrop where the fervor of national consciousness was tied to the mobilization of nationalism, both as a "principle of abstract solidarity" (Agnew 1989:13) and a contentious political force (Arnold 1973:1). It is somewhat ironic, therefore, that in new contexts, the sociological boundaries implied by national states were appropriated in attempts to engineer social constraint and order (Dennis 1984:285). In fact, it has been suggested that such calls upon tradition, however "invented," (Ranger 1983) are common during periods of social transition and transformation, largely because of the sense of continuity and security that such tradition conjures (Spiegel and McAllister 1991:1). At

Modderfontein, the call was to the immutability of Europe. This was marked most obviously by the parceling of land into national villages and the power of naming. Doreen Massey (1995: 186–187) has suggested that the construction of notions of the identity of place rely in some measure on resonance—points of reference inserted both materially and through words. Nations and the "places" within them suggest, at least notionally, both power and stability—a referenced physicality that posits social extensions. The Modderfontein landscape is, arguably, a reflection of this. Certainly it explains why Hamburg Village was not called "Germany," for a relatively recent union was a poor benchmark for colonial instabilities. It is likely, too, that the name "Germany" was rejected for political reasons. The strong presence of British capital in early Johannesburg and a strategic alliance with Kruger's Transvaal Republic was vital in stemming the advance of German imperialism (Rich 1983:414). Maintaining verbal distance from a colonial adversary was, minimally, an expedient doff towards the concession-granting powers of government.

Housing Ethnicity

These concerns with national identity and categorization were not confined to naming but were powerfully extended to the kinds of dwellings provided for workers. J. B. Jackson (quoted in Meinig 1979:228) has argued that in the study of landscape, "first comes the house," for it is the microcosm, the "most reliable indication of [people's] identity." At Modderfontein it is also an indication of the strength of ethnic perception.

The Victorian and Edwardian eras were the heyday of urban expansion and set the patterns for 20th-century development: the dominance of the single-family house (Power 1993:178). In England, however, by-law housing had set this pattern for all classes by the middle of the 19th century (Power 1993:175). Dr. Carus, physician to the King of Saxony, was struck in 1851 by English dwelling arrangements and the dominance of the single-family structure: "Every man's house is his castle. This is a feeling which cannot be entertained, and an expression which cannot be used in Germany or France, where ten or fifteen families often live together in the same large house" (quoted in Burnett 1978:200). Similarly, Anne Power (1993:102) notes for working-class Germany of the late-19th and early-20th centuries that "a strong and early preference for small dwellings with two to four units per house [was] common."

At Modderfontein the implementation of these precedents underlines the strength of ethnic design—the *perception* of who would come and how they would live. In the villages, back-to-back dwellings of four or six per unit and dormitory-like structures were built following an ideal European model of small, integrated communities (Power 1993:103). For English and Scottish workers, however, individual houses with street frontages and small, enclosed gardens were provided along Antwerp Avenue (Figure 2). British horror at the blockhouses is well expressed by Beveridge (1919:8):

> The stoep is tiny and the kitchen about two foot square and water is not laid on and there is no sink so water must be carried out too. The public room has one of those big cupboards in it and looks hideous though the room is big. I could hit the German who designed it ... there is no privacy about it and no through draft and no garden to speak of.

The failure of such modeling, and the point has been made for landscape studies in general, is the paradox of design and living, the fact that the element most overlooked in analyses of landscape is the people (Warren 1993:183). Yet when places are contextualized (Bender 1993) or considered in "living terms" (Meinig 1979:228), the interpretations, challenges, and redefinitions of a "dwelling perspective" (Ingold 1993:152) are prompted (Wynn 1992; Jarman 1993; Thomas 1993). At Modderfontein, such overturn of design is readily explicated in the documentation. Early photographs show apparently uncontrolled tented living arrangements (a photograph [ca. 1897] of Italy Village has a number of tents in the foreground) and moments of individual resistance and subversion of the empty spaces on maps can be cited. Company letter books record problems with squatters and David Allen (n.d.:26) narrates the tale of Old Scotch:

> an ancient Native pensioner who [took up] quarters in one of the arches of the sulphuric acid plant which had been enclosed to provide a store ... he did no work and refused to live in the compound, but he was obliged to

evacuate his quarters when the repair man turned up one Monday morning and found that during the weekend Scotch had butchered a sheep in his store and converted it into a shambles.

However embellished and inaccurate the story, it does suggest people were appropriating space outside the confines of the regulated dwelling areas. This may have been particularly true in the early years of development. In a letter dated October 1895, for example, Franz Hoenig, the general works manager, requests, "that the stables and coach house are glassed, painted, and quite finished so that we can occupy it" (Modderfontein Company Letter Book 1895:241). An April 1900 insurance claim records a galvanized iron "lean-to" structure attached to a dwelling (Modderfontein Company Letter Book 1900:771). Whatever the reasons for such accommodations, and they were surely varied, it is clear that day-to-day living had little to do with the appointed national clusters and tidy designations of design. Reality was infinitely less ordered. A staff list covering the period 1899 to 1901, for example, specifies 14 groups: Italian, German, Russian, Austrian, Dutch, Transvaal Burgher, English, Swiss, French, Danish, Cape Colonial, Swedish, Spanish, Turkish, Belgian, and Orange Free State Burgher (Behrens 1999). At least six of these, including the Russians, who were the third largest group, are not historically accounted for on the residential landscape. Indeed, their presence in popular recollections is generally forgotten. So too is the overcrowding, which at times must have been extreme. Early documentation, for example, records "66 houses for workpeople to accommodate 650" (Buckle 1900). Other sources note complaints about sanitation and generally poor living conditions (Modderfontein Company Minute Book 1899:182; *The Star* 1899; Allen n.d.:4) that, together with the reality of constant personal danger, may have contributed to the increasingly rapid employee turnover rates, which fell from an average of 553 days in prewar years (1895–1898) to 271 days during the period 1901–1903 (*Modderfontein Staff Register*).

The ultimate triumph of design then has been the creation of a symbolic landscape—as older residents of Modderfontein (including Karl Köhler [1980], grandson of the first factory workshop engineer) would have it, "a paradise lost." These accounts, selectively evacuated of historical context (Smith 1993) are reminiscent of England's 18th-century Romantic painters who found "the great furnaces and steam-belching mills" at night to be "sublime experiences" (Cosgrove 1984:232). At Modderfontein Köhler (1980) recalls how, on Saturday nights, residents of the northeastern parts of Johannesburg would make trips to Edenvale Hill by animal-drawn vehicles "to see this modern wonder where Modderfontein lay like a sparkling diamond necklace in the Modderspruit Valley."

The identities of places are bound up with the histories that are told of them, how those histories are told, and which history turns out to be dominant (Massey 1995:186). Modderfontein is a triumph of conservative endeavor, with the social boundaries of class, race, and ethnicity marking powerful and historically successful attempts to invent tradition in the style of what Massey (1994:92) has called a global construction of the local. If the reference was Europe, the contrast was Johannesburg—a city fraught with instabilities: economic booms and slumps, a rampant emerging middle class, and political disorder, exemplified in the Jameson Raid of 1895, when construction at Modderfontein was beginning, and the South African War of 1899. Olive Schreiner wrote in that year, "anything so appalling, so decayed I have never seen ... one realises in Johannesburg what the tone of society must have been in the reign of Charles II. The whole moral fibre decayed ... we are a city given over to lust ..." (quoted in Ricci 1986:58). Four years later, Emily Hobhouse wrote of "patchy streets ... big houses and semi-shanties alternately, the streets ill-kept, the shops nothing particular, not a single imposing edifice ... [emphasis in original]" (quoted in Ricci 1986:68).

At Modderfontein, concern with creating stability amid the perceived social, moral, and architectural disorder of Johannesburg resulted in a landscape of unique divisions and contrast. The interpretive challenge is to chart middle ground in understanding between collective context and individual response (Ley and Duncan 1993:329), for, as John Berger (1976:13–15) makes clear, "landscapes can be deceptive ... sometimes less a setting for the lives of its inhabitants than a curtain behind which their struggles, achievements and accidents take place." In the overbearing paternalistic landscape of 19th-century industry, this seems particularly pertinent and attempts to access the lived experience of the average resident fraught with difficulty. David Ley (1993:128) suggests it is "a problem of historical reconstruction, of retrieving the sources which would illuminate the routines and meanings of ordinary lives." It is precisely here, however, that the great strength of archaeological thinking resides: the potential to contribute history through an understanding of domestic, everyday events—social chronicles unavailable through any other avenue of enquiry (Hall 1992). At Modderfontein, a final perspective on landscape comes from this endeavor.

Archaeological Landscapes

At Modderfontein, an interest in the historically under-represented work force directed attention towards the early residential areas and associated middens as unique sources of social information. Extensive fieldwork was conducted across the property, and collections of domestic debris (ceramics, bone, glass, etc.) were recovered. These are discussed in greater detail elsewhere (Behrens 1999, 2004). Attention is focused here on work conducted at Italy Village (Figure 2), where excavations provided information on undocumented modifications of the built environment.

Constructed in 1896 and 1897, Italy Village consisted originally of eight main buildings: five residential blocks of four or six back-to-back units per structure, a community hall, and two undesignated buildings. Although the village was occupied continuously from the late 1890s to the late 1960s, individual residences were variously demolished, enlarged, and modernized as community requirements and circumstance prompted. A 1938 aerial photograph revealed that two of the residential blocks had been razed by this time, while the last standing structures were leveled in 1967. Successful growth of the primary colonizer *Mirabilis jalapa* over the earliest demolition areas prompted more detailed investigations and the in-situ foundation of one block was excavated (Behrens 1999). During this process, a concrete step, recessed below the footing horizon, was uncovered and an underground cellar, 2.9 × 2.2 m (9.5 × 7.2 ft.) in dimension, was unearthed. The cellar does

not appear on any official plans and was almost certainly built after the initial phase of construction, as it disrupts the stone foundation lines and uses building materials of a different type and superior quality to the main structure (Behrens 1999). Adjacent to this cellar, a second, smaller, brick-and-concrete-lined pit measuring 1.2 × 1.2 m (3.9 × 3.9 ft.) was uncovered. Access appears to have been via an external trapdoor, and a storage function is assumed. Taken together, these two features demonstrate an architectural competence perfectly in keeping with the village's artisan residents while pointing also to unofficial efforts to alter domestic space. Early photographs provide further evidence, showing the partial enclosure of verandahs with corrugated iron sheets. Interestingly, residents from the 1920s and 1930s have no recollections of such additions, intimating they were solutions to temporary problems (Behrens 1999). As Mary Beaudry and Stephen Mrozowski (1988:5) have pointed out in their work at the Boott Cotton Mills, research on the domestic environment and studies of working-class homes have shown that "domestic interiors were often ... areas over which workers exercised control." Plaster samples recovered from cellar excavations certainly suggest a degree of eclecticism in decoration as paint sequences of bright yellow, green and cornflower blue contrast with historical accounts of annual whitewashing (Modderfontein Company Minute Book 1899), uniform brown interiors, and the aesthetic disenchantment of Beveridge (1919:4): "the ... decoration everywhere is German and therefore hideous—pink and pale blue and gold you know the nearest approach to tawdriness that you could get ... ." At Italy Village, such additions and alterations served to enlarge the "small and cramped ... workmen's houses" (Beveridge 1919:4) and provided personal spaces beyond the paternalism of company-controlled dwellings. Karl Köhler (1980) recalls that entrances to cellars were often hidden with carpets and flowerpots, a disguise that was probably imperative given the sometimes-intrusive nature of management. As Allen (n.d.:53) recounts: William Cullen, the general works manager between 1901 and 1915, "took a great interest in the welfare of the workers and made frequent visits to the villages driving a high dog cart and inspecting gardens and praising or admonishing housewives."

Less tangible than built and brightly painted walls, a second, more equivocal act of social construction at Modderfontein is postulated in a material culture of leisure and invention, and hinges on an interweaving of turn-of-the-century attitudes towards recreation and photographic convention. Although a dream of the Enlightenment had been "to liberate time from the necessity of work and to force the physical world to meet consumer needs" (Cross 1993:17), political economists from the 18th century onwards were disquieted by the notion that improved material circumstances might negatively impact the willingness of laborers to work (Cross 1993:17; Jordan 2003:18). The assumption, as Gary Cross (1993:17) points out, was that "the motivation to work declined with higher wages [and that] the demand for leisure would increase with the meeting of basic needs." Left unchecked, the demand for leisure was, therefore, limitless, while the desire for goods was finite (Cross 1993:16). Although the 20th-century culture of "work and spend" (Cross 1993:16) was to prove the waywardness of such ideas, their currency in an age of ever-expanding industrialization, capital investment and mass mobilization, and control of large and diverse workforces was significant (Tagg 1988:62). At early Modderfontein, the pronounced heterogeneity of labor certainly attentioned managerial anxieties and explains, at least in part, an early policy to pay the man (or nationality) rather than the job: "Italians were prepared to work for 10 or 12 pounds per month while Germans and Scots, accustomed to a higher standard of living, expected at least 18–20 pounds per month" (Allen n.d.:3). Implicit in the philosophy of the day was the idea that leisure, as a by product of material prosperity, was best managed by elites rather than democratized. Thus, as early accounts suggest, free time was far from abundant: "Artisans seem to have worked seven days per week and up to ten hours per day as a matter of course" (Allen n.d.:3). "Annual holidays were not known until trades union [sic] was introduced ... tradesmen worked every Saturday afternoon and Sundays" (Fredricks n.d.:15,47). Official holidays, when they could not be avoided, were marked by extraordinary efforts at control:

There was great doings at the Dynamite Factory during the Christmas Holidays, when the factory was closed

.... A general committee representing both officials and employees was appointed to deal with the whole of the festivities ... a perfect round of amusements were provided ... on Christmas Eve a large Christmas tree and treat for the children ... on Christmas Day a service was held in the morning ... in the afternoon a Kafir dance took place in front of the Manager's house before a large crowd of spectators, in which about four hundred Natives took part, each tribe dancing separately and in its own peculiar way ... on Friday a picnic ... on Saturday sports were held at the Casino grounds, and an interesting and exciting programme of events was successfully carried out, the items including egg and spoon races, three-legged races, sack races, donkey races, bolster and bar, tilting the bucket, tug-of-war, and Kafir obstacle races, the latter causing great amusement to the large crowd of spectators present .... For the evening a concert and dance took place at the new Employees' Club, which was nicely decorated (Leader 1902).

The daily alternative for a working class unmanaged and unoccupied is absurdly conjectured by J. Fredricks (n.d.:15): "as there was no recreation for the worker it was just as well that they worked every weekend, otherwise they might have run wild all over the country. These tradesmen were accustomed to having jolly weekends at home, overseas, drinking, dancing and singing with picnics etc." However preposterous, the inherence of such attitudes carried some historical persuasion. That this was both understood and disregarded is suggested by the construction of village leisure facilities away from the officially sanctioned Workman's Club. Significantly, at Hamburg Village, the club and skittle alley was built some 500 meters beyond the village limits, outside the paternal gaze of the general works manager's house (Figures 2, 3). For others, the hire of a four-wheel trolley to picnic at an isolated dam was a frequent choosing—the importance of the event marked by the performance of photography (Sontag 1977:28). Although rare, photographs of workers picnicking away from the central factory areas (Figure 5) occur as loose inclusions in the photographic archive at Modderfontein (at least one was donated to the museum from a private collection) and are remarkably different from the official album collections, which exemplify the late-19th-century photographic traditions of controlled observation and record keeping (Tagg 1988:5,60; Schwartz and Ryan 2003:2). These official photographs consist chiefly of construction activities and factory views and

FIGURE 5. Picnicking at Modderfontein ca. 1897. (Courtesy of the Dynamite Company Museum Archive at Modderfontein, South Africa.)

include many of the conventional themes of the time: panoramic views, big trees, and modes of transportation (Jensen 1978:1). While a number of these photographs do show people, they are formal workplace pictures, focused on task and surroundings, rather than personal action (Stanley 1991:62–64) and typically carry labels that serve as prompts and guides to viewing: "packing dynamite," "unloading boxwood," and so forth. In contrast, the recorded excursions (Figure 5) lack written explanations. The oral narratives that once must have accompanied such records are now missing. What is intriguing then is the familiarity of such shots, the subjectity and style that seems historically distant yet immediately recognizable. This is the great mystery and the powerful allure of domestic photography. Democratized in the late 1880s with the advent of Kodak, it is the camera, Marianne Hirsch (1999:xvi) argues, that has become "the family's primary instrument of self-knowledge and self-representation—the primary means by which family memory is perpetuated, by which the family's story is told." The conundrum is that the very commonality of these images makes them difficult to interpret. They shore convention in static and circumscribed ways (Hirsch 1999:xvi), and, yet, like the ubiquitous sherds of ceramic and flakes of bone that litter historical sites, these images demand attention. Viewed as artifacts in their own right, these domestic snapshots should, as Patricia Holland (1991:10) argues for more contemporary situations, be understood as "part of the material with which we make sense of our wider world

... part of the detailed and concrete existence with which we gain some control over our surroundings and negotiate with the particularity of our circumstances." In historical contexts, this social latency carries added significance. As Susan Lalvani (1996:69) has shown, photography is entangled at the juncture of colonialism and industrialism—a complicity that photographic histories have not always recognized. More recent scholarship (Chambers 2003; Schwartz and Ryan 2003) has proven, however, that family photography can serve as witness to the colonization process. In this way the conventions of domestic photography become refocused (Hirsch 1999:xvi) and are revealed as densely ideological (Watney 1991:27).

At a practical level, this view is set off from the more customary use of photographs as marginal inclusions within a text "in order to provide a 'feel' or 'atmosphere' for the period, to identify a person or place, or simply because of their outright quaintness" (Hayes et al. 1998:2). Realigning the visual with the textual moves photographs away from the idea that they function as a kind of uncomplicated biography (Burgin 1982:2) or a neutral record of reality (Eco 1982:33). Instead, photography is understood as a "process of signification" (Burgin 1982:2), as an act deeply embedded in the social relations and "discursive system" of which all images are a part (Tagg 1988:4). For Joan Schwartz and James Ryan (2003:6) it is self-evident that photographs "play a central role in constituting and sustaining both individual and collective notions of landscape and identity." Importantly, the process of discerning meaning retrospectively is lodged in a close attention to history and context (Schwartz and Ryan 2003:6). At Modderfontein, therefore, the photographic archive cannot profitably be considered in isolation but must be linked to the wider social landscape. In this way, the leisure photographs of early Modderfontein artisans become a kind of foil to corporate design, a discrete moment of action in a larger lived experience. Of course, these private photographs have their own internal context, which is an important analytical starting place. To begin, they are couched in the photographic conventions of the day and reflect the use of photography as an important component of leisure in which conventional (but not everyday) domesticity was stressed. The scene outdoors and connected with outdoor rites (Williams 1991:187) was, moreover, a distinctively working-class code. As Susan Sontag (1977:61) writes, "laborers ... are usually photographed in a setting (often outdoors) which locates them, which speaks for them—as if they could not be assumed to have the kinds of separate identities normally achieved in the middle and upper classes."

Although clearly lodged within these visual traditions, such a circumscribed viewing of the leisure snapshots is, arguably, amiss. Importantly, the perspective is one that fails to register the irony and ambiguity inherent in such carefully executed moments of record or the resonances sparked by the context of debated leisure. As Rob Shields (1991:96) argues, "leisure is not simply the presence of what is pleasurable ... nor is it the absence of work ... Leisure is what is *licenced* as legitimate pleasure within an economy of coded micropowers [emphasis in original]." To picnic beyond the paternal eye and to frame the act materially speaks intriguingly of the social agency of labor. Daniel Miller (1995:1) suggests that what marks the mass consumer is the consciousness that one is living through objects and images not of one's own creation. The power of photographs, consciously posed and considered, is a tantalizing counter to more general productive forfeiture. This notion of deep-seated posturing is well explicated in an excerpt from the reminiscences of Fredricks (n.d.:60) (Figure 6):

> When a batch of foreigners arrived from overseas they were photographed at the weekends. The party consisted of a white man with six to ten natives. The man with a large hunter's helmet, shirt sleeves rolled up with open neck shirt, leggings and top boots. He stood in the centre of the group with natives on either side. The natives were armed with knobkieries and in a half sitting position, the end natives standing with assegais and shields. The man was armed with a strapped revolver hanging on one side. At the bottom of the photo it read, "In the Wilds of Africa" and "The natives of the veld." The photos were sent to relatives and friends.

For European artisans, displaced from the familiarity of home, a spirit of foreign adventure and "empire-building" was coupled with an acute awareness of new social opportunity in a time and place that permitted redefinitions of class and occupational status (Ranger 1983).

At least initially, it is tempting to suggest that the urge to convey these expanded horizons to an audience far removed was of primary significance. As Holland (1991:4) and Schwartz and Ryan (2003:6) suggest, one of the great powers of pictures is to contain the tension between ideal and lived experiences, and it is surely no small irony that as photography facilitated and encoded new celebrations of family, increased social and geographical mobility among Europeans accelerated disintegration (Chambers 2003:101). For Modderfontein workers then the photographs may have served not simply as a kind of personal and collective invention but also as a way to stake ownership in a new and still-unfamiliar land. In Sontag's (1977:9) words, "photographs ... help people take possession of space in which they are insecure." In blurring the distinction between the real and the imagined, these photographs draw attention to the overlaps between history and fantasy (Holland 1991:9; Schwartz and Ryan 2003:6). They provide a way to look behind and beyond the "curtained" landscape of corporate design, to glimpse the social actors at ease.

Conclusion

January 2nd 1896
Mr Hall
Modderfontein

Dear Sir

It has come to our knowledge that you have taken the liberty of taking from the tree some peaches that were not even ripe —

FIGURE 6. "In the Wilds of Africa," Modderfontein ca. 1895. (Courtesy of the Dynamite Company Museum Archive at Modderfontein, South Africa.)

We draw your attention to the fact that it is strictly forbidden to pluck any fruit growing on the grounds of the Company without a special permission from the Manager: this will be enforced by a fine.

Yours faithfully

Franz Hoenig
(Modderfontein Company Letter Book 1896:388)

Matthew Johnson (1999:34) has recently suggested that as historical archaeologists "we walk in a uniquely dangerous space of the human past, a space between often very powerful 'master narratives' of cultural and social identity and much smaller, stranger, and potentially more subversive narratives of archaeological material." At Modderfontein, this walk has worn a path between the planned spaces and architecture of 19th-century factory modeling and the lived reality of those who labored and leisured across these geographical contours. Following the ideas of David Landon, (1999: 90) it is suggested that the view realized is not one of simple "domination" and "resistance" but one of an active and purposeful negotiation that was, at different times and places, more or less successful. As Mr Hall's stolen peaches eloquently demonstrate, corporate efforts at control were never all-encompassing. It seems, however, equally important to note that our ability to recover these processes of social debate is also constrained. Archaeological residues are differentiated, favoring certain spaces and groups across the landscape and through time. While efforts have been made to tease meaning from multiple contexts, in the end they have slipped unevenly between the grandeur of European design precedents and small, fleeting moments of domestic pleasure. The lesson to be drawn is perhaps one of method. To access a fuller meaning of landscape, it seems that historical archaeologists must be willing to seek out and adopt methodologies unconstrained by traditional procedures and categories of analysis. To pursue Berger's metaphor, the piece just written should be read as simply a scene with other scenes and acts that both precede and follow this particular analytical performance. There are important voices missing from this Modderfontein script, most noticeably those of middle management and the non-European laborers who constituted the majority of the Dynamite Company's workforce. The challenge for the future is to find new ways to walk backstage.

ACKNOWLEDGMENTS

My sincere thanks to Simon Hall, who developed the Modderfontein archaeological project and encouraged my involvement. Martin Hall first suggested a landscape study, and I have benefited from discussions with Mandy Esterhuysen, Antonia Malan, Kim Sales, and Alex Schoeman. Work at the Dynamite Factory was funded by African Explosives and Chemical Industries, and I owe particular thanks to Boet Coetzee, Johnny Johnson, Suzette Kotze, Len Larsen, and Barry Sewell. Many of Modderfontein's older residents have given hours of their time to talk about the past, and I thank Mr Karl Köhler for his wisdom. Mark Cassell has been a gracious and patient editor, and I thank Simon Hall, Chris DeCorse, contributors to this volume, and anonymous reviewers for valuable comments on earlier drafts of this paper. All errors, of course, remain my own. I thank Sue Goode-Null and Rebecca Snyder for help with figures 1 and 2 and François Richard for proofreading at the last minute. All photographs are reproduced courtesy of the Dynamite Company Museum Archive at Modderfontein. Additional funding was provided by the University of the Witwatersrand and the Centre for Science Development, South Africa. The opinions expressed in this paper and the conclusions reached are those of the author and are not necessarily to be attributed to either institution.

REFERENCES

AGNEW, JOHN A.
1989 The Devaluation of Place in Social Science. In *The Power of Place*, John A. Agnew and James S. Duncan, editors, pp. 9–29. Unwin Hyman. London, UK.

ALLEN, DAVID F.
n.d. History of Modderfontein 1896–1953. Manuscript, The Dynamite Company Museum Archive, Johannesburg, South Africa.

ARNOLD, DAVID J.
1973 *Britain, Europe, and the World 1871–1971*. Edward Arnold Publishers, London, UK.

BEAUDRY, MARY C., AND STEPHEN MROZOWSKI
1988 The Archaeology of Work and Home Life in Lowell Massachusetts. An Interdisciplinary Study of the Boott Cotton Mills Corporation. *The Journal of the Society for Industrial Archaeology*, 14(2):1–22.

BEHRENS, JOANNA
1999 Ethnic Identity and Process: European Migrant Workers at Modderfontein Dynamite Factory. Master's thesis, Department of Archaeology, University of the Witwatersrand, South Africa.
2004 Navigating the Liminal. An Archaeological Perspective on South African Industrialisation. In *African Historical Archaeologies*, Paul Lane and Andrew Reid, editors, in press. Plenum Press, New York, NY.

Joanna Behrens

BENDER, BARBARA (EDITOR)
1993 *Landscape, Politics, and Perspective*. Berg, Providence, RI.

BERGER, JOHN
1976 *A Fortunate Man*. Writers and Readers, London, UK.

BEVERIDGE, ROBERT
1919 Personal correspondence, typed copies of originals held by Beveridge's son, The Dynamite Company Museum Archive, Johannesburg, South Africa.

BUCKLE, CAPTAIN [NO FIRST NAME]
1900 Report to the Transvaal Concessions Commission. South African National Archives, source AMPT PUBS, Volume 177, 19, Pretoria.

BURGIN, VICTOR
1982 Introduction. In *Thinking Photography*, Victor Burgin, editor, pp. 1–14. Macmillan, Hampshire, UK.

BURNETT, JOHN
1978 *A Social History of Housing* 1815–1970. David and Charles, Newton Abbot, UK.

CALLINICOS, LULI
1987 *Working Life 1886–1940*. Ravan Press, Johannesburg, South Africa.

CARTWRIGHT, ALAN P.
1964 *The Dynamite Company*. Hortors Printers, Johannesburg, South Africa.

CHAMBERS, DEBORAH
2003 Family as Place: Family Photograph Albums and the Domestication of Public and Private Space. In *Picturing Place: Photography and the Geographical Imagination*, Joan M. Schwartz and James R. Ryan, editors, pp. 96–114. I.B. Tauris, London, UK.

COSGROVE, DENIS E.
1984 *Social Formation and Symbolic Landscape*. Croom Helm, London, UK.

CROSS, GARY S.
1993 *Time and Money: The Making of Consumer Culture*. Routledge, London, UK.

DANIELS, STEPHEN
1988 The Political Iconography of Woodland in Later Georgian England. In *The Iconography of Landscape*, Denis E. Cosgrove and Stephen Daniels, editors, pp. 43–82. Cambridge University Press, Cambridge, UK.

DAVIES, DOUGLAS
1988 The Evocative Symbolism of Trees. In *The Iconography of Landscape*, Denis E. Cosgrove and Stephen Daniels, editors, pp. 32–42. Cambridge University Press, Cambridge, UK.

DAY, GRANT L.
1996 Finding Ethnicity in the Material Record. Paper presented at the 29th Conference on Historical and Underwater Archaeology, Cincinnati, OH.

DENNIS, RICHARD
1984 *English Industrial Cities of the Nineteenth Century: A Social Geography*. Cambridge University Press, Cambridge, UK.

ECO, UMBERTO
1982 Critique of the Image. In *Thinking Photography*, Victor Burgin, editor, pp. 32–38. Macmillan, Hampshire, UK.

EMERSON, MATTHEW C.
1987 *The Archaeology of a California Mining Town*, Somersville, CA.

FREDRICKS, J.
n.d. Reminiscences of an Old Timer. Manuscript, The Dynamite Company Museum Archive, Johannesburg, South Africa.

GAULDIE, ENID
1974 *Cruel Habitations: A History of Working-Class Housing 1780–1918*. George Allen & Unwin, London, UK.

HALL, MARTIN
1992 Small Things and the Mobile, Conflictual Fusion of Power, Fear, and Desire. In *The Art and Mystery of Historical Archaeology. Essays in Honor of James Deetz*, Anne E. Yentsch and Mary C. Beaudry, editors, pp. 373–400. CRC Press, Boca Raton, FL.

HAYES, PATRICIA, JEREMY SILVESTER, AND WOLFRAM HARTMANN
1998 Photography, History, and Memory. In *The Colonizing Camera: Photographs in the Making of Namibian History*, Wolfram Hartman, Jeremy Silvester, and Patricia Hayes, editors, pp. 2–9. University of Cape Town Press, Cape Town, South Africa.

HIRSCH, MARIANNE
1999 Introduction: Familial Looking. In *The Familial Gaze*, Marianne Hirsch, editor, pp. xi–xxv. University Press of New England, Hanover, NH.

HOLLAND, PATRICIA
1991 History, Memory, and the Family Album. In *Family Snaps: The Meaning of Domestic Photography*, Jo Spence and Patricia Holland, editors, pp. 1–14. Virago, London, UK.

INGOLD, TIM
1993 The Temporality of the Landscape. *World Archaeology*, 25(2):152–174.

JACKSON, PETER
1989 *Maps of Meaning*. Unwin Hyman, London, UK.

JARMAN, NEIL
1993 Intersecting Belfast. In *Landscape, Politics, and Perspective*, Barbara Bender, editor, pp. 107–138. Berg, Providence, RI.

JENSEN, OLIVER
1978 *America's Yesterdays*. American Heritage Publishing Company, New York, NY.

JOHNSON, MATTHEW H.
1999 Rethinking Historical Archaeology. In *Historical Archaeology: Back from the Edge*, Pedro Paulo A. Funari, Martin Hall, and Sian Jones, editors, pp. 23–36. Routledge, London, UK.

JORDAN, SARAH
2003 *The Anxieties of Idleness*. Bucknell University Press, London, UK.

KALLAWAY, PETER, AND PATRICK PEARSON
1986 *Johannesburg: Images and Continuities*. Ravan Press, Johannesburg, South Africa.

KÖHLER, KARL
1980 Some Aspects of Electricity at Modderfontein. Manuscript, The Dynamite Company Museum Archive, Johannesburg, South Africa.
1987 Some Aspects of the History of the Frakenwald Area of Modderfontein Factory. Manuscript, The Dynamite Company Museum Archive, Johannesburg, South Africa.

LALVANI, SUREN
1996 *Photography, Vision, and the Production of Modern Bodies*. State University of New York Press, Albany.

LANDON, DAVID B.
1999 Interpreting Social Organization at Industrial Sites: An Example from the Ohio Trap Rock Mine. *Northeast Historical Archaeology*, 28:89–103.

LEADER
1902 No title. *Leader*, 31 December 1902. Johannesburg, South Africa.

LEY, DAVID
1993 Co-operative Housing as a Moral Landscape: Re-Examining the Postmodern City. In *Place/Culture/Representation*, James S. Duncan and David Ley, editors, pp. 128–148. Routledge, London, UK.

LEY, DAVID, AND JAMES S. DUNCAN
1993 Epilogue. In *Place/Culture/Representation*, James S. Duncan and David Ley, editors, pp. 329–334. Routledge, London, UK.

MARSHALL, J. D.
1968 Colonisation as a Factor in the Planting of Towns in North-West England. In *The Study of Urban History*, Harold J. Dyos, editor, pp. 215–230. Edward Arnold, London, UK.

MASSEY, DOREEN
1994 *Space, Place, and Gender*. Polity Press, London, UK.
1995 Places and Their Pasts. *History Workshop Journal*, 39(Spring):182–192.

MEINIG, DONALD W. (EDITOR)
1979 *The Interpretation of Ordinary Landscapes*. Oxford University Press, Oxford, UK.

MILLER, DANIEL
1995 Anthropology, Modernity, and Consumption. In *Worlds Apart: Modernity through the Prism of the Local*, Daniel Miller, editor, pp. 1–22. Routledge, London, UK.

MODDERFONTEIN COMPANY LETTER BOOKS
1895–1900 *De Zuid Afrikaansche Fabrieken Voor Ontplofbare Stoffen Beperkt* (The South African Explosives Company), Letter Books, Nos. 2, 4, and 6, The Dynamite Company Museum Archive, Johannesburg, South Africa.

MODDERFONTEIN COMPANY MINUTE BOOKS
1899 *De Zuid Afrikaansche Fabrieken Voor Ontplofbare Stoffen Beperkt* (The South African Explosives Company), Minute Book, Number 3, The Dynamite Company Museum Archive, Johannesburg, South Africa.

MODDERFONTEIN STAFF REGISTER
1895 *Modderfontein Staff Register*, 1895–1904, The Dynamite Company Museum Archive, Johannesburg, South Africa.

MROZOWSKI, STEPHEN
1991 Landscapes of Inequality. In *The Archaeology of Inequality*, Randall H. McGuire and Robert Paynter, editors, pp. 79–101. Basil Blackwell, Oxford, UK.

POWER, ANNE
1993 *Hovels to Highrise. State Housing in Europe since 1850*. Routledge, London, UK.

PREGHILL, PHILIP, AND NANCY VOLKMAN
1993 *Landscapes in History: Design and Planning in the Western Tradition*. Van Nostrand Reinhold, New York, NY.

RAND DAILY MAIL
1902 No title. *Rand Daily Mail*, 23 September 1902. Johannesburg, South Africa.

RANGER, TERENCE O.
1983 The Invention of Tradition in Colonial Africa. In *The Invention of Tradition*, Eric J. Hobsbawn and Terence O. Ranger, editors, pp. 211–262. Cambridge University Press, Cambridge, UK.

RICCI, DIGBY
1986 *Reef of Time: Johannesburg in Writing*. Credo Press, Johannesburg, South Africa.

RICH, PAUL
1983 Milnerism and a Ripping Yarn: Transvaal Land Settlement and John Buchan's Novel "Prester John" 1901–1910. In *Town and Countryside in the Transvaal: Capitalist Penetration and Popular Response*, Belinda Bozzoli, editor, pp. 412–433. Ravan Press, Johannesburg, South Africa.

SCHWARTZ, JOAN M., AND JAMES R. RYAN
2003 Introduction: Photography and the Geographical Imagination. In *Picturing Place: Photography and the Geographical Imagination*, Joan M. Schwartz and James R. Ryan, editors, pp. 1–18. I.B. Tauris, London, UK.

SHIELDS, ROB
1991 *Places on the Margin: Alternative Geographies of Modernity*. Routledge, London, UK.

SMITH, JONATHAN
1993 The Lie That Binds: Destabilizing the Text of Landscape. In *Place/Culture/Representation*, James S. Duncan and David Ley, editors, pp. 78–92. Routledge, London, UK.

SONTAG, SUSAN
1977 *On Photography*. Penguin, London, UK.

SPIEGEL, ANDREW D., AND PATRICK A. MCALLISTER (EDITORS)
1991 *Tradition and Transition in Southern Africa*. Witwatersrand University Press, Johannesburg, South Africa.

STANLEY, JO
1991 Well, Who'd Want an Old Picture of Me at Work? In *Family Snaps: The Meaning of Domestic Photography*, Jo Spence and Patricia Holland, editors, pp. 60–71. Virago, London, UK.

THE STAR
1899 No title. *The Star*, March 1899. Johannesburg, South Africa.

SUNDELOWITZ, SELWYN
1987 The Modderfontein Civic Centre. An Opportunity for Cultural Continuity and Embellishment. Architecture thesis, Department of Architecture, University of Pretoria, South Africa.

TAGG, JOHN
1988 *The Burden of Representation: Essays on Photographs and Histories*. University of Massachusetts Press, Amherst, MA.

THOMAS, JULIAN
1993 The Politics of Vision and the Archaeologies of Landscape. In *Landscape, Politics, and Perspective*, Barbara Bender, editor, pp. 19–48. Berg, Providence, RI.

TRINDER, BARRIE
1982 *The Making of the Industrial Landscape*. J.M. Dent & Sons, London, UK.

TURRELL, ROB
1982 Kimberley: Labour and Compounds, 1871–1888. In *Industrialisation and Social Change in South Africa*, Shula Marks and Richard Rathbone, editors, pp. 45–76. Longman, New York, NY.

WARREN, STACY
1993 This Heaven Gives Me Migraines. In *Place/Culture/Representation*, James S. Duncan and David Ley, editors, pp. 173–186. Routledge, London, UK.

WATNEY, SIMON
1991 Ordinary Boys. In *Family Snaps: The Meaning of Domestic Photography*, Jo Spence and Patricia Holland, editors, pp. 26–43. Virago, London, UK.

WILLIAMS, VAL
1991 Carefully Creating an Idyll: Vanessa Bell and Snapshot Photography. In *Family Snaps: The Meaning of Domestic Photography*, Jo Spence and Patricia Holland, editors, pp. 180–198. Virago, London, UK.

WYNN, GRAEME
1992 Ideology, Identity, Landscape, and Society in the Lower Colonies of British North America, 1840–1860. In *Ideology and Landscape in Historical Perspective*, Alan R. H. Baker and Gideon Biger, editors, pp. 197–229. Cambridge University Press, Cambridge, UK.

ZUKIN, SHARON
1991 *Landscapes of Power: From Detroit to Disney World*. University of California Press, Berkeley, CA.

JOANNA BEHRENS
SCHOOL OF GEOGRAPHY, ARCHAEOLOGY, AND ENVIRONMENTAL STUDIES
UNIVERSITY OF THE WITWATERSRAND
P.O. WITS
JOHANNESBURG 2050 SOUTH AFRICA

Bradford Botwick
Debra A. McClane

Landscapes of Resistance: A View of the Nineteenth-Century Chesapeake Bay Oyster Fishery

ABSTRACT

The introduction of industrialized harvesting techniques to the Chesapeake Bay oyster fishery in the 19th century was resisted by communities of oyster tongers who represented traditional fishing methods. Maryland oyster tongers contested the advancement of industrial harvesting through various means. Important to this opposition was the development of an occupational identity that promoted traditional values and fishing practices and rejected wage labor. Natural and cultural landscapes of the working and domestic spheres helped shape and reproduce this occupational identity in part by placing constraints on aspects of the lifeways of oyster tonging communities. Ultimately, these landscapes became emblems of the distinctive life and economic choices of oyster tongers.

Introduction

During the second half of the 19th century, industrialization brought new technologies, capital, and labor organization to the Chesapeake Bay oyster fishery. The newer practices, represented by the oyster dredging industry, contrasted with hand tonging, a small-scale, owner-operated venture that represented traditional oyster harvesting practices. Faced with competition, Maryland oyster tongers resisted the domination of the fishery by dredgers. Central to this opposition was the development and maintenance of an occupational identity among oyster tongers whose value system appears to have rejected the wage labor economy of the dredging industry. The natural and cultural landscapes associated with the work and domestic settings of the oyster fishery helped to shape and reinforce this communal identity.

Aspects of landscape that helped define the social boundaries of oyster tonging are emphasized. To provide a framework for interpreting landscape, the context of the 19th-century Maryland oyster fishery and the basis of the oyster tongers' occupational identity is outlined. Next, the landscapes associated with the oyster fishery are described. Finally, to highlight the distinct cultural environments associated with the two harvesting techniques and illustrate how landscape helped shape the identity of oyster tongers, comparisons are made between a specific tonging community and one that participated in the dredging industry.

Historic Context

The time period between circa 1860 and 1920 saw expansion of the Chesapeake Bay oyster fishery and the introduction of industrialized harvesting, with consequent social and economic changes. Although oystering had been a regular occupation in the region since at least the 18th century, intensive commercial exploitation of oysters began in earnest around the time of the American Civil War (1861–1865) (Brewington 1956:171). Forces contributing to the growth of the oyster fishery at this time included the depletion of northeastern oyster beds; a depressed agricultural economy in the Chesapeake region that led farmers to turn to fishing; a national demand for seafood; and legislation that prohibited nonnative Marylanders from harvesting and exporting oysters, thereby encouraging participation and investment by natives. In addition, development of improved packing technology and infrastructure, such as the extension of rail lines to port towns, enabled more intensive harvesting and processing (Bayliff 1971:294; Wennersten 1978:81; Sharrer 1988). Combined, these influences led to a boom period that peaked at 15 million bushels in 1884–1885 (Sharrer 1988:5). By the 1890s overfishing, poor conservation, pollution, disease, and siltation contributed to declines in the productivity of the oyster beds (Bureau of Statistics and Information of Maryland 1911:262; Alford 1973). A resurgence of agriculture in the region may have also contributed to smaller oyster harvests as residents abandoned fishing to concentrate on farming (Sharrer 1988:10).

An important development in the history of the Chesapeake Bay oyster boom was the introduction of dredging, a harvesting technique that contrasted with traditional practices and that represented not only a technological dividing line but also a social and economic boundary. Dredging introduced industrial techniques for harvesting and processing the resource, as well as for organizing labor, capital, and technology. Opposition to these innovations became a basis of tongers' occupational identity. Important differences in the two harvesting techniques are summarized below.

Oyster Tonging:
A Traditional Technique

Shaft tonging, named for the implement used to collect oysters, was the traditional technique. Tongs were used for oystering in the region as early as 1700 and remained the dominant harvesting method through the 19th and 20th centuries (Witty and Johnson 1988:115–116). Shaft tongs consisted of a pair of hinged poles with basket-like metal rakes at their ends (Figure 1). Working from a small boat, tongers lowered the rakes to the oyster bed, scraping a load of oysters into each basket by opening and closing the shafts. Shaft tonging was physically demanding; a load of oysters could weigh as much as 70 pounds, and the oysterman hauled it in pulling the tongs up, hand over hand, and then swinging the full tong head into the boat (Witty and Johnston 1988:115). The oyster season spanned the months between autumn and spring. Typical workdays lasted from before dawn to nearly dark and were spent alternately tonging, culling the smaller oysters and other debris from the saleable catch, and delivering the harvest to packing houses or buy boats (large vessels that anchored at the oyster bars to purchase the catch directly from the tongers).

Hand tonging involved skilled or artisan-like qualities that contrasted with the requirements of dredging. While tonging demanded physical strength and stamina, it also required knowledge and intuition about the resource. Oyster tongers had to know where to find the most productive oyster beds and had to understand daily and annual natural or cultural influences that could affect the beds' locations and productivity. Reportedly, skilled tongers could also distinguish between oysters and rocks or other debris through feel (Lang 1961:35,39). These insights were often manifested as a sense that had to be gained through experience rather than as an objective set of rules (Carey 1988:30).

Capital and labor organization in the tonging trade also differed from that of the dredging industry. Tonging required relatively small capital outlays and had low maintenance costs. Boats used for tonging included canoes, skiffs, or other small vessels that could be rigged with one or two sails and typically were not decked (Ingersoll 1882; Brewington 1956:66; Wennersten 1978:84; Witty and Johnson 1988:175). The inexpensive and simple equipment used for tonging required relatively infrequent and less costly maintenance and repair (Witty and Johnson 1988:116). Tonging also had relatively

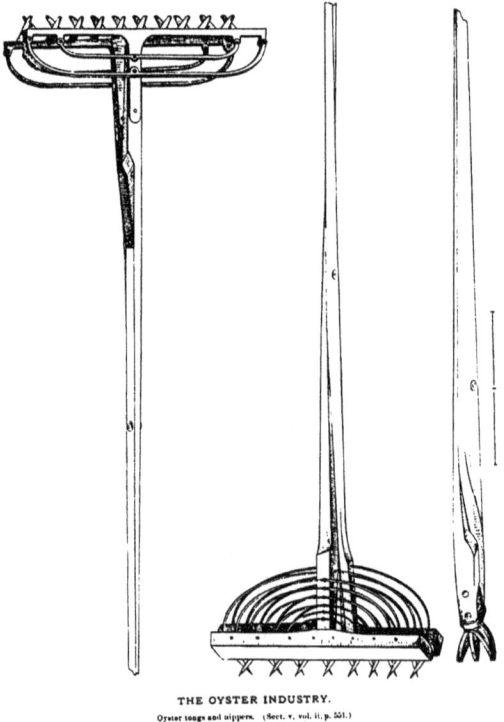

THE OYSTER INDUSTRY.
Oyster tongs and nippers. (Sect. v, vol. ii, p. 551.)

FIGURE 1. Oyster tongs. (Courtesy of the National Oceanic and Atmospheric Administration/Department of Commerce [1887].)

low labor costs, if any; it was usually conducted by an individual or pair of men in partnership, from small sailing vessels that the oyster tonger owned along with all his tackle. Finally, tongers made their own arrangements for marketing their catch and controlled all profits.

Oyster Dredging: An Industrial Pursuit

Although first used in the region as early as 1820, dredging became prominent in Maryland waters after the Civil War. Named for the large metal-framed scoops used for harvesting, dredges were dragged across the oyster bars by large vessels and when full, crewmen reeled them in with one- or two-handled windlasses

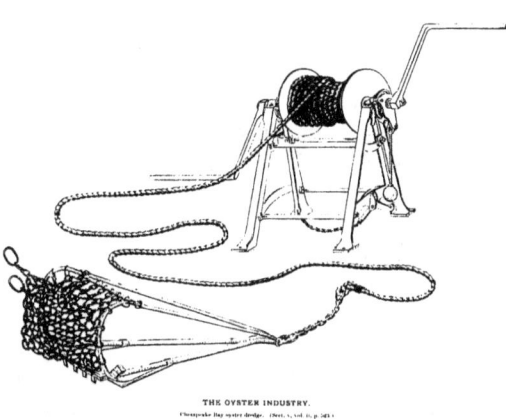

THE OYSTER INDUSTRY.
Chesapeake Bay oyster dredge. (Sect. 1, vol. ii, p. 543.)

FIGURE 2. Oyster dredge. (Courtesy of the National Oceanic and Atmospheric Administration/Department of Commerce [1887].)

(Figure 2) (Witty and Johnson 1988:126–129). Dredge boats normally operated two dredges simultaneously, each handled by two to four men. Dredge boat crews spent grueling winter days hauling in the wet, muddy catch, dumping it on the deck, and sorting through it (Wennersten 1981:35). Marketing the catch differed from tonging in that most dredge boats were owned and operated by oyster packinghouses located in Chesapeake Bay cities such as Baltimore, Crisfield, and Cambridge. At the end of a voyage, dredge boats unloaded at the docks of their parent packinghouses.

A dredging operation, including sailing of the boat (steam-powered vessels were prohibited) and performing the harvesting process, required an average crew size of about eight men (Ingersoll 1882:160; Goode 1887:[2] 550). Unlike tongers, these men were not necessarily professional fishermen. Moreover, they were wage laborers with no stake in the fishing operation. Dredge boat captains (frequently paid employees themselves) or labor contractors hired crews and were evidently willing to take anyone physically able to perform the work. Early on, African Americans often filled crew positions aboard dredge boats, but they began refusing to sign on due to the onerousness of the work. Regional labor agents then drew upon destitute individuals and newly arrived German and Irish immigrants (Wennersten 1978:86, 1981:56–58; Santopietro 1986:240). Ultimately, dredge boat crews were composed of men from lower socio-economic classes, those unable to find other work or those, like convicts, for whom dredging might be a preferable alternative.

While dredge boat crews filled largely unskilled positions, dredge boat captains were professional fishermen and managers. Dredge boat captains had to perform effectively as fishermen, sailors, and personnel managers, and for this responsibility they often received cash bonuses or profit shares on top of their salaries (Santopietro 1986:240).

The capital necessary to outfit a dredging operation was beyond the means of hand tongers. The boats had to be large and powerful enough to pull a dredge across the oyster bars while under sail. Vessels of 5 to 75 tons, such as bugeyes, pungies, and skipjacks, were used for this task (Ingersoll 1882:161; Chapelle 1935:257; Brewington 1956:63–64; Wennersten 1981:99–100; Kiener 1989). The dredges, winches, provisions, crew salaries, and other necessities also required a larger capital outlay than tonging. Consequently, the dredging industry was run mostly by partnerships that controlled one or more aspects of oyster harvesting, packing, and sales.

The preceding sketch of the oyster dredging industry highlights important differences between it and hand tonging. Where tonging was a small-scale, owner-operated affair, the organization and running of dredging followed an industrial model. Dredging required larger capital outlays than tonging, and used crews of unskilled wage laborers working under the management of dredge boat captains who often were also employees of the boat owners rather than owners themselves. Finally, the harvesting of the resource sometimes comprised only part of a larger enterprise that combined under a single-ownership concern the extraction, processing, and distribution of the final product.

Tonger's Response to Dredging

Like many 19th-century artisan and craft-based workers, Maryland oyster tongers did not view industrialization as a positive development. Specific responses to dredging varied. Some Maryland oystermen entered the dredging industry as laborers or possibly dredge boat captains; some entered partnerships as dredge boat owners; others rejected the dredging industry altogether and fought against its domination of the oyster fishery.

Legislation comprised one means of opposition. Ostensibly designed to conserve natural oyster resources, legislation in fact sought to impede competition from nonresident concerns and to protect Maryland oystermen from "technological unemployment" (Alford 1975:236; Sharrer 1988:9). As early as 1820, Maryland law banned dredging in response to the arrival of New England dredge boats, which took their catch away to northern markets, thus depriving locals of any gain from the fishery. Additional laws intended to protect native oystermen prohibited the export of oysters out of the region by nonresidents. This legislation led New Englanders to settle in Baltimore and establish processing and distribution facilities there.

Prohibitions on dredging held until 1854 when Somerset County removed restrictions on the technique. The ban was lifted altogether by an 1865 statewide law that permitted dredging between September 1 and June 1 but only in the state's public waters, which were generally too deep for tonging. County waters (up to 300 yards out from the low water mark) were reserved for tongers. Although the law opened a door to dredging, it forbade the use of steam-powered vessels or equipment, probably to hinder efficiency, and thus sustained overall policies of hobbling industrial harvesting techniques. Other laws shortened the length of the dredging

season and increased the legal size of oysters (Bayliff 1971:295; Santopietro 1986; Sharrer 1988:9). As noted, a number of the laws that restricted dredging protected tongers' livelihoods. The fact that tongers could push favorable legislation suggests that they possessed considerable political clout, which John Alford (1975:235) attributes to the overrepresentation of oyster-producing counties in the state legislature.

In addition to instigating legislation, Maryland tongers engaged in actual combat against dredgers as well as against Virginia oystermen. Tension arose from transgressions by dredge boats into harvesting areas reserved for tonging. Fights with Virginia fishermen stemmed from disputes over the location of the state line and which side had rights to the oyster beds along it. Dredging was not restricted in Virginia, and dredgers based there routinely poached Maryland oyster beds, sometimes meeting armed opposition by the natives. John Wennersten (1981) has labeled the violence associated with these conflicts the "Oyster Wars of the Chesapeake." Acrimony and antagonism lasted through the second half of the 19th century to the 1910s, peaking in intensity between 1883 and 1894 (Wennersten 1978:91). While dramatic, fighting was not unusual in commercial fisheries during this period; turn-of-the-century battles between gillnet and fish trap users in the northwest salmon fishery required intercession by Washington and Oregon National Guard units (Smith 1977:224). Violence was a frequent component of labor conflict during this era, and Maryland oystermen were not unique in their response to competition, changing labor conditions, and the industrialization of their trade.

Opposition to the new technologies and labor relationships of the dredging industry also helped create and reinforce an occupational identity among oyster-tonging communities. Milton Cantor (1979:15) notes that workers form communal identities on the basis of shared interests, which are also viewed as being different and opposed to others.

Responses to changing working conditions may include greater group coherence (Gilje 1995) and an emphasis by the group on traditional values and behaviors as well as the idealization of craft (Cantor 1979:6,8, 12; Faler 1979).

Resistance to dredging necessitated collective action, which, in turn, required some form of communal identity. Hand tongers developed an occupational identity based on their working conditions of tonging and rejection of the industrial disciplines related to dredging. This identity also emphasized a commitment to traditional harvesting practices. As discussed below, elements of the natural and cultural landscapes of the region helped to shape this identity.

Identity, Community, and Culture

Oyster tonging appears to have given rise to identities, communities, and cultures based on occupation in portions of the Eastern Shore of Chesapeake Bay. To clarify how these concepts interrelate and how they gave rise to an occupational community or subculture among oyster tongers, basic definitions and assumptions must be presented. For this analysis, relatively straightforward definitions of identity, community, and culture are used. The concept of identity is defined here as the set of behavioral or personal characteristics by which an individual is recognizable as a member of a group. This idea should be distinguished from concepts of personal or individual identity.

Definitions of community tend to emphasize both geographical proximity and shared interests (Robertson 1981). For this analysis, two concepts of community are considered. The first consists of the social groups with shared values, interests, objectives, and experiences that are not necessarily living together and might be termed a "community of interests." The second definition refers to groups of people living in relative proximity and could be referred to as "residential communities." For this analysis, the first type of community refers to oyster fishermen who participate in specific versions of the fishery and who view themselves as a distinct group linked by their interest in maintaining traditional work practices. Presumably, operators of the oyster dredging industry had their own interests with respect to the fishery and viewed themselves as a separate community from tongers. The residential community refers to people living together in specific locations but who might not possess the same interests and thus could belong to different communities of interest.

Basic definitions of culture refer to it as the totality of socially transmitted (nonbiological) behavior patterns, acts, beliefs, institutions, and all other products of human work and thought. The concept of culture also delineates the rules, norms, and customs of a particular society. These characteristics are unique to a society and distinguish it from other societies. Moreover, culture is learned, internalized, and transmitted to successive generations. Subcultures are groups that share many elements of a larger culture but also possess their own distinctive customs, values, norms, and lifestyles (Thompson and Hickey 1999).

Identity, community, and culture interrelate at different levels. Identity can be a product of the process of socialization to a particular community (whether one defined by shared interests or a residential group) and/or culture. An individual develops an identity as a member of a group through processes of socialization that teach the appropriate behavior, conduct, expectations, and other characteristics of the group. A community or culture can have a collective identity manifested as distinctive qualities that distinguish it from other communities or cultures. Of course these concepts are mutable and not fixed over time and space. These simplified definitions provide a context for examining developments in the Chesapeake Bay oyster fishery.

Changes in the oyster fishery during the second half of the 19th century gave rise to communities of interest with distinct identities composed of oyster tongers. As noted, hand tonging and its associated practices had developed before this time. However, friction with, and opposition to, the oyster dredging industry helped certain ideologies emerge that emphasized the maintenance of traditional work practices. These ideologies also placed a higher value on labor independence than on economic security, among other things. In turn, these ideologies and practices became a basis for communities of interest. The attitudes, values, practices, and lifestyles of the oyster tonging groups also appear to have become normalized to form a subculture. As discussed in a later section, this culture with its attendant ideologies had distinctive material expressions that could be seen in the natural and cultural landscapes of the region.

Work formed the basis for the emergence of oyster tonging communities and culture. It is therefore useful to examine these communities,

Oyster Tongers as an Occupational Community

Occupational communities or subcultures develop among some workers. Herbert Applebaum (1981) defines occupational communities as groups of people working in the same trade, craft, or occupation whose shared experiences and way of life form a basis of a distinct culture. Members of this culture can be expected to share ideas and beliefs and to engage in similar behavior. Further, an occupational community represents a particular relationship between work and nonwork life in that members of the community are affected by their work in such a way that their leisure time is permeated by work relationships and their associated value systems. In such situations, work can become the dominant force in people's lives, shaping their attitudes, beliefs, and actions at work and toward life in general (Thompson and Hickey 1999:515). Applebaum notes that this situation more often applies to craftsmen because they tend to lack separate work and leisure spheres, so their work spills over into their nonwork interests, social activities, ideas, and values (Applebaum 1981:100–101). The occupational identity of fishermen, and by extension Chesapeake Bay oyster tongers, is based on the shared type of work, the common experiences, specialized skills and knowledge, location of work, and the physical and economic risks involved. Identity is imparted to fishermen through the process of entering the trade and becoming a member of the group, and identity is reinforced through constant participation in the work (Kaplan 1987:491; Lloyd and Mullen 1990:11).

Chesapeake Bay oyster tongers shared a number of experiences that encouraged the development of an identity based on work. They possessed similar skills and knowledge; they worked together in the same locations using the same types of equipment; and they marketed their harvests through the same outlets. These circumstances would have helped foster a sense of shared identity. Furthermore, 19th-century legislative activity indicates that they possessed shared goals and could act together toward achieving them. In addition, oystermen chose to participate in the trade on their own terms (i.e., by avoiding wage labor). This inclination probably arose from and reinforced particular values and attitudes about work, further solidifying their cohesiveness as an occupational group.

Ideologies associated with the occupational subculture would have permeated into the domestic sphere of oyster tongers to family members who did not directly participate in oystering. In other commercial fisheries, wives develop a sense of identification with the trade through various activities not related to fishing. They are often knowledgeable about their husbands' occupation and frequently feel a commitment to the fishery. Further, they view domestic activities as contributing to their husbands' work by providing emotional and physical support (Thompson et al. 1983; Dixon et al. 1984; Davis 1986:135,138, 1988:217, 1993:458; Lloyd and Mullen 1990:11; Thiessen et al. 1992). Routine aspects of daily life take on meaning that can underscore the distinctiveness of fishing families. For example, the preparation of characteristically large meals for their husbands helps shape the identities of fishermens' wives (Lloyd and Mullen 1990). In addition, adjustments to daily and seasonal routines convey to family members an affinity to their husbands/fathers' occupation. These kinds of activities in the domestic sphere ultimately create and reinforce the identification that family members have with the occupation. It is reasonable to conclude that being raised and living in communities based on oyster tonging would engender among the families of oyster tongers a commitment to hand tonging as well as the same attitudes towards wage labor and resistance to it. Thus, the occupational subculture associated with the oyster-tonging fishery can be said to have included not only the fishermen but also their families. The subculture encompassed both residential communities of oyster tongers living in relatively separate locations from other social groups and the communities of interest made up of numbers of these residential groups. Growing up in these communities socialized members to their behaviors, beliefs, norms, and material life.

That 19th-century oyster tongers were perceived as a distinct social group is suggested by contemporary descriptions of them.

Accounts contrast the oystermen with "thrifty, intelligent, and industrious" Maryland Eastern Shore farmers (Wilson 1876). Ernest Ingersoll, in his 1882 study of the oyster industry, and George Goode, who paraphrased Ingersoll in his 1887 congressional report on the fisheries of the United States, characterized tongers as "indolent and improvident." Ingersoll polled Eastern Shore county clerks about the character of oyster tongers. Responses described the "moral and social condition" of tongers as "poor," "of a low order," and "in morals ... equal to any body of men similarly situated," while "a large majority [are] reckless and improvident" (Ingersoll 1882:162).

While these contemporary descriptions are biased by the dominant ideologies of 19th-century society and describe what was viewed as aberrant behavior, they also suggest the outlook and economic objectives of tongers. Hence, conduct that 19th-century observers call lazy and imprudent may have been a reflection of different cultural values. Oyster tongers appear to have favored autonomy in their work over material gain and financial security. Ethnographic accounts of modern fishing communities in the region (Ellis 1986; Forrest 1988) suggest that watermen do not view fishing as lucrative and that they realize one's economic and social circumstances could be improved by changing occupation. Nevertheless, contemporary fishers often opt to remain in the fishing trade despite lower economic prospects, rejecting regular hourly and daily participation in other jobs as confining (Ellis 1986). Nineteenth-century oyster tongers may have made similar tradeoffs. For instance, oystermen could enhance their economic position by working as dredge boat captains (Dize 1990); dredge captains earned an annual average of $2,000 during the 1880s compared to the tonger's average of $225 per season (Santopietro 1986:236). Less skilled fishers might have become crewmen aboard dredge boats, thus at least achieving a regular income. Yet, many tongers appear to have rejected these options, choosing to work when necessary or when they wanted to rather than working for others or maintaining strict regular hours. At the same time, they fought to restrict dredging and preserve their economic viability as small-scale owner operators. In return for the lower financial returns of these practices, tongers maintained control of their work schedules, oversight of production and marketing, and kept all profits.

Tongers seem to have entered the wage labor economy only seasonally as agricultural laborers, crew aboard freight carriers, or at other jobs. They could and did avoid doing so, however, by engaging in various activities during the year to make ends meet, such as other types of fishing, gardening, husbandry, and market hunting (Botwick and McClane 1998). That these kinds of activities may have been preferred to seasonal labor is suggested by John Forrest's (1988) study of a modern North Carolina fishing community. Here, folklore indicated that watermen admire the ability to hustle a living through whatever means were available while not giving up fishing as their primary occupation.

Landscape as Social Boundary in the Chesapeake Oyster Fishery

Landscapes helped shape and maintain the ideologies of oyster tongers by reinforcing their occupational identity. Principally, landscapes helped draw the boundaries between who was and was not a tonger and by extension became an assertion of opposition to industrialization. The natural and cultural, as well as working and residential environments could operate this way.

With respect to the working world of oystering, differences in the physical locations of dredging and tonging structured the working environments of the two fisheries oppositely and helped define the corresponding occupational groups. As noted, dredging was supposed to take place only in state waters while tongers usually had sole rights to county waters, extending up to 300 yards out from the low water mark (Bayliff 1971; Santopietro 1986; Sharrer 1988) and normally including rivers, tidal guts, straights, and inlets. Thus, in contrast to dredging, which took place in open water, tonging was conducted near shore in relatively sheltered locations. It should be noted that although tonging involved only one or two men working on a boat, it was not conducted in isolation; historic illustrations and photographs depict tongers working in groups, with clusters of boats being focused on individual oyster bars (Figure 3). This type of environment permitted communication, camaraderie, and other socialization necessary to produce an occupational identity.

More striking elements of the tongers' landscape are found in their domestic and residential communities. Bloodsworth Island, located in southern Maryland on the Chesapeake's Eastern Shore comprises an example of the landscapes associated with oyster tonging communities. Historic and archaeological research of this community provided a basis for inferences about the occupational identity of oyster tongers and their communities. The natural and cultural landscape of Bloodsworth Island can be contrasted to neighboring Holland Island whose residents participated in the dredging industry.

Oyster Tonging Landscapes: Bloodsworth Island

Bloodsworth Island currently consists of several hundred acres of marshland lying just over a mile from the nearest mainland point and encompassing only a few habitable high spots. Deeds show the island came under private ownership by 1672. Settlement up to this point, if any, appears to have been sparse. By the mid-19th century only two structures are known to have been present. During the 1870s about a dozen families occupied the island, representing its densest overall population. Island residents began moving to the mainland around the turn of the 20th century, the last residents leaving in 1918. Afterwards the island was utilized primarily as a crabbing and hunting station (Botwick and McClane 1998:39,42).

Historic maps document the development and extent of settlement on Bloodsworth Island. An 1843 plat shows the entire island under the ownership of Robert Bloodsworth and depicts settled portions of the island exclusively at its northeastern margin where two houses are shown. A notation on the plat indicates that only about 30 acres of the island are habitable, the rest (6880 ac.) being marsh. Further, the habitable land was prone to flooding at high tide, suggesting that by the 1840s the island already represented marginal real estate (Dorchester County Circuit Court 1843).

When the island's population reached its peak in the 1870s, however, settlement had

FIGURE 3. The working environment of oyster tongers. Tonging is taking place from the small sail canoes. The large vessel to the right is a buy boat (Scribner & Co. 1877).

expanded to all habitable locations, consisting of a few dispersed low ridges and rises within the marshes. Similar patterns of land use are noted on adjacent islands where apparently any piece of habitable land contained an isolated homestead. On all of these islands, settlement remained sparse, and no concentrations are noted anywhere on any island except Holland Island, which is discussed below (Figure 4) (Lake et al. 1877). This settlement pattern lasted until the island's final abandonment (Figures 5 and 6) (Maryland Shellfish Commission 1910).

Tax records, wills, and deeds indicate that most of the families occupying Bloodsworth Island during the last half of the 19th century made a living from watering activities. Census data record the occupations of island residents as "oysterman," "sailor," and "farmer," this last entry possibly reflecting seasonal or career cycles in watermens' work lives. That Bloodsworth Islanders were involved in the tonging fishery rather than dredging is suggested by the types of boats they owned during this period—smaller sailing canoes typically used for tonging. Besides, it appears unlikely that many occupations other than fishing were open to island residents, a situation that was partly an effect of the island's natural environment. The island seems to have always lacked enough tillable land to make farming viable full time. At most, island residents probably cultivated small garden plots for home consumption and kept livestock, which might have provided some cash as well as meat and wool for home use (Wilke et al. 1980; Botwick and McClane 1998:53). Notably, the highpoint in animal husbandry occurred during the 1850s, prior to the oyster boom, while by the 1870s island residents owned few farm animals beyond what might be necessary for home use. These changes suggest that before the oyster industry expanded, island residents may have experimented with agriculture and then decreased their emphasis on it as oystering became profitable. Conversely, rising sea levels and/or erosion caused by pasturing livestock could have decreased the viability of husbandry, leading island residents to seek opportunities presented by the oyster economy (Botwick and McClane 1998:54).

In addition to influencing occupational choices, the natural environment of Bloodsworth Island helped frame the identity of oyster tongers by emphasizing differences with the larger society. Many fishing communities are physically isolated, which helps to create boundaries and a sense of separation from the rest of society (Maril 1983:75,84–85; Peace 1996). In the Chesapeake region, tongers often lived on islands and in marginal areas divided from the mainland by extensive marshes (Dixon et al. 1984; Ellis 1986; Forrest 1988), so these communities were figuratively if not actually islands.

The physical environment of Bloodsworth Island likely helped to support this sense of separation. Notably, conditions on the island reflect both natural and cultural processes. Environmental studies (Wilke et al. 1980; U.S. Navy 1982) suggest that the island would have been drier and less marshy during the past few hundred years, despite rising sea levels. Past clearing and pasturing exacerbated natural processes, enabling erosion and colonization by salt marsh species and speeding the growth of wetlands. As noted, by the second half of the 19th century the island contained only a few small isolated habitable areas surrounded by vast marshes. These conditions contributed to the nature of the built environment.

The cultural landscapes of Bloodsworth Island and other tonging communities further influenced social identity. The built environment of Bloodsworth Island was never extensive and was confined to secluded homesteads on isolated high spots. The development of the island's built environment is not entirely clear. For instance, as noted above, island property owners raised livestock in relatively large numbers prior to 1870, but it cannot be said for certain if these property owners lived on the island at this time or only grazed livestock on it. It is reasonable to conclude that the cultural landscape before 1870 contained few permanent structures and possibly more extensive pasture than after 1870. Wood lots may also have been relatively large prior to 1870, although on the whole the landscape would have been flat, undifferentiated, and dominated by extensive salt marshes.

Despite expansion during the second half of the 19th century, the built environment remained characterized by sparse settlement restricted to relatively high ground. At the level of individual homesteads, archaeological data (Davidson 1982; Botwick and McClane 1998) and regional architectural studies (Glassie 1972,

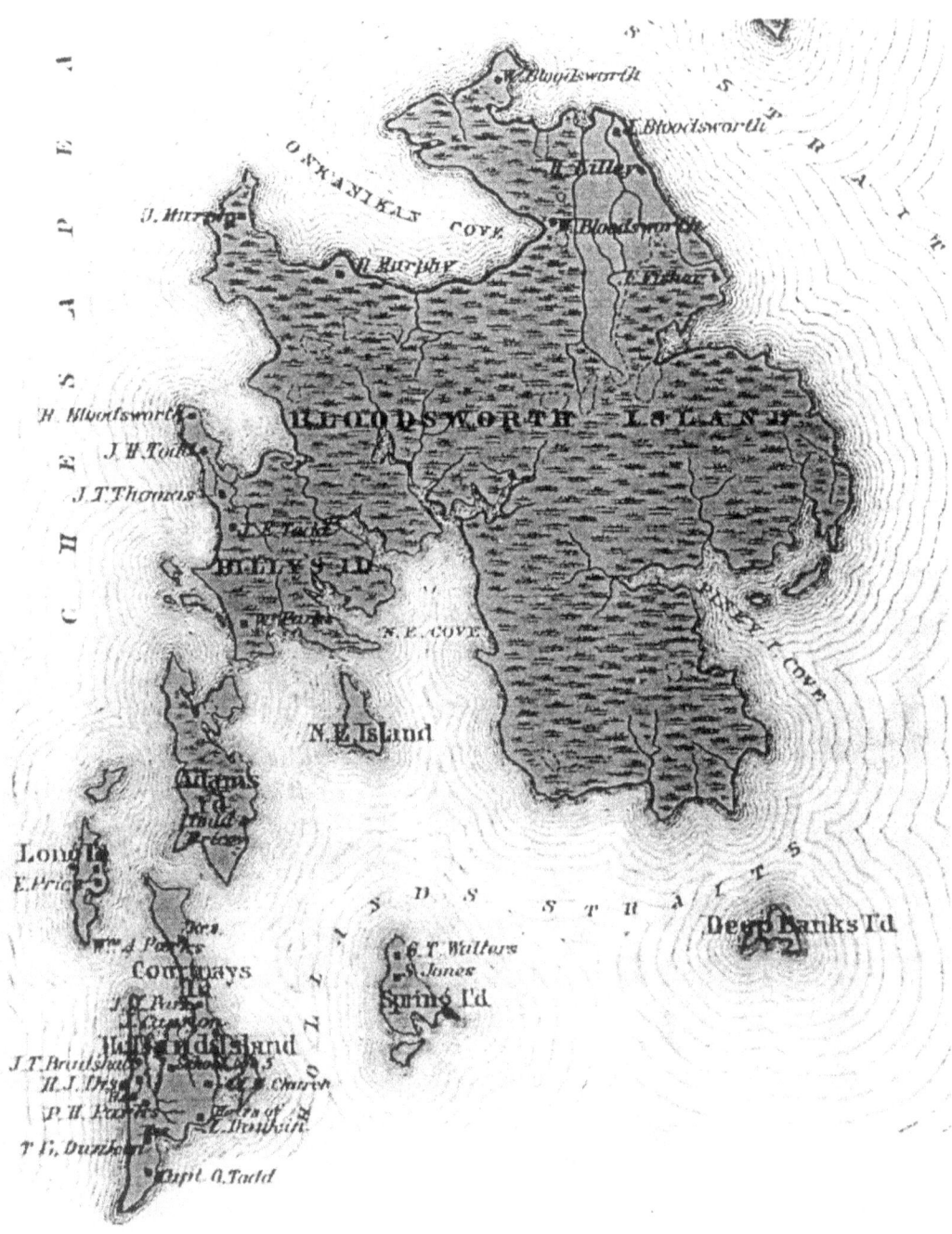

FIGURE 4. Detail of 1877 *Atlas of Dorchester County* showing settlement on Bloodsworth and adjacent islands in the 1870s. (Courtesy of the Chesapeake Bay Maritime Museum.)

1975; Weeks 1984; Lanier and Herman 1997) suggest that houses on the island consisted of one-room deep, two-room wide frame dwellings elevated on brick or wooden piers. Although archaeological and documentary evidence for them is lacking, a variety of barns, sheds, enclosures, and garden plots probably made up the rest of an oysterman's homestead. Domestic

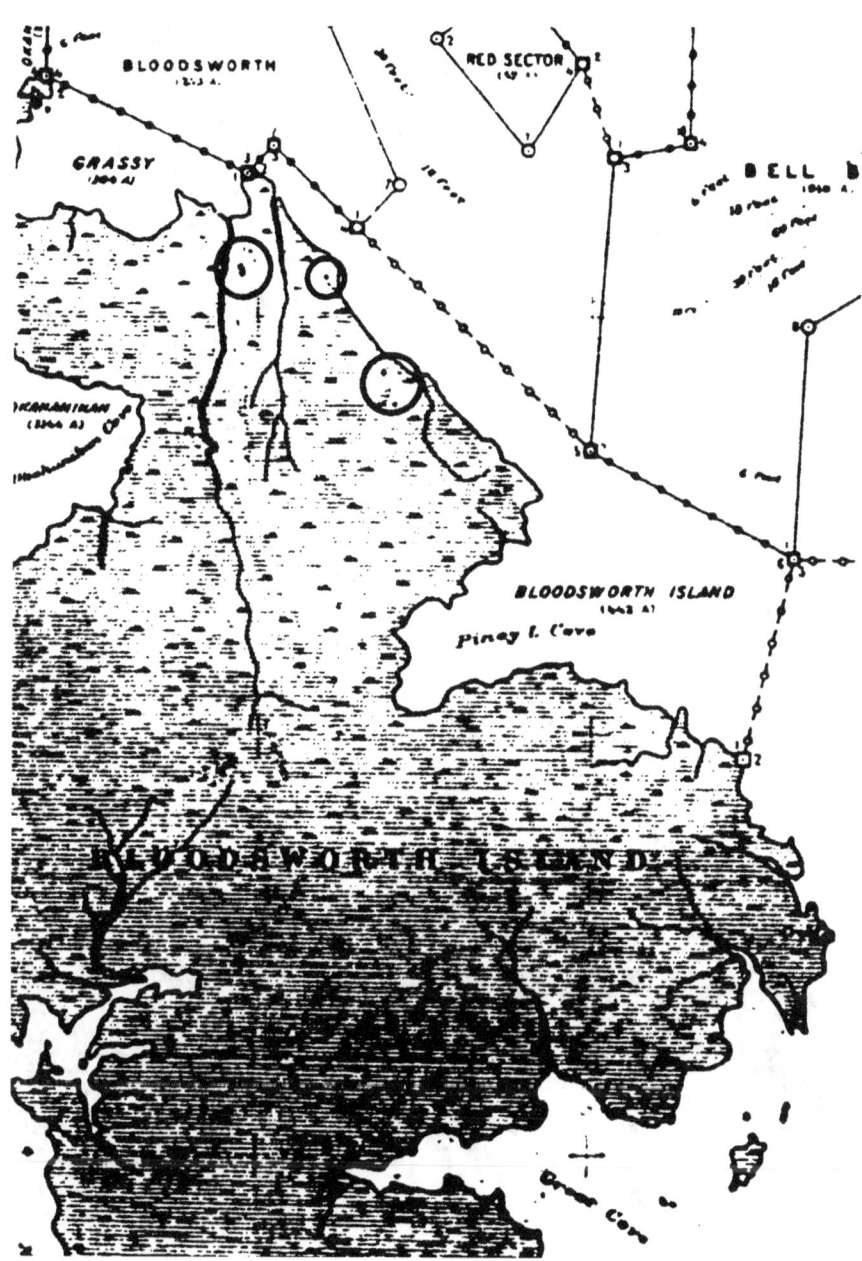

FIGURE 5. Detail of 1910 Maryland Shellfish Commission map showing early-20th-century settlement on the northern part of Bloodsworth Island. Mapped houses are circled. (Courtesy of the Chesapeake Bay Maritime Museum.)

locations also overlapped with working areas. The houses lay relatively close to boat landings, which probably consisted only of poles driven into shallow water to moor boats and possibly dumps of shell, wood, or brick on the bank to provide some solid ground. Work-related tasks, such as equipment maintenance, probably took place in residential yards.

Three house sites (sites 18D080, 18D081, and 18DO82) have been examined archaeologically

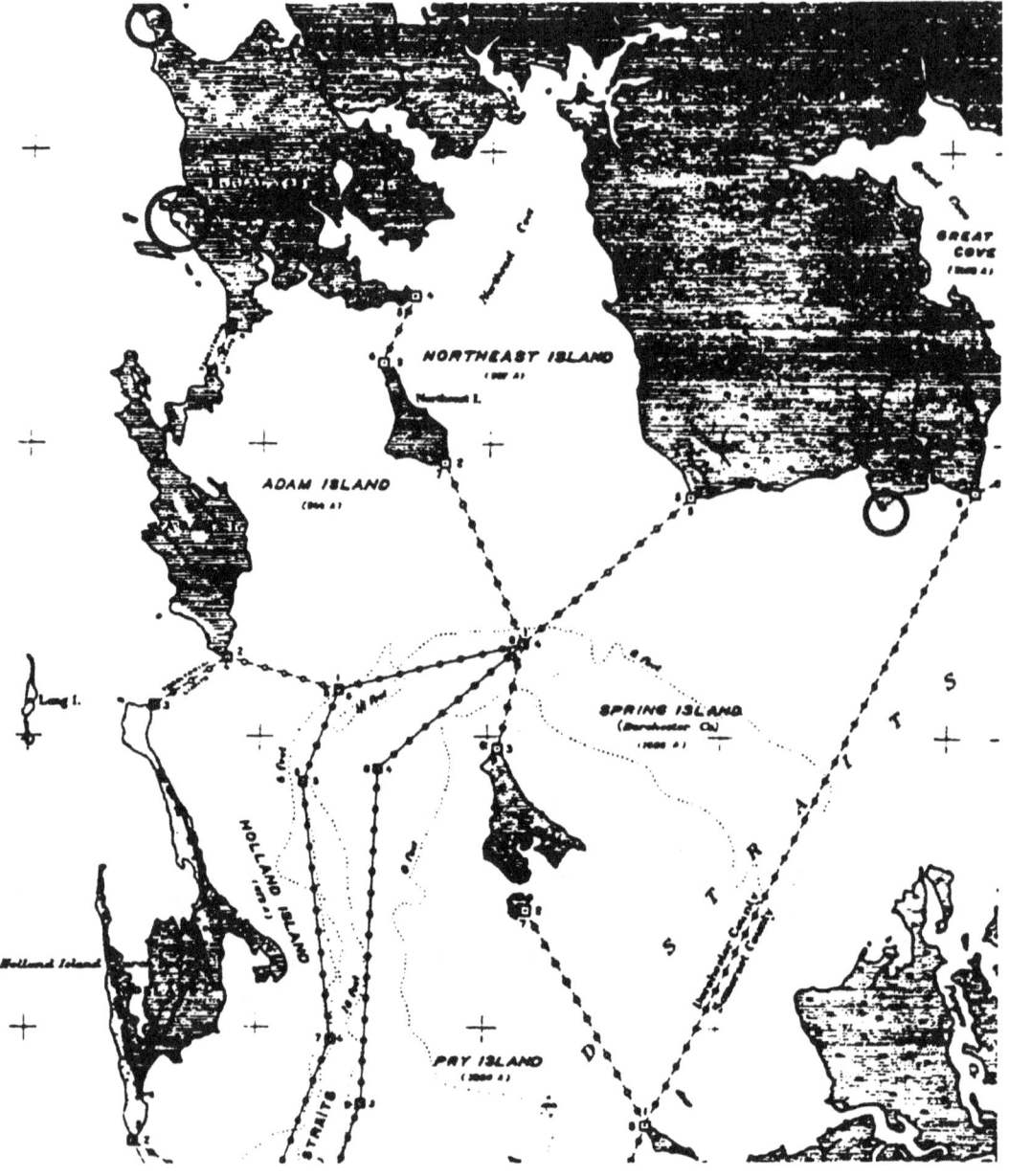

FIGURE 6. Detail of 1910 Maryland Shellfish Commission map showing early-20th-century settlement on the southern part of Bloodsworth Island. Mapped houses are circled. Holland Island is in the lower left corner. (Courtesy of the Chesapeake Bay Maritime Museum.)

on Bloodsworth Island and provide information about the organization of the island's homesteads (Wilke et al. 1980; Davidson 1982; Botwick and McClane 1998). Site 18DO80 is related to the John Bloodsworth household during the second half of the 19th century. Aspects of the site illustrate the nature of the domestic landscape associated with oyster tonging. The principal architectural features identified at this site include remains of a chimney base/hearth facing an open space flanked by two brick-paved areas. Presumably, the open space was the house location. Extrapolating from common house types in the Dorchester County region, it is reasonable to assume that the John Bloodsworth house consisted of a one-room deep frame structure with the rooms placed side by side and incorporating a two-room hall and parlor floor plan (Figure 7) (Botwick and McClane 1998:54,103–105). While the more formal central-hall plan became common in the region by the 18th century, the smaller hall-parlor plan persisted into the 20th century (Glassie 1975; Lanier and Herman 1997: 16) and had come to be mostly associated with

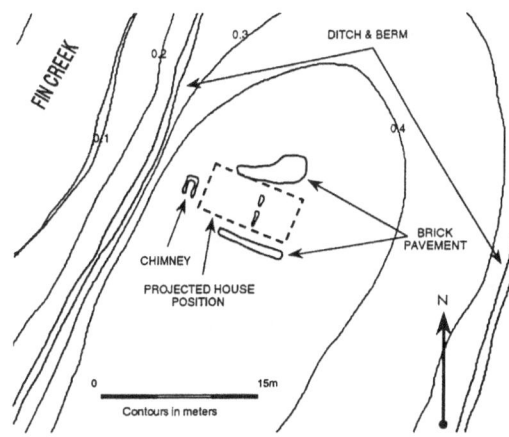

FIGURE 7. John Bloodsworth House Site (18DO180) (after Botwick and McClane 1998).

less affluent households by the latter part of the 1800s (Weeks 1984:209). The only detailed representation of houses on the island supports this interpretation. The 1843 plat of Robert Bloodsworth's holdings shows two houses on the island. Both are one-story, three-bay structures with a single chimney each.

Other aspects of the domestic landscape identified at this site are related to the immediate residential yard as well as a projected larger property. Domestic yard areas were not apparent from the fieldwork, although a system of dykes and ditches formed a large rectangular enclosure of the house site (Figure 7). Remains of a fence atop the dykes further defined this space. Beyond the immediate dwelling area, the

property included a family cemetery. The intervening area contained an embanked stock pond and a level clearing suitable for farm buildings, although no direct evidence of such structures was found.

Testing of a second site (18DO182), a house owned by William Parks's family between the 1840s and 1870s, exposed features that Thomas Davidson (1982) interpreted as a two-story, four-room dwelling. Davidson reconstructed the house's floor plan to encompass a narrow brick "floor" that he interpreted as a room. In fact, this feature resembles the paved areas identified at the John Bloodsworth house. If this is the case, then the Parks house probably represents a smaller two-room house like the one projected for John Bloodsworth's family. Davidson (1982:19) notes that ceramics from the site conformed to the lower end of Miller's cost index, suggesting a lower income household that might be expected to occupy the smaller and older style house type.

A third site (18DO81) represents a domestic occupation associated with William Bloodsworth's family during the second half of the 19th century. Archaeological work here revealed little direct evidence of the house but provided some information about the layout and landscape of the house lot. Features identified here include a brick pier, possibly marking the house location, segments of a dyke and ditch system, a fence line, and a stock pond. A pile of clamshells dumped at the edge of the creek flowing past the house appears to represent a makeshift boat landing. What is worth pointing out about this feature is its proximity to the projected house location. The landing and house are about 100 feet apart, and this short span emphasizes the overlapping domestic and work spheres at the site. Also important to note is that, rather than a shared community facility, the landing is exclusive to the house. This arrangement of individual household landings is viewed as an additional characteristic of oyster tonging landscapes.

Regarding landscapes associated with the entire island, historic maps (Lake et al. 1877; Maryland Shellfish Commission 1910) indicate that during the height of the oyster boom five widely spaced houses in the northeastern part of the island represented the greatest concentration of settlement (Figures 4, 5, and 6). Additional houses were distributed on isolated high spots in the island's marshes. It is important to note the aspects of the landscape that are missing from Bloodsworth Island. The island contained no structures or facilities related to social, economic, political, or religious activities that might create a focus of settlement or community. In addition, the island lacked roads. Travel within the island probably took place on muddy paths, sometimes built up with brick, shells, or planks. A possible causeway was identified on the island at Site 18DO80, but this feature only connected the dwelling and family cemetery and did not constitute part of an integrated island-wide transportation network (Botwick and McClane 1998). As with a road network, no central boat landing, harbor, or docks were present. Landings appear to have been associated only with individual dwellings and to have consisted of informal affairs built of shell or refuse dumps.

An Oyster Dredging Landscape: Holland Island

The rather stark landscape of Bloodsworth Island can be contrasted to the more crowded and busy scene on neighboring Holland Island, located within the group of smaller islands south of Bloodsworth. During the oyster boom it was occupied by fishermen involved in the dredging industry. Although much smaller than Bloodsworth Island, Holland Island contained slightly more habitable land and strikingly different natural and cultural landscapes.

Although not the focus of data collection for the present study, the history and development of Holland Island can be sketched here. Holland Island was occupied as early as the 1600s. Although subsequent developments are not clear, the settlement history may have paralleled that of Bloodsworth Island until after the Civil War. While the population of Holland Island reportedly peaked between 1890 and 1910 (Holland Island Preservation Foundation 1995), historic maps indicate that settlement already differed from Bloodsworth Island by the 1870s. In addition to being more densely settled, Holland Island possessed a church by this time, representing a socio-religious focus for the island's residents (Lake et al. 1877) (Figure 8). By the turn of the 20th century Holland Island's 300-plus residents lived in 64 houses. In addition,

the island contained several general stores, a grade school, baseball field, church, post office, full-time doctor and minister, and fraternal organization (Holland Island Preservation Foundation 1995). Historic maps indicate the presence of other community facilities, including an integrated road network linking all portions of the

FIGURE 8. Detail of 1877 *Atlas of Dorchester County* showing settlement on Holland Island in the 1870s. Note the school and church. (Courtesy of the Chesapeake Bay Maritime Museum.)

island and a central landing (Figure 9) (Maryland Shellfish Commission 1910). The harbor was occupied by a fleet of workboats, including 55 skipjacks (Holland Island Preservation Foundation 1995), which were the characteristic oyster dredge boats of Chesapeake Bay (Witty and Johnson 1988:175). Tax data for the period between 1876 and 1896 indicate that prior to the advent of the skipjack in the 1890s, Holland Islanders mostly owned bug eyes and pungies (Botwick and McClane 1998), heavy vessels used for oyster dredging.

Although Holland Island prospered during the last quarter of the 19th century, it began a physical decline that paralleled downturns

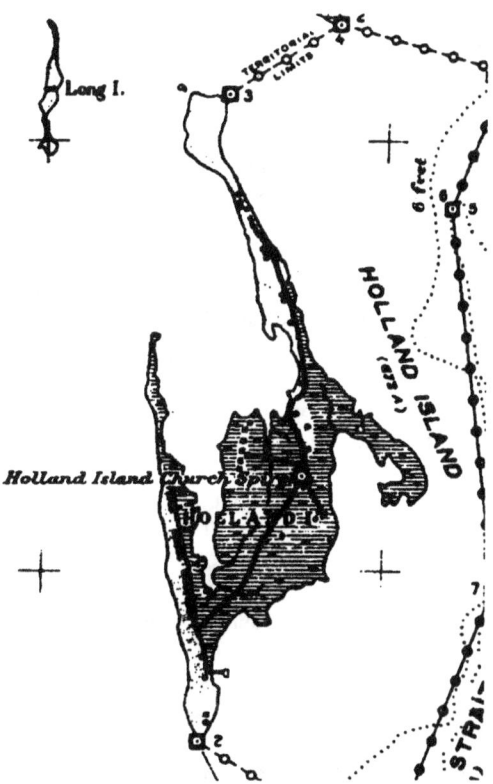

FIGURE 9. Detail of 1910 Maryland Shellfish Commission map showing early-20th-century settlement on Holland Island. Note the concentration of settlement along the island's main roads and the communal landing at the lower portion of the island. (Courtesy of the Chesapeake Bay Maritime Museum.)

settlement on Holland Island was much denser than on Bloodsworth Island. Historic maps and photographs show houses clustered along the island's main streets, and these neighborhoods presented a much different face than the relatively isolated homesteads of Bloodsworth Island (Figures 8 and 9).

In addition, the houses expressed a greater degree of affluence both in size and assessed value. Tax assessments for the period between 1876 and 1896, roughly corresponding to the period of the oyster boom, indicate that average values for buildings and improvements on Holland Island were $1,187.50. For the same period buildings and improvements on Bloodsworth Island averaged $82.72 (Dorchester Co. Board of Commissioners 1876–1896). These statistics suggest the landscape of Holland Island included larger and better quality houses, possibly the two-story, three-bay, gabled-roof dwellings that became associated with middle-income farmers and tradesmen in the region during the 19th century (Weeks 1984:209).

Photographs of Holland Island and a single extant house confirm this supposition, indicating large structures with two- or two-and-one-half stories and three or more bays. Rear ells, multiple chimneys, and front and rear porches were common. An historic photograph of the Todd house on Holland Island shows a porch on the rear ell and the yard enclosed by a white picket fence (Holland Island Preservation Foundation 1995). The scene evokes a very different feeling than the more forlorn picture of oyster tongers' homesteads.

In sum, map and tax data suggest very different landscapes on the two islands. The Holland Island community—and here we are referring to a residential community that also had a interests in common—was involved in the industrialized aspects of the oyster fishery. The island's landscape might be interpreted as a reflection of a different occupational identity and associated ideologies. The community exhibited a cohesive quality marked by houses set close together and connected by a network of roads. The commitment to ideologies of industrial order and discipline were reinforced by the presence on the island of church, school, and post office, all places where dominant social values could be introduced and disseminated (Cantor 1979:14). The central boat landing of

in the oyster economy. Around 1900, erosion worsened as severe floods ate away chunks of the island and exposed new areas to steady and severe erosion. Between 1915 and 1950 the island shrank from 160 to 80 acres. Beginning in the 1920s as the island's size continued to diminish, families started moving away. In the process they dismantled houses and rebuilt them on the mainland. By 1950 only one house remained.

Tax assessment data for Holland Island indicate that during the oyster boom individual homesteads contained the same range of structure types as those found on Bloodsworth Island: kitchens, smoke houses, stables, and hen houses. There were important distinctions, however. One difference, as noted, was that this island accommodated larger dredging boats, which also symbolized the commitment to the industrial oystering methods. Also, the island's landing area represented a discrete work sphere where activities related to fishing and shipping could be separated from activities associated with the domestic sphere, a practice in keeping with 19th-century developments that moved work out of the domestic realm. Finally, concentrated settlement and social facilities created a context within which community sanction and censure could exist.

Holland Islanders thus also had a community identity based on occupation. However, they clearly related to the oyster fishery in a different way than Bloodsworth Islanders and presumably had different views about work in general. It is probable that the identity of this community was oriented around its oyster dredging activities and, although it cannot be said for certain, they might have viewed themselves as more closely resembling the region's "thrifty, intelligent, and industrious" farmers in their attitudes and outlook than the "indolent and improvident" oyster tongers. They certainly would have had objectives and interests apart from Bloodsworth Islanders, and their ideologies had a much different material expression.

In contrast, Bloodsworth Island contained a small population living in isolated homesteads surrounded by marshes and connected by only rough paths, if at all. Archaeological remains and tax data suggest relatively rude homesteads whose value amounted to a fraction of those on the neighboring island. Landings here were informal and served individual residences rather than the community. Moreover, the proximity of landings to house sites created spaces where work and domestic spheres overlapped, a situation that more closely resembled older and more traditional patterns of labor and work organization. The situation appears summed up by George Goode (1887[2]:551): "having secured a house, [the oysterman's] ambition seems satisfied, and but little time or money is spent in beautifying or improving it."

Conclusion

Returning to the issue of resistance, we argue that differences in residential and working landscapes helped symbolize distinctions between oyster tongers and nontongers in a highly visible way. Goode's statement regarding the lack of domestic improvements among oyster tongers indicates that outsiders linked them to a particular cultural environment. Tongers would have also made the distinction. To resist the economic order that was invading their region, Maryland tongers adopted a set of values that emphasized traditional working and business practices, especially autonomy of labor and resistance to industrial work disciplines and relationships. Oyster tonging communities placed little value on the accumulation of profits and did not pursue strategies for achieving upward economic or social mobility. Instead, they accepted a lifestyle that barely rose above subsistence. This lifestyle, however, came to symbolize the occupational subculture associated with oyster tonging.

Landscapes such as that of Bloodsworth Island supported this identity and associated ideologies. The dispersed settlement patterns of marginal places like Bloodsworth Island reinforced ideas of separation, individuality, and autonomy. The lack of integrating facilities in such landscapes, such as roads and communal landings, provided similar reinforcement. Finally, the absence of churches, schools, post offices, and other facilities that integrate social and political authority, and which can compel conformity, enhanced the ability of oyster tonging communities to remain apart. Created and maintained by oyster tonging communities, these landscapes shaped the way oyster tongers and their families viewed the world and particularly their relationship to new oystering practices represented by dredging. While the tongers probably did not set out to live in an economically inferior way, their retention of traditional working practices, landscapes, and community patterns came to represent an assertion of resistance to the industrialization of the oyster fishery.

ACKNOWLEDGMENTS

This study was conducted as part of a research project sponsored by the United States Navy, Naval Facilities Engineering Command, Atlantic Division, and was performed for EDAW, Inc., Alexandria, Virginia. Kerri Culhane's research assistance greatly enhanced the project and this paper. We appreciate the comments made by Ken Mohney, our symposium colleagues, and the anonymous reviewers that have led us to strengthen and tighten our arguments. Of course, any omissions or errors in this paper are our responsibility.

REFERENCES

ALFORD, JOHN J.
1973 The Role of Management in Chesapeake Oyster Production. *The Geographical Review*, 63(1): 44–54.
1975 The Chesapeake Oyster Fishery. *Annals of the Association of American Geographers*, 65(2):229–239.

APPLEBAUM, HERBERT A.
1981 *Royal Blue: The Culture of Construction Workers.* Holt, Rinehart, and Winston, New York, NY.

BAYLIFF, WILLIAM H.
1971 Natural Resources. In The Old Line State: A History of Maryland, Morris L. Radoff, editor, pp. 267–307. Maryland Hall of Records Commission, *Publication*, No. 16. Annapolis, MD.

BOTWICK, BRAD, AND DEBRA A. MCCLANE
1998 Getting on with Living: History and Community of a Chesapeake Oystering Family; Phase II Investigations at Sites 18DO79, 18DO80, and 18DO81 aboard the U.S. Naval Reservation Bloodsworth Island, Dorchester County, Maryland. Report to EDAW, Inc., Alexandria, VA, from Gray & Pape, Inc., Richmond, VA.

BREWINGTON, M. V.
1956 *Chesapeake Bay: A Pictorial Maritime History.* Cornell Maritime Press, Cambridge, MD.

BUREAU OF STATISTICS AND INFORMATION OF MARYLAND
1911 *Twentieth Annual Report.* Baltimore, MD.

CANTOR, MILTON (EDITOR)
1979 *American Working Class Culture: Explorations in American Labor and Social History.* Greenwood Press, Westport, CT.

CAREY, GEORGE G.
1988 Watermen: Culture Heroes in Workboats. In *Working the Water: The Commercial Fisheries of Maryland's Patuxent River*, Paula J. Johnson, editor, pp. 21–33. The University Press of Virginia, Charlottesville.

CHAPELLE, HOWARD I.
1935 *The History of American Sailing Ships.* Bonanza Books, New York, NY.

DAVIDSON, THOMAS E.
1982 Archaeological Excavations at Site 18-DO-82 and Find Spot X21-X30, U.S. Naval Reservation, Bloodsworth Island. *Maryland Historical Trust Manuscript Series*, No. 23, Annapolis, MD.

DAVIS, DONA LEE
1986 Occupational Community and Fishermen's Wives in a Newfoundland Fishing Village. *Anthropological Quarterly*, 59(3):129–142.
1988 "Shore Skippers" and "Grass Widows": Active and Passive Women's Roles in a Newfoundland Fishery. In *To Work and To Weep: Women in Fishing Economies*, Jane Nadel-Klein and Dona Lee Davis, editors, pp. 211–229. Institute of Social and Economic Research, Memorial University of Newfoundland Press, St. Johns, Canada.
1993 When Men Become "Women": Gender Antagonisms and the Changing Sexual Geography of Work in Newfoundland. *Sex Roles*, 29(7/8):457–475.

DIXON, RICHARD D., ROGER C. LOWERY, JAMES C. SABELLA, AND MARCUS J. HEPBURN
1984 Fishermen's Wives: A Case Study of a Middle Atlantic Coastal Fishing Community. *Sex Roles*, 10(1/2): 33–52.

DIZE, FRANCES W.
1990 *Smith Island, Chesapeake Bay.* Tidewater Publishers, Centreville, MD.

DORCHESTER COUNTY CIRCUIT COURT
1843 Land Records. MSA C710, County Agency Series Listing. Maryland State Archives, Annapolis.

DORCHESTER COUNTY BOARD OF COMMISSIONERS
1876–1896 Assessment Records, District 10. MSA CM 419-1, County Agency Series Listing (Microfilm), Maryland State Archives, Annapolis.

ELLIS, CAROLYN
1986 *Fisher Folk: Two Communities on Chesapeake Bay.* University Press of Kentucky, Lexington.

FALER, PAUL
1979 Cultural Aspects of the Industrial Revolution: Lynn, Massachusetts, Shoemakers and Industrial Morality, 1826–1860. In *American Working Class Culture: Explorations in American Labor and Social History*, Milton Cantor, editor, pp. 121–148. Greenwood Press, Westport, CT.

FORREST, JOHN
1988 *Lord, I'm Coming Home: Everyday Aesthetics in Tidewater North Carolina.* Cornell University Press, Ithaca, NY.

GILJE, PAUL A.
1995 Identity and Independence: The American Artisan, 1750–1850. In *American Artisans: Crafting Social Identity, 1750–1850*, Howard B. Rock, Paul A. Gilje, and Robert Asher, editors, pp. xi–xx. Johns Hopkins University Press, Baltimore, MD.

GLASSIE, HENRY
1972 Eighteenth-Century Cultural Process in Delaware Valley Folk Building. *Winterthur Portfolio*, 7: 29–57.

1975 *Folk Housing in Middle Virginia.* University of Tennessee Press, Knoxville.

GOODE, GEORGE BROWN
1887 *The Fisheries and Fishery Industries of the United States: Section V, History and Methods of the Fisheries.* U.S. Bureau of Fisheries, Washington, DC.

HOLLAND ISLAND PRESERVATION FOUNDATION
1995 To Save an Island <http://www.intercom.net/local/holland>. Holland Island Preservation, Foundation, Salisbury, MD. 1995.

INGERSOLL, ERNEST
1882 *The History and Present Condition of the Oyster Industry.* John L. Murphy, Trenton, NJ.

KAPLAN, ILENE M.
1988 Women Who Go to Sea: Working in the Commercial Fishing Industry. *Journal of Contemporary Ethnography*, 16(4):491–514.

KIENER, ROBERT
1989 Can We Save the Skipjacks? *Historic Preservation*, 41(2):30–39.

LAKE, GRIFFING, AND STEVENSON
1877 *An Illustrated Atlas of Talbot and Dorchester Counties, Maryland.* Reprinted in *The 1877 Atlases and Other Early Maps of the Eastern Shore of Maryland.* Unaccessioned collection, Chesapeake Bay Maritime Museum, St. Michaels, MD.

LANG, VARLEY
1961 *Follow the Water.* John F. Blair, Publisher, Winston-Salem, NC.

LANIER, GABRIELLE M., AND BERNARD L. HERMAN
1997 *Everyday Architecture of the Mid-Atlantic: Looking at Buildings and Landscapes.* Johns Hopkins University Press, Baltimore, MD.

LLOYD, TIMOTHY C., AND PATRICK B. MULLEN
1990 *Lake Erie Fishermen: Work, Identity, and Tradition.* University of Illinois Press, Urbana.

MARIL, ROBERT LEE
1983 *Texas Shrimpers: Community, Capitalism, and the Sea.* Texas A&M University Press, College Station.

MARYLAND SHELLFISH COMMISSION
1910 *Oyster Charts No. 41 and 42 Charts of Maryland Oyster Survey, 1906–1912.* Accession No. 1966.117.001, Chesapeake Bay Maritime Museum, St. Michaels, MD.

PEACE, ADRIAN
1996 When the Salmon Comes: The Politics of Summer Fishing in an Irish Community. *Journal of Anthropological Research*, 52(1):85–106.

ROBERTSON, IAN
1981 *Sociology,* 2nd edition. Worth Publishers, Inc., New York, NY.

SANTOPIETRO, GEORGE D.
1986 The Evolution of Property Rights to a Natural Resource: The Oyster Grounds of the Chesapeake Bay. Doctoral dissertation, Department of History, Virginia Polytechnic Institute and State University, Blacksburg.

SCRIBNER & CO
1877 American Oyster Culture. *Scribner's Monthly*, 15(2):225–238. New York, NY.

SHARRER, G. TERRY
1988 The Patuxent Fisheries: Transformations of a Rural Economy, 1880–1985. In *Working the Water: The Commercial Fisheries of Maryland's Patuxent River,* Paula J. Johnson, editor, pp. 1–20. University Press of Virginia, Charlottesville.

SMITH, COURTLAND L.
1977 Fisheries as Subsistence Resources: Growth and Decline of the Columbia River Salmon Fishery. In *Those Who Live from the Sea: A Study in Maritime Anthropology,* M. Estellie Smith, editor, pp. 215–234. West Publishing Company, St. Paul, MN.

THIESSEN, VICTOR, ANTHONY DAVIS, AND SVEIN JENTOFT
1992 The Veiled Crew: An Exploratory Study of Wives' Reported and Desired Contributions to Coastal Fisheries Enterprises in Northern Norway and Nova Scotia. *Human Organization*, 51(4):342–352.

THOMPSON, PAUL, TONY WAILEY, AND TREVOR LUMMIS
1983 *Living the Fishing.* Routledge & Kegan Paul, London, UK.

THOMPSON, WILLIAM E., AND JOSEPH V. HICKEY
1999 *Society in Focus,* 3rd edition. Longman, New York, NY.

U.S. NAVY
1982 Environmental Assessment for Continued Use of the Bloodsworth Island Shore Bombardment and Bombing Range. Norfolk, VA.

WEEKS, CHRISTOPHER (EDITOR)
1984 *Between the Nanticoke and the Choptank: An Architectural History of Dorchester County, Maryland.* Johns Hopkins University Press and the Maryland Historical Trust, Baltimore.

WENNERSTEN, JOHN R.
1978 The Almighty Oyster: A Saga of Old Somerset and the Eastern Shore, 1850–1920. *Maryland Historical Magazine*, 74(1):80–93.
1981 *The Oyster Wars of Chesapeake Bay.* Tidewater Publishers, Centreville, MD.

WILKE, STEVE, RINITA DALAN, LORENA WALSH, JIM DEMAREST, WILLIAM HOYT, AND ROBERT STUCKENRATH
1980   Cultural Resource Survey of U.S. Naval Reservation, Bloodsworth Island, Dorchester County, Maryland. Report to Maryland Historical Trust, Annapolis, from Geo-Recon International, Seattle, WA.

WILSON, ROBERT
1876   On the Eastern Shore. *Lippencott's Magazine of Popular Literature and Science* 18. J. B. Lippencott and Co., Philadelphia, PA.

WITTY, ANNE, AND PAULA J. JOHNSON
1988   Catalog of Artifacts. In *Working the Water: The Commercial Fisheries of Maryland's Patuxent River*, Paula J. Johnson, editor, pp. 53–180. University Press of Virginia, Charlottesville.

BRADFORD BOTWICK
NEW SOUTH ASSOCIATES, INC.
1534 LEESBURG ROAD
COLUMBIA, SC 29209

DEBRA A. MCCLANE
RICHMOND, VA 23219

Thomas C. McErlean

Archaeology of the Strangford Lough Kelp Industry in the Eighteenth- and Early-Nineteenth Centuries

ABSTRACT

An archaeological survey of the maritime cultural landscape of Strangford Lough in Northern Ireland found rich and varied remains of structures relating to the kelp industry. Adding this information to historical documentation provided great insight into the rapid rise of an economic asset in the 18th century and its equally rapid decline in the early-19th century. Kelp provided an essential material for major industries of the industrial revolution and was a major source of income in coastal Ireland. This paper traces the imprint left on the foreshore and coastal archaeology of an Irish Sea lough by the exploitation of seaweed for making kelp.

Introduction

An archaeological survey of the maritime cultural landscape of Strangford Lough was undertaken by a contracted team of archaeologists on behalf of the government agency, Environment and Heritage Service, between 1995 and 2000 (Figure 1) (McErlean et al. 2002). The team was subsequently appointed to the staff of the Centre for Maritime Archaeology at the University of Ulster, Coleraine, Northern Ireland. From the outset of the survey, new types of archaeological sites were recorded. Evidence for the economic exploitation of seaweed around the shores of the lough led to the understanding that this was an activity of major importance for the Irish economy in the late-18th and early-19th centuries.

Seaweed was an important coastal resource in past settlement, and its exploitation is one of the many components of the maritime cultural landscape. Its use by people is probably as old as their exploitation of the seashore but is still imperfectly understood and under-researched, even though in historic times its importance becomes apparent. The eating of edible seaweed as a food supplement is still widespread throughout the world today and may be seen as a survival from the diet of prehistoric coastal dwellers. Its exploitation by coastal communities for livestock grazing and as a source for fodder for cattle, sheep, and pigs is well documented. Seaweed was used from an early period in coastal areas as a fertilizer for crops as it contains nitrogen, phosphate, and potash, and its application greatly enhances soil fertility. Because the shoreline has a high density of sandy soils, seaweed supplied a moisture-trapping compost, greatly improving soil texture. Its effects are short lived, and in areas where it was used, fresh applications were added every year. In Ireland, this resource, known as "wrack," was intensively used in coastal areas. With a rising population in the 18th and early-19th centuries, it was also a jealously guarded resource. In the 18th century around large parts of the Irish and Scottish coastlines, seaweed achieved

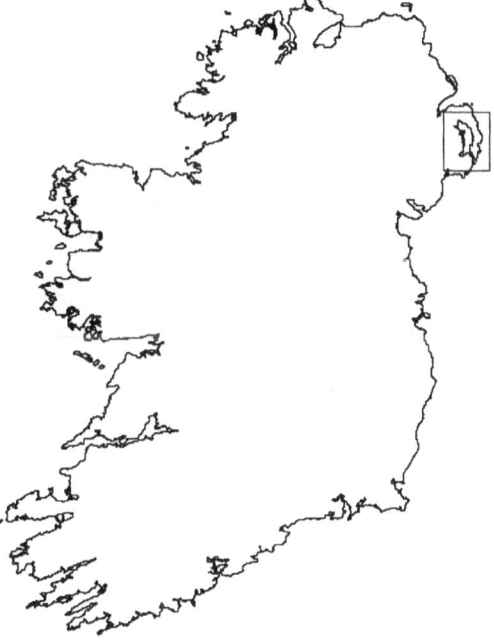

FIGURE 1. Strangford Lough location. (Map by Wes Forsythe, 2001.)

a new importance as the resource base for the production of kelp.

"Kelp" is the commercial name for the burned ashes of seaweed, which in the past was used as source of an impure form of soda (sodium carbonate) and of iodine. The name kelp causes some confusion because of its use both as a name for a family of seaweeds, the kelps (these being mainly the *Laminarias*) and as the name for seaweed slag. In origin, the term originally referred to the slag and later was applied to the plants. Soda, as an alkali, was in great demand in the 18th century for a large number of industrial processes, the most important of which were in the manufacture of glass and soap and as an agent in bleaching linen. Kelp making as a source of soda in the 18th century revolutionized the economy of the northern and western seaboards of Ireland and Scotland, providing a cash crop in an otherwise largely subsistence economy. The intertidal zone, previously exploited for wrack and fishing, now assumed a greater economic importance. The possession of "a kelp shore," as those parts of the coastline supporting suitable growth of seaweed for kelp production were named, was highly valued.

In the soda-ash stage of kelp making, which largely dates to the 18th century and the early years of the 19th century, the best seaweeds were the bladder wracks *Fucus vesiculosus* and *Ascophyllum nodosum*, which grow in the intertidal zone, mainly on the middle and lower shore. In the iodine stage, dating to the 19th and 20th centuries, kelp making turned almost exclusively to the drift weed, the *Laminarias*, or kelps, as they contain a larger amount of iodine (Chapman 1970:24). Because of its abundance on Irish and Scottish coasts, the most important of these was *Laminaria digitata*. As these species grow at extreme low water and in the subtidal zone, the focus of seaweed gathering in the 19th century shifted from the intertidal to the subtidal zone. In Strangford Lough, the great days of kelp making belong to the soda phase of the industry, and little evidence was found for any large-scale activity in the area of iodine production. One of the major discoveries of the survey was that the largest class of artificial structures on the foreshore and coastal edge were those relating to kelp production of the 18th- and early-19th centuries. Future intertidal surveys are likely to demonstrate a similar

component in the archaeology of many parts of the Irish and Scottish coastlines.

Kelp Industry in Ireland and Scotland

The use of seaweed slag as a source of soda may have a very ancient origin, but it is not until the 17th century that documentation starts to to demonstrate seaweed's widespread use. For centuries, potash, mainly extracted from wood ashes, had been the main source of alkali. It may have been the growing scarcity of wood that influenced the shift to seaweed as an alternative source of alkali. Much of the published material on Irish kelp making is concerned with the 19th- and early-20th-century iodine phase of the industry. There is little specific literature about Irish kelp production as a source of soda, so that only the broad outlines of its history are currently known. Production for industrial purposes seems well established in Irish coastal areas by the end of the 17th century, as it is recorded as an export item in 1702 (Harper 1974:22). Its origins would seem to lie in developments earlier in that century. During the 17th century, the production of kelp as a source of soda for glassmaking, especially in England and France, stimulated demand for the product (Godfrey 1975:159). In France, kelp making for glass manufacture on the coasts of Normandy and Brittany had become a well-regulated industry by the 1690s (Chapman 1970:25). In the early-17th century, a number of glasshouses were established in Ireland, and kelp is mentioned among the stock of one established by the first Earl of Cork at Ballynegeragh in County Waterford in ca. 1618 (Westropp 1920:25–30).

Another major stimulus appears to have been provided by the Irish linen industry, which was well established, especially in Ulster, by the end of the 17th century. The industry underwent a rapid period of development in the first decade of the 18th century, not least in terms of improved bleaching techniques (Crawford 1980:114–115). In 1698, Louis Crommelin and a group of French Huguenots settled in Lurgan in County Armagh and were one of the contributing forces in the improvement in linen technology, although the importance of their contribution has been questioned (Crawford 1980: 113). It is possible to speculate that, given the French influence in many aspects of the linen industry, the growth of Irish kelp production for bleaching may have been stimulated by French kelp making. In 1711, the Irish Board of Linen and Hempen Manufactures was established to promote and regulate linen production. Rewards and grants were given to develop new processes, amongst which kelp making may have been included (Crawford 1980:113).

There is certainly clear evidence that in County Antrim, kelp manufacture was being encouraged by County Grand Jury presentments (Harper 1974). In 1712, several individuals near Larne Lough and Island Magee were awarded a subsidy of 6s 9d (six shillings and nine pence) per ton for making kelp, and in that year they produced just over nine tons (Harper 1974:23). By 1716, the subsidy had dropped to 2s 6d (two shillings and six pence), perhaps suggesting that kelp making in the Antrim coast region was becoming more widespread. By about 1720, kelp was being made on the west coast of Ireland (O'Neill 1970). The impression is that it became a major activity on parts of the Irish coastline in the following two decades. The western and northern seaboards of Ireland and their offshore islands, with their rocky coastlines, support an abundant growth of seaweed, and it seems that these were exploited relatively quickly.

The story of Scottish kelp making mirrors that of Ireland. Some aspects of it are better documented and can be used to shed light on its Irish counterpart (Rymer 1974a, 1974b). It appears to have commenced in the Orkneys in 1722 and soon became a major industry. An idea of its economic importance can be ascertained from the fact that between 1722 and 1793, the Orkney landlords were calculated to have made £291,976 from kelp (O'Dell and Walton 1962: 194). Later, kelp making commenced in Western Scotland and the Isles and the influence of Irish kelp makers appears strong. Its introduction seems have taken place over a period of about 40 years from about 1730 to 1770. North Uist seems to have been the earliest Hebridean island to commence manufacture. It is believed that in 1735, an Irishman was brought in by MacDonald of Boisdale to teach kelp manufacture to the islanders (McKenzie 1974). By 1746 production had started in Tiree (O'Dell and Walton 1962: 195). In 1748, McLeod of Harris permitted some Irish to make kelp on his shore for the first time (Thompson 1973). In Lewis it started

about 1750 and on Coll, in 1764 (McKay 1980: 171). An Irish manufacturer is said to have introduced it to Jura in 1762 (McKay 1980: 125), followed by Barra in 1763. By about 1770, it would appear that any of the shores in Western Scotland and the Scottish Isles having sufficient seaweed was a site for kelp making. An idea of the scale and importance the industry in the 1760s in the Hebrides is given below in a table extracted from figures given in *The Rev. Dr. John Walker's Report on the Hebrides of 1764 and 1771* (Table 1) (McKay 1980).

The development of the kelp industry in Scotland had a tremendous impact on the marginal economies of the coastal fringe of the highlands and islands and led to considerable economic and social change, being one of the factors influencing the rapid rise in population. By the beginning of the 19th century, Scotland's kelp industry as a whole was producing about 20,000 tons annually. Its collapse had severe effects on coastal society and contributed to a subsequent depopulation and emigration (Rymer 1974a). The market price for kelp can be traced in more detail from the Scottish industry than the Irish one, but as the two industries were to some extent integrated, these are of direct relevance. Following the law of supply and demand, the price of kelp rose steadily throughout the 18th century. From 1740 to 1760, the average price of kelp was about £3 per ton, doubling to about £6 between the years 1760 to 1790. During 1790 to 1800, the price continued to rise, reaching £10, followed by a decline from 1800 to 1805. The years between 1807 and 1810 were the peak period in the price of kelp as the Peninsular War interfered with the import of the Spanish equivalent known as *barilla*. During this time, the price reached £16 per ton and above. From 1810 to 1820, prices dropped dramatically to those of 30 or 40 years previously. By the 1830s, the price had slumped to a level that made kelp making economically unviable, and the soda phase of the industry collapsed. The price of Irish kelp followed a very similar trend but, because of a perceived inferiority to the Scottish product, consistently at a slightly lower market price (Table 1).

During the 18th century, kelp faced a major competitor in the form of Spanish *barilla*, made from the ash of the shore plant, *Salsola sativa*. *Barilla* contained about 20% alkali as opposed

TABLE 1
KELP PRODUCTION IN THE HEBRIDES IN 1764

Island	Kelp Tonnage Produced in 1764 (unless otherwise stated)	Price per Ton	Export Value
Lewis	50	£3.5.0	£162.5.0
Harris	100	£3.5.0	£325.
North Uist	500	£3.5.0	£1625
Benbecula	200	£3.5.0	£650
South Uist	100	£3.5.0	£325.5.0
Barra	60	(£3.5.0)	(£195)
Islay	"some kelp"		
Jura	40 (1762)	(£3.5.0)	(£130)
Colonsay	40	£4	£160
Mull	100	£3.10.0	£350
Coll	40	£4	£160
Tiree	44	£3.5.0	£143.0.0
Skye	200	£3.15.0	£750.0.0
Total	1,384		£4,975.10.0

Note: Figures extracted from McKay 1980.

to 10% in Irish and Scottish kelp (Barker 1977: 488). To protect the home industry, heavy duties were imposed on kelp imports in the mid-18th century. In spite of this, the product was in great demand, and Belfast merchants imported large quantities from Spain to supply the local bleachers in the late-18th century. The pages of the *Belfast News Letter* during this period carried frequent advertisements announcing the arrival of cargoes of *barrilla* to be sold at auction on the quays. In the 1820s, two events took place, which had a direct result on Irish and Scottish kelp making as a source of soda. The first was the reduction of the import duties on *barilla* in Britain in 1822 and in Ireland in 1823 (U.K. Parliament 1824:238–239). The second was the abolition of the salt tax in 1825, which made it commercially viable to make soda chemically using the Leblanc method. During the next 10 years, kelp making for soda went into rapid decline, and its production ceased along major stretches of the coast. In 1812, Curtois discovered iodine as an element in seaweed slag. Its subsequent applications in medicine, dyes, and later in photography revived kelp making as a coastal economic activity during the 19th century. Some coastal communities continued kelp production to supply the iodine market, but its economic significance and extent was much more limited than that of the soda industry.

Kelp Industry in Strangford Lough ca. 1720 to 1820

Documentary evidence for kelp making in Strangford Lough is sparse and fragmentary, but a general overview can be constructed from brief comments by a number of authors, as outlined below. At present, it is unclear when kelp manufacture started in the Lough, but an early reference to the value of the seaweed resource, suggesting that the production of kelp had commenced, is found in the articles of sale of the Montgomery Estate at Greyabbey in 1717. In addition to the land and islands being transferred, it states, "and all kelp, wreck and sea-weed growing or being or that hereafter shall grow or be on the said manor, towns, lands, rocks and premises, or on the coasts or shores thereof or of any part thereof, or that belong or are reputed to belong to the same" (Hill 1869:420).

By the middle of the 18th century, production was well established, had become a major economic activity, and had produced significant revenue for the owners of the foreshore of the lough. Walter Harris (1744:154) noted, "The greatest and profitable manufacture carried on in these islands, and on the flat stony coasts surrounding the lake, is the burning of seaweed into kelp, which employs upwards of 300 hands, and is said to produce to the several proprietors neat profit upwards of £1000 per annum."

The impact of the introduction of kelp making sometime earlier in the century had, by this date, transformed the local coastal economy and considerably raised the profile of the foreshore as a zone for exploitation. Kelp making had taken precedence over the exploitation of seaweed as manure, and Harris (1744:43) further noted,

> This Peninsula produces large Quantities of Barley, and a kind of Oats, called the Light-Foot-Oats, as well from the Help of Marle abounding in the marshy Grounds, as from Ore-Weed, which they have in great Plenty, both from the Islands in the Lake, and the Eastern Shore. But this Vegetable is too precious to be used much as Manure; for they turn it to a better Account by burning it into Kelp, which they do in great Quantities, that they not only supply the linen manufacturers in this and neighboring counties, but export it in abundance for the use of the glass-houses in Dublin and Bristol, as appears in the custom-house books of Portaferry.

The economic importance of the foreshore affected land values of the adjoining shores. For instance, in 1757 when Judge Ward of Castle Ward was considering purchasing the townland of Audleystown on the southern coast of the Lough, one of the factors to be ascertained was the amount of kelp made over a three-year period (McErlean and Reeves-Smyth 1990:16). In his account of his economic fact-finding tour through the region in 1776, Arthur Young noted (Hutton 1892:139),

> All along the coasts of Ardes and in Strangford Lough sea wrack is collected by the country people with great diligence, for burning into kelp; it yields at present from 40s to 50s a ton, the bleach greens have much

of it, and the rest of it is exported to England. Some gentlemen, who keep their shores in their own hands, pay 20s a ton for collecting and burning: at other times they pay rent for the shore. In loch Strangford the kelp is better than the open shore.

As the demand for kelp rose steadily during the second half of the 18th century, Strangford Lough was advantageously placed near the heart of the Irish linen industry, in northern Down and Antrim, to supply the increasing demand for kelp from the linen bleachers. This branch of the industry had expanded rapidly from 1730 to 1750, and, by the middle of the century, there were local bleach greens around the lough at Newtonards, Comber, Ardmillan, Downpatrick, and Portaferry. The bulk of the Strangford kelp would have been sold locally but, as seen from the reference above, quantities were also shipped further afield to Dublin and Bristol to supply glass houses. On the eve of the rapid decline of the industry after 1823, A. Atkinson (1823) noted in reference to Portaferry:

> The manufacture of a seaweed called box-wrack, into kelp, may be considered as a part of the trade of this place, in common with every other part of the Strangford shore. About 1000 tons weight of this kelp is manufactured in the district just noticed, and disposed of chiefly in the markets of Dublin and Glasgow.

In the late 18th century, in common with much Irish kelp in general, Strangford kelp had acquired a poor reputation for quality in comparison to "highland kelp" as the Scottish product was normally called. One of the main accusations made against Irish kelp makers was that the product was frequently adulterated by the inclusion of stones to raise its weight. In 1802, J. Dubourdieu (1802:240–241) noted in reference to the Strangford kelp that

> A considerable quantity of kelp is made every summer along the coasts, but particularly on the Lough of Strangford; the whole quantity manufactured there ... amounts to between four and five hundred tons, whilst that made on the eastern coast does not amount to more than one hundred tons per annum; that on the shores of the lake is much superior in quality to that on the open shore, but neither the one nor the other are of so good a quality as formerly, owing to the avarice of the labourers employed in making it, who, to increase the weight, mix more than the proper proportion of gravel with the ashes, after they are reduced to a fluid state; the proper proportion is one to twenty,

but, by putting more than that quantity, the kelp is not so much in demand as it formerly was. If I recollect aright, there is a law against the adulteration of kelp, which directs it to be broken in pieces, and thrown upon the fields, excepting, however, the field of the person so adulterating it.

Decline of the Kelp Industry in Strangford Lough

The decline of the industry can be traced through the Ordnance Survey Memoirs of the 1830s for the parishes surrounding the lough (Day and McWilliams 1991, 1992). In 1833, kelp manufacture was still being carried out in Killinchy Parish, on the western side of the lough, where it is recorded (Dubourdieu 1802: 88) that

> Kelp is made on the main shore and on the islands off the parish. From the northern extremity to the road at White Rock 40 pounds per annum is paid for the privilege of burning kelp, not any lease granted. The renter gets 30 tons of kelp, which he sends to Liverpoole and obtains from 3 pounds 10 shilling to 9 pounds a ton according to the quality. From White Rock to the southern extremity of the shore at Ringhaddy the right of burning kelp on it is held by lease for 20 years of the rent of 60 pounds per annum. The same person also rents the adjacent island at 90 pounds per annum and manufactures on an average 120 tons of kelp, which he sends to Liverpoole and obtains the prices stated above.

As stated in the description of Ardglass Parish in 1835 (Dubourdieu 1802:2), the industry was declining rapidly.

> Kelp (an impure kind) mixed with sand and earthy matter was formerly obtained in great quantities from different species of Fucus but the price of article has declined so much of late as scarcely to defray the expense of preparing and bringing it to market. Soap boilers in the neighbourhood use it still in preference to barilla.

Elsewhere around the lough, surviving documentation suggests strongly that kelp making ceased in many areas during the 1830s. The loss of income from kelp making to landowners, tenants, and laborers must have been considerable. The industry was carried on for more than 100 years on its foreshores, and at no time, before or since, has there been so much human activity in the intertidal zone.

Kelp Shores of Strangford Lough

With the exception of the tidal sandflats at its northern end, most of the coast of the lough and its islands support a good growth of foreshore seaweed and were therefore commercially viable for kelp manufacture. The organization of kelp making varied on each estate, with some carrying out production directly. By at least the mid-18th century, others were letting out their shores separately from the adjoining land for kelp making. The *Belfast News Letter* periodically carried advertisements for the letting of kelp shores. For instance in 1754, the Delamont estate advertised the reletting of their shore for any period not exceeding 31 years (*Belfast News Letter* 1754:3). In 1773, James Bailie of Inishargie advertised the letting of the kelp shore at Gransha for three lives or 31 years. and in 1776 the Ardkeen estate advertised their extensive kelp shores on the islands of the middle section of the lough for up to 31 years (*Belfast News Letter* 1773:4). It would seem that it was the practice on many estates to rent out their shores in their entirety. The renter presumably acquired precedence over any traditional shore rights of tenants of the estate to cut seaweed for fertilizer, but one may assume that their rights to the cast weed was still intact. Little information has come to light about the cost of renting a kelp shore, except for the very late details given in the Ordnance Survey Memoirs, which record that in 1833, the renter paid £40 and £60 per annum for different parts of the shore in Killinchy parish. The islands off the shore of the parish, which contained a rich growth of seaweed, were let for £90 per annum (Day and McWilliams 1991:88).

Kelp Production on the Ringdufferin Estate 1779–1807

A search was made through papers of the main estates around Strangford Lough, but this proved disappointing as little of substance was found in reference to kelp-making activities. The survival of a kelp account book covering the period 1779 to 1807 and detailing kelp production on the Ringdufferin Estate over a 30-year time span has proved an extremely valuable source of information on the local organization of the industry. The book has been preserved at Ringdufferin House since the 18th century and was brought to the attention of the survey team by Mr. Paddy Mackie. Permission to use material from it was generously given by the current owners of the Ringdufferin estate, Mr. and Mrs. Martin Hamilton.

The estate is situated in the midsection of the western shore of Strangford Lough and has a long and well-documented history of occupation from medieval times to the present. The Bailie family owned the estate from the early-17th century to the middle of the 20th century. The kelp account book covers the period of ownership of James Bailie who held the estate from 1774 to 1819. He was a prominent man in local affairs, being at one time High Sheriff of County Down and a magistrate, as well as being a diligent landowner and substantial maritime trader. Bailie kept direct control of the kelp production on his shores through all of its stages—harvesting, burning, storing, and marketing. Analyses of his detailed accounts allow many observations to be made on how the industry was conducted at a local level in part of the lough in the late-18th century. The Bailie estate was comparatively small, and funds made from kelp production must have been a major source of income. The demesne, or home farm, consisted of the townland of Ringdufferin and nearby Pawle Island (pronounced "pole"). The shoreline of the island has an extensive boulder foreshore with a good cover of seaweed, which slopes down to an expanse of intertidal mud flats. There is a similar extensive fringe of seaweed-covered boulder foreshore on its eastern side.

Between 1779 and 1799, the accounts are detailed, and information may be extracted concerning the amount of kelp made each year, the location of the seaweed used, who it was sold to, and at what price. From 1799 to 1807, the recorded information is less precise. Table 2 notes some aspects of the accounts covering the period 1779 to 1799. An interesting feature is that for kelp making, the foreshore of the estate was divided into three sections: Warren Point to Grove Point, Castle Island to Danes Point, and Pawle Island (Figures 1, 2, 3).

The important point to emerge is that only one division on the estate was harvested each year. In 1779, for example, Warren Point to Grove Point was cut, followed in 1780 by the

Castle Island to Danes Point division, and in 1781 by Pawle Island. The same three-year cycle of cutting was repeated in 1782–1784, 1785–1787, and 1788–1790, demonstrating that each division was cut only once every three years. The Warren Point to Grove Point shore was cut in 1779, 1782, 1785, 1788, and 1791. This provides clear evidence of a three-year rotational system of cutting being practiced to allow the seaweed on each division three years to recover and grow to a sufficient size to make it economical to harvest. It seems probable that on other kelp shores around the lough a similar rotation system was practiced and that management of the resource entailed a division of the shore to facilitate this system (Table 2).

Using the formula that 20 tons of wet seaweed equals 1 ton of kelp (Chapman 1970: 45), it is possible to gain an impression of how much seaweed was cut annually for the kelp production on the estate by the team of four

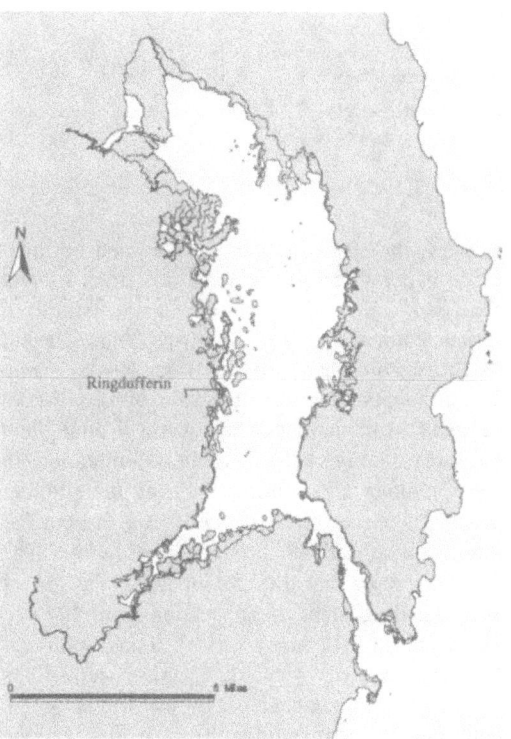

FIGURE 2. The location of the Ringdufferin Estate. (Map by author, 2001.)

Thomas C. McErlean

TABLE 2
KELP PRODUCTION (IN TONS) ON THE RINGDUFFERIN ESTATE 1779–1799

Year	Warren Point to Grove Point	Castle Island to Danes Point	Pawle Island
1779	31	-	-
1780	-	37.5	-
1781	-	-	26
1782	22	-	-
1783	-	35	
1784	-	-	20.5
1785	23	-	-
1786	-	35	-
1787	-	-	35
1788	21	-	-
1789	-	30.5	-
1790	-	-	Cut, amount NK
1791	26	-	-
1792	-	-	-
1793	-	40	-
1794	-	-	-
1795	31	-	-
1796	-	-	32
1797	-	36.5	-
1798	29	-	-
1799	-	37	20.5
Average Av. production (to nearest ton)	26 tons over 7 cuts	36 tons over 7 cuts	25 tons over 5 cuts
Probable weight of wet seaweed cut	520 tons per cut	720 tons per cut	500 tons per cut

kelpers who carried out the cutting and burning. Once every three years, some 720 tons of wet seaweed were cut from the Castle Island to Danes Point shore, 520 tons from Warren Point to Grove Point, and 500 tons from Pawle Island. The accounts show that the sale of kelp began in most years in late May or early June, and so, presumably, kelp making commenced in early summer and continued during the summer months. The net profit depended on the current market price and the production expenses. The accounts show that the cost of making a ton of kelp remained static at £1 per ton from 1779 to 1812, but in 1812 rose to £1 5s (one pound and five shillings) per ton. All of this cost appears to have been accounted for by the wages of the kelpers who were paid at £1 per ton. A note in the account book estimates that for the nine years from 1779 to 1787 inclusive, a profit of

£1,123 was made from making kelp and that the average yearly profit was £125. On a small estate like Ringdufferin, this figure demonstrates that kelp making provided an important source of income.

The sales accounts show that the market price of the kelp fluctuated over the period covered by the accounts, as shown in Figure 4. Sales were continuous from June to late September but largely ceased during the winter months. Small amounts of the remaining portion of the previous year's production were sold sporadically from February to May and fetched slightly higher prices, presumably as the product was becoming scarce. The accounts start on a high in 1779 and 1780 as a result of the British war with France and the American colonies, which interrupted the import of ashes from abroad and pushed up the price of home-produced

Perspectives from Historical Archaeology:

For the most part, the kelp was sold directly from the estate to the consumers. The local bleachers of Down, Armagh, and South Antrim were major customers with individuals in Tandragee, Dromore, Ballynahinch, Lisburn, Lambeg Belfast, Antrim, and elsewhere referred to in the account. Among those mentioned in the 1780s are Samuel Delacherois, the Mussens of Lisburn, and John Riddle of Comber. Some customers, such as Alexander Finlay of High Street and Mathew Steel of Castle Street in Belfast, were soap boilers. The only obvious glassmaker who can be identified is John Smylie and Co. of Belfast who was a customer in 1788. The kelp was normally sold by the hundredweight and transported inland by carriers who charged £1 for 6 hundredweight, or transported by boat to customers in Down, Strangford, Newry, and Dublin.

Archaeology of Kelp in Strangford Lough

Introduction: Stages in Kelp Making

The process of kelp making consisted of a number of well-defined stages: harvesting the seaweed on the foreshore where it was then dried, burning it in kilns, and storage of the product. Structures relating to all of these production stages have left their mark on the archaeology of the shore. A superb example of this range of activities is to be found at Chapel Island, to the west of Greyabbey, where there are kelp kilns and the ruins of a kelp house. Nearby on the foreshore to the east is a large kelp grid, which artificially extended the seaweed-growing area over a sandy zone near low water. Since kelp making on a large scale appears to have ceased around Strangford Lough before the middle of the 19th century, it is not surprising that there are no contemporary accounts of the process available from folk tradition in the area. There is much information, mostly of 19th-century date, from other parts of the coast of Ireland and from Scotland. A clear outline of how kelp making was carried out can be reconstructed (Evans 1957; Clark 1971; Thompson 1973; Harper 1974; Fenton 1978; Hamond 1991, 1998). Most of these descriptions relate to the production of kelp for iodine extraction in the later 19th century rather than to the production of soda

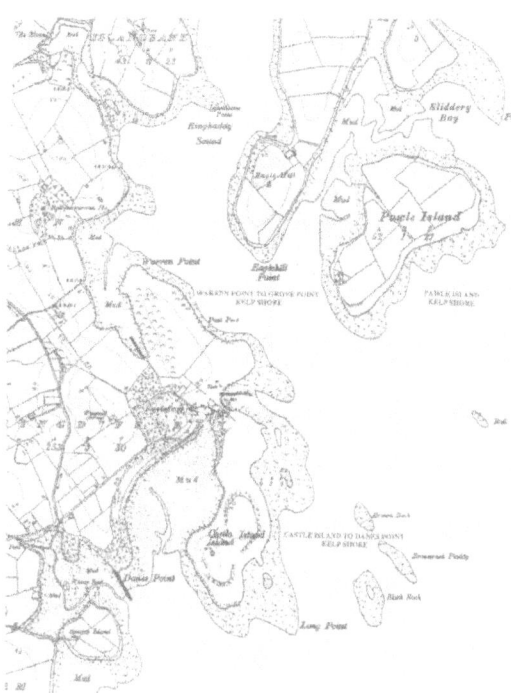

FIGURE 3. The Ringdufferin kelp shores. (Based on Ordnance Survey 6-inch map, sheet 24, Co. Down, 1920.)

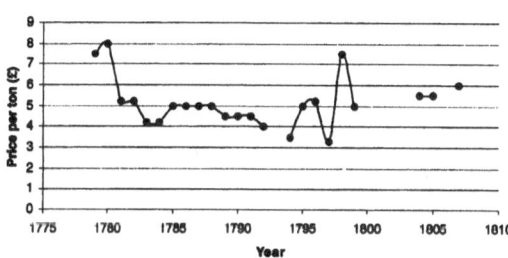

FIGURE 4. Price of kelp from the Ringdufferin accounts 1779 to 1807. (Graph by author, 2001.)

kelp. In 1780 the price reached £8 per ton, and a net profit of £240 was made. The only comparable year with such a high price during the period covered by the account was 1798, when it jumped from £3 10s (three pounds and ten shillings) to £7 10s (seven pounds and ten shillings). The rebellion in that year may have made local kelp scarce or resulted in difficulties in getting ashes from abroad, thus increasing the price.

in the 18th century. Nevertheless, apart from the change in the exploitation of the largely subtidal drift weeds, the main outlines of the process were very similar and can be used to throw light on how kelp making was carried out around the lough.

Harvesting the Seaweed and Shore Divisions

It is important to stress that in kelp making for soda, seaweed harvesting took place on the foreshore and was based largely on the bladder wracks. As these plants re-grow from their roots, they were cut rather than pulled. Cutting was carried out during the summer months by teams of kelpers and was a labor-intensive exercise. The removal of many tons of wet seaweed during the relatively short period between the tides would have required a considerable effort. The cut weed was removed from the foreshore in panniers or in carts if the boulder-strewn shore topography allowed. In Strangford Lough, based on the Ring-dufferin information, a three-year rotation cycle seems to have been the norm.

The most important impact of kelp making on the coastal archaeology of Stangford Lough is the subdivision of the foreshore by low stone walls, erected to define seaweed rights and probably to regulate rotational cutting. These intertidal walls normally commence at, or just below, the high water mark and continue down the low water mark or else at the junction of the boulder zone with the mud or sand. The walls, which have no corresponding land counterpart and relate only to the foreshore, are not shown on the large-scale Ordnance Survey maps. No awareness was found to exist in local knowledge about their significance or function. All are of dry stone construction and built using double boulders with infill. The walls vary in height from 0.5 m to a maximum of 1.5 m and are on average 1 m wide. Their length is governed by the width of the local boulder zones, which vary considerably. Almost all are in a ruinous state.

Some 150 examples were found during the survey and are mostly concentrated on the western and southwestern parts of Strangford Lough and adjacent islands. They are largely absent on the northern and eastern parts and nonexistent on the sand flats at the northern end of the lough. On a simple level, their overall distribution generally reflects that of the distribution of the seaweed-covered boulder foreshores present in the lough. Their absence on this type of terrain on the east and northeast requires comment. This apparent anomaly probably stems from differences in shore management among the estates around the lough. On those where the seaweed resource was kept directly under their own control, or leased out as a block to an outside contractor, there may have been little need to subdivide the foreshore. In contrast, it was the practice on many estates to give shore rights to tenants who held land on the adjoining shore, and this would have resulted in the need for a well-defined demarcation of the foreshore. On some parts of the coast, where the subdivision of the foreshore is intense with walls spaced closely along the foreshore, it is possible to suggest that an individual tenant would have held a number of these subdivisions, which were cut on a rotational basis.

Burning and Kelp Kilns

Before burning, the cut weed was dried to make it combustible and to prevent rotting, which would render it useless. The drying process for the seaweed appears to have been very similar to haymaking and took place along the shoreline. The weed was spread out on grass or draped on a sea wall and allowed to dry in the sun or wind, then stacked in conical ricks. When sufficient amounts were ready, a kiln was prepared. The burning process took on average 8 to 12 hours and required the constant attention of two to four people. The fire was started using whatever local source of fuel was available—turf, straw, or dried gorse, for example—and this was placed at the bottom of the kiln. The dried seaweed was added slowly to the smoldering fire, as fast burning at a high temperature could ruin the product.

After the initial firing, little or no additional fuel was needed. The residue gathered in the bottom of the kiln in a viscous, porridge-like mass, which had to be stirred frequently by the kelpers from the sides of the kiln using wooden poles (ash being the preferred wood) or iron rods.

During the burning, the kilns gave out large plumes of white, oily smoke, which could be smelled and seen from long distance. In an area like Strangford where, in the 18th century, kelp making was carried out intensively, a large part of the coastline during the summer months must have been clouded by smoke from the numerous kilns. Burning went on until the kiln was full, and it was then the kelp was raked and leveled and allowed to cool very slowly for 12 to 24 hours. As it cooled, the kelp formed into a very hard, dark blue mass, which was extremely heavy. When cooled sufficiently, it was broken up into easily handled blocks and removed from the kiln.

The term kiln is a rather grand title for what, in reality, was an open stone-lined pit. Kelp kilns were very simple structures, normally consisting of a circular, oval, or rectangular setting of stones, open at the top and enclosing a shallow pit. During the survey it was found that in the popular imagination, many of the large lime kilns around the shores of the lough were thought to be kelp kilns, and it is thus worth noting that there is little similarity between the two types. No contemporary descriptions of a Strangford Lough kelp kiln have come to light, but there appears to be surprisingly little variation in kiln structure during the soda phase of the industry throughout the kelp-making seaboard of Scotland and Ireland. In some areas rectangular- or oblong-shaped kilns seem to have been preferred, but in both Ireland and Scotland, circular or oval forms seem more prevalent.

Twenty-one examples or probable examples of kelp kilns were found during the survey. Their distribution bears little relationship to the extent of kelp production around Strangford Lough that appears to have been carried on everywhere a sufficient source of foreshore seaweed was available. Rather, it reflects factors of recognition and detection, as well as survival of remains. As most are only on average one course high, their detection is made very difficult by high summer vegetation. Field survey during the winter months would undoubtedly have yielded a much larger number. Most survive only as a low spread or setting of stones situated on the shoreline just above the high water mark, and a great many are likely to have been removed by subsequent cultivation. Many more possible kiln sites were observed along the coastal fringe

but without excavation, their identification is uncertain.

All of the surviving examples were found on islands, with eight on Salt Island, five on Green Island (both in the Quoile estuary), and eight on Chapel Island near Greyabbey. The kilns on Salt Island are all located within 8 m of the shoreline and are subcircular to oval in shape, with average maximum diameters ranging from 1.5 to 2.5 m, their heights ranging from 0.25 m to 0.45 m. The interiors of most kilns were full of stones or other debris, and excavation would be needed to reveal the depth. On Green Island, a cluster of five occurs close together, being separated by gaps of 4 to 5 m and located about 5 m above the shoreline. They are all subcircular with an average diameter of ca. 1.5 m and average heights of 0.2 m.

The kilns on Chapel Island are potentially the most interesting, as they appear larger and better preserved. Unfortunately, with one exception, they are covered by dense vegetation, making measurements impossible without substantial clearance. They are strung out along the shore edge of the raised beach on the eastern and western sides of the southern part of the island, each one being separated by a wide space. Their cover of brambles and blackthorn, which forms hummocks of dense vegetation in the otherwise treeless sheep pasture of the island, renders them very prominent and, from a distance, gives them the superficial appearance of cairn-like mounds. Closer inspection, although very limited by the overgrowth, shows them to be oval kilns in a relatively good state of preservation and larger than those on Salt or Green islands.

Their superficial resemblance to prehistoric burial cairns led the Belfast Natural History and Philosophy Society in 1925 to "excavate" five of them in a morning. At the bases of the "cairns," they found what they though were the dry stone foundations of small buildings "6 ft. square," which they interpreted erroneously as the remains of the "bothies" or shelters of kelpers (Lawlor 1925:35–26). One, located near the southern tip of the island, is shown and designated "kelp kiln" on the Ordnance Survey 6-inch map of Down, sheet 11, (Ordnance Survey 1858) and has the distinction of being the only kelp kiln in the lough shown on an Ordnance Survey map. The relative absence of overgrowth allowed examination, and it was found to consist of a wide, oval-shaped stone structure, approximately 1.4 m high with diameters of approximately 8.6 m and 7.8 m. The enclosed space consists of a central, subrectangular hollow measuring approximately 1.9 by 2.7 m. Superficially, those found tend to agree with those found elsewhere in the range of size and shape.

Storage of the Product and Kelp Houses

Soda is highly soluble, and rain and damp can cause rapid deterioration of the kelp, so that it was brought for storage immediately after production to a dry store called a "kelp house." Presumably, these were centrally placed to store the accumulated production of a season's burning from a wide foreshore area. Only a small number have left visible traces, but the former distribution of many of them can be ascertained from the very small buildings identified on remote and uninhabited islands and for which any other function seems highly unlikely. These are shown on the Ordnance Survey 6-inch map editions of 1833 to 1834 and 1858 to 1859. On the former, these structures are normally shown without a designation as to function, but the 1858 to 1859 edition occasionally names them as kelp houses.

Uninhabited buildings on small islands listed in the 1841 census are, in many cases, identifiable with those shown on the Ordnance Survey maps and provide a complementary source for the location of kelp houses. Almost all of these had gone by the time of the 1851 census and were presumably abandoned and left to fall into ruin with the collapse of the industry. The distribution of kelp houses shown on Figure 5 highlights clearly the importance of the islands and tidally submerged boulder areas or "pladdies," with their dense seaweed cover, in the northern part of the lough for kelp making in the 18th century. Some are located on tiny islands like Sheelah's Island, Boretree Island West, Bird Island, and Creagaveagh Rock.

The sites of kelp houses shown on the early Ordnance Survey maps or listed in the 1841 census were sought during field survey, but the majority have left no observable surface trace. Some have survived in altered form through reuse as animal shelters or as shooting hides. The ruins of a relatively large example

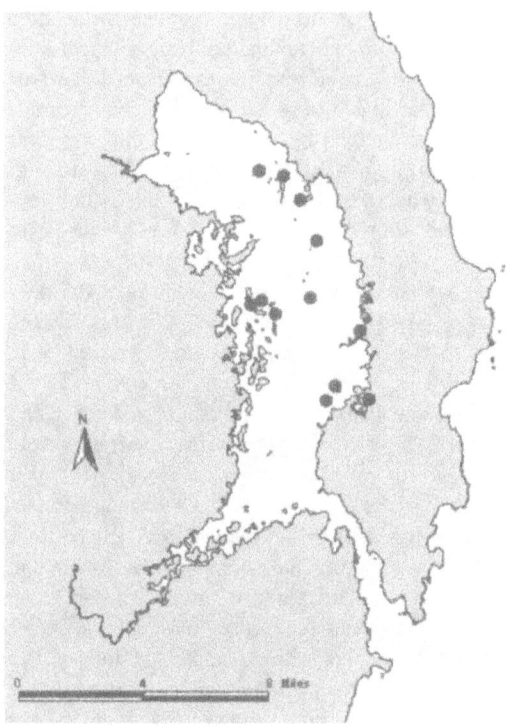

FIGURE 5. The distribution of kelp houses. (Map by Thomas McErlean and Wes Forsythe, 2001.)

have survived on the northeastern shore of Chapel Island (Greyabbey). It is stone built and measures approximately 13 by 3.5 m. Another example with some features surviving aboveground is located at the western end of South Island in Greyabbey Bay, consisting of the rectangular ruins of a small stone building measuring approximately 7.2 by 3.9 m. Documentary evidence suggests that some were substantially built structures. In 1773, for example when advertising a kelp shore at Gransha townland on the southeast of the lough, one of the inducements offered was "a large kelp house on the shore, newly built of stone and lime and slated" (*Belfast News Letter* 1773:4). This house is shown on the 1834 Ordnance Survey map (Ordnance Survey 1834) but has left no trace on the ground today.

Seaweed Cultivation and Kelp Grids

One of the most interesting aspects of the kelp industry in Strangford Lough is the 18th-century cultivation of seaweed as a crop in the intertidal zone. In order for the larger brown seaweeds to grow, they require stones or boulders to securely anchor their root-like base or "holdfast." Areas of the foreshore or seabed composed of bare, smooth rock or of sand or mud are generally devoid of seaweed growth, but growth can be encouraged by the placement of small boulders. This technique was adopted to extend the zones of natural growth. This practice was remarkable enough in Strangford Lough to merit a comment by Arthur Young on his agricultural tour of the country in 1776 when he wrote, "An instance of industry in this loch deserves to be recorded. It is not uncommon for the men to draw stones from their fields, and spread them on the shores in order to make wrack (fucus) grow; a good crop being only obtained from rocks and stones" (Hutton 1892:139).

Seventeen examples of artificial stone settings or kelp grids for seaweed cultivation were found around the foreshore of the lough (Figure 6). The true number is probably much greater as

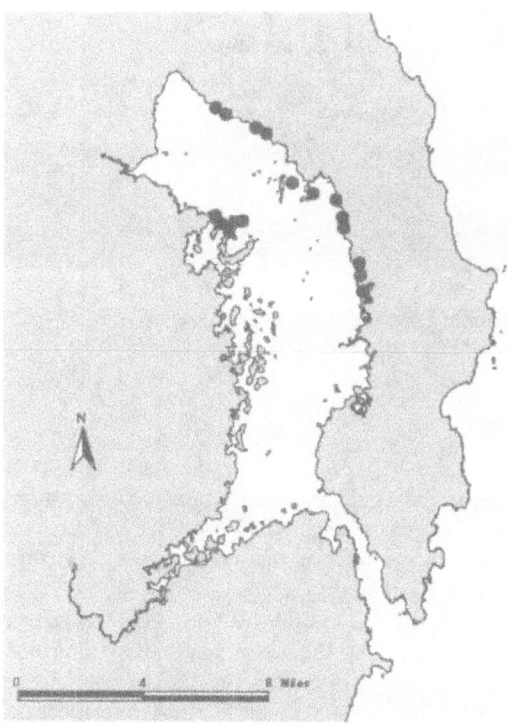

FIGURE 6. The distribution of kelp grids. (Map by Thomas McErlean and Wes Forsythe, 2001.)

their detection is sometimes difficult during field survey. Those now devoid of seaweed growth are easily detected because they are visually prominent on the foreshore as artificial stone settings, by virtue of their geometric plans. Other examples where the stones are set less regularly can be easily missed or dismissed as natural. The greatest problem for detection in many cases is concealment under a dense seaweed cover. Some examples were found almost completely submerged under mud or sand, caused by either sinking or deposition, and many have probably disappeared from view in this way. The distribution of kelp grids revealed during the survey shows a concentration on the northeastern section of the lough, with five good examples found on the western side of the lough in the Reagh Island to Ringneill area. All of the known examples are located on flat, sandy foreshores and are mostly to be found on the middle to lower shore.

Much of the distribution pattern can be accounted for in terms of foreshore terrain. The general absence of grids on the western and southwestern foreshores of the lough can be explained by the high content of mud where stones would sink. No examples were found on the extensive sand flats at the north of the lough, which is puzzling. It is interesting to observe that a relatively large number of the grids are presently devoid of seaweed growth. One explanation for this may be found in the limited information available on known cultivation techniques, which document that it was important to reset and turn the stones at regular intervals, and, since this has ceased, seaweed growth has been inhibited. Probably the most splendid example of a kelp grid in the lough is that at Herring Bay (Ballygarvan) whose outline is best viewed from the air or from the overlooking high ground (Figures 7 and 8).

This little horseshoe-shaped bay has a narrow fringing boulder zone that slopes down to a flat, sandy central area, covered by 2 to 3 m of water at high tide. The depth of water makes it ideal for growing the brown sea weeds of the middle and lower shore, but the absence of stones would have prevented natural growth and was rectified by the creation of a very regular grid of artificially placed stones. The grid occupies an area of some 5.4 acres and is composed of approximately 102 parallel rows

FIGURE 7. The Herring Bay kelp grid from the air. (Courtesy of Environment and Heritage Service, Department of the Environment, Northern Ireland, UK.)

FIGURE 8. The Herring Bay kelp grid from the east. (Courtesy of Environment and Heritage Service, Department of the Environment, Northern Ireland, UK.)

of stones. Spacing the rows from 0.9 to 1.7 m apart and placing the stones in adjoining rows in alternate positions allowed each plant to grow without competing with its neighbor.

The other examples of kelp grids around the lough (Figure 9) vary in extent from about 0.6 to 3.7 acres. It is possible that the smaller ones may represent small-scale cultivation by individual tenants, while the larger ones of more than 2 acres may have been created under estate management. The size of the stones used reflects the average size of the local shale and greywacke boulders on the immediate foreshore and are, on average, 0.35 by 0.25 by 0.10 m. The average spacing between stones and rows is about 0.6 m.

From the observation by Young quoted above, it appears that the kelp grids of Strangford Lough were in existence by the middle of the 1770s. This is one of the earliest references to seaweed cultivation in the country, and it is obvious that Young regarded it as something

FIGURE 9. Reagh Island kelp grid (Courtesy of Environment and Heritage Service, Department of the Environment, Northern Ireland, UK.)

quite singular. Another early reference to the practice in Strangford is contained in an advertisement in 1773 to let the kelp shore at Gransha on the southeast of the lough. One of the inducements offered to the prospective tenant was "the liberty to improve at least 50 acres, the bottom hard clay, and the stones very convenient ... If a tenant living at a distance takes the shore, he shall have the duty work of man, horses, and wheel cars to draw stones" (*Belfast News Letter* 1773:4). This suggests that the practice of "improving the shore" was well established by this date and may have commenced in the middle of the 18th century. The origins of this form of cultivation are obscure but are of great interest. One of the best contemporary 18th-century descriptions of the practice was made by Dr. John Walker in his *Report on The Hebrides,* dated 1764 to 1771, in which he advocated its introduction. Although lengthy, this is worth quoting in full:

> Besides the making of kelp, there is scarce anything in Sky, that can be called manufacture. The Island produces about 200 ton annually yet this is but a small quantity compared to what it might produce with proper improvement. The planting of sea weeds is the improvement here meant. The most simple of all kinds of cultivation, but if I mistake not, would turn out the most profitable. All submarine plants when burnt produce the lixivial Salt called Kelp, so

necessary in many extensive manufactures, and which already brings a great sum of money annually to the Western Coasts of Scoland. But nine tenths of all the kelp manufactured in the Hebrides, are produced from the three following plants. FUCUS serratus. Linn,. F. vescculosus Linn. F. nodosus. Linn. These three plants cannot grow either upon sand and sleech, but almost always be rooted upon stone. They generally cover all the fast rocks within ordinary Flood Mark, but the greatest crop of them is to be obseovered where a sandy or sleechy shore, is thick covered with loose rocks and stones of such a size, as to be seldom or never moved by the violence of the waters. It is also to be noticed, that they are of quicker and more vigorous growth, according as they are situated near the Mark of the lowest ebb; and gradually from a less luxurient crop, as they approach flood mark. Their growth also is greatly promoted by shelter; for they arrive at a larger size, in a landlocked bay where the water is calm, than upon an exposed shore. To cover the shores, especially near the Mark of Ebb, with loose stones from 50 lb to 200 Weight, is all that is required, to raise these profitable plants in great abundance. The sea is everywhere full of their seeds, and there adhaere to and grow upon every stone, capable of lying in the sea water, without mouldering. There are none of the Hebrides, in which, the quantity of kelp might not be greatly augmented by this improvement and in Sky in particular, it might be prosecuted to a great extent. In the lochs of Fallart, Arnisnisort, Snizort, Bracadale, Slapan, and Eyshort, there are some thousand of acres, on which no sea weeds grow at present, but which might all be planted in this manner for the production of kelp. The sides of these vast locks, like almost all the other shores in the Highlands, are thick covered with loose rocks and stones fit for the purpose, and all the trouble and expence attending this improvement, is to carry them off the ground, a few hundred yards within the Floodmark. The profit attending this simple piece of improvement, must be very extraordinary; yet it could not be exactly ascertained as in all the Islands, I could not find an accurate answer to this question how much kelp is produced from an acre of sea weeds. The Islanders employed in the manufacture have no idea of an acre, and they were as much at a loss, as to the weight of kelp, producible from any certain weight or quanity of sea weeds. I had the pleasure of finding this proposed cultivation of sea weeds, admitted by some of the most intelligent gentlemen in the Western Islands, both as practicable and highly profitable and upon enquiring into the most proper method of carrying it into execution, they all agreed in this. That if the great proprietors of the Islands, and who live all at a distance, did not think proper to engage in the trouble and expence of this improvement: their tenants might plant the shores, with stones, in the manner described above; upon the assurance of receiving from them three crops of sea weeds, rent free which would require about 12 years. In this way the landlords at the expiration of 12 years, might have the rental of their Estates greatly increased, without any trouble or expence whatever (McKay 1980:211–212).

There is very little historic documentation on Irish seaweed cultivation, save for at a few localities. A. D. Cotton (1911) described wrack cultivation on Clare Island, Achill Island, and Clew Bay in County Mayo. He coined the term *"Fucus* Farms" for these intertidal cultivation plots and remarked on the effectiveness of providing an artificial anchorage for certain species of seaweed, as demonstrated by rapid colonization and subsequent luxuriant growth (Cotton 1911:53). On Clare Island these were still in use in the early-20th century and Cotton (1911:153) described them thus:

> Where rocks are present Fucus grows naturally, but where, as is usually the case, the shore is composed of sand, the farmers set to work to obtain a growth of Wrack by artificial means. Stones about a foot square are disposed in rows a yard apart, with paths left between for carting. Sporelings speedily appear on the stones, and during the course of a year develop into good-sized plants. The following season the Wrack is cut. This operation takes place in February and March, was observed by the survey party of Easter, 1910. ... Owing to the symmetrical arrangement of the stones, the artificial plots are at once distinguishable from natural vegetation; but when the weed is in its second season and the plants inclined to overlap, the distinction might not strike the eye of the casual observer.

On Clare Island, the seaweed was cut after two year's growth, and the stones turned over for a new crop to develop. The dominant colonizing species was *Fucus vesiculosus* with only small numbers of *Ascophyllium* and *Fucus serratus*.

Perhaps the best-known and most impressive example of seaweed cultivation on the Irish coast is that at Mill Bay, on the northern shore of Carlingford Lough, County Down (Evans 1957:221–222). The cultivation is at its most impressive on air photographs from which can be seen more than a square mile of the intertidal sand flats, laid out in rectangular plots composed of rows of spaced boulders. In the latter half of the 19th century, there were 1,100 plots, each about half an acre in size. Like the County Mayo examples, the plots were used as a source of wrack and were cut about every two years. Maintenance of the bed was carried out every few years as the stones sank in the sand or were silted up, requiring the row to be raised and reset (Doran [1975]:56). Several hundred local farmers leased the beds from the landlord, and the seaweed was used on the potato crop.

The antiquity of these cultivation plots has not been established, but they were in existence in 1846 and continued in use to about 1940 (Evans 1957:221; Doran [1975]). The important difference between the Clare Island and Mill Bay beds and those of Strangford is that they were being used in the 19th and 20th centuries to grow seaweed as a fertilizer. Estyn Evans (1957:221) did not think the origin of seaweed cultivation arose out of the kelp industry "as the best species for kelp grow in deeper water." In this, he mistakes the earlier phase of the industry in the 18th century, which concentrated on the *Fucus* species, and the 19th century phase for iodine, which concentrated more on the *Laminaria* species. It seems highly probable that the practice originated in the commercial incentive offered by kelp making in the 18th century and was later used as a source of wrack.

Conclusion

The intertidal zone in Strangford Lough was harvested intensely for seaweed from about 1720 to 1830, and it is interesting to speculate on what the ecological impact of this annual loss of a large volume of algae must have been. There have been a number of proposals in recent times for the commercial harvesting of *Ascophyllum* and other algae in the lough on a relatively large scale, with a commercially viable figure of 3,000 tons per year being suggested. Research suggests that this would be damaging ecologically and that harvesting of key species would cause unacceptable environmental change (Davison and Boaden 1990: 2–8). In 1976, some small-scale cutting of *Ascophyllum* was carried out. Its effect was still observable three years later during quantitative investigation that demonstrated a noticeable ecological change between cut and uncut areas (Boaden and Dring 1980).

The effects included loss of shore cover, a reduction of canopy cover on the shore, an influx of nontarget algae from the upper zones, and changes and impoverishment of the subcanopy and under-boulder fauna—in other words, a reduction in the faunal biomass. It is clear that the brown algae on which the kelp industry was based makes a major contribution to the ecology of the lough. Its intense exploitation over a long period must have modified the ecology of the shore. Harris (1774:247) suggested that one of the reasons for the decline in the herring shoals in the lough may have been kelp burning during the spawning season and that the removal of seaweed in the sheltered bays where they spawned probably contributed to the declining numbers. He proposed, "Therefore seaweed ought not to be burned in the herring bays during the fishing season, nor until the young fish have growth and strength sufficient for their removal."

Others commentators during the 18th century expressed concerns about the environmental effect of kelp manufacture, providing an interesting avenue of future research. The fragmentary historical and archaeological evidence of the long-vanished kelp industry in Strangford Lough demonstrates that this resource was of prime importance in the economy of the region in the 18th and early-19th centuries and that this period witnessed the maximum exploitation of the intertidal zone.

References

ATKINSON, A.
1823 *Ireland Exhibited to England: In a Political and Moral Survey of Her Population.* Baldwin, Cradock, and Joy, London, England, UK.

BARKER, T. C.
1977 *The Glassmakers Pilkington: The Rise of an International Company, 1826–1876.* Weidenfell and Nicholson, London, England, UK.

BELFAST NEWS LETTER
1754 Delamont Estate: Advertisement. *Belfast News Letter,* 25 January:3. Belfast, Northern Ireland, UK.
1773 James Bailie: Advertisement. *Belfast News Letter,* 11 May:4. Belfast, Northern Ireland, UK.

BOADEN, PATRICK J. S., AND M. J. DRING
1980 A Quantitative Evaluation of the Effect of *Ascophyllum* Harvesting on the Littoral Ecosystem. *Helgolander Meersunters* 33:700–710.

CHAPMAN, V. J.
1970 *Seaweeds and Their Uses,* 2nd edition. Methuen, London, England, UK.

CLARK, W.
1971 *Rathlin, Disputed Island, Portlaw.* Volturna Press, Portlaw, Republic of Ireland.

COTTON, A. D.
1911 Algae, Marine, A Biological Survey of Clare Island in the County of Mayo and Adjoining District, Section 1. *Proceedings of the Royal Irish Academy* 31(B): 53–56, 151–154.

CRAWFORD, WILLIAM H.
1980 Drapers and Bleachers in the Early Ulster Linen Industry. In *Négoce et Industrie en France et en Irlande aux XVIIIe et XIXe Siècles, Franco-Irish Symposium on Social and Economic History,* L. M. Cullen and P. Butel, editors, pp. 113–119. Éditions du National de la Recherche Scientifique, Paris, France.

DAVISON, A. J., AND PATRICK J. S. BOADEN
1990 The Management of Strangford Lough: A Study of the Marine Environment, Its Conservation, and Its Exploitation. Report to the Department of the Environment (NI), Countryside and Wildlife Branch from the School of Biology and Biochemistry, Environmental and Evolutionary Biology Division, The Queen's University of Belfast, Belfast, Northern Ireland, UK.

DAY, ANGELIQUE, AND PATRICK MCWILLIAMS (EDITORS)
1991 *Ordnance Survey Memoirs of Ireland, Volume 7, Parishes of County Down II 1832–4, 1837, North Down and the Ardes.* Institute of Irish Studies, Belfast, Northern Ireland, UK.

1992 *Ordnance Survey Memoirs of Ireland, Volume 17, Parishes of County Down IV 1833–7, East Down and Lecale.* Institute of Irish Studies, Belfast, Northern Ireland, UK.

DORAN, JOSEPH. S.
[1975] *My Mourne.* Mourne Observer Press, Newcastle, Northern Ireland, UK.

DUBOURDIEU, J.
1802 *Statistical Survey of the County of Down with Observations on the Means of Improvement; Drawn up for the Consideration and by Order of the Dublin Society.* Graisburry & Campbell, Dublin, Republic of Ireland.

EVANS, E. ESTYN
1957 *Irish Folk Ways.* Routledge and Kegan Paul, London, England, UK.

FENTON, ALEXANDER
1978 *The Northern Isle: Orkney and Shetland.* Donald Publishers, Edinburgh, Scotland, UK.

GODFREY, E. S.
1975 *The Development of English Glass Making, 1560–1640.* University of North Carolina Press, Raleigh.

HAMOND, FRED
1991 *Antrim Coast and Glens, Industrial Heritage.* HMSO Belfast, Northern Ireland, UK.
1998 Water and Weed: The Exploitation of Coastal Resources. *Ulster Local Studies* 19(2):60–75.

HARPER, DOUGLAS
1974 Kelp Burning in the Glens. *The Glynns, Journal of the Glens of Antrim Historical Society* 2:19–24.

HARRIS, WALTER
1744 *The Ancient and Present State of the County of Down.* Dublin, Republic of Ireland.

HILL, GEORGE
1869 *The Montgomery Manuscripts, 1603–1706.* James Cleeland, Belfast, Northern Ireland, UK.

HUTTON, A. W. (EDITOR)
1892 *Arthur Young's Tour of Ireland, 1776–1779.* George Bell, London, England, UK.

LAWLOR, H. C.
1925 Archaeological Section, 9th Session, 1924–1925. *Proceedings of the Belfast Natural History and Philosophy Society, 1924–1925,* Belfast, Northern Ireland, UK.

McERLEAN, THOMAS, ROSEMARY McCONKEY, AND WESLEY FORSYTHE
2002 *Strangford Lough: An Archaeological Survey of the Maritime Cultural Landscape.* Northern Ireland Archaeological Monographs, No. 6, Environment and Heritage Service. Blackstaff Press, Belfast, UK.

McERLEAN, THOMAS, AND TERRENCE REEVES-SMYTH
1990 Castle Ward Demesne. Manuscript, National Trust Rowallane, Saintfield, County Down, Northern Ireland, UK.

McKAY, M.
1980 *The Rev. Dr. John Walker's Report on the Hebrides of 1764 and 1771.* John Donald Publishers, Edinburgh, Scotland, UK.

McKENZIE, W. C.
1974 *The History of the Outer Hebrides, Lewis, Harris, North and South Uist, Benecula and Barra.* Mercat Press, Edinburgh, Scotland, UK.

O'DELL, A. C., AND K. WALTON
1962 *The Highlands and Islands of Scotland.* Thomas Nelson and Sons, London, England, UK.

O'NEILL, T. P.
1970 Some Irish Techniques of Collecting Seaweed. *Folklife* 8:13–19.

ORDNANCE SURVEY
1834 Down sheet 18, Ireland, 6-inch map. Ordnance Survey of Ireland.
1858 Down sheet 11, Ireland, 6-inch map. Ordnance Survey of Ireland.

RYMER, L.
1974a A Note and Comments, the Kelp Industry in North Knapdale. *Scottish Studies* 18:127–132.
1974b The Scottish Kelp Industry. *Scottish Geographical Magazine* 90(3):142–152.

THOMPSON, F.
1973 *Harris and Lewis, Outer Hebrides.* David and Charles, Newton Abbot, England, UK.

UNITED KINGDOM (U.K.) PARLIAMENT
1824 Repeal of Duties. *Sessional Papers* (Commons).

WESTROPP, M. S. D.
1920 *Irish Glass.* Herbert Jenkins London, England, UK.

THOMAS C. McERLEAN
CENTRE FOR MARITIME ARCHAEOLOGY
SCHOOL OF ENVIRONMENTAL SCIENCES
UNIVERSITY OF ULSTER
COLERAINE BT52 1SA
NORTHERN IRELAND, UK

JAMES G. GIBB
DAVID J. BERNSTEIN
DANIEL F. CASSEDY

Making Cheese: Archaeology of a 19th Century Rural Industry

ABSTRACT

The concept of production strategies is employed to analyze the variety of organizational forms and technologies created by 19th century rural cheese makers. Archaeologically recovered data and historic documents are used to reconstruct the sequence of production strategies utilized at the Columbus Center Cheese Factory site in south-central New York State. Information on six changing aspects of plant operation is provided. These include ownership and management, marketing, materials procurement, manufacturing processes, expansion of production, and disposition of by-products.

Introduction

Rural industrial sites are an important resource for studying the role of the emergent factory system of production in the creation of new economies and social relations in nineteenth century hinterland communities. By considering both the archaeological and documentary data pertaining to these sites, it is possible to address such issues as the effect of changing rural-urban relationships on technology, the influence of transportation and marketing considerations on plant design and operation, and the effects of entrepreneurial activity (*sensu* Barth 1963) on household production.

In this paper it is suggested that the concept of production strategy is a useful tool for integrating archaeological and documentary information from industrial sites and relating it to broader issues of historical and anthropological importance. Research conducted at the Columbus Center Cheese Factory site in Chenango County, New York, is discussed in detail and presented as a case study in the use of this approach. First, the production strategy concept is introduced. A brief history of the regional cheddar cheese industry between 1850 and 1900 and of the Columbus Center factory follows. Next, archaeological findings at the site are described and, in conjunction with documentary data, are used to reconstruct the production strategies employed during the operation of the factory (1864 to ca. 1900). In the concluding section, it is suggested that knowledge of these strategies can be used effectively in analyses of rural depopulation, changing patterns in rural household production, and the development of agriculture and related industries.

Production Strategy

A production strategy is the body of organizational, marketing, and technological options that a producer selects and integrates in the operation of a business. Production strategies are not static. Changes may be prompted by perceived deficiencies of a strategy or by demands that arise from changing market conditions. Decisions regarding the product to be manufactured, its quantity and quality, expansion of facilities, marketing techniques, utilization of labor, and the technology to be used in production must constantly be made by the producer. Failure to account for changing conditions endangers the future of both the factory and the community that relies upon it for employment.

Reconstructions of production strategies, such as the one offered here, necessarily draw upon both archaeological and archival sources. Production technologies, episodes of facility expansion, and the addition or elimination of waste disposal systems are all archaeologically visible. Other decisions, especially those involving organizational changes in the production and marketing of the product, can only be approached through documentary research. Transfer of ownership, mergers, changes in patterns of capitalization and materials procurement, among other topics of interest, are matters of public record, and therefore are accessible through conventional documents (e.g., deeds, mortgages, corporate charters, newspapers and county histories). The documents are also required to reconstruct industry-wide trends, a necessary step if the production strategy in question is to be understood in a context other than the community. Manufacturers, after all, respond to conditions beyond as well as within the community in which they work. A brief history of the cheddar cheese industry in the United States, therefore, precedes the discussion of the production strategy reconstructed for the Columbus Center Cheese Factory.

Historical Background

In response to soaring cheese prices (Kennedy 1864:lxxxv) during the 1860s, the manufacture of cheddar cheese rapidly abandoned the household kitchen for privately and cooperatively owned factories (Pirtle 1933). Each factory was operated by a skilled cheese maker assisted by one or more workers. Many of the former were itinerant, contracting their services on a seasonal basis (roughly April through October) and were compensated based on the volume of cheese produced. The workers, a least some of whom were women (e.g., Lamphere in New York State Cheese Makers Association 1864:22; Rumsey 1954:18; Wickson 1875: 823), were paid wages by the cheese maker. Those cheese makers who owned factories either purchased the milk and claimed all profits from the sale of cheese or were compensated in the same way as the itinerants; i.e., they were paid by the farmers a set price per hundredweight of cheese produced. Farmers delivered milk on a daily basis from within a three mile radius of the factory (Gilbert 1896:37) and received payment or a dividend upon the eventual sale of the cheese; the form of compensation often dependent on whether the factory was privately or cooperatively owned (Willard 1865:22).

The most common cheese manufactured in central New York was cheddar, with Limburger, Swiss, and Neufchatel gaining in importance during the last two decades of the 19th century. Cheddar was in high demand, relatively simple to make, easy to transport, and preserved better than the soft cheeses. Cheese, regardless of type, was sold directly to wholesalers at dairy boards of exchange (Brunger 1954; Lampard 1963), or indirectly through urban based commission merchants (see Porter and Livesay 1971 for a discussion of the role of commission merchants in marketing rural produce). These wholesalers marketed the product in North America and as far away as Europe and Australia.

Whey, a highly nutritious but bulky by-product of cheese making (it amounted to 90% of the original weight of the milk used in the manufacturing process) could not be sold in non-local markets due to its low value-to-bulk ratio. This commodity has never been considered palatable by Americans, thus it was disposed of or used as animal feed. At some factories, farmers were entitled to a share of the whey, which they fed to their livestock, while at others the cheese maker claimed it as partial payment for services (Bartlett in NYSCMA 1864:28). Hogs owned by farmers and/or cheese makers were often kept at the factories, eliminating the need to transport whey (Judd 1865; DeAngelis in NYSCMA 1864:33). When not used as livestock feed, whey was drained out of the factory and into a nearby stream. For reasons of public health and sanitation, both the housing of farm animals at cheese factories (1890s) and the dumping of whey into waterways (1970s) were outlawed in New York. This created a disposal problem for small factories which continues today. (Today, many large establishments install dehydrating facilities and sell the dehydrated whey as filler to be used in processing foods.)

While 19th-century cheddar cheese factories varied greatly in terms of the structure of ownership and operation, the basic manufacturing process was relatively uniform. Each day milk was delivered to the plant where it was weighed and drained into double boiler curd vats (Figures 1 and 2). The milk was cooled overnight with spring water, only to be warmed the following morning with steam or hot water. Curd was then formed with the addition of rennet (an enzyme extracted from calves' stomachs) and the whey drained off (Figure 3). Next, the curd was rinsed, drained, and salted on a curd-working table, and then gathered and placed in cheese hoops where it was pressed overnight (Figure 4). The following morning, the

FIGURE 1. Delivery of milk at the factory (Wickson 1875: 818).

to accommodate large gang presses, it had to be spacious and its floor well-braced. Steam (from either an appended boiler room or a boiler located within the curd room) and cold water were transferred to the vats by a series of pipes and a drain was needed to remove the whey from the curd room. The curing room, like the curd room, required a spacious, well-braced floor. Wall and floor ventilators were critical for controlling humidity and maintaining the necessary uniform temperature of 64–70 degrees F (Willard 1865:29–30).

These structural requirements restricted plant expansion since it was difficult to integrate additions with already existing functionally discrete rooms and traffic patterns. In practice, limited milk supplies (a function of the number of dairy cows that could be supported on a fixed unit of land and the distance that milk could be transported on a daily basis) discouraged expansion, as there was little point in enlarging a facility unless milk contributions could be proportionately increased.

The issue of milk supply was critical because the success of manufacturers in securing lucrative contracts for their cheese, and higher returns for contributing farmers, was dependent on their ability to produce large quantities of a standard quality. New York State manufacturers attacked this problem by building additional factories and/or purchasing those of their competitors. These "combinations" (Russell 1926) proliferated throughout the state in the 1870s and 1880s. Little is known about the organization of labor and resources in the combinations, but it is possible that skilled labor, equipment, and storage space were shared among commonly owned factories. It is also probable that in the absence of cooperatives, milk would be purchased for a number of factories by a local cheese "magnate." As discussed below, the Columbus Center Cheese Factory was part of a combination.

"green" cheese was removed from its hoop, wiped clean, and bandaged with cheesecloth and paraffin. The cheese rounds were then placed in a curing room and turned over daily for several weeks to several months (Figure 5).

Each stage of cheese production—weighing the milk, making and pressing the curd, curing the cheese—made specific spatial and structural demands on the 19th-century cheese factory. Outside access to the weigh room was usually restricted to one or two windows, through which the milk was delivered, thereby discouraging dust-raising pedestrian traffic. The weigh room had to be elevated above the floor of the curd room as gravity was needed to convey the milk to the vats. The curd room was built with tightly fitted wall and floor boards to minimize dust entry and to facilitate cleaning (Blakelee 1885:480). In addition, in order

Documentary History of the Columbus Center Cheese Factory

The Columbus Center Cheese Factory site is located in the northeast corner of Chenango County

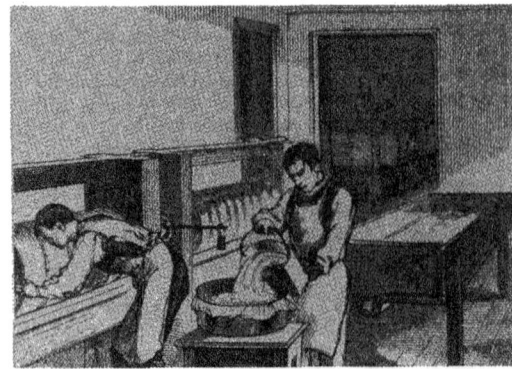

FIGURE 2. Weighing the milk (Wickson 1875:819).
FIGURE 3. The curd room (Wickson 1875:821).
FIGURE 4. The curd pressing room (Wickson 1875:822).
FIGURE 5. The curing room (Wickson 1875:823).

in south-central New York (Figure 6). It lies on the north side of NYS Route 80, several hundred feet west of the crossroads hamlet of Columbus Center. The nearest railroad stations are at New Berlin, five miles to the southeast, and Sherburne, seven miles to the west. The factory site is in the midst of a classic dairying region, characterized by rolling relief, rocky soil, spring-fed streams, and sparse settlement. Built into a hillside below a spring, the factory site overlooks the hamlet. Center Creek, a small, deeply incised stream, separates the site from Columbus Center.

The Columbus Center factory may have been established as early as 1864 by the partnership of Nicholas Richer and Henry Holmes (NYSCMA 1865:17). Richer was a cheese maker and Holmes a "dealer in butter, cheese, wool, etc." (Smith 1880:225). They produced an unknown quantity of cheese from the milk of approximately 600 cows (NYSCMA 1865:17). That partnership soon dissolved and, by 1869, Richer joined with George B. Whitmore, a local wholesaler in produce (Childe 1869; Biographical Publishing Company 1898: 21). The two were brothers-in-law by way of Richer's marriage to Ann Whitmore in the 1850s. By 1880 they owned six of the eight cheese factories in the Town of Columbus (Smith 1880:440) and as many as eight other factories in adjoining towns (Biographical Publishing Company 1898:81). The duration of their partnership has not been determined.

In 1869, shortly before or after the formation of

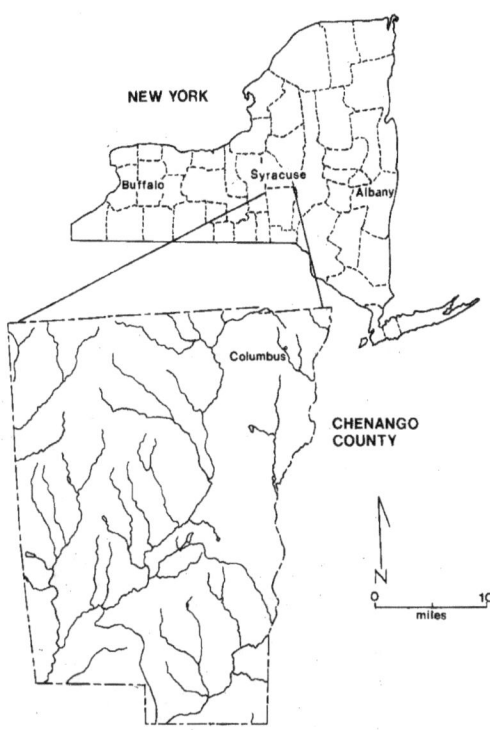

FIGURE 6. Location of the Columbus Center Cheese Factory site.

other hand, were prominent manufacturers in the neighboring town of New Berlin. In 1880, they owned at least four local creameries (butter factories), two of which they purchased from cooperatives (Smith 1880:383). By the end of the 19th century, the Sages owned most of the cheese factories and creameries in the Columbus-New Berlin area and they continued to operate the Columbus Center facility until around 1900. Unlike their predecessors, however, the Sages manufactured both butter and cheese and they shipped fluid milk from their five New Berlin factories (New York State Department of Agriculture 1895).

Table 1 summarizes data reported by the New York State Department of Agriculture in 1892 and 1894 for the Columbus Center Factory (NYSDA 1893, 1895). The NYSDA report for 1904 lacks any reference to factories in Columbus, indicating that the Columbus Center facility was defunct by this date (NYSDA 1904). An illustrated postcard (Figure 7), postmarked in 1908, shows the partially dismantled factory with the hamlet in the background. A local cheese company subsequently built a concrete milk receiving station on the site. It was eventually dismantled as well (Robbins 1972:1–2), although recent residents cannot recall when. The site has since reverted to pasture.

the partnership, Whitmore moved to New York City where he joined a commission firm of which he eventually became a senior partner. His biographer states that "at this day [1898] few commission houses in New York City do so large a business in general farm produce, while none handle more boxes of cheese" (Biographical Publishing Company 1898:24). While Whitmore prospered in New York City, Richer remained in Columbus where he acquired a general store, several large farms, and a saw mill located across the road from the cheese factory (Wilber 1967:618–620). The mill produced shingles, lumber, cheese boxes, and butter tubs (Anonymous 1886).

The Columbus Center Cheese Factory was sold to the partnership of Wilcox and Sage (later E.A. Sage and Sage and Brown) in the late 1880s. Of Wilcox, little is known. The Sage family, on the

Archaeological Excavations

Archaeological investigation of the Columbus Center Cheese Factory site was undertaken in 1986 by the Public Archaeology Facility of the State University of New York at Binghamton, under the sponsorship of the New York State Department of Transportation. Immediate goals of the fieldwork were to establish the extent and integrity of the cultural deposits and to demonstrate that the site could contribute to a better understanding of local and regional history. The site, found during an initial survey of a highway right-of-way, is endangered by a proposed realignment of Route 80, a situation which prompted the archaeological investigations described in this section. On the basis of this research, the New York State Historic Preservation Office determined that the site is eligible for

TABLE 1
NEW YORK STATE DEPARTMENT OF AGRICULTURE PRODUCTION FIGURES FOR THE COLUMBUS CENTER CHEESE FACTORY

Year	Proprietors	Pounds Produced		Cows[a]	Milk[b]
		Butter	Cheese		
1892	E.A. Sage	47,894	136,452	Not Available	
1894	Sage, Brown & Co.	87,357	214,507	750	2,976,499

[a]Average number of cows from the neighborhood supplying milk. [b]Total weight of milk, in pounds, delivered to the factory.

FIGURE 7. 1908 postcard showing partially dismantled cheese factory.

inclusion in the National Register of Historic Places. Its fate, as of this writing, has not been determined.

The factory site occupies a pair of terraces on the eastern slope of a small hill (Figure 8). Each of the terraces measures approximately 20 m (65.6 ft) north-south by 10 m (32.8 ft) east-west. A small brook skirts the base of the hill at a distance of some 50 m (164 ft) east of the site. The southern edge of the site is defined by a modern roadway (NYS 80). To the west is pasture and to the north is a small ravine which ultimately enters the creek.

Three major soil horizons were identified at the site. The uppermost is an unplowed A horizon con- sisting of a friable brown loam that contains large quantities of recent refuse including nails, window glass, domestic artifacts, and large deposits of coal ash and cinders. Clearly defined layers of ash, brick rubble and cinders are present in the interior of the factory buildings. These deposits result from 20th-century dumping. Beneath the A horizon is yellow-brown clayey loam containing moderate quantities of rocks. This stratum, as well as the underlying grey clay, is culturally sterile.

The cheese factory was initially tested with a series of shovel test pits during a standard highway right-of-way survey. These test pits revealed struc- tural remains below extensive 20th-century refuse

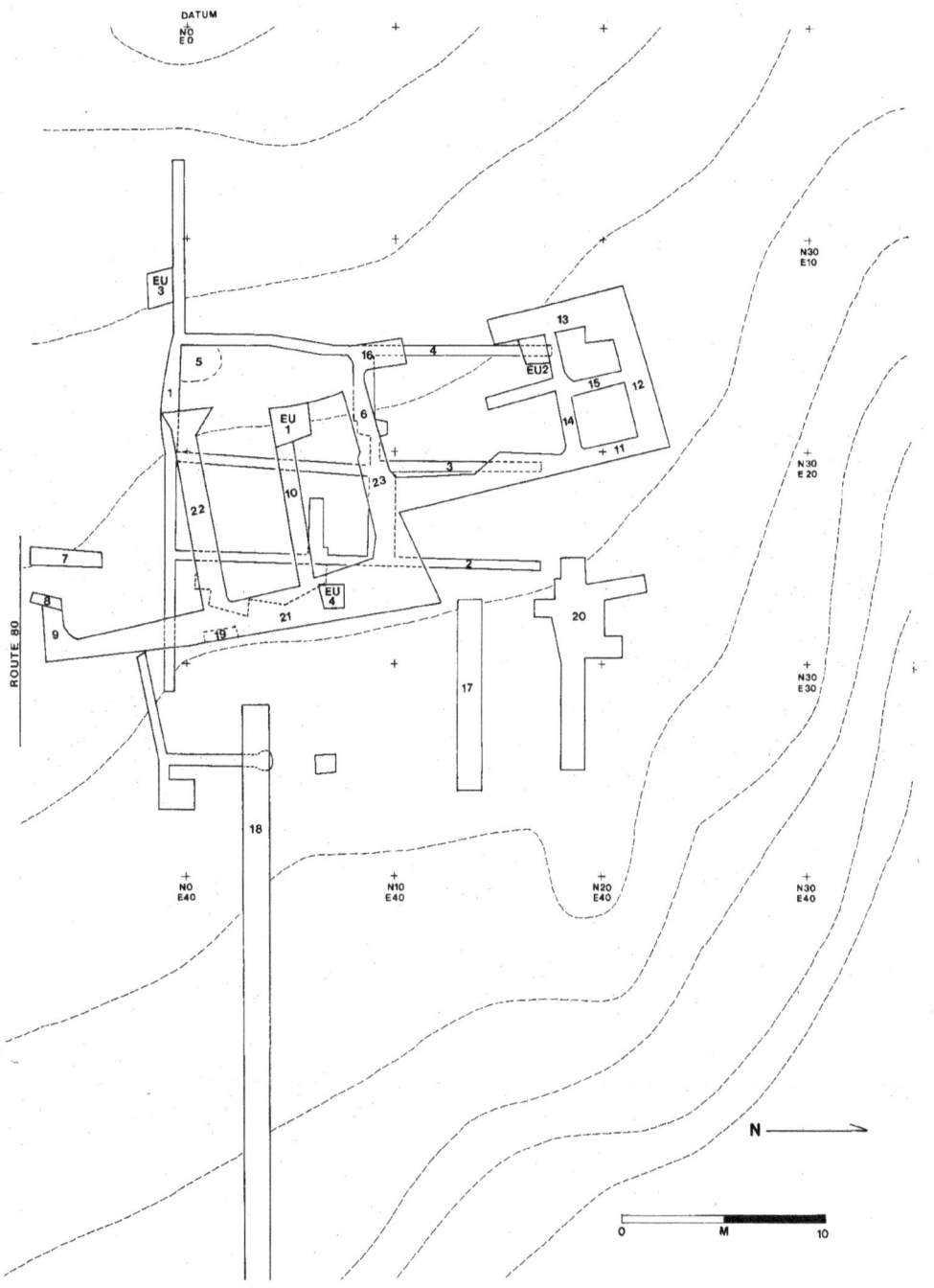

FIGURE 8. Topographic map (1 m contour intervals) showing location of archaeological excavations at the Columbus Center Cheese Factory site.

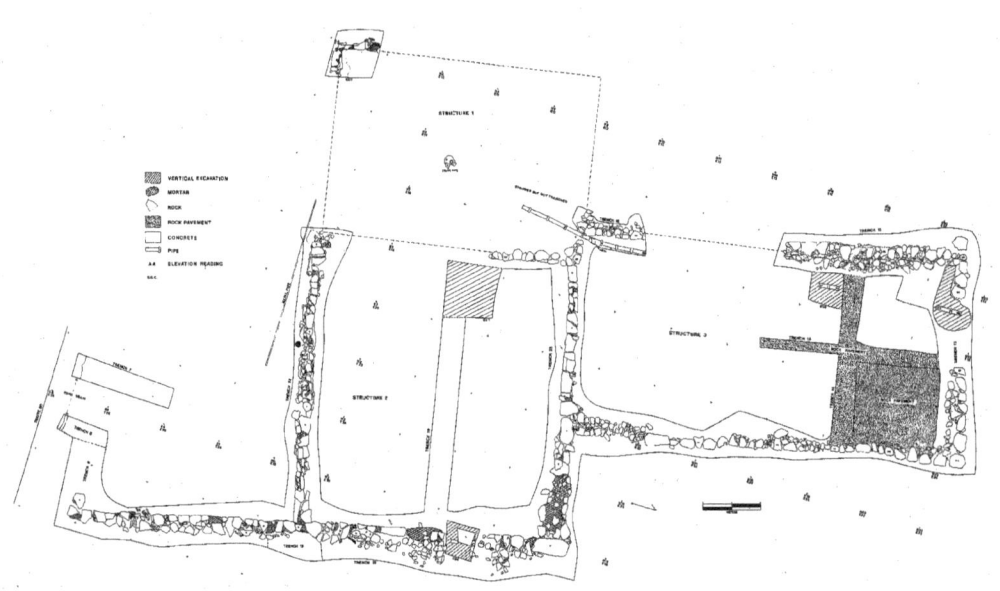

FIGURE 9. Structures 1-3.

deposits. A series of six narrow trenches of variable length (numbers 1–6 in Figure 8) were then excavated to determine the extent of the structure. Although inadequate for exposing the full extent and configuration of the foundations, they confirmed the presence of intact walls beneath the refuse. Accordingly, an additional 16 trenches, some overlapping and incorporating the original trenches, were excavated (Figures 8–10). These units were placed where surface features (rises, depressions, or vegetational anomalies) indicated the presence of foundation walls and were frequently extended horizontally in order to determine whether foundations lacking in surface indicators were present.

In addition to exposing stratigraphy and foundations, the trenches were designed to uncover evidence of building expansion and, through the recovery of machine parts and structural features, the presence of function-specific rooms. All of the trenches were excavated with shovels, trowels, and whiskbrooms. With the exception of Trench 10 and the four excavation units (EUs in Figures 8 and 9), the trenches were excavated by stripping away sod and sweeping or shoveling off the cinders from the tops of the foundation walls. Soil from the trenches was not screened, but nails, window glass, coal stove parts, and electric insulators were readily discernible. They were collected and assigned provenience designations. Trench 10 and EU 1 were placed within the structure and were dug to sterile soil in order to expose stratigraphy and document the recent dumping at the Cheese Factory site.

Four excavation units (designated EU1–EU4 on Figures 8 and 9), each measuring approximately 2 m^2, were excavated within the exposed foundations to discover if floors had survived and to recover stratigraphic information useful for interpreting features, construction sequences, and post-abandonment transformations of the deposits. In order to document site topography and to examine vertical relationships among structures and other features, a contour map was also produced. Together, the trenches, excavation units, and the contour map provide data on the organization of space within the factory, maintenance and expansion of the facility, disposition of manufacturing by-products, and abandonment and subsequent reuse of the site.

During fieldwork, a total of five structures, three of which are contiguous, were encountered (Figures 9 and 10). Each of these is described below in terms of its size, construction, internal differentiation, and probable function. A metal water pipe and a terra-cotta pipe (the latter presumably for draining off whey) were also uncovered. Remnants (surface depressions) of a small road encircling the facility were also identified. Recognizable post-abandonment processes include factory dismantling, land filling, construction and demolition of a 20th-century building, and the return of the area to pasture.

Structure 1, the westernmost of the five buildings, is located on the highest terrain (Figure 9). Although its foundation was not completely exposed, definition of three corners indicates that it is rectangular and measures 9 × 7 m (30 × 23 ft). These building measurements, and all others reported here, are necessarily approximate due to the crudeness of the foundation walls and their incomplete state of preservation. The foundation is composed of mortared fieldstone and lacks well-defined coursing. The 2 m² unit (EU3) excavated in the southwest corner of Structure 1 revealed a rubble fill, but no floor. A mortar lip found below the top of the west wall and a rectangular dark stain in the subsoil (remains of a joist) are all that remain of the original floor. Presumably, it was removed when the factory building was dismantled in the early 1900s.

The 1908 photograph of the factory (Figure 7) shows the superstructure of Structure 1. Window sashes had been removed by that time as had other portions of the facility. (An informant noted that her father, a local farmer, reused the lumber in a nearby barn.) The photograph does reveal that Structure 1 was a two and a half story framed building with a gabled, shingled roof and horizontal siding. Imitation quoins appear on the southwest corner of the structure. A small, gabled ell with two windows is supported by posts and appended to the west wall. The rectangular aperture

in the eastern half of the ridgeline shows the location of a dismantled chimney.

Stripping of the sod within Structure 1 revealed a j-joint terra-cotta pipe set into concrete near the approximate center of the building. A length of fitted segments of pipe of the same material, oriented toward the center of the structure, exits at the northeast corner (Figure 9). There is no evidence of a holding tank in the narrow strip between the factory and the ravine. The pipe segments are 61 cm (24 in) in length and 14 cm (5.5 in) in diameter and have both a plain and flaired end for fitting. A number of the pipe joints are mortared in place. One broken length, patched with a piece of sheet metal, was found just outside Structure 1. This terra-cotta pipe probably served to drain whey from Structure 1 to the ravine north of the factory.

It is likely that Structure 1 served as the curd room. The elevation of the structure (allowing gravity to be employed in transferring milk), the terra-cotta drain pipe for removing whey, and the presumed delivery of milk through the west wall ell (compare Figures 1 and 7) all indicate that early steps in the cheese manufacturing process took place here.

Structure 1 shares its east wall with Structure 2, the foundations of which were almost completely exposed during excavation. Structure 2 measures approximately 10 × 9 m (33 × 30 ft) and its foundation was also constructed of mortared fieldstone. A large flat stone (exposed in EU4), set some 60 cm (24 in) below the top of the foundation, suggests an east wall doorway. Some poorly preserved wood fragments were found above sterile subsoil on the interior side of the door, but no floor was discernible. A series of large flat stones set along the north wall of Structure 2 may indicate the presence of a bay door. This opening is roughly 3 m (10 ft) in length and leads to the adjoining structure (Structure 3). A widening and deepening of the exploratory trench in which this threshold was found (Trench 23, Figure 9) also failed to reveal traces of a floor.

Trench 10 and EU1 were excavated to determine if a floor survived in Structure 2. Neither unit yielded structural remains. In each, ash, cinders and rubble were observed above sterile subsoil. As with Structure 1, the floor seems to have been removed from Structure 2 and the resulting depression filled with debris.

The east wall of Structure 2 extends some 8 m (26 ft) south of its intersection with the south wall, makes a right angle to the west, and abruptly ends. The east and south walls bond at their intersection; that is, there is no seam separating the two walls to indicate that the south extension is an addition. Construction and modification of the modern highway may have destroyed a portion of the wall and, unfortunately, the 1908 photograph of the factory (Figure 7) gives no direct clue as to the wall's function. Whether it is the remains of another structure or a retaining wall cannot be determined with confidence, although the limited archaeological and photographic evidence tends to support the latter interpretation. The photograph depicts a hand pump to the right (south) of Structure 1, suggesting that this area may have been used for cleaning cheese implements, as well as for other, as yet undetermined, activities.

Sharing the north wall of Structure 2 is Structure 3 (Figure 9). This structure's foundation was almost entirely exposed during excavation. It measures approximately 14 × 7 m (46 × 23 ft). Unlike Structures 1 and 2, Structure 3's fieldstone foundation is unmortared and only one course in height. While the west wall of this structure bonds with the north wall of Structure 1, its east wall abuts (a seam is formed) the north wall of Structure 2. Ordinarily, the appearance of such a seam would suggest that the structures were not built at the same time, however, the nature of the intersection at the southwest corner suggests differently. Structure 3 was built at the same time as Structures 1 and 2; it was simply finished after the completion of the foundation of Structure 2. Structures 1 and 2 share a continuous north wall.

Movement between Structures 2 and 3 was permitted by means of the bay door described above. There was no direct access between Structures 1 and 3 and, as suggested in Figure 7, Structure 1 may have lacked exterior doorways. These two structures were connected by a short length of common wall and by the terra-cotta drain pipe that

entered Structure 3 through its southwest corner (Figure 9). The pipe runs roughly parallel to the west wall of Structure 3 and exits through a 2 m (6 ft) gap in the north wall, some 20 m (66 ft) from its origin in Structure 1. The missing central portion of the north wall may represent an exterior bay door, but there is no evidence of a stone or wood threshold to confirm this interpretation. Throughout its course in Structure 3, the terra-cotta pipe is covered by a stone pavement. The pavement extends across the entire interior of the structure just beneath the sod and a thin layer of soil.

The 1908 photograph of the factory depicts a balloon-framed gabled structure of two and one half stories on the north side of Structure 1 (to the left of the light colored central building). This partly dismantled structure undoubtedly corresponds to Structure 3. Like Structure 1, it bore a shingled roof. All of the exterior siding had been removed by the time the photograph was taken, revealing (when the photograph is magnified) horizontal, carvel-built interior siding (the horizontal planks are set on edge to form a tight, flush seam). A small aperture is visible on the west side of the gable just beneath the ridgeline and it is likely that a chimney, since dismantled, was located here. There is no archaeological evidence, however, for such a placement.

Structure 3 probably served as a curing room. The stone pavement beneath the wood floor would have permitted relatively dust free ventilation through floor registers and the heat retaining properties of the stones would help maintain uniform temperatures. Furthermore, cured cheeses could be easily loaded on a waiting wagon outside the north doorway. Access to Structure 1 was possible only by passing through the bay door in the south wall of Structure 3 (north wall of Structure 2) and then crossing Structure 2 (Figure 9). This configuration suggests that Structure 2 was the curd working and pressing room since these activities would not require direct outside access. They would, however, require direct access to both the curd and curing rooms.

In sum, the layout of Structures 1, 2, and 3 corresponds well with the tripartite division of cheese factories (outlined above) described in the

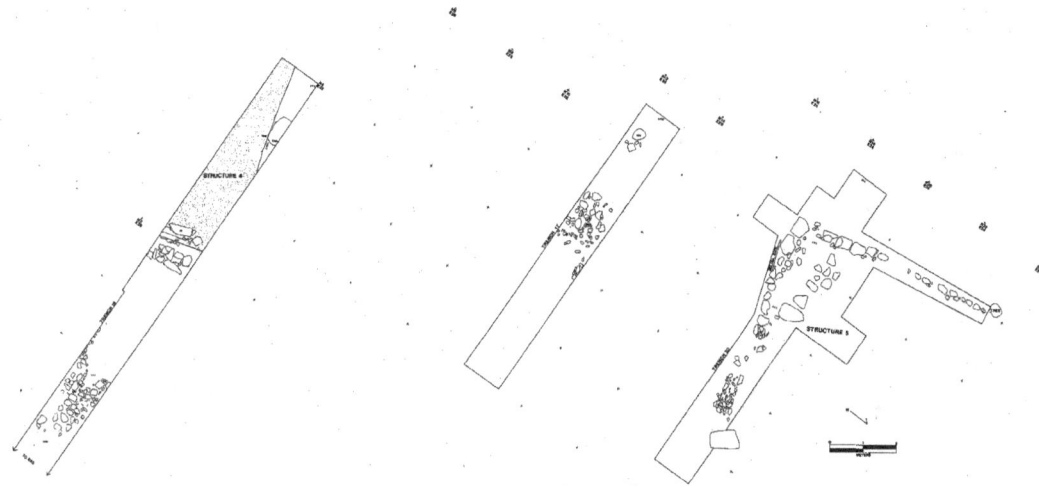

FIGURE 10. Structures 4 and 5.

19th- and 20th-century literature. The reconstructed configuration of the Columbus Center Cheese Factory would allow for the efficient segregation of tasks, as well as the smooth movement of raw materials and finished product. Based on the presence of only one seam in the walls of the foundation it is reasonable to conclude that the facility was built in one episode.

Two additional disconnected structures were uncovered at the site (Figure 10). Structure 4 is located approximately 5 m (16.5 ft) downhill (east) of the main complex and is marked by a concrete floor measuring 7.4 × 6.4 m (24 × 21 ft). The floor is oriented at a slight angle to the axes of the other buildings. Remnants of a concrete wall and a fieldstone footing located along its eastern edge were identified. Structure 4 is probably the remains of the concrete milk receiving station, in use from approximately 1910 to 1940, described by local informants. Hundreds of machine-cut, machine-headed nails recovered from the surface of the structure suggest an earlier date; however, the use of such nails continued long after the widespread introduction of wire nails. Cut nails are still used to affix lumber to concrete.

North of Structure 4 and east of Structure 3 are the remains of a fifth building, designated Structure 5 (Figure 10). Limited testing here revealed a square structure measuring approximately 6 × 6 m (20 × 20 ft). The foundation appears to be of a single course of dry-laid fieldstone, though multiple courses may exist on the downslope (eastern) portion of the foundation. Removal of the sod from above the west and south walls revealed a dark brown sandy humus containing dense quantities of cinders, brick fragments, nails and glass. Due to time and contractual restraints, no further testing of this structure was undertaken. There is insufficient evidence to identify the function, date of construction, or date of dismantling of Structure 5. This is unfortunate since its construction could represent a significant shift in production strategy by Richer and Whitmore or their successors. It is also possible that it predates the initial establishment of the cheese factory.

Artifacts directly associated with the operation of the Columbus Center Cheese Factory are few and most of the cultural material found in the fill post-dates the plant's operation. These include large quantities of cinders and ash, plate glass, brick fragments, wire, and parts of a coal stove. A concentration of broken bottles, ceramics, brick,

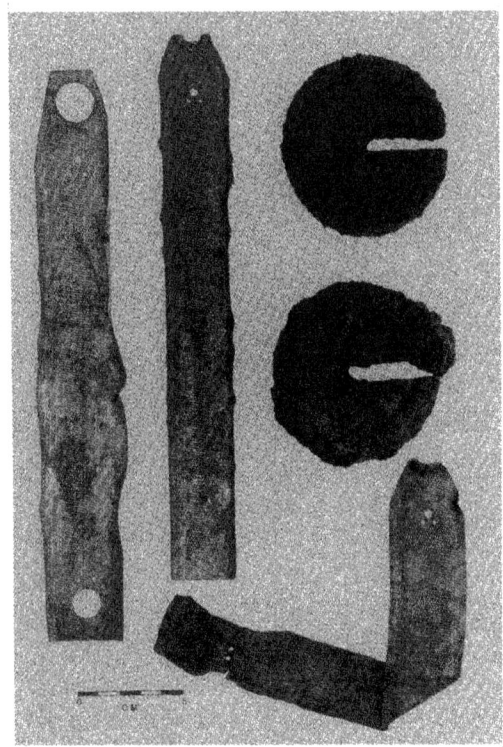

FIGURE 11. Thermometer backplates (*left* and *bottom*) and balance scale weights (*upper right*) found at the Columbus Center Cheese Factory site.

makers' mark'' ''Whitman and Burrell, Little Falls, NY'' is seen on one of the backplates.

The structures and artifacts of the Columbus Center Cheese Factory are interpreted with the aid of 19th-century descriptions of cheese factories and of the cheddaring process. Wagons from local farms delivered milk to the receiving ell on the west side of the complex. Here the milk was weighed, tested for quality, and drained into the curd vats in Structure 1. In this structure, the milk was cooled with spring water brought down to the factory in metal pipes (the remains of which lie just south of the south wall of the complex). Heat was then applied to the milk by means of a steam boiler or fire box beneath the vats. After the curd formed the whey was drained off through the terra-cotta pipe. Next, the curd was gathered up and brought into Structure 2 for salting and pressing. Finally, the green cheese rounds were stored in Structure 3 where they were cured, weighed, and after several weeks, loaded on wagons for shipment.

Production Strategies at the Cheese Factory

Archaeological and documentary data reveal at least five production strategies employed at the Columbus Center Cheese Factory. Each change of strategy marked an increase in the geographical scope and organizational complexity of the operation. In this section, six aspects of plant operations are described for each strategy. These include plant ownership and management, marketing, materials procurement, manufacturing processes, expansion of production, and disposition of by-products.

The Columbus Center Cheese Factory was built by Henry Holmes and Nicholas Richer in 1863 or 1864. In 1864, the partners joined the newly organized New York State Cheese Manufacturers' Association. Richer was the cheese maker and he supervised the daily operations of the factory. Holmes, a local merchant, probably was responsible for marketing the cheese. With access to the milk of approximately 600 cows, Richer could have manufactured as much as 200,000 pounds of cheddar cheese each season. (This figure is based

and nails was uncovered above the intersection of the north wall of Structure 1 and the west wall of Structure 3, but it too appears to post-date the factory. The site appears to have been used as a trash dump during the early 20th century.

Five artifacts were found that can be firmly associated with cheese making: two balance scale weights and three thermometer backplates (Figure 11). One of the weights was found along the south wall of Structure 2, the other in the fill above Structure 5. Thermometer backplates were found in Structures 1 and 5, and in a sheet deposit of refuse between Structures 4 and 5. All of the backplates bear the inscriptions ''Freezing,'' ''Churning'' (62 degrees F), ''Cheese'' (86 degrees F), ''Scalding'' (150 degrees F), and ''Boiling.'' The on reported yields from other factories in the region with comparable milk supplies.) Documents relating to the purchase of milk have not been identified, but it is likely that the farmers were paid monthly or seasonally for the quantity of milk delivered to the factory. Arrangements for the sale of the cheese were probably made with itinerant agents or, through the post, with commission merchants in Utica and New York City. It was then transported by wagon to Chenango Canal at Sherburne or to the railroad at New Berlin. Materials such as cheesecloth, cheese boxes, salt, and annota (a coloring agent) were probably procured through Holme's mercantile network or directly from cheese manufacturing supply houses in Utica.

The tripartite configuration of the factory, retained throughout its existence, is in keeping with standard practices. This suggests that Richer and his successors used the normal cheddaring process described by their contemporaries. Evidence of factory expansion is wholly lacking, with the possible exception of Structure 5. Determination of this structure's date of construction and function, however, awaits further excavation. The termination of the terra-cotta pipe above the ravine indicates that none of the cheese makers sought to profit from control of the whey. These efforts would have required a holding tank in which the by-product could be collected and stored. As mentioned above, there is no archaeological evidence of any such structure.

By 1869, Holmes left the partnership and was replaced by his fellow merchant and Richer's brother-in-law, George B. Whitmore. Soon after the new partnership was formed, Whitmore joined a commission firm in New York City, therby initiating a new strategy. His move facilitated sales and increased the partnership's access to capital. Materials procurement practices seemingly changed little, although Richer's purchase of a local general store may have facilitated access to producer goods. There is no evidence of change in the manufacturing process or of factory expansion in the late 1860s or early 1870s. The patched drain pipe suggests that whey dumping continued.

Richer and Whitmore effected a major shift in strategy (the third in the sequence) in the middle to

late 1870s. Perhaps employing outside capital, Richer erected a sawmill directly across the road from the cheese factory. The mill produced, among other things, cheese boxes, presumably used to package cheese from the Columbus Center Factory. Also at this time, the partners purchased five of the remaining six cheese factories in the town. By the mid-1880s, they acquired eight additional factories in adjoining towns. Clearly, Richer and Whitmore pursued a strategy of integrating and expanding production without altering the original factory. The process of integration began, as described above, with Whitmore moving to New York City. It did not end with the third strategy described here, but continued under the direction of new owners. This new strategy entailed the use of capital to acquire neighboring facilities. It did not include, in the case of Columbus Center, investment in the physical expansion of the factory.

In the middle to late 1880s, Richer and Whitmore sold all of their factories to the Sage family. As of 1880, the Sages owned four of the six creameries (butter and cheese factories) in the neighboring town of New Berlin. By 1892, they introduced butter making into four of their Columbus factories, including the one at Columbus Center. (The Sages appear to have closed the other two Columbus plants.) Butter making at Columbus Center may account for Structure 5. Other aspects of the Sage operation—marketing, materials procurement, and by-product disposition—have not been determined. It is probable, however, that practices in these areas became more complex as the Sage combination grew. There is evidence that the Sage family had a succession of partners, but this probably had more to do with plant acquisition and capitalization than with other aspects of the operation. Archaeological and archival research into the extensive Sage operations should clarify these practices and further develop the interpretation of the Columbus Center factory.

By 1894, the Sage corporation owned 13 operating creameries in the towns of Norwich, Columbus, and New Berlin and had sold or shut down at least two of the Columbus factories. They initiated a new strategy (the fifth in this series) with the shipment and sale of cheese, butter, and fluid milk from six of their plants, one of which was located in the town of Columbus. Milk was not shipped from the Columbus Center factory, perhaps due to its location miles away from the nearest railroad. Cheese and butter remained its sole products.

Between 1894 and 1904, many of the factories in the area closed, including the one at Columbus Center. A clue to understanding the causes of this decline is provided in an 1898 statement by then Secretary of the Utica Board of Trade, Benjamin Gilbert:

> In the valleys of Stockbridge and Chenango I could tell you of a dozen factories which two years ago produced from one half to a ton of cheese per day, but which railroad companies have bought up, turned the key in the door and have said to the dairymen, ''Bring your milk to the station, we are not going to run this factory'' (Gilbert quoted in Poese 1985:34).

It appears that the practice of shipping fluid milk, begun by the Sages and other manufacturers, was taken over by the railroads. Creameries were closed down and the milk transported to urban markets. Remote communities like Columbus Center, with higher transportation costs for their produce, lost the market for their dairy products. The result was economic decline and depopulation. Widespread adoption of the automobile during the first two decades of the 20th century eventually undermined the railroad's monopoly. Cheese factories thrived once again, albeit as large, corporately owned facilities supplied by networks of milk receiving stations dispersed across the countryside. The Columbus Center Factory, no longer needed, was dismantled in 1908 and replaced by one of these masonry milk receiving stations.

Summary and Discussion

Excavations at the site of the Columbus Center Cheese Factory revealed a main building containing three rooms and two detached structures. The functions of the three rooms within the main structure are readily identified based on their spatial relationships and the postion and course of a terra-cotta drainpipe. Oral accounts and evidence of rel-atively modern construction techniques indicate that Structure 4 is an early 20th-century milk receiving station. Structure 5 sustained only very limited archaeological testing, thus its function cannot be positively determined. However, archival evidence suggests that butter-making was introduced at the factory in the late 1880s or early 1890s and Structure 5 may have housed a cream separator and churns for the manufacture of this commodity.

It is also interesting to note what testing failed to reveal. The terra-cotta pipe, presumably used to drain whey out of the curd room (Structure 1), passed through the curd and curing rooms and terminated at the edge of a deep ravine. There is no trace of a holding tank at the end of the pipe and the slope below is too steep to have supported livestock pens. Not only does it appear that whey was dumped into the ravine, but the patch on the pipe suggests that this practice continued for some time. Evidence of building expansion is also lacking. With the exception of Structure 5 and the early 20th-century milk receiving station (Structure 4), the foundations for the factory all appear to have been built at the same time. Any additions to the core structure either lacked foundations or were built on top of the existing structure. Adding floors to the structure (there is no evidence of this in the ca. 1908 photograph) would have increased storage and curing capacity, but would not have increased work space in the critical curd-working area.

Rather than expand the existing facility or diversify into such enterprises as hog raising, Richer, Whitmore, and the Sage family removed their capital from the community. Throughout its 40 years of operation, the main factory building remained substantially unchanged. As noted above, there is no evidence of livestock pens or a holding tank having been constructed at the end of the drainpipe in order to utilize whey. Apparently no effort was made to use this byproduct as livestock feed or in the manufacture of products such as ricotta cheese or whey butter.

Archival and archaeological data from the Columbus Center Cheese Factory site reveal at least five successive production strategies as well as overall trends of capital exportation and the loss of local control over production. Understanding production strategies such as those described here provides a valuable interpretive framework in which community level processes such as economic and agricultural development, rural depopulation, and the effect of entrepreneurial activities can be examined. Further, it provides an effective means of organizing and synthesizing data on rural industries collected from archaeological and documentary sources.

ACKNOWLEDGMENTS

Funds for research at the Columbus Center Cheese Factory site were provided by the New York State Department of Transportation. The maps in this article were drawn by Beth Cassedy and John Pryor and the photographs were taken by the late Bruce Wrighton. We would like to thank Chris Hays, Susan Pollock, and three anonymous reviewers for commenting on early versions of this paper.

REFERENCES

ANONYMOUS
  1886 History of Columbus. Columbus Argus 1(1). Reprinted in New Berlin Gazette, September 8, 1960.

BARTH, FREDERICK
  1963 The Role of the Entrepreneur in Social Change in Northern Norway. Univesitetsforlaget Bergen, Oslo.

BIOGRAPHICAL PUBLISHING COMPANY
  1898 Biographical Sketches of Leading Citizens of Chenango County, New York. Biographical Publishing Company, Buffalo.

BLAKELEE, GEORGE
  1885 Blakelee's Industrial Cyclopedia for the Mechanic, Housewife, and Children of Every Household. J.S. Olgilive Publishing Company, New York.

BRUNGER, ERIC
  1954 Changes in the New York State Dairy Industry, 1850–1880. University Microfilms, Ann Arbor.

CHILDE, HAMILTON P.
  1869 Gazetteer and Business Directory of Chenango County, New York, for 1869–1870. H. Childe, Syracuse.

GILBERT, BENJAMIN DAVIS
  1896 The Cheese Industry of the State of New York. U.S. Government Printing Office, Washington, D.C.

JUDD, ORANGE
  1865 The Associated Dairy or Cheese Factory System. American Agriculturalist 24(1):340.

KENNEDY, JOSEPH
  1864 Agriculture of the United States in 1860; Compiled from the Original Returns of the Eighth Census. U.S. Government Printing Office, Washington, D.C.

LAMPARD, ERIC
  1963 The Rise of the Dairy Industry in Wisconsin: A Study in Agricultural Change, 1820–1920. The State Historical Society of Wisconsin, Madison.

NEW YORK STATE CHEESE MANUFACTURERS' ASSOCIATION (NYSCMA)
  1864 The Report of the New York State Cheese Manufacturers' Association. NYSCMA, Utica.
  1865 The Report of the New York State Cheese Manufacturers' Association. NYSCMA, Utica.

NEW YORK STATE DEPARTMENT OF AGRICULTURE (NYSDA)
  1893 Summary of the Butter and Cheese Made in Factories in the State of New York During the Season of 1892. Argus Company, Albany.
  1895 Summary of the Butter and Cheese Made in Factories in the State of New York During the Season of 1894. Argus Company, Albany.
  1904 Summary of the Butter and Cheese Made in Factories in the State of New York During the Season of 1904. Argus Company, Albany.

PIRTLE, T.R.
  1933 A Handbook of Dairy Statistics. U.S. Government Printing Office, Washington, D.C.

POESE, LAUREN SUE
  1985 The History and Design of Specialized Architecture: Cheese Factories in Central New York. Unpublished M.A. thesis, Cornell University, Ithaca, New York.

PORTER, GLENN, AND HAROLD C. LIVESAY
  1971 Merchants and Manufacturers: Changes in the Structure of Nineteenth-Century Marketing. Johns Hopkins University Press, Baltimore.

ROBBINS, FRANCES BRIGHAM
  1972 Columbus. Ms. on file, Chenango County Historical Society, Norwich, New York.

RUMSEY, MARION W.
  1954 The Old Cheese Factory: Pungent Memories of Long Ago. Courier Magazine 3(10):17–19.

RUSSELL, E. H.
  1926 Letter of M.C. Bond, Extension Professor in Marketing, dated June 6, 1926. Ms. on file, Mann Library, Cornell University, Ithaca, New York.

SMITH, JAMES
  1880 History of Chenango and Madison Counties, New York. Mason and Company, Syracuse.

WICKSON, EDWARD J.
  1875 Butter and Cheese. *Harper's New Monthly Magazine* 51(306):813–827.

WILBER, FLOYD
  1967 *Glimpses of Early New Berlin and Related Facts.* F. Wilber, New Berlin, New York.

WILLARD, XERXES
  1865 Annual Address to the New York State Cheese Man-ufacturers' Association. *Second Annual Report of the NYSCMA, with Accompanying Papers, etc., for the Year 1864.* New York State Cheese Manufacturers' Association, Utica.

JAMES G. GIBB
DAVID J. BERNSTEIN
DANIEL F. CASSEDY
DEPARTMENT OF ANTHROPOLOGY
STATE UNIVERSITY OF NEW YORK
BINGHAMTON, NEW YORK 13901

DEBORAH A. HULL-WALSKI
FRANK L. WALSKI

There's Trouble a-Brewin': The Brewing and Bottling Industries at Harpers Ferry, West Virginia

ABSTRACT

During the late 19th and early 20th centuries, a brewery and bottling plant operated in the town of Harpers Ferry, West Virginia. Archaeological excavations recovered beer and soft drink bottles once used by these industries. Considering that the brewery was operational in Harpers Ferry for over 10 years and bottled soft drinks and beer, it was surprising that relatively few bottles attributable to the brewery were recovered from the excavations. In order to understand this phenomenon, this study examines the historical context of the brewery, its associated bottling plant, and the people who worked in these industries. The Harpers Ferry brewery bottles recovered from the excavations are described and compared with bottles from regional breweries and bottling plants. Various possibilities for the lack of bottles are considered, including financial problems of the brewery, popularity of the product, and temperance.

Introduction

Archaeological excavations conducted in 1989 and 1990 as part of restoration work at Harpers Ferry National Historical Park, West Virginia, recovered over 140,000 artifacts from the backyards of buildings located in Lower Town Harpers Ferry. Approximately 1,800 bottles, representing various products, were recovered from three backyard privies. Only 52 of these bottles were attributable to the brewery and bottling plant at Harpers Ferry.

This study considers the reasons that such a small percentage of Harpers Ferry brewery bottles was recovered. In order to understand the context of the Harpers Ferry bottles, a history of the brewery and bottling plant, focusing mainly on the owners and workers, is presented. Beer and soft drink bottles found in the excavations, including bottles from regional breweries and bottling plants, in ad-

dition to those from Harpers Ferry, are described. The bottles and their products are considered in terms of disposal methods for returnable bottles, popularity of product, and alcohol consumption during a time of temperance. The possible relationship between the brewery's financial instability and the lack of Harpers Ferry bottles recovered during the excavations is addressed.

Only sketchy glimpses about brewery operations and brewery workers could be gathered from newspapers, deed books, brewery journals, corporation records, census records, and historical maps. The business records of the brewery and bottling plant, which would have produced a better insight into the operations, have not yet been located. General histories on breweries and brewery workers were used to help understand how the Harpers Ferry brewery may have functioned.

Historical Background

In 1895, the year the Harpers Ferry brewery was built, 1,732 breweries in America produced a total of 33,237,650 barrels of beer (Friedrich and Bull 1976:306). Beer had been made in America since the earliest American settlement, but it was not until the mid-1800s that the production of beer accelerated. The American public's response to lager beer, coupled with technological advances in beer making, led to an increase in beer production and the number of breweries. When bottled beer became a feasible commercial proposition for breweries after pasteurization was perfected in 1875, bottling plants became a common industry associated with a brewery (Kroll 1976:1). A large proportion of beer bottling plants commonly marketed carbonated beverages as a sideline (Riley 1972[1958]:133). In the case of Harpers Ferry, a bottling plant that marketed beer and soft drinks led to the construction of a brewery that produced lager beer.

The brewery and bottling plant located at Harpers Ferry began as a small beer and soft drink bottling operation established by James McGraw, a local merchant. McGraw began his beer bottling business around 1885, a date established by an

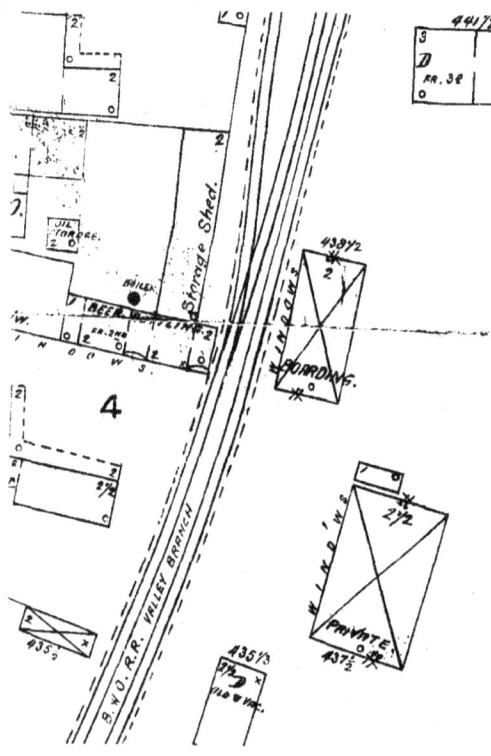

FIGURE 1. Sanborn Fire Insurance map (Sanborn Map Company 1894) illustrating the McGraw bottling plant and the pre-brewery building. (Courtesy of Harpers Ferry National Historical Park.)

advertisement in a local newspaper which noted Milwaukee Lager Beer being bottled for trade by McGraw (*Spirit of Jefferson* [*SoJ*] 1885:2).

Apparently bottled beer was well received at Harpers Ferry, for in 1888 McGraw built a bottling plant behind his business in Block B, Lot 3 (Figure 1). In 1890 he turned over his bottling business to his son James C. (*SoJ* 1890:3). During the next three years, advertisements in the *Spirit of Jefferson* noted James C. as agent for Sachs Puden ginger ale, Pilsner export beer, and Pabst Milwaukee beer. The Pabst advertisement indicated how brewers wanted beer perceived: "Pure, Healthful, Nourishing and—Refreshing Pabst's Milwaukee Beer . . . As a Beverage unsurpassed, As a Tonic unexcelled, As a Nervine unapproachable is Pabst's Beer" (*SoJ* 1892:3).

James McGraw died in 1893 and James C. became the administrator of an estimated estate of $155,000 (*SoJ* 1893:3). J. C. soon began to expand the beverage business, adding new equipment and an ice machine (Jefferson County Deed Book [JCDB] 1894; *SoJ* 1894:3). Two years after his father's death, James C. announced his intention to build a large brewery in Harpers Ferry (*SoJ* 1895a: 2). The brewery was to be constructed in Block C, Lot 11, land previously purchased by his father (JCDB 1885). The land, containing a brick and stone building, was located between the Shenandoah River and the B & O Railroad, approximately 75 ft. southwest from the bottling plant (Figure 1). The entire cost of the brewery, including machinery, was $30,000 (*SoJ* 1895b:2).

McGraw named the brewery the Harpers Ferry Brewing Company (Figure 2). It was expected to produce up to 10,000 barrels a year, although the brewery had the ability to expand to 30,000 (*SoJ* 1895b:2). The steam-bottling plant owned by McGraw was associated with the brewery, packaging not only beer made in the brewery, but also soft drinks (JCDB 1897:494). By 1897, J. C. McGraw's beverage business included beer brewing, beer and soft drink bottling, and soft drink and ice manufacturing (JCDB 1897:497).

Although left a large estate by his father, J. C. apparently over-extended himself financially by assuming loans to pay for the building of the brewery and other investments. In October 1897, three months after a fire at the brewery incurred $6,000 worth of damages, J. C. McGraw declared bankruptcy (*Western Brewer* 1897:1372; JCDB 1897: 493–498). McGraw's brewery and bottling plant were soon offered for sale. The estimated worth of the industries at the time of the bankruptcy was $50,000 (*SoJ* 1897:2).

James M. Mason, Jr., the lawyer handling the bankruptcy, kept the brewery operating from October to January while looking for buyers. Mason stated that he first offered the brewery for $35,000, but, "then dropped to $30,000, later to $25,000, later to $20,000, and finally as low as $12,000. I finally even offered to let any one have the Brew-

FIGURE 2. Photograph of the Harpers Ferry brewery, ca. 1895. The brewery is located in the right corner of the photograph between the railroad tracks and river; an arrow points to the brewery. (Courtesy of Harpers Ferry National Historical Park.)

ery [*sic*] without any cash payment, provided, this [*sic*] the party would give me collateral or some security . . ." (Jefferson County Court Records [JCCR] 1906).

The brewery was finally sold in February 1898 to August Krueger of Cincinnati, Ohio, a bad decision as Mason soon discovered (JCDB 1898a). Krueger, according to Mason, turned out to be an "ex-Convict and consumate [*sic*] adventurer" who borrowed the collateral from "ignorant work-

TABLE 1
OWNERS OF THE HARPERS FERRY BREWERY AND BOTTLING PLANT

Owners	Date of Purchase	Purchase Price ($)
James McGraw	1888 (built bottling plant on Lot 3)	unknown
James C. McGraw	1895 (built brewery on Lot 11)	30,000
August Krueger (Krueger and Schafer)	14 February 1898	17,700
(1st) Belvidere Brewing Company; Krueger and Schafer, stockholders	16 May 1898	17,200
(2nd) Belvidere Brewing Company; Abner and Drury, stockholders	June 1898 (unofficial); 19 December 1899 (legal)	14,000
Leder-Weideman Brewing Company	17 February 1903 bottling plant Lot 3 not purchased; building sold to Ella Doran 1907	14,360.28
Jefferson Brewing Company	1 November 1905	12,215.96
German Brewing Company	14 June 1909	4,000
Charles T. Smith (Harpers Ferry Bottling Works)	24 November 1916; bottling works continued until destruction in 1942	1,000

men,'' promising them jobs at the brewery (JCCR 1906). This enterprise resulted in failure by June of the same year (*SoJ* 1898:2).

During the following years the ownership of the brewery, as well as the bottling franchise and ice manufacturing concern, changed hands many times (Table 1). The bottling plant probably was moved in 1903 to a location inside the brewery complex after the Leder-Weideman Brewing Company failed to purchase the Block B, Lot 3 building. Stockholders of the Belvidere Brewing Company retained title to the Lot 3 building until it was sold to Ella Doran in 1907 (JCDB 1907).

In addition to financial problems, the brewery suffered from a series of disasters. Fires were common in brewery complexes and three major fires are known to have affected the brewery. In July 1897, while McGraw owned the brewery, a fire burned the contents of the brewery stable. Another during the Leder-Weideman period destroyed portions of the brewery stable and bottling plant (*Farmers Advocate [FA]* 1906:3). A final fire in January of 1909 caused $50,000 to $70,000 worth of damages. The Jefferson Brewing Company's ice plant and main brew house burned, but the bottling plant and stable escaped the fire (*FA* 1909a:2). Although most of the deeds of trust required the brewery owners to carry insurance, it was not enough to cover a major disaster. In fact, the Jefferson Brewing Company had insured the brewery for only one-third of its worth (*SoJ* 1909:3). When the fire of 1909 destroyed the ice plant and brew house, the owners were unable to rebuild (*SoJ* 1909:3).

The brewery also suffered from other disasters. A short time after the sale of Krueger and Schafer's Belvidere Brewing Company to the new stockholders secured by James Mason—the brewery was still called the Belvidere Brewing Company—a local newspaper announced several hundred barrels of beer had been spoiled in the brewing process and subsequently emptied into the river (*FA* 1898a:3). Apparently the beer in the brewery, which had been made prior to Krueger's purchase, was not stored at the appropriate temperature and, as a result, was entirely spoiled (JCCR 1906).

Although various owners of the brewery owed significant amounts of money on loans, they continued to pour money into improvements. The Belvidere Brewing Company, Leder-Weideman Brewing Company, and Jefferson Brewing Company purchased land around the brewery, adding outbuildings and offices. The companies also made additions and improvements within the brewery complex. Belvidere Brewing Company added a refrigerating plant, the Leder-Weideman Brewing Company moved the bottling plant into the brewery complex, and the Jefferson Brewing Company made improvements on the ice plant (*FA* 1898b:3, 1909b:3).

The brewing operation at Harpers Ferry was finally suspended following the fire in 1909, which destroyed most of the brewery complex. Although the stockholders of the Jefferson Brewing Company planned to rebuild the ice factory and operate a bottling works which would sell beers "that made Milwaukee famous," they instead sold the brewery lands to the German Brewing Company (*FA* 1909b:3; JCDB 1909:37). The German Brewing Company probably used the Harpers Ferry brewery as a distribution point for the beer it manufactured in Cumberland, Maryland. The beer may have been bottled in the bottling plant, which had withstood the fire. This operation apparently continued until 1914 when prohibition became effective in West Virginia.

By 1916, all the land owned by the German Brewing Company, including the fire-damaged remains of the brewery, was sold to Charles Smith, a local resident who had acted as a bottling salesman to the German Brewing Company. Smith continued the bottling operation of the brewery, selling soft drink products. The new operation, called the Harpers Ferry Bottling Works, continued to operate until its destruction by flood in 1942.

The numerous changes in the brewery's ownership were indicative of the time period in which the brewery operated. Many small breweries failed in the latter half of the 19th century and the first half of the 20th century due to the vast amount of capital needed to run brewing operations:

> In the particular case of the brewing industry, there had been a huge outlay of capital between 1880 and 1890 for new equipment, new buildings, new processes, new personnel. Only the most soundly based firms could survive this investment (Baron 1962:272).

The Harpers Ferry brewery was never soundly based. The selling of the brewery every few years was probably a way to clear title and escape losses. Corporations were formed to separate individuals from personal liability and to acquire additional

capital. Brewers from other states with well-established firms were brought in to help the floundering Harpers Ferry brewery, but with no success.

In 1910 there were over 1,500 breweries in the United States. The majority of the breweries were small, local enterprises which made their deliveries by horse-drawn wagons. It was, however, the "few large, highly mechanized factories, with merchandising chains extending beyond their own neighborhoods or towns, that controlled the major part of the market" (Baron 1962:256). Consolidations became common and large, stable firms absorbed the small, local companies.

While the brewery was unsuccessful, the bottling operation was a survivor. The bottling concern, begun by James McGraw around 1885, went through numerous changes. The operation began by bottling beer, then added soft drinks. Beer bottling was discontinued from 1914 to 1933 during state and national prohibition, but soft drink bottling continued. The bottling plant was always linked with the brewery during the brewery's years of operation, but emerged as an individual operation following the brewery's destruction in 1909.

Intertwined with the history of the owners is the story of the workers. The following section discusses those individuals who worked at the brewery and bottling works and the conditions under which they labored.

The Brewery and Bottling Plant Workers

Some documentary evidence exists about the people who worked at the brewery and bottling works. In 1895 J. C. McGraw hired Fritz Jensen of Chicago, Illinois, as brewmaster of the Harpers Ferry Brewery. Jensen, according to the *Spirit of Jefferson* (1895b:2), came "with one of the best recommendations in the country." The same newspaper article listed Matthew Volk of Philadelphia, Pennsylvania, and P. Schaupert of Brooklyn, New York, as associates of Jensen. No other employees are known for that year, but an 1896 newspaper article mentioned a McGraw's brewery employee named Adolph Schmidt (*SoJ* 1896:2). The United

States census of 1900 did not list any of these men. By 1899 Mathew Volk owned a brewery in Bellefonte, Pennsylvania (Bull et al. 1984:250).

When the 1900 census was taken, Belvidere Brewing Company owned the brewery. The census listed 12 men employed at a brewery: an engineer, two clerks, four laborers, two bottlers, a brewmaster, a brewery second man, and a brewery apprentice. Most of the employees were natives of West Virginia or the surrounding states. The brewmaster, second man, and apprentice, however, were from Germany and a bottler was from England (United States Bureau of the Census [USBC] 1900: 73–75, 79, 81).

According to the 1900 census, approximately half of the employees listed, including all the natives of Germany and England, boarded near the brewery, while the others had homes in the Harpers Ferry area. The brewery workers probably boarded in private households or in boardinghouses in Lower Town Harpers Ferry. The brewery, at least during Leder-Weideman years of operation, may have provided a residence for some of the workers. An entry in a 1903 deed of trust indicated the Leder-Weideman Brewing Company wanted to "replace the buildings called the office and brewery residence" (JCDB 1903:506). These buildings were probably located in Block C, Lot 1 directly north of the brewery and on the west side of Market Street. It is unknown how long this residence was in use; however, a stockholder of the Belvidere Brewing Company had purchased a portion of Lot 1 in 1898 and this land was subsequently passed on to the Leder-Weideman company when the brewery was sold (JCDB 1898c, 1903:503–504). Providing a place of residence for their employees was common practice for brewery owners (Baron 1962:278).

When the 1910 census was taken, one year after the brewery was destroyed, only two brewery workers listed in the previous census were still working in Harpers Ferry. One man was now a mill laborer and the other a saloon barkeeper. The 1910 census did list two men employed in bottling operations. Charles T. Smith was listed as a salesman at a bottling establishment, while the second man was a bottling works laborer (USBC 1910:186,

189, 190). These men were probably working for the German Brewing Company.

It is very probable that more people worked at the bottling plant and brewery than were listed in the census of 1900, but no corroborating evidence could be found. Only those individuals listed with brewery or bottling related occupations were included in this study. Individuals called laborers or day-laborers by census-takers may have worked at the brewery, but they were not considered because they could not be identified as brewery workers or bottlers.

Individuals employed in the brewery worked under difficult conditions. Brewery work by the end of the 19th century was very mechanized, and steam power had replaced many hand operations. The introduction of new operations, including ice manufacturing and bottling, led to a diversified labor structure. In addition to those individuals who specialized in brewing beer, there were engineers to operate the ice machinery, general laborers, bottlers to package the product, and drivers to distribute the beer (Baron 1962:274).

The brewery workers toiled in an environment where they were subjected at times to extreme temperature changes. The brew house itself averaged a temperature of 68°F, while the cooling rooms were 41°F and the malt kiln rooms 176°F. The brewery in Harpers Ferry, according to 1902 and 1907 Sanborn Insurance maps, was not equipped for heat so during cold winter months the brew house was probably much colder than 68°F (Figures 3, 4). In addition to the varying temperatures, the workers breathed air that contained carbonic acid, sulfuric acid, and other substances. The polluted air combined with radical changes in temperature led to many lung diseases (Schulter 1910:260–268).

In addition to diseases caused by polluted air and varying temperatures, many brewery workers suffered from alcohol abuse. The "free beer" system employed by most breweries led not only to an increase in accidents, but also to many "cases of drunkenness" (Schulter 1910:259–263).

Brewery employees worked an exceptionally long day in an industry only semi-automated. Many operations, including bottle- and keg-washing, were done by hand. The average work day for

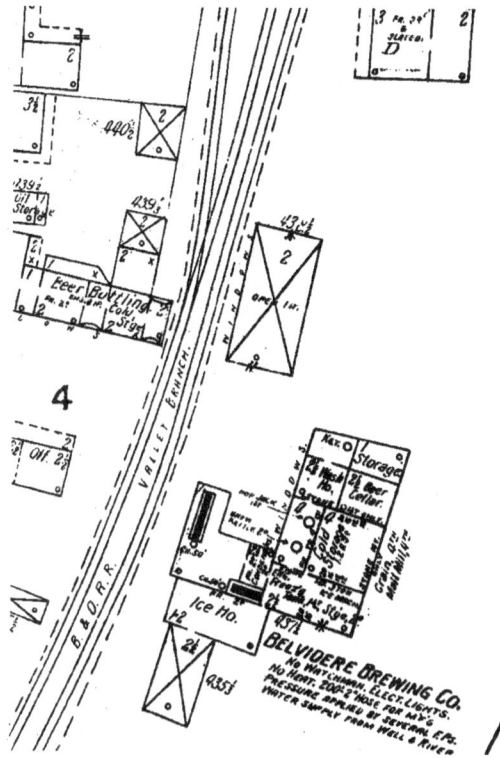

FIGURE 3. Sanborn Fire Insurance map (Sanborn Map Company 1902) illustrating the Harpers Ferry brewery during Belvidere Brewing Company's years of ownership. Note that the bottling operation is not yet within the brewery complex. (Courtesy of Harpers Ferry National Historical Park.)

a brewery worker was 14–18 hours, and the work week was usually six days long with some work on Sundays. The Sunday work day was usually 6–8 hours long (Schulter 1910:92–93). It is probable that the brewery employees worked shifts because the 1907 Sanborn map notes the brewery ran day and night (Figure 4). According to a union spokesperson, working conditions prior to union organization in the 1880s, were

> as bad as can be imagined. It was not only that the wages paid were the smallest possible and that the working time was confined only by the natural limits of human endurance, but besides this the treatment of the workmen was of such a kind that it seems impossible today to understand how

they could submit to it. Cuffs and blows were everyday occurrences (Schulter 1910:89).

The labor movement of brewery workers began in the 1870s. In 1886 the National Union of the Brewers of the United States was formed, and changed its name a year later to the National Union of United Brewery Workmen of the United States (Baron 1962:281). The union strove to obtain a minimum wage and reduced working hours for the workers (Baron 1962:283).

In 1899 the National Brewery Workers Union began an investigation into working conditions of its members in Baltimore. It was discovered that engineers and drivers in various breweries worked a 16- to 18-hour day during the busy seasons with brewery laborers working a 12- to 14-hour day (Kelley 1965:547).

The Brewery Workers Union instituted a strike in the Baltimore area following its investigation. The agreement reached between the union and the brewery owners was:

> engineers should be on duty 12 hours; that the work day for the brew-workers should be 9 hours from October to March and 10 hours for the remainder of the year, or the summer season . . . the wage scale gave the brew-workers at kettles $15 a week; in the fermenting rooms and storage and packing cellars $15; in the wash-houses $13; apprentices $9; regular drivers $12; engineers not less than $18; oilers and helpers $2 a day. The scale was the same that had been in force, but a concession was made by the brewers agreeing to give double pay for work on Sunday (Kelley 1965:548).

Wages and hours for Harpers Ferry employees are not known. It is probable the individuals who worked at the brewery were subjected to the same long hours as those workers in Baltimore. The brewery at Harpers Ferry was unionized during Leder-Weideman's 1903–1905 period of ownership. A 1903 newspaper article noted that employees of the Leder-Weideman Brewing Company had organized and joined the brewers union (*FA* 1903:2). It is not known whether the workers ever attempted to strike for better wages and working conditions. The fact they unionized does suggest that they were dissatisfied with their working conditions. The 1900 and 1910 censuses (USBC 1900, 1910) indicate brewery workers did not stay long in the Harpers Ferry area. If conditions in Balti-

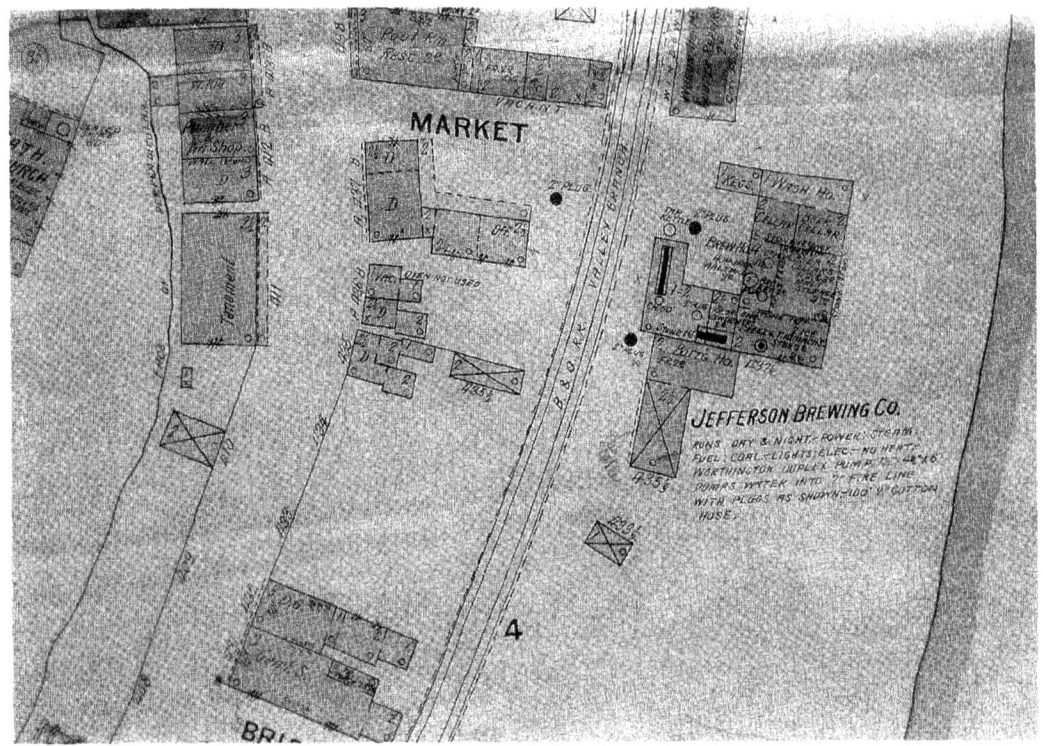

FIGURE 4. Sanborn Fire Insurance map (Sanborn Map Company 1907) illustrating the Harpers Ferry brewery with the bottling operation within the brewery complex during Jefferson Brewing Company's ownership. (Courtesy of Harpers Ferry National Historical Park.)

more breweries may be applied to the Harpers Ferry operation, it may be supposed that long hours, an unfavorable working environment, low wages, and uncertainty about management changes made the brewery at Harpers Ferry an unsatisfactory place to work.

From 1888 to 1903 the bottlers worked in the bottling plant built by James McGraw (Figure 1). The plant was apparently steam operated; the 1894 Sanborn map (Sanborn Map Company 1894) depicted a boiler located next to the building. The plant was moved to the brewery complex in 1903 when the Leder-Weideman Brewing Company purchased the brewery, but not the Lot 3 bottling plant (Figure 4).

The beer produced by the brewery was usually lager, but ale was also brewed. The soft drinks known to be bottled included ginger ale, sarsaparilla, and lemon sours (Jefferson County Book of Corporation 1898). McGraw obtained new and modern equipment for the bottling plant in the mid-1890s, and this equipment was passed down to subsequent owners. Some bottling equipment used included a loop seal bottling machine, a bottling table with a Hutchinson attachment and syrup gauge, and a steamtank bottle washing machine (JCDB 1894, 1898b:441; *Brewers Journal* 1895: 1372). Although modern equipment was used, much of the bottlers' work was done manually. The bottles were washed and dried by hand, while filling and capping were done partly by hand and partly by machine. The bottlers' working environment from 1888 to 1914 was probably not much better than that of the brewers. The bottling oper-

Perspectives from Historical Archaeology:

ation, at least after 1903, took place in the same unheated building as the brewing operations. The job also could be hazardous; attempting to seal a bottle with pressurized contents was a dangerous occupation, especially when most of the work was done by hand.

The bottlers probably worked the same long work day and work week as the brewery workers. When the Baltimore brewery went on strike in 1899, so did the bottlers, asking for shorter hours and more pay. Some concessions were made to the brewery workers, but none to the bottlers. Their organization was composed mainly of young men and boys with little influence. The brewery owners believed there was little profit in the bottling trade and that this profit would be wiped out with a pay increase (Kelley 1965:548).

The brewery and bottling plant at Harpers Ferry encountered numerous obstacles during its operational years: ownership changes, possible worker unrest, and natural disasters. Another problem encountered was prohibition.

Prohibition

The temperance movement in the Harpers Ferry area began around 1831, and by the 1890s approximately four different temperance groups operated in the area (*Virginia Free Press [VFP]* 1831:3). By the early 1900s the temperance movement had become a strong and vocal force circulating petitions to have liquor licenses suspended and saloons closed (*VFP* 1912:5).

The residents of the Harpers Ferry area took sides on the prohibition issue. Elections were declared either "wet" or "dry." Liquor licenses were granted if the county court was considered a wet one. If the elected members were for prohibition, no liquor licenses were granted.

In April of 1911 all of Jefferson County, West Virginia, went completely dry with the exception of Charles Town and Harpers Ferry (*VFP* 1911a: 3). In June 1911, however, the county court voted Jefferson County dry by a unanimous vote, closing three saloons and a beer depot, probably belonging to the German Brewing Company, in Harpers Ferry (*VFP* 1911b:4). No liquor licenses were granted from July 1911 to January 1913 when a new county commissioner, elected in 1913, reissued the licenses. According to *Virginia Free Press,* a dry newspaper, the decision was forced by liquor interests in Harpers Ferry (*VFP* 1913:2). By 1 January 1914, Harpers Ferry was one of only three towns in the Shenandoah Valley that were still wet (*VFP* 1914a:2). On 1 July 1914, the state of West Virginia went completely dry, five years before national prohibition (*VFP* 1914b:3).

The temperance movement must have had an effect on brewery operations because the owners were never sure whether or not their licenses would be renewed or revoked. Harpers Ferry townspeople may also have been affected by the temperance groups, curbing their consumption of alcoholic beverages. Saloons were required to "keep their windows uncovered so activity within [could] be observed from the street" (*SoJ* 1908:2). Temperance groups in the area were very visible with numerous petitions and speeches. As early as 1887, 2,000 people attended prohibition speeches at Island Park in Harpers Ferry (*VFP* 1887:3).

With all the pressure from the temperance movement and the constant threat of state and national prohibition, brewery owners must have been continually worried about their business. If local residents were not drinking much in the way of alcoholic beverages, the brewery's business was probably never substantial.

The evidence from the archaeological excavations in Block B, Lots 2 and 3, indicates that despite the temperance movement Lower Town Harpers Ferry residents were drinking beer not only from the brewery at Harpers Ferry, but from other regional breweries. The following section discusses the beer and soft drink bottles recovered during recent archaeological work at Harpers Ferry.

The Bottles

Excavations conducted in 1989 and 1990 at Harpers Ferry as part of a major restoration program yielded over 140,000 artifacts. Most of the artifacts were recovered from three privy features

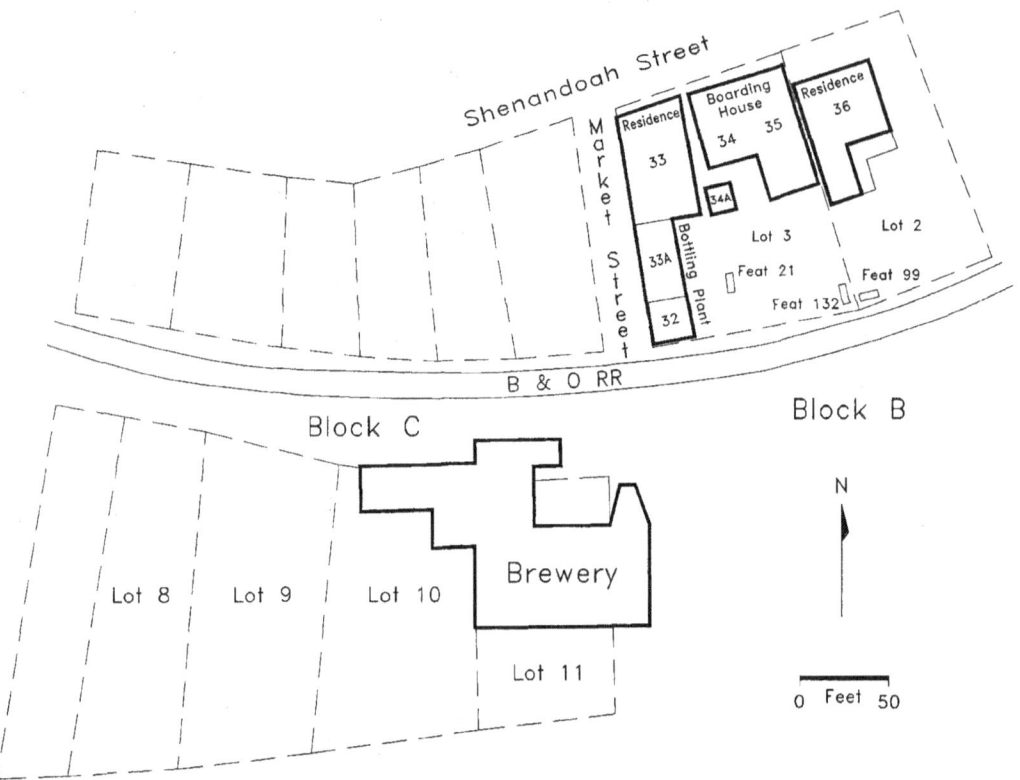

FIGURE 5. Map showing the location of the Hurst, boardinghouse, and Feature 21 privies associated with the boardinghouse, bottling plant, and brewery.

in Block B, Lot 3 (Figure 5); Ford (this volume) provides a detailed description. According to Ford (this volume), a privy—Feature 132—situated in the southeast corner of Lot 2 originally served the McGraw/Doran boardinghouse and shops ca. 1891–1910. Secondary use continued through the 1950s. A second, later privy, Feature 21, on Lot 2 contained artifacts dating from approximately the 1920s to the 1950s (Ford, this volume). The third privy, Feature 99, situated in the southwest corner of Lot 2, was used primarily by the J. Garland Hurst household. Artifacts recovered from the privy indicate two periods of use. The first included artifacts dating to the last quarter of the 19th century; the second dated after the 1930s. The boardinghouse and Hurst privies were in use dur-

ing the years the Harpers Ferry brewery and bottling plant were operational. Only the bottling plant was functioning when Feature 21 was used.

Approximately 130 beer and soda bottles, dating from the 1880s to the 1920s, were recovered from the three privies. These bottles belonged not only to the Harpers Ferry bottling plant, but also to regional breweries and bottling works. The bottle counts used in the following discussion were determined through minimum vessel analysis.

Harpers Ferry Bottles

One James McGraw bottle and 49 bottles attributed to J. C. McGraw were found within the board-

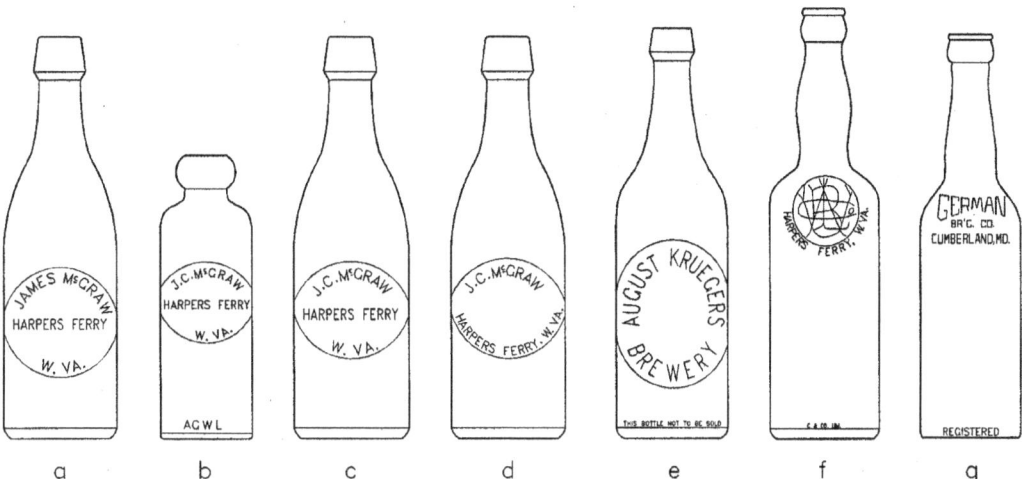

FIGURE 6. Harpers Ferry bottles: *a*, James McGraw beer bottle; *b*, J. C. McGraw soda bottle; *c–d*, J. C. McGraw beer bottle; *e*, August Krueger beer bottle; *f*, Leder-Weideman Brewing Company beer bottle; *g*, German Brewing Company beer bottle.

inghouse privy. The James McGraw bottle was aquamarine in color and probably contained beer (Figure 6a). It was made in a two-piece plate mold and tool-finished; it probably required a swing-type stopper. The bottle was fragmented so all marks were not present. The base of the bottle, which probably had the glass manufacturer's mark, was missing. The back of the bottle contained the warning:

THIS BOTTLE/NOT TO/BE SOLD.

This McGraw bottle probably dated between 1885, when James McGraw began his business, and 1893, when he turned the bottling business over to his son, James C.

The J. C. McGraw bottles found in the boardinghouse privy were in two forms: beer and soda. Thirty-six soda bottles had finishes that accommodated Hutchinson stoppers. The bottles, aquamarine in color, were manufactured in two-piece plate molds and tool-finished. Figure 6b illustrates marks found on the bottles. All the soda bottles were manufactured by American Glass Works Limited, Pittsburgh, Pennsylvania. The glass manufacturer's mark (A.G.W.L.) was used 1880–1905

(Toulouse 1971:43). The bottles were also embossed with the warning:

THIS BOTTLE NOT/TO BE SOLD.

Thirteen J. C. McGraw bottles probably contained beer. The bottles were all manufactured in two-piece plate molds and tool-finished. The finish styles differed on the beer bottles. One bottle had a loop seal finish, while the remainder were blob top finishes requiring swing-type stoppers. The low number of loop seal finishes is interesting considering J. C. purchased a loop seal machine for his business in 1895. In addition, numerous rubber seals, used with loop seal closures, were found during the excavations.

The J. C. McGraw beer bottle company embossments were in two styles (Figure 6c, 6d). The bottles also carried one of two warnings:

THIS BOTTLE/NOT TO/BE SOLD or
THIS/BOTTLE/IS NEVER SOLD.

There does not appear to be any correlation between the different slug plates and the warning label. The majority of the bottles were manufactured by American Glass Works Ltd. Two bottles, however, had unidentifiable glass manufacturer marks:

D and F.B. & F.J. Co.

No bottles were found in the Block B, Lots 2 and 3, excavations for Krueger and Schafer, Belvidere Brewing Company, Leder-Weideman Brewing Company, or Jefferson Brewing Company. The Harpers Ferry National Historical Park Museum contains an embossed Leder-Weideman Brewing Company bottle, and subsequent archaeological excavations in Lower Town Harpers Ferry have recovered fragments of such bottles (Figure 6f). Only one bottle representing the Krueger and Schafer Company has been located, and it is in a private collection (Figure 6e). Both companies utilized two-piece plate molds with tooled finishes. The Krueger bottle was colorless with loop seal finishes; the Leder-Weideman bottles were brown with crown closures.

The German Brewing Company was represented by two bottles recovered during the excavations (Figure 6g). One was found in Feature 21 and one in the boardinghouse privy. Based on manufacturers' marks, it is possible that these bottles may date to the years the German Brewing Company owned brewery land. The bottles were brown in color and made by an automatic bottle machine with crown finishes. One bottle, marked 17 N 13, may represent the American Bottle Company, Chicago, Illinois. The "N 13" part of the mark may indicate the bottle was made at the company's Newark, Ohio, plant in 1913 (Toulouse 1971:30). Many glass manufacturers used this code structure, however, so the date cannot be confirmed. If the date is accurate, the bottle was in use during the time the German Brewing Company operated a beer depot out of the burned brewery in Harpers Ferry.

Unmarked Beer Bottles

Approximately 20 beer bottles, found in the boardinghouse privy, had no company embossments. The bottles, aquamarine and colorless, were manufactured in two-piece plate molds. The fin-

ishes, all tool finished, accommodated crown, loop seal, and swing-type stoppers. Most of the bottles were embossed with the following warnings:

THIS BOTTLE NOT TO BE SOLD/RETURN
WHEN EMPTY and
THIS BOTTLE IS NEVER SOLD.

These bottles may have been used with paper labels by the Harpers Ferry brewery. It is possible that J. C. McGraw, Krueger and Schafer, Belvidere Brewing Company, Leder-Weideman Company, Jefferson Brewing Company, and German Brewing Company all used paper labels at one time or another. Considering the short amount of time brewing companies stayed in business at Harpers Ferry, it would not be surprising to find they did not spend money on embossed bottles.

Regional Brewery Bottles

Twenty-seven bottles recovered during excavations represented 15 brewing companies. These companies were all contemporaneous with the brewery at Harpers Ferry and were located in Baltimore, Maryland; Washington, D.C.; Cumberland, Maryland; Indianapolis, Indiana; Alexandria, Virginia; Milwaukee, Wisconsin; New York; and Illinois. Some brewing companies, located in distant states, had branches or beer depots in the local area. For example, Pabst Milwaukee Beer had branches in Washington, D.C., and Hartford, Connecticut; the Great Western Star Brewing Company in Illinois had a branch office in Baltimore.

The non-local brewery bottles were found in various excavation units, but most (n = 26) were from the three privies. The boardinghouse privy contained the most (n = 18); Feature 21 had 3 and the Hurst privy had 5. The manufacturing techniques included two-piece plate molds and automatic bottle machines. The closure types were swing-type, loop seal, and crown. The colors included aquamarine, brown, and colorless. Variations of the inscribed warning

THIS BOTTLE NOT TO BE SOLD

were embossed on the majority of the bottles.

Regional Bottling Works Bottles

Twenty-eight bottles from contemporaneous regional bottling companies were recovered during excavations. The bottles were found in all three privies, but the majority (n = 26) were from the boardinghouse privy. Based on bottle shape, it is probable that 18 of the bottles contained beer and 10 held soft drinks. All the beer bottles were found in the boardinghouse privy. The two-piece plate mold beer bottles used loop seal and swing-type closures while the soda bottles had Hutchinson and crown closures. With the exception of two automatic bottle machine bottles, all were made using two-piece plate molds. The two automatic bottle machine bottles were found in Feature 21 and the Hurst privy.

The bottling works were located in: Washington, D.C.; Hagerstown, Frederick, and Baltimore, Maryland; Charles Town and Martinsburg, West Virginia; Roanoke and Harrisonburg, Virginia; and Hanover and Chambersburg, Pennsylvania. Many of the bottles were marked:

THIS BOTTLE NOT TO BE SOLD or
THIS BOTTLE IS NEVER SOLD.

Summary

The bottles used by the brewery and bottling works at Harpers Ferry were all returnable, as were most of the regional breweries and bottling works containers. The majority of the bottles were embossed with such warnings as

THIS BOTTLE IS NEVER SOLD.

Returnable soda bottles became common after the invention of the Hutchinson stopper. Returnable beer bottles were also common after the 1870s, when lager beer could be bottled successfully (McKearin and Wilson 1978:242–243; Busch 1987:70).

Returnable bottles were considered the legal property of the bottler, and customers were required to return them to the bottler for refilling. As a result, the cost of the bottle was not included in the price of the product. For example, in the early 1900s a bottle of soda pop cost five cents; selling the bottle along with the contents would have added an additional two and one-half cents (Busch 1987:70). Although the returnable bottle system was to the advantage of the consumer, it was still difficult to get people to return bottles to the bottler. Housewives used bottles to can goods. Bottle dealers appropriated bottles and sold them to other companies. Many bottles were simply discarded, thrown away with last night's dinner (Busch 1987:71–72).

The returnable bottles recovered during excavations provide an interesting observation of disposal methods. Supposedly returnable bottles were practical when distribution was localized (Busch 1987:70). Fifty McGraw bottles were found in the boardinghouse privy. This privy was used from approximately 1891 to 1910, which coincides with the use of nearby buildings as a bottling plant for the McGraw, Krueger and Schafer, and Belvidere companies.

If returnable bottles were practical when distribution was localized, why were so many J. C. McGraw bottles found in the boardinghouse privy, a structure located only steps away from the bottling department? There are a number of possibilities to explain the dumping of 50 returnable bottles. One explanation may be the bottles were dumped following McGraw's bankruptcy in 1897. The new brewing company would have had no use for bottles with J. C. McGraw's name. Another reason may be the bottles were thrown away after McGraw purchased the loop seal machine in 1895. Only one of the bottles recovered had a loop seal finish. Perhaps the bottling department tossed out the no-longer-needed Hutchinson and swing-type closure bottles. Vandalism may also be a possibility. Discontented workers at the bottling plant may have simply thrown away the bottles when management was not looking. Considering how expensive bottles were, the loss of 49 containers at one time would have been significant. It is also possible the residents of the boardinghouse simply discarded the bottles after the contents were consumed. This seems unusual considering how close

Deborah A. Hull-Walski and Frank L. Walski

the bottling department was to the boardinghouse. Another reason may be that workers at the bottling plant were sneaking bottles of beer and soda and depositing the empty bottles in the privy, a result perhaps of the "free beer" system (James Gibb 1992, pers. comm.).

The archaeological evidence indicates the bottles were found in various levels of the privy fill. This would suggest the bottles were thrown out over a period of time rather than disposed of in one episode. It is very probable the residents of the boardinghouse or workers in the store or bottling plant were depositing bottles in the privy after the bottles were empty rather than returning them to the bottling department. Again, this practice of throwing away bottles seems unusual considering the proximity of the bottling plant and is suggestive of secrecy, sabotage, or laziness.

Conclusions

The artifactual evidence from the three privies seems to suggest the brewery was never a successful venture. With the exception of the J. C. McGraw and the German Brewing Company bottles, no beer or soft drink bottles were found that would indicate even the existence of a brewery and bottling plant in Harpers Ferry from 1897 to 1909. Although it is possible that 20 unmarked beer bottles may have contained Harpers Ferry beer, no unmarked soft drink bottles were found. It is also surprising that no embossed bottles with the Leder-Weideman Company logo were found, as this company was in existence for two years and did use a bottle with an embossed logo.

Although there is no supporting evidence, it is possible that the brewery at Harpers Ferry dealt more with selling beer in barrels and kegs than in bottles. The Sanborn maps of 1902 and 1907 (Sanborn Map Company 1902, 1907) do indicate the presence of bottling departments, and the 1900 census (USBC 1900) does list two men employed as bottlers. Financial problems, however, may have kept the owners from hiring a full staff for the bottling department. As stated earlier, brewery owners believed there was little profit in the bot-

tling trade. If the brewery owners did not use their bottling department as a full-scale operation, it would be expected that few Harpers Ferry bottles would be found.

The lack of Harpers Ferry bottles found in the backyard privies may also indicate that the beer and soft drinks were never well-received by the townspeople, or at least not popular with the Hurst family or among the people who lived in the boardinghouse. The archaeological evidence suggests that, with the exception of the products produced by McGraw, soft drinks and beer produced by non-Harpers Ferry companies were more popular.

The brewery at Harpers Ferry was fraught with problems from the very start, which seems evident in the archaeological record. Combined with the possibility that the products of the brewery and bottling works were unpopular, the lack of capital, competition from local and national brewers, worker unrest, and destructive fires could only lead to the brewery's failure. Prohibition finally closed down the brewery from all activities dealing with beer. The bottling plant, however, continued in use until its destruction by flood in 1942.

ACKNOWLEDGMENTS

We are grateful to a number of people for their assistance in producing not only this article, but the larger research report from which it is drawn. We would like to thank Susan E. Winter and Paul A. Shackel for their help in reviewing and editing our work. Without their enthusiasm for the Harpers Ferry project, the opportunity to produce this research would never have occurred. We owe a debt of gratitude to Pat Chickering, Mike Jenkins, and Stan Bumgardner, historians at Harpers Ferry National Historical Park, for all their help in searching through the local newspapers and deed records of the late 19th and early 20th centuries for any reference to the Harpers Ferry brewery. Nancy Potts, a librarian at the Harpers Ferry Center, continuously provided us with out-of-print sources on brewery operations. Ken Kulp, an archaeologist at Harpers Ferry National Historical Park, spent weekends at libraries helping us track down one of the brewery owners, and John Ravenhorst, another Harpers Ferry archaeologist, redrew our bottles using Autocad, producing quality line drawings. Many people reviewed our larger research report for content and style. Especially helpful were Stephen R. Potter, Robert C. Sonderman, and Bernard K. Means. Finally, we would like to thank Craig W. Davis who shares our enthusiasm about 19th-century breweries and who provided us with a number of references.

REFERENCES

BARON, STANLEY
   1962   *Brewed in America: A History of Beer and Ale in the United States.* Little, Brown, Boston, Massachusetts.

BREWERS JOURNAL [Chicago]
   1895   No title. *Brewers Journal,* 15 July:1372.

BULL, DONALD, MANFRED FRIEDRICH, AND
ROBERT GOTTSCHALK
   1984   *American Breweries.* Bullworks, Trumbull, Connecticut.

BUSCH, JANE
   1987   Second Time Around: A Look at Bottle Reuse. *Historical Archaeology* 21(1):67–80.

FARMERS ADVOCATE [Charles Town, West Virginia] (*FA*)
   1898a   No title. *Farmers Advocate,* 25 June:3.
   1898b   No title. *Farmers Advocate,* 6 August:3.
   1903   No title. *Farmers Advocate,* 31 October:2.
   1906   No title. *Farmers Advocate,* 17 February:3.
   1909a   Fire at Harpers Ferry. *Farmers Advocate,* 16 January:2.
   1909b   No title. *Farmers Advocate,* 23 January:3.

FRIEDRICH, MANFRED, AND DONALD BULL
   1976   *The Register of United States Breweries: 1876–1976.* N.p., Trumbull, Connecticut.

JEFFERSON COUNTY BOOK OF CORPORATION
   1898   Jefferson County Book of Corporation 2, 11 May: 21. Jefferson County Courthouse, Charles Town, West Virginia.

JEFFERSON COUNTY COURT RECORDS (JCCR)
   1906   Jefferson County Court Records, Envelope No. 135, Case of James C. McGraw, Charles Town, West Virginia. Records on file, West Virginia and Regional History Collection. Charles C. Wise, Jr., Library, West Virginia University, Morgantown.

JEFFERSON COUNTY DEED BOOK (JCDB)
   1885   Jefferson County Deed Book P, 16 December:54. Jefferson County Courthouse, Charles Town, West Virginia.
   1894   Jefferson County Deed Book 77, 25 April:47. Jefferson County Courthouse, Charles Town, West Virginia.

   1897   Jefferson County Deed Book 83, 1 October:493–498. Jefferson County Courthouse, Charles Town, West Virginia.
   1898a   Jefferson County Deed Book 84, 14 February:364. Jefferson County Courthouse, Charles Town, West Virginia.
   1898b   Jefferson County Deed Book 84, 31 March:441–442. Jefferson County Courthouse, Charles Town, West Virginia.
   1898c   Jefferson County Deed Book 86, 28 November:105. Jefferson County Courthouse, Charles Town, West Virginia.
   1903   Jefferson County Deed Book 92, 17 February:503–509. Jefferson County Courthouse, Charles Town, West Virginia.
   1907   Jefferson County Deed Book 98, 1 January:384. Jefferson County Courthouse, Charles Town, West Virginia.
   1909   Jefferson County Deed Book 103, 14 June:37. Jefferson County Courthouse, Charles Town, West Virginia.

KELLEY, WILLIAM J.
   1965   *Brewing in Maryland: From Colonial Times to the Present.* William J. Kelley, Baltimore, Maryland.

KROLL, WAYNE L.
   1976   *Badger Breweries: Past and Present.* Wayne L. Kroll, Jefferson, Wisconsin.

MCKEARIN, HELEN, AND KENNETH M. WILSON
   1978   *American Bottles and Flasks and Their Ancestry.* Crown, New York.

RILEY, JOHN J.
   1972   *A History of the American Soft Drink Industry: Bottle Carbonated Beverages, 1807–1957.* Reprint of 1958 edition. Arno Press, New York.

SANBORN MAP COMPANY
   1894   *Fire Insurance Map of Harpers Ferry, West Virginia.* Sanborn Map Company, New York. Map on file, Harpers Ferry National Historical Park, Harpers Ferry, West Virginia.
   1902   *Fire Insurance Map of Harpers Ferry, West Virginia.* Sanborn Map Company, New York. Map on file, Harpers Ferry National Historical Park, Harpers Ferry, West Virginia.
   1907   *Fire Insurance Map of Harpers Ferry, West Virginia.* Sanborn Map Company, New York. Map on file, Harpers Ferry National Historical Park, Harpers Ferry, West Virginia.

SCHULTER, HERMANN
   1910   *The Brewing Industry and the Brewery Worker's Movement in America.* International Union of United Brewery Workmen of America, Cincinnati, Ohio.

SPIRIT OF JEFFERSON [Charles Town, West Virginia] (*SoJ*)
   1885   Advertisement. *Spirit of Jefferson,* 28 April:2.

1890   No title. *Spirit of Jefferson*, 13 May:3.
1892   No title. *Spirit of Jefferson*, 5 July:3.
1893   No title. *Spirit of Jefferson*, 21 November:3.
1894   No title. *Spirit of Jefferson*, 10 June:3.
1895a   No title. *Spirit of Jefferson*, 12 March:2.
1895b   Harpers Ferry Brewing Company. *Spirit of Jefferson*, 4 June:2.
1896   No title. *Spirit of Jefferson*, 15 December:2.
1897   No title. *Spirit of Jefferson*, 5 October:2.
1898   No title. *Spirit of Jefferson*, 14 June:2.
1908   No title. *Spirit of Jefferson*, 16 June:2.
1909   No title. *Spirit of Jefferson*, 19 January:3.

TOULOUSE, JULIAN H.
1971   *Bottle Makers and Their Marks.* Thomas Nelson, New York.

UNITED STATES BUREAU OF THE CENSUS (USBC)
1900   *Population Statistics; Harpers Ferry, West Virginia.* On file, Harpers Ferry Library, Harpers Ferry, West Virginia. Microfilm.
1910   *Population Statistics; Harpers Ferry, West Virginia.* On file, Harpers Ferry Library, Harpers Ferry, West Virginia. Microfilm.

VIRGINIA FREE PRESS [Harpers Ferry, West Virginia] (*VFP*)
1831   No title. *Virginia Free Press,* 1 September:3.
1887   No title. *Virginia Free Press,* 28 July:3.
1911a   No title. *Virginia Free Press,* 13 April:3.
1911b   No title. *Virginia Free Press,* 8 June:4.
1912   No title. *Virginia Free Press,* 19 December:5.
1913   No title. *Virginia Free Press,* 16 January:2.
1914a   No title. *Virginia Free Press,* 1 January:2.
1914b   No title. *Virginia Free Press,* 9 July:3.

WESTERN BREWER [Chicago]
1897   Bungs. *Western Brewer,* 15 July:1372.

DEBORAH A. HULL-WALSKI
DEPARTMENT OF ANTHROPOLOGY
NATIONAL MUSEUM OF NATURAL HISTORY
SMITHSONIAN INSTITUTION
WASHINGTON, D.C. 20560

FRANK L. WALSKI
OFFICE OF REPATRIATION
NATIONAL MUSEUM OF NATURAL HISTORY
SMITHSONIAN INSTITUTION
WASHINGTON, D.C. 20560

Sophia E. Kelly

The Role of Technological Transitions in the Development of American Ceramic Industries: Elijah Cornell and the Shift from Redware to Stoneware Production

ABSTRACT

In the mid-1800s, the construction of canal and rail networks profoundly affected ceramic manufacturing in New York State by lowering the cost of transporting stoneware clay and finished vessels. Consumer demand for stoneware storage containers, energized by lower prices and increased availability, spurred the development of stoneware potteries across the state. Many American earthenware potters shifted partially or entirely over to stoneware production. This paper contends that the difficult transition between ceramic manufacturing technologies played a role in the decline of the handicraft pottery industry in the early 20th century. Stoneware production required firsthand instruction, large capital investments and resource networks, new labor structures, and an understanding of changing consumer expectations. The analysis uses documentary and archaeological evidence from the potter Elijah Cornell as a case study of technological change in the operation of a traditional American earthenware business.

Introduction

Technological transitions in manufacturing processes often catalyze widespread changes to the organization of labor and the types of goods manufactured. In the mid-1800s, a shift from the widespread production of earthenware (i.e., redware) storage containers to that of similar containers made of stoneware marked one such critical juncture in American manufacturing history (Barber 1891:152; Guilland 1971; Osgood 1971; Webster 1971; Greer 1999). Prior to this time, the comparatively simple techniques and readily available raw materials used in redware manufacturing enabled widespread local production of earthenware vessels (Ketchum 1970:7, 1987:5; Pendery 1985; Starbuck and Dupre

1985; McConnell 1999:18; Lindsey 2004:423). The spatially restricted sources of clay necessary for stoneware production, on the other hand, facilitated the development of stoneware manufacturing in only a few places before the development of better transportation systems. Access to high-quality stoneware clay and the technological complexity of stoneware manufacturing compared to low-fired earthenware production contributed to specialized pottery production and the early industrialization of stoneware manufacturing (Webster 1971:38; Ketchum 1991b:1).

The expansion of canal and rail transportation starting in the 1820s dramatically altered the American ceramic industry by lowering shipping prices for both stoneware clay and finished vessels. Potters along the new transportation corridors were able, for the first time, to produce stoneware pottery profitably to fill local consumer demands. Many redware potters began to make stoneware pottery in addition to their accustomed wares. Some potters even shifted completely to stoneware production (Ramsay 1947:42,47; Watkins 1950:247–248; Ketchum 1970:5, 1987:228–229; Lasansky 1979:3,17; Myers 1984:51; Mullins 1992:187; Broderick and Bouck 1995:176,201–202; Schaltenbrand 1996:23; Burrison 2008:57). By the late 1800s, most household food-storage vessels were no longer redware containers but were instead made of more durable and less toxic stoneware and glass (Ketchum 1991b).

This article argues that the technological difficulties encountered in the transition from redware to stoneware production may have contributed to the failure of some traditional potteries sooner than would have been expected from the pressures of market competition alone. As Schaltenbrand (1996:7) notes: "Unlike the making of low-fired redware (earthenware), stoneware production demanded special knowledge and technical proficiency. Considerable risks were involved in starting a stoneware business, and those who hoped for success faced formidable challenges." This analysis uses documentary and archaeological evidence from the potter Elijah Cornell to examine the technological shift from redware to stoneware production. Although Cornell is just one individual, his reactions to changes during this pivotal period in history provide a glimpse into the motivations of a traditional American potter.

Tra sitionf romR edwa et oS tonewn e

Rapid shifts in American ceramic industries during the mid-19th century, preceded by an extended period of slow growth, served to intensify the effects of technological change on traditional producers. Pottery production in the United States was late to industrialize, and the industrialization process was more conservative than in other industries, such as textiles (Barber 1891; Postlewaite 1940; Ramsay 1947:95; Myers 1980:2). Potters themselves were reluctant to adopt new technologies or to change their organization of production (Pendery 1985). Traditional potters often selectively adopted aspects of the industrial manufacturing processes while retaining many long-established labor practices (Faulkner 1982; Myers 1984:52; Mullins 1992; Schaltenbrand 1996:159).

American ceramic production prior to the 19th-century was characterized by small-scale household industries that manufactured predominantly simple and inexpensive utilitarian earthenware vessels. Redware pottery was produced using common brick clay that could be mined locally at little expense. In addition, redware kilns could be built fairly quickly from simple materials (Ketchum 1991a:1; Lindsey 2004:423). These kilns were easier to operate and maintain in comparison to the kilns used for high-fired ceramics, because they were typically restricted to temperatures between 1,000°C and 1,200°C (Osgood 1971:33).

By the mid-1800s, stoneware storage containers replaced redware containers in many American households when transportation networks allowed for the shipment of stoneware clay and pottery across the East Coast (Myers 1984:53; Branin 1988:18). In addition to lower prices and greater availability of stoneware, consumers preferred stonewares over redwares for several functional reasons. First, redware pottery is less durable than stoneware, because it is fired at a lower temperature and the clay was often filled with impurities that contributed

to a weaker material that fractured more easily (Ketchum 1970:13; Branin 1988:19; McConnell 1999:15–17; Groover 2003:231). Second, stoneware clay is structurally nonporous when fired correctly. In contrast, redware containers are naturally permeable and must be covered with glazes to hold liquids (Baldwin 1993:11). These glazes easily chip or craze, which makes cleaning more difficult (Watkins 1950:54,160; Osgood 1971:40; Bensch 1987:9; Branin 1988:19). Finally, stoneware pottery is nontoxic because it did not require the use of lead-based glazes to produce watertight vessels. Earthenware containers were traditionally rendered waterproof through the application of glazes made of clay, fine sand, water, and red lead. By the late 18th and early 19th centuries, people had begun to realize that lead poisoning was induced by lead leaching from the glazes of redware ceramics (Watkins 1950:11,80,127; Tunis 1965:121; Ketchum 1970:12; Myers 1984:56; Bensch 1987:9; Mullins 1992:187; Baldwin 1993:13; Skerry and Hood 2009:212).

For many 19th-century potters, the decision to transition to stoneware manufacture from redware manufacture was an economic necessity. Stoneware commanded higher prices than earthenware and New York State households provided an eager market for these sturdy and nontoxic vessels (Watkins 1950:79; Myers 1984:64; Comstock 1994:15). Cities located along major waterways and canals, such as Geddes, Rochester, and Utica, quickly became centers for stoneware production. The transition from redware to stoneware containers in American households was not monolithic, however, and was heavily influenced by location. For instance, families in isolated, rural communities often continued to use redware well after their urban counterparts. The primary reason for a lag in redware replacement in rural areas was more limited access to transportation networks that could import stoneware clay and pottery from the coast (McConnell 1999:27). In addition, locally made earthenwares were often the only pottery available in rural areas because they were the only type a local potter knew how to make (Guilland 1971:47). Poorer families in both rural and urban settings also often opted to buy cheap redwares in lieu of more expensive stoneware alternatives (Rinzler and Sayers 1980:79; Zug 1986:209; Baldwin 1993:13; McConnell

1999:27; Groover 2003:231–232; Burrison 2008:91). By the 1840s, however, transportation improvements compelled traditional craftsmen in even the most remote areas to adopt new production methods to satisfy changing preferences (Webster 1971:37; Bensch 1987:5).

Factors Affecting the Successful Adoption of Stoneware Technologies

Historians and archaeologists have argued that market competition from industrial manufactories was the proximate cause for the demise of traditional American potteries (Webster 1971; Myers 1980; Ketchum 1991b). These models are based primarily on data from urban, coastal regions where economic changes occurred first and had a more immediate effect on small-scale producers (Turnbaugh 2002:528). Industrialization took a slightly different course in inland regions where population densities were smaller and economies were locally based. While competition from industrial potteries eventually destabilized the market base of rural potters, some initially tried to master the techniques required for high-fired ceramic manufacturing in order to satisfy local consumer demand for stoneware containers (Watkins 1950:247–248, 1974:73; Baldwin 1993:16; Broderick and Bouck 1995:176,201–202; Schaltenbrand 1996:23). Others experimented with stoneware production but ultimately decided to return to full-time redware production (Ramsay 1947:57).

This paper analyzes the technological transition from redware to stoneware manufacture through the decisions made by one 19th-century redware potter. In particular, the study postulates four primary reasons that explain why technological transitions posed an obstacle to redware potters learning to produce high-fired pottery:

1. *Instruction and the Learning Process*: First-hand instruction concerning stoneware manufacturing techniques was pivotal to successful mastery of the process. The shortage of available and willing potters who could teach these techniques presented significant obstacles to some traditional potters.

2. *Capital Investments and Resource Networks*: Stoneware production required substantial capital investments, including large initial outlays for clay, which had to be imported from a few, localized stoneware-clay deposits.

3. *Organization of Production*: Although the successful implementation of stoneware technologies did not necessarily involve changes to the traditional organization of labor, the stoneware manufacturing process encouraged task segmentation and expansion beyond that of a small-scale kinship-based industry.

4. *Expectations*: Transportation networks across New York State enabled potteries across a wide region to produce and ship competitively priced stoneware containers. With stiff competition in stoneware manufacturing, traditional producers had to master the techniques to form and fire stoneware vessels, as well as the skills to make their new products durable and attractive.

These issues provide an analytical framework through which to consider one potter's response and compare it to the experiences of other contemporary redware potters. An individual potter's reaction to these factors is conditioned by his knowledge base, perseverance, adaptability, and monetary assets. Some factors may pose little problem to some potters, while others may present a significant obstacle.

Case Study: Elijah Cornell

Elijah Cornell is among a handful of 19th-century American potters for whom detailed records have survived (Starbuck and Dupre 1985; Worrell 1985; Mullins 1992). His journal and the collection of Cornell family correspondence are the most complete extant records of a New York 19th-century redware potter (Ketchum 1987:319). Archaeological data from an excavation of Cornell's pottery supplement the documentary record to provide an understanding of the role of technological change in Cornell's production decisions. The following section briefly details Cornell's life before his venture into stoneware production in 1841.

Cornell (Figure 1) was the first well-documented potter in Ithaca, New York, and the father of the telegraph entrepreneur Ezra

FIGURE 1. Photographic portrait of Elijah Cornell, ca. 1840. (Photo courtesy of the Kroch Rare Book Library, Cornell University.)

Cornell. Like other contemporary potters, Elijah Cornell was able to profit from redware manufacture until the mid-1800s by focusing on the production of storage vessels and other utilitarian forms (Myers 1980:47). Cornell family biographers note that, aside from a few personal matters that necessitated relocation, Cornell's frequent moves during his early career (1793–1819) were in response to the changing market for redware containers (Figure 2). In 1819 he established a more permanent home in the rural community of DeRuyter, New York, where, in 1824, he constructed a building devoted to his pottery business (Dorf 1852:4–10; A. Cornell 1884:25–32; Parton 1891:126; Engeln 1917:107; Watkins 1950:78). DeRuyter offered Cornell a steady market for his redware pottery (A. Cornell 1884:31). The construction of canal and rail transportation networks in New York during the 1830s and 1840s, however, presented both opportunities and challenges to traditional potters in inland, rural areas. After 1840, Cornell found

it difficult to compete with potteries situated closer to transportation systems (A. Cornell 1884:31–32; Ketchum 1987:268–269).[1]

In the winter of 1841, Cornell wrote to his oldest son Ezra, who was living in Ithaca, from his home in DeRuyter: "I should like to be again settled with a small pottery on a small but good piece of land" (Dorf 1852:42). Soon after this letter was written, Cornell moved to Ithaca, situated at the southern end of Lake Cayuga in the Finger Lakes District. Ithaca's population of approximately 5,000 people and connection to the Erie Canal system through the Cayuga and Seneca Canal offered a larger potential pottery market and efficient transportation networks.

Cornell began redware pottery production in Ithaca in the summer of 1841 and started producing stoneware pottery during the following summer (E. B. Cornell, Sr. 1841–1842). Although local consumer demand in Ithaca likely induced Cornell to begin stoneware production, Cornell did not stop producing low-fired earthenwares. Excavations at the Cornell Pottery in Ithaca suggest that Cornell operated a small earthenware kiln at the same time as a main stoneware kiln (Bliss 1977:10). Cornell family documents suggest that Cornell continued to produce redware until he retired in 1848 (D. Cornell 1847; A. Cornell 1884:32).

Documentary evidence suggests that Cornell may not have been sufficiently prepared to amass the labor and resources necessary for stoneware manufacture, nor did he possess knowledge of the techniques required to produce high-fired pottery. When he moved to Ithaca in 1841, Cornell did not entertain the idea of shifting to stoneware production. On 27 December 1839, Cornell's sentiments about the prospect of a pottery in Ithaca were revealed in a letter to his children:

> And now for business I want that my boys[2] should exercise some real reflection—consider in the first place the vast space or vacancy that there is for a pottery in Ithaca and likewise that the business can be carried on with less outgoes than any other good business that can be mentioned. It can be made to support its self without on[e] dollar cash expense and gives as much pay for the labour as any other business, the stock is under foot in the earth and the fine trees in the vicinity and there is nothing wanted but to set it in motion in the right way and it would succeed to admiration. The whole business might be got under way with only a little family labor and a great share can be done by boys which I have and have

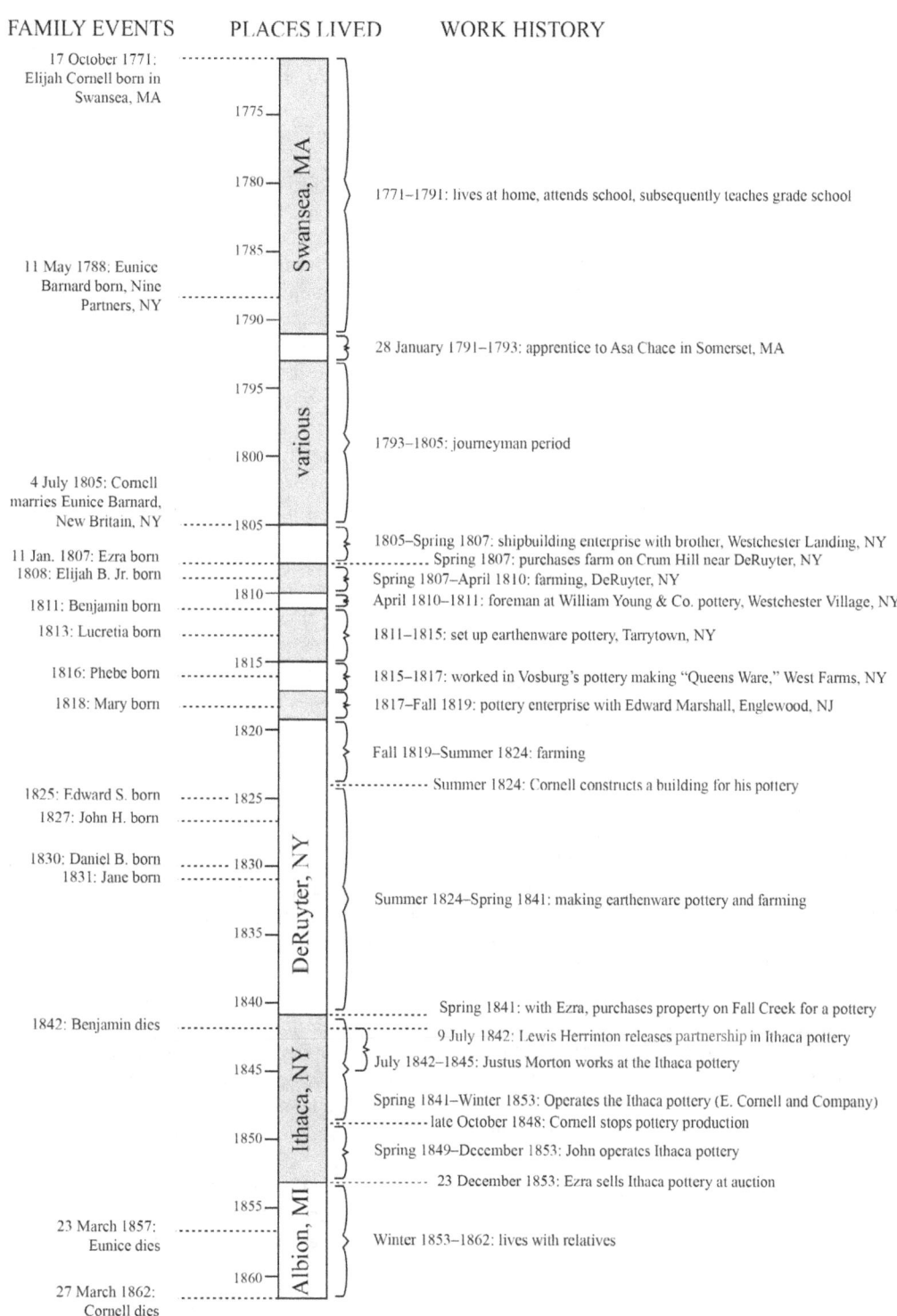

FIGURE 2. Timeline of events in Elijah Cornell's life. (Chart by author, 2011.)

to support and surely they will be better than new hands and I have every tool and convenience that is necessary to start it which would be of but little use without using—Now I do not know as I shall ever be able to do much, but that makes no difference, the business stands good independent of any one man (E. B. Cornell, Sr. 1839).

Cornell mentioned that the necessary clay is "under foot," which indicates that he had not yet considered the prospect of shifting to stoneware manufacture, which would require clay imported from the New Jersey/New York area. In addition, Cornell stated that a pottery is a good investment because it has "less outgoes than any other good business," "can be made to support its self without on[e] dollar cash expense," "gives as much pay for the labour as any other business," and "stands good independent or any one man" (E. B. Cornell, Sr. 1839). Although all of these statements may be true of earthenware production during its heyday, the United States pottery industry was changing markedly by 1839. As Cornell would soon learn, a successful stoneware pottery can hardly stand "good independent of any one man."

The Process of Technological Adoption

Several critical factors may have affected Elijah Cornell's technological transition from redware to stoneware pottery production. The present analysis relies on four principal sources of information. First, Cornell's journal of the first two years of pottery manufacture in Ithaca provides notes on the number and types of pottery he produced, expenditures for the pottery, the sale price of some of his vessels, and labor input by people working in the pottery (E. B. Cornell, Sr. 1841–1842). Second, Cornell family correspondence provides information about the operation of the pottery. Third, surviving Cornell vessels are material evidence of his redware and stoneware production. Five redware pieces associated with the Cornell family are housed in repositories (Figure 3). In addition, three marked Cornell stoneware pieces and one possible Cornell stoneware piece have been identified in private collections. Although only one of these pieces has been located, historical photographs of the remaining pieces offer a small, but important, sample of the potter's work (Figures 4, 5, and 6). Finally, notes, reports, and artifact collections

from excavation of the Ithaca pottery site provide data on Cornell's occupation of the pottery (Bliss and Kruse 1976; Bliss 1977).

1. Instruction and the Learning Process

The first factor that may have influenced Cornell's success in stoneware manufacture was the availability of knowledgeable instruction. The transition from redware to stoneware production was difficult for traditional potters who had already undergone their formal training, as it required new skills (Greer 1999:37,41,48; Kille 2009:40–43). In addition to the difficulty of adopting new techniques midcareer, redware potters may have found it difficult to receive training in the art of high-fired ceramics. Prior to the mid-1800s, itinerant potters who traveled between pottery shops played an important role in the spread of techniques and technologies (Baldwin 1993:99,114,136,169; Sweezy 1994:23,117,203; Brown 2006:21; Burrison 2008:9). British and German immigrants with knowledge of stoneware pottery production, but lacking resources to start their own potteries, were another valuable source of instruction (Woodhouse 1974:205; Sweezy 1994:19; Perry 2004:7). With the establishment of large stoneware factories in the mid-19th century, however, the tradition of the semi-itinerant folk potters began to wane. Potteries more often employed semiskilled workers who operated machinery, or specialists who focused their attention on one part of the production process (Ketchum 1987:13). Fewer and fewer mobile potters who were well versed in all aspects of stoneware pottery production were available to potters seeking instruction. In addition, many successful stoneware potteries throughout American history depended on the specialized knowledge and skills of one or two experts trained in making high-fired ceramics. These experts sometimes guarded their trade secrets closely; the simplest techniques were difficult to access (Watkins 1950:35; Franco 1971:875; Guilland 1971:47; Ketchum 1987:11; Schaltenbrand 1996:23; Speight and Toki 2003:131). As a result, potters who were not connected to a knowledge base for high-fired ceramics learned through experimentation and often relied on methods used in redware manufacturing to compensate for their lack of expertise (McConnell 1999:27). Experimentation, however, was costly in time, materials, and money.

FIGURE 3. Redware pottery produced by Elijah Cornell: (*a*) large flowerpot and redware jar (Collection of the Kroch Rare Book Library, Cornell University; photo by author, 2003.), (*b*) plate initialed by Ezra Cornell when he was a boy working in his father's pottery in DeRuyter, New York (Photo courtesy of the History Center in Tompkins County, Ithaca, New York, 2011.), (*c*) redware pitcher (Photo courtesy of the History Center in Tompkins County, Ithaca, New York, 2011.), and (*d*) redware pitcher. (Collection of the Kroch Rare Book Library, Cornell University; photo by author, 2003.)

History of Cornell's Partnerships

Cornell appears to have realized that he required training and partnered with two experienced stoneware potters. Documentary evidence suggests that Cornell collaborated with and may have been instructed in stoneware techniques by Lewis Harrington (Herrinton) from 1841 until 1842, and Justus Morton from 1842 until 1844 (E. B. Cornell, Sr. 1841–1842; Herrinton 1842). Harrington had operated a stoneware pottery in Utica in 1829 before he became Cornell's initial partner in the Ithaca pottery in 1841 (Ketchum 1987:537). On 9 July 1842,

FIGURE 4. Salt-glazed and wood-fired stoneware jar produced by Elijah Cornell. Likely marked: E CORNELL & CO / ITHACA. (Courtesy of a private collection; photo ca. 1990s.)

Harrington relinquished his partnership in the Ithaca pottery to Cornell, which at that time was referred to as "E Cornell and Company of Ithaca Falls," in exchange for $150 of earthenware (Herrinton 1842).

Cornell's business relationship with Morton appears to have coincided directly with Harrington's departure. Cornell did not appear to pay Morton a salary, so Morton must have received a share of the pottery's profits in compensation. Morton's association with Cornell continued until at least the spring of 1844. Morton left the Ithaca area to work in Nathan Clark's pottery in Lyons sometime after 1845 and continued to work there until 1848 (Ketchum 1987:301,368).

Morton's Role in Stoneware Instruction

The Cornell letters reveal that while Morton worked in Ithaca, his assistance and advice were influential in Cornell's transition to stoneware production. Morton's experience likely stemmed from his training at the large Athens stoneware pottery on the west bank of the Hudson River (Ketchum 1987:368). Although family correspondence suggests that Cornell began to produce stoneware on his own (E. B. Cornell, Jr. 1845; D. Cornell 1848a, 1848b), Morton may have initially made most of the stonewares at the Ithaca pottery. Cornell appears to have been an active part of the stoneware production process

FIGURE 5. Salt-glazed and wood-fired stoneware jug by Elijah Cornell. Likely marked: E CORNELL & CO / ITHACA. (Courtesy of a private collection; photo ca. 1990s.)

and likely learned techniques from Morton as they worked together. In a letter from Cornell to his son Ezra on 29 August 1842, Cornell implied that he and Morton were coordinating their efforts:

> I would write a few lines informing that we have burned a kiln of stoneware and had good luck as we could expect for the first kiln and Morton will likely have another made this week and likewise we have an earthen kiln about glazed and am going to burn this week (E. B. Cornell, Sr. 1842).

Nevertheless, despite Morton's training, he and Cornell had trouble obtaining and using proper materials for stoneware production. In particular, they faced three critical issues. First, they struggled to obtain the correct clays to produce functional stoneware containers. Second, they grappled with mastering firing conditions that would produce bright gray stonewares. Finally, they encountered problems with the salt-glazing process.

High-Temperature Clays

After burning their first stoneware kiln in late August 1842, Cornell noted that they produced saleable ware. However, the family letters suggest that they were still experimenting with

FIGURE 6. Salt-glazed and wood-fired stoneware jug by Elijah Cornell. Marked: E CORNELL & CO / ITHACA. (Courtesy of a private collection; photos by author, 2011.)

different clays. In a letter to his brother, Ezra, on 29 September 1842, E. B., Jr., discussed their father's experimentation with clay and temper:

> They say you must not fail to see about some more clay before you come home. ... They have tried some clays but find none that will stand the fire with out melting down. I believe they think that the lake sand will answer as well as any other sand to mix with the clay (E. B. Cornell, Jr. 1842).

As a potter lacking experience in stoneware production, Cornell might not have known which clays would sustain the high heat (1,200°C–1,400°C) of a stoneware kiln. While South Amboy stoneware clay becomes densest around 1,200°C–1,250°C (Ries et al. 1904:459), earthenware clay, which is fired at temperatures less than 1,100°C, would

collapse in the heat of a stoneware kiln (Turnbaugh 1985:11). According to some historians, other potters learning to produce stoneware pottery struggled to produce saleable wares with clays unsuitable for high temperatures (Watkins 1959:16). In the mid-1700s, James Duché, son of the famous potter Andrew Duché of Philadelphia, attempted stoneware manufacture in New England with clays from Martha's Vineyard. An account of Duché's failures to produce stoneware pottery noted that the pottery "shrank from the Heat, & fell to pieces" (Watkins 1950:247–248). Lura Woodside Watkins (1959:15) writes that "only after a third trial did the potter realize that the trouble could not be attributed to any lack of knowledge on his part, but that the clay itself was at fault." Despite James Duché's training, he was unable to produce stoneware pottery successfully with locally available clay.

Surviving examples of Cornell's stoneware production were likely manufactured using a mixture of redware and stoneware clay, e.g., Figures 5 and 6, and possibly Figure 4. The mixture of stoneware production techniques, such as salt glazing with redware clays, indicates experimentation by a potter unacquainted with high-fired pottery manufacture. The fact that Cornell was able to fire pottery, not made of pure stoneware clay, to temperatures capable of vaporizing the salts for salt glazing suggests that he probably engaged in some amount of trial and error, and most likely encountered a great deal of initial trouble.

Discolored Stoneware

Cornell's letters and examples of his stoneware pottery (Figures 4, 5, and 6) suggest that he may have had trouble producing light, even-colored wares. A comparison between a Cornell vessel and vessels produced by later potters at the Ithaca pottery demonstrates that Cornell's is the darkest and dingiest of the collection. Other earthenware potters learning to produce stoneware pottery may have encountered similar problems. For instance, Abraham Hodgson in Galway, New York, initially produced dark-colored stonewares (Broderick and Bouck 1995:202). Cornell may not have anticipated these problems when he began stoneware manufacture because he was highly skilled at controlling kiln temperatures for earthenware production. His failure to produce attractive stoneware illustrates that firing techniques were not easily transferable. The undesired darkness was most probably the result of one or more of the following factors: (1) extensive reduction firing, (2) inferior stoneware clay, and (3) mixing stoneware and earthenware clay. Cornell's inexperience with stoneware clay and high-temperature firing most likely meant that one or all of these factors were an issue in his pottery production.

Extensive reduction firing could have been a major reason why Cornell's pottery was "dingy" and discolored. Stoneware kilns were often operated at a slight reduction, which produced a characteristic gray color (Speight and Toki 2003:439). Potters typically sealed their air flow vents after salt glazing to reduce the amount of oxygen in the kiln (Searle 1930:222; Kirk and Othmer 1947:536; Dewar 2002:46).

A beneficial reducing atmosphere, however, can easily shift to an oxygen-choked atmosphere that produces dinginess and inconsistencies in color. Clay with high iron content is particularly susceptible to discoloration. The reduction firing sometimes turns unglazed surfaces of stoneware a pinkish color with brown freckles. Impurities such as coal or wood dust, salts, and lime can cause blistering and discoloration as well (Searle 1930:202; Nigrosh 1994:14; Cuff 1996:64; Jeremiah Donovan 2003, pers. comm.).

The unattractive appearance of Cornell's surviving stoneware pottery may be due to low-quality stoneware clay with high iron content. Stoneware clay typically has low iron levels relative to clays used for earthenwares (Ries 1900:793,820; Baldwin 1993:11; Comstock 1994:65). In addition to perhaps using low-quality clays, it appears that Cornell never established a steady source for his stoneware clay. Cornell's son Daniel, who worked for a merchant in Union Springs, New York, for two months, wrote to his father on 3 October 1848, "I will see about that clay and send some if I can" (D. Cornell 1848a).

Another possible reason for the dull color of Cornell's surviving stonewares may be his mixing of stoneware and redware clays, which can result in a dingy appearance—see, e.g., Figures 5 and 6, and possibly Figure 4 (Ketchum 1970:14, 1987:11–12; Webster 1971:38). Waster sherds and kiln furniture excavated from early levels at the Cornell pottery suggest that local clay was added to high-quality imported clay (Bliss and Kruse 1976:12). However, in later levels, kiln furniture was made predominantly of the same stoneware clay as the vessels. These levels may correspond to Cornell's last years at the Ithaca pottery or to later potters.

The impetus to mix stoneware clay with redware clay was most likely to stretch the expensive imported clay (Bliss 1977:4). Potters located farther from clay sources or from efficient transportation routes were more likely to mix clays than those who were closer (Ramsay 1947:60; Ketchum 1970:14; Mullins 1992:187; Broderick and Bouck 1995:23,202).

Salt Glazing

Salt glazing is a common surface treatment on stoneware pottery, but is very rarely applied to redware pottery due to the temperatures required to vaporize salt (Ramsay 1947:121; Comstock 1994:26,40,290; Snodgrass 2004:774). Although salt glazing was relatively simple, it required potters to control carefully the timing of salting, kiln temperature, and how they stacked pottery within their kilns (Greer 1999:180–192). According to Webster (1971:42), stoneware potters were often secretive about their salt-glazing techniques and rarely wrote them down.

As a redware potter unaccustomed to the salt-glazing technique, Cornell appears to have struggled with the salt-glazing process. In August 1842, E. B., Jr., wrote to his brother, Ezra, about their father's troubles. He noted that the pottery "glazing looks rather dingy owing to the kiln taking so great portion of it" (E. B. Cornell, Jr. 1842). From this letter it might be surmised that Cornell and Morton were unacquainted with how much salt to add during the firing process, when to add it, or how much of the salt vapor would adhere to the kiln's walls. The appearance of the pottery as well as the description of the glaze in the letters suggest that the pottery was not exposed to enough salt, which resulted in minimal gloss on the pottery's surface. It is likely that Cornell and Morton did not introduce the salt at the right temperature, did not salt enough, or did not stack the kiln so that the salt vapor could circulate through it.

2. Resource Networks and Capital Investments

The second factor that may have contributed to Cornell's issues with shifting from redware to stoneware production may relate to the costs associated with stoneware manufacture. Stoneware potteries required more capital investment to be successful than redware manufactories (Skerry and Hood 2009:185). In particular, purchasing the optimum raw materials for stoneware manufacture presented a significant obstacle to potters transitioning to new types of ceramic production. In order to start and continue his pottery, Cornell relied on the financial assistance of his sons, particularly Ezra. The following discussion focuses on two nonlocal materials that traditional potters had to obtain to manufacture stoneware pottery successfully: (1) stoneware clay and (2) cobalt oxide pigment.

Clay

Cornell received advice about what type of clay to purchase and how to obtain it through his collaboration with Justus Morton. In a letter to Ezra in August 1842, Cornell noted that

> I have through Morton advise wrote to Morgan to know of him as he will let us have a load of clay on credit until spring and then we shall want another load and will make payment for this and we think it would be well if thee on thy way home to see and negotiate with him about it if it is convenient as we shall be wanting clay through the winter. We are enjoying good health and am in haste to get to work (E. B. Cornell, Sr. 1842).

The Morgan that Cornell mentioned in the letter was likely Charles Morgan (1808–1852), whose family owned extensive clay beds in South Amboy, New Jersey (Branin 1988:34; Veit 2002:144). Clay from Morgan's banks was shipped to New England and mid-Atlantic potteries. Cornell might not have been using South Amboy clay until two years later, however. In a letter written on 15 March 1844, Cornell told Ezra that he preferred to use South Amboy clay:

> As respects the clay ... I can say South Amboy clay on many accounts. Firstly, the potters in these parts are more acquainted with it and better know how to make and burn it and as Morton told us about Baltimore Clay that it must be made thicker and larger to have its bigness when burnt which unacquainted hands would not know how to make the allowances (E. B. Cornell, Sr. 1844).

Cornell seems to have responded to a suggestion from his son Ezra that he use Baltimore clay. This would be plausible because at this time Ezra was involved in business in Baltimore and Washington, D.C. Ezra wrote back to his father from Washington on 24 March to agree with the decision to buy South Amboy clay instead: "In regard to the clay, on more mature reflection I should have come to the same conclusion that thee has that the Amboy Clay is the safest" (E. Cornell 1844).

Although stoneware clay from South Amboy became an industry standard among New York potteries, its high price was often an encumbrance to small businesses (Webster 1971:38; Ketchum 1987:13,140,316). Inland potters like Cornell had to shoulder shipping costs. In a letter to Ezra from E. B., Jr., from Ithaca on 29 August 1842, E. B., Jr., noted that Ezra ordered the clay and that their father (Elijah) paid the $25 freight fee (E. B. Cornell, Jr. 1842). The value of $25 in 1842 would be approximately $681 in 2008 (Officer and Williamson 2010). Cornell could not pay for the clay and the freight on his own, and relied on his sons to provide him with enough capital. The Ithaca pottery would have to manufacture enough wares to pay off the purchase price of the clay.[3]

Cobalt Oxide

In addition to clay, Cornell also had to acquire cobalt oxide for decorations. Cobalt decorations on stoneware were extremely popular in New York State during the 1700s and 1800s. Although stonewares were utilitarian containers, the quality of cobalt decorations most probably influenced how consumers selected which containers to purchase. In particular, cobalt decorations added to the value of stoneware vessels (Franco 1971:875; Skerry and Hood 2009:202), and these decorations became almost essential to stoneware sales in the competitive pottery market (Webster 1971:55; Schaltenbrand 1996:121,130).

High-quality cobalt oxide, however, was sometimes difficult to find. In 1842, Cornell and Justus Morton appear to have encountered some trouble obtaining cobalt oxide. Cornell himself was likely not familiar with the use of cobalt oxide and where to obtain it because redware potters rarely used cobalt decoration (Ramsay 1947:14). In contrast to the red lead and manganese used in redware decoration (Ketchum 1970:11), cobalt was one of the most costly coloring materials that a stoneware potter had to buy (Schaltenbrand 1996:121).[4]

Cornell obtained some low-quality cobalt pigment from an undocumented source, but soon realized that he needed a more concentrated version. In a letter to his son, Ezra, in August 1842, Cornell asked him to help him obtain "some powder blue that is of a deep color as this that we have is very pale" (E. B. Cornell, Sr. 1844). Cornell's "powder blue" was probably pale because it was heavily diluted. In line with the scarcity and high price of cobalt Cornell appears to have been restrained in his use of blue decoration. On the surviving pieces of Cornell's pottery, cobalt is used exclusively to highlight the potter's mark, except for one jug on which there are small dabs of cobalt at the top of the handle and one other location (Figures 4, 5, and 6).

3. Organization of Production

The third factor that may have influenced the success of Cornell's transition to stoneware production may have involved the organization of labor associated with high-fired ceramic manufacture. Although new technologies could often be accommodated within the labor relations of nonindustrial potteries, some production processes, such as the change from redware to stoneware manufacturing, encouraged a shift in the organization of pottery manufactories (Webster 1971:52; Myers 1980; Ketchum 1987:13; Stern 1994). The specialized materials and skills required for stoneware production contributed to its industrialization in Europe and the United States (Ketchum 1970:15; Lasansky 1979:5; Skerry and Hood 2009:185). In contrast, redware production began and, for the most part, continued to be produced on a small scale by individual potters (Ketchum 1970:4; Starbuck and Dupre 1985; McConnell 1999).

During the mid-1800s, potters adjusted to the labor requirements of stoneware manufacturing in several different ways. First, some potters found work in larger manufactories that employed dozens of laborers (Ketchum 1970:4). Second, many stoneware potteries increased the practice of segmenting production tasks so that each worker specialized in a particular part of the production process. Clay preparation, throwing, firing, and decoration were often completed by different groups of workers (Greer 1999:37). Finally, industrializing potteries mechanized portions of the production process through time-saving technologies, such as the jigger and the jolly (Postlewaite 1940; Greer 1999:52).

Cornell did not respond adequately to the need for new labor organization when adopting stoneware technologies. His pottery business depended on the labor of his nuclear family, and he did not mechanize any part of his production process. Although Justus Morton worked in the pottery from 1842 to 1844, there is no evidence that Cornell hired a replacement after Morton left. Cornell's letter to his children on 27 December 1839 implied that he considered the family workshop as the model for a pottery business: "The whole business might be got under way with only a little family labor and a great share can be done by boys which I have" (E. B. Cornell, Sr. 1839).

Cornell's eldest son, Ezra, helped his father in the DeRuyter pottery almost year round, with the exception of the winter when he went to school (Dorf 1852:7). In Ithaca, Cornell relied on the labor of his younger sons Daniel (age 11–12), John (age 14–15), and Edward (age 16–17). The second-oldest son, E. B., Jr., probably did not contribute directly to the Ithaca pottery when it was first established, but communicated frequently with his brother, Ezra, about the operation. By 1846, E. B., Jr.'s letters suggest that he was more involved in the day-to-day operation of the pottery.

Analysis of Cornell's journal reveals distinct changes in the amount of labor that his family invested in the pottery business. Figure 7 shows the number of days that Cornell and his three younger sons worked in the pottery business from June 1841 until November 1842 and the jobs they performed. The records demonstrate that although Cornell did the majority of the work at the pottery, his sons provided significant assistance. Cornell produced the majority of his wares in the summer and early fall. However, when Cornell began stoneware production, family time investment in pottery manufacture increased dramatically. Cornell worked every day of August 1842 in the pottery. He took only 6 or 7 days off per month in the following September, October, and November.

The dashed line on Figure 7 illustrates the number of redware pots that Cornell produced in his first seven kilns. Redware production increased until Cornell's sixth redware kiln and then dramatically dropped in his seventh. The drop in redware production directly follows the beginning of stoneware production. Therefore, the large peak in labor by Cornell and his sons in August and September 1842 was likely related to the beginning of stoneware production at the pottery. Unfortunately, documentary evidence does not reveal the number or forms of stoneware vessels produced.

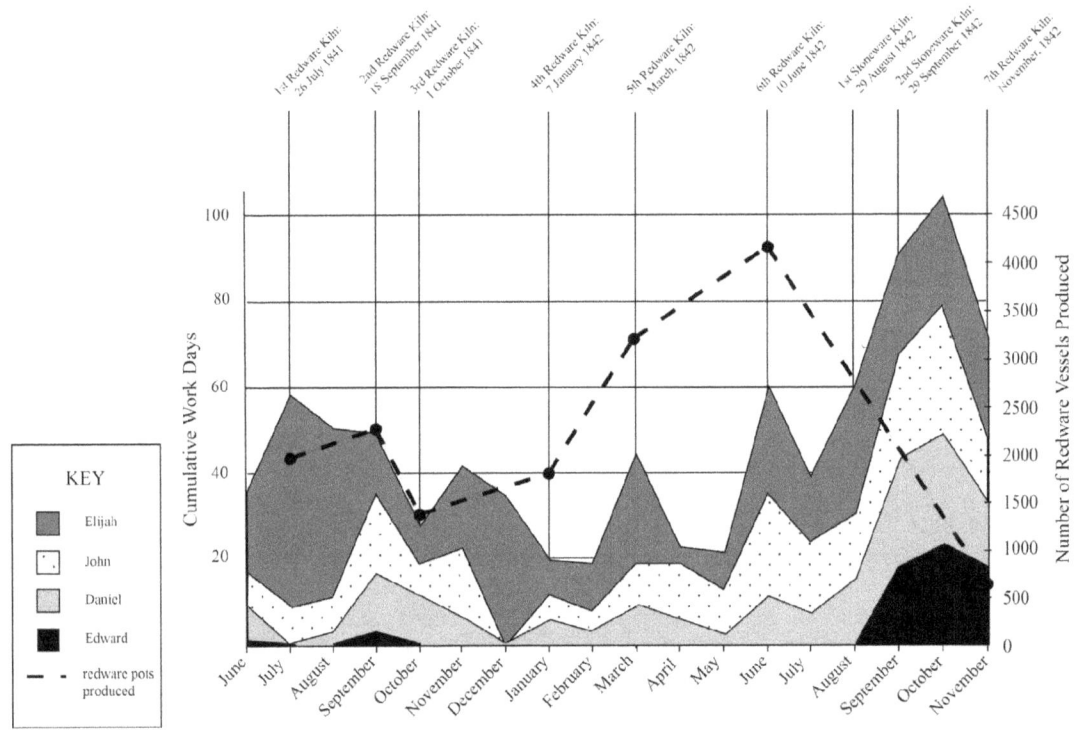

FIGURE 7. Cornell family labor on Ithaca pottery business and cumulative redware production from June 1841 to November 1842. (Graph by author, 2011.)

4. Consumer Expectations

The final factor that may have impacted Cornell's success in transitioning from redware to stoneware production was consumer expectations. The popularization of stoneware over earthenware storage containers in the late 19th century was a large part of the reason many redware potters either ceased production or shifted to stoneware manufacturing (Ketchum 1970:4–5, 1987:17). Although the origin of consumer demand can be debated—either stemming from a desire for nontoxic and durable household pottery, or as a result of technological and economic changes to the pottery industry—it seems clear that, once consumer preferences were oriented toward stoneware vessels, these predilections had a significant impact on the New York pottery industry.

Consumer expectations may have been a particular problem for Elijah Cornell because New York households may have had higher standards for stoneware containers than other regions of the United States. New York households were among the first to replace redware storage containers with stoneware containers because they could easily access high-quality stoneware potteries adjacent to stoneware-clay deposits in South Amboy, Staten Island, and Long Island (Ketchum 1970:3). New York State became one of the largest stoneware producers by volume in the United States starting in the early 18th century (Ketchum 1987; Janowitz 2008). While Cornell operated his Ithaca pottery, more potters were working in New York State than before or after that time (Figure 8). The long history and high quality of New York State stonewares created heavy competition among stoneware manufacturers in the region.

Consumer expectations for stonewares differed considerably from expectations for redwares in three critical ways. First, the color of stoneware pottery varied considerably less than redware pottery (Broderick and Bouck 1995:22–23). Variation in stoneware pottery was often caused by low-grade stoneware clays that included impurities. These impurities often signaled that the clay fabric was not as strong as clay that lacked these inclusions (Ries 1897:72, 1900:767;

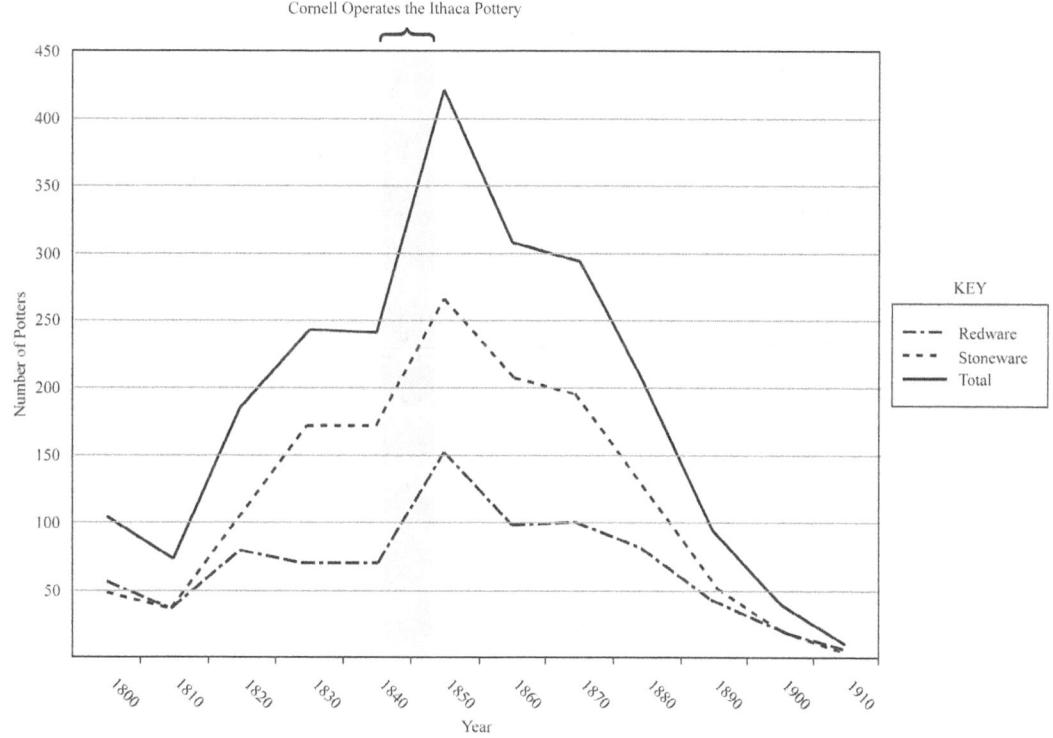

FIGURE 8. Number of potters working in New York State from 1800 to 1910. Data based on Ketchum (1987:511–580). (Graph by author, 2011.)

Geijsbeek 1902:84–85; Nigrosh 1994:14). Consumers might have expected little variation in the color of stoneware vessels because discoloration in the wares typically suggested a product made of low-quality materials or a product that was less durable (Ketchum 1970:14; Comstock 1994:67; Drake 2000:249). Reddish colored stonewares were sometimes called redwares and were sold for less than their gray counterparts (Drake 2000:249). Even in the less competitive stoneware industries of the Shenandoah Valley, Comstock (1994:67) notes that "customers accustomed to the usual gray hue of stoneware would discriminate against the red." In addition, the high quality and quantity of New York State stonewares provided consumers with many attractive selections from which to choose.

Second, because stoneware vessels were primarily used as utilitarian storage containers, consumers expected a narrow range of stoneware vessel forms and standardized shapes. Although records of Cornell's stoneware vessel forms are not available, detailed notes of his redware production provide an indication of his preparations to switch from redware to stoneware forms (Table 1). Of the redware vessel forms that Cornell produced the most frequently, only one group, jugs/pitchers/jars, was a common stoneware vessel form. A photograph of a redware preserve jar produced by Cornell demonstrates that the form is almost identical to a stoneware jar of the same size (Figure 3a). The other groups—flowerpots, bowls/cups, and plates—were either still made using redware (flowerpots) or were increasingly made of other materials such as refined earthenwares, porcelain, and glass. Through time, Cornell reduced the range of redware vessel forms that he manufactured and may have devoted more time and attention to stoneware production to meet client demand.

Finally, consumers desired competitively priced stoneware. Although consumers also expected competitive prices for redwares, the competition present in the stoneware industry was particularly steep. Advertisements issued by stoneware manufacturers often mentioned that they would undercut any price offered by their competitors. Improved transportation networks during the 1800s enabled the efficient and cost-effective movement of goods across New York State and the entire Eastern Seaboard, which opened previously isolated rural markets to increased competition from coastal sources. The completion of the Erie Canal in 1825 and the Cayuga and Seneca Canal in 1828 connected Ithaca to major transportation systems across the state. In 1834, Ithaca's imports and exports, including household pottery, were valued at over $1.5 million (Mayer 1956:20–21).

Although Cornell was the only potter in Ithaca, his business was affected by regional competition. Family letters suggest that sales to consumers living outside Ithaca were an important component of Cornell's business. His journal indicates that, in addition to sales in Ithaca, he sold earthenwares in Trumansburg (12 mi. from Ithaca) and Scipio (25 mi. from Ithaca). It is likely that Cornell also expected to distribute his stonewares to these same customers. During his production years in Ithaca (1841–1848), however, several nearby potteries operated in the Finger Lakes region (Ketchum 1987:appendix C) (Table 2, Figure 9). In particular, the number of potteries supplying stonewares increased significantly through time. Figure 10 presents the number of operational potteries during Cornell's years in Ithaca. These potteries had distribution spheres that overlapped with that of the Ithaca pottery and competed for rural markets. Stoneware potteries in Cortland and Homer, for example, sold their wares throughout New York as well as in Pennsylvania and Delaware (Ketchum 1987:316).

Cornell's pottery prices were not particularly economical. His journal notes the type, number, and wholesale prices of wares he produced from 1841 until 1842 (Table 1). For instance, Cornell asked $0.37 for a 1 gal. redware jug in 1841, while other redware potteries charged only $0.125 to $0.25 for the same item. Cornell's retail prices for 1 gal. redware jugs also exceeded wholesale prices for 1 gal. stoneware jugs listed by other New York State stoneware potteries ($0.08–$0.31) (Table 3). Stoneware is more expensive to manufacture than earthenware, and an equivalent-sized redware vessel should cost less. Consumer reactions to Cornell's prices suggest that he was asking more than the local market would support. Records of the actual sale price for Cornell's pottery from 1841 to 1842 indicate that he was often unable to obtain his full asking price (Table 4). Inconsistencies in the prices of some redwares through time imply that Cornell attempted to adjust his prices to the Ithaca market.

TABLE 1
REDWARE VESSEL FORMS PRODUCED BY CORNELL

Ware Form, Size	First Kiln		Second Kiln		Third Kiln		Fourth Kiln		Fifth Kiln		Sixth Kiln		Seventh Kiln	
	Number	Item Price	Number	Item Price	Number	Item Price	Number	Item Price	Number	Item Price	Number	Item Price	Number	Item Price
Basons	—	—	—	—	—	—	—	—	24	0.23	—	—	—	—
Basons, large	60	0.42	—	—	—	—	—	—	—	—	—	—	—	—
Bowl/cup, pint	30	0.08	144	0.09	—	—	144	0.08	60	0.08	96	0.08	96	0.08
Bowl/cup, small	24	0.06	216	0.06	—	—	144	0.06	126	0.05	120	0.06	72	0.48
Bowls, 2 gal.	—	—	72	0.12	—	—	96	0.18	—	—	92	0.18	—	—
Bowls, 1/2 gal.	—	—	—	—	—	—	102	0.12	—	—	—	—	96	0.12
Bowls, quart	30	0.29	78	0.13	—	—	24	0.40	72	0.40	66	0.13	—	—
Butter pots	159	0.25	—	—	—	—	—	—	96	0.24	48	0.40	—	—
Chamber pots, large	—	—	100	0.25	—	—	78	0.22	60	0.18	83	0.24	96	0.24
Chamber pots, small	—	—	—	—	—	—	84	0.24	—	—	—	—	—	—
Crocks, large	—	—	—	—	—	—	84	0.16	—	—	—	—	—	—
Crocks, middling	—	—	—	—	—	—	84	0.12	—	—	—	—	—	—
Crocks, small	—	—	—	—	—	—	—	—	—	—	—	—	—	—
Flat pots	—	—	51	0.21	—	—	—	—	—	—	84	0.24	—	—
Flower pots w/ stationary stand, 1st size	—	—	—	—	—	—	—	—	—	—	60	0.28	—	—
Flower pots w/ stationary stand, 2nd size	—	—	—	—	—	—	—	—	—	—	—	—	—	—
Flower pots w/ stationary stand, 3rd size	—	—	—	—	—	—	—	—	—	—	60	0.24	—	—
Flower pots, large	—	—	50	0.29	300	0.13	—	—	60	0.24	180	0.20	—	—
Flower pots, 2nd size	—	—	100	0.25	300	0.17	—	—	240	0.06[a]	180	0.28	—	—
Flower pots, 3rd size	—	—	100	0.21	192	0.18	—	—	120	0.16	180	0.20	—	—
Flower pots, 4th size	—	—	100	0.16	—	—	—	—	60	0.20	468	0.16	—	—
Flower pots, 5th size	—	—	100	0.12	—	—	—	—	—	—	180	0.12	—	—
Flower pots, 6th size	—	—	100	0.09	300	0.09	—	—	120	0.09	180	0.09	—	—
Flower pots, not specified	72	0.23	—	—	—	—	—	—	—	—	—	—	—	—
Ink stands, small	120	0.04	—	—	—	—	—	—	300	0.04	—	—	—	—
Jugs/pitchers/jars, gallon	28	0.37	33	0.37	—	—	36	0.14	180	0.24	96	0.40	—	—
Jugs/pitchers/jars, 1/2 gal.	72	0.25	—	—	—	—	90	0.09	138	0.16	270	0.20	—	—
Jugs/pitchers/jars, quart	120	0.11	72	0.15	—	—	48	0.08	38	0.12	252	0.16	—	—
Jugs/pitchers/jars, pint	—	—	78	0.12	—	—	20	0.24	120	0.08	60	0.12	—	—
Jugs/pitchers/jars, small	—	—	36	0.08	—	—	78	0.20	—	—	132	0.10	—	—
Milk pans, large	48	0.27	—	—	—	—	—	—	104	0.24	96	0.24	—	—
Milk pans, small	100	0.21	—	—	—	—	—	—	93	0.20	132	0.20	—	—
Moodies, 12 in.[b]	—	—	—	—	96	0.19	—	—	—	—	—	—	—	—
Moodies, 11 in.[b]	—	—	—	—	105	0.16	—	—	—	—	—	—	—	—

TABLE 1 (CONTINUED)
REDWARE VESSEL FORMS PRODUCED BY CORNELL

Ware Form, Size	First Kiln		Second Kiln		Third Kiln		Fourth Kiln		Fifth Kiln		Sixth Kiln		Seventh Kiln	
	Number	Item Price	Number	Item Price	Number	Item Price	Number	Item Price	Number	Item Price	Number	Item Price	Number	Item Price
Moodies, small[b]	—	—	—	—	90	0.09	—	—	—	—	—	—	—	—
Mugs, quart	—	—	—	—	—	—	—	—	48	0.16	—	—	—	—
Mugs, pint	—	—	—	—	—	—	—	—	36	0.12	—	—	36	0.12
Mugs, 1/2 pt.	—	—	—	—	—	—	72	0.08	72	0.08	—	—	36	0.08
Mugs, bilged, w/covers	—	—	—	—	—	—	—	—	36	0.25	—	—	—	—
Pipkins	—	—	—	—	—	—	—	—	—	—	144	0.21	—	—
Plates, 11 in.[c]	151	0.15	—	—	—	—	—	—	—	—	—	—	—	—
Plates, large	114	0.08	144	0.08	—	—	216	0.08	240	0.08	225	0.08	144	0.06
Plates, middling	72	0.06	108	0.06	—	—	120	0.06	102	0.06	141	0.06	72	0.04
Plates, small	72	0.04	72	0.04	—	—	—	—	—	—	—	—	—	—
Platters, small	108	0.14	96	0.15	—	—	92	0.13	96	0.16	144	0.16	—	—
Pots, large	28	0.37	6	0.36	—	—	5	0.38	—	0.36	14	0.40	—	—
Pots, 2 gal.	81	0.32	120	0.33	—	—	90	0.32	96	0.36	176	0.30	—	—
Pots, gallon	40	0.21	48	0.21	—	—	87	0.25	144	0.24	48	0.24	—	—
Pots, 1/2 gal.	—	—	—	—	—	—	—	—	48	0.16	48	0.16	—	—
Pots, small	36	0.15	21	0.15	—	—	36	0.14	—	—	—	—	—	—
Preserve pot, 1/2 gal.	—	—	144	0.26	—	—	—	—	—	—	—	—	—	—
Preserve pot, quart	—	—	48	0.17	—	—	—	—	—	—	—	—	—	—
Pudding pans, high	84	0.24	—	—	—	—	—	—	—	—	—	—	—	—
Pudding pans, small	30	0.08	36	0.08	—	—	—	—	—	—	—	—	—	—
Wash bowls, 1/2 gal.	40	0.37	—	—	—	—	—	—	102	0.18	120	0.18	—	—
Wash bowls, quart	204	0.10	—	—	—	—	—	—	84	0.12	—	—	—	—
Wash bowls, pint	90	0.07	—	—	—	—	—	—	184	0.06	—	—	—	—

[a]Price may be an error in the journal.
[b]Moodies were likely saucers for flowerpots.
[c]Called dishes in Elijah Cornell's journal.

TABLE 2
POTTERIES IN THE FINGER LAKES REGION DURING CORNELL'S PRODUCTION YEARS IN ITHACA
(1841–1848)

Location of Pottery/Potteries	Distance from Ithaca (miles)	Duration of Redware Production	Duration of Stoneware Production
Aurora	22	1835–1842	N/a
Baldwinsville	50	1848–1876	1848–1876
Cortland	20	1835–??	1835–1885
Dundee	25	N/a	1845–1860
Homer	24	N/a	1832–1844
Lyons	50	1825–1835	1830–1904
Penn Yan	33	1830–1849	(1830?) 1850–1876
Syracuse	45	1840–1915	1840–1887
Waterloo	35	1820–1894	ca. 1850

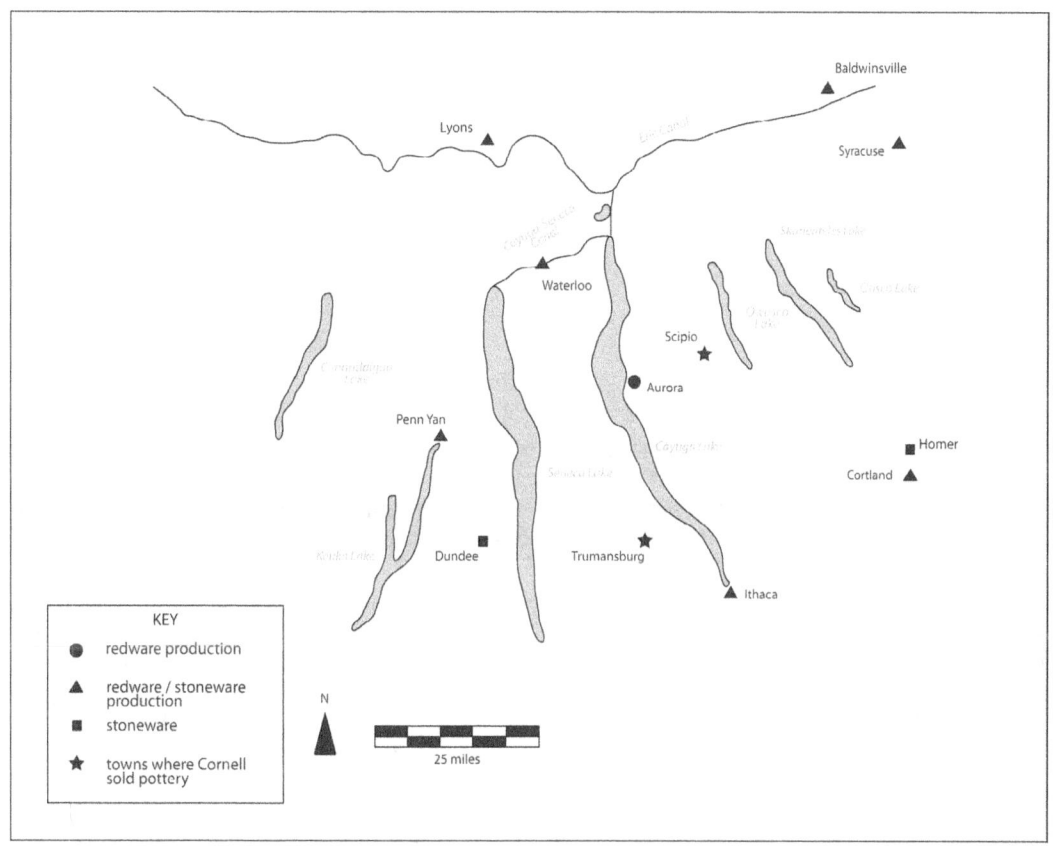

FIGURE 9. Map of redware and stoneware manufactories in the vicinity of Ithaca, New York, during Cornell's production years (1841–1848). (Map by author, 2011.)

Sophia E. Kelly

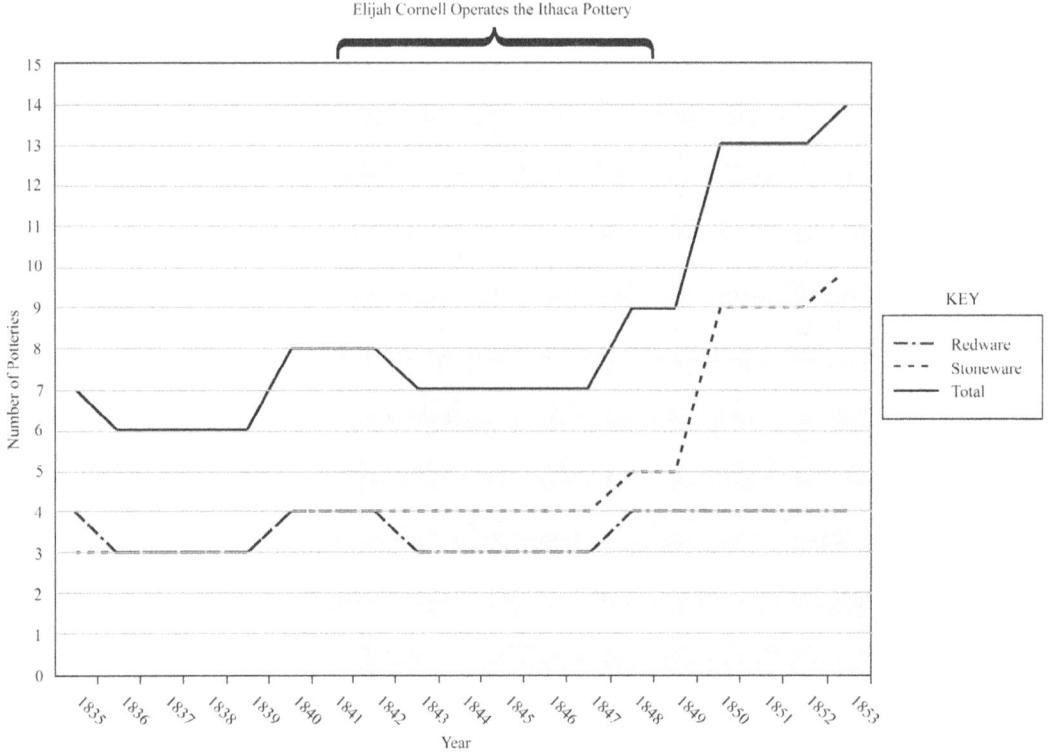

FIGURE 10. Number of redware and stoneware potteries within 50 mi. of Ithaca during Cornell's production years (1841–1848). Shading denotes period of ownership of the Ithaca pottery by the Cornell family. (Graph by author, 2011.)

In summary, if more attractive gray-and-blue stoneware were available for reasonable prices, local consumers might have purchased it in lieu of Cornell's wares. During the early years of his Ithaca pottery, Cornell was able to sell his stoneware vessels despite the fact that they may have been less attractive than the products of other nearby manufactories. On 29 August 1842, E. B., Jr., wrote to Ezra that their father's pottery "goes off well and people seem to be satisfied with it and with the excuse for the glaseing not being any better" (E. B. Cornell, Jr. 1842). A month later, E. B., Jr., wrote to Ezra that their father "has burnt the second kiln of stone ware and had good luck he has sold it all out on short credit for cash & has taken some store pay & they are getting a first rate runn" (E. B. Cornell, Jr. 1842). The fact that people bought "dingy" stoneware probably indicates a lack of competition early in Cornell's stoneware career. As noted above, this competition increased dramatically through the mid-1800s.

Discussion

This study contends that Elijah Cornell's transition from redware to stoneware production, like that of some other American potters, was fraught with difficulties (Osgood 1971:54; Broderick and Bouck 1995:202–203; Schaltenbrand 1996:11). Cornell's technical troubles were exacerbated by rising inter- and intraregional competition. While the Ithaca pottery struggled to produce a profit, Ezra Cornell was finding it increasingly difficult to subsidize his father's business. On 24 March 1844 Ezra asked his father to pay the freight on the clay that he bought for him:

I shall try to send a store [of clay] home by earliest navigation and hope you will be able to make such arrangements for the payment of freight as well not embarass by requiring money for that purpose for if [Linn][7] should fail in getting his claim adjusted now funding before Congress it may be difficult for me to get at this time what he owes me in which case it

284

Perspectives from Historical Archaeology:

TABLE 3
PRICE COMPARISON: CORNELL AND HIS COMPETITORS

Pottery Type	Pottery Name	Location	Date	Price of 1 Gal. Jug[a] (US$)	Price in 2008[b] (US$)
Stoneware	Seymour & Co.	Troy, NY	1827	0.25	5.57
	Clark & Fox	Athens, NY	1837	0.20	4.65
	Syracuse Stoneware Co.	Syracuse, NY	1837	0.08	1.68
	Thomas D. Chollar	Cortland, NY	Ca. 1840	0.25	6.42
	Julius Norton Pottery	Bennington, VT	1849	0.25	7.26
	Albany Stone Ware Factory	Albany, NY	Ca. 1850	0.31	8.82
	T. Harrington	Lyons, NY	1857	0.25	6.36
	Albany Stone Ware, E. B. Orcutt	Albany, NY	1858	0.25	6.75
	Thompson & Tyler	Troy, NY	1858	0.25	6.75
	Albany Stone Ware Factory, Staudinger	Albany, NY	Ca. 1860	0.25	6.68
	Eagle Pottery	Olean, NY	1860	0.25	6.68
	John Burger	Rochester, NY	1860	0.30	8.01
	Satterlee & Russell	Fort Edward, NY	1860	0.25	6.68
	E. & L. Norton Pottery	Bennington, VT	1862	0.25	5.52
	Albany Stone Ware Factory	Albany, NY	1864	0.25	3.53
	Satterlee & Mory	Fort Edward, NY	1864	0.29	4.10
	Charles Hart	Sherburne, NY	1865	0.30	4.09
	J. A. and C. W. Underwood	Fort Edward, NY	1866	0.29	4.06
	J. A. and C. W. Underwood	Fort Edward, NY	1867	0.29	4.35
	Hart Brothers	Fulton, NY	Ca. 1870	0.29	4.94
	Haxtun, Ottman & Co.	Fort Edward, NY	1871	0.29	5.27
	Haxtun, Ottman & Co.	Fort Edward, NY	1872	0.29	5.27
	A. J. & J. L. Russell	West Troy, NY	1878	0.29	8.09
	Hart Brothers	Fulton, NY	1879	0.29	6.46
	Ottman Brothers and Company	Fort Edward, NY	1879	0.29	6.46
	Macumber & Mood	Ithaca, NY	1886	0.30	7.08
	Syracuse Stoneware Co.	Syracuse, NY	1899	0.08	2.14
	Fulper Bros. Pottery	Flemington, NJ	Ca. 1880	0.29	6.30
	Syracuse Stoneware Co.	Syracuse, NY	1887	0.08	1.87
Redware	Thomas O. Goodwin	West Hartford, CT	1834	0.18	4.67
	Cornell Pottery	Ithaca, NY	1841	0.37	9.42
	Ahrens Pottery	Paris, ON	1874	0.25	4.88
	Conestogo Pottery	Conestogo, ON	Ca. 1890	0.125	3.05

[a]Prices are based on price lists distributed by individual potteries.
[b]Prices standardized to dollar amount in 2008 (Officer and Williamson 2009).

TABLE 4
ACTUAL SALE PRICES FOR CORNELL'S POTTERY FROM 1841 TO 1842

Date	Item Description in Cornell Journal	Wholesale Price from Production List	Sale Price Noted in Journal	Obtained Asking Price (YES/NO)
22 July 1841	1 Two Gallon Pot & 3 pint bowls	$0.55–$0.61 (price varies through time)	$0.43	NO
23 July 1841	Bowl & Cup	$0.16 (if both are pint sized)	$0.16	YES
4 October 1841	Quart Jar	$0.14	$0.13	NO
Fall 1841	1 Half Gallon jar	$0.25	$0.19	NO
16 December 1841	Jar	$0.25 (if jar is ½ gallon-sized)	$0.25	YES
31 December 1841	Ink stand	$0.04	$0.06	YES
24 July 1842	Small Chamber	$0.19	$0.13	NO
9 August 1842	Small Chamber	$0.19	$0.13	NO

would pinch me even to get the clay and must seek of my other engagements as cannot be put off although able the pottery to pay its way if nothing more (E. Cornell 1844).

From 1844 until 1846 E. B., Jr., wrote a series of letters to his brother Ezra about their father's continued financial woes (E. B. Cornell, Jr. 1844, 1845, 1846a, 1846b). In particular, Cornell was perennially behind in rent for the pottery to his landlord Jeremiah Beebe, who was becoming increasingly impatient. On 8 March 1846 E. B., Jr., wrote to his older brother that he feared that the pottery was financially doomed:

Father read a letter from Mr Beebe yesterday respecting rent the whole contents of which was Friend Cornell I cant wate any longer. What course he will take I don't know. Father is very uneasy about the matter. I think if the business will not support itself you had better come home & assist him in setting it up so as to try and save what little there is left of his farm for it will be rather hard for him to be striped of everything he has got at his advanced age (E. B. Cornell, Jr. 1846a).

Four years after Cornell began to make stonewares, E. B., Jr., wrote to Ezra on 8 March 1846 that their brother John wanted to leave their father's pottery:

The business is managed so that the boys have got discouraged and are determined not to remain at home any longer. John says if they would get a good stoneware potter he would be glad to stay at home & learn the trade but as it is he can learn nothing and is discouraged and means to go ware he can learn the trade. It is impossible the way the business is managed to get money enough to pay the rent (E. B. Cornell, Jr. 1846a).

The letter indicates that while Cornell was still producing stonewares, he was still not "good" at the craft and could not provide sufficient instruction to his son. The situation did not improve and, eight months later (19 November), E. B., Jr., wrote to Ezra to tell him that John had left Ithaca to become a potter in Cortland. In the same letter E. B., Jr., told Ezra that he also wanted to leave their father's pottery (E. B. Cornell, Jr. 1846b).

Family correspondence suggests that Cornell retired from the pottery in October 1848 (D. Cornell 1848a, 1848b). On 9 November John wrote to Ezra to ask about purchasing the pottery from their father, as he was no longer using it (J. Cornell 1848). The Cornell pottery was abruptly sold at auction on 23 December 1853 when Ezra overextended his finances with the development of a telegraph system. Elijah Cornell and his wife Eunice spent the rest of their lives living with relatives in Michigan (Sisler 1975).

Conclusion

This study suggests that the technological transition from redware to stoneware production may have presented one of the first challenges to traditional potters in rural areas of the United States. Demand for stoneware containers preceded the intense competition from industrializing potteries on the East Coast. The difficulty in transitioning between two types of manufacturing technologies was part of a series of obstacles that affected the success of these craft producers. This paper has highlighted the role of (1) instruction and the learning process, (2) capital investments, (3) the organization of pottery production, and (4) consumer expectations as four factors that influenced the ability of redwares potters to transition to stoneware production. The study findings suggest that Elijah Cornell likely found that improvements in transportation networks, manufacturing equipment, and the development of competitive materials presented insurmountable hurdles to a stoneware pottery business.

Although Cornell may have struggled to enter the stoneware business, ample evidence also suggests that his career—which spanned 57 years until he was 77 years old—weathered the changing tides of the 19th-century American economy remarkably well. Cornell kept the Ithaca pottery running in a highly competitive region for almost seven years and was among the longest owners of the pottery. The challenges that his business ultimately faced were shared by traditional potters at a national level. In particular, the local markets that supported individual craftsmen were increasingly supplied by the output of large factories (Ketchum 1991a:15). By the end of the 1800s, both redware and stoneware production were reduced to a few functional or industrial forms, or to collectible miniatures, flowerpots, tile, and decorative terra cotta (Ketchum 1987:18).

Acknowledgments

The author is indebted to Sherene Baugher for valuable instruction on American pottery production during the 1800s. Scott Thompson and John Kille provided insightful reviews of the manuscript. William C. Ketchum, Jr., offered expert advice about historical stoneware production and suggested several helpful sources. Jeremiah Donovan was an important consult on traditional pottery production methods. Carol Griggs provided access to her Ithaca pottery excavation reports. Scott Stull organized the rough-sort analysis of the Ithaca pottery artifact collections and supplied background information on the pottery. Ann Cline Kelly provided expertise on reading and interpreting the Cornell family correspondence. The author is grateful to the staffs at the Ithaca History Center and the Koch Library at Cornell University for their assistance with archival materials. Finally, the manuscript substantially benefited from suggestions by Meta Janowitz, Chris Espenshade, and an anonymous reviewer. All remaining errors and omissions are the author's sole responsibility.

References

BALDWIN, CINDA K.
1993   *Great and Noble Jar: Traditional Stoneware of South Carolina.* University of Georgia Press, Athens.

BARBER, EDWIN ATLEE
1891   The Rise of the Pottery Industry: The Development of American Industries since Columbus. *Popular Science Monthly* 40(12):145–170.

BENSCH, CHRISTOPHER
1987   *The Blue and the Gray: Oneida County Stoneware.* Munson-Williams-Proctor Institute, Utica, NY.

BLISS, CAROL
1977   The Cornell Pottery in Ithaca, N.Y.: A Preliminary Report. Manuscript, DeWitt Historical Museum, Ithaca, NY.

BLISS, CAROL, AND SUSAN KRUSE
1976   The Stoneware Industry in Ithaca, N.Y. Manuscript, Department of Anthropology, Cornell University, Ithaca, NY.

BRANIN, M. LELYN
1988   *The Early Makers of Handcrafted Earthenware and Stoneware in Central and Southern New Jersey.* Fairleigh Dickinson University Press, Madison, NJ.

BRODERICK, WARREN F., AND WILLIAM BOUCK
1995   *Pottery Works: Potteries of New York State's Capital District and Upper Hudson Region.* Associated University Presses, London, UK.

BROWN, CHARLOTTE VESTAL
2006   *The Remarkable Potters of Seagrove: The Folk Pottery of a Legendary North Carolina Community.* Lark Books, New York, NY.

BURRISON, JOHN A.
2008   *Brothers in Clay: The Story of Georgia Folk Pottery.* University of Georgia Press, Athens.

COMSTOCK, HAROLD E.
1994   *The Pottery of the Shenandoah Valley Region.* Museum of Early Southern Decorative Arts, Winston-Salem, NC.

CORNELL, ALONZO B.
1884   *"True and Firm": Biography of Ezra Cornell, Founder of the Cornell University.* A. S. Barnes & Co., New York, NY.

CORNELL, DANIEL B.
1847   Letter to Elijah Cornell, 30 March. Ezra Cornell Papers, Kroch Rare Book and Manuscript Library, Cornell University, Ithaca, NY.
1848a Letter to Parents, 3 October. Ezra Cornell Papers, Kroch Rare Book and Manuscript Library, Cornell University, Ithaca, NY.
1848b Letter to Parents, 10 October. Ezra Cornell Papers, Kroch Rare Book and Manuscript Library, Cornell University, Ithaca, NY.

CORNELL, ELIJAH B.
1839   Letter to Children, 27 December. Ezra Cornell Papers, Kroch Rare Book and Manuscript Library, Cornell University, Ithaca, NY.
1841–1842   Journal of Pottery Kiln Production. Manuscript, DeWitt Historical Museum, Ithaca, NY.
1842   Letter to Ezra Cornell, 29 August. Ezra Cornell Papers, Kroch Rare Book and Manuscript Library, Cornell University, Ithaca, NY.
1844   Letter to Ezra Cornell, 15 March. Ezra Cornell Papers, Kroch Rare Book and Manuscript Library, Cornell University, Ithaca, NY.

CORNELL, ELIJAH B., JR.
1842   Letter to Ezra Cornell, 29 September. Ezra Cornell Papers, Kroch Rare Book and Manuscript Library, Cornell University, Ithaca, NY.
1844   Letter to Ezra Cornell, 2 April. Ezra Cornell Papers, Kroch Rare Book and Manuscript Library, Cornell University, Ithaca, NY.
1845   Letter to Ezra Cornell, 23 July. Ezra Cornell Papers, Kroch Rare Book and Manuscript Library, Cornell University, Ithaca, NY.
1846a Letter to Ezra Cornell, 8 March. Ezra Cornell Papers, Kroch Rare Book and Manuscript Library, Cornell University, Ithaca, NY.

1846b Letter to Ezra Cornell, 19 November. Ezra Cornell Papers, Kroch Rare Book and Manuscript Library, Cornell University, Ithaca, NY.

CORNELL, EZRA
1844 Letter to Elijah Cornell, 24 March. Ezra Cornell Papers, Kroch Rare Book and Manuscript Library, Cornell University, Ithaca, NY.
1865 Letter to Ch. Beverley, Esq., 4 September. Ezra Cornell Papers, Kroch Rare Book and Manuscript Library, Cornell University, Ithaca, NY.

CORNELL, JOHN
1848 Letter to Ezra Cornell, 9 November. Ezra Cornell Papers, Kroch Rare Book and Manuscript Library, Cornell University, Ithaca, NY.

CUFF, YVONNE HUTCHINSON
1996 *Ceramic Technology for Potters and Sculptors.* University of Pennsylvania Press, Philadelphia.

DEWAR, RICHARD
2002 *Stoneware.* University of Pennsylvania Press, Philadelphia.

DORF, PHILIP
1852 *The Builder: A Biography of Ezra Cornell.* MacMillan Company, New York, NY.

DRAKE, PAUL
2000 *What Did They Mean by That?: A Dictionary of Historical and Genealogical Terms, Old and New.* Heritage Books, Westminster, MD.

ENGELN, OSCAR D.
1917 *Concerning Cornell.* Geography Supply Bureau, Ithaca, NY.

FAULKNER, CHARLES H.
1982 The Weaver Pottery: A Late Nineteenth-Century Family Industry in a Southeastern Urban Setting. In *The Archaeology of Urban America: The Search for Pattern and Process*, R. S. Dickens, Jr., editor, pp. 209–235. Academic Press, New York, NY.

FRANCO, BARBARA
1971 Stoneware Made by the White Family in Utica, New York. *Antiques* 95(6):872–875.

GEIJSBEEK, SAMUEL
1902 Clay as a Commercial Commodity. *Clay Worker* 37&38:193–195.

GREER, GEORGEANNA H.
1999 *American Stonewares: The Art and Craft of Utilitarian Potters*, 3rd ed. Schiffer, Atglen, PA.

GROOVER, MARK D.
2003 *An Archaeological Study of Rural Capitalism and Material Life: The Gibbs Farmstead in Southern Appalachia, 1790–1920.* Kluwer Academic/Plenum, New York, NY.

GUILLAND, HAROLD F.
1971 *Early American Folk Pottery.* Chilton Book Company, Philadelphia, PA.

HERRINTON, LEWIS
1842 Statement Relinquishing Claims to Partnership in E. Cornell and Company of Ithaca Falls, 9 July. Manuscript, DeWitt Historical Museum, Ithaca, NY.

JANOWITZ, META
2008 New York City Stonewares from the African Burial Ground. *Ceramics in America* 4:41–67.

KETCHUM, WILLIAM C., JR.
1970 *Early Potters and Potteries of New York State.* Funk & Wagnalls, New York, NY.
1987 *Potters and Potteries of New York State, 1650–1900.* Syracuse University Press, Syracuse, NY.
1991a *American Redware.* Henry Holt and Company, New York, NY.
1991b *American Stoneware.* Henry Holt and Company, New York, NY.

KILLE, JOHN E.
2009 *The Cultural Landscape of Baltimore's 19th-Century Working Class Stoneware Potters.* Doctoral dissertation, Department of American Studies, University of Maryland, College Park. University Microfilms International, Ann Arbor, MI.

KIRK, RAYMOND ELLER, AND DONALD FREDERICK OTHMER
1947 *Encyclopedia of Chemical Technology: Carbon (cont'd) to Cinchophen.* Interscience Encyclopedia, New York, NY.

LASANSKY, JEANNETTE
1979 *Made of Mud: Stoneware Potteries in Central Pennsylvania 1831–1929.* Pennsylvania State University Press, University Park.

LINDSEY, JACK L.
2004 Redware. In *Encyclopedia of American Folk Art*, Gerard C. Wertkin, editor, pp. 423–424. Routledge, New York, NY.

MAYER, VIRGINIA W.
1956 *Ithaca Past and Present.* Art Craft of Ithaca, Ithaca, NY.

McCONNELL, KEVIN
1999 *Redware: America's Folk Art Pottery.* Schiffer, Atglen, PA.

MORSE, SAMUEL F. B.
1843 Letter to Archibald L. Linn, 23 January, with Morse Alphabet Added by Ezra Cornell, 18 February 1873. Kroch Rare Book Library, Cornell University, Ithaca, NY.

MULLINS, PAUL R.
1992 Defining the Boundaries of Change: The Records of an Industrializing Potter. In *Text-Aided Archaeology*, Barbara J. Little, editor, pp. 179–193. CRC Press, Boca Raton, FL.

MYERS, SUSAN H.
1980   *Handcraft to Industry: Philadelphia Ceramics in the First Half of the Nineteenth Century.* Smithsonian Institution Press, Washington, DC.
1984   The Business of Potting, 1780–1840. In *The Craftsman in Early America*, Ian M. G. Quimby, editor, pp. 190–233. W. W. Norton & Co., New York, NY.

NIGROSH, LEON I.
1994   *Claywork: Form and Idea in Ceramic Design.* Davis Publications, Worcester, MA.

OFFICER, LAWRENCE H., AND SAMUEL H. WILLIAMSON
2010   Seven Ways to Compute the Relative Value of a U.S. Dollar Amount—1774 to Present. MeasuringWorth <http://www.measuringworth.com/calculators/uscompare/index.php>. Accessed 15 December 2010.

OSGOOD, CORNELIUS
1971   *The Jug and Related Stoneware of Bennington.* Charles E. Tuttle, Rutland, VT.

PARTON, JAMES
1891   *Captains of Industry.* Houghton, Mifflin and Co., Boston, MA.

PENDERY, STEVEN R.
1985   Changing Redware Production in Southern New Hampshire. In *Domestic Pottery of the Northeastern United States 1625–1850*, Sarah Peabody Turnbaugh, editor, pp. 101–118. Academic Press, Orlando, FL.

PERRY, BARBARA STONE
2004   *North Carolina Pottery: The Collection of the Mint Museums.* University of North Carolina Press, Chapel Hill.

POSTLEWAITE, DONALD E.
1940   The Mechanization of the Ceramic Industry. *Ohio State Engineer* 24(1):14–18.

RAMSAY, JOHN
1947   *American Potters and Pottery.* Tudor Publishing Co., New York, NY.

RIES, HEINRICH
1897   *Clay Deposits and Clay Industry in North Carolina: A Preliminary Report.* North Carolina Geological Survey Bulletin No. 13. Guy V. Barnes, Raleigh.
1900   *Clays of New York: Their Properties and Uses.* Bulletin of the New York State Museum 7(35). University of the State of New York, Albany.

RIES, HEINRICH, HENRY BARNARD KÜMMEL, AND GEORGE N. KNAPP
1904   *The Clays and Clay Industry of New Jersey.* MacCrellish & Quigley, Trenton, NJ.

RINZLER, RALPH, AND ROBERT SAYERS
1980   *The Meaders Family, North Georgia Potters.* Smithsonian Institution, Smithsonian Folklife Studies No. 1. Washington, DC.

SCHALTENBRAND, PHIL
1996   *Stoneware of Southwestern Pennsylvania.* University of Pittsburgh Press, Pittsburgh, PA.

SEARLE, ALFRED BROADHEAD
1930   *An Encyclopædia of the Ceramic Industries.* E. Benn, London, UK.

SISLER, CAROL U.
1975   Elija Cornell's Pottery, 1841. *Historic Ithaca Newsletter* 4. Ithaca, NY.
1994   Cornell Pottery. *Then & Now—Ithaca Journal* 1 January. Ithaca, NY.
2002   Cornell Family Pottery Site Uncovered. *Then & Now—Ithaca Journal* 24 August. Ithaca, NY.

SKERRY, JANINE E., AND SUZANNE FINDLEN HOOD
2009   *Salt-Glazed Stoneware in Early America.* Colonial Williamsburg Foundation, Williamsburg, VA.

SNODGRASS, MARY ELLEN
2004   *Encyclopedia of Kitchen History.* Fitzroy Dearborn, New York, NY.

SPEIGHT, CHARLOTTE F., AND JOHN TOKI
2003   *Hands in Clay*, 5th ed. McGraw-Hill, New York, NY.

STARBUCK, DAVID R., AND MARY B. DUPRE
1985   Production Continuity and Obsolescence of Traditional Redwares in Concord, New Hampshire. In *Domestic Pottery of the Northeastern United States, 1625–1850*, Sarah Peabody Turnbaugh, editor, pp. 133–152. Academic Press, Orlando, FL.

STERN, MARC JEFFREY
1994   *The Pottery Industry of Trenton: A Skilled Trade in Transition, 1850–1929.* Rutgers University Press, New Brunswick, NJ.

SWEEZY, NANCY
1994   *Raised in Clay: The Southern Pottery Tradition.* University of North Carolina Press, Chapel Hill.

TUNIS, EDWIN
1965   *Colonial Craftsmen and the Beginnings of American Industry.* World Publishing Co., Cleveland, OH.

TURNBAUGH, SARAH PEABODY
1985   Introduction. In *Domestic Pottery of the Northeastern United States, 1625–1850*, Sarah Peabody Turnbaugh, editor, pp. 1–28. Academic Press, Orlando, FL.
2002   Redware. In *The Encyclopedia of Historical Archaeology*, Charles E. Orser, Jr., editor, pp. 526–529. Routledge, New York, NY.

UNITED STATES CONGRESS
2005   *Biographical Directory of the United States Congress, 1774–2005.* United States Congress, Joint Committee on Printing, Washington, DC.

VEIT, RICHARD
2002   *Digging New Jersey's Past: Historical Archaeology in the Garden State.* Rutgers University Press, New Brunswick, NJ.

WATKINS, LURA WOODSIDE

1950 *Early New England Potters and Their Wares.* Harvard University Press, Cambridge, MA.

1959 *Early New England Pottery.* Old Sturbridge Village, Sturbridge, MA.

1974 New England Pottery in the Smithsonian Institution. In *The Art of the Potter: Redware and Stoneware*, Diana Stradling and J. Garrison Stradling, editors, pp. 70–74. Main Street Press, New York, NY.

WEBSTER, DONALD BLAKE

1971 *Decorated Stoneware Pottery of North America.* Charles E. Tuttle Company, Rutland, VT.

WOODHOUSE, CHARLES PLATTEN

1974 *The World's Master Potters.* David & Charles, London, UK.

WORRELL, JOHN

1985 Ceramic Production in the Exchange Network of an Agricultural Neighborhood. In *Domestic Pottery of the Northeastern United States, 1625–1850*, Sarah Peabody Turnbaugh, editor, pp. 153–169. Academic Press, Orlando, FL.

ZUG, CHARLES G., III

1986 *Turners and Burners: The Folk Potters of North Carolina.* University of North Carolina Press, Chapel Hill.

Endnotes

[1]"Gradually the introduction of the celebrated Amboy clay, from New Jersey, by water transportation, enabled potteries located on the line of the canal to produce stoneware at prices which proved injurious to the sale of earthenware; and owing to the isolated location of De Ruyter, it was found impossible to compete successfully with manufactories more favorably suited" (A. Cornell 1884:31–32).

[2]In 1839, the male Cornell children were Ezra, age 32; Elijah B. (E. B., Jr.), age 31; Benjamin, age 28; Edward, age 14; John, age 12; and Daniel B., age 9.

[3]The importance of clay resources to the success of potteries continued to influence the thinking of Cornell's eldest son, Ezra. In 1865, a businessman contacted Ezra soliciting his thoughts about the construction of a porcelain pottery in Ithaca. Ezra noted that he had knowledge of the pottery business since his father was a potter and told the man he was enthusiastic about the business venture. However, Ezra specifically noted potteries should only be constructed "if it is found that suitable materials are accessible" (E. Cornell 1865). His statement was likely guided by his experience with helping his father obtain nonlocal clay for his pottery.

[4]Donald Webster notes that the famous Athens potter Nathan Clark paid 38¢ per pound for cobalt oxide in 1836 (Webster 1971:55). Cobalt oxide was either obtained through European importers or from East Haddam, Connecticut, after 1787 (Ramsay 1947:19). Most imported cobalt typically originated in Eastern Europe (Broderick and Bouck 1995:23).

[5]Family biographers note that, early in his career, Cornell impressed his employer, Vosburg, at the Queens Ware Pottery in West Farms, New York, with his knowledge of firing techniques for earthenware pottery. In 1812, while a French consultant hired by the pottery struggled to produce bright white earthenware pottery, Cornell controlled the kiln conditions to reduce discoloration and mottling on the pottery surfaces. Cornell soon replaced the expert and secured a firm position in the pottery for approximately four years until it went out of business around 1817 (Dorf 1852:6; A. Cornell 1884:25).

[6]Prices are wholesale and are based on advertised pricelists published by individual potteries.

[7]Linn likely refers to Archibald Ladley Linn who served in the 27th Congress (1841–1843) as chairman of the Committee on Public Expenditures. In 1844, he was elected to the New York State Assembly (United States Congress 2005). Linn was involved, along with Ezra Cornell, with the beginning of telegraph communication in the United States (Morse 1843).

SOPHIA E. KELLY
7 EAST REDONDO DRIVE
TEMPE, AZ 8

Part V:
Transport Enterprises

RICHARD J. DENT

On The Archaeology of Early Canals: Research on the Patowmack Canal in Great Falls, Virginia

ABSTRACT

The Patowmack Canal is an important artifact of early post-colonial development in the United States. Under construction in 1785 the canal system utilized the channel of the Potomac River in conjunction with five canals built to by-pass rapids and falls. This paper examines the historical context of this undertaking along with archaeological investigations at the Great Falls by-pass canal in Virginia. Archaeological excavations were employed to reveal the various technological elements of this first generation canal system. This technology is also shown to be a reflection of the institutional milieu which produced this artifact.

Introduction

For many years, historical archaeology was a discipline concerned, to a great degree, with the colonial past. Recently, however, many archaeologists have also turned toward study of the post-colonial period. As research horizons have broadened, archaeologists have been obliged to excavate and understand artifacts of early commercial and industrial development. This paper examines such an artifact, the Patowmack Canal, begun in 1785 and completed in 1802.

Construction of the Patowmack Canal was undertaken by the Patowmack Company, chartered by the General Assemblies of both Maryland and Virginia, respectively, in 1784 and 1785. This infrastructure project was championed by George Washington, and it was he that served as the company's first president. According to the Acts and Resolutions of Virginia and Maryland, the project was to open and extend navigation on the Potomac River from the tidewater (Port of Georgetown) to the highest point practicable on the North Branch.

This effort was the first extensive canal construction attempted in the United States. Over the sometimes precipitous 218 mile-long Potomac River, safe navigation was to be provided where possible in the river channel itself through removal of bars and loose rubble, the blasting out of bedrock, and, in some cases, by constructing sluices or walled channels in shallow water. At certain locations, by-pass or skirting canals were necessary to overcome rapids or falls. From surveys it was determined that there were five locations where such by-pass canals would be needed—House's Falls, Shenandoah Falls, Seneca Falls, Great Falls, and Little Falls (see Figure 1). At the latter two locations, Great and Little Falls, by-pass canals with locks were ultimately necessary to overcome the drop of the river bed.

Archaeological excavations were undertaken at the Great Falls by-pass canal which was completed by the Patowmack Company in 1802. This by-pass canal, the largest and most complex in the overall system, today contains, among its many features, some of the earliest surviving essentially intact canal locks. The remains of this by-pass canal are especially significant in that they represent the first generation of canal technology in this country. Extensive excavations were undertaken on the lower gate pocket of Lock 1 (this lock was completed by 1798) to recover the remains of the lock gates (Dent 1983). Earlier excavations undertaken by the National Park Service (Comer 1977; Ziek 1979 and 1980) also provided additional information on Lock 1 as well as on the canal prism and its various elements.

The goals of this research are as follows. First, the major emphasis is on employing archaeology to rediscover and document early canal technology. At present little is known about the technology employed in the first generation of canals constructed in the United States. Written records are scarce. While some early European technical literature survives and was used to guide early canal builders, it is evident that conditions in this country were unique and often resulted in undocumented experimentation and invention. Later ca-

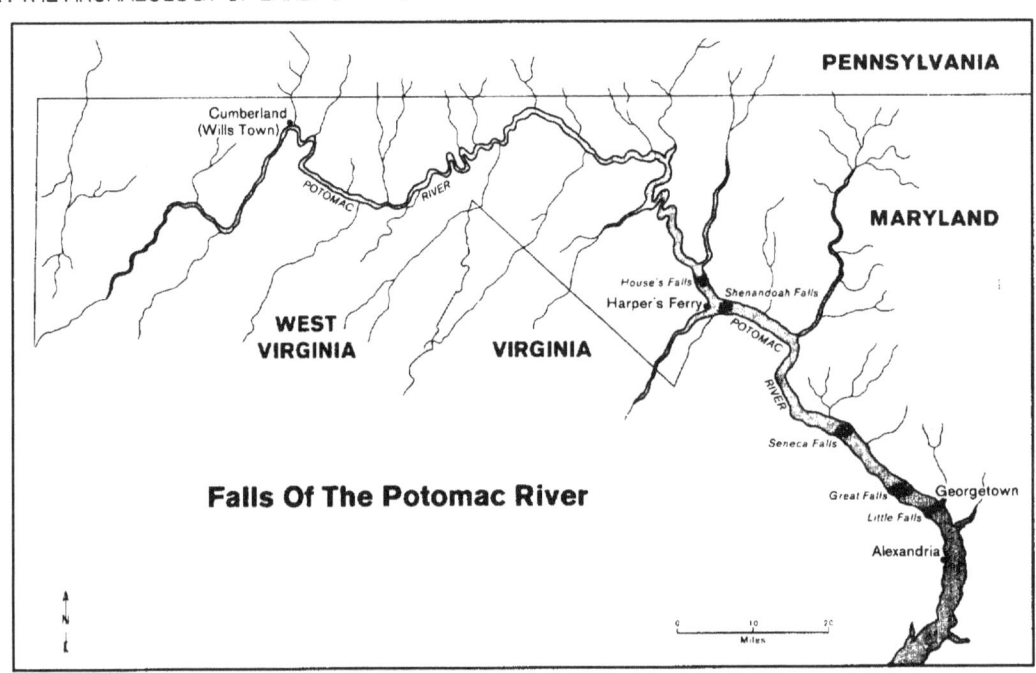

Falls Of The Potomac River

FIGURE 1. By-Pass Canals of Patowmack Canal Company. Map by Cartographic Services, University of Maryland.

nal systems, such as the Chesapeake and Ohio Canal, Erie Canal, and others, have been archaeologically investigated but are artifacts of the second generation of canal building and cannot directly be compared to earlier efforts. The Great Falls by-pass canal of the Patowmack Company therefore represents an opportunity to archaeologically explore the genesis of canal technology in this country.

Second, this research also examines the Patowmack Canal as an artifact of early commercial and industrial development in post-revolutionary times. The project was a precedent and many of its elements can be seen as a reflection of the institutional milieu within which the undertaking was conceived and carried out. While the Patowmack Canal was a financial failure, it was a useful experiment (albeit unintended) in both a technological and developmental sense. By viewing the effort as a product of the times, one can begin to see how the many problems its builders faced and solved did ultimately create the proper environment for future successful transportation development in the United States.

Historical Context

Canal construction for transportation purposes has been undertaken since ancient times. In England, the oldest known canal is an artifact of Roman times. Certainly, however, in England and on the continent, the period of greatest canal construction can be associated with the industrial revolution. Although industrial and commercial development in the United States somewhat lagged behind that of the Old World countries, canal building here had started before the end of the 18th century. Some canals were built east of the Appalachians for the purpose of connecting various bodies of water. The South Hadley Falls Canal in Massachusetts and the Dismal Swamp Canal in Virginia were opened by 1794 (Hadfield 1968:192). Both, however, were level water canals running from one body of water to another. Technologically, the greater challenge was to construct canals with locks capable of allowing watercraft to traverse elevated terrain. An ultimate goal of such a canal in the United States would be to cross the Appalachian Mountains thus linking the Atlantic Coast with the western interior.

Various plans and schemes had been advanced, as early as 1749, for transforming the Potomac River into such a transportation artery. The Patowmack Company, however, was the first sustained effort at building a permanent transportation network that would link the east coast of the United States with the trans-Appalachian western interior (see Bacon-Foster 1912; Littlefield 1979; Torres-Reyes 1970 for complete histories of this company). This project marked the beginning of a national redefinition. Stagnation was inevitable without expansion and instead of looking only toward reestablishing trade with England, the young post-revolutionary nation was set to unify itself and tap the riches of its own frontier.

The Patowmack Company was formed and promoted by a cadre of individuals with political power and financial resources. Influential company officers, such as Washington and others, were successful in lobbying both the Maryland and Virginia legislatures for the necessary charter. This was no minor feat given local political rivalries and the lack of a strong federal government to support interstate projects. The company was to be funded by the issue of joint stock. The pay-as-you-go purchase plan, unfortunately, required only a minimal initial pledge for stock purchase. This ultimately proved disastrous in the post-war economic climate when stock holders could often not make further installments (Littlefield 1985:4). As construction costs doubled, the company was forced to turn to sponsoring lotteries and heavy borrowing.

A critical reading of the surviving documentary record indicates two precepts were to guide this undertaking. There is little doubt that at least some of the forces behind the project, as witnessed by the passage below, saw the undertaking as part of a larger cause. Washington, in a letter to the Marquis de Lafayette, poetically stated:

> I wish to see the sons and daughters of the world in peace and busily employed in the more agreeable amusement of fulfilling the first and great commandment, Increase and Multiply: as an encouragement to which we have opened the fertile plains of the Ohio to the poor, the needy and the oppressed of the Earth; anyone therefore who is heavy

laden, or who wants land to cultivate, may repair thither and abound, as in the Land of Promise, with milk and honey: the ways are preparing, and the road will be made easy thro' the channels of the Potomac (cited in Metcalf 1982:112).

While there is no need to cast doubt on such noble intentions, the venture also had other purposes that are a reflection of the institutional milieu within which this undertaking was conceived and carried out.

The Patowmack Company was also a speculative venture designed to produce profits for its investors. Funds generated by the gentry were employed in an effort to bind the Maryland and Virginia region to the markets and raw materials of the western interior. Washington, himself, succinctly revealed the contradiction between ideology and reality when he wrote:

> We shall not only draw the produce of western settlers but the fur and peltry of the lakes also, to our ports (being the nearest and easiest of transportation) to the amazing increase of our own exports, while we bind these people to a chain which will never be broken (cited in Fitzpatrick 1938:188).

The basic formula to accomplish this goal, of course, was to build a transportation system that would allow watercraft to pass safely over the Potomac River at a quicker pace and therefore at less cost than any other competing form of transportation.

The Potomac River was recognized as one of the shortest routes to the waters of the Ohio River from any part of the Atlantic Coast. It was also central to the original 13 states and adjacent to politically powerful Virginia (Littlefield 1979:6). Once organized the Patowmack Company set about opening up navigation of the Potomac River. As stated earlier, the plan was to clear the natural river channel and utilize it wherever possible. At five locations, however, by-pass canals would be necessary to avoid rapids or falls (Figure 1). In most instances the company was able to complete its obligations without undue difficulty. The exception to this rule proved to be the construction of by-pass canals with locks at Little Falls and Great Falls. Little Falls was finally circumvented in 1795 with the construction of wooden locks that over-

TABLE 1

SUMMARY DATA ON BY-PASS CANALS OF PATOWMACK CANAL COMPANY

Location	Locks	Drop	Length	Date Completed
Little Falls	3	37 1/2 ft	11,442 ft	1795
Great Falls	5	76 9/12 ft	3,600 ft	1802
Seneca Falls	—	7 ft	3,960 ft	1790
Shenandoah Falls	—	15 ft	5,280 ft	1790
House's Falls	—	3 ft	150 ft	unknown

came a drop of 37 ½ feet. The Great Falls by-pass canal remained the final obstacle to the completion of the system and ultimately turned the project into a 17-year effort. Table 1 offers summary data on the individual by-pass canals.

To his credit, Washington realized the task of making the cataract at Great Falls navigable would require an effort of the highest order. His personal surveys indicated that a drop in the river of over 76 vertical feet within 1 mile at this location would dictate a by-pass canal with at least several locks. Excavations of the by-pass prism had begun in 1786. By 1794 work could proceed no further without setting the locks. With Lock 1 completed in 1798, the company became financially insolvent. When funding became available again in 1800, work resumed and the remaining four locks were built in short order. All locks were ready for gate installation in December of 1801. And the entire transportation system was finally operating in February 1802.

By the standards of the time, the project was a technological marvel. The Patowmack Canal allowed watercraft to move goods 218 miles, overcoming an almost 2000-foot drop in the Potomac River. The elevation overcome by this system was over three times that of the much later Erie Canal. The Patowmack Canal is all the more remarkable when one realizes that it was built completely by untrained personnel with little or no formal knowledge of hydrology or canal engineering.

Unfortunately, the undertaking was never a financial success. A series of severe droughts shortly after its completion allowed the system to sometimes only operate about 45 days of the year. For this and other reasons, the entire transportation system remained officially in operation only until

1828. It is probable that the works saw use for a year or so after this date. Salvage rights were soon conveyed to the newly formed Chesapeake and Ohio Canal Company that started work on a canal on the opposite shore of the Potomac River. This new canal would not employ the natural river channel and thus was a great improvement over the Potowmack Canal system. It is therefore probable that around 1830 the works of the Patowmack Company started their tenure as a ruin.

As early as 1929 local officials recognized the significance of this artifact. In 1969 the by-pass canal at Great Falls was declared a National Historic Civil Engineering Landmark. It is also a Virginia State Landmark and is included on the National Register of Historic Places. Most recently it has been declared a National Historic Landmark. The remainder of this article will focus on the most notable feature of the system, the Great Falls by-pass canal, and on the archaeological excavations at that location.

Great Falls By-Pass Canal

As completed in 1802, after 17 years of labor, the Great Falls by-pass canal was 3600 feet long. From upstream entrance to downstream exit this by-pass canal overcomes an elevation drop of 76 ¾ feet. The remains of this canal are perhaps the best surviving example of early canal technology. In this section of the paper a detailed description of its features, based on field surveys and archaeological excavations, will be presented. The reader may refer to Figure 2 for a map of the works.

At the upstream end of the by-pass canal the first feature encountered was a wing-dam which once

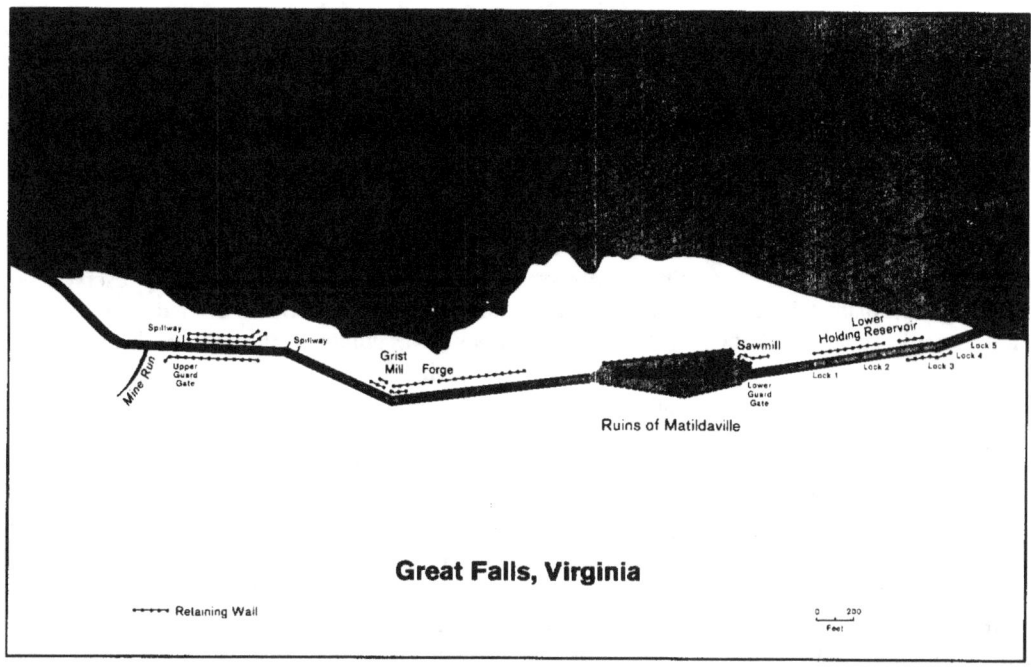

FIGURE 2. By-Pass Canal Works at Great Falls, Virginia. Field Measurements by R. J. Dent and Map by Cartographic Services, University of Maryland.

angled out from the entrance of the waterway to a low-lying island in the Potomac River. A major concern, given the frequent droughts in the area, was to insure a constant supply of water for the works. This wing-dam originally consisted of a timber crib filled with large stones. It forced some of the stream flow into the by-pass canal and allowed excess water to run over its top and escape downstream. Another function was to ease turbulence around the entrance, thus allowing watercraft to maneuver into the by-pass canal.

The actual by-pass canal prism was 12 feet wide at the bottom and 30 feet wide at the top (Comer 1977:53). This prism was 6 feet deep, and a water depth of 4 feet was the norm. In most prisms standard practice was to coat the prism bed with a mixture of clay and sand, known as puddle, to preclude water percolation through the bottom. Trenches were usually also filled with this puddle in the canal banks. This technique was first perfected by the great English canal builder, James Brindley (Burton 1972:89). Archaeological exca-

vations, however, indicate that no puddle, either lining the bottom or in the form of puddle gutters, was present (Comer 1977:59). The builders apparently realized that such features were not necessary given the fact that water-charged bedrock formed the prism base. This bedrock also further served to recharge the by-pass canal prism with groundwater. Archaeological excavations also indicate a gravel revetment was installed on the banks of the prism to minimize wave-action damage (Comer 1977:20–21).

Approximately 700 feet down the by-pass canal a small stream, Mine Run, was captured to provide an additional source of water for the system. Some 210 feet further down the by-pass canal the first relief mechanism was encountered. This consisted of a spillway that allowed surplus water to exit the prism and flow back toward the Potomac River. The spillway, actually a low masonry dam built into the prism wall, was 25 feet wide.

Slightly further down the by-pass canal a guard gate was placed. The purpose of this mechanism was to allow operators to stop the flow of water into most of the by-pass canal for maintenance purposes and to also restrict water flow in periods of flood. Concern for possible flood water damage was evident with construction of large masonry retaining walls built of dry-laid stone on both sides of the upper by-pass canal prism. This upstream end of the canal had to withstand the brunt of force delivered by seasonal floods. Another spillway was placed approximately 550 feet downstream from the guard gate as an additional relief mechanism.

Further downstream, from the spillways and guard gates, two late 18th century industrial operations drew water from the by-pass canal prism. A flume was once present to feed a grist mill (later converted to a sawmill) erected by Samuel Briggs. Slightly further downstream an iron forge, operated by John Potts and William Wilson, also removed water to power a trip-hammer. Archaeological excavations indicate the masonry walls of the canal prism were narrowed in this area to restrict available water, thus maintaining an acceptable depth (Comer 1977:61). Such a practice helped to compensate for water drawn off from the prism by the mill and forge. Archaeological testing at both the mill and forge was undertaken by Southside Historical Sites (Troup, Barnes, and Barka 1978 and 1979).

The next major feature of the by-pass canal was located at about its mid-point. Here a holding reservoir ponded water to supply the lift-locks below. The holding reservoir, based on excavations (Comer 1977:58), was about 1175 feet long and 210 feet wide and had a mean water depth of a little over 9 feet. A spillway at its lower end allowed excess water to escape and also powered a sawmill. At the reservoirs extreme terminus a feeder gate let water travel to a lower reservoir. The nearby lower guard gate allowed water to flow directly to the first lock.

The village of Matildaville was also located along the southern perimeter of the holding reservoir. General "Light Horse" Harry Lee speculated on this land, and the village was chartered in 1790. Although this settlement never met the expectations of its developer, it once contained several

industries as well as storehouses, domestic structures, inns, and Patowmack Canal Company offices. The most extensive archaeological excavations of this location were completed by Southside Historical Sites (Barnes 1978; Troup 1979a, 1979b and 1979c; Troup and Barnes 1979; Troup, Barnes, and Barka 1978 and 1979).

The first lock was located a short distance below the lower guard gate of the holding reservoir. This lock was set by Leonard Harbaugh in 1797–98. Lock 1 was unique on the Great Falls by-pass canal given the dimensions of its chamber, 14 feet wide versus the standard 12 feet, and the fact that accommodations were made in the gate pocket for a guillotine type of sluice door. Its uniqueness was a reflection of a set of plans delivered by Harbaugh's predecessor, Christopher Myers, before his dismissal as well as of the experimental nature of canal building in this country at that point in time. More specific observations on Lock 1 will be offered in the next section of this article. Nominal specifications for all locks, based on field measurements, are given on Table 2.

Lock 2 was reached by a passage through a short channel below Lock 1. The masonry walls of this lock are dressed Triassic sandstone, as are those of Locks 1 and 3, and reflect the standard width of 12 feet. No allowances were made in the gate pocket for guillotine sluice doors and a letter written by an early visitor specifically points out that the newer butterfly type of door was installed on this and the lower three locks (cited in Metcalf 1982:116). In short, a definite evolution in canal technology is evident between Locks 1 and 2.

Below Lock 2, the prism entered the tripartite combination of Locks 3, 4, and 5. By linking these three locks the need for one set of gates (2) was eliminated. A disadvantage of such linked systems, however, was water loss, especially for watercraft travelling upstream. To compensate for this water loss, a lower holding reservoir, fed by water from the upper reservoir, but by-passing Locks 1 and 2, was constructed. Water from this lower holding reservoir was diverted directly into Lock 3, thus insuring an adequate water supply for the three-lock combination.

Lock 3 also had a chamber that was wider at the

TABLE 2

SUMMARY DATA ON BY-PASS CANAL LOCKS OF PATOWMACK CANAL COMPANY

Lock	Length	Width	Lift	Volume	Date	Material	Condition
1	100 ft	18 ft	11 ft	23,400 cu ft	1795	Wood	Destroyed
2	100 ft	18 ft	11 ft	23,400 cu ft	1795	Wood	Destroyed
3	100 ft	18 ft	11 ft	23,400 cu ft	1795	Wood	Destroyed
By-Pass Canal at Great Falls							
1	100 ft	14 ft	10 ft	18,200 cu ft	1797	Stone*	Intact
2	100 ft	12 ft	16 ft	22,800 cu ft	1801	Stone*	Intact
3	100 ft	12 ft	14 ft	20,400 cu ft	1801	Stone*	Intact
4	100 ft	12 ft	18 ft	25,200 cu ft	1801	Stone**	Intact
5	100 ft	12 ft	18 ft	25,200 cu ft	1801	Stone**	Intact

*built with dressed stone
**cut from natural bedrock

downstream end than at the upstream entrance. This feature compensated for a 20 degree bend in the by-pass canal. The need for such a turn was probably the result of the constant realignment of the by-pass canal path during construction. Such an allowance for a watercraft to turn within a lock is unique for this country.

Locks 4 and 5 were the most spectacular on the by-pass canal system. Both were cut and blasted directly into natural bedrock. This latter activity involved the first extensive use of black powder for excavation purposes in the United States. Each of these two locks had a tremendous lift (see Table 2) and each was set some 47–65 feet into solid bedrock. Bedrock formed the walls, or cheeks, of the locks, with masonry added at the points where gate apparatus was needed.

After exiting Lock 5, the last at the Great Falls by-pass canal, a watercraft would have overcome an elevation drop of 76 ¾ feet from the upstream entrance, thus avoiding the cataract within the gorge. The watercraft would be eased back into the Potomac River behind the protection of a small wing-dam built to lessen water turbulence. It would then travel downstream to the Little Falls works, pass through, and eventually arrive at the tidewater port of Georgetown (now part of the District of Columbia) or possibly move further down the Potomac River to Alexandria, Virginia. Most of these watercraft were broken up for their

timber, but a few were taken back up through the system in a return westward.

Archaeological Excavations at Lock One

In 1979 the National Park Service made the decision to stabilize and desilt Locks 1 and 2 on the Great Falls by-pass canal (Ziek 1979). When sediment was removed from the lower gate pocket of Lock 1, the partial remains of the guard gates were encountered. An exploratory excavation to determine the extent and condition of the gate remains was undertaken shortly thereafter (Ziek 1980). Preliminary findings indicated that the lower portions of the gates along with the miter-sill had survived. It was also determined that desilting had disturbed the site environment enough that the wooden gates and associated artifacts were in danger of decay and eventual destruction.

With the support of the National Park Service, the University of Maryland at College Park, Department of Anthropology, undertook the excavation and recovery, under the direction of the author, of guard gate apparatus. Lock 1, completed in 1797–98, is the earliest known surviving example of such an engineering feature. Although the gate remains discovered were not completely intact, it was thought that the recovery of those portions remaining and the resulting analysis of these objects would still provide invaluable information on early canal design, construction, and operation.

Exploratory tests within Lock 1 indicated soil matrix extended to a depth of 3 to 4 feet. Plans called for excavation of a 40 × 14 foot area within the interior of Lock 1. Excavation was by natural stratigraphic layers, and all artifacts recovered were plotted in their exact position with elevations below site datum also provided. A gasoline pump and siphon hoses were utilized to keep the canal as dry as possible. As excavations proceeded a detailed photographic documentation of the effort was undertaken. Soil samples were also collected and analyzed in order to understand depositional processes. Complete architectural drawings were also produced for the entire lock structure as well as gate remains.

When excavations were complete, the remains of the guard gates and the miter sill which the gates butted up against were recovered. A plan view of the gates and miter sill **in situ** is included on Figure 3, and Figure 4 illustrates elevations of the guard gate remains. A detailed discussion of these artifacts can be found in Dent (1983); all objects recovered are currently undergoing conservation. This section of the article will give a brief description of the lock apparatus recovered and will then turn to an examination of how these objects relate to an understanding of early canal technology.

Each guard gate recovered is 9.4 feet wide from the hinge post (where it was secured to the lock walls) to the miter post (where it joined the opposite gate). Structurally, these gates were framed with white oak and faced with vertical planks, cut in random widths, from yellow pine (Lamb 1980:1). Everything seems to have been coated with pitch to halt decay. John Sullivan (1824:39) indicates such coating techniques were adopted from the wood preservation experiments of the British Navy. The major horizontal and vertical members were pit-sawn and then joined with mortise-and-tenon joints. An exception to this method of dressing was the hinge post which retained part of the circular shape of the original log.

All major horizontal timbers were tapered to-

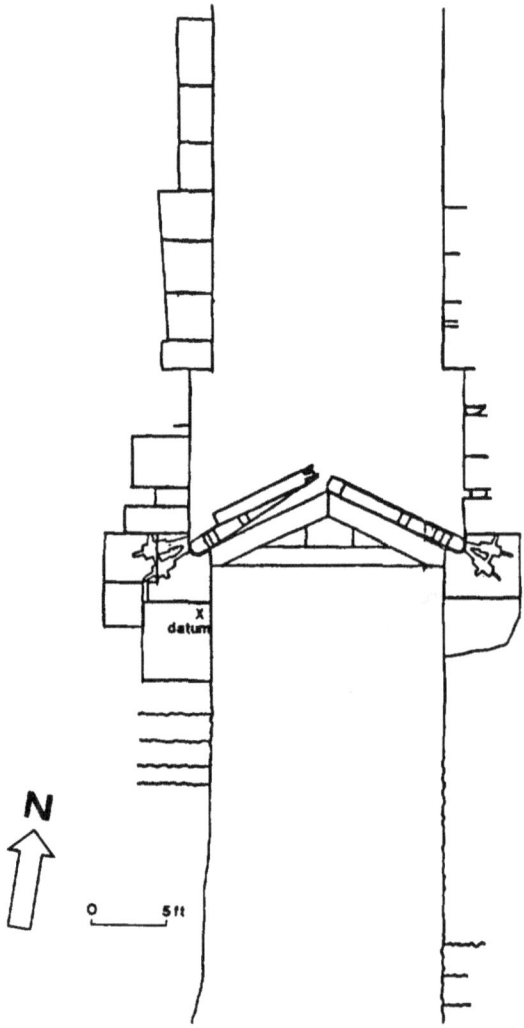

FIGURE 3. Plan View of Guard Gates and Miter Sill *In Situ.* Datum is 148 ft Above Sea Level. Drawing by Barbara Siegel.

ward the miter post. This design feature was a weight saving innovation. Two small vertical timbers outline the sluice openings near the hinge post. Hardware present in the sluice openings indicates that a butterfly type of sluice door, which turned on a pivot, had been installed on these gates. The east gate also shows evidence of structural repairs. Each guard gate turned on a substantial iron pin held secure in the bottom of the lock chamber by a large timber. The bottom of the lock

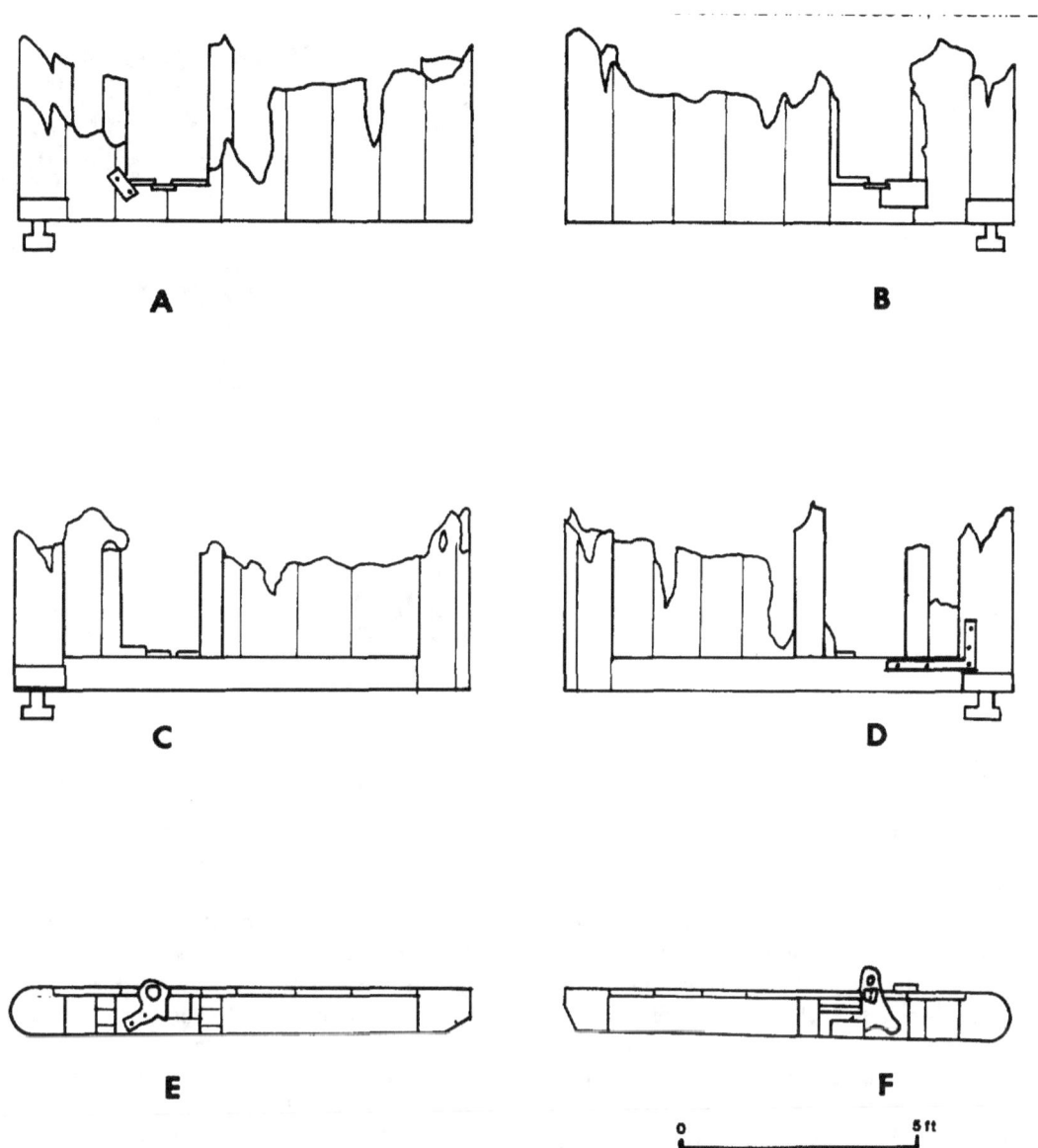

FIGURE 4. Guard Gate Remains—A) Upstream Side of East Gate, B) Upstream Side of West Gate, C) Downstream Side of West Gate, D) Downstream Side of East Gate, E) Plan of West Gate, and F) Plan of East Gate. Drawings by Barbara Siegel.

chamber was formed in bedrock and no wooden flooring, as employed in many canal locks, was present.

After the gates were removed, the miter sill, which formed a stop for the guard gates, was recovered. This unit (Figure 5), also cut from white oak, was 15 feet wide at the downstream edge and culminated in a triangular apex upstream. The miter sill assembly contained at least 24 separate pieces of timber with each piece covered

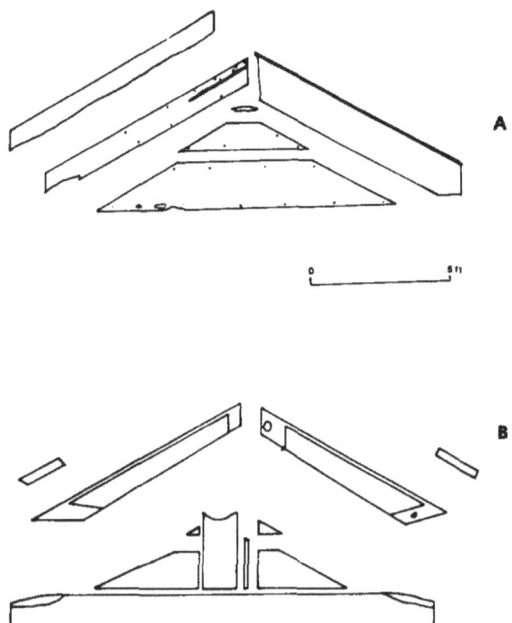

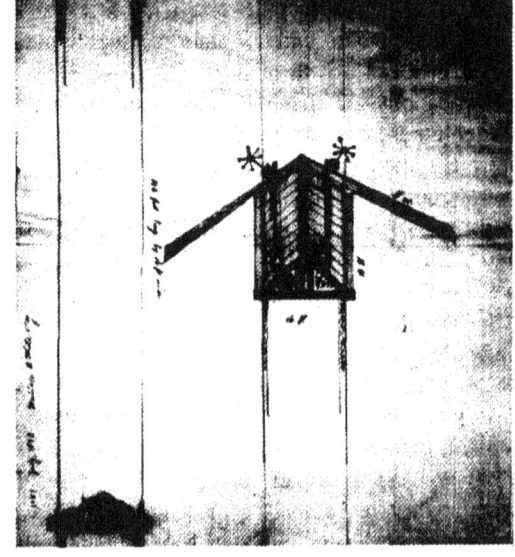

FIGURE 5. Miter Sill Remains—A) Top Level, B) Lower Framing.

FIGURE 6. Cartographic Proposal of 1785. Produced by Thomas Johnson and Enclosed in a Letter to George Washington. George Washington Papers, Minnesota Historical Society. Reproduced with Permission of Minnesota Historical Society. Scale Unknown.

with what appears to be tar paper. The separation of wood by sheathing was believed to inhibit fermentation and rot (Sullivan 1824:40). Major timbers were fastened by mortise-and-tenon joints and spiked together in three discrete layers. The entire assembly fit into notches cut in the lock walls and was also anchored into bedrock.

Evidence suggests Lock 1 was planned and built circa 1797–98. Harlan Unrau (1976:5) notes it was probable that there were only 20 reference works known in the United States by 1819 that dealt, at least in part, with canal engineering. With Lock 1 completed over two decades before this date, an even smaller corpus of literature was available to the builders of the Patowmack Canal. In addition to recovering artifacts of this early canal project, it is also possible to examine European technological transfer to the Patowmack Company project and acceptance or modification in this context.

The earliest and only known cartographic representation of design features associated with the Patowmack Canal was produced by Thomas Johnson, an investor and officer of the company, in 1785 (Figure 6). While Johnson's sketches were proposals, they illustrate guard gates and a miter sill of standard European design. Similar gates and miter sills are illustrated in the standard European reference works of the time written by Charles Vallancey (1763), John Phillips (1792), Robert Fulton (1796), and the compilers of the *Encyclopedia Britannica* (1771).

Excavations at Lock 1 indicate that Johnson's proposals, mirroring European technology, were followed closely in the design of the lock. The miter sill recovered was a facsimile of Johnson's plans and the gates were close copies. Guillotine sluice doors, which slide up and down instead of pivoting, were employed as evidenced by allowances for them where the guard gate folded back into the lock walls to allow watercraft to enter and exit the lock. The unique 14 feet width of lock one, vis-a-vis the other locks at Great Falls, was an intermediate downsizing step between the enormous and unnecessary 18 feet wide locks at the Little Falls works and the later 12 feet standard width of locks two through five at Great Falls.

Indications are that the guard gates recovered through these excavations are not the originals but were installed just prior to 1821. An 1819 company report states the original guard gates at Great Falls were deteriorating (Bacon-Foster 1912:216), and a letter written in 1821 implies all guard gates had been replaced (Bacon-Foster 1912:221). Repairs on these guard gates were undertaken in 1827–28 (Patowmack Company Annual Report of 1828). Added support braces were present on the east gate and probably are an artifact of these repairs. Cut nails in the guard gates also post-date 1790 and are a further indication that the gates recovered were 1820–21 replacements. Hardware present on the gates indicates the original guillotine sluice doors had been replaced by butterfly doors which pivoted instead of lifted. This butterfly type of sluice door was easier to operate and, based on its presence on other locks at the Great Falls works, was available by the very early 19th century.

In summary, excavations at Lock 1 allowed the recovery of unique artifacts and data on early canal construction and operation. With Lock 1 designed before 1797 it is evident that European technology influenced its construction. However, this lock assembly also fits into a continuum of experimentation with available technology when viewed in relationship to other locks on the Patowmack Canal system. Lock widths were gradually decreased to fit the circumstances of water transportation in this country, and as new innovations, such as improved sluice doors became available, they were rapidly incorporated into the system. After the initial success with this lock, the Potowmack Company engineers seemed even more willing to experiment with new technology in the remaining four locks on the Great Falls works. While the guard gates recovered from Lock 1 were not the originals, they still remain the earliest known examples of canal guard gates. Their construction date of 1820–21 indicates such objects in use lasted about 20–25 years. Because the gates were recovered and are being preserved by the National Park Service, they will be available for further study and comparison.

Conclusion

The research reported on through this article has been concerned with archaeological excavations at the Patowmack Company's Great Falls works and the institutional milieu under which the project was conceived and carried out. In an ideological sense this canal system has always been viewed as an important artifact of early post-colonial development given its first-of-a-kind nature and George Washington's association with the project. This research, however, illustrates that its importance goes beyond such a limited perspective. The Patowmack Company was both a precedent and unintended laboratory for infrastructure development in this country. A critical evaluation of its successes and failures is best approached from the standpoint of the development of early canal technology as well as early transportation development in the United States.

Archaeological excavations have provided a window through which the genesis and evolution of first generation canal technology may be viewed. While some European technology did transfer, there was also a large amount of experimentation and innovation. Canal prisms were built without features that most engineers saw as necessary, and locks were set with greater lifts than European engineers of the time thought possible. Lock designs were sometimes so unconventional that many feared they would not operate. The very idea of clearing a natural river channel and only by-passing major obstacles was, in itself, a redefinition of traditional European canal transportation.

Some of this technological experimentation and innovation can be seen as a reflection of the institutional milieu within which its creators worked. Wallace (1982:149–154) correctly points out that entrepreneural environments create situations where speculative efforts are directed toward completing the task at hand rapidly and often in a non-traditional manner. Sheer natural obstacles, unique to this country, also dictated a different canal technology.

Much of the canal technology which was employed on the Patowmack Company system was successful. The Great Falls by-pass canal, for example, was a technological triumph that caused visitors of the time to stand in awe at the effort it represented and the physical obstacles it overcame. Unfortunately, however, the use of the natural river channel in the system was a risk that proved disastrous. For much of the transportation system's life, it could only operate for about 45 days a year due to low water in the Potomac River's upper channel. This mistake would be corrected in later canal projects with the construction of still-water canals with separate dedicated channels.

The organization of the Patowmack Company itself also held important lessons for future transportation systems. Joint-stock undertakings, such as the Patowmack Company, could not carry out major internal improvements without substantial and reliable government aid. A strong federal government would also be needed to handle interstate politics. The obstacles encountered by the Patowmack Company did much to encourage a Federalist vision of a country united by a well-integrated, government supported system of internal commerce and transportation (Littlefield 1985:4). The Patowmack Company also illustrated that transportation systems would be most successful when they were built to connect already existing markets. The Patowmack Company, unfortunately, connected two regions before a strong demand for either region's products was in existence. This did much to limit revenue, through tolls, to the system (Littlefield 1985:3).

In closing, the Patowmack Company and its transportation system represents one of the grandest experiments of the age. Although the lessons learned were harsh, ultimately turning construction into a 17 year ordeal, the undertaking was the beginning of ambitious infrastructure development in this country. The project also united two regions for the first time and did much to help develop the young country's self-image. While the Patowmack Company itself was not a total success, the vision of the project and its sponsors was ultimately fulfilled by later canal systems.

ACKNOWLEDGEMENTS

The excavations at Great Falls were sponsored by the George Washington Memorial Parkway Unit of the National Capital Region, National Park Service. Research funds were provided through contract number CX-3000-1-0138. Nick Veloz of the George Washington Memorial Parkway Unit ultimately deserves much of the credit for his recognition of the significance of the gate remains and his efforts to insure that they were properly excavated and conserved. Stephen Potter, National Capital Region Archaeologist, also aided greatly in this research. Douglas Comer, Denver Service Center, undertook earlier excavations important to this research. Special thanks are also due Karen Orrence, Tricia McGuire, Barbara Siegel, and Jonathan Wright for their assistance in the recovery of the gates. Edward Duffey, Brian Adams, Jim Putnam, Jerry Hall, and Ray Kelly of Great Falls Park were also instrumental in completing this research. Valuable suggestions were also made by Douglas R. Littlefield, University of California at Los Angeles, and anonymous reviewers.

REFERENCES

BACON-FOSTER, CORRA
1912 Early Chapters in the Development of the Potomac Route to the West. *Records of the Columbia Historical Society* 15:96–323.

BARNES, ARTHUR G.
1978 *History of the Patowmack Canal: Matildaville*. Southside Historic Sites, Williamsburg.

BURTON, ANTHONY
1972 *The Canal Builders*. Eyre Methuen, London.

COMER, DOUGLAS C.
1977 Archeological Test Excavation of the Patowmack Canal. Ms. on file, National Park Service, Denver Service Center.

DENT, RICHARD J.
1983 Report of Investigations at Lock Number One of the Patowmack Canal. Ms. on file, National Park Service, National Capital Region, George Washington Memorial Parkway.

ENCYCLOPEDIA BRITANNICA
1771 Canals and Canal Building. Britannica Publishing Company, Edinburgh.

FITZPATRICK, JOHN C.
  1938 *The Writings of George Washington*. Government Printing Office, Washington, D.C.

FULTON, ROBERT
  1796 *A Treatise on the Improvement of Canal Navigation*. Privately Published, London.

HADFIELD, CHARLES R.
  1968 *The Canal Age*. Frederick A. Praeger, New York.

LAMB, FREDERICK M.
  1980 Report on Wood Identification. Letter on file, National Park Service, National Capital Region, George Washington Memorial Parkway.

LITTLEFIELD, DOUGLAS R.
  1979 *A History of the Potomac Canal Company and its Colonial Predecessors, 1748–1828*. Masters Thesis, University of Maryland. University Microfilms, Ann Arbor.
  1985 The Potomac Company: A Misadventure in Early American Internal Improvements. In Press, *Business History Review*.

METCALF, PAUL
  1982 *Waters of the Patowmack*. North Point Press, San Francisco.

PHILLIPS, JOHN
  1792 *A General History of Inland Navigation*. Privately Published, London.

POTOWMACK CANAL COMPANY
  1828 Annual Report of the Patowmack Canal Company. Privately Published, Georgetown.

SULLIVAN, JOHN L.
  1824 Suggestions on the Canal Policy of Pennsylvania in Reference to the Effects of Inland Navigation of the Adjoining States on the Commerce of Philadelphia. Report for the City of Philadelphia.

TORRES-REYES, RICARDO
  1970 *Patowmack Company Canal and Locks*. United States Department of Interior, National Park Service, Washington, D.C.

TROUP, CHARLES G.
  1979a *Archeology of the Patowmack Canal: Matildaville*. Southside Historic Sites, Williamsburg.

1979b *Ruins of the Old Jail*. Southside Historic Sites, Williamsburg.
1979c *William Dickey House*. Southside Historic Sites, Williamsburg.

TROUP, CHARLES G. AND ARTHUR G. BARNES
  1979 *The Springhouse*. Southside Historic Sites, Williamsburg.

TROUP, CHARLES G., ARTHUR G. BARNES, AND NORMAN F. BARKA
  1978 *The Potts and Wilson Iron Forge/Foundry*. Southside Historic Sites, Williamsburg.
  1979 *The Samuel Briggs Grist Mill*. Southside Historic Sites, Williamsburg.

UNRAU, HARLAN D.
  1976 Survey of Canal Construction Technology. Ms. on file, National Park Service, Denver Service Center.

VALLANCEY, CHARLES
  1763 *A Treatise on Inland Navigation, or, the Art of making Rivers Navigable, of making Canals in all sorts of Soils, and of Constructing Locks and Sluices*. Privately Published, Dublin.

WALLACE, ANTHONY F. C.
  1982 *The Social Context of Innovation*. Princeton University Press, Princeton.

ZIEK, ROBIN D.
  1979 Archaeological Testing Lock #1 Patowmack Canal. Ms. on file, National Park Service, Denver Service Center.
  1980 Archeological Investigations of the Lock Gates in Lock #1, Patowmack Canal. Ms. on file, National Park Service, Denver Service Center.

RICHARD J. DENT
DEPARTMENT OF ANTHROPOLOGY
UNIVERSITY OF MARYLAND
COLLEGE PARK, MARYLAND 20742

Lucy Taksa

The Material Culture of an Industrial Artifact: Interpreting Control, Defiance, and Everyday Resistance at the New South Wales Eveleigh Railway Workshops

ABSTRACT

The Eveleigh Railway Workshops operated between the 1880s and the late 1980s in Sydney, Australia. Using an interpretive approach and drawing on the concept of the cultural landscape, the relationship between the spatial arrangement of Eveleigh's nonportable structures, its operations management strategies, and the material-cultural practices of its employees are investigated. In addition, archival and oral sources are related to the site's material culture in order to explain how patterns of work and interaction gave rise to discourses and practices of control and defiance. On this basis, attention to such intangible and ephemeral dimensions of the archaeological record as workers' resistance can provide an effective means for understanding how one group of people actively shaped their physical environment.

Introduction

In 1879 the New South Wales (NSW) Government bought 62 acres at Eveleigh, 4 kilometers from Sydney's central business district, for a new railway workshop complex. Clearing of the site began the following year on both sides of the main rail line leading to the city's rail terminus. The locomotive workshops and the running sheds were erected on the southern side, together with engine and boiler houses, engine drivers' quarters, a sand house, and furnace and shunting yards. The buildings on the northern side of the railway line included two large timber stores, a stores manager's office, carriage and wagon workshops, a paint and trimming shop, a tender shop, and a grand locomotive (later chief mechanical) engineer's office. Subsequently, more structures were added. In 1898–99 a large erecting shop and a foundry were built on the western end of the locomotive workshop. After the turn of the century, further construction occurred on the site's eastern boundary, including a new locomotive workshop in 1906. A new foundry and spring shop, made of currugated iron rather than brick, came later (Commissioner for Railways 1881:11–12,29–31, 1882:12–13, 1898:7,14; NSW Railways and Tramways Dept. [NSW R&T] 1930:105–107).

The Eveleigh Railway Workshops are one of Australia's oldest industrial artifacts. For a century they assembled, maintained, and repaired imported and locally manufactured locomotives and other railway rolling stock. Not only were they arguably the largest and most advanced of their kind by Australian standards, in their first 50 years of operations they were one of the country's largest employers (Taksa 1996). The spread of dieselization during the 1950s resulted in major changes to Eveleigh's operations and a substantial decrease in its workforce. From the 1960s it was seen to be a technological backwater. As the 1980s progressed, its operations were wound down and finally terminated in 1989. These latter developments resulted in a growing appreciation of Eveleigh's heritage value. Its architectural and technological significance was recognized by numerous heritage studies and heritage mangement plans, which provided the framework for the conservation of the site's built fabric and its remaining machinery and tool collection (Don Godden & Associates 1986; Godden Mackay 1990, 1996; Schwager Brooks and Partners 1993; Thorp 1994; NSW Dept. of Works and Services, Heritage Group, 1995, 1999; White 1995; Rappaport 1997; Simpson Dawbin 2003). Unfortunately, only one of these reports gave any attention to the relationship between the site's material culture, its workforce, and the social fabric of everyday life (Taksa 1996). In supporting the needs of cultural resource management, this body of work has relied on a taxonomic approach to industrial heritage that is informed by positivist assumptions, an empiricist orientation, and a technologically deterministic teleology. In short, it reflects what Iain Stuart

(1992:140) refers to as the "object fetishism" that has come to be associated with industrial archaeology are eschewed here.

Such assumptions and orientations are eschewed here. Instead of using an inventory of Eveleigh's buildings and artifacts to assess the nature and impact of its material culture, it adopts an interpretative approach that emphasizes the historical and cultural context, extending the gaze beyond "things material and particular" (Beaudry et al. 1991:152) and also beyond the vision of urban space as a "topographically neutralized celled grid" (Upton 1992:69). In other words, the paper presents Eveleigh as a cultural lansdcape in which "the relationship of behavior to the material world is far from passive" (Beaudry et al. 1991:150) because humans play "an active role in creating meaning and in shaping the world around them" (Beaudry et al. 1991:152). This approach provides a rationale for combining the use of material culture with documentary and oral sources to analyze how spatial, strucural, and administrative arrangements, as well as "boundaries defined by bricks and mortar" (Upton 1992:56), influenced patterns of work, interaction, and "discourses of control and defiance" (Beaudry et al. 1991:168).

The assumptions and methodologies that have underpinned the site's adaptive reuse and heritage management are described. A broader interpretative approach provides the best means for teasing out the connections between Eveleigh's layout and physical structures and the human activities that took place within its boundaries. On this basis, attention is given to the way (a) Eveleigh's built fabric and spatial and administrative arrangements defined its operations and relations among its employees; (b) management strategies adopted during and after World War I affected patterns of work, working conditions, and interactions among employees; and (c) management's efforts to control behavior were resisted by employees. These three layers of Eveleigh's cultural landscape not only throw light on connections between the physical environment and human behavior but also on such intangible aspects of material culture as the workshops' impact on everyday life and employees' behaviors, ideas, and "acts of everyday resistance" (Beaudry et al. 1991:169).

How can these ephemeral dimensions of the archaeological record be effectively uncovered and analyzed? An interpretative approach is used in identifying how workers negotiated the site's layout and buildings and the management of its operations by appropriating particular spaces inside Eveleigh and on its boundaries. Their ability to organize mass meetings was central to this process of negotiation and appropriation and, therefore, also to their resistance. Through this device, the workers challenged existing relations of power and remapped both the material and symbolic boundaries within Eveleigh and between it and the surrounding public space (Mrozowski 1991:94; Lofland 1998:10).

Looking beyond Railway and Industrial Landscapes

Eveleigh's buildings and its operations reflected the grandeur and dominance of the steam era. During the 1930s, about 540 steam locomotives were overhauled in the workshops each year (Preston 1997:15–17). Up to the present time, Eveleigh's "evocative group of rambling buildings" (Capon 1996:9) remain a constant feature of Sydney's industrial landscape. Although parts of Eveleigh have been redeveloped, its main structures have been retained and reused, mainly as a result of the site's continued public ownership and the NSW Government's compliance with its own heritage laws and regulations (Figure 1). Both the main locomotive and the new locomotive workshops are now managed by the Sydney

FIGURE 1. Eveleigh locomotive workshops. (State Library of New South Wales Government Printing Office [1] Collection: 06678, with permission from State Library of New South Wales & State Records, NSW, Australia.)

Perspectives from Historical Archaeology:

Harbour Foreshore Authority and occupied by the Australian Technology Park, which promotes the development of information technologies (Taksa 2000, 2003). Other parts of the site continue to be used for railway purposes by the State Rail Authority (Schwager Brooks 1993:1) and also by 3801 Limited, a community-based organization that leases the Large Erecting shop to restore heritage trains (Figure 2) (Hocking 1998). The fate of the site's 8.6 hectare northern portion has been similarly fragmented. Future

FIGURE 2. Eveleigh large erecting shop. (State Library of New South Wales Government Printing Office [1] Collection: 12019, with permission from State Library of New South Wales & State Records, NSW, Australia.)

use of the Rail Authority's paint shops and the chief mechanical engineer's office has yet to be resolved. In late 2002, the NSW Government decided to establish an arts and theater center in the carriage and wagon shops under the jurisdiction of the NSW Ministry for the Arts (Hallett 2002:5), revoking an earlier plan to redevelop this building as a transport or railway heritage park (NSW Government 2000).

Government ownership and heritage laws are not the only factors that have shaped Eveleigh's fate. Unlike most other large disused factories in Australia, Eveleigh's heritage value has been recognized because of its association with the steam era of railway transportation and that dominant icon of 19th-century technology, the steam locomotive. On 26 April 1988 the entire Eveleigh Railway Workshops complex was listed on the Register of the National Estate as a site of national significance. On 17 November 1995

seven buildings within the complex were listed as heritage items on the NSW Regional Environment Plan. After changes were made to the state's heritage legislation, the entire complex was listed on the State Heritage Register as an item of state significance on 2 April 1999. The workshops are also listed on the SRA State Rail Section 170 Register as a heritage item of state significance (Simpson Dawbin 2003).

As in other parts of the world, such recognition of heritage value draws on the popularity of railway antiquarianism (Cattell and Falconer 1995), the roots of which can be found in the late-19th century, and the railway preservation mania that emerged in the United Kingdom and Australia after World War II when dieselization accompanied railway modernization (Samuel 1996:236,243–245,254,302–303). Its effect has been a narrow focus on the preservation of railway structures and railway technology. All that remains at Eveleigh are buildings and machines. In the early 1990s, most of its remaining machinery and tool collection was moved into bays 1 and 2 of the locomotive workshop, which were excluded from redevelopment by the Heritage Council of NSW (Taksa 2001, 2003). In 2003 some machines were placed in different parts of this building, where they now form a backdrop for the high-tech companies that lease space from the Australian Technology Park. Their conservation was recently completed (Figure 3) (Sydney Harbour Foreshore Authority 2003).

This emphasis on built fabric and mechanical artifacts reflects and reinforces authorized views

FIGURE 3. Eveleigh tools in Bay 1, Eveleigh locomotive workshops building. (Photograph by Peter Murphy; © Lucy Taksa and the University of New South Wales.)

about the site's value. In 1993, the Eveleigh Precinct Conservation Policy reiterated the argument for conservation mounted by one of Australia's leading industrial heritage consultants (Godden 1990:13) when it attributed the site's significance to the fact that it "contained the finest examples of late Victorian large industrial buildings in NSW" and "the most complete set of late nineteenth and early twentieth century light and medium engineering workshop technology in Australia ... the United Kingdom or the USA" (Schwager Brooks 1993:9) (Figure 4). One year later, this view was also reinforced in the archaeological assessment that was undertaken before redevelopment of the site began. In the absence of any excavation, the archaeologist concluded,

while the residential occupation of the later nineteenth century would have created a cumulative and extensive archaeological resource, the cutting and filling carried out to level the site for railway purposes is likely to have extensively disturbed and possibly destroyed that evidence leaving, at best, fragmentary features and deposits. The railway occupation, apart from the filling material, may also be represented by some industrial relics within the site. Those demolition programmes and preparation works for ... the railway ... may be viewed as site formation processes that are the principal "artefacts" of twentieth century evolution (Thorp 1994:16).

Accordingly, Wendy Thorp (1994:17) argued that the "principal significance of the Eveleigh Precinct ... is its association with and demonstration of railway history and technological development associated with that industry."

This way of assessing Eveleigh's material culture is extremely problemmatic. Without serious attention to Eveleigh's cultural landscape, all this emphasis on the relics associated with the railway industry and its technology tells us little about the site's physical environment and the employees that sustained its industrial operations and the state's railway transport system for just over 100 years. As numerous scholars have noted, railways had a profound impact on national destinies, the growth of cities, and the texture of everyday life. Railway structures like railway lines, bridges, stations and railway workshops also fundamentally altered natural and urban landscapes (Patmore 1994:135,141; Divall and Coulls 1999:7–10). These broader factors draw attention to the importance of context. More specifically, from an historical persepctive they highlight the fact that railway workshops constituted an important cultural context in their own right since they encompassed both the factory system and the railway system, two of the most prominent elements of the industrial revolution (Olssen and Brecher 1992:350–351).

Attention to material remains alone provides little understanding of the way they were modified "through culturally determined behavior" (Deetz 1977:24–25). As Dell Upton (1992:52) pointed out, material culture needs to be seen more broadly as something that extends beyond individual, tangible artifacts or discrete collections of artifacts. To effectively interpret the impact that people have had on physical environments like Eveleigh and how their culturally determined behaviors were shaped by and also shaped such

FIGURE 4. 1,500 ton "Davy" steam and hydraulic forging press installed in Bay 1, Eveleigh locomotive workshops building in 1923. (Photograph by Peter Murphy; © Lucy Taksa and the University of New South Wales.)

environments, there is a need to "investigate the reciprocal relationships among selves and human alterations of the environment" and "take into account both intention and reaction, action and interpretation" (Upton 1992:52). From this broader perspective, material culture can be seen "as a medium of communication and expression that can condition and at times control social action" (Beaudry et al. 1991:153).

Action, interpretation, communication, and expression are not, however, only pertinent to material culture but also to culture more generally (Denning 1997:423,453). Raymond Williams (1989b:36) claims "the culture of a people can only be what all its members are engaged in creating in the act of living." It is "a condition in which" people "participate in the articulation of meanings and values." Hence, he stressed,

> We are brought up with certain ideas about communication which on the whole I think mislead us. We think of it as an activity which takes place after the important things have happened ... Communication is secondary, just as people think of art as secondary, as marginal activity, because first there is life and then there is art. First there is reality and then there is communication about reality (Williams 1989a:21).

To overcome this misconception Williams (1989a:21) suggested that attention had to be given to (a) patterns of communication, some of which we are barely conscious of because they are so deeply ingrained in "our minds and the shape of our society"; and (b) both formal and informal communication systems. Among the latter, he included the institutions of the state and education as well as the features of the places in which people live—the prominent buildings or aspects of the natural landscape that somehow express "the meaning of what it is to live in that place, and around that building, around that feature" (Williams 1989a:22). From this perspective, Eveleigh itself can be viewed as a center of communication because the mass meetings held inside its gates, as well as those held on its boundaries, provided forums for the exchange of ideas and a recognition of shared interests.

Cultural Landscapes

Landscapes are "the richest historical record we possess" (Hoskins 1955:14). They form an integral part of our intellectual and cultural baggage (Taylor and Winston-Gregson 1992: 101). When we add the word *cultural* as a prefix to landscape we extend the frame of reference to include what Sharon Zukin (1991: 16) has described as the "architecture of social ... relations imposed by powerful institutions." Yet the idea of *landscape* needs some further exposition because it contains a multitude of meanings and its common use varies greatly (Mitchell 2000:99). Although originally used to refer to a genre of painting, it now encompasses the idea of place and also the institutions and the "ensemble of material and social practices and their symbolic representations" that occur in places (Zukin 1991:16). Because landscape stretches the imagination beyond physical surroundings, it has become a popular conceptual tool, particularly for cultural geographers. As Zukin (1991:18) pointed out over a decade ago, cultural geographers now "regard all landscapes as symbolic, as expressions of cultural values, social behavior, and individual actions worked upon particular localities over a span of time." For Zukin (1991:19) they are microcosms of social relations, in which power, coercion, and collective resistance are defining themes. In short, Zukin (1991:12,18) argues that landscape is "a cultural artifact of social conflict and cohesion" and "a field of impact between authority and resistance."

This conceptualization of the cultural landscape encourages us to acknowledge that questions about spatiality are central to questions about resistance (Pile 1997:27) and that "resistance opposes power ... through specific geographies" (Pile 1997:1). It also creates a good foundation for mapping spatial practices of domination and resistance (Pile 1997:2). How can these practices be effectively mapped and, further, how can mapping spatial practices in one cultural landscape enhance our understanding of workers' "acts of everyday resistance"? (Beaudry et al. 1991:169). Steve Pile (1997:14) suggests that mapping spatial practices has to begin with "the context in which acts of resistance take place" because this draws our attention to the fluidity, inconsistency, and ambiguity of power relations and the fact that in certain circumstances power relations "produce discontinuous spaces," which can be transgressed. By contextualizing and mapping spatial practices the

Lucy Taksa

interplay between behavior and environment and the relationship between the tactics of domination and resistance and the spaces of domination and resistance can be appreciated.

According to Pile (1997:27), "once passive, inert and singular notions of spatiality ... are abandoned, then it becomes clear that resistance is as much defined through the struggle to define liberation, space and subjectivity as through the elite's attempts to defeat, prevent and oppress those who threaten their authority." This perspective draws attention to the material effects of power and what Pile (1997:27) refers to as the "the politics of lived spaces" and the "politics of location."

In order to map the spatial practices of domination and resistance, we need to begin with the premis that location is both "the ground which defines struggle and a highly contested terrain." At the same time, the politics of location is informed by notions of unity and difference and that spaces of domination are created through the imposition of boundaries by those in power who seek to circumscribe and regulate the use of space (Pile 1997:28–29). According to Pile (1997:16), however, such efforts to control spaces of resistance can only ever be partial because "the spatial practices of resistance" involve not only the mobilization of particular interest groups in particular places but also a process of insinuation. As Pile (1997:16) explains, "resistance does not just act on topographies imposed through the spatial technologies of domination, it moves across them under the noses of the enemy, seeking to create new meanings out of imposed meanings, to re-work and divert space to other ends." Such insinuation occurs when people occupy strategic locations in order to challenge the boundaries that dominate their lives, and it results in the repositioning, the opening up, or even the closing down of physical and symbolic boundaries (Pile 1997:28–29). In other words, "tactics of resistance have at least two 'surfaces': one facing towards the map of power, the other facing in another direction" (Pile 1997:16).

By directing attention to the spatial geographies of control and defiance, this conceptual framework enhances the interpretative approach elaborated earlier. Workers actively negotiated Eveleigh's spatial and structural arrangements as well as material and symbolic boundaries

by occupying strategic locations as part of their daily acts of resistance.

The Geography of Eveleigh's Cultural Landscape

Eveleigh's cultural landscape was shaped by the public ownership and control over railway transportation, which began in 1855, and the NSW Government's acquisition of the Chisholm Estate in 1879 (Commissioner for Railways 1880:11; Lee 1988:26,92). Clearing of the land began the following year and the plan adopted divided operations into four main sections: carriage and wagon shops, paint shop and stores, locomotive shops, and running sheds. Construction of the necessary structures took six years. Beside the two-story chief mechanical engineer's office building, the railway stores and the paint and trimming shops on the northern side of the railway line, the carriage and wagon repairing shops contained wood working machine and fitting, turning, and smiths' shops. On the southern side of the railway tracks, the 16 bays of the main locomotive workshop included boiler, steam-hammer and smiths' shops, an iron and brass foundry, a tin and coppersmiths' shop, engine and tender repairing shops, wheel machine and fitting shops, joiners' shops, and a small store. The point of this plan was to enable each of the divisions to communicate with the main lines without interfering with each other or interrupting traffic (Figure 5) (Commissioner for Railways 1881:11–12,29–31, 1882:12–13, 1898:7,14; NSW R&T 1898:172, 1930:105–107; Forsyth [1955]:3).

From 1887 the workshops assembled, repaired, and maintained railway rolling stock and steam locomotives imported from Britain and the United States (Commissioner for Railways 1891:19–20, 1893:20–21; Oliver et al. 1899:50; Burke 1995:82,86–89). By the early 1890s, 2,500 people worked there at a time when the NSW railways' permanent workforce had reached 11,827 (Markey 1988:99–100). By the turn of the century, Eveleigh's employees made up 10% of the department's workforce (NSW R&T 1900:239). After manufacturing was added to its functions in 1908 (Burke 1986:39; Gunn 1989:250), the number of workers increased to 3,270 (Blacket 1912:6–10,13). In 1955 departmental histories of the workshops

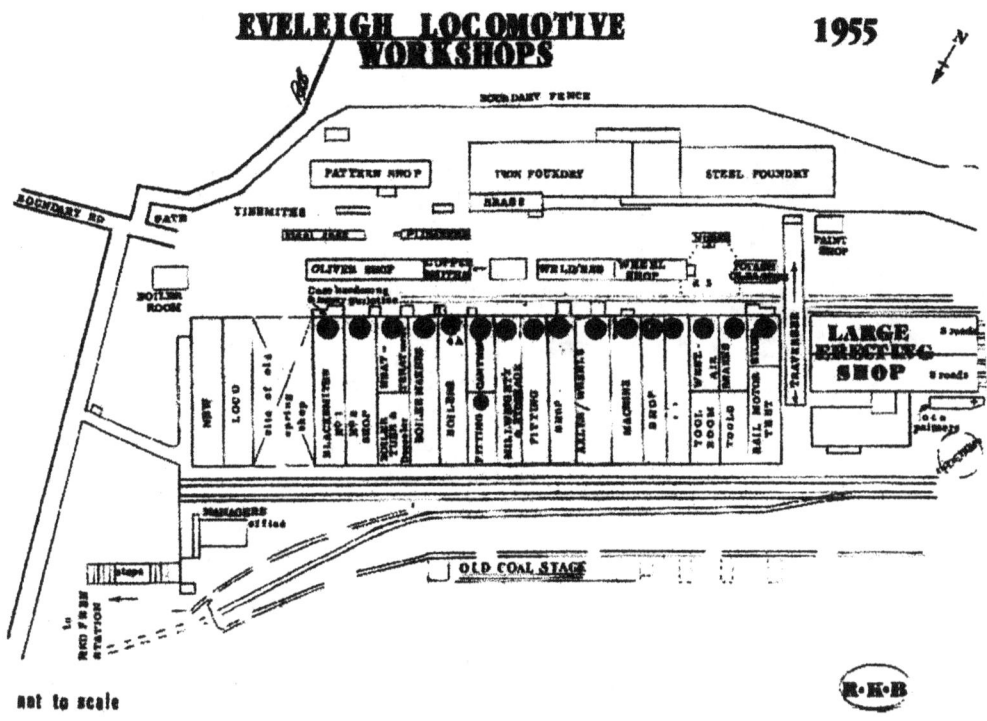

FIGURE 5. Plan of Eveleigh Locomotive Workshops, ca. 1955. (© Richard Butcher, with permission.)

claimed that the total staff remained at an average of 3,000 (Commissioner for Railways 1955:5; Guthrie 1955:7).

Eveleigh workers were divided by the department's bureaucratic structure, by occupation, and by formal operational and spatial arrangements. Speaking of the 1950s, Brian Dunnett (1996) commented that the workers' "identity was very much related to their working situation" and "the type of work they were doing ... If they were actually working on the steam engines well then they identified with that piece or equipment, if they were working on carriages then they would identify there." Hal Alexander (1996), who worked in the carriage shops at this time, also pointed out that the spatial, administrative, and occupational divisions between workers in the locomotive shops and the carriage and paint shops created jealousies among them; although only separated by a "dozen train tracks," the distance was "a mile wide."

Divisions also occurred on the same side of the railway tracks between the running sheds and

the locomotive workshops. John Willis (1996), who worked in the former put it this way:

> The Running Sheds were a different set-up from the (Locomotive) workshops, very close to one another, walking distance, but we weren't really attached to them, we had our own section. Our Running Sheds were mostly wooden and tin structures whereas the workshops were all brick. They had a lot cleaner situation than we had. We had about 300 steam engines going out every day and it was very dirty, very dirty.

This spatial and occupational segregation prevented interaction not just in relation to work activities but also social activities. At Christmas both groups would have their own "break up parties." According to Willis (1996), the running shed and locomotive workshop staff would certainly exchange Christmas greetings, but those employed in the latter shops "never sort of came down and interfered with ours and we never interfered with theirs" (Figure 6).

Yet despite these differences and divisions, spatial isolation, shiftwork, craft traditions,

FIGURE 6. Eveleigh locomotive running sheds. (State Library of New South Wales Government Printing Office [1] Collection: 12017, with permission from State Library of New South Wales & State Records, NSW, Australia.)

and membership of trade unions encouraged collectivism among workers. The Royal Commission appointed by the government in 1904 to inquire into the possibility of locomotive manufacture at Eveleigh found that employees had succeeded in enforcing collective norms on output and that their unions had prevented the introduction of piecework and bonus payment systems (McAllister et al. 1904:12–17). Solidarity of this nature sustained industrial action over the ensuing decade (Patmore 1985: 305–306,335,338–340).

To deal with escalating industrial action between 1916 and 1917, railway management introduced a new card system of recording work times on 20 July 1917, which not only altered patterns of work and spatial and operational arrangements but also traditional work practices. For the workers, the card system was the same as the system popularized in the United States by Frederick Winslow Taylor, known as "scientific management" (NSW Labor Council 1917; Holme 1918:6; Childe 1964:154; Turner 1979:141). On 2 August 1917, 3,000 Eveleigh employees walked off the job. They were soon followed by 5,780 other railway workers who were employed in various branches of the department, and by the end of the week, the number of strikers increased to 10,000. Only 15,000 of the Railways and Tramways Department's 48,000 employees did not strike (Patmore 1985:343). The dispute soon escalated to a general strike throughout NSW, which in

the railways and tramways alone lasted for six weeks (Taksa 1991).

Workers opposed the system because of the way it increased management's control over their job performance and ability to interact and collaborate. They complained about its reliance on the employment of additional foremen "to supervise and strictly watch every few men" and to "exhort men to further effort." They disliked the way their every movement was timed and that their movements were restricted to certain machines and benches because they were no longer allowed to get their tools and materials. Under the new system, they were "provided with the means of communication with the tool store" and everything was brought to them by others (NSW Parliament 1917–1918:448,491,495–496,500; *Sydney Morning Herald* 1917; Holme 1918:65).

The government's response to their industrial action was belligerent. Its coercive measures undermined the workers' resistance and led to a comprehensive defeat for the labor movement. The railway dispute officially ended on 10 September 1917, and the terms of settlement were extremely harsh. The notorious card system was retained, strikebreakers kept their new jobs, and trade union officials were blacklisted. In all 2,000 strikers were refused re-employment. Those who regained their jobs lost their seniority and other rights (Holme 1918:44a,103–106a; Hearn 1990:31; Taksa 1991: 23–24, 1997:38–39).

Besides introducing the card system, the railways department also made other "physical changes," basically in line with Taylor's system. These included sequential operations, the reorganization of supervisory procedures, a routing system that designated the order of work and the grouping of machines and tools, and a carefully organized and controlled tool room to enable the supply of specific materials for specific tasks (Taylor 1903, 1906, 1911; Taksa 1997:52–54). These changes to workshop layout and processes destabilized traditional work practices, limited interaction and communication among workers, and involved spatialized practices of domination. New foremen employed to supervise the card system were given control over the sequential ordering of task performance (Curlewis 1918:57,65).

Previously workers had been allocated tasks every morning by leading hands. Late in the afternoon, a timekeeper would walk through the works and ask employees, "Well, what have you been on to-day?" Workers would respond by dividing up the total hours of the day worked and then apportioning the eight and three-quarter hours to each job they had performed (Curlewis 1918:10). By contrast, after the card system was introduced, the time it took each individual to perform each task could be calculated from the cards, which contained information on the precise work performed, rates of pay, and job numbers (Curlewis 1918:14). From the workers' perspective, the system put them on "trial for every hour of the day" (Curlewis 1918:39).

Planning and control over job performance was also accompanied by a rudimentary routing system. The machine shop was "sectionalized" in a way that reduced transportation during manufacture and allowed "complete concentration on the requirements of a particular section ... by those employed in that section" (NSW R&T [1918]:8). The adoption of high-speed steel tools, which were also closely associated with Taylor's system of management (Taylor 1906), further reinforced constraints on workers whose technical control over their jobs was reduced alongside their ability to work collectively. One railway department report noted that those who operated lathes, drilling, and other machines were no longer allowed to grind their own tools; clearance angles were standardized, rather than being "left to the whims of the particular man using the tool"; and workers no longer had to congregate around a grindstone because a damaged or a blunt tool could be "passed in and a sound one received in lieu in a few moments" (NSW R&T [1918]:8). The department's new tool room also had significant implications for spatial practices. As one coach painter told Justice H.R. Curlewis during the hearings of the Royal Commission appointed to investigate the card system in 1918: "For the last thirty years I have always been in charge of a job; any material I wanted I obtained from the store myself." But after the new system was adopted, he had to first obtain "an order from the sub-foreman" (Curlewis 1918:27).

These changes prevented workers from exercising discretion, interacting, communicating, and collaborating with one another. By looking closely at their spatial consequences an account can be taken of intentions and reactions, actions and interpretations (Upton 1992:52). Eveleigh's employees negotiated changes to the physical environment of their workplace and those negotiations provided a cultural expression of everyday life (Beaudry et al. 1991:150).

Overcoming Spatial and Industrial Constraints

In an effort to overcome the new constraints on their labor and interactions, workers established rank-and-file shop-floor committees during the 1920s, which continued to function until the 1970s (Wilson 1971:39–40, 1980:45–46; Patmore 1985:357–358,439–446; Jones 1988). Through their campaigns for improved working conditions, these committees had a profound impact on the fabric of everyday life, mainly because the mass meetings they organized shaped workers' cultural practices. Initially, these meetings sought to increase union membership by overcoming divisions between the skilled and unskilled (*OBU* 1919; *Railway Union Gazette* 1925:15, 1926:11; *The Magnet* 1935a:2). Increasingly, however, their focus extended to control over the labor process. Most attacked the card system that had been implemented in 1917 (Federated Society 1925:346; *The Ironworker* 1928:7; *The Railroad*, 1931a:10, 1931b:5). They also campaigned for improved sanitary facilities, like doors on lavatory cubicles and wash basins in place of buckets. Such efforts eventually met with success (*The Magnet* 1933:4, 1935b:2, 1944a:2, 1944b:2; *Eveleigh News* 1954).

The wash basins introduced in the 1950s were to outlast the workshops themselves. Following the transformation of the new locomotive shop into the Australian Technology Park's National Innovation Centre in the mid-1990s, one remaining row of wash basins was placed on display in the building's foyer. The accompanying miniscule plaque provides no insight into the social meaning of this artifact. Noting only that the basins replaced the buckets in which workers had washed off the grime of their labor for decades, this interpretative device conceals the years of struggle that were required to obtain them. Instead, this display provides a testimony to the "object fetishism" (Stuart 1992:140)

FIGURE 7. Wash basins located in the National Innovation Centre, Australian Technology Park, Eveleigh (originally the New Locomotive workshop building). (Photograph by Peter Murphy; © Lucy Taksa and the University of New South Wales.)

that has come to dominate the conservation of Eveleigh's material culture (Figure 7).

The meaning of this artifact is found in its relationship with Eveleigh's material culture and the material-cultural practices through which Eveleigh employees interacted with their environment and succeeded in shaping the world around. Beaudry et al. (1991:160) note, "Recovery of meaning is predicated in recovery of context ... context not only frames meaning by tying it to actual situations and events, but it is inextricably bound up with meaning... ." In this way, the key to explain the archaeological record can be found.

Spatial Struggles of Resistance

The campaigns mounted by the shop committees centered on the organization of mass meetings. Although such meetings did not overcome divisions caused by occupational differences, administrative arrangements, and spatial segregation, they did provide opportunities for regular contact among workers and an avenue for communication in a context in which interaction was being tightly controlled by management. Early industrial meetings were held at the entry gates to the workshops during lunchtimes. Those employed on the southern side of the railway tracks met at the Boundary Street gate, while those employed on the northern side met at the gate on the junction between Codrington and Wilson streets (Bruce

1996; Dunnett 1996; Johnson 1996; Matthews 1996; Cavaliere 1997; Bollins 1998; Rhymes 1998; Russo 1998). From 1926, such meetings were being held weekly under the auspices of the shop committees or various unions. Not only did these meetings forge networks among workers from disparate occupations, they also physically brought together the officials of the 12 trade unions that operated at Eveleigh at this time (*Railway Union Gazette* 1925:15, 1926:11; *The Ironworker* 1928:14; Jones 1939). But while workers could exercise autonomy on the streets outside the gates, their rights over space inside Eveleigh were limited and had to be fought for.

In order to overcome such limits, workers employed on the locomotive side began to organize meetings in a large open area in front of the first-aid station that was halfway along the main workshop building and therefore accessible to all employed on the site's southern portion. Meetings were also held in the buildings on the northern side of the railway line. In the carriage workshops, employees would assemble on a massive deck in the timber mill (Bollins 1998). Those employed in the main railway store held their meetings in their meal room. Both these places provided an important locus of conflict. In 1926 the head storekeeper and the controller of stores informed a union organizer who was addressing a lunchtime meeting in the meal room that he "had no right to be there," a directive the organizer ignored (*Railway Union Gazette* 1926:11). This encounter marked the first of many efforts to control the workers' spatial practices (Federated Society 1929:137). Three years later the Australian Railways Union reported that the superintendent of stores "almost developed apoplexy" when he was told that the union's state secretary had arrived to address a lunchtime meeting there (*The Railroad* 1929:5). At this stage, workers were only allowed to gather together for social activities authorized by management, as occurred in 1929 when a formal farewell for Railway Chief Commissioner James Fraser was held in the open area adjacent to the Boundary Street gate (Figure 8) (Gunn 1989:324–325).

It would, however, be a mistake to conclude that continued use of the gate area for mass meetings reflected the department's total power over space. For although the railway

James Fraser's farewell.
Chief Commissioner of Railways, 1917-29.

FIGURE 8. James Fraser's farewell near Eveleigh's Boundary Street gate, 1929. (John Barnes private collection, with permission.)

commissioners certainly tried to impose and police spatial boundaries during this period by issuing formal memoranda prohibiting union representatives from addressing meetings of employees on railway premises, as occurred on 11 March 1930, the Australian Railways Union continued its campaign to obtain the right to hold lunch-hour meetings inside the workshops (*The Railroad* 1930:22). Indeed, this ban did not stop meetings from being held. On 4 December 1931, a joint meeting of railway and engineering union members was disrupted by several of the department's managers on the grounds that special "permission" had not been granted, as had been decreed necessary after an earlier mass meeting. Such obstruction was a prominent feature of the 1930s. In February 1933, a combined union deputation to the railway commissioner and his chief staff supervisor criticized another circular that prohibited union meetings on departmental premises (The Railroad 1931b:5, 1933:8, 1935a:10, 1935b:12). Two years later, when railway officials again affirmed their refusal to grant permission for mass meetings, the shop committees organized a protest meeting for 6 April, which was attended by hundreds of workers. In June alone, four were held and others followed throughout the ensuing years (*The Magnet* 1935b:1–2, 1935c:2,4, 1935d:2, 1936a:4, 1937a:1, 1937b:1; *The Railroad* 1935a:10, 1935b:12). In 1938,

when the railway commissioners issued an edict prohibiting workers from taking their traditional morning tea break at 9 a.m., the workers immediately held a large meeting in the carriage and wagon works. Instead of staying there, however, "a flood of men poured on Wilson Street gate," where shop committee delegates and also representatives from three different unions foreshadowed a combined union campaign against this attack on their "30-year-old custom" (*Labor Daily* 1938:5; *The Railroad* 1938:14) (Figure 9).

Clearly, the field of contact between authority and resistance had territorial implications. Workers not only resisted management's increasing efforts to define appropriate behavior and authorized boundaries but also challenged them by marking out strategic locations in which they could exercise some degree of autonomy (Pile 1997:14). In effect, the shop committee meetings enabled Eveleigh's workers to remap the terrain on which they engaged in struggle over their rights.

Remapping the Ground for Struggle

Spatial practices of resistance formed an important cultural practice in the everyday life of the workshops. Despite their struggles to obtain the right to hold meetings inside the workshops, the workers and their representatives continued to move their meetings to the Boundary Street gate "where the Eveleigh Loco workshops were situated" and to the Codrington Street gate on "the carriage side" because discussions could take place there "unhindered by any kinds of

FIGURE 9. The mass meeting of Eveleigh workers (*The Railroad*, 43, 15 November 1938:1). (Courtesy State Library of New South Wales.)

bans" (Jones 1988). This movement supports Pile's (1997:15) argument that resistance occurs not only "where space is denied, circumscribed and/or totally administered" but also "between the spaces authorized by authority" (Pile 1997: 13). The gate areas, technically viewed as outside of departmental property, provided precisely such spatial interstices.

On these borders between Eveleigh and the surrounding public space, Eveleigh's cultural landscape intersected with Sydney's political landscape. For it was here during the late 1920s and 1930s that politicians from the Australian Labor Party, like Australia's Prime Minister Jim Scullin, and the NSW Labor Premier Jack Lang addressed Eveleigh workers at the gates as part of their election campaigns (State Library of NSW 1934). Similarly, in 1936, William Joseph Carlton and William John McKell, two Labor members of the NSW Parliament who represented the nearby working-class localities, addressed a huge mass meeting at the Wilson Street gate about the conservative government's attack on railway workers' superannuation rights (*The Magnet* 1936b:4). These political meetings tended to focus on broad policy issues. Yet they had immense ramifications for daily resistance at Eveleigh. On the one hand, they emphasized the fact that the department's power did not extend to the public space outside Eveleigh's boundaries. On the other, they provided a means for employees to challenge management's efforts to enforce Eveleigh's material and symbolic boundaries.

A case in point occurred in 1937 just before the NSW state election when Lang attempted to present his industrial policy speech to a mass meeting at the Boundary Street gate using an amplifer that relied on the department's electricity supply from the Eveleigh gatehouse (*The Railroad* 1937c:2). To the horror of all concerned, Lang was effectively silenced when the gatehouse attendent cut the electricity. Recalling this event many decades later, Stan Jones (1988) said that he and the other shop committee activitsts responded by agitating for "the right of free speech in the workshops themselves," and he concluded that this right "was finally attained in practice if not in open acknowledgment, by the authorities."

How was this outcome achieved? Despite persistent management bans, the committees continued to organize mass meetings as part of their struggles to prevent conditions from deteriorating, for better pay (*The Railroad* 1932:2, 1937a:11, 1937b:1, 1941b:5, 1941c:1, 1941d:1; *Eveleigh News* 1954), against an employer's union that was formed in 1939 (*The Railroad* 1939a:1, 1939b:2, 1939c:2), against the introduction of a new bonus and timekeeping system in the same year (*The Railroad* 1939d:2), and dangerous working conditions, particularly in the munitions annex that was added to the locomotive workshops during World War II (*The Railroad* 1939e:5, 1939f:7, 1941a:1, 1941d:3). These struggles over space were pivotal in formalizing one particular meeting place, which became known as Red Square during the Cold War when the federal government undertook measures against the Communist Party of Australia and its members, some of who were prominent and active in the Eveleigh shop committees (Buckley and Wheelwright 1998:238–242,247–252).

Eveleigh's Red Square

Originally known as Ambulance Square because of its location beside the first-aid station, Red Square provides a cogent example of "the ways in which power relations are incomplete, fluid, liable to rupture, inconsistent, awkward and ambiguous" (Pile 1997:14). Its very existence, as much as its renaming, shows how spatial practices of resistance and their symbolic representations not only involve mobilization but also a process of insinuation (Pile 1997:16).

Red Square is remembered by all those who were employed in the locomotive workshops, large erecting shop and running sheds, as well as by union delegates who worked in the carriage and wagon shops (Alexander 1996; Driver et al. 1996; Bollins 1998). Red Square, according to Bob Matthews (1996) "was where all the meetings were held." Jack Bruce (1996) elaborated, "Ambulance Square was Red Square because all the union meetings were held there and the union movement was pretty heavily into communist control. So it became communist, communist—red, Red Square." For those who were involved in the shop committees and the Communist Party, it was "where the revolutionaries met" (Aldridge et al. 1999).

Red Square provided an extremely important "medium of communication and expression" that conditioned and controlled "social action"

(Beaudry et al. 1991:153). According to Syd Kain (Aldridge and Kain 1999), delegates would let workers know that a meeting was being held by chalking a notice up on a board or "on the floor in the middle rows," which would inform workers that there was "a meeting on up at the Square at 10 past 12, or something like that, so everyone would turn up. So everyone would know." Similarly, Jeff Aldridge (Aldridge and Kain 1999) remembered that this system of communication "worked through the whole workshops." He himself wrote notices up "outside the toilets at the end of Nine Bay," and he told "other blokes where to write" notices in the boiler shop, the blacksmiths shop and in the new loco shop. Bob Rhymes (Driver et al. 1996), who became a union shop steward and an active shop committee member in the early 1950s after arriving from the United Kingdom, said that the shop committees would then send two delegates to address mass meetings in the Square once a month. In the main these would be attended by those workers who "paid about 10 pence a year" to be affiliated to the committees, as well as "other interested people" (Driver et al. 1996). By the 1950s workers had won the right to hold mass meetings at Red Square albeit "purely for domestic issues," like the appalling amenities (Aldridge et al. 1999), which were unlikely to cause strike action (Cavaliere 1997) or which provided information to workers that was deemed to be "beneficial to the management" (Russo 1998).

The shop committees were not the only organizations to hold meetings at Red Square. The two engineering unions, the Boilermakers' Society, the Blacksmiths' Union, and the Australian Railways Union organized them to raise issues directly pertinent to their members. Combined union meetings were held here as well to enable consideration of industrial matters that affected the whole of the workforce (Driver et al. 1996). According to Jack Bruce (1996), "If some proposal was up, you were going to have a stoppage or something like that over some issue, it may be pay related, if there was a campaign developing ... options would be put up to you in Ambulance Square and the opposition to it was aired .... They were fairly aggressive speakers and they fairly aggressively got people behind them." Once a vote was taken, remarked Bob Rhymes (Driver

et al. 1996), "generally the majority decision was accepted as ... binding."

Yet workers still "had to make application to the Works Manager for permission to hold a meeting" (Driver et al. 1996). If management withheld permission because the meeting centered on an existing or impending dispute, the workers would proceed to the entry gates (Driver et al. 1996). Similarly, if the combined unions recommended a stoppage during a meeting or if a meeting was still in progress when the last lunch whistle blew, Rymes (1998) recalled that the meeting would be adjourned. The workers would proceed to the Boundary Street gate, while the shop stewards would call out those who had not attended the meeting, and in most cases they "came out because they were involved." Once at the gates, added Aldridge (Aldridge et al. 1999), "you had to stand outside ... and the microphones were just placed inside the gate and connected to the watchman's humpy to allow the people to be addressed."

Red Square was clearly a strategic location in which workers contested management's control and sought to exercise power over the site. It was part of the cultural landscape that had been appropriated by the workers during the 1920s and 1930s, not just for meetings but also for lunchtime games of rugby (Barnes 1999). The entry gate areas were also important strategic locations. Both the square and the gates were taken up by workers in their struggles against spatial control and surveillance. As the earlier mentioned meeting addressed by Lang in 1937 showed, at a time when collective resistance inside the workshops was being prohibited, railway management tried to maintain its authority by defining who could and who could not occupy various places in and around the workshops (Pile 1997:28–30).

Yet management's ability to control and regulate the spaces and practices of resistance was limited by the "discontinous spaces" that resulted from the fluidity, inconsistency, and ambiguity of power relations between the workers and their managers and the workers' ability to transgress authorized boundaries (Pile 1997: 14). By the 1950s the railway commissioner accepted the gates "as not being on the premises" (Driver et al. 1996). Both Bruce (1996) and Keith Johnson (1996) agreed that at this time meetings were technically considered not to be on railway property if the speakers remained outside the physical boundaries of the workshops, which led Louie Cavaliere (1997) to comment, "look how silly they were": the workers were able to use the department's electricity for loudspeakers, even though they generally "stood inside the gate." Indeed, he recalled that the management "was always telling us, 'Go outside.'"

Viewing these negotiations over space at "the more mundane, micrological level of everyday practices and choices about how to live" shows "how contested and embattled terrains can be reinscribed, redefined, remapped" (Moore 1997:88–89). The mass meetings held at Red Square and the various gates illustrate the way workers reacted to the department's tactics of domination. Far from succeeding in regulating the workers' movements and confining them to highly circumscribed areas, such tactics gave rise to resistance that effectively created "autonomous" social domains (Moore 1997:91).

The Politics of Location

The numbers of workers attending meetings varied according to which bodies organized them and which issues were being addressed. Dunnet (1996) recalled that during the 1950s, union meetings inside the workshops usually attracted 50 to 60 people. But when "a major issue" or "a big political event" of "national importance" arose, the "major political players of the day" from the Australian Labor Party and the Australian Communist Party would address crowds of around two or three thousand at Red Square or in the various canteen and meal rooms. Meetings of this scale occurred mainly during state and federal elections (Bruce 1996; Aldridge 1999; Aldridge and Kain 1999). For Dunnett (1996), they illustrated that Eveleigh "was always a political area." Indeed, he thought that the employees' "industrial muscle" was enhanced by their ability to "put on a demonstration outside of Parliament in half an hour or so, which they did do very effectively," particularly in December 1947 and June 1961 when campaigns for wage increases culminated in combined union demonstrations and mass stoppages (Tribune 1947:6; Gunn 1989:440).

Mass meetings and demonstrations inside Eveleigh, on its boundaries, and also beyond them drew on the ensemble of spatial practices of resistance, which evolved after the 1917 strike as workers negotiated the site's layout and structures as well as the management strategies that shaped patterns of work and interaction. These practices reflected the interplay among intentions, reactions, actions and interpretations (Upton 1992:51–52).

Mass meetings certainly provided a means of resistance, yet, as importantly, they enabled participants to interact and communicate with each other, to identify common experiences and interests, and to articulate and share their own collective meanings and values. These outcomes would become particularly significant for Eveleigh's cultural landacape during the 1950s and 1960s, after the federal Labor government implemented its postwar mass migration policy, which resulted in the employment of thousands of immigrant workers, initially from Southern Europe and later from the Middle East and Eastern Europe at Eveleigh (Hearn 1990:146–147; Fox 1991:151–53; Alexander 1996; Bruce 1996; Cavaliere 1997; Russo 1998; Aldridge 1999). Mass meetings played an important role in helping the newcomers become what Bruce (1996) referred to as "part and parcel of the workshop." In Dick Nichols (1999) view, meetings helped to minimize cultural differences by encouraging migrants to become involved in union activities.

These meetings provided a social anchor for new employees. One Italian immigrant remembered:

> People used to help each other in the old days because people … had a lot of suffering. That's why we come the Red Square. Actually Red Square existed before I ever went there. There in the '50s and '40s and really during the war … There used to be always trouble with the working people. That's how the camaraderie start through the trade union and through the Shop Committee that we had there … And, er, that's how people got the thing solved (Russo 1998).

The first meeting Cavaliere (1997) attended at Red Square in the early 1950s dealt with poor sanitary facilities. In recalling the motion put by the shop committee representative to hold a stop-work meeting for 15 minutes, he commented, "I said to myself, 'Fifteen Cminutes. What that going to achieve, fifteen minutes.' That achieve a lot of things." This experience led Cavaliere into a life of industrial activism.

Initially, he was recruited by the shop committee to help translate union notices. Afterwards, he attended delegates' meetings "in the back of Red Square" where, according to Jack Lloyd (Aldridge et al. 1999), "an old railway carriage that had been de-wheeled and placed on blocks" was "turned into an office" and meeting room for delegates in the late 1950s.

The installation of this carriage, with management's approval, marked an important change in its spatial policy. Known as "The Kremlin," this carriage was initially used by shop stewards for meetings to decide on industrial tactics. At this stage, meetings were only allowed at lunchtimes, and they were held every Tuesday (Russo 1998; Aldridge and Kain 1999; Aldridge et al. 1999). Subsequently, during the 1970s and 1980s, by the time Vince Russo (1998) became a shop steward, management permitted meetings to be held during working hours. The use of this carriage, in the area that had come to be associated with industrial mobilization, resistance, and recreation, extended workers' rights over space within the workshops. From here they negotiated directly with management. It was in this carriage that they produced and printed the shop committee newsletter, *Eveleigh News*, at lunchtimes and after work. Issued fortnightly, this organ was not only used for what Jack Lloyd (Aldridge et al. 1999) called union propaganda but also for "more social things like garden clubs and hiking clubs, and various other things—chess clubs—and things like that that would make it an interesting little paper."

Today, all vestiges of this vibrant material culture and its practices have gone. Only the buildings and a small collection of machinery remain. The less tangible features of everyday life that came to dominate work at Eveleigh are buried in the memories of those who once worked there and in the rapidly deteriorating pages of the shop committee and union newspapers held by the State Library of NSW and the Noel Butlin Archives of Business and Labour at the Australian National University. Only when these oral and documentary sources are studied in conjunction with Eveleigh's remaining material structures and artifacts can a glimpse be gained of the employees' spatial practices and the strategic locations they occupied, both of which remained a constant feature of their struggles with management even up to and including their opposition to Eveleigh's closure in the late 1980s.

Conclusion

The Eveleigh Railway Workshops were a contested terrain in which workers and managers engaged in the politics of location. In this cultural landscape, workers reacted to management's efforts to control their labor and regulate their use of space by organizing mass meetings, which enabled them to express their interests and values and pursue improvements. Such material-cultural practices provided a medium for communication and conditioned action. Red Square, together with the other spaces used for meetings inside the workshops' buildings and on their boundaries, formed a crucially important aspect of Eveleigh's material culture. Over time, spatial struggles between management and labor transformed this environment as workers succeeded in circumventing the arrangements of domination that were imposed on them during the course of their work.

REFERENCES

ALDRIDGE, JEFF
　1999　Taped interview by author. Sydney, Australia, 16 March.

ALDRIDGE, JEFF, AND SPENCER (SYD) KAIN
　1999　Taped conversation with author. Sydney, Australia, 14 March.

ALDRIDGE, JEFF, SPENCER (SYD) KAIN, JACK LLOYD, JOHN LEE, BOB RHYMES
　1999　Group taped interview by author. Sydney, Australia, 5 March.

ALEXANDER, HAL
　1996　Taped interview by Joan Kent. Sydney, Australia, 15 April.

BARNES, JOHN
　1999　Taped interview by author. Sydney, Australia, 31 March.

BEAUDRY, MARY C., LAUREN J. COOK, AND STEPHEN A. MROZOWSKI
　1991　Artifacts and Active Voices: Material Culture as Social Discourse. In *The Archaeology of Inequality: Material Culture, Domination, and Resistance*, Randall H. McGuire and Robert Paynter, editors, pp. 150–191. Blackwell, Oxford, England.

BLACKET, WILFRED
  1912 *Report of the Royal Commission of Inquiry as to Whether the Supply of Locomotives is Adequate for Traffic Purposes and if inadequate, to inquire into the causes and reasons of such inadequacy, and as to how far future Locomotive Requirements can be met at Eveleigh Works.* NSW Parliament [State Rail Authority Archives], Sydney, Australia.

BOLLINS, FRANK
  1998 Taped interview by author. Sydney, Australia, 10 August.

BRUCE, JOHN (JACK) ROBERT
  1996 Taped interview by author. Sydney, Australia, 25 March.

BUCKLEY, KEN, AND TED WHEELWRIGHT
  1998 *False Paradise: Australian Capitalism Revisited.* Oxford University Press, Melbourne, Australia.

BURKE, DAVID
  1986 *Man of Steam: E. E. Lucy—Gentleman Engineer in the Great Days of the Iron Horse.* Iron Horse Press, Sydney, Australia.
  1995 *Making the Railways.* State Library of New South Wales Press, Sydney, Australia.

BUTCHER, RICHARD K.
  1992 A Report on the Preservation of Eveleigh Railway Workshops, Redfern. Manuscript, Architecture Department, University of Sydney, Australia.

CAPON, EDMUND
  1996 Introduction. In *Railways, Relics and Romance: The Eveleigh Railway Workshops, New South Wales,* Suzanne Falkiner, editor, pp. 9–11. Caroline Simpson, Sydney, Australia.

CATTELL, J., AND K. FALCONER
  1995 *Swindon: The Legacy of a Railway Town.* HMSO, London, England.

CAVALIERE, LOUIE
  1997 Taped interview by author. Sydney, Australia, 5 November.

CHEONG, PUI SHVEN
  1988 The Eveleigh Railway Locomotive Workshops at Redfern, Sydney: Significance and Recommendations. Manuscript, School of Architecture, University of New South Wales, Australia.

CHILDE, V.G.
  1964 *How Labour Governs.* Melbourne University Press, Melbourne, Australia.

COMMISSIONER FOR RAILWAYS
  1880 *Annual Report.* State Rail Authority Archives R8/2, Sydney, Australia.
  1881 *Annual Report.* State Rail Authority Archives R8/3, Sydney, Australia.
  1882 *Annual Report.* State Rail Authority Archives R8/4, Sydney, Australia.
  1891 Report Appendix II, from Chief Mechanical Engineer to Commissioner for Railways. In *Annual Report 1890–1891.* State Rail Authority Archives R9/4, Sydney, Australia.
  1893 Report Appendix II, from Chief Mechanical Engineer to Commissioner for Railways. In *Annual Report 1892–1893,* State Rail Authority Archives R9/4, Sydney, Australia.
  1898 *Annual Report,* including Chief Mechanical Engineer's Report. State Rail Authority Archives R9/10, Sydney, Australia.
  1955 Letter to F.P.H, Fewtrell Works Manager, from Assistant Chief Mechanical Engineer, 14 April. State Rail Authorities Archives, A88/44, Box 3, Sydney, Australia.

CURLEWIS, J. J.
  1918 *Royal Commission of Inquiry into the Effects of the Workings of the System known as the Job and Time Cards System introduced into the Tramways and Railways Workshops of the Railways Commissioners.* New South Wales Parliamentary Papers, Vol. 5–6, State Library of NSW, Sydney, Ausralia.

DEETZ, JAMES
  1977 *In Small Things Forgotten: The Archaeology of Early Modern Life.* Anchor, New York, NY.

DENNING, MICHAEL
  1997 *The Cultural Front: The Labouring of American Culture in the Twentieth Century.* Verso, London, England.

DIVALL, COLIN, AND ANTHONY COULLS
  1999 Railways as World Heritage Sites. *Locality, Special Issue—Industrial Heritage,* 1(10): 7–10.

DON GODDEN & ASSOCIATES
  1986 *A Heritage Study of Eveleigh Railway Workshops.* Don Godden & Associates for the New South Wales Government, Sydney, Australia.

DRIVER, BILL, FRANK BOLLENS, GORDON NORTH, BOB MATTHEWS, BILL LEECH, JACK BRUCE, AND BOB RHYMES
  1996 Taped group interview by Lucy Taksa. Sydney, Australia, 17 November.

DUNNETT, BRIAN
  1996 Taped interview by Joan Kent. Sydney, Australia, 10 May.

EVELEIGH NEWS (OF EVELEIGH LOCO CENTRAL SHOP COMMITTEE)
  1954 *Eveleigh News,* 9 June.

FEDERATED SOCIETY OF BOILERMAKERS AND IRON SHIPBUILDERS OF AUSTRALIA
  1925 Redfern Branch Report. *Quarterly Report of the Federated Society of Boilermakers and Iron Shipbuilders of Australia,* 42(4):346.

1929 Redfern Branch Report. *Quarterly Report of the Federated Society of Boilermakers and Iron Shipbuilders of Australia*, 59(6):137–140.

FORSYTH, J. H.
[1955] Railway Development in Relation to the Mechanical Branch 1855 to 1955. Manuscript, State Rail Authority Archives B271, Sydney, Australia.

FOX, CHARLIE
1991 *Working Australia*. Allen & Unwin, Sydney, Australia.

GODDEN, DON
1990 Eveleigh: Sydney's Rail Era Relic of World Standing. *The National Trust Magazine*, 54:[n.p.].

GODDEN MACKAY
1990 White Bay to Blackwattle Bay, Central to Eveleigh Heritage Study, Vol. 1. Report for the New South Wales Government, from Godden Mackay, Sydney, Australia.
1996 Eveleigh Workshops Management Plan for Moveable Items and Social History. Report for the New South Wales Government, from Godden Mackay, Sydney, Australia.

GUNN, JOHN
1989 *Along Parallel Lines: A History of the Railways of New South Wales, 1850–1986*. Melbourne University Press, Melbourne, Australia.

GUTHRIE, [NO FIRST NAME] MR.
[1955] History of Eveleigh Workshops. Unpublished Notes, State Rail Authority Archives, A88/44, Box 3, Sydney, Australia.

HALLETT, BRYCE
2002 Railyard Becomes Arts Central as Theatre Companies Roll in. *Sydney Morning Herald*, 21 March:5.

HEARN, MARK
1990 *Working Lives: A History of the Australian Railways Union (New South Wales Branch)*. Hale & Iremonger, Sydney, Australia.

HOCKING, KEN
1998 Travel: Highland Fling. *The Sun-Herald*, 27 December, Sydney, Australia.

HOLME, J. B.
1918 The New South Wales Strike Crisis of 1917. Report by the Industrial Commissioner of the State, commissioned by the NSW Parliament. New South Wales Legislative Assembly, Sydney, Australia.

HOSKINS, W. G.
1955 *The Making of the English Landscape*. Hodder and Staughton, London, England.

HOUGHTON, T. H.
1917 Presidential Address. *Proceedings, Royal Society of New South Wales*, 51:1–70.

THE IRONWORKER (OF IRONWORKER'S UNION)
1928 *The Ironworker*, 1 January. State Library of NSW, Sydney, Australia.

JOHNSON, KEITH
1996 Taped interview by author. Sydney, Australia, 23 February.

JONES, STAN
1939 Eveleigh—The Heart of the Transport System. *Daily News* 19 January:[n.p.]
1988 Taped interview by Russ Herman. Combined Railway Unions Cultural Committee's Oral History Project, Sydney, Australia.

THE LABOR DAILY [OF AUSTRALIAN LABOR PARTY, NSW BRANCH]
1938 *The Labor Daily*, 11 November. State Library of NSW, Sydney, Australia.

LEE, ROBERT
1988 *The Greatest Public Work: The New South Wales Railways—1848 to 1889*. Hale & Iremonger, Sydney, Australia.

LOFLAND, LYN H.
1998 *The Public Realm: Exploring the City's Quintessential Social Territory*. Aldine De Gruyter, New York, NY.

THE MAGNET [OF CENTRAL COUNCIL OF THE NSW RAILWAYS SHOP COMMITTEES]
1933 *The Magnet*, 11 November:2. National Library of Australia, Canberra.
1935a *The Magnet*, March:2. National Library of Australia, Canberra.
1935b *The Magnet*, April:1–2. National Library of Australia, Canberra.
1935c *The Magnet*, July:2,4. National Library of Australia, Canberra.
1935d *The Magnet*, December:2. National Library of Australia, Canberra.
1936a *The Magnet*, March:4. National Library of Australia, Canberra.
1936b *The Magnet*, May:4. National Library of Australia, Canberra.
1937a *The Magnet*, February:1. National Library of Australia, Canberra.
1937b *The Magnet*, March:1. National Library of Australia, Canberra.
1944a *The Magnet*, June:2. National Library of Australia, Canberra.
1944b *The Magnet*, July:2. National Library of Australia, Canberra.

MARKEY, RAYMOND
1988 *The Making of the Labor Party in New South Wales, 1880–1900*, New South Wales University Press, Sydney, Australia.

MATTHEWS, BOB
1996 Taped interview by Joan Kent. Sidney, Australia, 20 February.

McAllister, C., T. Roberts, G. Nutt, T. H. Woodroffe, and W. Thow
    1904 *Royal Commission of Inquiry into the Practicability of the Construction of Locomotives by the Government, or by Private Enterprise, in this State.* New South Wales Parliament [State Rail Authorities Archives], Sydney, Australia.

Mitchell, Don
    2000 *Cultural Geography: A Critical Introduction.* Blackwell Publishers, Oxford, England.

Moore, Donald S.
    1997 Remapping Resistance: Ground for Struggle and the Politics of Place. In *Geographies of Resistance*, Steve Pile and Michael Keith, editors, pp. 87–106. Routledge, London, England.

Mrozowski, Stephen A.
    1991 Landscapes of Inequality. In *The Archaeology of Inequality: Material Culture, Domination, and Resistance*, Randall H. McGuire and Robert Paynter, editors, pp. 79–101. Blackwell, Oxford, England.

New South Wales Department of Works and Services, Heritage Group
    1995 *Eveleigh Railway Yards Locomotive Workshops Conservation Management Plan.* New South Wales Government, Sydney, Australia.
    1999 *Eveleigh Carriage Workshops Conservation Analysis.* New South Wales Government, Sydney, Australia.

New South Wales Government
    2000 Press Release, 7 March. NSW Premier's Department, Sydney, Australia.

New South Wales Labor Council
    1917 *Report.* 31 December. State Library of NSW, Sydney, Australia.

New South Wales Parliament
    1917–*1918* *Parliamentary Debates,* Vol. 67. State Library of NSW, Sydney, Australia.

New South Wales Railways and Tramways Department (NSW R&T)
    1898 The New Erecting Shops, Eveleigh. *New South Wales Railway Budget,* 20 June. State Library of NSW, Sydney, Australia.
    1900 The Locomotive Shops at Eveleigh. *New South Wales Railway and Tramway Budget,* 21 July. State Library of NSW, Sydney, Australia.
    [1918] *Report on Eveleigh Locomotive Workshops.* State Rail Authority Archives, B253, Sydney, Australia.
    1930 The Origin and Growth of Eveleigh. *The Staff,* 18 February:103–107.

Nichols, Dick
    1999 Taped interview by author. Sydney, Australia, 11 May.

OBU (One Big Union)
    1919 *OBU (One Big Union):* Official Organ of the Workers' Industrial Union of Australia, 1 April. State Library of NSW, Sydney, Australia.

Oliver, Charles, W. M. Fehon, David Kirkaldie
    1899 Ten Years' Retrospect. In *Annual Report 1899,* Commissioners for New South Wales Railways. State Rail Authority Archives R9/11, Sydney, Australia.

Olssen, Erik, and Jeremey Brecher
    1992 The Power of Shop Culture: The Labour Process in the New Zealand Railway Workshops, 1890–1930. *International Review of Social History,* 37:350–75.

Patmore, Allan
    1994 Railways and Landscapes. In *Common Roots - Separate Branches: Railway History and Preservation, Proceedings of an International Symposium Held at the National Railway Museum, York, from 8 to 12 October 1993,* Rob Shorland-Ball, editor, pp. 13–22. Science Museum for the National Railway Museum, York, United Kingdom.

Patmore, G. A.
    1985 A History of Industrial Relations in the New South Wales Government Railways: 1855–1929. Doctoral dissertation, University of Sydney, Australia.

Pile, Steve
    1997 Introduction. In *Geographies of Resistance*, Steve Pile and Michael Keith, editors, pp. 1–32. Routledge, London, England.

Preston, R. G.
    1997 *The Eveleigh Locomotive Workshops Story.* Australian Railway Historical Society, New South Wales Division, Sydney, Australia.

The Railroad [for the Australian Railways Union]
    1929 *The Railroad,* 10 June. State Library of NSW, Sydney, Australia.
    1930 *The Railroad,* 10 April. State Library of NSW, Sydney, Australia.
    1931a *The Railroad,* 10 March. State Library of NSW, Sydney, Australia.
    1931b *The Railroad,* 10 December. State Library of NSW, Sydney, Australia.
    1932 *The Railroad,* 10 February. State Library of NSW, Sydney, Australia.
    1933 *The Railroad,* 10 April. State Library of NSW, Sydney, Australia.
    1935a *The Railroad,* 10 April. State Library of NSW, Sydney, Australia.
    1935b *The Railroad,* 10 May. State Library of NSW, Sydney, Australia.
    1937a *The Railroad,* 29 June. State Library of NSW, Sydney, Australia.
    1937b *The Railroad,* 27 July. State Library of NSW, Sydney, Australia.

1937c *The Railroad*, 17 August. State Library of NSW, Sydney, Australia.

1938 *The Railroad*, 15 November. State Library of NSW, Sydney, Australia.

1939a *The Railroad*, 7 February. State Library of NSW, Sydney, Australia.

1939b *The Railroad*, 14 February. State Library of NSW, Sydney, Australia.

1939c *The Railroad*, 21 March. State Library of NSW, Sydney, Australia.

1939d *The Railroad*, 4 April. State Library of NSW, Sydney, Australia.

1939e *The Railroad*, 23 May. State Library of NSW, Sydney, Australia.

1939f *The Railroad*, 30 May. State Library of NSW, Sydney, Australia.

1941a *The Railroad*, 11 March. State Library of NSW, Sydney, Australia.

1941b *The Railroad*, 1 April. State Library of NSW, Sydney, Australia.

1941c *The Railroad*, 8 April. State Library of NSW, Sydney, Australia.

1941d *The Railroad*, 1 July. State Library of NSW, Sydney, Australia.

1941e *The Railroad*, 15 July. State Library of NSW, Sydney, Australia.

RAILWAY UNION GAZETTE [FOR THE AUSTRALIAN RAILWAYS UNION]

1925 *Railway Union Gazette*, 11 July. State Library of NSW, Sydney, Australia.

1926 *Railway Union Gazette,* 10 September. State Library of NSW, Sydney, Australia.

RAPPAPORT, PAUL

1997 Chief Mechanical Engineer's Building: 327 Wilson Street, Chippendale, Eveleigh Locomotive Workshops Conservation Management Plan. Report for the Railway Authority, New South Wales Government, Sydney, Australia.

RHYMES, BOB

1998 Taped interview by author. Sydney, Australia, 31 July.

RUSSO, VINCE

1998 Taped interview by author. Sydney, Australia, 30 October.

SAMUEL, RAPHAEL

1996 *Theatres of Memory: Vol. 1, Past and Present in Contemporary Culture.* Verso, London, England.

SCHWAGER BROOKS AND PARTNERS

1993 Eveleigh Precinct Conservation Policy. Report for the New South Wales Government, from Schwager Brooks and Partners, Sydney, Australia.

SIMPSON DAWBIN

2003 Large Erecting Shop Conservation Management Plan. Report for the New South Wales Government, from Simpson Dawbin, Sydney, Australia.

STATE LIBRARY OF NEW SOUTH WALES

1934 Mass Rally of Eveleigh Railway Workers Listen to an Election Speech from Jack Lang at Redfern, August 22, 1934. In *Sydney: At Work and Play Photographic Collection.* Photo caption, Still 00354, State Library of New South Wales, Sydney, Australia.

STUART, IAIN

1992 Stranger in a Strange Land: Historical Archaeology and History in Post Contact Australia. *Public History Review,* 1:136–147.

SYDNEY HARBOUR FORESHORE AUTHORITY

2003 Sydney Harbour Foreshore Authority, NSW Government <http://www.shfa.nsw.gov.au/contents/news_display> 10 April.

SYDNEY MORNING HERALD

1917 *Sydney Morning Herald,* 8 August, Sydney, Australia.

TAKSA, LUCY

1991 Defence not Defiance: Social Protest and the New South Wales General Strike of 1917. *Labour History,* 60:16–33.

1996 Social and Oral History. In Eveleigh Workshops Management Plan for Moveable Items Vol. 2, pp. 1–73. Report to the New South Wales Government, from Godden Mackay, Sydney, Australia.

1997 Scientific Management and the General Strike of 1917: Workplace Restructuring in the New South Wales Railways and Tramways Department. *Historical Studies in Industrial Relations,* 4:37–64.

2000 Not Simply a Geographic Location: The Future of Eveleigh. *The State of History,* 2(May). History Council of New South Wales, Sydney, Australia.

2001 Workplace, Community, Mobilization and Labor Politics at the Eveleigh Railway Workshops. In *Labour and Community: Historical Perspectives,* Ray Markey, editor, pp. 51–79. University of Wollongong Press, Wollongong, Ausralia.

2003 Machines and Ghosts: Politics, Industrial Heritage, and the History of Working Life at the New South Wales Eveleigh Railway Workshops. *Labour History,* 85, in press [November].

TAYLOR, F. W.

1947 Shop Management. In *Scientific Management,* pp. 17–207. Harper & Brothers, New York, NY. [originally published in 1903.]

1906 On the Art of Cutting Metals. *Transactions, American Society of Mechanical Engineers,* 28:31–58.

1911 *The Principles of Scientific Management.* Harper & Brothers, New York, NY.

TAYLOR, KEN, AND JONATHAN WINSTON-GREGSON

1992 Cultural Landscapes as a Historical Resource: A Case Study at Windmill Hill, Appin, New South Wales. *Public History Review,* 1:81–102.

Lucy Taksa

THORP, WENDY
1994   Heritage Assessment: Archaeological Resources, ATP Master Plan Site Eveleigh. Report for City West Development Corporation, Sydney, Australia.

TRIBUNE (OF COMMUNIST PARTY OF AUSTRALIA)
1947   Tribune, 20 December:6. State Library of New South Wales, Sydney, Australia.

TURNER, IAN
1979   Industrial Labour and Politics: The Dynamics of the Labour Movement in Eastern Australia, 1900–1921. Hale and Iremonger, Sydney, Australia.

UPTON, DELL
1992   The City as Material Culture. In The Art and Mystery of Historical Archaeology: Essays in Honor of James Deetz, Anne Elisabeth Yentsch and Mary C. Beaudry, editors, pp. 51–73. CRC Press, Boca Raton, FL.

WHITE, CAMERON
1995   Eveleigh Railway Yard: The Adaptive Re-Use of Heritage. Masters thesis, University of Sydney, Australia.

WILLIAMS, RAYMOND
1989a   Communications and Community, 1961. In Raymond Williams Resources of Hope Culture, Democracy, Socialism, Robin Gable, editor, pp. 19–31. Verso, London, England.

1989b   The Idea of Common Culture, 1968. In Raymond Williams Resources of Hope Culture, Democracy, Socialism, Robin Gable, editor, pp. 32–38. Verso, London, England.

WILLIS, JOHN
1996   Taped interview by author. Sydney, Australia, 5 February.

WILSON, ALAN
1971   Australia's First Shop Committees. The Modern Unionist, (June):39–40.
1980   The Railway Shop Committees' Struggle. In Sixty Years of Struggle: A Journal of Communist and Labour History, 1:45–6. Red Pen Publications, Sydney, Australia.

ZUKIN, SHARON
1991   Landscapes of Power: From Detroit to Disney World. University of California Press, Berkeley.

LUCY TAKSA
SCHOOL OF ORGANISATION AND MANAGEMENT
THE UNIVERSITY OF NEW SOUTH WALES
SYDNEY, NEW SOUTH WALES, AUSTRALIA 2052

Michael R. Polk (迈克 • 波克)

Interpreting Chinese Worker Camps on the Transcontinental Railroad at Promontory Summit, Utah

试论犹他突顶山上的中国劳工营

ABSTRACT

The first transcontinental railroad was completed at Promontory Summit, Utah, on 10 May 1869. Unique to this construction was the employment of thousands of ethnic Chinese railroad workers. The Promontory Mountains portion of the route had the largest concentration of railroad construction camps. Of 19 camps recorded during an inventory of the Golden Spike National Historic Site, four appear to be of Chinese ethnic origin. These camps were smaller than European American camps, with fewer features. Both Chinese and European American artifacts were found at Chinese worker camps, revealing the practicality of and need for locally produced and railroad-issued items, as well as the workers' desire to use ethnically familiar items. A comparison with Chinese construction camps in Nevada and California reveals important similarities, suggesting that up to 500 Chinese construction laborers may have lived at the four Utah sites. A multifaceted explanation is provided for the separation of Chinese camps from other workers' camps.

1869年五月10日，第一条横贯大陆铁路在犹他州的突顶山峻工。这一工程的独特之处，在于它雇佣了成千上万的中国工人。突顶山路段聚集了该铁路工程中最多的劳工营。在金色道钉国家历史纪念地的目录所记载的19个营地中，有四个属于中国工人。这些营地比欧美营地规模小，而遗迹较少。在中国劳工营，来自中国与欧美的文物均有出土。这既显示出当地产品和铁路周边物品的实用性以及他们对这些物品的需求，也显示出他们对故乡熟悉物件使用的渴望。内华达州与加州境内类似的中国劳工营相比较，显示了两者重要的相似之处。据估计，有多达500名中国劳工曾居住在这四个营地内。本文还将对中国劳工营与其它国家劳工营的分隔提供多面向的解释。

Introduction

Promontory Summit lies in a cold, windswept, high-desert environment in rural northern Utah. It is a place far removed from the urban population of the nearby Wasatch Front and lacks significant water resources. The area remains sparsely populated nearly a century and a half after the completion of the transcontinental railroad, one of the most significant events to occur in the United States. Such a construction feat had never before been undertaken anywhere. Not only was the achievement a technological marvel, but it had equally important social, political, and economic significance for the country and the world as a whole. This railroad stretched from Omaha, Nebraska, westward to the Pacific Ocean, ending at Oakland, California. It bridged the vast unknown spaces of the Great American Desert and accelerated the processes whereby the American frontier was eventually eliminated. It opened the great western lands to settlement, hastening the creation of western territories and states. It united East and West. Instead of taking six weeks to cross the nation by pony express, mail now took six days from coast to coast. The railroad led to the almost complete annihilation of the American bison, changing Native American lifeways. Historians count the completion of the transcontinental railroad among the most significant and far-reaching events in the nation's history.

The area surrounding the Last Spike location was the site of the most intense construction activity undertaken during the period from 1868 to 1869. There construction culminated when the Union Pacific Railroad (UPRR) from Omaha and the Central Pacific Railroad (CPRR) from Sacramento, California, eventually met to join their railroads in a grand celebration on 10 May 1869. The area set aside in 1957 as a national historic site was designated the Golden Spike National Historic Site (GSNHS) to commemorate the completion of the first transcontinental railroad and to acknowledge the tremendous historical consequences that occurred as a result (Public Law 89-102). On 30 July 1965, it became part of the U.S. National Park System. The site was listed in the National Register of Historic Places in 1966, and its significance was documented for the register in 1986 (Hendricks 1986). In addition, the "Joining of the Rails/Transcontinental Railroad" was designated a National Civil Engineering Landmark in 1969 by the American Society of Civil Engineers.

Within this historic site are a great many historical resources, including railroad grades and cuts along the eastern slopes of the Promontory Mountains, along with railroad workers' camps, all dating from late 1868 to May 1869 (Figure 1). It also includes remains of the former town site of Promontory, along with the former roundhouse and associated railroad structures. The GSNHS was the subject of a multiyear investigation to document and understand these resources (Polk 2013). In 2001 the U.S. National Park Service's Western Archaeological and Conservation Center (WACC) initiated a survey and inventory of resources, followed by similar efforts by Sagebrush Consultants, LLC (Sagebrush) from 2002 to 2008. This effort built upon previous studies and investigations, including Robert Utley's (1960) early documentation of the park's national historical significance; James Ayres's (1982) archaeological investigation of the town site of Promontory Station; Homstad et al.'s (2000) preparation of a cultural landscape report; and Sagebrush's overview of the archaeology and history of the

Promontory route (Polk 1998). The most recent work culminated in a series of interim reports covering each year of fieldwork, followed by a compilation of the information in a report entitled: "From Lampo Junction to Rozel: The Archeological History of the Transcontinental Railroad across the Promontory Mountains, Utah" (Polk and Simmons-Johnson 2012).

Of the many books and articles that have been published about the transcontinental effort, very few have focused on the archaeology, and even fewer on the construction workers themselves, those who were largely responsible for completion of the world's first transcontinental railway. The focus of this article is on the workers' efforts to complete the final section of the transcontinental railroad during late 1868 and early 1869. The politics and story of the actual construction leading up to the railroads' arrival at Promontory have been told many times, in works such as Klein (1987), Bain (1999), Francaviglia (2008), Ambrose (1990), Galloway (1950, 1989), Kraus (1969), and Utley (1969). Particularly valuable for an overview of Promontory Summit during this time

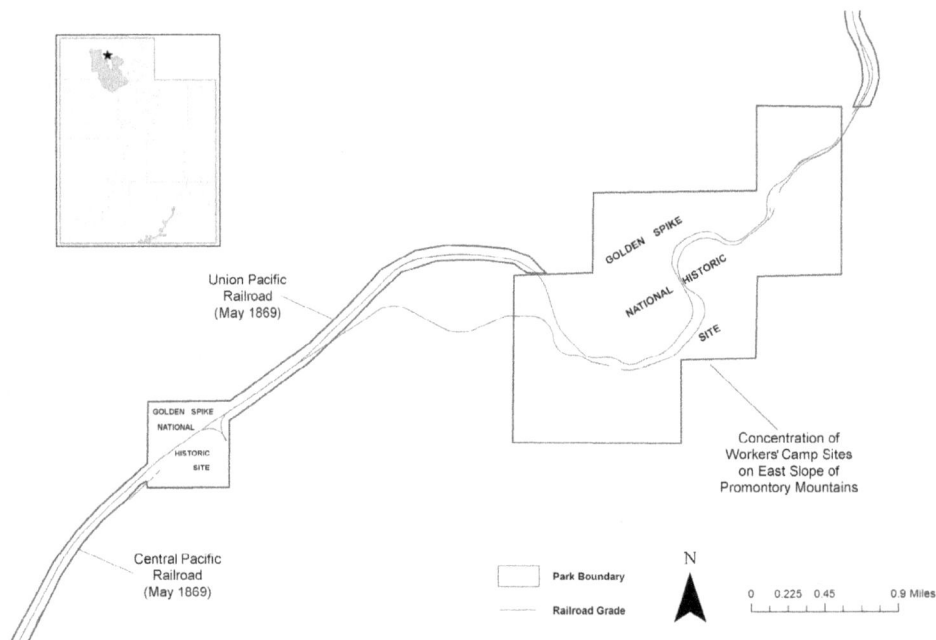

FIGURE 1. Map showing the Promontory Summit area in the Golden Spike National Historic Site where the Central Pacific Railroad and the Union Pacific Railroads united, May–November 1869. (Map developed from USGS 7.5' quadrangles: Sunset Pass [1968], Lampo Junction [1972], Golden Spike Monument [1967], and Thatcher Mountain SW, Utah [1966], by Jamie Morrison, Sagebrush Consultants, 2014.)

is Francaviglia's *Over the Range: A History of the Promontory Summit Route of the Pacific Railroad* (Francaviglia 2008). The broad history will not be repeated here, other than to provide context where it is critical to an understanding of the construction and workers at Promontory, Utah. However, a brief contextual history is necessary to understand better the local activities carried out by workers of the UPRR and CPRR, and the archaeology discussed later.

Promontory Summit

GSNHS, which straddles the area of Promontory Summit, contains the largest concentration of worker camp archaeological sites along the routes of both the UPRR and CPRR. Not only are these camp sites sources of information about railroad company activity, but also about the cultural and ethnic origins of the workers

who lived in those camps and labored on the railroads (Figure 2).

It is estimated that during the final push to complete the line in 1868–1869 as many as 6,000 workers toiled across northern Utah (Francaviglia 2008:88–89). Goodwin (1991:181) indicates that during the final construction phase of CPRR work on the transcontinental, the railroad had 12,000 Chinese construction workers on its payroll. Where all these men were working is not clear, although it is likely that most would have been in the Promontory area, where both railroads concentrated most of their resources in May 1869. This was a multicultural effort that included, almost entirely, men who were Irish, Cornish, Chinese, German, African American, English, and Native American, as well as Mormons and former Civil War officers and soldiers. There were also some women who contributed. The

FIGURE 2. Big Trestle, photo by A. J. Russell, May 1869. This trestle, just east of Promontory Summit, Utah, lies on the east slope of the Promontory Mountains, where intensive construction took place in early 1869. Note the remaining worker camp tents on the ridge in the *upper right* of the photograph. (Courtesy Utah State Historical Society.)

magnitude, significance, and very nature of the effort has encouraged historians to focus on the powerful men who were behind the building of the railroad, and on its economics and politics. Few have spent much time picking out bits of information from histories, documents, diaries, and, especially, archaeology to examine and understand better the role of common workers in the effort. Legends about the Union Pacific's Irish track layers, construction contractor "General" John Casement's work gangs, and the Central Pacific's loyal Chinese workers have become part of historical lore and overshadow the many other individuals and groups who participated in the construction effort. For example, the fact that Brigham Young's Mormon work crews, as contractors to both the UPRR and the CPRR, built most of the grade across northern Utah has been generally obscured (Galloway 1950:103; Strobridge 2002:3). There is also a smattering of information suggesting Native American involvement was not only in construction, but also in maintenance operations along the

transcontinental railroad. Davis (1894:153) writes that at the 10 May 1869 ceremony "[c]urious Mexicans, Indians and half-breeds, with the Chinese, Negro, and Irish laborers, lent to the auspicious little gathering a suggestive air of cosmopolitanism." George Kraus, cited in Fike and Raymond (1981: 9), notes that "Indians, indigenous to the area, also worked alongside the Chinese" (Figure 3).

Despite the fact that there are many published anecdotal accounts about transcontinental railroad workers of a variety of ethnicities, it is known that a significant segment of the workforce was from a number of backgrounds other than European American. By far the largest single group was ethnic Chinese, the extraordinary contribution of whose members was largely in support of CPRR construction from California to Promontory Summit during the years 1865 to 1869. Most of the 19 construction camps recorded at GSNHS were dominated by European Americans and likely represented groups associated with the UPRR construction. Four or five camps contain

FIGURE 3. Site 42BO1134, Chinese workers' camp, on the edge of the Central Pacific Railroad grade near Promontory Summit. The image shows the location of a tent platform and rock clusters. The view is to the east southeast with Great Salt Lake in the background. (Photo by Heather Weymouth, Sagebrush Consultants, 2002.)

artifacts of ethnic Chinese, the predominant material culture present. The distinct artifact assemblage, the moderate size, and other evidence strongly indicate occupation by Chinese railroad workers during 1868 and 1869. Almost certainly these camps were occupied by the Chinese who worked for the CPRR. There is no indication that the UPRR hired Chinese crews for its work, and, according to Strobridge (2002:2): "No Chinese ever worked east of Promontory," a further indication that the UPRR did not hire Chinese railroad workers. The Chinese who worked on the railroad at Promontory were the most documented ethnic group there. The presence of these men in Utah was the result of a chain of events dating back to the late 1840s in China and California.

Railroad Construction Approaching Promontory Summit

The CPRR and UPRR could operate independently when their respective construction sites were hundreds or thousands of miles apart, but the federal government, the promoter and funder of a significant part of this effort, expected cooperation to fulfill the ultimate goal of the project. This came into play as construction entered the Territory of Utah. Initial examinations of possible routes for the proposed railroad line through the northern portion of Utah were carried out as early as 1863 and 1864 (Rigdan 1951:1480). Following these initial reconnaissance efforts, more detailed surveys were carried out by UPRR engineers in 1867. During 1868 final location surveys were made from the mouth of Weber Canyon to Humboldt Wells in Nevada. At the same time, the CPRR was making its own surveys for the transcontinental route through the area. In 1867 CPRR engineers explored the Wasatch Range, its valleys and basins, and as far as the Ham's Fork River in Wyoming. In 1868 the CPRR engineers filed their preliminary survey with the U.S. Department of the Interior (Rigdan 1951:1481).

While grading and laying track moved rapidly along for the UPRR, the CPRR also pushed its crews to move more quickly. Both railroads, using Mormon contract laborers, undertook grading along the Promontory route from Corinne (east of Promontory) to Rozel

(just west of Promontory). The UPRR did not begin construction west of Ogden until February 1869 (Utley 1960:46). By March 1869, construction activity by both railroads was moving at a frenzied pace. The UPRR tracks reached Ogden on 8 March 1869 (*Salt Lake Daily Telegraph* 1869). A letter to the *Deseret Evening News* dated 25 March 1869 provided a firsthand account of this activity in the area between Corinne and Junction City (now known as Lampo Junction):

> Work is being vigorously prosecuted ... both lines running near each other and occasionally crossing. Both companies have their pile drivers at work where the lines cross the [Bear] river [near Corinne]. From Corinne west thirty miles, the grading camps present the appearance of a mighty army. As far as the eye can reach are to be seen almost a continuous line of tents, wagons and men. (*Deseret Evening News* 1869)

The CPRR tracks did not reach Promontory from the west until 30 April 1969 (Dodge 1910:943). Track was not completed to the summit by the UPRR until 9 May (Ames 1969:336). On 10 April, Congress ratified the railroad agreement to join the rails at Promontory Summit. The rails were officially joined on 10 May 1869.

Railroad Construction Camps

Thousands of workers were involved in this construction. Closer inspection of the archaeology of construction camps from a relatively early time period for the intermountain West provides fascinating, though limited, insights into camp structure, ethnicity, group dynamics, and labor relations among large corporate entities, their subcontractors, and the workers. Reaching the "end of the line" for both railroads at Promontory, in the latter half of 1868 and early 1869, resulted in a number of unique circumstances, certainly something that had not been encountered anywhere else up to that time. At least three of these are significant:

> 1. The topographic challenges for the railroads were considerable. The east slope of the Promontory Mountains is very steep and rocky. Except for tunnels, this location posed the greatest challenge for construction anywhere along the 86 mi. stretch of the UPRR from Promontory Summit eastward to Echo, Utah (Morris 1876:6). This alone resulted in an enormous expense for both railroads, as well as in the use of an army of workers.

2. Congress had not yet established a meeting point for the railroads. Each company had been working to gain advantage by building past and far beyond the other. In early 1869, CPRR crews were grading as far east as Echo Summit, near the Wyoming border, while Union Pacific crews were working in the vicinity of Humboldt Wells, in eastern Nevada (Utley 1960:18), a distance of about 250 mi. More local to Promontory Summit, each railroad spent enormous sums of money building railroad grades and culverts, filling washes, and even building trestles more than 25 mi. past the other in order to gain the advantage mentioned above. It was not until 10 April 1869, when Congress chose Promontory Summit as the meeting place, that this frenzied work ceased, and both railroads worked toward a logical joining of their respective tracks. The competition prompted both railroads to expend far more resources and men than would have normally been the case.

3. The close proximity of each railroad's crews (at least 19 camps located within a few miles of one another), coupled with the difficult terrain, strategic maneuvering for position by each railroad, and the fact that all resources available were called upon with little concern for cost, created an unusual mix of elements. Every construction crew, including the Irish, Cornish, Native Americans, Chinese, African Americans, Germans, English, Mormons, and Civil War veterans, was represented and interacted at this place to some degree, (McCague 1964:117).

It was at Promontory that the track layers caught up with the graders, those responsible for blasting rock ledges, spanning the arroyos, filling the washes, and leveling the terrain upon which to lay the ties and track. Histories of the great effort to cross the continent often gloss over the details of how it was done and who was responsible for the backbreaking jobs of construction that were completed in an era with few machines to ease the process. Picks, shovels, pry bars, and horse- and mule-drawn carts and wheelbarrows, coupled with blasting powder, were the commonly used tools.

During the GSNHS archaeological inventory between 2002 and 2008, 19 railroad construction sites were recorded. It is certain that more camps exist outside the park boundary. Site locational data indicate that a construction camp was established every 3 to 5 mi. and even closer together on the eastern slopes of the Promontory Mountains. Identification of sites by company, subcontractor, or ethnicity will require more historical research and analysis than has been possible as part of this project, but some interesting details have emerged from the basic data recovered. At least two camps

can almost certainly be tied to a particular railroad. The largest two workers' camp sites lie adjacent to particular company track lines, providing evidence of the railroad with which they were affiliated. Site 42BO851, closest to the "Big Fill" structure built by the CPRR, is likely to have been a Central Pacific camp. Site 42BO852, located closest to the UPRR-constructed "Big Trestle," is probably a Union Pacific camp (Figure 4).

Features common to almost all of the camps in the area include dugouts, some with dry-laid rock walls and many larger ones with collapsed dry-laid chimneys. There are tent platforms at all of the camps as well. Artifacts found at all of the sites are consistent with occupation during the construction period, and, at many, evidence of much later occupation suggests that they may have been used as maintenance camps. A wide variety of bottle glass, much of it reflecting beer and wine consumption; clothing fasteners; a lot of unidentifiable metal; and some wood were found across the sites. Many cut nails were found around a dry-laid stone building foundation, but none were found around dugouts or tent platforms. There were four brass military buttons found, one U.S. Army cavalry button dating to before 1861, and three Civil War–era general-service buttons issued by the U.S. Army. While some artifacts that can be attributed to ethnic Chinese were present on several sites, four sites in particular contain the best evidence of being exclusively Chinese construction camps (Polk 2013).

The 19 railroad construction sites were recorded as part of the research project undertaken by the U.S. National Park Service and Sagebrush during the early 2000s (Giles and Frost 2001; Weymouth and Southworth 2002; Weymouth, Pagano, and Garrison 2006; Weymouth, Pagano, Williamson et al. 2006). Within these 19 sites 219 features were recorded, including 144 depressions, 26 room blocks, 18 tent platforms, 12 rock shelters, and 2 blacksmith platforms. Other features identified were hearths, collapsed-chimney rubble/rock piles, an earthen mound, check dams, and a diversion ditch.

Excavation was not a part of the investigation. The aridity of the region has limited the vegetation present on the surface, making it possible to gain considerable insight into the

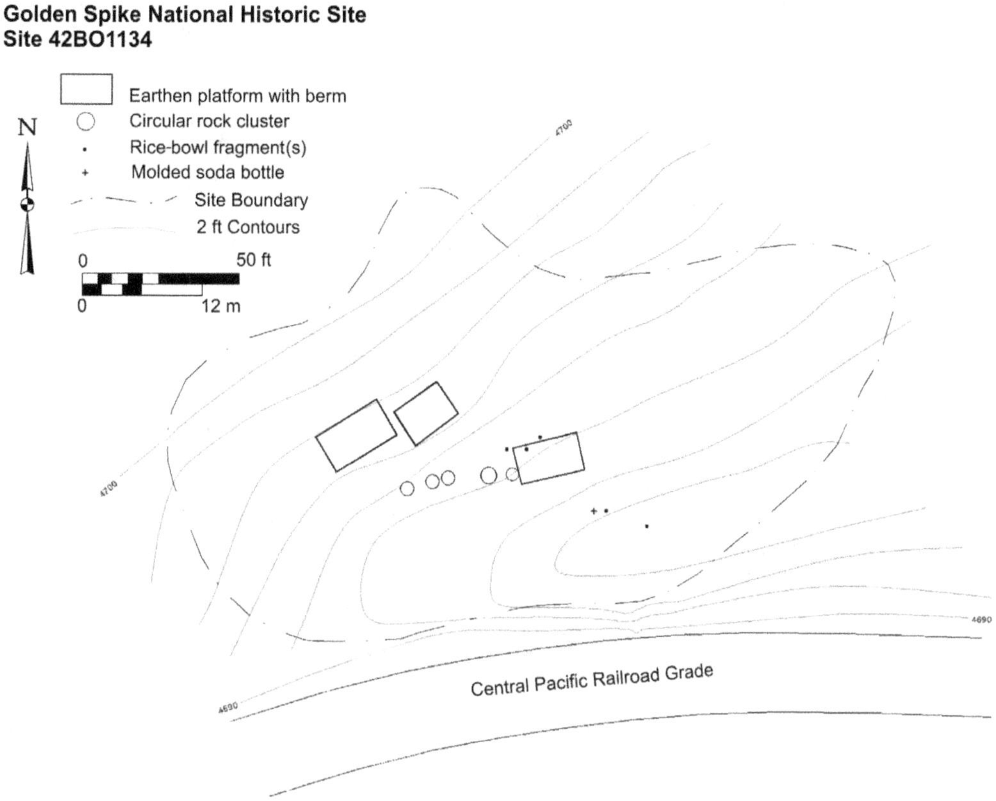

Golden Spike National Historic Site
Site 42BO1134

▭ Earthen platform with berm
○ Circular rock cluster
· Rice-bowl fragment(s)
+ Molded soda bottle
-- · -- Site Boundary
—— 2 ft Contours

N

0   50 ft

0   12 m

Central Pacific Railroad Grade

FIGURE 4. Sketch map of Site 42BO1134, Chinese worker camp, near Promontory Summit, Utah. (Map by Heather Weymouth, Sagebrush Consultants, 2002.)

nature and function of the archaeological sites. Fifteen of the camps have evidence strongly associating them with European American occupation. This includes stoneware jar fragments and earthenwares; nails; soda, liquor, and medicine bottles; cartridges; fasteners; utensils; buttons; blasting powder–can fragments; cast-iron pot fragments; and many other commonly discarded artifacts dating to the 1868–1869 period. These camp sites are distinct in other ways. Most contain habitation features. Habitation structures include small-to-large housing units; and large, rectangular structures likely representing barracks, communal mess halls, and Union Pacific or Central Pacific corporate structures. Other moderately sized structures may represent supply sheds, machinery sheds, and stores. Specific types of ground structures at Promontory have been described by Anderson (1983:227–236):

1. Pit structures, largely circular in shape with a pile of stone off to one area where a fireplace was built;
2. Square-to-rectangular masonry foundations or rooms consisting of foundations made of unshaped rocks, which were dry laid;
3. Dugout features, excavated into the sides of hills, with pits that were lined or reinforced with rock; and
4. Tent platforms, a very common feature, with the largest in area measuring 12 × 36 ft. The largest could represent mess tents, corporate headquarters, or areas to park wagons.

These features, along with others, such as check dams, mounds of indeterminate origin, and hearths, account for 138 formal features within 15 sites, averaging about 9 features per camp. The largest site, 42BO852, alone has 67 features.

One other significant physical characteristic of these camps is their size. The sites range from about 0.1 ac. to more than 24 ac. in area, averaging about 2.4 ac.

Chinese Worker Camps at Promontory

Four camp sites were identified as Chinese, largely through ethnically identifiable artifacts. The fact that only superficial evidence could be examined limited interpretation and comparison, but there are still useful metrics to describe and ponder. These sites tended to be much smaller in size and have fewer visible features than the European American sites in the area. Despite years of locals collecting artifacts along the railroad, a significant number of artifacts were still present, likely eroding out of the ground over time. Table 1 lists the site identification numbers, features, and size for each of the identified Chinese sites.

Selected artifacts were collected, and others were noted at the sites. These artifacts provide a broader understanding of occupation here. Many artifacts of European American manufacture appear to have been for domestic use and were likely purchased or supplied by the railroads for the workers. Also, at least a small portion of the artifact assemblage includes work-related artifacts associated with railroad construction (i.e., blasting-can fragments and nails). Most significantly, however, a high percentage of ethnic Chinese artifacts was found. A summary of those artifacts that were collected as part of this research follows.

White porcelain tableware fragments, most commonly rice bowls, were found at each of the sites. Most fragments could be identified as having painted blue (dominant) or polychrome patterns with a clear glaze finish. Specific designs could be identified on fewer fragments. The most common pattern identified was Bamboo, followed by the Double Happiness pattern. There were also a few examples of the Four Seasons pattern. More fragments of rice bowls and other tableware ceramics exist at Site 42BO1070 than any of the other sites (Figure 5). About the same number were found at Sites 42BO1068, 42BO1060, and 42BO1134. Other ceramic fragments found at the sites were stoneware rice wine– and soy sauce–bottle, or ginger-jar fragments, and many fragments of orange earthenware opium-pipe bowls.

At Site 42BO1060, opium-tin fragments were found, along with a cast-brass Chinese coin from the reign of Emperor Zhi He (A.D. 1054–1055) of the Song Dynasty, which lasted from 960 to 1279 (Kevin Aiken 2014, pers. comm.). While this is not a Chinese coin commonly found in western North America, apparently it is not unusual, even though it dates to a very early time period (Figure 6).

Comparisons with Other Railroad Construction Camps with Chinese Components

While not numerous, there have been studies carried out at a number of railroad construction camps in Nevada and California, from the same general time period, that included Chinese workers who almost certainly followed a living pattern similar to those workers at Promontory in 1868 and 1869. A few of those studies are discussed below.

Investigations and excavations with ethnic Chinese components have been undertaken at a transcontinental railroad site called Summit Camp in California (Baxter and Allen, this issue), a workers' camp site known as Lakeview Camp on the Virginia & Truckee Railroad (V&TRR) in western Nevada, dating to 1872 (Rogers 1997; Furnis and Maniery,

TABLE 1

FEATURES AND SIZES OF ETHNIC CHINESE WORKER CAMP SITES NEAR PROMONTORY SUMMIT

Site Number	Features	Site Size
42BO1060	2 dugouts, 2 hearth remnants	60,500 sq. ft. (1.4 ac.)
42BO1068	Unknown (disturbed)	54,000 sq. ft. (1.2 ac.)
42BO1070	1 possible tent platform, 2 wooden posts	1,450 sq. ft. (0.03 ac.)
42BO1134	3 tent platforms, 5 limestone rock clusters	46,170 sq. ft. (1.1 ac.)

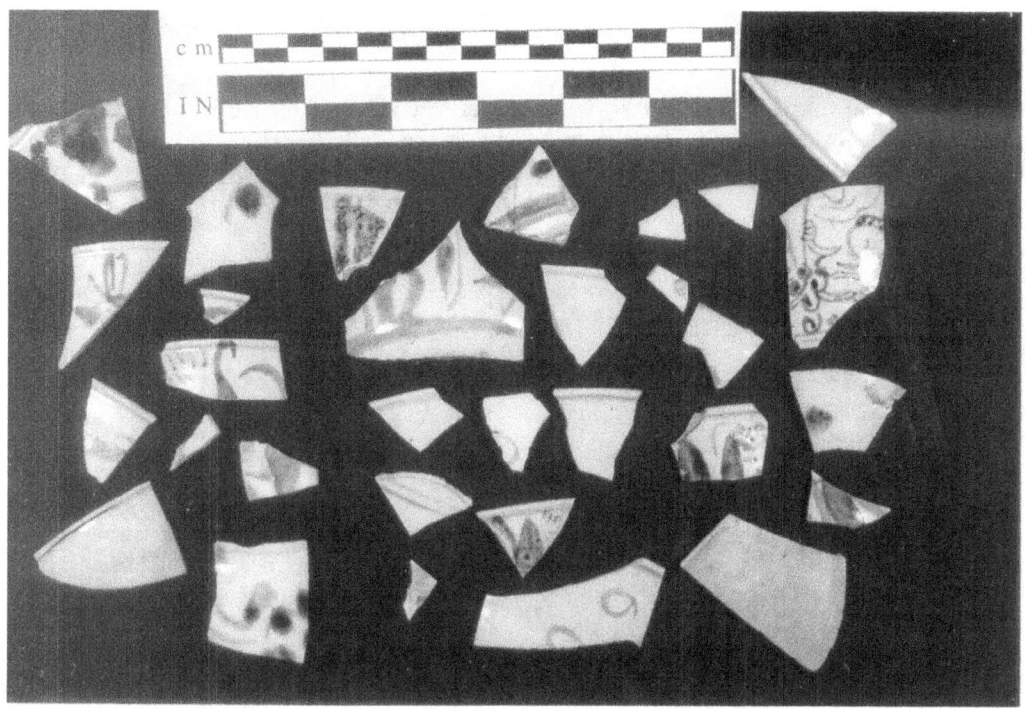

FIGURE 5. Porcelain utilitarian-ware bowl fragments from Chinese worker camps on the east slope of the Promontory Mountains, where the most intense construction activity on the transcontinental railroad took place. (Photo by Heather Weymouth, Sagebrush Consultants, 2002.)

FIGURE 6. Chinese coins recovered from a National Park Service excavation of an 1869 Central Pacific Railroad stone culvert headwall (Hutchinson 1988). This work was done in support of restoration efforts.

this issue), and a workers' camp associated with construction of the Eureka & Palisade Railroad in central Nevada in 1875 (Zier 1985). All of these investigations seem to suggest that similar occupation patterns and activities took place in each of these disparate areas over a fairly short period during or shortly after completion of the transcontinental railroad (1865–1875).

The Summit Camp site shows some similar traits, including the kinds of domestic and Chinese artifacts present at Promontory sites and a hearth feature, but the length of occupation and the fact that a cabin was once present on the site make meticulous comparisons difficult.

The Lakeview Camp was occupied for several weeks in 1872. Studies of the site reveal that the camp was certainly a temporary camp, probably occupied by a large group of Chinese individuals during the construction of the V&TRR (Rogers 1997; Furnis and Maniery, this issue). No evidence of permanent structures or of extensive ranch features was found at the site. The archaeological deposits are fairly shallow (approximately 50 cm below surface) and limited in their artifact quantities and functional types, suggesting short-term occupation of a domestic nature. The Lakeview Camp report (Rogers 1997) further elucidates that the overwhelming majority of artifacts found were manufactured in China. Also, it indicates that the site was organized into public and private, socializing and work areas.

The worker camp in central Nevada, 26EU790, on the Eureka & Palisade Railroad offers particularly useful comparisons to Promontory (Zier 1985). Occupied for what appears to have been only a few days in 1875, there were three artifact clusters found. Cluster A measured 90 × 100 ft. (9,000 sq. ft.), Cluster B measured 60 × 100 ft. (6,000 sq. ft.), and Cluster C measured 75 × 100 ft. (7,500 sq. ft.). These probably represent occupation by 12 to 20 workmen for one or two nights (Zier 1985:149). Artifact categories found at the site were similar to those at the Lakeview Camp. Also similar to Lakeview, relatively few artifacts were present on the site.

With the exception of Summit Camp (where remains of a permanent building were found), the sites discussed lacked evidence of permanent structures. Also, all the sites had few artifacts present, and most of those artifacts were

of Chinese origin. Cultural features present (except at the central Nevada site) consisted of hearths or stone concentrations. Of particular note here are the three measured areas of activity at site 26EU790. Using this as a guide and extrapolating from the Lakeview Camp, which likely represented multiple gangs congregating in a central place over time, a similar projection could be made for the Promontory Chinese sites. For instance, if Site 42BO1060, measuring 60,500 sq. ft., was divided into separate, adjacent camps of 12- to 20-man work gangs (Goodwin 1991:184), one could speculate that up to eight different worker groups congregated at this site; similarly, for 42BO1068, seven work gangs; for Site 42BO1070, perhaps only one; and for 42BO1134, six. Adding these together, one could project that as many as 250 to 500 Chinese, and possibly more, may have lived at these sites during railroad construction.

Further Thoughts about Construction Camps

Despite the limited survey and surface-collection information about the sites at Promontory, more comparative analyses between similar sites along other western railroads can provide valuable insights on and important understanding of these camps. Even various demographic and sociological analyses may offer more insights. For instance, the fact that Chinese workers are known to have built distinct camps, separate from other railroad workers, is an important subject to explore. In addition to environmental and technological variables influencing camp layout, social-structure variables created conventions for behavior in many construction camps (Buckles 1983). Buckles argues that native-born laborers would not tolerate the presence of the nonnative laborers employed, such as Chinese, Italians, Mexicans, and African Americans, and suggests that ethnic separation in camps was common and even enforced by management. This would also apply to Mormons, who made up a large percentage of the construction crews at Promontory. Their strict moral code and religious beliefs, not to mention attachment to separate construction companies (and railroads), would almost certainly have led them to set up camps physically separated from others working in the area. These ideas are supported and enhanced by Goodwin and colleagues, who describe in detail the reasons for separation of the Chinese, including those described above, as well as the fact that the Chinese bosses and workers themselves chose this pattern (Goodwin 1991:182–183). Labor contractors found it easier to maintain discipline this way, and naturally workers sought familiar company and the customs of their fellow countrymen.

These and other important aspects of railroad workers' camps will be difficult to tease out without further archaeological investigation. It is expected that more detailed analyses of the features and artifacts from the construction camps found on the Promontory Mountains slope will allow a better understanding of who occupied each camp. These analyses will also help identify camp affiliation with either UPRR or CPRR, the amount of ethnic diversity at each camp, and more information concerning the origin of camp occupants.

References

AMBROSE, STEPHEN E.
1990 *Nothing Like It in the World: The Men Who Built the Transcontinental Railroad, 1863–1869*. Simon & Schuster, New York, NY.

AMES, CHARLES U.
1969 *Pioneering the Union Pacific: A Reappraisal of the Builders of the Railroad*. Appleton-Century-Crofts, New York, NY.

ANDERSON, ADRIENNE
1983 Ancillary Construction of Promontory Summit, Utah: Those Domestic Structures Built by Railroad Workers. In *Forgotten Places and Things: Archaeological Perspectives on American History*, Albert E. Ward, editor, pp. 225–238. Center for Anthropological Studies, Albuquerque, NM.

AYERS, JAMES E.
1982 *Archaeological Survey of Golden Spike National Historic Site and Record Search for Promontory, Utah*. Arizona State Museum, Tucson.

BAIN, DAVID HAWARD
1999 *Empire Express: Building the First Transcontinental Railroad*. Viking, New York, NY.

BUCKLES, WILLIAM G.
1983 Models for Railroad Construction Related Sites in the West. In *Forgotten Places and Things: Archaeological Perspectives on American History*, Albert E. Ward, editor, pp. 213–223. Center for Anthropological Studies, Albuquerque, NM.

DAVIS, JOHN P.
1894 *The Union Pacific Railway; A Study in Railway Politics, History, and Economics*. S. C. Griggs, Chicago, IL.

DESERET EVENING NEWS
1869 No title. *Deseret Evening News* 7 April:5. Salt Lake City, UT.

DODGE, GRENVILLE M.
1910 *How We Built the Union Pacific Railway: And Other Railway Papers and Addresses*. U.S. Congress (Senate), Washington, DC.

FIKE, RICHARD E., AND ANAN S. RAYMOND
1981 *Rails East to Promontory: The Utah Stations*. Bureau of Land Management, Cultural Resource Series No. 8. Salt Lake City, UT.

FRANCAVIGLIA, RICHARD V.
2008 *Over the Range: A History of the Promontory Summit Route of the Pacific Railroad*. Utah State University Press, Logan.

GALLOWAY, JOHN DEBO
1950 *The First Transcontinental Railroad: Central Pacific and Union Pacific, 1863–1869*. Simmons-Boardman, New York, NY.
1989 *The First Transcontinental Railroad*. Dorset Press, New York, NY.

GILES, RALPH B., AND DAWN A. FROST
2001 Golden Spike National Historic Site: Systemwide Archeological Inventory Program Fiscal Year 2000 Interim Report. Manuscript, National Park Service, Western Archeological and Conservation Center, Tucson, AZ.

GOODWIN, VICTOR
1991 Transportation. In *Nevada's Northeast Frontier*, Victor Goodwin, Edna B. Patterson, and Louise A Ulph, authors, pp. 133–206. University of Nevada Press, Reno.

HENDRICKS, RICKY
1986 Golden Spike National Historic Site, UT. National Register of Historic Places Registration Form, Utah State Historic Preservation Office, Salt Lake City.

HOMSTAD, CARLA, JANENE CAYWOOD, AND PEGGY NELSON
2000 *Cultural Landscape Report Golden Spike National Historic Site Box Elder County, Utah*. National Park Service, Intermountain Region, Cultural Resources Selections, No. 16. Denver, CO.

HUTCHINSON, SAYRE
1988 List of Classified Structures, Stone Box Culvert, Record 11858. National Park Service, List of Classified Structures <http://hscl.cr.nps.gov/insidenps/report.asp?STATE=&PARK=&STRUCTURE=&SORT=1&RECORDNO=11858>. Accessed 9 August 2014.

KLEIN, MAURY
  1987   *Union Pacific: Birth of a Railroad, 1862–1893.*
         Doubleday, Garden City, NY.

KRAUS, GEORGE
  1969   *High Road to Promontory: Building the Central
         Pacific (Now the Southern Pacific) across the High
         Sierra.* Castle, New York, NY.

McCAGUE, JAMES
  1964   *Moguls and Iron Men: The Story of the First
         Transcontinental Railroad.* Harper & Row, New
         York, NY.

MORRIS, ISAAC N.
  1876   *Condition of the Union Pacific Railroad.* 44th
         Congress (House), 1st sess., Executive Document
         180. Washington, DC.

POLK, MICHAEL R.
  1998   Cultural Resources Overview and Preservation
         Recommendations, Promontory Route Corinne to
         Promontory, Utah, Report No. 1134. Manuscript,
         Sagebrush Consultants LLC, Ogden, UT.
  2013   The History and Influence of Chinese Railroad
         Workers on the Transcontinental Railroad: A View
         from the End of the Line at Promontory Summit.
         Paper presented at the Archaeology Network of
         the Chinese Railroad Workers in North America
         Workshop, Stanford University, Stanford, CA.

POLK, MICHAEL R., AND WENDY SIMMONS-JOHNSON
  2012   From Lampo Junction to Rozel: The Archeological
         History of the Transcontinental Railroad across the
         Promontory Mountains, Utah, GOSP Synthesis
         Report. Manuscript, Golden Spike National Historic
         Site, National Park Service, Promontory, UT.

RIGDAN, PAUL
  1951   Historical Catalogue: Union Pacific Historical
         Museum. Manuscript, Western Heritage Museum,
         Omaha, NE.

ROGERS, C. LYNN
  1997   Making Camp Chinese Style: The Archaeology of a
         V&T Railroad Graders' Camp, Carson City, Nevada.
         Manuscript, Archaeological Research Services,
         Virginia City, NV.

SALT LAKE DAILY TELEGRAPH
  1869   No title. *Salt Lake Daily Telegraph* 15 March:2. Salt
         Lake City, UT.

STROBRIDGE, EDWIN
  2002   Fiction or Fact? Did the Chinese and Irish RR Workers
         Really Try to Blow Each Other Up? Central Pacific
         Railroad Photographic History Museum <http://cprr
         .org/Game/Interactive_Railroad_Project/Fiction_or
         _Fact.html>. Accessed 10 September 2002.

UTLEY, ROBERT M.
  1960   The National Survey of Historic Sites and Buildings,
         Special Report on Promontory Summit, Utah (Golden
         Spike National Historic Site). Manuscript, United
         States Department of the Interior, National Park
         Service Region 3, Santa Fe, NM.
  1969   *Golden Spike National Historic Site, Utah.* National
         Park Service, Historical Handbook Series No. 40.
         Washington, DC.

WEYMOUTH, HEATHER M., SANDY CHYNOWETH PAGANO,
AND ANGELA L. GARRISON
  2006   Archaeological Inventory of Golden Spike National
         Historic Site and Adjacent Bureau of Land
         Management Railroad Rights-of-Way Fiscal Year
         2002 Interim Report, Report No. 1279. Report to RMC
         Consultants, Inc., Wheat Ridge, CO, and National Park
         Service, Lakewood, CO, from Sagebrush Consultants
         LLC, Ogden, UT.

WEYMOUTH, HEATHER M., SANDY CHYNOWETH PAGANO,
ANDREW WILLIAMSON, AND ANGELA L. GARRISON
  2006   Golden Spike National Historic Site Systemwide
         Archaeological Inventory Program Fiscal Year 2003
         Interim Report, Report No. 1303. Report to RMC
         Consultants, Inc., Wheat Ridge, CO, and National Park
         Service, Lakewood, CO, from Sagebrush Consultants
         LLC, Ogden, UT.

WEYMOUTH, HEATHER M., AND DON SOUTHWORTH
  2002   Golden Spike National Historic Site Systemwide
         Archaeological Inventory Program Fiscal Year 2001
         Interim Report, Report No. 1225. Report to RMC
         Consultants, Inc., Wheat Ridge, CO, and National Park
         Service, Lakewood, CO, from Sagebrush Consultants
         LLC, Ogden, UT.

ZIER, CHARLES D.
  1985   *Archaeological Data Recovery Associated with the
         Mt. Hope Project, Eureka County, Nevada.* Bureau
         of Land Management, Cultural Resource Series, No.
         8. Reno, NV.

MICHAEL R. POLK
SAGEBRUSH CONSULTANTS
QUINCY AVENUE, SUITE
OGDEN, UT

Ryan P. Harrod (瑞安·哈罗德)
John J. Crandall (约翰·克朗达)

Rails Built of the Ancestors' Bones: The Bioarchaeology of the Overseas Chinese Experience
祖先白骨建成的铁轨：对海外华人生活经验的生物考古学

ABSTRACT

Between 1865 and 1869, thousands of Chinese immigrants came to the United States to construct the transcontinental railroad. Their impact went beyond labor and helped to develop the social and economic landscape of the country through their ingenuity. Archaeological analyses are especially important for understanding the Chinese in historical America because of the lack of written records. Bioarchaeology can contribute by providing a glimpse into the lives of these resourceful and diverse laborers who toiled to contribute to the development of the railways in the 19th century. The reanalysis of the remains of 13 Chinese men recovered from a cemetery in Carlin, Nevada, reveals that most individuals exhibited widespread musculoskeletal development suggesting frequent, repeated bodily strain. Additionally, all 13 individuals exhibited skeletal trauma or pathologies. The men recovered from Carlin reveal the extent to which Chinese railroad workers endured exploitative oppression and racism, while simultaneously embodying resilience.

在1865至1869年间，成千上万的中国移民来到美国修建横贯大陆铁路。他们所带来的影响远不止其劳动力。他们的创造力促进了整个美国社会与经济的发展。由于缺少文字记载，考古学分析对我们理解这些中国工人十分重要。生物考古学则尤为重要，因为它可以展现这些工人的足智多谋、多样化的生活。本文对内华达州卡林镇一处公墓中发掘的13具中国工人遗骸进行了重新分析。分析结果显示，这些人的肌骨骼发展暗示了频繁和重复性的身体劳损。除此之外，这13个人都显示出骨骼的损伤与病兆。卡林工人的遗骸揭示了中国铁路工人所受的剥削性压迫和种族歧视的程度，却也同时展现了他们不屈不挠的精神。

Introduction

In the 19th century, hundreds of thousands of people left their homelands in and around Guangdong Province in China to find work and build more prosperous lives. This mass emigration of laborers from China would have a profound impact on the rest of the world, as these individuals facilitated development in the Americas, Caribbean, Australia, New Zealand, and Asia. In the United States, the importance of the labor performed by these individuals is most readily apparent in the construction of the first transcontinental railroad between 1865 and 1869.

The reality is that these Chinese immigrants, or overseas Chinese, were not simply laborers, but individuals that, beginning in the early to mid-1800s, would transform the social, economic, and political landscape of the United States countless times (Chan 1991; Takaki 1998; McKeown 1999; Chang 2003). Often characterized as a single group, this vast diaspora was complex. Historical research has found that some individuals would stay in the countries to which they had migrated, but others often returned to China (Chen 2000). Regardless of how long individuals lived in the United States, their presence helped to shape and transform Sino-American relations for generations to come. Yet historians and archaeologists know relatively little about the individual lived experiences of these laborers.

One of the main reasons so little is known about Chinese laborers in the United States is because researchers have only recovered traces of their lives in this foreign land. Beyond the material culture they left behind, historians and others have had, in general, only the records and perspectives of non-Chinese Americans to rely on. Unfortunately, these accounts often offer a biased, superficial account from which to reconstruct the lives of Chinese laborers.

Recently, a number of archaeologists have increasingly sought to bring all Asian immigrant laborers, including the Chinese, into focus in their research on a wide variety of topics and using a variety of lines of evidence (Voss and Allen 2008; Ross 2013). The focus of this special issue is a specific demographic of Chinese immigrant laborers, the men who helped to build the transcontinental railroad and its tributaries. The contribution of this article is to explore the ways in which data derived from the skeletal remains of the laborers themselves can provide some insight into the lives of Chinese laborers working on the construction of the railroads in the historical American West.

A review of the bioarchaeological research conducted on Chinese railroad workers to date reveals that data derived from contextualized analyses of the human remains have played a minimal role in the efforts to understand the importance of the Chinese in the development of the United States during the 19th century. In fact, most of what is known about Chinese immigrants is based on only 13 burials, recovered from a cemetery in the town of Carlin, in Elko County, Nevada (Figure 1).

According to Chung et al. (2005:107), several of the burials were accidentally discovered by the landowner during construction of a new home. The archaeological analysis of the site and mortuary context was carried out by Eugene Hattori and Fred Frampton (Chung et al. 2005:107), while the initial osteological analysis of the bodies was conducted by a team from the National Museum of Natural History that included Douglas Owsley, Kari

Bruwelheide, Juliet Brundige, David Hunt, Chip Clark, and Rebecca Redmond (Owsley et al. 1997). Currently, the remains are housed in the Sheilagh Brooks Laboratory in the Department of Anthropology at the University of Nevada, Las Vegas. Given the important nature of the burials, in terms of what they can reveal about Chinese railroad workers, the skeletal remains have been analyzed previously by several other researchers, including the authors. The focus of these past research projects has been on enhancing understanding of cultural retention and transformation among Chinese Americans (Chung et al. 2005), the assessment of the geographic origin in China and biological affinities of the individuals (Schmidt 2006; Schmidt et al. 2011), and, most recently, the identification of systems of inequality and violence (Harrod et al. 2013).

This article reviews the findings obtained from these analyses of the remains of the 13 burials excavated from Carlin. Relying on the detailed historical reconstructions established by Chung et al. (2005) and expanding on the

FIGURE 1. Map of Carlin, Nevada, in relation to the railroads of the American West. Image adapted from a map of the Central Pacific Railroad of California (Crofutt 1872:193). (Map by Ryan P. Harrod, 2014.)

work done by Harrod et al. (2013), the goal is to provide a more complete picture of the lives of these individuals. The focus is on analyses of skeletal injuries, muscle strain, osteoarthritis or degenerative joint disease, dental health, and mortuary treatment, because these skeletal markers provide an indication of the overall health and well-being of these men who spent a portion of their lives as railroad workers. The findings from the skeletal analysis are contextualized against historical and archival research, and the extent of muscle strain, widespread trauma, and disease testify to the cycles of suffering faced by early Chinese immigrants to America.

Historical Context

After learning of the discovery of gold in California, Chinese immigrated to the western United States by the thousands. According to archival work by Chung et al. (2005:108), the *Virginia City Territorial Enterprise* from 1871 suggests that, from the placer mines in California in the 1850s, Chinese traveled eastward into Nevada and worked near Gold Hill. Chinese immigration to Nevada only increased with the discovery of the Comstock Lode in 1859, which led to Chinese laborers engaging in a number of occupations throughout the state (Chung et al. 2005).

The construction of the Central Pacific Railroad (CPRR) began in 1868. With many Chinese in the state already, and more immigrating across the West as railroad construction rose and fell, many Chinese worked the rails and stayed into the 20th century to form immigrant communities in Nevada. Chung et al. (2005:108) noted that at least 10,000, and up to 17,000, Chinese were hired to lay track across northern Nevada. It was these Chinese who encountered the land that became Carlin, Nevada, in Elko County. After the completion of the transcontinental railroad in 1869, many of the railroad laborers stayed in Nevada as maintenance men and construction workers.

Chung et al. (2005:109) discussed some of the other occupations in which Chinese laborers engaged after the construction of the railroad was completed, including crop farmers, restaurant and laundry owners, miners, and laborers in the lumber and mining industries. All of these

occupations were related to the railroad to some degree, as they often provided services for the people still working on the railroad or were subsidized directly by the railroad companies. In an interview by Chung in 2000, John Fong recollects operating, in the late 1800s, a restaurant in Carlin that was subsidized by the CPRR and used produce grown by Chinese farmers/gardeners whose plots of land were along the rail line (Chung et al. 2005:109). His oral testimony, as well as the documentary record (Carter 1976), provided testimony of the presence of the Chinese in a number of industries in Carlin after May 1869, when the railroads in the region had been completed. Carlin had a Chinatown, complete with merchants and networks tying the local Chinese community into the larger district and benevolent associations. The associations were responsible for moving remittance and the bones of the dead back to the provincial community, while bringing Chinese wares to Nevada (Chung et al. 2005). Thus, the cemetery sample discussed in this article represents a subsection of the Chinese who lived in Carlin in the 19th century. First, these men survived railroad work and were buried in a small segregated cemetery away from the European American cemetery in town. Second, they represent men who lived in Carlin after the railways were completed. Third, they were, curiously and for unknown reasons, not shipped back to their provincial community by district associations. While they likely worked on the railways and thus ended up in Carlin, the life histories of these individuals likely do not represent the full diversity of the experiences Chinese railway workers had. The information collected from these human remains offers a data set that will help to enhance what is known of railroad workers from China.

It is important to understand that, in general, the men who labored to construct the railroads in the United States during the 19th century were at greater risk of poor health and early death. Labor statistics about industrial accidents recorded by regional bureaus reveals that being a railroad worker in the mid-19th century was a dangerous job. Friedman and Ladinsky (1967:60), investigating historical industrial accidents in Wisconsin, found that during the 1800s injury incidence among rail line workers was higher than for any other industry, including mining and manufacturing-related occupations.

They also found that the number of individuals injured laboring on the railroad increased over time, and, by 1906, 5 out of every 100 workers had an accident at work (Friedman and Ladinsky 1967:60).

The assumption that being a railroad worker in the 19th century was hard and potentially lethal is corroborated by the few records Chinese laborers left behind in other countries where railways were developed in the 19th and 20th centuries. Wong Hau-hon, writing in 1926 from Canada, provided testimony to the terrors of railway construction (Yung et al. 2006). Working on the Canadian Pacific Railroad in the 1880s, Wong came from Guangdong Province, like the men from Carlin, Nevada, and discussed his experience in great detail. This man's account of his experiences working the rails in Canada informs reconstructions of the experiences of Chinese laborers in the United States. He writes:

> The work was very dangerous. ... Dynamite was used to blast a rock cave. Twenty charges were placed and ignited, but only eighteen blasts went off. However, the white foreman, thinking that all of the dynamite had gone off, ordered the Chinese workers to enter the cave to resume work. Just at that moment the remaining two charges suddenly exploded. Chinese bodies flew from the cave as if shot from a cannon. Blood and flesh were mixed in a horrible mess. On this occasion about ten or twenty workers were killed. (Yung et al. 2006:39–42)

If these same dangerous conditions existed for railroad laborers in the 19th-century United States, then risks of accidents and death were intimately tied to the building of the CPRR. The risks would have included more than just accidents along the rail line, but also death and suffering resulting from surveying the land, cutting the trees, and maintaining the railway. Eleven tunnel projects were also part of the Central Pacific railway (Baxter and Allen, this issue), and Chinese workers were the majority of those who worked the most dangerous tasks of blasting and drilling these tunnels. Fatalities and injuries no doubt abounded in such situations, as Wong's account illustrates.

Death and direct occupational injury were not the only risks facing the Chinese who built the railways running through northern Nevada. They would have also experienced fatigue, food shortages, dehydration, and exposure due to cold weather. While not all of these stressors can be inferred from bones directly, putting human skeletal remains in their larger archaeological and cultural context can help reveal if the stressors did, in fact, have an impact on the lives of Chinese railroad workers. Evidence of starvation, inferred from the degree of processing seen in the animal remains recovered from archaeological contexts, such as rail camps in Montana (Ellis et al. 2011), indicates that there were times when people appeared to be attempting to obtain as many nutrients from food sources as possible. In terms of parasites, research on the prevalence of the bacterium *Helicobacter pylori* among modern Chinese immigrants in Australia reveals that there was a differential exposure to this bacteria. The authors found that the risks were primarily cultural, and included factors such as socioeconomic status and, surprisingly, the use of chopsticks (Chow et al. 1995). The authors suggest that the use of chopsticks increased the risk of transmitting the bacteria through communal eating and sharing of chopsticks. The cultural practice of sharing utensils was common enough among Chinese in the 1930s that a health program to combat tuberculosis was started to promote ideas of individuality in eating and sleeping, including more hygienic practices at table (Lei 2010). Given that communal food practice still existed in the 1930s, it is likely that it was also common among Chinese immigrant laborers in the late 1800s.

To make up for the scarcity of written records concerning the hazards Chinese workers faced on railways in the United States, one approach is to look at the effects of hard labor and the health of contemporaneous workers involved in similar tasks. Tüchsen et al. (2005) evaluated the hospital records of 5,123 bridge and tunnel laborers and 109,383 other types of construction workers in Denmark. The researchers looked at workers who were involved in a large multiphase project, called the Green Belt Fixed Link, between 1989 and 1998. The median employment length for these workers was about two years (Tüchsen et al. 2005:24), so the workers only performed intensive labor for a relatively short period of time. Similar to their Chinese counterparts who built the transcontinental railroad over 100 years earlier, these workers were organized into labor gangs, worked strenuous and long hours, lived in camps, and were exposed to poor weather conditions. Based on hospital records, these workers had a risk of poor health and death similar to other construction workers, but were admitted to the hospital more often. They were hospitalized for a wide range of ailments, including musculoskeletal injuries, infections, parasites, cardiovascular disease, and digestive issues (Tüchsen et al. 2005:22,25–26). The indication of this study is that the relatively short period of intensely hard labor resulted in long-term consequences to the bodies of these Danish bridge and tunnel laborers that resembled, and in some ways exceeded, the consequences for workers who had done hard labor over a much longer period. Thus, the short period that the Chinese railroad workers labored to build the transcontinental railroad would most likely have significantly affected their health, and the impact should be evident on their bodies. The reality is that the Chinese men working on the railroads were at risk, not only during their relatively short times as laborers, but also long after the work on the railroads was completed.

Bioarchaeological Reanalysis of the Carlin Chinese

The value of a bioarchaeological approach to the 13 Chinese men recovered from Carlin, Nevada, is that a comparative, situated analysis of skeletal data sheds light on the dynamic relationship that human health plays with the environment, both social and natural (Table 1).

Investigating the bodies of these men provides a direct window through which to assess many of these stressors and to understand how they affected survivors, who would likely be buried later at Carlin's Chinese cemetery. Shifting ecologies, which can include changing international policy, racial sentiment, changes in the local ecology, seasonality, or changes in diet, can all alter one's skeletal health, growth, development, and risk of injury. Thus, when used creatively, skeletal data can illuminate anthropological understandings of a wide variety of biosocial processes, such as urbanization, immigration, trade, shifts in social hierarchy, increasing sociopolitical inequality, racism, and other processes that would all have affected the Chinese differently.

Mortuary Context and Demography

The first step of any analysis of burials is to reconstruct the context in which the burials were located and the demographic profile of the sample, creating the "bioarchaeological profile" (Harrod 2013:65). The 1870 U.S. census notes that about 25% of Chinese in Carlin were railroad workers, and the period the cemetery was in use includes the time of the census. Chung et al. (2005) also suggested that transient Chinese were buried elsewhere, supporting our claim that these men likely represent railroad workers who made Carlin their home after the rails were finished in 1869. The cemetery was in use in Carlin from 1885 until 1924. Thus, these remains record both injury and survival after the end of labor on, at least, the Central Pacific Railroad, and likely in other hard industries, such as logging or mining.

Located approximately two city blocks away from the public cemetery of Carlin, Nevada (Chung et al. 2005:107), the mortuary context of Carlin is not well documented historically, but a great deal of information is known about the site as a result of the detailed archaeological reconstructions by Hattori and Frampton, and historical research conducted by Chung. Burial 1 is the only exception to this, as it was removed during the construction of a new house, and the landscape was altered (Chung et al. 2005:120). A chapter in *Chinese American Death Rituals: Respecting the Ancestors* by Chung et al. (2005) provides an exhaustive account of the mortuary context of these burials that goes beyond the scope of this article. What is important to note here is that the coffin type and material, along with the associated grave goods, show that, although there was some degree of homogeneity among the Chinese men living in Carlin, there were also distinct differences, including but not limited to evidence of varying degrees of social status within the community.

The demographic profile of the men buried at Carlin, Nevada, illuminates the risks Chinese males underwent during the late 1800s and early 1900s in the American West. That Chinese men suffered marginalization, increased risks of injury, and early death in historical northern Nevada is supported by local newspaper articles (Chung et al. 2005:115–116), the establishment,

TABLE 1

SUMMARY OF AGE, PATHOLOGY, DEGENERATION, AND TRAUMA FROM 13 BURIALS RECOVERED FROM CARLIN, NEVADA

Demography		Pathological Conditions		Stress-Related Degenerative Changes		Trauma and Injury	
Burial	Age	Skeletal Pathologies	Dental Pathologies	Entheseal Development	Osteoarthritis	Antemortem Trauma	Perimortem Trauma
1	45–50+	N/A	Periodontal disease, 2 caries, and 1 abscess[a]	Moderate to robust development of upper limb, moderate development of lower limb	Slight to moderate degenerative joint and disk disease and several Schmorl's nodes on thoaracic vertebrae	1 small cranial depression fracture	N/A
2	30+	Periosteal reaction on tibia (L/R)[b]	Not scored	Not scored	Osteolitic lesions on lumbar vertebrae and iliac crest (L)[b]	Broken humerus (L), radius (L), rib (R), and metatarsal (L)[b]	N/A
3	35–45	Periosteal reaction on cranium	Periodontal disease[a]	Robust development of upper limb, robust development of lower limb	Fused sacroiliac joint and moderate degenerative disk disease	Facial fracture and broken rib (R)	N/A
4	50+	N/A	N/A	Moderate to robust development of upper limb, moderate to robust development of lower limb	Slight to moderate degenerative disk disease and several Schmorl's nodes on thoracic and lumbar vertebrae	2 large cranial depression fractures and broken tibia and fibula (L)	N/A
5	35–45	N/A	5 caries and 5 abscesses[a]	Moderate development of upper limb, moderate development of lower limb	Slight degenerative disk disease and moderate degenerative joint disease of the humerus (L/R)	2 small cranial depression fractures and broken humerus (L)	N/A

TABLE 1 (CONTINUED)

SUMMARY OF AGE, PATHOLOGY, DEGENERATION, AND TRAUMA FROM 13 BURIALS RECOVERED FROM CARLIN, NEVADA

Demography		Pathological Conditions		Stress-Related Degenerative Changes		Trauma and Injury	
Burial	Age	Skeletal Pathologies	Dental Pathologies	Entheseal Development	Osteoarthritis	Antemortem Trauma	Perimortem Trauma
6	30–40	N/A	13 caries and 7 abscesses[a]	Moderate to robust development of upper limb, moderate to robust development of lower limb	Spondylolysis (L5) and osteoarthritic changes and shortening of the clavicle (R)	2 large linear fractures of the cranium and 1 facial fracture	N/A
7	40–50	Slight to moderate porotic hyperostosis	Enamel hypoplasia, 9 caries, and 4 abscesses[a]	Moderate development of upper limb, moderate development of lower limb	Slight degenerative disk disease	1 large cranial depression fracture with reactive bone around it	N/A
8	30–40	N/A	Periodontal disease[a]	Robust development of upper limb, moderate development of lower limb	N/A	1 small cranial depression fracture, a facial fracture, and broken ribs (L/R), metatarsals (L)	Broken ribs (L/R), sternum, lumbar (L-5), sacrum, and os coxae (L/R)
9	20–30	Slight to moderate porotic hyperostosis	Periodontal disease, enamel hypoplasia, and two caries[a]	Moderate development of upper limb, moderate development of lower limb	N/A	1 large linear fracture of the cranium	N/A
10	40–50	Slight to moderate porotic hyperostosis, severe periosteal reaction on femur, tibia and fibula (L/R)	Periodontal disease, 5 caries. and one abscess[a]	Robust development of upper limb, robust development of lower limb	Slight to moderate degenerative joint disease, moderate degenerative disk disease, and several Schmorl's nodes on thoracic and lumbar	1 small and 1 medium cranial depression fracture	A severe panfacial fracture involving multiple cranial bones, rib (L/R), sternum, and cervical vertebrae (C6–C7)

TABLE 1 (CONTINUED)
SUMMARY OF AGE, PATHOLOGY, DEGENERATION, AND TRAUMA FROM 13 BURIALS RECOVERED FROM CARLIN, NEVADA.

Demography		Pathological Conditions		Stress-Related Degenerative Changes		Trauma and Injury	
Burial	Age	Skeletal Pathologies	Dental Pathologies	Entheseal Development	Osteoarthritis	Antemortem Trauma	Perimortem Trauma
11	40–50	N/A	2 abscesses[a]	Moderate to robust development of upper limb, moderate to robust development of lower limb	Slight degenerative joint disease, slight to moderate degenerative disk disease, several Schmorl's nodes on thoracic and lumbar vertebrae	1 small and 1 large cranial depression fracture	N/A
12	50+	Slight to moderate porotic hyperostosis and periosteal reaction on femur, tibia, and fibula (L/R)	N/A	Moderate development of upper limb, slight to moderate development of lower limb	Slight to moderate degenerative disk disease, several Schmorl's nodes on thoracic and lumbar vertebrae	2 small cranial depression fractures	N/A
13		N/A	4 caries[a]	Moderate to robust development of upper limb, robust development of lower limb	N/A	1 small and medium cranial depression fracture and broken rib with lytic lesion	N/A

Note: Data based on the analysis by Harrod et al. (2013), Vilos et al. (2010), and Thompson et al. (2002). The findings presented support prior research by Owsley et al. (1997) and Schmidt (2006, 2009).
[a]Vilos et al. (2010).
[b]Thompson et al. (2002).

in the nearby town of Virginia City, of an anti-Chinese league that wanted to close Chinese laundries (James et al. 1994:170), and the vote in 1880 that was 17,259 to 183 in support of banning Chinese immigration (Wren 1904:82).

Analysis of demography indicates each individual is an adult male ranging in age from 20 to over 50 years, which matches the profile of the individuals who would have been living in the area at this time. The young age of some individuals at time of death suggests that these men faced hardships that were common among men who, in the United States by 1880, were typically living only into their 30s or 40s (Infoplease 2012).

With this in mind, bioarchaeological analysis goes beyond demographic data and looks at "biocultural identity" (Harrod 2013:70), which involves reconstructing disruptions in growth and development, or identifying the overall well-being of an individual, identifying stress-related degenerative changes to the body, and summarizing trauma and injury patterns (Figure 2). The value of incorporating these other markers on the bones is that they provide a way to overcome the limitations of relying on mortuary context, which is often a reflection of the people who buried an individual and not the person who was buried. Additionally, reconstructing the biocultural identity of each burial allows a better interpretation of the demographic trends seen in this unfortunately small skeletal assemblage.

Ov rh l Well-Being

All the individuals have indicators on their bones that reveal widespread health stress. Four individuals (Burial 7, Burial 9, Burial 10, and Burial 12; 4 of 13, 30.7%) have some form of porotic hyperostosis, which has been consistently shown to develop in childhood (Stuart-Macadam 1985; Walker et al. 2009; J. Morgan 2014). The importance of porotic hyperostosis is that it indicates some form of nutritional stress during childhood that left a lasting impact on the body. This can be seen into adulthood, but can also develop in adulthood (Walker et al. 2009; Crandall and Martin 2012). This suggests that, prior to coming to work on the railroad in America, these men had already experienced some degree of physical stress in their lives. Three individuals

(Burial 2, Burial 10, and Burial 12; 3 of 13, 23.1%) have some form of periosteal reaction, which is a nonspecific indicator of bony irritation. This type of reaction generally arises due to infection and can be seen as a measure of immunocompetence. The fact that 3 of 13 individuals (Burial 2, Burial 10, and Burial 12) exhibit periosteal reaction indicates the likelihood of infection among the Carlin men during a time when tuberculosis was the leading cause of death in the United States. Finally, one individual (Burial 5; 1 of 13, 7.6%) has degenerative changes throughout the body consistent with joint breakdown due to hard labor.

Focusing on nutrition, it appears that, in terms of height, the men at Carlin were shorter than average. This is based on a recent study of the height of people in China between 1880 and 1929 (S. Morgan 2004:210). What Morgan found was that male height averaged between 166.0 and 167.5 cm; in contrast, the average height of individuals from Carlin was 162.8 cm. The difference is interesting, however, because when Morgan looked at subsets of the population, he found that men working in occupations that required less skill but more labor, such as railroad workers, had a stature that was on average 1.1 cm shorter (S. Morgan 2004:211). Stature is largely a function of childhood health. Looking at data collected during a longitudinal study of a cohort of 2,879 people in Great Britain all born in 1946, Wadsworth et al. (2002) found that leg length and, as a result, stature, were positively correlated with nutrition and overall health during the early years of childhood. Taken alongside the evidence of nutritional stress indicated by porotic hyperostosis, the reduced stature of the individuals from Carlin supports the theory that these men had had rough childhoods in China. The importance of evidence of poor health during the earliest years of life is that it may lend support to the historical evidence that people were migrating to the developing world, including the United States, in order to flee the hardship and strife that engulfed Guangdong in the late 1800s.

Stress-Relh edD eg nerh iv C hn g s

Ancient skeletal remains provide evidence of degenerative diseases, such as osteoarthritis, or excess development of muscle attachments

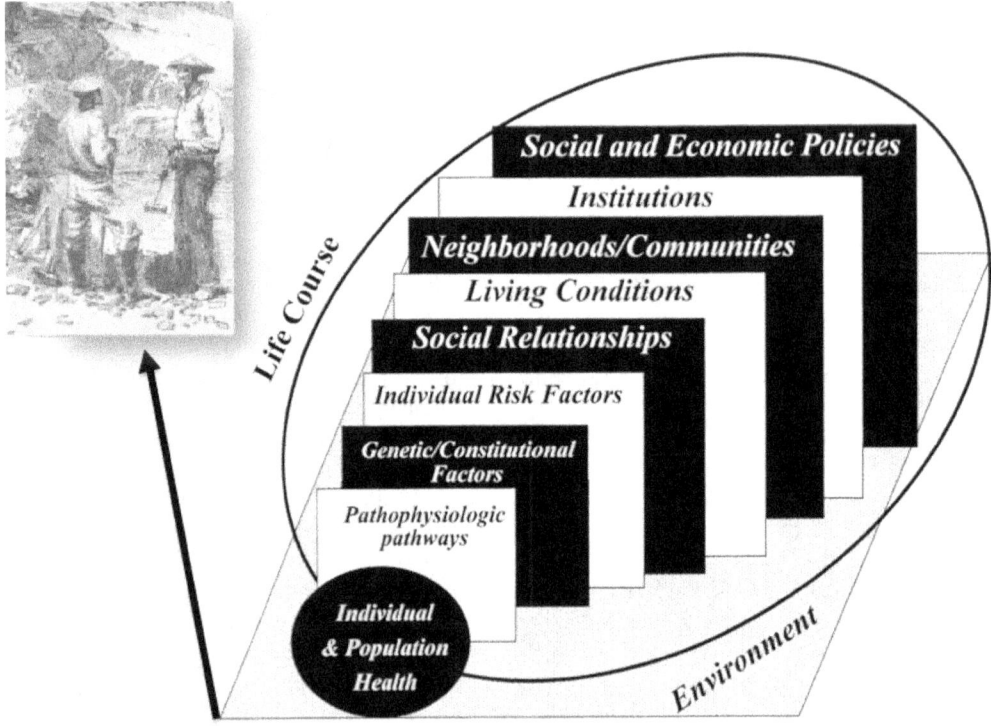

FIGURE 2. Reconstructing the biocultural identity of a Chinese railroad worker. Images modified from *Harper's Weekly* (1867) and Kaplan (2000:43). (Figure by Ryan P. Harrod, 2014.)

(entheses) that commonly affects humans, especially laborers. Analyses of degenerative joint disease, the collapse of vertebrae in the spine, or the buildup of abnormal bone at muscle attachment sites throughout the body can all shed light on the biomechanical stressors faced by past humans (Woo and Pak 2013). When contextualized, these data can be used to understand how subsistence changes, economic shifts, or transformations in industry differentially affect communities (Henderson and Cardoso 2013). The remains can also be useful for identifying patterns of violence and repeated exposure to injury, either accidental or as a result of occupational activities.

Measures of activity at Carlin are also interesting because, in general, the bones of the individuals were not more robust when compared to the mean robusticity of a sample of modern Chinese males. Yet the development of entheses among these individuals was fairly pronounced, which suggests that they were not necessarily engaged in more weight-bearing activities, but doing different, or at least more, activities that put strain on attachment sites in the limbs. This is consistent with the historical accounts of labor endured by the Chinese in a variety of industries, including railroad construction and tunnel mining.

Trauma and Injury

There is evidence of some form of antemortem trauma on each individual from the Carlin cemetery. These injuries range in severity from small divots on the surface of the cranial vault to the complete fracture of both the tibia and fibula. The presence of even slight trauma is significant, as it illustrates that these individuals were a population that was at greater risk of injury due to accidents and violence.

Two of the thirteen buried individuals (Burial 8 and Burial 10; 2 of 13, 15.4%) show evidence of suffering injuries that were severe enough to have caused their deaths. These two burials were the focus of Schmidt's (2009) article about interpersonal violence. Burial 8 has extensive perimortem trauma, but lacks trauma to the head, which led Schmidt (2009), as well as Chung et al. (2005), to conclude that the injuries were likely related to occupational trauma. Burial 10, however, has perimortem trauma to both the body and the head that appears more likely to be the result of violence. The cranial trauma is especially indicative of violence because there is a severe panfacial fracture or trauma that involves numerous bones of the face. Additionally, research on contemporary coroner's reports, conducted by Chung et al. (2005:136–137), discovered an individual of the same approximate age as Burial 10, named Yee Hong Shing, who the coroner reported as killed by a blow to the head.

Ov rh lQ uh ityf L ife

The analysis of health, in addition to the nutritional and activity-related findings, suggests that the Chinese men living in Carlin were working hard and, as a result, showed signs of stress and strain on their bones. They grew up in communities facing nutritional strife and left only to find more hardship, albeit of a different kind. These men had improved diets in the United States; however, trauma and musculoskeletal development data suggest that they were vulnerable to the strains of hard labor and the risk of violent injury, and likely suffered violence as racial minorities during a time of great racial tension.

Particularly interesting are the individuals who have either multiple pathological conditions or a pathology with associated traumatic injuries. For example, Burial 10 and Burial 12 have both porotic hyperostosis and periosteal reactions. The combination of childhood nutritional stress with evidence of adult infection and trauma may not be incidental, as prior developmental pathologies may increase an individual's vulnerability to infection as an adult (Clark et al. 1986; Danese et al. 2007). In terms of the co-occurrence of trauma and pathology, Harrod et al. (2013) found that three burials (3 of 13, 23.1%) had both a pathological condition that likely occurred during their adult lives and some form of traumatic injury that was more likely also to have occurred when they were adults. Burial 5 had osteoarthritis and cranial trauma, while

Burial 10 and Burial 12 had cranial trauma in association with periosteal reactions.

Harrod et al.'s (2013) recent analysis provides evidence that the pattern of skeletal injuries and stress seen among the Carlin men is similar to other ethnographic and historical cases of racialized labor exploitation, the most contemporary example being the greater risk of trauma and inequalities faced by Mexican migrant laborers in the United States today (Holmes 2013). The findings also support the fact that not all Chinese immigrants had the same experience, a finding that Chung et al. (2005) clearly showed in the historical reconstruction.

Conclusionn dF utureP rospects

Revealing the lived experience of the Chinese men who helped to build the railroad networks in the American West is an ongoing project that relies on multiple perspectives and a wealth of interdisciplinary data, including that from the analysis of other Chinese remains. Future bioarchaeological research will continue to contribute to this growing body of knowledge. Author Crandall is currently working on a more holistic project that incorporates a larger regional perspective and cross-cultural data to analyze the overall well-being of these laborers. His research compares the Carlin individuals with data from other Chinese migrant populations, as well as European American individuals from that same general period. The goal of the project is to put health in context, continue examining labor exploitation, and understand how diverse and different life was for Chinese laborers in the United States compared to that of other Americans. Additionally, both authors Crandall and Harrod are interested in looking at burials of individuals who remained in their home communities or whose bodies were sent home to China. Examination of the bones that made it back to China can reveal much about shifting health and identity, and the importance of funerary rituals in maintaining the transnational community across the Pacific.

Outside the research performed by the authors, there is a need for bioarchaeologists interested in asking other questions, including those revealing the more nuanced indications of sociopolitical identity, gender roles, and family relationships among the Chinese men who immigrated to the

United States and other industrialized countries in the 19th century. The focus of this article has been on the experiences of the adult men who contributed to the labor force, and, while this is important, our research only scratches the surface. To understand the lived experience of these Chinese workers it is imperative that the research incorporate more historical records and family stories passed down to descendants. Historical bioarchaeologies, in conjunction with data derived from the human remains, would expand the questions that we archaeologists are able to ask. Perhaps this could allow studies of social differences in labor camps and between merchants who supplied railroad workers with food and the workers themselves. Some potential avenues of research include ascertaining how certain occupations (mining and the use of explosives) compare to more generalized labor, determining whether some individuals did indeed hold higher status than others, and assessing whether the status a person held shifted over time. Perhaps health was bad and trauma severe for all men early on, but their status shifted as permanent communities were established. Bioarchaeological analysis often obscures rapid social transformation, making the incorporation of historical documentation more crucial to understanding whether social status was enough to buffer some individuals from poor health and traumatic injury.

The importance of women and children is woefully under-examined in this project because the burials from Carlin do not include skeletal remains from female Chinese immigrants and their children. While women and children are not often represented in documentary evidence of this period, they still played an important role in Asian American history. Additionally, with the establishment of communities like the one in Carlin came the development of families. Bioarchaeological analyses of childhood and family structure would enable discussions of kinship and U.S. "race" formation to be enriched with empirical data.

The value of continued bioarchaeological research is that it will help to illustrate the complex and often fluid nature of Chinese migration to and labor in the United States at the turn of the century. It will also provide one more line of evidence for reconstructing the history of Chinese immigrants, including

understanding how and why they engaged and incorporated American cultural practices as they settled in the United States.

There are still a lot of unanswered questions regarding the Chinese who emigrated from Guangdong Province, particularly railroad workers. Did they all experience the kinds of injury and violence seen at Carlin? How did laborers experience exploitation differently among labor industries? Did merchants or different types of laborers have different experiences? Where did laborers come from, and how did they move across the United States? What about drug use (e.g., opium) and the use of medications (e.g., mercury)? We argue that bioarchaeology can, at minimum, help answer all of these questions. Research produced thus far has already revealed the lives of this poorly understood group. Future skeletal analyses can only enhance the picture of life on (and off) the rails that is emerging from the work in this issue.

Acknowledgments

The authors would like to thank the organizers of this issue and all the participants at the Chinese Railroad Workers in North America Project Conference held in October 2013. The research and wisdom of the other participants have been invaluable in shaping our research.

References

CARTER, GREGG L.
  1976 Social Demography of the Chinese in Nevada: 1870–1880. *Nevada Historical Society Quarterly* 18(3):85–86.

CHAN, SUSCHENG
  1991 *Asian Americans: An Interpretive History*. Twayne, New York, NY.

CHANG, IRIS
  2003 *The Chinese in America: A Narrative History*. Penguin, New York, NY.

CHEN, YONG
  2000 *Chinese San Francisco, 1850-1943: A Trans-Pacific Community*. Stanford University Press, Stanford, CA.

CHOW, TONY K., JOHN R. LAMBERT, MARK L. WAHLQVIST, AND BRIDGET H. HSU-HAGE
  1995 *Helicobacter pylori* in Melbourne Chinese Immigrants: Evidence for Oral–Oral Transmission via Chopsticks. *Journal of Gastroenterology and Hepatology* 10(5):562–569.

Chung, Sue F., Fred P. Frampton,
and Timothy W. Murphy
2005 Venerate These Bones: Chinese American Funerary and Burial Practices as Seen in Carlin, Elko County, Nevada. In *Chinese American Death Rituals: Respecting the Ancestors*, Sue F. Chung and Pricilla Wegars, editors, pp. 107–146. AltaMira Press, Lanham, MD.

Clark, George A., Nicholas R. Hall,
George J. Armelagos, Gary A. Borkan,
Manohar M. Panjabi, and F. Todd Wetzel
1986 Poor Growth Prior to Early Childhood: Decreased Health and Life-Span in the Adult. *American Journal of Physical Anthropology* 70(2):145–160.

Cohen, Mark N., and George J. Armelagos (editors)
1984 *Paleopathology at the Origins of Agriculture.* Academic Press, Orlando, FL.

Crandall, John J., and Debra L. Martin
2012 On Porotic Hyperostosis and the Interpretation of Hominin Diets, 9 October. PLOS ONE <http://plosone.org/annotation/listThread.action?root=55385>. Accessed 18 February 2015.

Crofutt, George A.
1872 *Crofutt's Trans-Continental Tourist's Guide.* Geo. A. Crofutt, New York, NY.

Danese, Andrea, Carmine M. Pariante, Avshalom
Caspi, Alan Taylor, and Richie Poulton
2007 Childhood Maltreatment Predicts Adult Inflammation in a Life-Course Study. *Proceedings of the National Academy of Sciences* 104(4):1325–1330.

Ellis, Meredith A. B., Christopher W. Merritt,
Shannon A. Novak, and Kelly J. Dixon
2011 The Signature of Starvation: A Comparision of Bone Processing at a Chinese Encampment in Montana and the Donner Party Camp in California. *Historical Archaeology* 45(2):97–112.

Friedman, Lawrence M., and Jack Ladinsky
1967 Social Change and the Law of Industrial Accidents. *Columbia Law Review* 67(1):50–82.

Harper's Weekly
1867 Central Pacific Railroad—Chinese Laborers at Work. *Harper's Weekly* 7 December:772.

Harrod, Ryan P.
2013 *Chronologies of Pain and Power: Violence, Inequality, and Social Control among Ancestral Pueblo Populations (AD 850–1300).* Doctoral dissertation, Department of Anthropology, University of Nevada, Las Vegas. University Microfilms International, Ann Arbor, MI.

Harrod, Ryan P., Jennifer L. Thompson,
and Debra L. Martin
2013 Hard Labor and Hostile Encounters: What Human Remains Reveal about Institutional Violence and Chinese Immigrants Living in Carlin, Nevada (1885–1923). *Historical Archaeology* 46(4):85–111.

Henderson, Charlotte Y., and F. Alves Cardoso
2013 Entheseal Changes and Occupation: Technical and Theoretical Advances and Their Applications. *International Journal of Osteoarchaeology* 23(2):127–134.

Holmes, Seth M.
2013 *Fresh Fruit, Broken Bodies: Migrant Farmworkers in the United States.* University of California Press, Berkeley.

Infoplease
2012 Life Expectancy by Age, 1850–2011. Infoplease <http://www.infoplease.com/ipa/A0005140.html>. Accessed 28 May 2014.

James, Ronald M., Richard D. Adkins,
and Rachel J. Hartigan
1994 Competition and Coexistence in the Laundry: A View of the Comstock. *Western Historical Quarterly* 25(2):164–184.

Kaplan, David
2000 The Darker Side of the "Original Affluent Society." *Journal of Anthropological Research* 56(3):301–324.

Lei, Sean Hsiang-lin
2010 Habituating Individuality: The Framing of Tuberculosis and Its Material Solutions in Republican China. *Bulletin of the History of Medicine* 84(2):248–279.

McKeown, Ashley
1999 Conceptualing Chinese Diasporas, 1984 to 1949. *Journal of Asian Studies* 58(2):306–337.

Morgan, Jennifer A.
2014 The Methodological and Diagnostic Applications of Micro-CT to Paleopathology: A Quantitative Study of Porotic Hyperostosis. Doctoral dissertation, Department of Anthropology, University of Western Ontario, London.

Morgan, Stephen L.
2004 Economic Growth and the Biological Standard of Living in China, 1880–1930. *Economics and Human Biology* 2(2):197–218.

Owsley, Douglas W., Kari Bruwelheide,
Juliet Brundige, David Hunt, Chip Clark,
and Rebecca Redmond
1997 Preliminary Report: Osteology and Paleopathology of the Carlin Chinese Cemetery. Manuscript, National Museum of Natural History, Smithsonian Institution, Washington, DC.

Ross, Douglas E.
2013 Overseas Chinese Archaeology. In *Encyclopedia of Global Archaeology*, Claire Smith, editor, pp. 5675–5686. Springer, New York, NY.

SCHMIDT, RYAN W.
   2006   The Forgotten Chinese Cemetery of Carlin, Nevada:
          A Bioanthropological Assessment. Master's thesis,
          Department of Anthropology, University of Nevada,
          Las Vegas.
   2009   Perimortem Injury in a Chinese American Cemetery:
          Two Cases of Occupational Hazard or Interpersonal
          Violence. *Internet Journal of Biological Anthropology*
          3(2). Internet Scientific Publications <https://ispub
          .com/IJBA/3/2/13579>. Accessed 19 February 2015.

SCHMIDT, RYAN W., NORIKO SEGUCHI, AND JENNIFER L.
THOMPSON
   2011   Chinese Immigrant Population History in North
          America Based on Craniometric Diversity.
          Anthropological Science 119(1):9−19.

STUART-MACADAM, PATRICIA
   1985   Porotic Hyperostosis: Representative of a Childhood
          Condition. *American Journal of Physical Anthropology*
          66(4):391−398.

TAKAKI, RONALD
   1998   *Strangers from a Different Shore: A History of Asian
          Americans.* Back Bay, New York, NY.

THOMPSON, JENNIFER L., BERNARDO T. ARRIAZA,
A. GALLEGOS, SUE F. CHUNG, VICKI CASSMAN,
J. CONLOGUE, AND R. BECKETT
   2002   A Preliminary Report on the Chinese Immigrants
          from Carlin, Nevada. Paper presented at the Annual
          Meeting of the Nevada Archaeological Association,
          Reno.

TÜCHSEN, FINN, HARALD HANNERZ, AND SØREN
SPANGENBERG
   2005   Mortality and Mobidity among Bridge and Tunnel
          Construction Workers Who Worked Long Hours and
          Long Days Constructing the Great Belt Fixed Link.
          *Scandinavian Journal of Work, Environment, and
          Health* 31(S2):22−26.

VILOS, JAMIE D., JENNIFER L. THOMPSON,
AND DEBRA L. MARTIN
   2010   Dental Morphology and Pathologies of Chinese
          Immigrants from Historic Carlin, Nevada. *American
          Journal of Physical Anthropology* 14(S50):236.

VOSS, BARBARA L., AND REBECCA ALLEN
   2008   Overseas Chinese Archaeology: Historical
          Foundations, Current Reflections, and New
          Directions. *Historical Archaeology* 42(3):5−28.

WADSWORTH, MICHAEL E. J., R. J. HARDY, A. A. PAUL,
S. F. MARSHALL, AND T. J. COLE
   2002   Leg and Trunk Length at 43 Years in Relation to
          Childhood Health, Diet and Family Circumstances;
          Evidence from the 1946 National Birth Cohort.
          International Journal of Epidemiology 31(2):383−390.

WALKER, PHILLIP L., RHONDA R. BATHURST,
REBECCA RICHMAN, THOR GJERDRUM,
AND VALERIE A. ANDRUSHKO
   2009   The Causes of Porotic Hyperstosis and Cribra
          Orbitalia: A Reappraisal of the Iron-Deficiency-
          Anemia Hypothesis. *American Journal of Physical
          Anthropology* 139(2):109–125.

WOO, EUN J., AND SUNYOUNG PAK
   2013   Degenerative Joint Diseases and Enthesopathies
          in a Joseon Dynasty Population from Korea.
          HOMO—Journal of Comparative Human Biology
          64(2):104−119.

WREN, THOMAS (EDITOR)
   1904   *A History of the State of Nevada: Its Resources and
          People.* Lewis, New York, NY.

YUNG, JUDY, GORDON H. CHANG,
AND HIM M. LAI (EDITORS)
   2006   *Chinese American Voices: From the Gold Rush to the
          Present.* University of California Press, Berkeley.

RYAN PATRICK HARROD
DEPARTMENT OF ANTHROPOLOGY,
UNIVERSITY OF ALASKA ANCHORAGE
⒫   ROVIDENCE DRIVE
ANCHORAGE, AK ⓿

JOHN JOSEPH CRANDALL
DEPARTMENT OF ANTHROPOLOGY
UNIVERSITY OF NEVADA, LAS VEGAS
⒮   . MARYLAND PARKWAY, MAILSTOP ⓿
LAS VEGAS, NV ⓿   ⓿

Part VI:
Kilns and Metallurgy

PRUDENCE M. RICE
SARA L. VAN BECK

The Spanish Colonial Kiln Tradition of Moquegua, Peru

ABSTRACT

Twenty-six kiln locations have been identified in association with Spanish colonial *bodegas* (wineries) in the Moquegua valley of southern Peru. The kilns are variable in size, design, and construction, and their differences may relate to the two probable functions of the kilns: firing earthenware vessels used in fermenting and transporting wine and brandy, and calcining calcium minerals or other materials. The Moquegua kilns show similarities to the *hornos árabes* (Moorish kilns) of Spain, as well as some features common to Spanish technological transfer in the New World.

Introduction

Spanish settlement of Peru, in the southern part of their colonial empire, began in the early to middle 16th century. Colonists established themselves in highland river valleys and along the coast of the western Andes with an economic base similar in many ways to that of their homeland. Grapes, olives, wheat, sheep, goats, and cattle formed the agricultural basis for settlement in this region, along with sugar cane. One valley where Spanish colonial agro-industrial development occurred—the Moquegua valley—has been the focus of recent historical archaeology investigations.

Moquegua is located on the Osmore River, which flows southwestward through mountainous desert terrain into the Pacific Ocean. The "Moquegua valley" is the central section of the Osmore, formed at the confluence of three tributaries, where the steep, narrow rivercourse levels out slightly between 1,500 and 1,000 m elevation. Although this mid-valley sector is less than 30 km long, it represents the largest area of arable land in the drainage. The town of Moquegua was founded near the upper end of this valley in 1541, and by

Historical Archaeology, 1993, 27(4):65–81.
Permission to reprint required.

the end of the century at least four *haciendas* with vineyards had been established by Spanish colonial settlers. Because the soils and dry climate of the area were well suited to the growing of grapes, Moquegua quickly developed into a viticultural center, producing large quantities of wine and brandy for supply to the Potosí silver mines in Upper Peru (modern Bolivia) (Brown 1986).

The Moquegua Bodegas Project, directed by the senior author from 1985–1990, was an investigation of the remains of the colonial *bodegas*, or winery sites, in the Moquegua valley (Rice 1987a; Rice and Ruhl 1989; Rice and Smith 1989). The project included survey and recording of surface remains, which comprise adobe buildings, auxiliary structures, and large fermentation jars (*tinajas*), and excavations at four of the 130 *bodega* locations identified in the valley (Figure 1). One of the "auxiliary structures" associated with the Moquegua viticultural agro-industry—kilns—was the subject of a study undertaken by the junior author in 1989 (Van Beck 1990, 1991). This study had the objectives of describing a sample of the kilns and their construction in greater detail, identifying traces of indigenous Peruvian influences in this introduced technology, and evaluating the functions of kilns in the economic operations of the *bodegas*. Because the Moquegua *bodegas* did not incorporate bricks or tiles into their construction, the authors initially assumed that these kilns were used to fire the earthenware *tinajas* and *botijas* (i.e., "olive jars") used in transporting wine and brandy. Variations in size, construction, and other features of the kilns, however, plus analysis of residues in the interior of two of them, suggested that some kilns may have functioned in calcining calcium minerals.

Kiln Technology: Spanish, Spanish Colonial, and Peruvian

Spanish kiln technology had its origins in Near Eastern and Mediterranean traditions, carried to the Iberian peninsula by early maritime trading cultures (e.g., Phoenicians, Greeks, Romans). These groups brought with them other aspects of

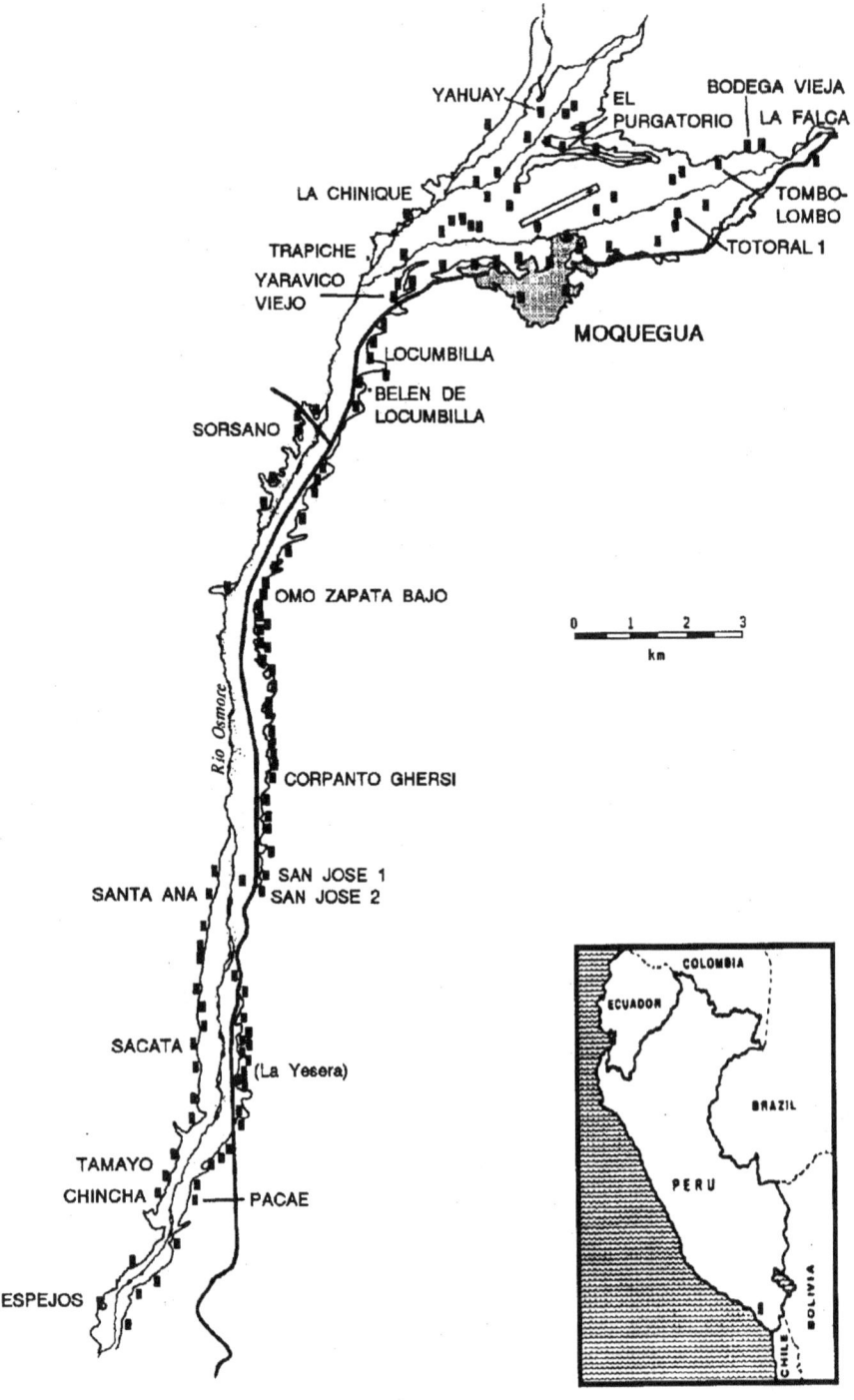

FIGURE 1. The Moquegua valley. Small black rectangles mark the 130 *bodega* locations identified in the valley. The named *bodegas* are locations of kilns.

Mediterranean culture, such as *amphorae* and agricultural products, and know-how, including grapes and wine-making. By the late 15th century, Spain's kiln technology was a hybrid with Iberian, Roman, and Moorish influences (Rhodes 1981: 55–56; Lister and Lister 1987:51–53; Mossman and Selsor 1987).

Remains of a few medieval and earlier kilns have been identified in Spain, but they have not been well described, and researchers often disagree as to the cultural origin of some of the features and how the kilns were fired. Kilns in Spain's colonial empire also reveal a mixture of traits. Roman influences (McWhirr 1979) can be recognized in a Spanish colonial kiln at Mission San Antonio in California (Costello 1985), but this was a rectangular kiln built of fired brick and used in firing construction tiles. As such, it is not directly comparable to the round, unfired adobe kilns of Moquegua, where tiles were not used extensively in construction—except occasionally for flooring.

For purposes of comparison with the kilns of Moquegua, it is probably most useful to highlight the Moorish ceramic kilns, or *hornos árabes,* of Spain. These are described (Rhodes 1981:55; Lister and Lister 1987:51–52) as domed, circular updraft kilns, built of bricks, stones, sherds, and clay, with diameters of 2–5 m, and height of 3 m. The firebox is usually large, to accommodate the bulky brush used as fuel, and is often partially buried in a hillside to support the walls and provide insulation, although completely above-ground structures are known. The perforated ware chamber floor is made of stone or clay, supported by arches or a central pillar. Rhodes (1981:56) illustrated a modern kiln in Egypt, similar to the medieval Spanish kiln, that has a shallow open area in front and a tunnel-like entrance to the firebox for stoking. The Listers (1987:51–52) suggest that the Spanish kilns achieved a firing temperature of approximately 1,050°C, and were probably fueled with agricultural by-products such as olive tree or grapevine prunings, olive oil-pressing by-products, or brush.

Some modern Spanish kilns provide analogs to those of Moquegua. In Villarobledo and Colmenar de Oreja, kilns used to fire huge earthenware *tinajas* are still standing, although the *tinajas* themselves

are no longer manufactured. In Colmenar, five large square kilns with domed roofs were noted, roughly 8 m on a side and 6.5 m in height, with subterranean fireboxes extending about 3 m below ground (Rice 1987b). It is assumed that these kilns were fired in a manner similar to those at Villarobledo, where *tinajas* were placed mouth-to-mouth and end-to-end in the kiln, the spaces between them being filled with smaller vessels (Cabasa 1990:48). Firing lasted from 10 to 24 hours.

An ethnographic survey of modern South America (Litto 1976) indicated that although most pottery firings were done in open "clamp firings," some ceramic kilns are similar to Spanish and Moorish designs. In Pucará, high in the southern Peruvian *altiplano* near Lake Titicaca, two types of updraft kilns were noted. One is a simple double-chambered circular structure of adobe brick, with a semi-subterranean firebox and arches supporting the floor of the ware chamber; it is loaded from the top through an entrance cut into the wall (Figure 2; Litto 1976:37–40). The second is also a double-chambered updraft type, but the circular chamber is surrounded by a square structure, and has an outer stairway for top-loading; the firebox has a double-arched entrance and is stoked from an "anteroom" (Litto 1976:40).

In the prehispanic New World, where it was traditionally believed that kilns were unknown, several recent archaeological projects in Mesoamerica and the Andes have uncovered evidence of pottery kilns dating well before the arrival of the Spaniards. In northern Peru, for example, more than 50 pottery kilns dating to the 8th century B.C. have been found in the Leche River valley; while a variety of types are represented, most are partially subterranean, double-chambered updraft kilns (Shimada 1989–1990:19–20). Prehispanic Peru also had a sophisticated metallurgical pyrotechnology, although few prehispanic ore-smelting furnaces have been identified in the Andes. The distinctive *huaira* or "wind furnace" reported by early Spanish chroniclers is of unknown antiquity; it is a small, circular furnace commonly located on windy slopes of hills to take advantage of strong prevailing winds (Peele 1893; Lechtman 1976:7–8).

The technology of lime calcination (Vitruvius

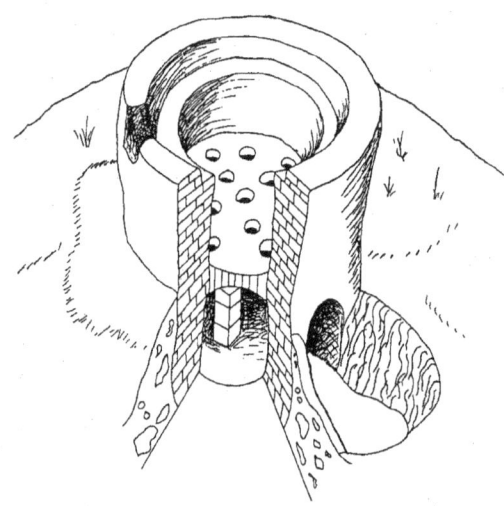

FIGURE 2. Cutaway drawing of a double-chambered updraft kiln in Pucará, Peru (after Litto 1976:38). Built into a hillside, the kiln has a perforated brick floor supported by brick arches, a semisubterranean firing chamber, a pit (*lower right*) to facilitate stoking the fire, and a niche in the upper wall for easier top-loading. The diameter of the firing chamber is 1.2 m.

Pollio 1960) has been less investigated archaeologically than has the firing of pottery. Lime kilns have been found at several mission sites in the Southwest U.S. and California (Costello 1977: 26): set into hillsides, they may be single- or double-chambered. A kiln for calcining lime, probably dating to the Spanish colonial period, has been investigated at Coamo, Puerto Rico; it is a circular, single-chambered updraft kiln, 5.6 m high with an internal diameter of approximately 4.5 m (Eikenholz 1983). It was constructed on a hillside and partially supported by earth, with the open face supported by two buttresses, and the mouth facing into the prevailing wind.

The Moquegua Kilns: Overview

Of the 26 Moquegua kiln locations, 23 are remains of standing kilns while one buried kiln was revealed in excavations; two other locations of former kilns were identified by informants, one of these being confirmed by burned deposits in a bulldozer cut. (Another kiln, referred to as *Fundición* kiln, was noted on a *hacienda* on the coast near Ilo. It was included in the kiln study and descriptions [Van Beck 1991:97–98], but is not included in the present discussion because it is outside the *bodegas* district of the Moquegua valley proper.)

Time and logistic constraints precluded visiting, measuring, mapping, and excavating at all 23 sites of standing kilns in the Moquegua valley. Twelve kilns were selected for study on the basis of degree of preservation and ease of access, and were visited and photographed during the 1989 kiln project; two kilns were also test excavated. Observations on the kilns included: details of construction technique, including number and thickness of "tiers" (multiple concentric courses of varying height) and buttresses; number of mouths and their arch construction; data on adobes, including patterns of courses, size, and inclusions; kind and location of repairs; presence of plastering; and general condition. Measurements included internal and external diameters and height; where possible two measurements were recorded to establish the internal diameter of the firing chamber, taken at approximately 1.25 m above current ground level. Wall thickness was recorded at the present top of the chamber wall. Orientation was established by compass. In addition, the ground plans of four kilns—Tamayo, Omo Zapata Bajo, Yahuay, and Espejos 1—were drawn using nails, string, 25-m tapes, and two protractors (a functioning transit was not available).

Location

The 26 kiln locations identified in the Moquegua valley are shown in Figure 1. Kilns are found throughout the valley, although more of them lie in the less accessible western and extreme northern parts of the valley, perhaps as a consequence of preservation. Four *bodegas*—La Chinique, Sorsano, Chincha, and Espejos—had two kilns; the remainder had one, or at least only one that is identifiable today. Given the extensive damage to the *bodegas* by modern occupants and constructional activities, it is not unlikely that other kilns once existed in the valley but have since been destroyed. Additionally, some very early kilns may be buried, as at Locumbilla, as discussed below.

Seventeen of the 26 kilns are built against hillsides and/or situated in *quebradas* (small pockets or extensions of the bottomlands at the margins of the valley); four kilns are situated out in the open, three of these atop the bluffs that edge the valley. Placement on or into hillsides is a useful strategy—seen earlier in both Roman and Moorish kilns as well as in the Andean wind-furnace for smelting—for strengthening and insulating the walls, thus increasing heat-retaining capabilities, and for capturing prevailing winds. Hillside settings also facilitate loading and unloading fired materials from the top of the kiln.

The siting of the kilns within the valley affects their functioning, because of their position relative to changing winds. Moquegua's location on the western slopes of the Andes means that the area experiences wind cycles typical of mountain regions, with daily "valley breezes" that blow upslope (or from the south, in Moquegua) after midmorning and nightly "mountain breezes" that flow downslope. The alignment of kilns relative to these prevailing winds, together with the size and position of their mouths, influences the draw of air for combustion and hence the amount of heat entering the kiln. In theory, the kilns' mouths should be positioned to capture these winds, in order to enhance combustion and economize on the use of scarce fuels in the valley. The precise firing schedules of the kilns are not known, but surely long firings of 24 hours or more were needed to fire the large, thick-walled *tinajas* and *botijas*. It is not surprising, therefore, that the largest kilns have two or more mouths placed to catch both the strong prevailing daytime (southerly, upvalley) winds as well as breezes flowing downhill along the slopes of the *quebradas*.

Design and Construction

The Moquegua kilns are all round, updraft kilns built of unfired adobes typically set in all-header courses. Some of them incorporate rounded river cobbles as part of the construction material, most commonly as exterior facings on the lower construction tiers and buttresses, but also occasionally as foundation courses below the adobe walls. Three of the four kilns that were excavated (Rice 1994) were constructed in or above depressions in the underlying sterile subsoil.

Mouth and arch construction of the Moquegua kilns is of poor quality by today's standards, as many recommendations for modern kiln construction (e.g., Rhodes 1981:151–156) were not observed. For example, the adobes were typically set unevenly, and specially formed adobes functioning as skewbacks or keystones were absent; instead, different thicknesses of mortar or even fragments of *tinajas* served these functions. Also, relatively flat arches (i.e., having greater span per unit rise) were placed over broad spans, contradicting modern structural advice. This practice makes for a structurally weak arch at a place in the kiln—a break in the continuous wall—that is already weakened. Nevertheless, despite these design flaws the Moquegua kilns seem to have been strong enough to fulfill their intended purpose.

The kilns are highly variable in size and construction detail, but this variability may be more apparent than real, and could have several causes: the small number of kilns surviving, changes over time, possible re-use, or a lack of strong tradition or rules governing their construction. Two groups of kilns, large and small, can be distinguished (Table 1).

Large kilns have interior chamber diameters averaging 5.47 m (range 4.6–7.3 m; n = 8) and generally thick walls averaging 2.6 m (range 0.50–5.05 m; n = 7). They are often constructed with multiple tiers and are heavily buttressed; buttresses are mostly of runner-header construction. Clay plaster lines the interior firing chamber of four kilns, and the exterior of three. Most kilns are built into hillsides or in *quebradas*, although two kilns are free-standing out in the open atop bluffs. None of the kilns has a permanent roof, and only Bodega Vieja kiln has any indications of a roof having once been present. Most of the kilns appear to have had multiple mouths, although frequently

TABLE 1
MEASUREMENTS (IN METERS) OF MOQUEGUA KILNS

Kilns	Height	Interior Diameter	Wall Thickness	Volume[a]	No. of Mouths
Large Kilns					
Yahuay	7.05	5.30	2.00	156.4	3
El Purgatorio					
La Falca[b]					
Bodega Vieja[b]					1+
Trapiche[b]					
Locumbilla	3.47	4.60	.40	15.95	?
Belén de Locumbilla	1.75	5.00	5.05	35.0	1+
Sorsano 2		7.30	.50		
Omo Zapata Bajo	4.62	5.00	1.10	75.2	2
Corpanto Ghersi		5.30	3.30		
Tamayo	4.90	5.25	1.50	107.1	1+
Espejos 2	4.10	6.00	2.18	116.3	2
Mean ($\bar{X}$)		5.4	2.0		
Small Kilns					
Totoral[b]					
La Chinique 1	3.20	2.45	1.20	15.1	1
Sorsano 1	2.56	2.30	0.55	10.8	
San Jose 2[b]					
Santa Ana	1.16	1.98	0.66	3.8	1
Sacata	1.87	2.38	0.67	8.3	1
Chincha 1	2.21		0.60		1+
Chincha 2	2.87	2.60	1.97	15.2	1+
Pacae	1.59	2.45	0.67	7.5	1
Espejos 1	3.67	1.98	2.62	11.3	2
Mean ($\bar{X}$)		2.3	1.1		

Note. Kiln locations not visited in 1989 survey include: Tombolombo (kiln destroyed), La Chinique 2, Yaravico Viejo (kiln destroyed), and San Jose 1.

[a]Minimum volumes of the kilns calculated on the basis of existing measurements of height using the formula for the volume of a cylinder:

$$V = \pi r^2 H$$

[b]Not measured

Source: Data from Van Beck (1991:Appendix 1).

the collapsed walls of the kiln make it difficult to determine.

Two large kilns appear to be double-chambered: the excavated kiln at Locumbilla, and possibly the kiln at Bodega Vieja. In contrast, most of the large kilns lack evidence of a floor at the base of the ware chamber, and so are assumed to be single-chambered—although it is possible that floors originally existed in the kilns and are now destroyed. In these presumed single-chambered kilns, one or more of the mouths functioned as fireboxes. This notion is supported by soot on the sides of some of the mouths, vitrification of the inner chamber walls around the opening of the mouths, and the position of the mouths themselves, one of which is oriented into the dominant wind to improve combustion efficiency.

Smaller kilns have interior chamber diameters averaging 2.3 m (range 1.98–2.60 m; n = 7); wall thickness averaged 1.1 m (range 0.55–2.62 m; n = 8). Unlike the multi-mouthed large kilns, these smaller kilns usually have only one small arched entrance, which is oriented perpendicular to (rather than into) the prevailing daily wind. Except for Espejos 1, small kilns are usually built with only one construction tier (indeed, often with only a single thickness of adobes) and only one has buttresses. All these characteristics—position of the single mouth, thinner walls, lack of external supports—suggest lower draft, less thermal stress on the adobes, slower rates of fuel consumption, and lower firing temperatures.

Functions

Little in the way of surface remains—such as artifact scatters—was found around these kilns that would divulge their use. Surface waster deposits and sherds were virtually non-existent, owing, no doubt, to the heavy occupation of the *bodega* sites by people and animals since colonial times, and the continued use of adjacent agricultural fields. Only the Belén de Locumbilla kiln area had surface scatters of *botija* fragments and overfired adobe fragments around the kiln. Buried waster deposits were noted around the Locumbilla kiln.

Differences in size as well as other details of the kilns' construction led to inferences of functional differences (without secure dating of these kilns, however, one cannot eliminate the possibility that they could also represent design changes over time). These authors thus hypothesize that the large kilns in Moquegua were primarily used in firing ceramics and the smaller kilns—whose constructional characteristics are better suited to low temperature firings—may have been used in calcining. It is possible, too, that the kilns were used for both activities, and ceramic kilns could have been re-used as calcination kilns after *tinajas* and *botijas* ceased to be made in the valley (compare Costello 1985:142).

Within the category of large kilns, the two designs, single- and double-chambered, may be related to the size of the ceramics to be fired in them. Small vessels, such as *botijas*, could have been top-loaded and fired in double-chambered kilns with underlying fireboxes. The large size of the *tinajas*, on the other hand, with diameters of ca. 1

m, suggests that these heavy vessels would have been fired in the large kilns with external fireboxes. These huge vessels are probably too large and heavy to be top-loaded, and instead could have been loaded into the lower portion of the kilns' firing chambers by carrying them in a cloth sling through a wide mouth in the side of the kiln. In general, the kilns' mouths have a span of 2 m or more (Van Beck 1991:148), ample space for a moving crew to carry a vessel inside. Once inside, the *tinajas* may have been stacked two-high, as in modern Spanish kilns (Cabasa 1990:48; see also Voyatzoglou 1973:16 for Greece), or in a single tier on the floor of the kiln. The firing capacity for *tinajas* was limited, as a kiln with a ware chamber diameter of 5 m could probably have held only five to seven *tinajas* in one level.

In actual practice, both vessels may have been fired together. After *tinajas* were in place, smaller vessels such as *botijas* could be placed in, around, and on top of them, being loaded from side entrances and the top. When loading was finished, a temporary wall would have been constructed across the loading mouth in order to seal it for firing, and a temporary roof built on top with adobes and sherds. This wall and temporary roof would have been dismantled after the kiln had cooled in order to unload the fired wares.

The small kilns, which generally had thin walls and a single mouth, are hypothesized to have been used primarily in calcining calcium minerals, a process in which rock, such as limestone or gypsum, and fuel are layered in a kiln and heated to remove chemically-combined water and produce a fine white powder. Gypsum deposits outcrop in thin strata along hillsides in the southern part of the valley; local geological sources of calcite have not been identified. White mineral deposits were found in numerous kilns, small and large, and two samples were analyzed by x-ray diffraction (Van Beck 1991:180–182, Appendices 2, 3). Both were found to be products of calcining calcium minerals. The sample from the small kiln at Pacae was identified as anhydrite (from gypsum) while the sample from the Espejos 1 kiln seemed closer to Portland cement (the original mineral may have been calcite rather than gypsum).

The uses of the calcined minerals—whether gypsum, calcite, or some other mineral—in Moquegua are unknown, although there are numerous possibilities (Rice 1994). Both lime and gypsum can be used in making constructional mortars, and plastered walls and floors are found at the *bodegas*. In agriculture, lime and gypsum are useful as soil additives to enhance fertilizer uptake and alter soil pH. Gypsum and lime also could have had specific uses in viticulture. At Locumbilla, *botija* fragments were recovered with their mouths stoppered with plugs of a white lime- or gypsum-like substance. Powdered gypsum may be sprinkled over grapes before or after crushing, an ancient process known as "plastering." Known from Roman times, plastering is associated with sherry-making in southern Spain (Amerine et al. 1972:411–412).

Unfortunately, the dates of construction and use of most of these kilns are unknown, and thus chronological and functional variations in kiln design cannot be differentiated. On the basis of what is known about the history of the wine industry in Moquegua, however, it is unlikely that kilns were constructed to fire ceramics after the mid- to late 19th century. In the 1860s and 1870s Moquegua experienced several upheavals that devastated the vineyards and wineries, including an earthquake, war with Chile, and a phylloxera epidemic. After these disasters, earthenware vessels for fermentation and storage began to be replaced with wooden barrels (Kuon Cabello 1981:180–181, 381, 394). Calcining, on the other hand, could have continued into the 20th century as needs for lime and gypsum likely did not disappear, and abandoned ceramic kilns may have been re-used in calcination. None of these kilns is a recent construction, as kilns used in Moquegua today are square or rectangular, and are used in firing bricks or in calcining gypsum as at La Yesera in the southern valley.

Fuel

Substantial quantities of fuel would have been necessary to fire the kilns. Although kiln firings are more thermally efficient than open firings, much of the heat generated in firing a kilnload of ceramics is used just to heat the structure itself or is lost through radiation and convection. The types of fuel that were available in colonial Moquegua were relatively limited, given that the hills surrounding the valley were bare of vegetation and most of the valley itself was devoted to agricultural use. No samples of the charcoal in the kilns were analyzed to give an idea of the fuel used to fire the kilns, but several logical guesses can be made. Cane growing along the river edges could have been used, although it is valued for roofing buildings. Animal dung is another possibility, suggested by ethnographic practice (Litto 1976:34, 40). The modern gypsum kiln at La Yesera *bodega* is fired with *yareta* (*Azorela yareta*), a resinous shrub of the high mountains. Agricultural by-products, including grapevine prunings and grape pressings, are a choice that seems more likely on the basis of analogies with firing practices in Mediterranean grape-growing areas. Also, two Frenchmen sent by the Peruvian government to study the failing Moquegua wine industry around the turn of the century reported the use of grape prunings as well as branches of trees growing in the valley bottomland as fuel for brandy distilleries (Chabert and Dubosc 1905:37).

The Moquegua Kilns: Examples

The following descriptions provide information on 12 of the best preserved kilns of the Moquegua bodegas. The other 14 kilns in the valley are noted on Figure 1 and Table 1, but without detailed descriptions in the text. Kilns are described here as they are located from north to south in the valley.

Yahuay Kiln

The kiln at Yahuay *bodega* (Van Beck 1991: 114–128) is a large, well-preserved, single-chambered, free-standing structure (Figure 3) located in a cornfield to the northeast of the *bodega* complex, beyond an open corral area. It has two construction tiers, five buttresses flanking its three mouths, and cobblestone facing on the lower tier. It is possible

FIGURE 3. The large, relatively well-preserved, free-standing kiln at Yahuay *bodega*, view to the east. The large piles of adobe debris are from collapse of the buttresses flanking the mouth visible in this picture. (Photo by the authors.)

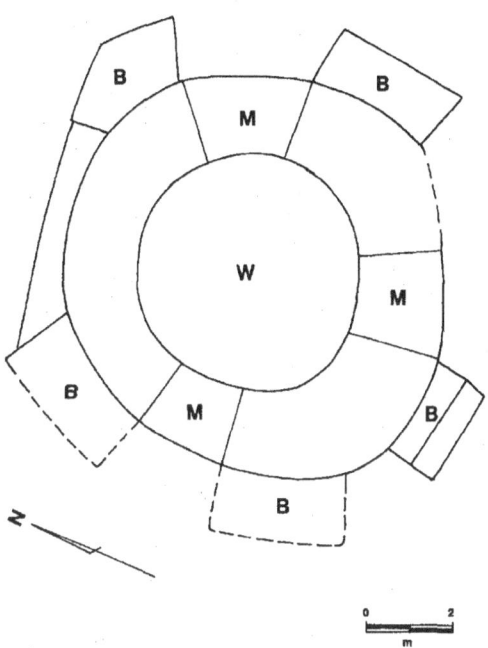

FIGURE 4. Plan drawing of the Yahuay kiln: B, buttress; M, mouth; W, ware chamber.

that a stairway exists by the east mouth, but it is in very poor condition; because it begins about 1.25 m above ground surface, rather than at ground level, it may simply be an artifact of selective removal of adobes. Two large mouths open to the south and east. A third mouth, double-arched and with a small span open to the west, effectively constitutes a tunnel through the thick kiln wall and between flanking buttresses (Figure 4). It creates a strong draft by capturing the prevailing afternoon winds. In general, the arches of this kiln were well constructed, and made use of keystones. The walls comprise three concentric tiers of adobes laid in an all-header pattern; in some places the outermost tier has separated from the central one, presumably as a consequence of thermal stress, or perhaps from the not-infrequent earth tremors of the region.

Although its large size and construction suggest that the Yahuay kiln originally functioned as a ceramic kiln, excavations revealed deposits suggesting that its most recent activity might have been in calcining. This accords with information supplied by the present inhabitants of the *bodega*, who referred to it as a lime kiln. Two adjacent test units were excavated, one outside and one inside the chamber. Interior deposits in the lower 50 cm in-

cluded layers of alternating charcoal/carbon and white powdery material (samples were not taken for analysis). Unfortunately, carbon samples taken from the kiln were insufficient for radiocarbon dating so these deposits remain undated. Excavations in the *bodega* itself yielded primarily 18th-century artifacts (Smith 1990, 1991).

Bodega Vieja Kiln

Built against a hillside, the kiln at Bodega Vieja (Van Beck 1991:95–97) has about half of its structure preserved (Figure 5). The kiln is estimated to be 2.2 m in height, and about 5 m exterior diameter (it was not measured). Bodega Vieja is the only kiln with evidence of roof construction remaining: four courses of headers angle inward over the wall of the ware chamber. Seven vents are visible at the top of the chamber wall, just at the

FIGURE 5. The interior of the Bodega Vieja kiln, showing the incurving adobes marking a domed roof over the ware chamber. View to the northeast. (Photo by the authors.)

FIGURE 6. The western half of the Locumbilla *bodega* kiln as revealed in 1989 excavations. The burned adobe floor of the ware chamber with its lines of flues is surrounded by a thin wall of unfired clay. Cobble paving covers fill in the area to the north and west around the kiln wall. (Photo by the authors.)

join with the roof, and would have helped increase draw. Because the adobes and mortar used in the roof differ from those in the walls, the roof appears to be a late addition. The interior walls show "luting," or plastering. The one existing mouth faces northeast, into the *quebrada*, with buttresses on either side. A second mouth may have existed in the part of the wall that is now destroyed. Although a floor was not clearly visible, it is possible that Bodega Vieja kiln was double-chambered.

La Chinique Kiln 1

The kiln at La Chinique (Van Beck 1991:175–176) is located on a hillside in a *quebrada*. It appears to have only one mouth which is at the upper level of the slope; the chamber of the kiln lies downslope. This mouth faces southeast, more-or-less perpendicular to the prevailing winds, but would capture downvalley, nightly breezes. The kiln has a stone buttressing tier around the lower exterior. Compared to other kilns in Moquegua, the La Chinique kiln is unusual in having a square base with a circular structure above; in this it is similar to a modern kiln used at Pucará in the highlands (Litto 1976:39). (It also faintly resembles the smaller kiln described by the mid-16th-century Italian writer Piccolpasso [1980:89] for use

in firing luster wares.) The upper part of the interior chamber seems to slope slightly inward, partially enclosing the chamber, and this may have increased draft, improving heat circulation. Indeed, the entire interior was vitrified.

Locumbilla Kiln

The kiln at Locumbilla *bodega* was discovered during excavations in a low area at the northern part of the site, at the margins of the architectural complex (Rice 1988; Rice and Smith 1989:47; Van Beck 1991:99–114). Excavations (see Rice 1994 for details) revealed the western half of a large, roughly circular ware chamber of a double-chambered kiln (Figure 6). The kiln was constructed in a large pit, roughly 6 m in north-south diameter by 3 m deep and gently sloping in the east, that had been excavated into sterile, rocky subsoil. Much of the kiln would have been situated below ground level. Constructed of unfired adobes, the ware chamber walls were only 95 cm high above the surface of the chamber floor and only 40 cm thick. This wall probably stood considerably higher originally, but it may have been intentionally cut at the time the kiln was abandoned. The interior diameter was approximately 4.6 m. No in situ clay plastering was found on the surface of this wall, although several sections of fire-reddened adobe facing had fallen into the chamber, as had many burned adobes. No evidence of roofing was found.

The floor of the ware chamber was constructed of adobes set on their sides in clay mortar. Three lines of round flues in the chamber floor were spaced approximately 30 cm apart; between the flues the floor was well-worn, and may have provided a walking area for loading and unloading the kiln. The floor was supported by three parallel modified bond-type arches spanning the lower chamber or firebox from north to south resting on low walls 1.1 m in height. The firebox was 2.2 m high, its floor being the sterile rocky substratum of the site. Thin deposits of carbon, white powdery material, and burned soil lay on a thin layer of sand on the firebox floor, and the rest of the chamber was filled with damp clay containing burned adobe fragments and few artifacts. A charcoal sample from under the firing floor (Beta-33725) yielded an age of 230 ± 70 ^{14}C years B.P., calibrated to A.D. 1656 (Stuiver and Becker 1986).

Around the northern and western sides of the kiln, and perhaps around parts of the southern side as well, the surface of the subsoil and fill surrounding the upper kiln walls was paved with a layer of large rounded river cobbles. This paving facilitated access to the ware chamber for loading and unloading. The eastern edge of the kiln pit served as the stoking area. It lacked the cobble paving, and instead, the floor of the pit sloped down (westward) to the floor of the firebox at 3.5 m b.s. The Locumbilla kiln may have resembled the kiln at Tamayo in having a short (3.5 m) tunnel leading into the firebox on the east side. Although considerably shorter than the Tamayo kiln tunnel, the Locumbilla tunnel is similarly oriented to capture downslope breezes. Outside the mouth of this tunnel, thin ashy layers overlay sterile subsoil, probably from raking ash out of the firebox during periodic cleanings. Waster deposits were noted in test pits all around the kiln, especially to the east. Considerable effort was expended in excavating test units around the kiln in hopes of finding evidence of pottery workshops or other activity areas related

to use of the kiln—perhaps datable—but these efforts were unsuccessful.

Belén de Locumbilla Kiln

This kiln is situated approximately midway between two *bodegas*, Belén de Locumbilla and Gaston, on the hill of a *quebrada* on the eastern midvalley (Van Beck 1991:93–95). Three types of clay are mined nearby, and part of the kiln is sometimes used today for firing adobes, which at the time of the visit were stacked against the southern wall. The kiln is in poor repair, although four tiers and two buttresses could be distinguished. Both interior and exterior surfaces had a clay plaster coating. Although a mouth is presumed to have existed on the east side, the only mouth visible today faces to the west between two buttresses, capturing the afternoon winds blowing up the *quebrada*. The kiln was unusual in having an exterior ramp constructed of adobes that sloped downward toward the western mouth. Vitrified adobes and occasional wasters were found northwest of this ramp.

Omo Zapata Bajo Kiln

The well-preserved kiln at Omo Zapata Bajo *bodega* (Van Beck 1991:86–90) is built into the south side of a hill in a *quebrada* on the east side of the middle valley. The kiln has two construction tiers, generally all headers, set on a course of stone (Figures 7, 8). Three large, stepped buttresses flank the two mouths opening to the south and west. Prevailing winds blow into the western mouth. Arches are bond type and lack keystones.

Pacae Kiln

The small kiln structure at Pacae (Van Beck 1991:177) sits in a *quebrada* on the east side of the river in the southern part of the valley, by the side of a road. Its walls are only partially visible, most

FIGURE 7. The kiln at Omo Zapata Bajo, west mouth. (Photo by the authors.)

FIGURE 9. The large free-standing kiln on the bluff at Tamayo *bodega,* view to the northwest. Note buttresses and stairway. The tunnel, which is not visible in this view, lies behind the kiln to the left. (Photo by the authors.)

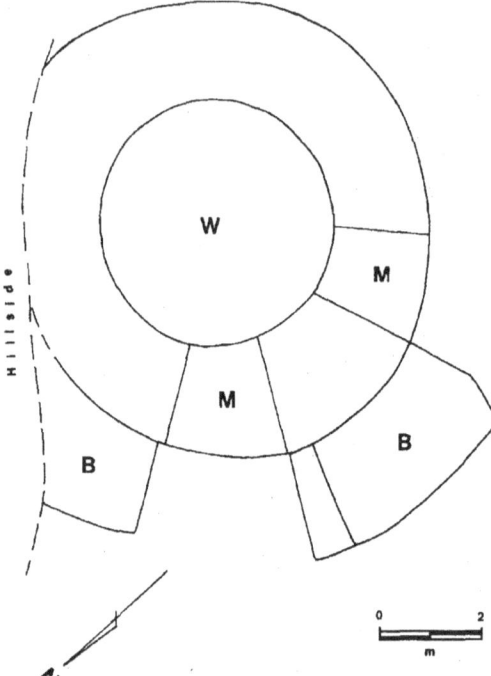

FIGURE 8. Plan drawing of the Omo Zapata Bajo kiln: B, buttress; M, mouth; W, ware chamber.

of the structure having either collapsed or been buried by accumulations of dirt, guano, and constructional debris. On the interior of the kiln, thick layers of guano reach up to the top of the walls, revealing that it had been used as an animal pen for some time. A prepared clay floor is visible under the kiln. The adobe wall is of runner construction, with two concentric rows of adobes and perhaps a cobble facing (now destroyed). Only a single mouth remains, with buttresses on either side; the mouth faces to the north, perpendicular to the winds blowing through the *quebrada.* A thick (ca. 12–15 cm) buried stratum of white powdery material lies to one side of the kiln; a sample was analyzed (Van Beck 1991:182) and proved to be anhydrite, a calcination byproduct of gypsum.

Tamayo Kiln

Tamayo kiln (Van Beck 1991:82–86) is a large, single-chambered kiln in the southern part of the valley, sitting on the western bluffs overlooking the valley floor, fully exposed to the strong southerly afternoon winds. An exterior stairway leads from ground level to the top of the chamber (Figure 9). The walls were constructed of two concentric courses of all-header adobes, and they are supported by five tall, thin, tapered buttresses constructed of runner-header patterns. The walls appear to curve inward slightly at the very top. The interior is luted with clay in two layers, 5.1 and 2.5

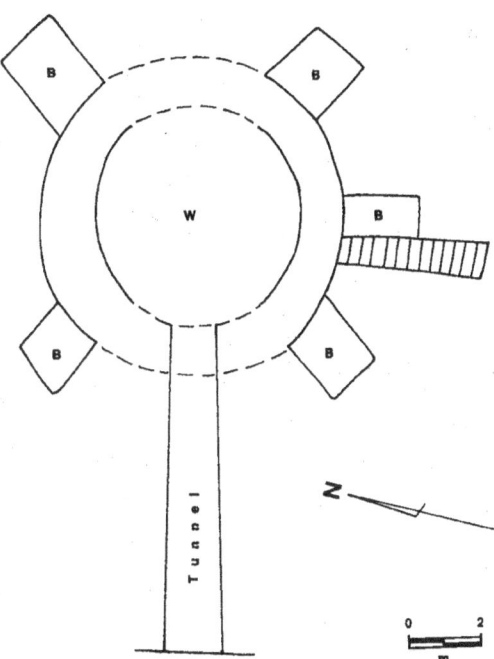

FIGURE 11. The kiln area at Chincha *bodega,* view to the south, showing the two kilns in a *quebrada* north of the *bodega* structures. The small kiln and associated grinding platform are in the background. (Photo by the authors.)

FIGURE 10. Plan drawing of the Tamayo kiln, showing the tunnel: B, buttress; W, ware chamber.

cm thick; this luting is burned orange, but vitrification is evident only around the firemouth. The exterior also was plastered with clay.

This kiln is unusual in having a long buried tunnel on the west side leading into the interior (Figure 10), with another arch in the chamber wall positioned directly above the tunnel; a second mouth exists at ground level on the east face, opposite the tunnel. The arches at both ends are running bond arches; the arch above the tunnel mouth is a ring type of all-header construction. The tunnel is on the kiln's west side, perpendicular to this wind, but it receives mountain (downslope) breezes. It is not certain how this kiln might have operated: fuel could have been burned in the tunnel or at the join of the tunnel to the mouth. The tunnel would have greatly increased draft into the kiln, while allowing more careful control of its draw than is possible with the normal position of the mouth facing the wind.

Chincha Kilns 1 and 2

Two kilns at Chincha *bodega* were located in a *quebrada* to the north of the bluff on which the structure complex sits (Figure 11). Although both kilns had small interior diameters, they are very different in wall thickness and construction, and both were test-excavated during the 1988 season. Chincha kiln #2 (Van Beck 1991:170–173) has an internal diameter of 2.6 m and thick (nearly 2.0 m) walls. It lacks buttresses. Its single entrance faces east, perpendicular to the prevailing winds, and is spanned by a bond arch. Excavations in an exterior mouth revealed that the kiln had been built on a foundation of rounded river cobbles set directly on bedrock. The interior was full of soil and trash, and could not be investigated.

Chincha kiln #1 (Van Beck 1991:173–175) is located to the south of Chincha 2, and has been nearly destroyed, with only a portion of its wall remaining. The wall is approximately 60 cm thick and is constructed of three lower courses of runners and headers; the upper courses are headers only. The standing wall is approximately 2.2 m high; internal diameter was not measurable. A single mouth remains, facing to the east (perpendicular to the prevailing winds). Deposits in the

FIGURE 12. East mouth of the Espejos 1 kiln. (Photo by the authors.)

dished interior of the kiln consisted of layers of ash, carbon, and a white material that was presumed at the time to be lime (but could also be gypsum). Artifacts recovered in excavations suggest a late 19th-century date: an 1865 Peruvian coin, a cigarette wrapper dated 1892, and a newspaper fragment from 1900 (Smith 1991:238).

East of Chincha 1 a stone feature on a low adobe structure is believed to be the basal platform for grinding calcined lime or gypsum into a powder. This circular mosaic of flagstone-like slabs of stone had a wooden post in the center and a raised rim. No millstone or grinding wheel (*arrastra*) was found nearby, although such wheels have been noted at other *bodegas*.

Espejos Kilns 1 and 2

The small kiln at Espejos *bodega* (Van Beck 1991:166–170), Kiln #1, is built on the southern hillside of a *quebrada* branching westward off the southern valley (Figure 12). This kiln has a number of features that set it apart from the other small kilns in the valley. Well-preserved, with unusually thick walls (2.62 m) and small chamber diameter (1.98 m), this kiln has four tiers, while an extension of the stone and adobe buttresses functions as a lower or fifth tier. Two mouths face east and southwest. The easternmost mouth, which showed some sooting, would capture afternoon winds

blowing up the *quebrada*. The southwestern fire-mouth has two poorly-built bond arches which lack keystones. Some interior luting is evident, and the interior chamber wall is heavily vitrified, the adobes glassy and olive green in color. A sample of a hard white-to-vitrified green deposit in the interior of the kiln near the southwest firemouth was analyzed by x-ray diffraction (Van Beck 1991:180–182, Appendices 2, 3); it was composed of a mixture of calcium and aluminum minerals, possibly resulting from lime or gypsum bonding with clay during calcination.

The larger of the two kilns at Espejos, Kiln #2, is set on the edge of a hill overlooking the vineyards. It is currently in poor repair and has been heavily modified for use in storing agricultural equipment (Van Beck 1991:90–93). The only visible mouth faces to the north, has a modified bond-type arch, and is buttressed on both sides; most of the southern wall, which has another mouth, has been obliterated. Because of damage, many construction details, such as numbers of tiers and concentric courses, could not be reliably obtained for this kiln.

Discussion

Kilns are an important part of the technological complex associated with viticulture that was transferred to the Andes by the Spanish colonists. Like the wine industry itself, the kilns retain many elements of their Spanish and Moorish and earlier Roman heritage. Kilns were used to fire the earthenware fermentation and transportation vessels associated with the wine industry, and travelers' accounts mentioning early 17th-century vineyards in coastal Peru (e.g., Vázquez de Espinosa cited in Lister and Lister 1987:332n322) note their presence. It is unlikely that every one of the recorded 130 *bodega* locations in the Moquegua valley originally had its own kiln or kilns, however. In the Pisco valley on the central Peruvian coast, for example, only four potteries supplied the needs of all the vineyards. Unfortunately, in his travels through Moquegua in about 1618, Vázquez de Espinosa (1987:28–29) did not mention kilns, although he noted the agricultural—especially viticultural—productivity of the valley. Early accounts do not specifically mention calcining activities.

Some of what has been presented here about the Moquegua kilns—such as their function—is simply conjecture. There is a great deal that is not known, such as their dates of construction and use (or re-use), and who built and fired them (Spaniards? Indians?). These problems are compounded by the variability in size, design, and construction technique of the surviving Moquegua kilns. This variability, combined with the generally inexpert construction of the kilns' arches, suggests that most of the structures were created by builders lacking experience in or a strong tradition of kiln design, or both. The builders seem to have enjoyed considerable license concerning how kilns were constructed, where they were placed, and what features were incorporated.

As a consequence, the Moquegua kilns seem to be hybrid designs created by selectively incorporating elements from a broad menu of choices. They share many traits with colonial kilns elsewhere in the Andes (particularly with the kilns in Pucará, near Lake Titicaca) and with Spanish (Moorish) kilns, and these similarities have been noted above. Placement of kilns into hillsides and the lack of a permanent roof contrasts with kilns used to fire *tinajas* in modern Spain, but provides points of comparison not only with indigenous metallurgical pyrotechnologies, but also with some Roman kilns (McWhirr 1979:99) and Spanish colonial kilns in Mexico. The Listers (1987:220) note that in the transfer of Spanish ceramic technology to New Spain techniques and styles were also selectively adopted or modified, and kilns were altered to suit the purposes of native users, particularly by leaving the tops open in place of constructing permanent roofs. Moquegua differs from other regions of the Spanish colonial empire in the absence of square or rectangular kilns for firing tiles and the apparent lack of use of tiles in building construction in the rural valley.

These similarities and differences in the processes of syncretism call attention to more general issues of technology transfer in remote peripheries

of colonization. The kilns built as part of Moquegua's viticultural agro-industry seem to exemplify the non-standardized or idiosyncratic "appropriate technologies" that commonly develop in industrial frontiers to meet the demands of specific local adaptations (Hardesty 1985:119). The kilns' variability makes it difficult to distinguish chronological, functional, and perhaps cultural or ethnic influences reflected in their construction, and it is hoped that future study might help resolve these issues.

ACKNOWLEDGMENTS

The research in Moquegua was funded primarily by the National Endowment for the Humanities and the National Geographic Society, and we are very grateful for this support. Permits for archaeological work in Peru were granted by the Comision Nacional de Arqueología and the Instituto Nacional de Cultura. Of the many people who assisted this project over the years, we would particularly like to single out the following: Greg Smith, who supervised excavations at the kilns and elsewhere; Donna Ruhl, who shared in the initial *bodega* site survey in 1985–1986; and Luis Watanabe and Gloria Salinas, who provided all manner of assistance in Moquegua. Special thanks to Julia Costello, who provided helpful comments on an earlier draft of this paper, and to Don Rice for preparation of the figures.

REFERENCES

AMERINE, M.A., H.W. BERG, AND W.V. CRUESS
1972   *The Technology of Wine Making.* Second edition. AVI, Westport, Connecticut.

BROWN, KENDALL
1986   *Bourbons and Brandy: Imperial Reform in Eighteenth Century Arequipa.* University of New Mexico Press, Albuquerque.

CABASA, SANTI
1990   The Last Tinajeros. *Ceramics Monthly* (March):44–48.

CHABERT, F., AND L. DUBOSC
1905   *Estudio sobre el viñedo de Moquegua y su reconstitución. Boletín del Ministerio de Fomento* 9(2):1–83. Tipografía de "El Lucero," Lima, Perú.

COSTELLO, JULIA G.

1977 Lime Processing in Spanish California, with Special Reference to Santa Barbara. *Pacific Coast Archaeological Society Quarterly* 13(3):22–32.

1985 The Brick and Tile Kiln. In Excavations at Mission San Antonio, 1976–1978, edited by Robert L. Hoover and Julia G. Costello. *Monograph* 26:122–145. Institute of Archaeology, University of California, Los Angeles.

EIKENHOLZ, JAMES C.

1983 A Spanish Colonial Lime Kiln. *Proceedings of the Ninth International Congress for the Study of the Pre-Columbian Cultures of the Lesser Antilles,* Santo Domingo, 2–8 August 1981. Centre de Recherches Caraibes, Université de Montréal, Montréal, Canada.

HARDESTY, DONALD L.

1985 Evolution on the Industrial Frontier. In *The Archaeology of Frontiers and Boundaries,* edited by Stanton W. Green and Stephen M. Perlman, pp. 213–229. Academic Press, Orlando, Florida.

KUON CABELLO, LUIS E.

1981 *Retazos de la historia de Moquegua.* Editorial Abril, Lima, Perú.

LECHTMAN, HEATHER

1976 A Metallurgical Site Survey of the Peruvian Andes. *Journal of Field Archaeology* 3:1–42.

LISTER, FLORENCE C., AND ROBERT H. LISTER

1987 *Andalusian Ceramics in Spain and New Spain; A Cultural Register from the Third Century B.C. to 1700.* University of Arizona Press, Tucson.

LITTO, GERTRUDE

1976 *South American Folk Pottery.* Watson-Guptill, New York.

McWHIRR, ALAN (EDITOR)

1979 Roman Brick and Tile: Studies in Manufacture, Distribution and Use in the Western Empire. *B.A.R. International Series* 68. Oxford, England.

MOSSMAN, BEAL M., AND MARCIA SELSOR

1987 The Three Story Kilns of Agost, Spain. Paper presented at the Annual Meeting of the American Anthropological Association, Chicago, Illinois.

PEELE, ROBERT, JR.

1893 A Primitive Smelting-Furnace. *School of Mines Quarterly* 15:8–10.

PICCOLPASSO, CIPRIANO

1980 *The Three Books of the Potter's Art,* translated by Ronald Lightbown and Alan Caiger-Smith. Scolar Press, London.

RHODES, DANIEL

1981 *Kilns Design, Construction, and Operation.* Chilton, Radnor, Pennsylvania.

RICE, PRUDENCE M.

1987a The Moquegua Bodegas Survey. *National Geographic Research* 3(2):136–138.

1987b Preliminary Report, Survey of Moquegua Bodegas (Wineries) and Their Spanish Background. Ms., Project files, Department of Anthropology, Southern Illinois University, Carbondale.

1988 Interim Report, Moquegua Bodegas Project, Fourth Season, 1988. Ms., Project files, Department of Anthropology, Southern Illnois University, Carbondale.

1994 The Kilns of Moquegua, Peru: Technology, Excavations, and Function. *Journal of Field Archaeology* 21(2), in press.

RICE, PRUDENCE M., AND DONNA L. RUHL

1989 Archaeological Survey of the Moquegua Bodegas. In Ecology, Settlement, and History in the Osmore Drainage, Peru, edited by Don S. Rice, Charles Stanish, and Philip R. Scarr. *B.A.R. International Series* S545:479–503. Oxford, England.

RICE, PRUDENCE M., AND GREG C. SMITH

1989 The Spanish Colonial Wineries of Moquegua, Peru. *Historical Archaeology* 23:41–49.

SHIMADA, IZUMI

1989– Research Report. Willay *Newsletter of the Andean*
1990 *Anthropological Research Group* 32/33:17–21.

SMITH, GREG C.

1990 Bodegas Excavations. In Interim Report, Moquegua Bodegas Project, Fifth Season, 1989, edited by Prudence M. Rice, pp. 9–38. Project files, Department of Anthropology, Southern Illinois University, Carbondale.

1991 Heard It Through the Grapevine: Andean and European Contributions to Spanish Colonial Culture and Viticulture in Moquegua, Peru. Unpublished Ph.D. dissertation, Department of Anthropology, University of Florida, Gainesville.

STUIVER, MINZE, AND BERND BECKER

1986 High-Precision Decadal Calibration of the Radiocarbon Time Scale, A.D. 1950–2500 B.C. *Radiocarbon* 28(2B):863–891.

VAN BECK, SARA L.

1990 Kiln Excavations. In *Interim Report, Moquegua Bodegas Project, Fifth Season, 1989,* edited by Prudence M. Rice, pp. 39–49. Project files, Department of Anthropology, Southern Illinois University, Carbondale.

1991 Spanish Colonial Kilns of Moquegua, Peru. Unpublished M.A. thesis, Department of Anthropology, University of Florida, Gainesville.

VÁZQUEZ DE ESPINOSA, ANTONIO

1987 Moquegua en el siglo XVII. Selection from *Compendio y descripción de las Indias Occidentales*

(1617–1618). In *Pequeña antología de Moquegua*, edited by Ismael Pinto Vargas, pp. 28–29. Ediciones El Virrey, Lima, Perú.

VITRUVIUS POLLIO, MARCUS
1960   *Vitruvius; The Ten Books on Architecture*, translated by M.H. Morgan. Dover, New York.

VOYATZOGLOU, MARIA
1973   The Potters of Thrapsano. *Ceramic Review* 126:13–16.

PRUDENCE M. RICE
DEPARTMENT OF ANTHROPOLOGY
SOUTHERN ILLINOIS UNIVERSITY
CARBONDALE, ILLINOIS 62901

SARA L. VAN BECK
SOUTHEASTERN ARCHAEOLOGICAL CENTER
NATIONAL PARK SERVICE
FLORIDA STATE UNIVERSITY
TALLAHASSEE, FLORIDA 32306

STEVEN L. DE VORE

Fur Trade Era Blacksmith Shops at Fort Union Trading Post National Historic Site, North Dakota

ABSTRACT

Fort Union Trading Post National Historic Site, North Dakota, represents the major outpost of the American Fur Company on the Upper Missouri between 1829 and 1867. Seven seasons of archaeological excavations conducted at the site for the purpose of obtaining structural information about the fort prior to reconstruction produced a variety of blacksmithing tools and features. Historical and field data indicate that four different locations were occupied by the blacksmith shops during the fort's existence. The present discussion is concerned with the structural layout and associated artifacts recovered from the 1850s blacksmith shop and the final smithy, built by the U.S. Army in 1864.

Introduction

Fort Union Trading Post National Historic Site is located approximately two miles from the confluence of the Missouri River and its tributary, the Yellowstone, near the boundary dividing North Dakota and Montana. The fort site lies on the left (north) bank of the Missouri River in Williams County, North Dakota (Figure 1). The fort and surrounding area was established as a National Historic Site in 1966 to commemorate the significant role played by Fort Union as a fur trading post on the Upper Missouri River. The initial operation of the fur trade at Fort Union started ca.1829 by the Upper Missouri Outfit of the American Fur Company. The fort existed until 1867 when it was sold to the U.S. Army for materials utilized in the construction of nearby Fort Buford (Thompson 1968:126).

Fort Union represented the major trade distribution and collection center in the Upper Missouri region between 1829 and the late 1850s when it was replaced in importance by Fort Benton. It was the pre-eminent post of the American Fur Company's western trade in the 19th century (Thompson 1986:1). The impressive complex was enclosed by a 16 ft. (4.88 m) high wooden palisade set on a stone foundation. The perimeter measured 226 ft. (69 m) by 220 ft. (67 m). Two stone bastions at the northeast and southwest corners of the fort served as mute sentries in this wilderness area. The major structures inside the fort were also placed on stone foundations. They included the Bourgeois' House, Dwelling Range, Store Range, Indians' and Artisans' House, Blacksmith Shop, and stone Powder Magazine.

The fort's primary role was to exploit the rich fur resources of the Yellowstone region and the upper reaches of the Missouri. The site was selected near the traditional homelands of the Blackfoot Indians in order to conduct trade with them (Chittenden 1986:332–333). The Company also procured trade with the Crow in the Yellowstone region and with the Assiniboine of the Upper Missouri. The fort also served as a supply depot and administrative center for support to Company trapping ventures into the Rocky Mountains. In order to support its vast enterprises along the Upper Missouri, the American Fur Company was also instrumental in establishing steamboat navigation to the mouth of the Yellowstone by 1832.

Historical Background

During the early years, the Company traded Euro-American goods for beaver pelts. Depletion of the beaver and the decline of the beaver hat as a status symbol in the east and in Europe led to a reduction for the demand of beaver by the early 1830s (Phillips and Smurr 1961:23; Mattison 1962:18). During this period, approximately 100 people were employed at Fort Union with another 400 employed in the Upper Missouri region (Mattison 1962:191). The post was self-sufficient with numerous artisans (e.g., blacksmiths, carpenters, joiners, coopers, tailors, shoemakers, hatters, and gunsmiths), company clerks and managers, hunt-

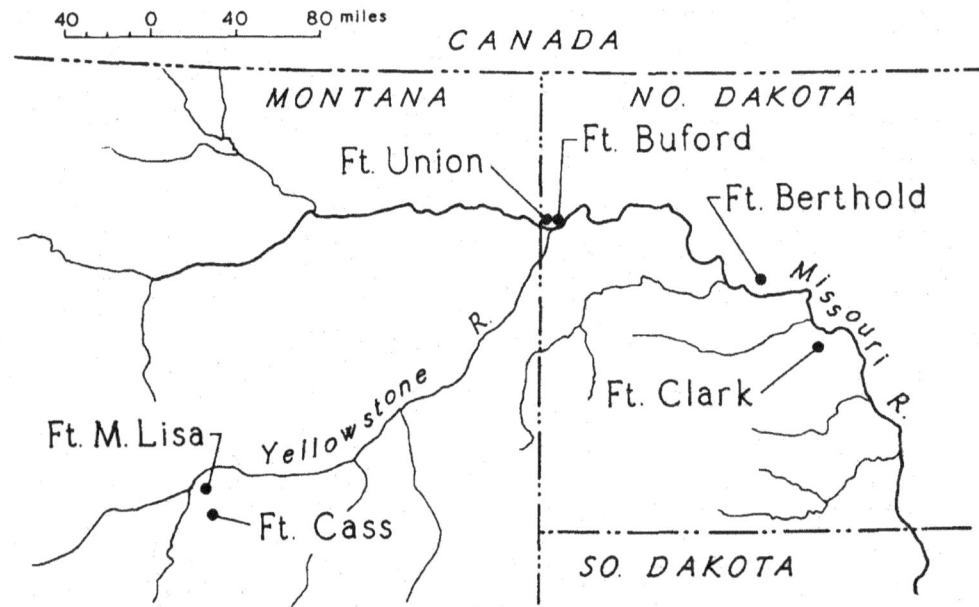

FIGURE 1. Location of Fort Union Trading Post National Historic Site, North Dakota.

ers, and engagées (common laborers) under employment.

As the beaver trade declined, the demand for bison robes brought a shift in the trade from pelts to robes. John Jacob Astor, head of the American Fur Company, upon noting this decline decided to retire from the business. In 1834, the Western Department, including the Upper Missouri Outfit, was sold to Pratte, Chouteau & Company. A change in management, in 1838, resulted in the formation of Pierre Chouteau, Jr., & Company (Mattison 1962:196). Despite Astor's retirement from the trading business, the name of the American Fur Company remained with the new company throughout its history. During the remainder of the fort's existence, trade centered primarily on bison robes acquired from Native Americans (Nute 1945:525). The chief trade goods included awls, beads, hawk bells, blankets, kettles, vermilion, guns, lead, gun powder, gunflints, combs, flannel shirts, buttons, and cloth. Coffee and sugar were also popular items along with the forbidden liquor (Mattison 1962:191–192).

In addition to its importance in the fur and robe trade, Fort Union was a focal point for the U.S. Government in its dealings with the Northern Plains tribes. The 1851 Treaty of Fort Laramie established Fort Union as a distribution point for annuities for some of the Upper Missouri tribes (Mattison 1962:200). It was also an important rendezvous point for the 1853 Northern Pacific Railroad Survey (Mattison 1962:199).

By the late 1850s, increased hostility from the Sioux and smallpox epidemics reduced the numbers of Native Americans trading at Fort Union. Declining trade at the fort diminished its importance as the major supply and administrative depot in the region. The Chouteaus lost their fur trade license during the Civil War since many of the Company's management were southern sympathizers (Mattison 1962:200). In 1865, they sold their interest in the Company to the Northwestern Fur Company.

When General Alfred Sully arrived at Fort Union in 1864, the old fort was in dilapidated shape. The increased concern over the Sioux depredations in the region caused the U.S. Army to station a company of infantry, composed of former Confederate prisoners-of-war, at the fort; however, the location and severe deterioration of the fort resulted in the construction of Fort Buford east of Fort Union at the confluence of the Missouri and Yellowstone Rivers. In 1867, the Army purchased Fort Union and salvaged what materials it could from the old fort in order to complete Fort Buford.

During its lifetime, Fort Union contributed significantly to the history of exploration, economics, sociology, and transportation along the American frontier. As headquarters of the Upper Missouri Outfit, the outpost had played a substantial role in one of the most important capitalistic enterprises (i.e., the fur and robe trade) of the 19th century in America. The wealth obtained from the sale of the furs and robes allowed the owners of the American Fur Company and its successors to exert considerable influence in the highest political circles, in turn affecting the development of commercial laws and policies towards the Native Americans (Nute 1945:528–530; Phillips and Smurr 1961). It also served as a prominent American presence on the northern border in order to exert the sovereignty of the young United States government (Phillips and Smurr 1961:348–429).

In addition to the numerous Native American customers, the fort also hosted eminent Euro-American visitors, many of whom recorded their impressions of this proud citadel in the western wilderness (Thompson 1986). Noted artists, such as Karl Bodmer, George Catlin, Rudolph Kurz, Carl Wimar, John Mix Stanley, and William Hayes, have left vivid records of Fort Union, as have the frontier photographers Illingworth and Bill. Scientists and sportsmen included John J. Audubon, Prince Maximilian of Wied, Sir George Gore, and Paul Wilhelm, Duke of Wurttenburg. In 1853, Isaac I. Stevens led a railroad survey crew past the fort on their way to the Pacific Ocean. Jesuit missionaries under Father Pierre DeSmet visited the fort. Military personnel and explorers who delayed at the fort included General Alfred Sulley, Lt. G. K. Warren with F. V. Hayden, and Capt. William F. Raynolds and Lt. Henry E.

Maynadier. Fort personnel, including Charles Larpenteur and Edwin Thompson Denig, left accounts of their daily activities and ethnographic studies of the Native Americans. They also collected artifacts, fossils, fauna, and flora at the request of American and European museums, universities, and zoos.

Archaeological Investigations

Although an excellent description (Thompson 1968) of Fort Union's architectural history was compiled shortly after the site's acquisition by the National Park Service, specific details needed for proposed reconstruction were missing. Archaeological methods were selected to elucidate the architectural features at the old fort site. Beginning in 1968, a series of four field seasons (Figure 2) was conducted either directly by National Park Service archaeologists between 1968 and 1970 (Moore 1968; Husted 1970,1971) or through a contractual agreement with the University of Colorado in 1972 (Gillio 1973). The earliest excavations may have occurred during the 1930s (Hummel 1938). The later investigations focused upon delineation of structures marked for reconstruction or which may be significant to site interpretation (Husted 1970:1).

Approximately 60 years of popular support for the reconstruction of Fort Union resulted in a Congressional mandate to the National Park Service in 1965 to reconstruct portions of the fort. The decision for onsite reconstruction resulted in three further seasons (1986–1988) of archaeological investigations in order to mitigate the destructive impact of construction upon existing archaeological resources at the site. In 1986, National Park Service personnel from the Midwest Archeological Center and volunteers commenced excavations at the site. The initial work centered on the Bourgeois' House, Kitchen, and surrounding area (Hunt and Peterson 1988). The 1987 field season focused on the East and North Palisades and associated bracing system and features (Peterson and Hunt 1990). The Northeast and Southwest Bastion foundations were also excavated. The final season of intensive

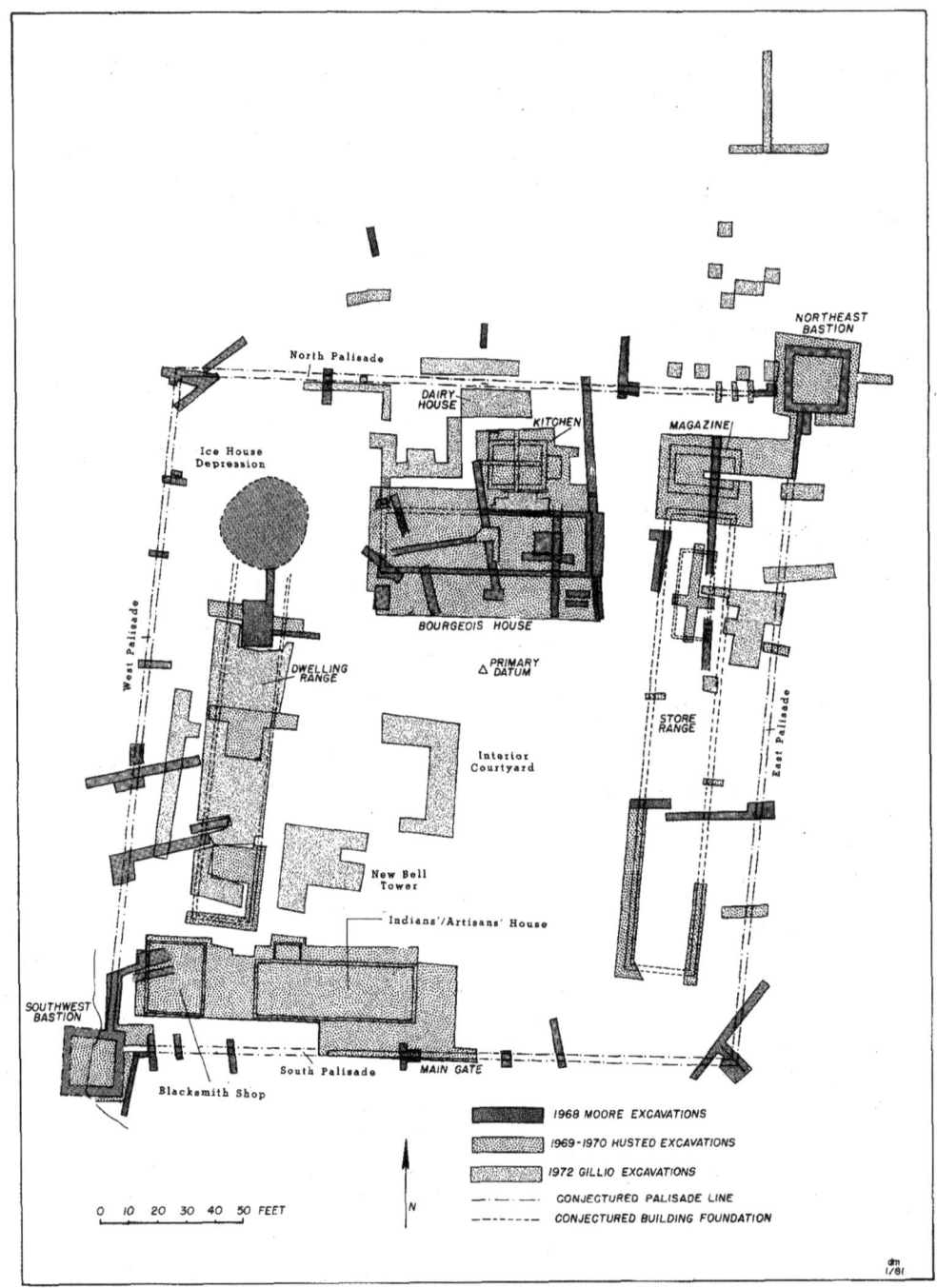

FIGURE 2. Reconstructed site map of the 1968–1972 archaeological investigations at Fort Union Trading Post.

FIGURE 3. View of the Indians' and Artisans' House (view toward the west with the Blacksmith Shop in the background).

archaeological investigations, in 1988, resulted in the excavation of the West and South Palisade lines, palisade bracing system, numerous archaeological features, and the Indians' and Artisans' House (Figure 3). In addition to the structure excavated as the Indians' and Artisans' House by Husted (1970, 1971), an earlier structure also used as Indian reception room and artisans' workshop was identified. Beneath these structures, one of the earliest structures at Fort Union, a blacksmith shop, was also located. The investigations provided detailed information concerning the early fort palisade (1829–1833).

Analysis of materials recovered during the 1968–1972 field seasons resulted in a series of reports (*Fort Union Trading Post National Historic Site [32WI17] Material Culture Reports*) focusing on specific categories of artifacts recovered at the site: food related materials (Hunt 1986b); personal and recreation materials (Hunt 1986c); firearms, trapping, and fishing equipment (Hunt 1986d); and buttons (Hunt 1986e). Additional reports include building hardware, construction materials, tools, and fasteners (De Vore 1988), trade goods, tools, transportation, and miscellaneous materials (De Vore 1990a); tobacco pipes (De Vore 1990b); and trade beads (De Vore 1990c). Another volume covered the analysis of the vertebrate fauna (Angus and Falk 1986). The initial report in the series presents a critical appraisal of the archaeology conducted at Fort Union prior to the 1986–1988 investigations (Hunt 1986a). When completed, the analysis of the hundreds of thousands of objects recovered between 1986–1988 will provide additional insight into the daily activities at Fort Union.

Blacksmithing at Fort Union

During the occupation of Fort Union, several artisans played a major role in the daily activities. These included stone masons, coopersmiths, gunsmiths, carpenters, tinsmiths, tailors, painters, farriers, and blacksmiths (Maximilian 1906:337). They were responsible for the making and mending of domestic materials, and for the construction activities at the fort. They also engaged in the manufacture of a variety of goods for trade with the Native Americans and free Euro-American trappers. Of these artisans, the blacksmith was probably the most important metal worker during the entire span of the fort's operation.

The blacksmith was the least specialized artisan and yet the most important for daily activities (Hogg 1964; Watson 1977; McRaven 1981; Bealer 1984). The smith made tools and other materials along with repairing broken items. The blacksmith was probably the fort's farrier, an occupation usually associated with the blacksmith especially on the frontier. The blacksmith's training in iron/metal working also may have meant the smith might spend some of his time engaged in coopering, tinsmithing, repairing small domestic objects, and gunsmithing (Armour 1976:25–26; Light 1984:38).

Although the Company records mention several blacksmiths employed by the Upper Missouri Outfit, only one is specifically named at Fort Union. In 1863, Joseph Goudereau, a Metis or French Canadian, became the fort's blacksmith (Boller 1868:382), serving also as a hunter during his stay. Other blacksmiths, stationed at Forts Clark, Atkinson or Berthold II, Pierre, and Benton, served as hunters, guides, boatmen, clerks, voyagers, and/or common laborers in addition to their main duties as the fort's blacksmith (William J. Hunt, Jr. 1989, pers. comm.).

Thompson (1968) described three separate blacksmithing shops at Fort Union. A fourth was mentioned in the diary of Maximilian, Prince of Wied-Neuwied (1832–1833). The successive fur-trade-era blacksmith shops were each located in the southwest quarter of the fort. The earliest blacksmith shop, mentioned by Maximilian (1832–1833), was situated near the main gate along the south palisade. The 1840s shop occupied the western end of the 1830s–1840s Indians' and Artisans' House. The 1850s Blacksmith Shop was placed in the southwest corner of the fort near the Southwest Bastion. The 1860s Army smithy was apparently located in the western end of the 1850s–1860s Indians' and Artisans' House (William J. Hunt, Jr. 1989, pers. comm.).

The blacksmith shops at Fort Union appear to have been generally similar to other frontier shops. Any blacksmith shop requires at least three functional areas (Light 1984:11–12). These areas may vary in complexity and spatial orientation; however, they are all necessary for the operation of the blacksmith shop. The main working area centered around the forge. Associated shop items included the forge itself, the bellows, the anvil, a slack tub to quench hot iron, a grindstone to sharpen tools, and a workbench with vise (Light 1984:11). Nearby, there should be a storage area where tools, mandrels, and swages are kept along with a supply of iron and charcoal fuels. Finally, there is a domestic area where the smith may socialize and conduct business with friends and clients. The arrangement of these areas is based on the personal preferences of the artisan, the structural dimensions of the shops, and the type and complexity of the activities conducted within the shop.

1829–1833 Blacksmith Shop

Maximilian's (1832–1833) depiction of the forge in a sketch from his diary indicated the location of the fort's first blacksmith shop to the west of the main gate. This location was confirmed during the 1988 National Park Service archaeological investigations (William J. Hunt, Jr. 1988, pers. comm.). The area contained a thick charcoal layer and numerous metal artifacts. The analysis of the excavations is presently underway.

1840s Blacksmith Shop

During the 1830s and 1840s, the second blacksmith, along with the gunsmith and tinner, occupied the western portion of the Indians' and Artisans' House. Edwin Denig (1986:185), the fort's chief clerk in 1843, describes the Indians' and Artisans' House as containing the reception-room for the Native Americans in addition to the work area for these artisans. Denig's usage of the term "shop" suggests the three artisans were utilizing one large room. Besides Denig's discussion of the western end of this structure, little historic information is available concerning the smithy in the Indians' and Artisans' House despite the importance of the artisans' work concerning the fur trade and domestic activities at the fort. By 1851, the blacksmith shop was moved to a separate building between the Indians' and Artisans' House and the West Palisade. During the 1988 excavation of the Indians' and Artisans' House identified by Husted (1970,1971), an intermediate structure was found between this structure and the early smithy. It is highly probable that this structure represents the one mentioned by Denig. Analysis of this structure, like the 1829–1833 smithy, is also underway.

1850s Blacksmith Shop

Sketches by Rudolph Kurz, a clerk between 1851 and 1852, illustrated a small portion of the north end of a gable roof (Thompson 1968:Illustration 10–11; Kurz 1986). Excavations in 1970 (Husted 1971:29–34) confirmed the existence of a third blacksmith shop in the structure with the gable roof. Since Denig makes no mention of this structure in 1843, one assumes the structure was built sometime between 1843 and 1851.

Archaeological Investigations

The archaeological investigations of the 1850s fur trade era smithy location were conducted by the National Park Service in 1968 by J. W. "Smokey" Moore, Jr. (1968) and in 1970 by Wilfred M. Husted (1971). Moore's excavations involved two northeast-southwest oriented trenches across the west wall of the Blacksmith Shop. Husted's excavations included the entire Blacksmith Shop.

In 1968, Moore (1968) identified a stone chimney base belonging the the Blacksmith Shop, approximately 10 ft. (3.05 m) east of the West Palisade and 12 ft. (3.66 m) north of the Southwest Bastion. He suggested that the chimney base might belong to an 'H' fireplace or to a forge. Although not completely exposed, the feature appeared to be approximately 6 ft. (1.83 m) square. The chimney base was built above a heavy stratum of charcoal, ash, and burned fill. Moore indicated the feature was apparently not one of the original fort structures but may have replaced an earlier feature.

In 1970, Husted (1971) identified this stucture (Figure 4) as the 1850s Blacksmith Shop illustrated by Kurz. The excavations of the Blacksmith Shop (Figure 5) exposed a foundation measuring 25 ft. (7.62 m) by 20.5 ft. (6.25 m). Since Husted's purpose was to delineate the structural foundations, the structures were excavated in 6 ft. (1.83 m) wide, north-south trenches which extended across the entire length of the building. This area was originally excavated in 1970 in order to define the western extent of the Indians' and Artisans' House. Husted (1971:30) indicated that the footings of the structure were in poorer condition, of lighter construction, and generally less substantial than those of other structures investigated during the 1968–1970 field seasons. The corners of the structure utilized wooden beams rather than stone for the foundation. It is possible that these corner beams formed the sills for openings in order to ventilate the building (Husted 1971:31).

Two forges and one fireplace were identified (Husted 1971:32). One forge was located along the west wall near the northwestern corner of the building. It measured 6.25 ft. (1.91 m) by 2.75 ft. (0.84 m). Iron tool fragments, fittings, implements, and other objects were found beside the eastern edge of the forge foundation. The other forge was near the center of the eastern wall. It was approximately 7 ft. (2.14 m) by 3.75 ft. (1.14 m). Several gun parts, gun flints, cartridge cases, and shot were recovered next to this forge, in addition to numerous blacksmithing and construction materials. Recovery of these items suggests that this forge was utilized by the fort's gunsmith and blacksmith. A hollow log set on its end was lo-

FIGURE 4. View of excavated Blacksmith Shop (view toward the north).

cated in the west central portion of the shop between the two forges. The log was 1.2 ft. (0.37 m) in diameter and was set approximately 1 ft. (0.31 m) into the floor of the smithy. It probably supported an anvil for one or both forges. The log was approximately 6 ft. (1.83 m) from the western forge and 5 ft. (1.52 m) from the eastern forge. Along the southern wall, a fireplace foundation was exposed. It measured 6 ft. (1.83 m) by 4 ft. (1.22 m). The hearth area was heavily burned.

Evidence for a wood floor existed along the southern half, the western edge, and the northern portion of the smithy. The area around the log apparently was left bare, which further suggests that the log supported the anvil since hot iron on a wooden floor would present a fire hazard. In the northeastern corner of the shop, an area of rocks was laid between the floor joists. Husted (1971:34) suggested that the rocks represented a foundation or support for a heavy piece of equipment or large weight. In the northwestern corner, a large concentration of charcoal mixed with ash was uncovered. This feature may represent a storage bin for the charcoal inside the shop, although a coal shed existed under either the south or the west gallery (Thompson 1968:221). Metal objects from the structure included building hardware, blacksmithing and construction tools, harness hardware, wagon parts, gun parts, trap hardware, scrap metal, and horse, mule, and oxen shoes. A variety of domestic artifacts from the structure included ceramic sherds, bottle and window glass fragments, can fragments, clay pipes, and faunal remains.

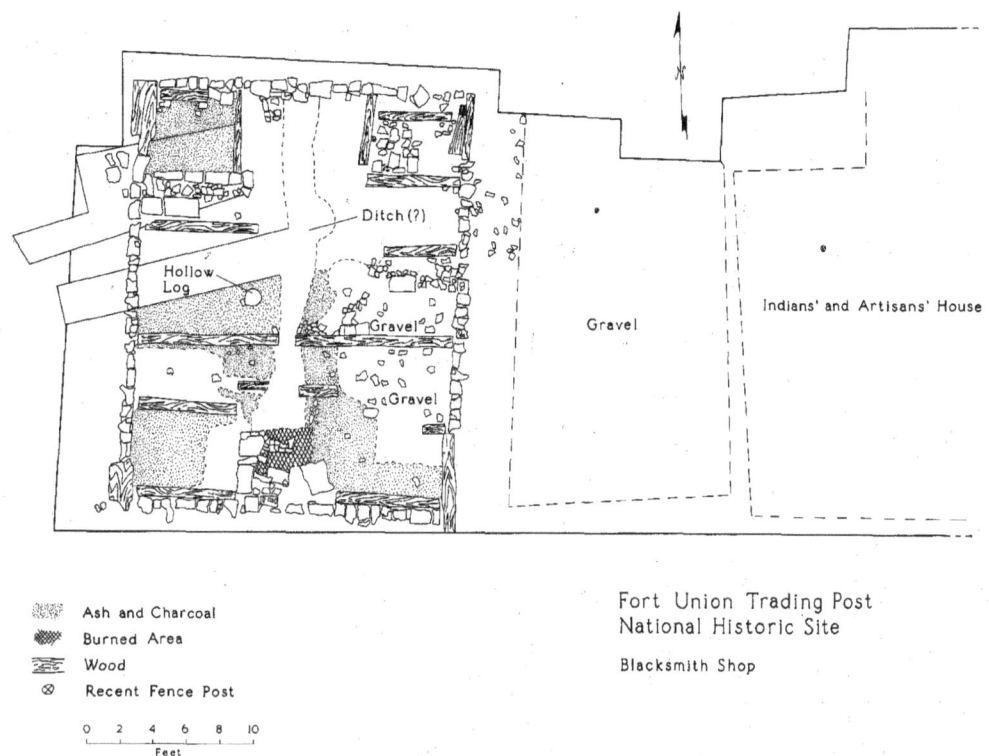

Ash and Charcoal
Burned Area
Wood
Recent Fence Post

0 2 4 6 8 10
Feet

Fort Union Trading Post
National Historic Site

Blacksmith Shop

FIGURE 5. Plan view of the 1850s Blacksmith Shop.

Shop Layout

Since Husted's purpose was to delineate the structural foundations, the structures were excavated in 6 ft. (1.83 m) wide, north-south trenches which extended across the entire width of the two buildings. This method of excavation prevented the analyst from learning a great deal about the way the shops were utilized. Although the Blacksmith Shop contained two forges, a fireplace, and the probable base for an anvil, the location of other items is unknown (Figure 6). The small forge in the northwestern corner of the Blacksmith Shop was probably a farrier's forge, based on its size and location near the entrance. The main forge was located on the east side of the building. Artifacts from the vicinity of the main forge indicated it was utilized by the fort's gunsmith as well as the blacksmith. The northwestern corner of the structure, adjacent to the smaller farrier forge, probably represented the charcoal bin since it contained a high concentration of charcoal. Charcoal is mentioned in the literature as being made at the fort by the blacksmith (Larpenteur 1835). Charcoal was the dominant forge fuel until the last quarter of the 19th century when it was superseded by coal (Light 1987:659).

Artifact Analysis

The assessment of the shop layout is also based on the analysis of the associated artifacts. The artifacts are described by functional categories

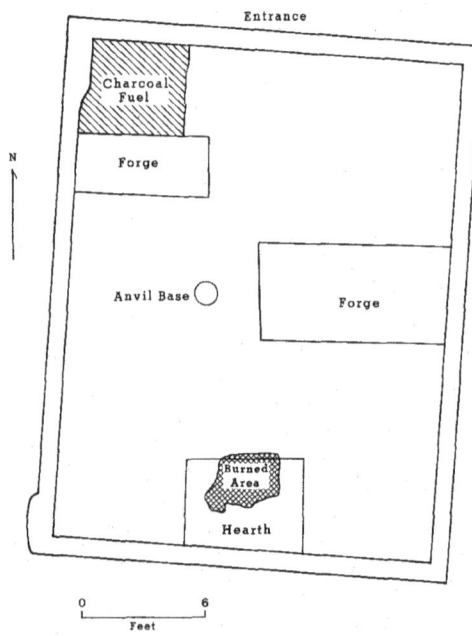

FIGURE 6. Shop layout of the 1850s Blacksmith Shop.

TABLE 1
ARTIFACTS RECOVERED FROM THE 1850S
BLACKSMITH SHOP

Functional Category	Field Season		
	1968	1970	Total
ARCHITECTURE			
Construction Material	93	210	303
Construction Hardware	178	605	783
COMMERCIAL			
Agriculture	0	11	11
Hunting	6	31	37
Fishing	1	2	3
Trapping	2	17	19
Construction Tools	5	30	35
Blacksmithing Tools	0	39	39
Miscellaneous Hardware	29	98	127
Scrap Metal	219	679	898
Slag	1	4	5
Shipping/Storage	1	0	1
Measurement	0	1	1
Communications	0	5	5
TRANSPORTATION			
Vehicles	4	29	33
Husbandry	27	104	131
DOMESTIC ITEMS			
Furnishings	0	0	0
Culinary	3	25	28
Gustatory	33	172	205
Portable Illumination	0	1	1
Home Information	0	0	0
Sewing	1	1	2
PERSONAL ITEMS			
Clothing	0	22	22
Footwear	0	0	0
Adornment	1	541	542
Body Ritual and Grooming	0	2	2
Medical and Health	5	4	9
Indulgences	3	11	14
Past Time and Recreation	0	0	0
Pocket Tools and Accessories	0	0	0
TOTAL	612	2644	3256

(Sprague 1980:251–261) with reference to the activities of the blacksmith (Table 1). Five basic functional categories of artifacts were recovered during the 1968 and 1970 archaeological investigations in the 1850s Blacksmith Shop: 1) architectural, 2) commercial, 3) transportation, 4) domestic, and 5) personal.

Architectural items include construction materials and hardware. The construction materials, including window glass, wooden board fragments, lime mortar, adobe, and common brick, represent artifacts used in the construction of the shop. Although some of the building hardware may have been used in the construction of the shop, the diversity of these artifacts indicated that the blacksmith probably made several of the objects for other buildings located at the fort. Among the items recovered were padlocks, surface mounted locks, and keys; latches; strap and butt hinges; hinged hasps; flanges; a T-brace; shutter holdback and pintles; rafter hangers; and a window sash lift.

Various fasteners were also recoverd including hand-wrought, machine cut, and wire nails; bolts, nuts, and washers; wire; rivets; wood screws; and staples. Although most of the items were probably made by the fort's blacksmith, some items were imported from St. Louis or from other eastern manufacturing centers (Missouri Historical Society 1983).

The commercial items include numerous objects

made by the blacksmith for use by the fort's personnel and for the trade operations. In addition, by-products of the actual forge operation (slag and scrap metal) are included in the commercial category. Several firearm related parts were found in the vicinity of the large forge including springs, breech plugs, side plates, lock plates to Northwest guns and Kentucky rifles, frizzens, and sears, which suggests that a gunsmith was present or the blacksmith was skilled in the manufacture of gun related parts (Hunt 1986c). In addition to these gun parts, percussion cap box fragments, lead balls, sprues or waste lead, and cast iron grapeshot were also found in the Blacksmith Shop. Several trap fragments, including jaws, spring, and posts, were present along with a fishhook and two fishing rod ferrules.

The majority of the blacksmithing tools recovered from the 1968–1972 excavations were from the Blacksmith Shop, along with numerous carpenters' and other artisans' tools. Blacksmithing tools include anvil tools, chisels, hammers, punches, files, and a reamer (described in detail in a later section of this paper). A toeing knife indicates farrier activities which the blacksmith may have undertaken. Carpenters' tools and tools designated for trade have also been recovered. These include pit saw and carpenter saw blade fragments, wedges, American and trade axes, froes, log chains, auger bits, hammers and pry bars, and wood chisels. Several tool tangs are also among the tools from Fort Union. Fragmented hardware and scrap metal comprise the major groups within this functional category. Barrel straps and steelyard poise represent the shipping/storage and measuring activities related to the fort's operation. In addition, the presence of chalk and ink containers suggests that the blacksmith may have maintained records concerning what jobs were done for the company and individuals (Hunt 1986c).

Transportation is divided between vehicles and husbandry. Vehicles include various wagon parts and steamboat equipment. Wagon axle, brake, pole/tongue, bed/box, and wheel hardware are present in the artifact collection. Broken steam engine parts may represent attempts to repair items on the steamboat or the salvaging of metal for later

use by the blacksmith. Husbandry relates to artifacts associated with draft animals (horses, mules, and oxen) used by the fort employees, including harness and saddle elements, shoes and shoe nails, and oxen yoke hardware. Several of these items may have been produced in the fort's blacksmith shop.

Domestic and personal items from the Blacksmith Shop reflect both personal activites of the smith and trade related manufacturing processes. Several culinary and gustatory items relate to food consumption. These include table/kitchen utensils, kettle or pot fragments, and other kitchen equipment (Hunt 1986b:1–13). Tin cans and alcoholic containers, including wine, beer/ale, whiskey, and brandy bottle fragments, were recovered from the Blacksmith Shop (Hunt 1986b:14–72). Condiment bottle fragments found in the shop were from Lea and Perrins Worcestershire Sauce containers (Hunt 1986b:95–97). Two Albany slipped, stoneware fragments and several whiteware fragments were also recoverd (Hunt 1986b:110–183). The whiteware included seven transfer printed vessel fragments, an edged plate fragment, and an undecorated plate. Faunal remains from the shop are primarily composed of mammalian species although birds and fish are also present (Angus and Falk 1986). The majority of the faunal material apparently represents food remains. The major sources of meat include *Bison bison, Odocoileus virginianus, Antilocapra americana, Bos taurus,* and *Sus scrofa.* Other mammalian species, with the exception of the rodents, may have been used as food or were procured for their fur or skins, including *Erethizon dorsatum, Canis* spp., *Vulpes vulpes, Taxidea taxus,* and *Sylvilagus* spp. *Gallus gallus, Pedioecetes phasianellus,* and *Anas* spp. served as food sources and, with the exception of *Gallus gallus,* may have been hunted for their feathers along with *Aquila chrysaetos.* Fish remains from the Blacksmith Shop consist of elements from *Ictalurus* spp. In addition to the food related items, part of a lantern and two scissors were found in the shop.

Personal items included buttons and beads. Other items such as hawk bells and tinkling cones may represent trade items made in the shop.

Grooming activities are represented by a toothbrush and a shaving cream pot lid fragment (Hunt 1986c). Bitters and patent medicine bottle fragments are included in the personal items category. Fragments of Drake's Plantation Bitters comprise the majority of the medical and health artifacts recovered during the excavations of the shop (Hunt 1986b:73–90). White ball clay and terra cotta tobacco pipe fragments represent the indulgence items recovered from the shop.

The artifacts recovered from the Blacksmith Shop are similar in their diversity to those recovered from Fort St. Joseph (1796–1812), Ontario (Light 1984:13–37). Activities at both blacksmith shops included the manufacture of both fort materials and trade related items, farriering, and coppering or at least general domestic repair. The domestic area in the shops, although not physically identified, was apparently present. Ceramics, bottle glass fragments, eating utensils, and faunal remains are indicators of such an area within the shops.

The blacksmith shop (ca.1834/36–1860) at Fort Vancouver, Washington (Ross et al. 1975), contained two forges and work areas. The size of this Hudson's Bay Company shop is approximately twice the size of the 1850s Blacksmith Shop at Fort Union or the smithy at Fort St. Joseph. Its artifact assemblage is also larger; however, when the assemblage is viewed within a functional framework, there is a definite similarity in functional activities (Ross et al. 1975:57–67). Architectural artifacts from Fort Vancouver include several types of hardware (e.g., hinges, pintles, locks and keys, latches, and hooks) and construction material (i.e., brick, mortar, putty, paint, concrete, asphalt, and tile). Commercial activities include the manufacture and/or repair of numerous domestic and trade related items. Agricultural items, trap parts, and several gun parts are also present. Both construction and blacksmithing tools are represented among the artifacts from the shop. Scrap iron and miscellaneous hardware fragments comprise a major portion of the artifact assemblage recovered from the structure. The transportation items indicate that both horses and mules were used as beasts of burden. Domestic and personal items from the shop suggest that the blacksmiths also ate and met with their clients in the shop area. Domestic and personal items found at the shop indicate the manufacture of items for the trade operations of the Hudson's Bay Company.

Army Blacksmith Shop

Fort Union's fourth smithy was constructed by the military in 1864 near the end of its occupation. Charles Larpenteur, the fort's bourgeois during the last few years, mentions the Army's building its own smithy in the fall of 1864 and daubing it (Thompson 1968:183,255). During the 1988 investigations at Fort Union, it became apparent that the structure identified and excavated by Husted (1970, 1971) was not the Indians' and Artisans' House described by Denig (1986:185), but rather a later version constructed over that foundation. Reexamination of the artifacts and the literature concerning the U. S. Army's presence at Fort Union between 1864 and 1866 suggested that the western end of the Indians' and Artisans' House may have been the location of the Army's blacksmith shop. Husted's mis-identification is understandable when one views the complexity of the construction episodes in the vicinity of the Indians' and Artisans' House.

Archaeological Investigations

In 1970, Husted (1971) continued the excavations in the Indians' and Artisans' House started in 1969. The 1969 excavations (Husted 1970) were concerned with the eastern end of the structure, a portion of the western room, and with the Main Gate area. The 1970 excavations included the work area in the western end of the Indians' and Artisans' House (Figure 7). The excavations of the Indians' and Artisans' House revealed a foundation of 60 ft. (18.29 m) by 20–20.5 ft. (6.10–6.25 m).

The western half of the structure (Figure 8) occupied by the artisans measured 31 ft. (9.45 m) by 20 ft. (6.10 m). A fireplace, or more likely a forge

FIGURE 7. View of Army smithy in the western portion of the Indians' and Artisans' House (view toward the south-southwest).

foundation, was located at the western end of the structure. It was slightly offset to the north of the center of the building and measured approximately 9 ft. (2.74 m) north-south by 6 ft. (1.83 m) east-west (Husted 1971:10). There was no obvious indication of a partition between the reception room and the artisans' shop although the probable division occurs near the mid-line of the building's central, H-shaped hearth which served to heat both rooms (Husted 1971:9). A series of wooden floor joists was oriented across the width of the structure and spaced 2.5–3 ft. (0.76–0.91 m) apart. Some badly deteriorated floor boards were uncovered immediately west of the fireplace. A rectangular (10 ft. [3.05 m] by 5 ft. [1.52 m]) stone feature on the exterior of the northern wall apparently repre-

sented a porch foundation similar to the front porch foundation of the Bourgeois' House. In addition to the blacksmithing tools, materials, and construction debris, domestic materials recovered from the structure included ceramic sherds, bottle glass fragments, clay pipe fragments, and a variety of faunal elements.

Shop Layout

The forge, hearth, and porch are the main indicators of the activities within the artisans' work area in the Indians' and Artisans' House (Figure 9). Apparently, the Indians' and Artisans' House mentioned in Denig's (1986:185) 1843 description of Fort Union was torn down and rebuilt sometime

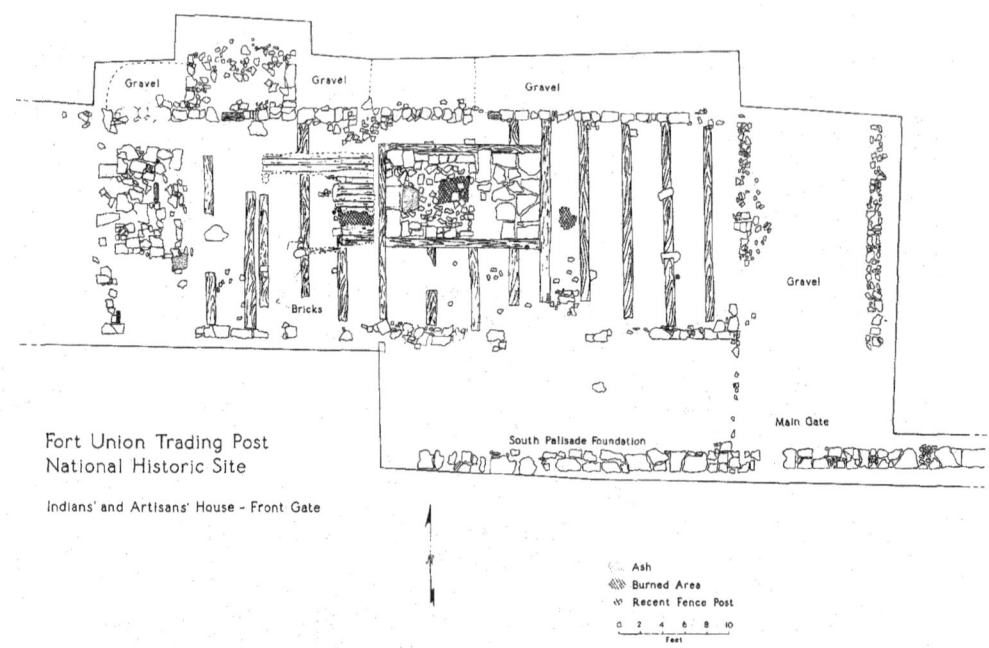

FIGURE 8. Plan view of the Indians' and Artisans' House.

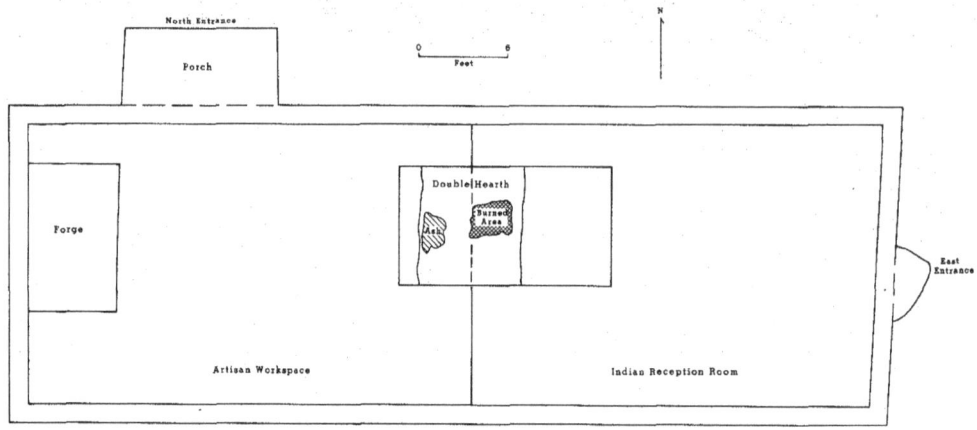

FIGURE 9. Shop layout of the Army smithy in the Indians' and Artisans' House.

after the artisans or the blacksmith moved into the 1850s Blacksmith Shop previously discussed. The 1988 excavations revealed that the second Indians' and Artisans' House was set on a stone foundation. Prior to the use of the west room by the Army for a smithy, the room probably served as a storeroom for trade with the Native Americans (William J. Hunt, Jr. 1988, pers. comm.).

TABLE 2
ARTIFACTS RECOVERED FROM
THE ARMY SMITHY IN THE INDIANS' AND
ARTISANS' HOUSE.

Functional Category	Field Season		
	1969	1970	Total
ARCHITECTURE			
Construction Material	271	419	690
Construction Hardware	20	70	90
COMMERCIAL			
Agriculture	0	0	0
Hunting	59	80	139
Fishing	0	0	0
Trapping	0	3	3
Construction Tools	6	3	9
Blacksmithing Tools	1	13	14
Miscellaneous Hardware	12	26	38
Scrap Metal	91	308	399
Slag	12	32	44
Shipping/Storage	0	5	5
Measurement	0	0	0
Communications	1	1	2
TRANSPORTATION			
Vehicles	1	4	5
Husbandry	4	9	13
DOMESTIC ITEMS			
Furnishings	3	1	4
Culinary	6	8	14
Gustatory	844	631	1475
Portable Illumination	0	0	0
Home Information	1	0	1
Sewing	0	13	13
PERSONAL ITEMS			
Clothing	42	39	81
Footwear	7	0	7
Adornment	1712	3817	5529
Body Ritual and Grooming	3	4	7
Medical and Health	10	10	20
Indulgences	102	144	246
Past Time and Recreation	4	3	7
Pocket Tools and Accessories	0	1	1
TOTAL	3212	5644	8856

Comparisons with 1850s Blacksmith Shop

Since the west room of the second Indians' and Artisans' House was used by the Army blacksmith for only two years, a comparison of the artifact categories with those from the 1850s Blacksmith Shop offers some contrast. Nevertheless, the presence of a large quantity of scrap metal, fragmented

hardware, and several blacksmithing tools certainly confirms that the room served, at least for a limited time, as the Army smithy (Table 2).

Architectural materials, including common bricks, wood, window glass, mortar, nails, and other fasteners are more prevalent in this smithy, which probably reflects the multiple construction episodes in this area. However, the number of architectural hardware items is substantially lower, perhaps because the west room in the Indians' and Artisans' House was used as a storeroom rather than for manufacturing materials for the fort. The commercial artifact category likewise contains fewer items than that of the 1850s Blacksmith Shop. The number of transportation items is also low when compared to those from the 1850s Blacksmith Shop.

The increase in items in the domestic and personal categories is undoubtably related to the primary use of the room for storage prior to the Army converting it to a smithy. Objects such as buttons, gaming pieces, beads, and numerous trade items, indicate the long term usage of this room as a storage area. The quantitative differences in other categories, such as culinary and gustatory, medical and health, and indulgences, may also reflect the multiple functions of the west room of this Indians' and Artisans' House.

Blacksmithing Tools

In addition to the basic equipment including the forge, bellows, anvil, and slack tub (Bealer 1984: 74), the blacksmith also had a variety of other tools. The ancillary tools were needed to make other tools and hardware necessary for daily activities. These tools were used to shape, cut, and bend the hot iron from the forge into the required items. Besides tools, the blacksmith generally kept a supply of iron for the raw material from which the various tools and hardware were manufactured.

The blacksmithing tools recovered from the 1968–1972 archeological investigations at Fort Union included anvil tools, hammers, tongs, hacksaw blades, chisels, punches, files, and reamers.

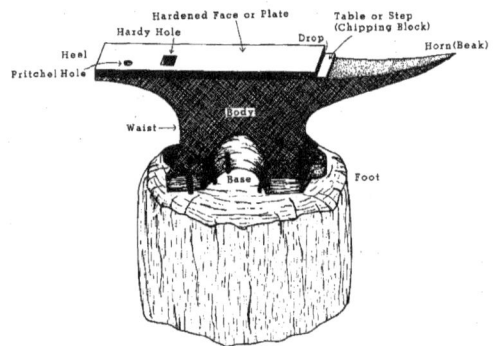

FIGURE 10. English or London anvil.

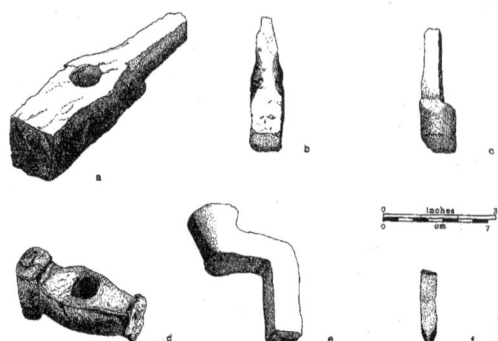

FIGURE 11. Anvil tools from Fort Union.

Anvil Tools

The anvil was one of the major implements of the blacksmith (Hogg 1964:40). The forge was used to heat the iron, but it was on the anvil that the blacksmith made his tools and other products. While the forge represented the heart of the typical blacksmith shop, the anvil was its soul (Watson 1977:23). The anvil was one of the few tools/implements that the blacksmith did not make. Until 1843 when Mark Fisher manufactured the first anvil in the United States, all anvils were imported from Europe (Smith 1966:64). While several varieties existed, the British and American smiths preferred the English or London pattern (Figure 10).

It was on the anvil that the blacksmith at Fort Union made the majority of iron tools and hardware required by the fort's inhabitants. A variety of ancillary tools were utilized in conjunction with the anvil to shape, cut, and bend the hot iron from the forge. The anvil tools were often linked to the anvil by a square shank which fitted into the hardy hole. Anvil tools were often made by the smith to fulfill specific functions or personal preferences (Bealer 1984:75). Three types of anvil tools are among the materials recovered at Fort Union: 1) swages, 2) fullers, and 3) hardies.

Swages

Swages are forming or shaping anvil tools (Smith 1966:121). Swages consist of a large diver-sity of shapes designed for specific purposes. They include top swages, bottom swages, drifts, and heading tools (Bealer 1984:95). Five specimens/fragments of swages were recovered.

Top and *bottom swages* consist of matched pairs. The bottom swages have square shanks which fit into the hardy hole on the anvil. The top swages have handles which fit into the eye that extends through the head of the tool. The metal to be shaped is placed between the swages, and the top swage receives the blows from either a sledge or heavy hand hammer. Top and bottom swages may also be used separately (Smith 1966: 121–122). A single square top swage was recovered during the excavations (Figure 11a). It is manufactured from hand-forged wrought iron. The larger end is slightly battered from repeated hammer blows. The handle would have fit in the circular eye.

Drifts are internal, one-piece swages used to shape and finish eyes of adzes, axes, hammers, and other eyed tools. Their shape varies from circular to rectangular depending upon the type of eye utilized in the tool. Two square and one oval cross-sectional drifts were recovered. They have a short taper at the end struck by the hammer with the long taper inserted into the partially formed eye (Bealer 1984:95–96). One square drift has a notched midsection which may have been utilized for the gripping of the drift by a pair of tongs, or it may have been wrapped with an iron rod to act as a handle

(Figure 11b). The ends opposite the working surface of these drifts exhibit battering resulting from repeated hammer blows. The drifts appear to be hand-forged from wrought iron.

Heading tools are used to make nail or bolt heads and come in a variety of sizes depending upon the dimension of the required nails or bolts. The tools are made from an iron bar which has holes punched into it corresponding to the nail or bolt size being manufactured (Bealer 1984: 96–97). Other bolt heading tools are solid swages used to make the head of a bolt or rivet while at the same time preventing the head from flattening or spreading (Smith 1966:124–125). The heading tool from Fort Union is of the second type and has a cylindrical head with a square shank (Figure 11c).

Fullers

Fullers are also shaping tools and, like the swages, they come in top and bottom pairs (Smith 1966:122). Top fullers have blunted, wedge-shaped, or rounded ends that fit in the groove of a bottom fuller. The fuller is used to draw out large pieces by indenting the surface of the hot iron which is subsequently smoothed with a heavy hammer or flattener (Bealer 1984:136). Besides drawing large pieces, they are also used to form grooves, collars, or other depressions in hot metal (Smith 1966:122). Two specimens were recovered at Fort Union. The Fort Union top fuller has a working edge that resembles a wide-edged chisel which has been rounded, and the opposite end exhibits heavy battering from numerous hammer blows (Figure 11d). The bottom fuller is bent into an S-shape (Fugure 11e). The head is slightly flared and circular in shape while the body is square in cross section. The bottom fuller is designed to fit into the hardy hole of the anvil.

Square Hardy

Hardies are anvil tools which are used to cut or create holes in both hot and cold metal (Smith 1966:122). A square hardy is made from a cut

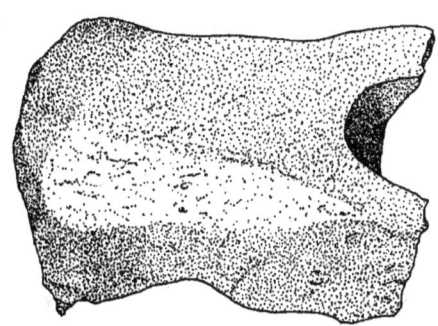

a

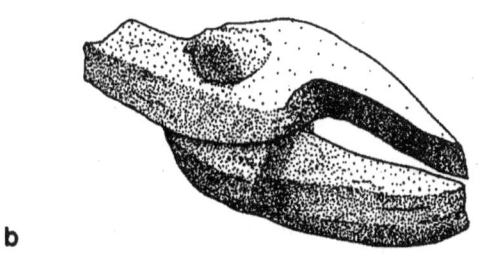

b

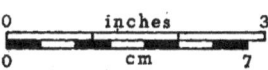

FIGURE 12. Sledge hammer and tong fragment, Fort Union.

piece of square, wrought iron rod. The tip tapers to a point for more accurate placement of the hardy. One hardy specimen recovered at Fort Union was used to produce a square hole by punching the hardy through the metal (Figure 11f).

Hammers

The hammer is not only an essential blacksmithing tool but also is used by a variety of other artisans including carpenters, tinsmiths, coopers, and farriers. The hammer is used to apply the force necessary to shape, cut, or punch metal or wood. By utilizing hammers of different weights, the blacksmith could produce the force required for a job by controlling the mass and acceleration of the hammer blow. The blacksmith, as well as other artisans, also used numerous hammers of various shapes. Some may be made of iron or steel while others may be manufactured from copper or lead to provide the worker with hard or soft heads as required (Bealer 1984:81).

The two hammers among the blacksmithing tools from Fort Union include an octagonal, 14 lb. (6.35 kg) sledge hammer fragment (Figure 12a) and a blank tinner's hammer. The sledge hammer is designed for both light and heavy forging (Smith 1966:103). It may also be used to drive wedges for felling trees and splitting logs, and to drive spokes into wheel hubs, etc. (Salaman 1975:233,235). The tinner's hammer, on the other hand, is a light hammer used in delicate work such as the shaping of tinned sheet metal or cupric metal. The bell of the Fort Union hammer is square, as is the face. The peen tapers from the eye; however, the oval eye is not completely punched through the body. Apparently, the hammer broke during the forging and shaping process.

Tongs

Tongs are large pincer-like tools used by the blacksmith to handle hot metal while it is being shaped (Smith 1966:136). These tools also vary in size and shape, and the majority are probably forged by the individual smith to meet his needs (Hogg 1964:49–52). There are three flat, straight-lip tone fragments in the Fort Union collection (Figure 12b). They consist of the head portion of the tongs with the handles broken near the pivot where the handle rods were forge welded to the head. The break occurs at a 45 degree angle which is typical of a forge weld.

Hacksaw Blades

Two hacksaw blade fragments were recovered during the previous archaeological investigations

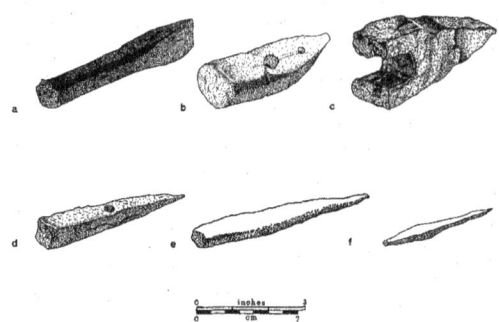

FIGURE 13. Chisels (*a–c*) and punches (*d–f*) associated with Fort Union blacksmiths.

at Fort Union. The hacksaw is a metal-cutting bow saw which has a shallow metal frame and a separate saw blade. The saw blade is attached to the frame by two metal pins which fit through the holes at the ends of the blade. The blade is tensioned in place by a thumbscrew in the saw frame (Salaman 1975:421). The fragments consist of the mid-sections of the hacksaw blade.

Chisels

Chisels represent metal cutting "set tools" that are set in place and struck with a hammer (Bealer 1984:460). Chisels are divided into set and hand-held chisels. Set chisels have handles and may be used for either hot or cold work. Hand-held chisels are designed for cold work. Chisels are also called cutters or rod chisels in the literature (Smith 1966: 115). Hot set chisels, or cutters, are utilized to cut hot metal. The angle of the cutting edge (approximately 30 degrees) is generally less than a cold chisel since heating the metal makes it softer so the cutting angle of the chisel does not have to be as great (Smith 1966:115). The cold chisels are used to cut the metal when it is cold and generally have cutting angles of 60 degrees. They are also generally heavier and wider than a hot chisel of comparable size since cutting harder, cold metal requires greater force and strength (Smith 1966:115). Twelve hand held, cold chisels (Figure 13a); one cold set chisel (Figure 13b); and two hot set chisels (Figure 13c) are represented in the artifact collections from Fort Union.

Punches

Blacksmith punches are used on hot metal to crease or produce holes. The punches taper to a point in order to spread the metal as they are driven through (Smith 1966:112). Blacksmith punches are easier and quicker to use than drills (Bealer 1984:87). They may also be used to drive keys into or from shafts and to mark holes on metal for drilling (Salaman 1975:383–385). Punches, like chisels, come in two forms: 1) set, or handled; and 2) hand held. The tips of the punches come in a variety of shapes in order to made circular, square, heart-shaped, and diamond-shaped holes. Other types of holes can be made by special shaped punches, including holes shaped like arrowheads or fleurs-de-lis (Bealer 1984:89). The tips may be pointed or blunt.

The 18 punches recovered from Fort Union consist of both the set and the hand held varieties. The punches appear to have been hand forged or made from old files. Twelve punches taper along the entire length of the shank from the butt to the point. Two of these are set punches (Figure 13d) but 10 are hand held (Figure 13e). Six additional specimens are shaped similarly to a brace bit with the widest part of the shank below the butt (Figure 13f). The point tapers from the widest part of the shank. They have either round or square points or blunt tips and are hand held. The specimens show little battering on their heads, probably evidence for resharpening to avoid the possibility of splintering (Smith 1966:113).

Files

Files are metal bars which have a series of raised teeth or cutting edges designed to cut metal or wood by abrasion. Although the smith could put a finish on a piece of work with a hammer and flatter, he often utilized a file to shape the pieces for the final fitting and for pieces which could be made by filing easier than by forging (Bealer 1984:110). Files are also used to sharpen other tools. Files are generally made from cast steel or hardened iron with the cuts applied by hand or by machine (Smith 1966:244–250). Cast steel, in this sense, refers to the process of casting the steel in ingots to be forged later, and not to the process of molding the tool directly from molten steel (Bealer 1984: 39).

Files are graded by their shape, size, fineness of cut, and purpose (Knight 1875:840). The blacksmith, as well as other artisans, would have numerous files of every shape, size, and cut (Bealer 1984:110). Files can be divided into three basic categories: 1) rasps which have separate, large pointed teeth; 2) mill files which have cuts resembling grooves on a mill wheel; and 3) mill bastard files with slanting cuts that follow the bar sinister of medieval heraldry (Bealer 1984:110–111). Cuts on a file may be single (float), double (crisscross), or rasp tooth. A variety of shapes also exist including rectangular (flat), round, half round, square, triangular, and fusiform (cigar-shaped).

The files from Fort Union appear to be factory manufactured. Two flat files have manufacturers' marks stamped on their tangs, but only one file (Figure 14a) has decipherable words (" . . . ST STEEL"). The words probably are "CAST STEEL," indicating the manner of manufacture of the metal utilized to make the file (Salaman 1975: 246). The process was invented in 1740 by Benjamin Huntsman of Sheffield, England. The term "cast steel" has come to indicate a tool of high quality. Two rat-tail tangs were also stamped. One fragment bore the lettering ". . . ANTE" over "ST86 . . ." which probably refers to the manufacturer and lot number. The second fragment has the partial word ". . . MTES" over "STEEL." The first word probably refers to the manufacturer and the second word to the mode of manufacture of the steel (i.e., cast steel) used in the file.

A total of 58 files/fragments of various sizes, shapes, and cuts have been recovered from the previous excavations at Fort Union. These include 15 flat files, 9 triangular files, 8 half round files, 2 frame saw files, 4 square files, 1 round file, and 19 rat-tailed file tangs. The majority of the files re-

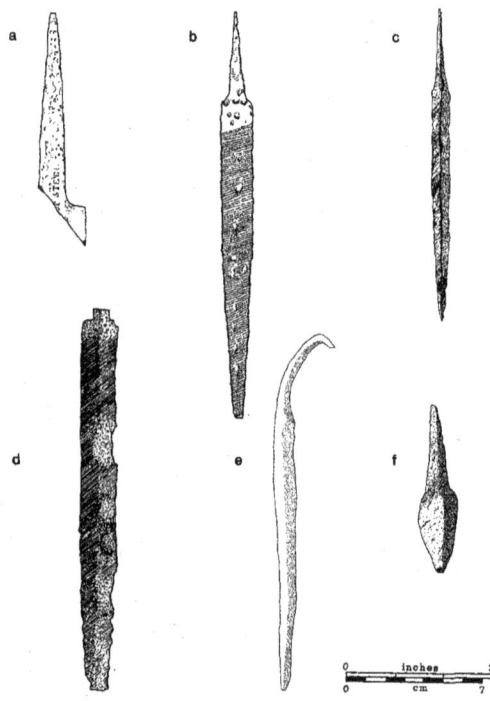

FIGURE 14. Files (*a–e*) and reamer (*f*).

square corners (Clark and Lyman 1974:48). The half round files (Figure 14d) have a semi-circular cross section and seven have a single cut as opposed to the double cut seen on the eighth. This type of file is another general purpose file which can be used on both flat and curved surfaces (Knight 1875:840; Clark and Lyman 1974:48; Philbin and Ettlinger 1988:52). Half round files have also been used to sharpen pit saws (Salaman 1975:439). The frame saw files are thick files used to sharpen the teeth of large saws (i.e., the pit saw). The square files taper along all four sides to a point at the tip (Figure 14e). These files are designed to enlarge rectangular-shaped holes and slots; smooth square corners; and for starting keyways and grooves for cotters, splines, or wedges (Knight 1876:2294; Clark and Lyman 1974:48; Philbin and Ettlinger 1988:52). The mid-section of the round file also appears to taper. While files represent metalworking, woodworking, or farriering tools, worn files also provide a source of high grade steel for the blacksmith (Light 1984:20).

Reamers

Reamers are utilized to enlarge or true an existing hole which was previously bored, or punched, into the metal (Smith 1966:221). The three reamers recovered from the 1968–1972 excavations at Fort Union are hand forged. They are made from square rods which flare near the mid-section and taper towards one end to facilitate the starting of the reamer in the hole to be enlarged (Figure 14f). The reamers may have fitted in a wooden handle or the chuck of a brace.

Final Remarks

Two of the four blacksmith shops at Fort Union have been excavated and the artifacts analyzed. The 1968–1972 excavations revealed the structural remains of the foundations, forges, fireplaces, and, in the 1850s Blacksmith Shop, the location of the anvil base and the charcoal bin. Other evidence for the shop layouts is lacking; however, a mini-

covered appear to be mill files, although the blunt, double-cut, tapered flat file; one triangular file; a double-cut, half round file; and the framing saw files are bastard-style files.

The flat files consist of 11 single-cut, parallel-sided files; one single-cut, tapered file; and three blunt, double-cut, tapered files (Figure 14b). Flat or rectangular files are typically general purpose files used for a variety of shaping and sharpening activities. The flat, single-cut files, also called mill files, are designed for general purpose metal work or tool sharpening (Philbin and Ettlinger 1988:52). The double-cut, flat files are designed for rough work with the single-cut, flat files used for fine precision work of the final smoothing of a metal object (Clark and Lyman 1974:48). The triangular files taper to a point (Figure 14c). These files are especially designed for sharpening saws (Knight 1876:2626; Salaman 1975:439), although they can be used to file acute interior angles and clean out mum of three functional areas probably existed in the structures. These include the forge area, storage area, and domestic area. In addition to the structural evidence, a variety of blacksmithing tools are among the materials recovered from these excavations. The tools represent steps in the manufacture of materials and implements from the initial shaping of the iron to the finished product. The 1988 excavations have also clarified the nature of the smithy identified in the western end of the Indians' and Artisans' House as relating to the U.S. Army occupation during the mid-1860s. Analyses of the 1829–1833 smithy and the 1840s shop are presently in progress.

ACKNOWLEDGMENTS

The author would like to thank Dr. F. A. Calabrese and the staff of the Midwest Archeological Center for their support during the project. The author would especially like to thank Dr. Douglas D. Scott, Rocky Mountain Division Archaeologist, for his helpful insight and guidance during the analysis portion of the project. The author would also like to thank William J. Hunt, Jr., Fort Union Project Director, and Carol Raish, the Center's editor, for their editorial comments and assistance. The author appreciates the work of Carrol Moxham and Mary Johnson in the preparation of the illustrations and photographs for this paper. While all of these people provided invaluable assistance, the author alone takes all responsibility for any errors contained herein.

REFERENCES

ANGUS, CAROLE A., AND GARL R. FALK
1986   *Fort Union Trading Post National Historic Site (32WI17) Material Culture Reports, Part VI: Preliminary Analysis of Vertebrate Fauna from the 1968–1972 Excavations.* Midwest Archeological Center Reports, Lincoln, Nebraska.

ARMOUR, DAVID A.
1976   Jean-Baptiste Amiot: A Blacksmith at Michilimackinac. In *Firearms on the Frontier: Guns at Fort Michilimackinac, 1715–1781,* edited by T. M. Hamilton, pp. 25–26. Reports in Mackinac History and Archaeology No. 5. Mackinac Island State Park Commission, Mackinac Island, Michigan.

BEALER, ALEX W.
1984   *The Art of Blacksmithing.* Third ed. Harper and Row, New York.

BOLLER, HENRY A.
1868   *Among the Indians, Eight Years in the Far West, 1856–1866.* T. Ellwood Zell, Philadelphia.

CHITTENDEN, HIRAM MARTIN
1986   *The American Fur Trade of the Far West.* 2 vols. Reprint of 1935 edition. University of Nebraska Press, Lincoln.

CLARK, STEPHEN, AND DANIEL LYMAN
1974   *The Incredible Illustrated Tool Book.* Pathfinder Publications, Boston.

DENIG, EDWIN
1986   Description of Fort Union. In *Audubon and His Journals,* Vol. 2, edited by Maria R. Audubon, pp. 180–188. Reprint of 1897 edition. Dover Publications, New York.

DE VORE, STEVEN L.
1988   *Fort Union Trading Post National Historic Site (32WI17) Material Culture Reports, Part VII: Building Hardware, Construction Materials, Tools, and Fasteners.* Midwest Archeological Center Reports, Lincoln, Nebraska.

1990a   *Fort Union Trading Post National Historic Site (32WI17) Material Culture Reports, Part VIII: Trade Goods, Tools, Transportation, and Miscellaneous Materials.* Midwest Archeological Center Reports, Lincoln, Nebraska, in press.

1990b   *Fort Union Trading Post National Historic Site (32WI17) Material Culture Reports, Part IX: Tobacco Pipes.* Midwest Archeological Center Reports, Lincoln, Nebraska, in press.

1990c   *Fort Union Trading Post National Historic Site (32WI17) Material Culture Reports, Part X: Trade Beads.* Midwest Archeological Center Reports, Lincoln, Nebraska, in press.

GILLIO, DAVID "A"
1973   1972 Excavations at Fort Union Trading Post National Historic Site, North Dakota. Contract No. 4970B20155, Department of Anthropology, University of Colorado, Boulder. Report submitted to National Park Service, Midwest Archeological Center, Lincoln, Nebraska.

HOGG, GARRY
1964   *Hammer and Tongs: Blacksmithery Down the Ages.* Hutchinson & Co., London.

HUMMEL, EDWARD A.
1938   Special Report, Fort Union, North Dakota. Ms. on file, Midwest Archeological Center, Lincoln, Nebraska.

HUNT, WILLIAM J., JR.
1986a   *Fort Union Trading Post National Historic Site (32WI17) Material Culture Reports, Part I: A Critical*

Review of the Archeological Investigations. Midwest Archeological Center Reports, Lincoln, Nebraska.

1986b *Fort Union Trading Post National Historic Site (32WI17) Material Culture Reports, Part II: Food Related Materials.* Midwest Archeological Center Reports, Lincoln, Nebraska.

1986c *Fort Union Trading Post National Historic Site (32WI17) Material Culture Reports, Part III: Personal and Recreational Materials.* Midwest Archeological Center Reports, Lincoln, Nebraska.

1986d *Fort Union Trading Post National Historic Site (32WI17) Material Culture Reports, Part IV: Firearms, Trapping, and Fishing Equipment.* Midwest Archeological Center Reports, Lincoln, Nebraska.

1986e *Fort Union Trading Post National Historic Site (32WI17) Material Culture Reports, Part V: Buttons as Closures, Buttons as Decoration: A Nineteenth Century Example from Fort Union.* Midwest Archeological Center Reports, Lincoln, Nebraska.

HUNT, WILLIAM, J., JR., AND LYNELLE A. PETERSON
1988 *Fort Union Trading Post Archeology and Architecture: Fort Union, The 1986 Excavations.* Midwest Archeological Center Reports, Lincoln, Nebraska.

HUSTED, WILFRED M.
1970 1969 Excavations at Fort Union Trading Post National Historic Site, North Dakota: A Progress Summary. Ms. on file, Midwest Archeological Center, Lincoln, Nebraska.

1971 1970 Excavations at Fort Union Trading Post National Historic Site, North Dakota: A Progress Summary. Ms. on file, Midwest Archeological Center, Lincoln, Nebraska.

KNIGHT, EDWARD H.
1875 *Knight's American Mechanical Dictionary: Being a Description of Tools, Instruments, Machines, Processes, and Engineering; History of Inventions; General Technological Vocabulary; and Digest of Mechanical Appliances in Science and the Arts.* Vol. 2(Felt-Per). J. B. Ford and Company, New York.

1876 *Knight's American Mechanical Dictionary: Being a Description of Tools, Instruments, Machines, Processes, and Engineering; History of Inventions; General Technological Vocabulary; and Digest of Mechanical Appliances in Science and the Arts.* Vol. 3(Per-Zym). Hurd and Houghton, New York.

KURZ, RUDOLPH FRIEDERICH
1986 *The Journal of Rudolph Friederich Kurz: The Life and Work of this Swiss Artist.* Reprint of 1937 edition. Ye Galleon Press, Fairfield, Washington.

LARPENTEUR, CHARLES
1834– Journals of Charles Larpenteur, Vol. 1. Ms. on file,
1837 Minnesota Historical Society Archives, St. Paul.

LIGHT, JOHN D.
1984 Tinker, Trader, Soldier, Smith: A Frontier Fur Trade Blacksmith Shop, Fort Joseph, Ontario, 1796–1812. In *A Frontier Fur Trade Black Smith Shop, 1796–1812,* revised ed., edited by John D. Light and Henry Unglik, pp. 3–49. Studies in Archaeology, Architecture and History, Natural Historic Parks and Sites. Environment Canada-Parks, Ottawa.

1987 Blacksmithing Technology and Forge Construction. *Technology and Culture* 28(3):658–665.

MATTISON, RAY H.
1962 Fort Union: Its Role in the Upper Missouri Fur Trade. *North Dakota History* 29(1–2):181–208.

MAXIMILIAN, PRINCE OF WIED
1832– Diary of a Journey in North America in the Years
1833 1832, 1833, and 1834. Ms. on file, Great Northern Natural Gas Collections, Joslyn Art Gallery, Omaha, Nebraska.

1906 Travels in the Interior of North America. In *Early Western Travels 1748–1846: A Series of Annotated Reprints of Some of the Best and Rarest Contemporary Volumes of Travel, Descriptive of the Aborigines and Social and Economic Conditions in the Middle and Far West, During the Period of Early American Settlement-Part I of Maximilian, Prince of Wied's, Travels in the Interior of North America, 1832–1834,* Vol. 22, edited by Reuben Gold Thwaites. Reprint of 1843 edition. Arthur H. Clark Company, Cleveland.

McRAVEN, CHARLES
1981 *Country Blacksmithing.* Harper and Row, New York.

MISSOURI HISTORICAL SOCIETY
1983 *American Fur Company Account Books.* Missouri Historical Society, St. Louis. Microfilm.

MOORE, JACKSON "SMOKEY" W., JR.
1968 Summary of Archeological Investigations, Fort Union Trading Post National Historic Site. Memorandum, (dated 10/9/1968) on file, Midwest Archeological Center, Lincoln, Nebraska.

NUTE, GRACE L.
1945 The Papers of the American Fur Company: A Brief Estimate of Their Significance. In *Annual Report of the American Historical Association for the Year 1944,* Vol. 2, pp. 519–538. Reprint of 1927 edition. United States Government Printing Office, Washington.

PETERSON, LYNELLE A., AND WILLIAM J. HUNT, JR.
1990 *The 1987 Investigations at Fort Union Trading Post: Archeology and Architecture.* Midwest Archeological Center Reports, Lincoln, Nebraska, in press.

PHILBIN, TOM, AND STEVE ETTLINGER
1988 *The Complete Illustrated Guide to Everything Sold in Hardware Stores.* Macmillan, New York.

PHILLIPS, PAUL C., AND J. S. SMURR
1961 *The Fur Trade.* 2 vols. University of Oklahoma Press, Norman, Oklahoma.

Ross, Lester A., Bryn H. Thomas,
Charles H. Hibbs, and Caroline D. Carley
1975 Fort Vancouver Excavations—X: Southeastern Fort Area. Ms. on file, Fort Vancouver National Historic Site, Vancouver, Washington.

Salaman, R. A.
1975 Dictionary of Tools Used in the Woodworking and Allied Trades, ca.1700–1970. Macmillan, New York.

Smith, H.R. Bradley
1966 Blacksmiths' and Farriers' Tools at Shelburne Museum—A History of Their Development from Forge to Factory. Museum Pamphlet Series, Number 7. Shelburne Museum, Shelburne, Vermont.

Sprague, Roderick
1980 A Functional Classification for Artifacts from 19th and 20th Century Sites. North American Archaeologist 2(3):251–261.

Thompson, Erwin N.
1968 Fort Union Trading Post Historic Structures Report, Part II, Historical Data Section. Office of Archeology and Historic Preservation, Division of History, National Park Service, U.S. Department of the Interior, Washington, D. C.
1986 Fort Union Trading Post: Fur Trade Empire on the Upper Missouri. Theodore Roosevelt Nature and History Association, Medora, North Dakota.

Watson, Aldren
1977 The Village Blacksmith. Second ed. Thomas Y. Crowell Company, New York.

Steven L. De Vore
Interagency Archeological Services
Rocky Mountain Regional Office
National Park Service
12795 W. Alameda Parkway
P.O. Box 25287
Denver, Colorado 80225

Mary Van Buren
Brendan J. M. Weaver

Contours of Labor and History: A Diachronic Perspective on Andean Mineral Production and the Making of Landscapes in Porco, Bolivia

ABSTRACT

The first Spanish silver mines in South America were located in Porco, Bolivia, and while these were rapidly eclipsed by the spectacular output from nearby Potosí, Porco has remained an important mining center until the present. The long-term history of mineral production is embodied in the landscape, which bears evidence of a diverse set of labor practices and technologies deployed at different scales to process ore. A decade of archaeological research at Porco demonstrates the role this landscape has played in mediating the relationship between indigenous workers and the broader political and economic forces that prevailed under the Inka, Spanish, and Republican regimes.

Introduction

Like much of southern Bolivia, Porco (Figure 1) has been the focus of mining activities for the last 500 years. Silver from this region transformed not only the Spanish Empire, but also sparked a metamorphosis of the European financial system that resulted in the emergence of a truly global economy. The history of Bolivian mining cannot be understood as a development that paralleled but lagged behind its northern counterparts; it was not characterized by a linear march towards large-scale industry, nor did the formation of the workforce follow the same trajectory as it did in Europe or even other parts of Latin America (Zulawski 1987; Langer 1996). In contrast to the development of mining in the United States and other affluent nations, the process that unfolded in Bolivia consisted of a complex series of interactions between workers and "foreign" elites that involved both competition and interdependence. This resulted in production at different scales and for different purposes, and—from the viewpoint of mine owners—a labor force that was undisciplined and unreliable. The present study investigates these issues from the perspective of Porco, a mining center located 35 km to the southwest of the infamous city of Potosí, and attempts to complement historical research on Bolivian mining by examining the deployment of labor at a single locale over the long term.

A decade of archaeological research at Porco has revealed that, rather than a progressive shift to highly capitalized mining, large- and small-scale projects have coexisted over the past five centuries. These activities have formed a continuum of sites, a landscape that was both produced by and structured labor, the product of a "taskscape" as Ingold (1993) has called it. The landscape played a key role in mediating the relationship between indigenous workers and the broader political and economic forces that prevailed under the Inka, Spanish, and Republican regimes, a process that resulted in a distinctive historical trajectory constituted by the annual or seasonal influx of people within a larger-scale cycle of investment in and abandonment of mine workings. The very nature of Porco as a place must be confronted in order to understand how seasonal movement, the coexistence of multiple scales of mineral exploitation, and a regular influx of newcomers have produced unique landscapes in various political and economic contexts (Agnew 1989:25; Anschuetz et al. 2001). While the creation of these landscapes unfolded across a temporal continuum, we argue that a critical disjuncture occurred in the 19th century when industrial mining followed in the wake of independence. This did not result in the independence of a fully proletarianized labor force, but instead promoted agro-pastoral occupation of the surrounding area that allowed families to work both on the farm and in the mine. Access to wage labor in combination with agricultural production provided households with a buffer against the vagaries of each and also led to the development of a permanent community shaped by its engagement with the local landscape.

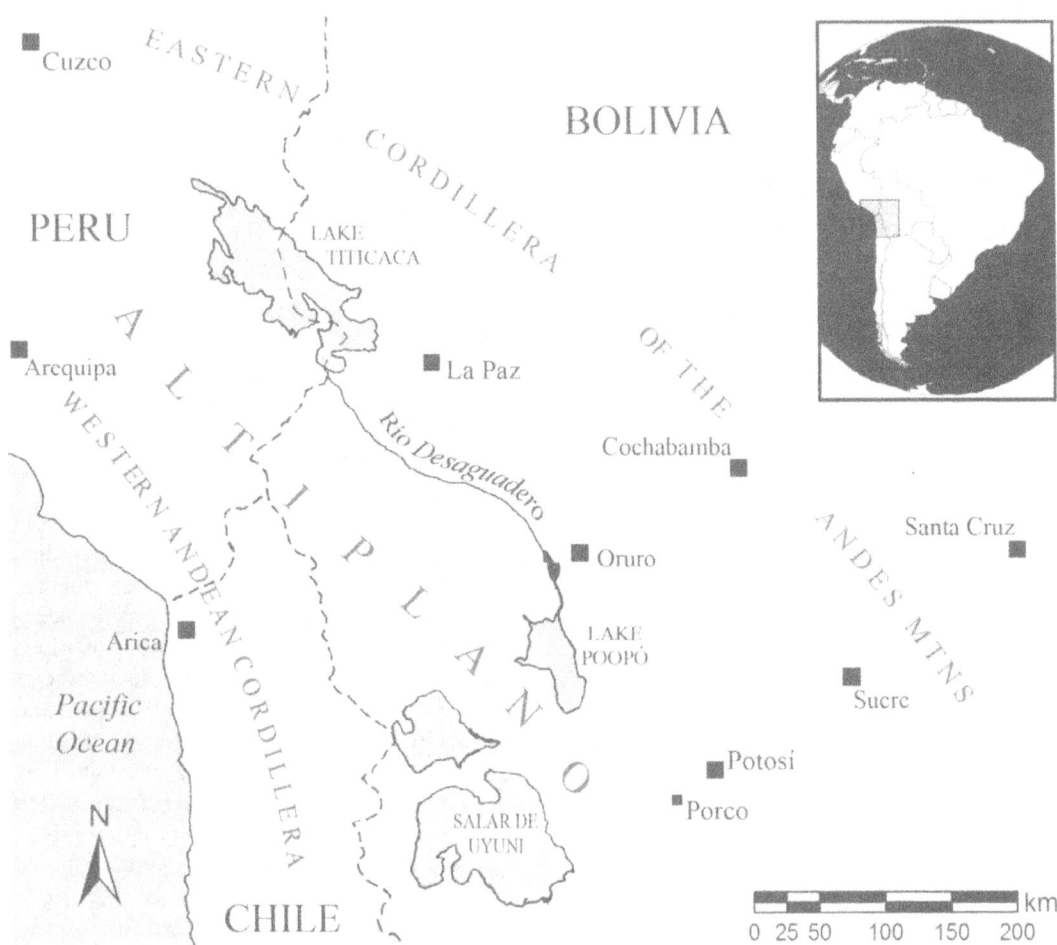

FIGURE 1. Map of the south-central Andes indicating the location of Porco, Bolivia. (Map by Brendan J. M. Weaver, 2011.)

Landscapes and the Global Economy

Investigating the relationship between the local and global, especially when simultaneously considering "nature" and "culture," poses the common conceptual challenge of analyzing phenomena that are typically understood in Western societies as being static and separate, but which are actually mutually constituted and in a constant process of change. An examination of landscape provides one means for negotiating this challenge. A central theme unifying Tim Ingold's work (Ingold 2000, 2011) is the breaking down of conceptual barriers that impede understanding of the dialectical relationships that constitute much of what is viewed

as concrete reality. Ingold's (1993) conceptualization of landscape is tied to the notion of a taskscape. He defines landscape as "the world as it is known to those who dwell therein, who inhabit its places and journey along the paths connecting them." A task is "any practical operation, carried out by a skilled agent in an environment, as part of his or her normal business of life," and each task is positioned in relation to others within an interlocking array of tasks that together form a taskscape (Ingold 1993:156). Landscapes are, then, embodied or concrete taskscapes that are generated by life and particularly by the movement of people through space. They are created by living and moving in a time frame consonant with an

Perspectives from Historical Archaeology:

individual's lifespan but are also concretized in a semidurable form that allows the discernment of long-term change. The advantage, then, of adopting Ingold's perspective on landscape is that it overcomes the conceptual tension between culture and nature (or meaning and the environment), and also provides a means to examine large-scale changes without excluding the daily lived experiences bundled through social practices (Keane 2003:414), such as labor, that occur at a much smaller temporal and geographic scale. Landscape, as a unit of analysis, connects what is often thought of as distinct domains of scale in terms of space and time.

In this study, landscape is understood as mediating the relationship between the larger political economy and the people who worked at Porco. These global forces, which included the shifting meaning of metals, the cyclical demand for minerals, and the changing nature of labor organization, impinged upon the local taskscape through the movement of pilgrims, workers, managers, and material culture into and out of Porco. The historical processes that ensued are similar to those that occurred elsewhere in the Andes, but the specificity of the landscape shaped the unique way that they unfolded over time.

Archaeological Research at Porco

Porco is on the edge of the altiplano in the Cordillera Oriental of southwestern Bolivia, at an elevation of 4,000 m above sea level. Its location on the landscape is marked by Cerro Apu Porco, or Lord Porco, a distinctive flat-topped peak that reaches almost 5,000 m in height. From the summit one looks down on Cerro Huayna Porco, or Young Porco; this mountain is connected to Apu Porco by a ridge and was the source of the silver produced here in Inka and colonial times (Figure 2). Turning to the south and east one can see mountains

FIGURE 2. Cerros Apu Porco and Huayna Porco. (Photo by Brendan J. M. Weaver, 2006.)

unfolding towards the horizon with a few equally distinctive peaks protruding above them: Potosí to the northeast, Chorolque and others to the south. All contain mines, and, like many Andean peaks, they are considered powerful animate residents of the landscape. From this height little evidence of human activity is visible, except to the north where the landscape has been thoroughly shaped by mining. The modern zinc mines and concentration plant now owned by Sinchi Wayra, a subsidiary of Glencore, have transformed the north slope of Apu Porco into a platform for industrial mining, and a large tailings pond dominates the plain to the northwest. The village of Porco sits at the base of Huayna Porco, and a few kilometers in the distance, at the junction of a river, a railway, and a dirt road that connects Potosí and the town of Uyuni, the village of Agua Castilla can be seen. Together Porco and Agua Castilla have a population of about 7,000, and although they are not company towns, all of the people who live in them are somehow connected to the mines.

Today most human activity in Porco is tethered to the two mountains that dominate the landscape, and this appears to have been the case for at least the last 500 years. A number of colonial sources refer to Inka exploitation of the mines, whose silver was transported to Cuzco (de Cieza de León 1984:372). In fact, the summit of Apu Porco is crowned by an irregularly shaped stone platform that is similar to other high-altitude shrines constructed by the Inka on important peaks in the southern Andes (Cruz 2009), in addition to smaller platforms and buildings of uncertain date.

From the summit of Apu Porco only the manifestations of what de Certeau (1984) has characterized as strategies can be seen: the walls of the Inka shrine; the offices, concentration plant, and tailings pond built by foreign companies; and the gridded villages and roads constructed by the state. These landscape features were planned and imposed by powerful entities whose goal was to control local resources—material, spiritual, and human. The vestiges of everyday, often tactical, practices— paths, homes, independent mines—are almost invisible from this distance. Only by descending and investigating the landscape can the ways in which both strategic and everyday activities were carried out in Porco be understood.

From this perspective it becomes clear that even powerful, external institutions had to accommodate local practice, and that both were shaped by historical precedent.

Archaeological research was initiated at Porco because unlike neighboring Potosí it was known to have been exploited in Inka times, if not earlier. In 1995 Proyecto Arqueológico Porco-Potosí was established by Mary Van Buren to examine continuities and disjunctions in the organization of labor and technology at Porco under distinct political regimes, with a particular emphasis on the Inka and colonial periods. Archaeological data were collected over the course of eight field seasons of various lengths using pedestrian surveys, mapping, excavation, and observation of traditional metallurgical techniques. Concurrently, archival research was conducted in Bolivia, Argentina, and Spain by Dr. Ana María Presta (Presta 2008). This paper examines project findings in terms of the ways in which landscapes were constructed over the course of five centuries of mineral exploitation and associated activities. The discussion is divided into two parts. The first examines labor practices under the Inka and Spanish regimes, which were characterized by the movement of workers and pilgrims in and out of Porco from distant provinces, and the shift from state control of production to individual entrepreneurship during the colonial period. The second section considers the ways in which industrial mining reshaped these practices and, perhaps ironically, resulted in a residential population that was more firmly rooted in the village and surrounding countryside.

Spatial Practices under the Inka and Spanish Regimes

The Inka and Spanish empires were organized in profoundly different ways, with wage labor, individual entrepreneurship, the secularization of production, and other aspects of incipient capitalism among the more salient characteristics of the latter. During the colonial period, though, similarities also existed, especially as Spaniards adapted a number of Inka practices for their own purposes. Key among these was the *mita*, a rotating labor tax that often required subjects to leave their agricultural communities in order to work on state-sponsored projects in other regions. At Porco, these differences and continuities are reflected in the ways in which space was organized under both empires.

Inkaic Porco: An Economic and Sacred Center

Much of the Potosí hinterland, including the region of Porco, was within Qaraqara territory when the Spaniards arrived. The Qaraqaras were part of the Charkas Federation, a loose political alliance that occupied what is now south-central Bolivia and which resisted the Inka conquest (Bouysse-Cassagne 1975; del Río 1995). While historical research suggests that Porco may have been an important ceremonial site and that its mineral resources may have been exploited prior to the Inka (Platt et al. 2006:126), archaeological evidence to date has not identified an occupation in the period immediately preceding its annexation by Tawantinsuyu in the 15th century (LeCoq and Cespedes 1996, 1997; Van Buren et al. 2006, 2007). The absence of material remains predating the Inka conquest may be the result of the limited occupation of Porco during this period, which would have consisted of seasonal use by pilgrims or by miners sent by their *mallku*, or ethnic leaders.

Sixteenth-century chroniclers reference the mines at Porco as perhaps the richest in the empire during the Inka period (de Cieza de León 1984:372), attracting particular attention from administrators in Cuzco. However, recent ethnohistorical and archaeological investigations challenge the long-held belief that the rich deposits at Potosí were unknown to the Inka. While there is little doubt that Porco was a particularly valued source of silver, this research suggests that it might actually have been of less importance than Potosí, which appears to have been the site of some metallurgical and ritual activity during Inka times (Platt and Quisbert 2007; Cruz and Absi 2008). Porco's significance may have been exaggerated by the indigenous elite, becoming a proverbial red herring to throw the Spaniards off the track of a more important mining center.

Although Porco was rich in mineral wealth, its elevation, extreme cold, and aridity (Montes de Oca 1989) severely limited its agro-pastoral potential. Today some households supplement their diets with fava beans and tubers grown in small plots along the San Juan River 6 km to the west of Porco, and others maintain small herds

of sheep and llamas, but most food is purchased in the markets of Potosí. During the Inka period, provisions and supplies for the mining operation were probably imported from an administrative center located 35 km to the southwest at Visijsa (near modern-day Yura), which was also an important pre-Inka settlement (Cespedes and LeCoq 1998). Then, as now, there was little except mineral exploitation to attract a permanent population to Porco.

Platt and his colleagues (Platt et al. 2006:135–235) argue that under the Inka, both mining and regional ritual practices were concentrated on the mines themselves, as well as the peaks of Apu and Huayna Porco, shaping the landscape of Porco's environs (Basso 1995; Ashmore and Knapp 1999; Potter 2004). Landscape as a referent is not simply a system of signs or a metaphor, but structures how relationships between entities in space are conceived (Morphy 1995:186). The Inka mining project at Porco was apparently connected to the solar cult at the focal point of the state religion of Tawantinsuyu, and the use of silver from Porco on temples in Cuzco created an indexical link between the center of imperial power and an important natural phenomenon, the rich vein, near the edge of the empire. Documentary evidence suggests a semiotic relationship, deeply seated in Andean dualism, between the silver from Porco and the life-giving light of the sun, the former being the "light" of the inner-world and therefore representing solar dominion (Platt et al. 2006:171). The supernatural entity or *huaca* called Tata Purqu in colonial documents, whose body is the mountain today called Apu Porco, was a deity of war and of the silver-rich mines that revealed the world's inner light (Platt et al. 2006:173). According to ethnohistorical sources, the powers of the animated peaks and mines at Porco were linked to a secondary body, a cultic icon, that was one of the principle foci of religious activity, attracting pilgrims from throughout the region of Charkas, perhaps according to the state ritual calendar. A document produced by Hernán González de la Casa (*Petición del Bachiller Hernán González de la Casa*), a priest in the parish of Toropalca from 1572 to 1577, describes the *huaca* of Porco as composed of three stones and a piece of very rich worked silver, weighing an *arroba*, or 11 kg (Abercrombie 1998:435–6; Platt et al. 2006:184). Platt and his colleagues propose that around the time of the arrival of the Spaniards in Porco in 1538, the idol was moved from its shrine in Porco to the nearby valley of Caltama, where its cult could be preserved in secret (Platt et al. 2006:139). Whether or not the veins at Porco were exploited prior to the region's conquest by the Inka, the *huacas* of Porco represented a source of hegemonic power for the Inka state, but also took on a primordial political role in the region among members of the Qaraqara-Charka Confederation, as a spatial and symbolic expression of a community united in a singular "cosmovision" (Platt et al. 2006:169) and woven together by the regular movement of worshippers to and from the area.

Inka settlement of Porco was not constructed over a preexisting community but consisted of an entirely planned space (Figure 3). However, given the apparent importance of the mines, the Inka transformation of the region was quite modest. The Inka-built environment consisted of a small administrative center (Jalantaña), a complex with 45 storage structures (the Huayrachinas site), a site for refining silver (Site 80) that had been previously smelted in nearby indigenous wind furnaces known as *huayrachinas* (Huayrachina Alta), two residential compounds at the foot of Cerro Huayna Porco (Uruquilla and Cruz Pampa), and the shrine on the summit of Apu Porco. Metallurgical production seems to have been centralized but spatially and functionally differentiated, most likely because distinct social groups were assigned to different tasks.

The limited range of materials recovered archaeologically suggests temporary occupation focused on specific mining-related activities rather than a permanent settlement by colonists moved by the state from another part of the empire. While these materials do not allow for precise identification of the specific ethnic groups and polities from which the workers came, the documentary record indicates that Lupaqas and Carangas were among them. The homelands of both of these groups lie outside Qaraqara territory and at some distance from Porco, in the western Titicaca Basin and to the southwest of Lake Poopó, respectively.

The seasonal nature of metallurgical labor meant constant movement between subject communities and the mining center, resulting in a large annual influx of people coming from distant provinces. The settlement at Porco, although temporary and seasonal, would have taken on a unique and cosmopolitan character. With a very limited native population in the vicinity, the Inka state would have brought *mit'a* workers and *yanakuna*, or skilled retainers, whose positions were often hereditary (Rowe 1982), from various parts of the empire together in an unfamiliar and temporarily occupied space. This is significant because native Andeans in many agrarian communities today (and in the past) conceptualize their living landscape in terms of a complex relationship between kin group, polity, production, and sacred places,

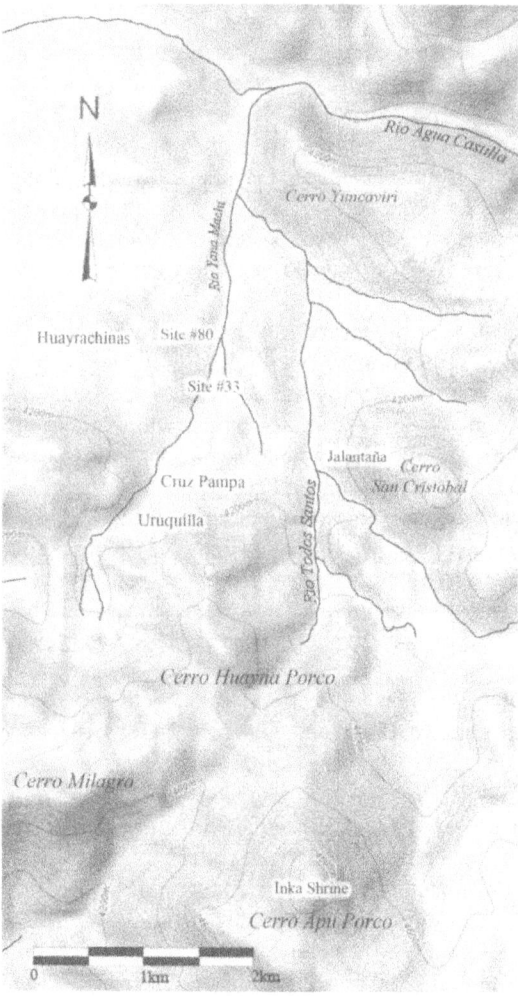

FIGURE 3. Major Inka sites located during survey. (Map by Brendan J. M. Weaver, 2011.)

or *huacas* (Urton 1981:37; Bastien 1985:190; Abercrombie 1998:322; Allen 2002:35). While the temporary residents of Porco would not have understood the local landscape to have been generative of their own social groups, they probably would have conceptualized their engagement with the mines and its products as a metaphorical extension of agricultural labor, much as the Inka did (Berthelot 1986) and some communities do today (Platt 1983).

Mining in the prehispanic Andes was a sacred act, transforming the fruit of the earth through human energy into a product imbued both with labor's and the mineral's own inherent properties (Lechtman 1996, 2007; Lechtman and Klein 1999). There is no archaeological evidence for the production of finished objects at Porco. Instead, refined silver was transported to Cuzco where it was used to adorn the Korikancha—the sacred center of the empire—and the litter upon which the Inka emperor, a descendant of the sun, was carried. The movement of metals from a distant corner of the Inka Empire into Cuzco, where it was used in part to decorate the litter on which the Inka traveled, is analogous to the movement of other sacred elements across the Andean landscape, both in the prehispanic past as well as today. Modern-day Andean pilgrimages are often described as sharing features with a deeply rooted, yet diversely expressed, cosmology that associates the ritualized movement of people across sacred landscapes with the cycling of water and sacred fluids (Bastien 1985; Allen 2002), the pathways of sacred celestial bodies (Urton 1981), the cycling of offices, and local ritual processions (Abercrombie 1998).

Michael Sallnow (Sallnow 1981, 1987) has examined the way ritualized and routine movement through Andean spaces plays on social memory, mapping social relationships, including cohesion and disjuncture, onto local landscapes and broad social geographies. The movement of sacred objects and pilgrims from their places of origin to sacred centers creates what Sallnow calls a "translocal landscape," which links the local pilgrim's community to the shrine itself across space through an appropriation of the shrine as local (Sallnow 1987:204). The *capacocha* (*capac ucha*) rite, a ceremony in which provincial youth traveled to the Korikancha to be received by the Inka and then returned to

their homelands to be sacrificed (Besom 2009), in some ways mirrors the movement of metals from Porco to Cuzco. The *capacocha* and other Inka rites where persons and objects moved across provincial divisions likely played a crucial role in fomenting social bonds, but also in how boundaries were constructed between persons and groups, and how symbols became multivalent through engagement (Rostworowski de Diez Canseco 1988:65–66). The procession of these children and precious metals into and out of the sacred imperial center wove the empire together in a process that physically acknowledged both the value of the periphery and its subordination to the center.

Spanish Porco: The Potosí Hinterland

After Francisco Pizarro defeated Atahuallpa and usurped authority over Tawantinsuyu (1531 to 1539) he was free to begin to assimilate its territories. The southern region (Qollasuyu) was incorporated into the Spanish Empire in 1538–1539 as the Inka threat receded. Francisco Pizarro's brothers, Hernando and Gonzalo, were shown the Inka project at Porco by Kuysara, the leader of the Charka. In Andean terms, this act recognized Castilian sovereignty in the transmittal of a "pact of reciprocity" that the Charka previously had with the Inka state (Platt et al. 2006:126–127). Porco immediately became the center of Spanish silver-mining operations in the Andes, but it fell into relative obscurity by the end of the 16th century after the discovery of the immense deposit at Cerro Rico, Potosí, in 1545.

In its first few years as a Spanish town (Figure 4), Porco's wealth drew great interest, and there were as many as 100 Spanish households in the settlement by the mid-16th century (Capoche 1959:125). However, as the notoriety of Potosí's famous Cerro Rico grew the number of Spaniards in Porco declined, and by 1600 only about 30 *vecinos*, or Spanish residents, remained (de Ocaña 1969:182). The mines of Porco, staffed mostly with draft labor supplemented by enslaved Africans, made very profitable holdings for several prominent Spaniards (Presta 1992, 1999, 2000:160). Skilled labor was provided through the institution of *yanaconaje*, which, roughly based on the Inka system of retainership, brought in individuals and families tied to specific Spaniards and, in theory, divorced from Andean

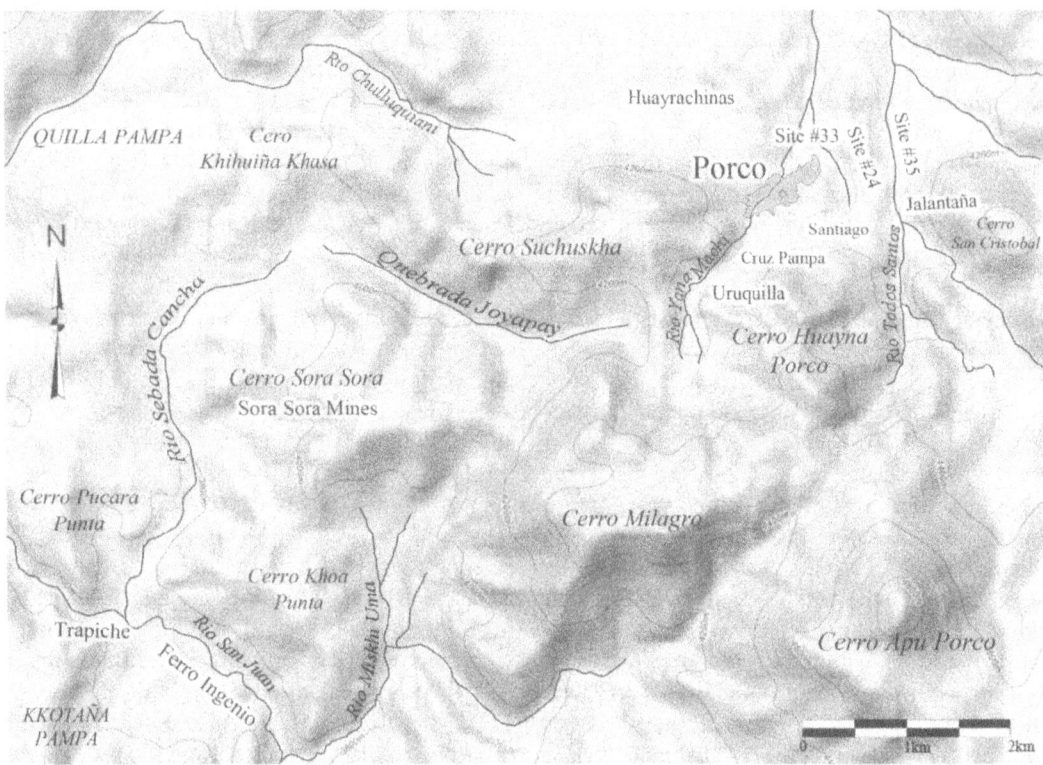

FIGURE 4. Major colonial-period sites located during survey. (Map by Brendan J. M. Weaver, 2011.)

ayllu (community and kinship) structures (Weaver 2008:118–120). This system called for large numbers of relatively unspecialized workers organized into small teams under the supervision of *yanaconas*. As the mining economy of Potosí and its hinterland gained strength around mid-century, Spanish administrators began to experiment with more-formalized labor structures, drawing workers from across the viceroyalty. By the 1570s securing sufficient inexpensive labor for the mines was still a considerable problem, and resolving this issue was one of the principal goals of reforms issued by Viceroy Francisco de Toledo. Toledo's response was an expansion of the *mita*, a labor obligation in which indigenous communities throughout the Viceroyalty of Peru provided a portion of their population on a rotation. However, while the *mita* remained the foundation of a system which famously supplied the majority of the mining labor to the silver mines of Potosí until the 18th century, its application at other mines on the altiplano

was less consistent, leading to large numbers of wage laborers in places like Porco (Cole 1985; Tandeter 1993).

With the arrival of the Spaniards, the landscape of Porco underwent radical reorganization, bringing out the stark differences in race and class, mapping labor onto the geological contours of the area in new ways, and transforming the use of sacred space. Inkaic Porco consisted of several clusters of habitation nestled at the foot of Apu and Huayna Porco, while the earliest incarnation of the Spanish town reproduced an urban core on a grid plan around a central plaza, catering to its first *encomenderos* and entrepreneurs. In contrast to the Spanish administration, Inka production seems to have been arranged by different tasks accomplished by distinct categories of workers. Under the Spaniards, this form of compartmentalization gave way to redundant task groups which reused Inka infrastructure. While the Spaniards concentrated their residences in the newly founded European-style village, the archaeological record in the surrounding area reflects both the residential separation of Indians and Europeans, as well as the decentralization of the labor process that followed the collapse of the Inka state (Van Buren and Presta 2010). With one exception, there was a lack of investment in new industrial infrastructure; instead, every building constructed during the Inka period was reused. Excavations in Uruquilla, Cruz Pampa, Jalantaña, and Huayrachinas yielded domestic debris as well as features and artifacts associated with the production of silver. While the Inka period was characterized by space that was differentiated by distinct tasks coordinated by a centralized administration, the division of this single large-scale mining project into individual mining claims belonging to specific Spaniards fractionalized the landscape into repeating undifferentiated spaces. The same tasks, both industrial and domestic, where carried out in every compound by workers associated with individual mining claims. The only new site established in the early colonial period, outside the Spanish village, was Santiago, a complex built at the foot of Hundimiento, the primary vein exploited at the time. Excavations conducted in 1999 revealed a compound comprised of a series of rectangular rooms surrounding a central patio; the walls were thick and whitewashed on the interior, and the two rooms tested were largely devoid of remains except for a few concentrations of tin-bearing ore, likely the gangue that remained after the silver ore was removed. In the mid-20th century locals referred to this site as "Pizarro's house," but it was probably used to store minerals and, perhaps, equipment rather than as a residence.

By the mid-16th century, several wealthy individuals, companies of individuals, and the Church were working the principal vein of Porco, named for its Spanish "discoverer," Hernando Pizarro. A second vein, the Veta de Los Zoras, located in the Cerro de Sora Sora about 5 km to the southwest of town, also seems to have been very profitable (Capoche 1959:126–127; Weaver 2008:106–116). In the late 16th century many claims were granted to the Sora Sora deposit, among them one held by the family of the indigenous man, Alonso Zora, who apparently had discovered the vein. The mines at Sora Sora consist of three formal adits and

numerous shallow pits and tunnels, and extend for 700 m along an east–west trending ridge at an elevation of about 4,200 m. A series of stone buildings, many of which appear to be contemporaneous, were constructed along the southern base of the ridge, adjacent to a ravine. These include housing for workers, storage, a corral, and a number of buildings of unknown function. The extremely low density of diagnostic artifacts at Sora Sora makes the dating of these occupations difficult. A few *botija* fragments, sherds from a small number of indigenous vessels, and a *tupu*, a type of woman's pin—all of which are commonly found at contact-period sites in the region—suggest use during early colonial times, corroborating the historical documents that indicate that these mines were first opened by the Spaniards in the late 16th century.

The Sora Sora mines are linked to most of the mineral processing sites in the San Juan Valley, which lies just to the southwest of Porco. Excavations and architectural survey carried out in 2006 and 2007 at the site of Ferro Ingenio (Figure 5) revealed multiple occupations (Weaver 2008), following a cycle of use and reuse common to many sites in Porco. The earliest colonial occupation, dated by material culture, including a coin (Po-153) minted in Potosí between 1596 and 1612 (Menzel 2004:266), coincides with the initial period of exploitation of the mines in Cerro Sora Sora. This component of the site consists of about 12 to 15 small rectangular structures that were used for domestic purposes as well as for refining silver. This early occupation seems to have followed the larger trends in Porco of seasonal use by a skilled class of workers, probably indigenous *yanaconas*, tied by tribute obligations to particular Spaniards. These workers triturated high-grade ore using manual grinding technology called *quimbaletes*, in conjunction with *huayrachinas* and cupellation hearths, or *tocochimbos*, to smelt and refine the ore (Van Buren and Mills 2005). The remains of *huayrachinas* are located on a hill just above the site. The modest affluence of the workers in the late-16th- and early-17th-century occupation of Ferro Ingenio is demonstrated by the presence of a small number of luxury items, such as silver *tupus*, a tassel of silver-wrapped thread, a European-style leather shoe, provincial Inka vessels, and a small number of imported ceramics such as majolicas and

FIGURE 5. Map of Ferro Ingenio. (Map by Brendan J. M. Weaver, 2007.)

Chinese porcelain. These objects were likely utilized by members of this special class of workers to negotiate their status within colonial society, drawing on symbols of both Inka and Spanish elite material culture (Weaver 2008:132–136; Van Buren and Weaver [2012]).

At the same site, a large stamp mill, or *ingenio*, driven by an overshot wheel powered by water diverted from the San Juan River, was constructed in the early to mid-18th century to pulverize ores of lesser quality. Indigenous workers mixed the pulverized ore with mercury on a large stone patio. The resulting amalgam was then heated to drive off the mercury and produce a *piña*, or lump, of pure silver. Two batteries of reverberatory furnaces at the site were probably used for this purpose and to directly smelt higher-grade ore that was also encountered on occasion. Both the mill complex and the early colonial antecedences at the site of Ferro Ingenio and Sora Sora represent formal operations that required considerable capital investment in infrastructure and labor.

The mining and processing of silver at Sora Sora and Ferro Ingenio were largely controlled by well-funded individuals from outside the valley who were motivated by the potential for large profits. The veins at Sora Sora were initially exploited by many of the same wealthy Spaniards who had claims in Porco, as well as the family of Antonio Zoras. When silver production fell off after 1600, Potosí and the surrounding region went into a steep decline. The reopening of Sora Sora and the construction of the stamp mill at Ferro Ingenio appear to have been catalyzed by a change in Spanish tax policy. In 1736 the tax on silver production was reduced from the *quinto*—or fifth—to the *diezemo* or tenth (Garner 1988). This reduced operational costs and promised greater potential profits, generating increased investment in the rehabilitation of old mines and the opening of new ones.

In addition to large mining operations that would have made use of *encomienda*, *mita*, slave, and some wage labor, the small-scale production of silver, often illicit or quasilegal, played a significant role in the economy of the Potosí region (Tandeter 1981, 1993; Stern 1988). Smaller mining and refining enterprises were run mostly by indigenous people or mestizos, and were sometimes viewed as direct competition by wealthier mine and mill owners, particularly when the price of mineral was high. In Porco, *yanaconas* who exploited relatively large holdings owned primarily by Europeans coexisted at times with independent miners who worked at a much smaller scale. Called *"kajcheo"* until recently, this form of mineral exploitation ranged from a fully legal form of sharecropping, in which a mine owner was given part of the mineral produced in exchange for access to the mine, to outright ore theft conducted by individuals or groups, often on the weekends or at night (Tandeter 1981; Rodríguez 1989; Platt 2000).

Site 35, a small metallurgical complex at the foot of Cerro San Cristobal that is clearly visible from the road to the mines is most likely a place where a legal form of *kajcheo* was practiced. The site includes six rectangular foundations, two small grinding platforms with rocker stones for triturating ore, and two crudely made buildings that contain a hearth and small furnaces for refining silver. Excavation of three structures at Site 35 in 2002 yielded a range of tools and technologies utilized in silver refining, small amounts of domestic debris in one building, and the disturbed burial of an indigenous woman. The ceramics consisted mostly of jars, but fragments of cooking vessels and serving bowls were also found; a small percentage of the sherds are from provincial Inka vessels, a type that appears to have lasted until approximately the mid-17th century in this region (Van Buren and Weaver [2012]). Archaeomagnetic samples from one hearth yielded a date of 1650 to 1800 (Lengyel et al. 2010); the provincial Inka sherds, a Nueva Cadiz bead (Smith and Good 1982; Lapham 2001) recovered from the burial, as well as a chevron bead and hawksbell (Mitchem and McEwan 1988; Deagan 2002:145) found in the L-shaped structure suggest that the first part of this range—or perhaps earlier—is most likely.

Site 35 probably housed a small residential population—perhaps just one or two families—that was engaged in the production of metal. The small cupellation hearth would have been appropriate for processing the ore produced by a modest family operation acting independently. Low artifact density and diversity suggest a short-term, seasonal occupation, an interpretation that gains support from the recovery of a cached set of grinding stones hidden in the floor of one of the structures. The residents of the site were probably independent workers, perhaps *k'ajchas* who were exploiting the small mines on the upper slopes of Cerro San Cristobal.

The colonial landscape in Porco was clearly marked by multiple scales of metallurgical production, a reality which would have created noticeable divisions among social spaces. In addition to small-scale production by independent households, *trapiches*, hand-powered mills employing rocker stones that were usually owned by mestizo or wealthy native silver merchants, competed with stamp mills for silver ores generated in large quantities. *Trapiches* were regarded by mine owners as "schools of depravity for the peon" (Rodríguez 1989:134) because of their association with ore thieves and independent miners whose use of alcohol and participation in fiestas and agricultural activities impeded the development of a disciplined workforce. Enrique Tandeter, a historian of colonial mining, estimates that in 1759 high-grading, or ore theft, accounted for almost 38% of the silver produced in Potosí (Tandeter 1993:92), and most of this was processed in native *trapiches*.

One such *trapiche* is located about a kilometer upriver from Ferro Ingenio, near the confluence of the San Juan and the Cebada Cancha rivers. However, as no diagnostic artifacts were recovered from the site, and it was not functioning within the historical memory of local residents, its chronological relationship to Ferro Ingenio remains unknown. Still, regardless of the actual chronological relationship between these sites, Ferro Ingenio and the San Juan *trapiche* represent two different scales of metallurgical production in operation throughout much of the Spanish colonial period, providing a narrative of local competition and class and racial conflict.

The history of Spanish colonial Porco from the 16th to the 18th century was characterized by competition over resources by mine owners, mill operators, and workers. The decentralization of the mining operations and metallurgical production that followed the collapse of the Inka state opened spaces for such competition on multiple scales, creating a fractionalized landscape. What can be seen on the ground across the *porqueño* landscape is the result of local agents engaging both their own geological environment and a far-reaching economy. Still, despite the distinct spatial organization of labor in the Inka and Spanish empires, Apu and Huayna Porco remained central, both in terms of the focus of seasonal economic activity and as an important *huaca* for the largely indigenous workforce.

Industrial Mining in the 19th and 20th Centuries

In 1826, a year after Bolivia gained independence from Spain, the Irish geographer Joseph Pentland initiated a two-year journey through southern Bolivia with the goal of producing a detailed map and an eye towards identifying worthwhile prospects for British investors. He described Porco as having been completely abandoned for some time (Pentland 1975:78), an assessment that is confirmed by the archaeological record. With the exception of Sora Sora and Ferro Ingenio in the San Juan drainage, no remains dating to the 18th or early 19th century have been identified in Porco.

Pentland's expedition presaged a revitalization of silver mining in the region that was stimulated by foreign as well as national capital (Mitre 1981; Platt 1996, 1997), and which was closely followed by the tin boom of the late 19th and early 20th centuries. The opening of the mining industry to foreign investors and the adoption of liberal economic policy transformed the nature of mineral extraction over the course of the century. Although the process was uneven and shaped by regional conditions (Langer 1996), new modes of finance, mechanized processes for extracting and dressing ore, and the replacement of llama and mule trains by railways are among the innovations that transformed Bolivian mining during this era. From the perspective of workers, one of the most important changes was the abolition of the *mita*, accompanied by attempts on the part of mining companies to create a disciplined, resident labor force. In Porco these factors had a profound effect on the relationship between miners and the surrounding landscape (Figure 6). Instead of the annual and temporary influx of *mita* laborers from distant provinces (accompanied, most likely, by wage laborers from Potosí), Porco saw—perhaps for the first time—the settlement of the surrounding countryside by a small but permanent agro-pastoral population who also worked in the mines. These people, whose seasonal and even daily routines took them from tunnels deep within Apu Porco to fields in the surrounding area where they pastured llamas and cultivated tubers, were probably among the first who actually identified themselves as *porqueños*.

The changes set in motion by independence are not apparent at Porco until late in the 19th century after the colonial law restricting the export of silver to coinage was overturned, making silver production more profitable (Smale 2010:18). The earliest indication that mining had resumed comes from the diary of J. B. Williams, a Cornish miner who was hired to supervise local workers in Porco from 1884 to 1887 (Gale and Williams 2001). Although he does not identify the company that employed him, he was transferred to Porco from Tatasi where he had worked in a mine controlled by the Guadalupe Mining Company, which was owned by Gregorio Pacheco, the president of Bolivia from 1884 to 1888. It is thus likely that some of Porco's mines were operated by Guadalupe at that time.

J. B. Williams, like many of his countrymen, had emigrated from Cornwall in the wake of the expansion of globalized British capital in order to seek employment in the region's burgeoning mining industry. A Methodist and self-described teetotaler, he was constantly frustrated by the natives' frequent refusal to work and indulgence in alcohol. His laconic diary entries document the challenges posed by the local labor force—which were similar to the ones faced by colonial mine owners—and also provide oblique insight into the community of Porco. For instance, on 30 August 1885, he wrote: "Feast Sta Rosa. A grand procession parading the Plaza, dressed in all kinds of hideous colours and fashion, more like a Circus than anything else," and on the next day: "No men at mine today. I hear they are all drunk at Porco so I don't expect we shall get any men this week." On 9 March of the following year he observed the beginning of carnival, writing that "[a]ll the folks came up here after breakfast, drinking, dancing and spreeing. I went down in the evening and it was a grand sight to see the Indians dressed up in wings of some large birds and dancing, etc." (Gale and Williams 2001).

The two fiestas that Williams describes are still observed by the residents of Porco and

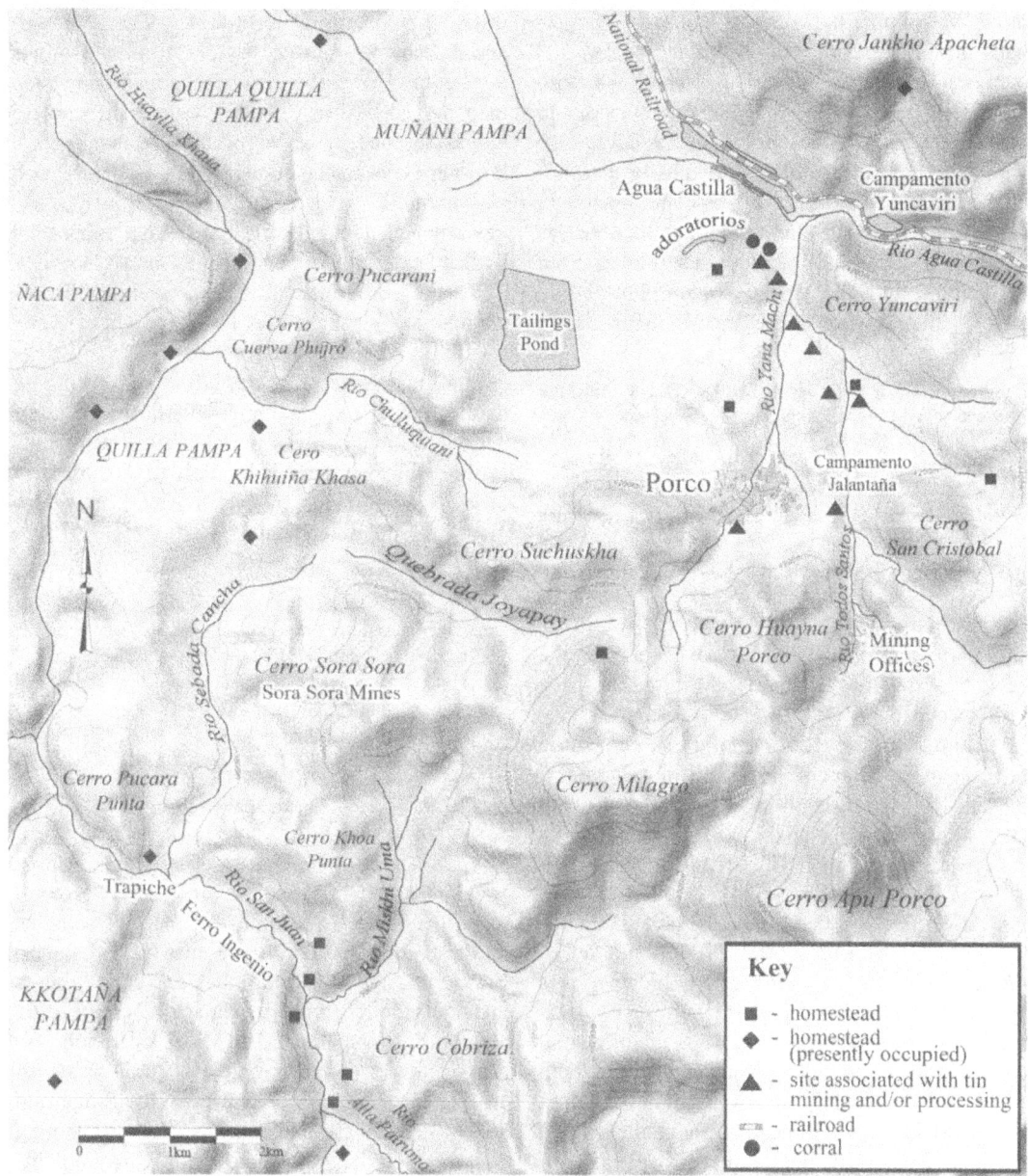

FIGURE 6. Major 19th- and early-20th-century sites located during survey. (Map by Brendan J. M. Weaver, 2011.)

are key events in the community's ritual cycle. The feast day of Santa Rosa honors the first Catholic saint of the Americas, who, according to residents, was born in Porco and moved to Lima as an infant (Jaimes 1905:345–350), and the condor dance is still performed at carnival; both are emblematic of a *porqueño* identity.

Williams's diary entries also provide some sense of the way in which the landscape was configured at the time, at least from his perspective. His house, which he shared with another English miner, was up on the mountain, close to the mine, most likely in the ravine at the foot of Apu Porco; other British workers that he mentions in his diary may have lived close by. A few mine staff, native miners, and perhaps the priest resided in the village below, and many of his entries describe interactions with them. He descended to the village in order to have breakfast with the priest on Sundays, dine with his supervisor, watch the dancing on holidays, and help pay the workers. The tension in his relationship with the community stemmed as much from the nature of labor relations as from the cultural gulf that separated them. On 19 July 1885 Williams wrote (Gale and Williams 2001):

> I went down town again pretty early but could not get anyone to work, but after pay succeeded in getting 17 to start for the mine, but when they got up on the mountains 7 started to run like deers and when we got to the mine we only had 9. I sent one of the dependentries back to tell Mr Pascoe, so he mounted his mule and captured 3 and sent up here, which I kept in the mine 3 days and 3 nights.

Apparently the labor force was not yet "free" and may even have included workers on the haciendas that the Guadalupe Mining Company also owned (Langer 1996).

Although the outline of a new economic order can be discerned in Williams's diary, the shift to industrial mining at Porco did not take place until the arrival of the tin barons a few decades later. In 1912—the year the railroad arrived—Porco Tin Mines, Ltd. was first advertised on the London Stock Exchange with capital of £125,000 (*Mining and Scientific Press* 1912:538). The original owner was Arturo Arana, and Avelina Aramayo & Co. was the commercial agent. Arana was an influential entrepreneur from Sucre who engaged in both silver and tin mining, and was among the first shareholders in the Banco Nacional de Bolivia (Serrano 2004:129); the Aramayos were one of the three most-influential families controlling tin production in Bolivia during the first half of the 20th century. The concession included 400 ac. of mining properties and 30 ac. adjacent to the Agua Castilla River, with associated water rights (*Weekly Sun* 1912:3). Arana had constructed a 10-stamp mill in Agua Castilla that was expanded by Porco Tin Mines (*Mining and Scientific Press* 1912:538). By 1915 a concentration plant was under construction at the site, and the complex was reported to be "one of the most up to date in Bolivia, the plant including

stamps, sand and slime tables and a Hardinge mill for regrinding" (Bullock 1915:421). An aerial tram transported the ore from the mines to the mill, and the resulting concentrate was then moved by rail to Antofagasta, Chile, where it was shipped to New York (Henderson 1916). By these means the mineral produced in Porco was virtually spirited out of the country, conveyed by cables and rails rather than carried by llamas under the supervision of native drivers. The large corrals that had been constructed near the marshy meadow just to the south of Agua Castilla were abandoned.

The infrastructure and labor requirements that characterized tin mining in Porco up until nationalization of the mines in 1952 were thus in place by the second decade of the 20th century. A report made by North American geologists in 1917 noted that

> Porco Tin Mines Ltd. is the only operator in the district, and its property includes the whole of the mineralized area of Apu Porco and a large part of Huayna Porco, but it is mining only the tin veins of Apu Porco. The mine offices are situated in a ravine between the two mountains on the north side of Apu Porco at the tunnel of the old Pie de Gallo mine, which was the most important of the silver mines on Huayna Porco (Singewald and Miller 1917:331).

Agua Castilla became a settlement almost equaling Porco in size as a result of its proximity to the railway and mill, and the mill complex itself eventually developed into Campamento Yuncaviri, a gated camp that currently houses managers and engineers who reside there only temporarily. The Porco Tin Mines operation was thus centralized, large scale (the mill was processing 50 t. of ore per day in 1917 [Singewald and Miller 1917]), and legally precluded mining by others in the immediate vicinity without the company's permission. Small-scale production was restricted to the smelting of silver from ores acquired illegally in company workings and the extraction of tin by cooperatives after the 1930s, both of which are addressed below.

While the extant documents provide a relatively clear view of mining operations from the perspective of management, they rarely include observations of the miners or the community in which they lived. A notable exception is Singewald and Miller's (1917:330) dismissive description of Porco as a small Indian village that was "a most primitive and picturesque place, consisting entirely of crude houses built of boulders collected from the stream and hill slopes and covered with thatched roofs." These visitors perceived Porco from afar, much like a landscape painting, the quaint backdrop from which a natural resource, a commodity, originated. Singewald and Miller's description is highly romanticized, conjuring an almost idyllic image of a fleeting rural past (Cosgrove 1984). Ironically, as a consequence of this new form of extractive economy, at least some of the miners and their families became more strongly rooted in Porco than ever before.

The formation of a community in Porco during the late 19th and early 20th centuries is suggested by data acquired during the archaeological survey of the area surrounding Porco, including a small stretch of the San Juan River that lies within the municipality's jurisdiction. The pedestrian survey revealed that the area immediately surrounding Porco (within approximately 3 km of the current village) was occupied by households engaged in agro-pastoral pursuits at only two points in history. Eight sites were identified that date to the regional-developments period, prior to the Inka conquest. These consist of small quantities of domestic debris that are sometimes associated with the stone foundations of one or two rectangular buildings. All of these sites are located along the Yana Machi River between Porco and Agua Castilla, close to three critical resources: a small *bofedal*, or marshy meadow, that could have provided pasture; sandstone outcrops on the western flank of Cerro Yuncaviri that were used to make grinding implements; and, most importantly, an outcrop of metamorphic sandstone that occurs along the contact of the Porco caldera and surrounding sedimentary rock, and was used extensively for manufacturing lithic tools. No evidence of agricultural fields occurs nearby, and the primary attraction appears to have been the metamorphic sandstone, as good tool stone is rare in the region

The second agro-pastoral occupation of the area occurred during the 19th and 20th centuries. A total of 10 estancias, or rural households, were identified, and these cluster in two areas: near the streams descending from Cerros Apu and Huayna Porco to Agua Castilla, and along the Río San Juan. These sites are comprised of

one to four rectangular structures constructed of stone or, more recently, adobe, and probably housed nuclear or small extended families. The domestic trash surrounding these homes includes plain and lead-glazed ceramics, bottle glass, and a variety of other items indicative of recent occupation such as tin cups, shoes, spoons, and recycled lard cans; one also contains *botijas* and Panamanian majolica, which indicate an early colonial component. Many are associated with small corrals, and the estancias in the San Juan drainage are located near abandoned agricultural terraces or small riverside fields encircled by stone walls.

The lack of an earlier agro-pastoral occupation and the temporal correspondence between the use of these sites and industrial mining in Porco strongly suggests that the latter enabled the former. While sustaining a purely agro-pastoral community in the vicinity of Porco would be difficult, if not impossible, miners could have raised llamas and crops to supplement their diet, sell in town, and provide a buffer against the vagaries of employment in the mines. This interpretation is supported by information from people who still maintain estancias near Porco; they are all miners or retired miners who have homes in Porco as well, and the food they produce complements what is purchased in the market. Today only the elderly reside in estancias for long periods, but in the past, prior to the availability of electricity, running water, and especially schools in Porco, entire families probably did so, at least for some parts of the year. The number of households who depended on both mining and agriculture for their livelihoods may never have been sizeable, but the population would certainly have been larger than the archaeological data suggest, both because currently occupied estancias were not documented, and because villagers today report maintaining estancias far beyond the area covered by the survey.

A number of scholars (Platt 1983; Contreras 1987; Langer 1996) have identified peasant participation in the mining economy as the reason Andean miners did not follow the same route towards proletarianization as workers in more developed countries. For centuries a large portion of the labor force has been drawn from the countryside, enabling workers to return to agrarian pursuits when there was no work in the mines and providing mine owners with a reserve labor pool that could be employed or dismissed in response to mineral prices and the availability of ore. Langer (1996) argues that a key factor shaping proletarianization in Bolivia was the availability and nature of labor in the local area and notes that this varied by region. Using these criteria he divides Bolivian mining operations into four types: (1) mines located in the high altiplano in areas that were sparsely populated by herders, (2) mines near large urban centers such as Potosí, (3) mines close to indigenous communities, and (4) mines near haciendas. Porco, like the much-better studied Huanchaco operation at the Pulacayo mines just to the west (Mitre 1981), falls into the first category. But, while Pulacayo eventually became a company town, Porco took a different path. Miners there developed the very modest agrarian potential of its hinterlands, allowing the movement between mine and field characteristic of other areas where agricultural settlement preceded the establishment of mines.

The interpenetration of mining and agriculture is also reflected in the silver-processing features that are often associated with rural estancias in the Porco area. This type of technology consists of a *huayrachina*, located on a hill or ridge for smelting ore, and a cupellation hearth constructed in a protected, hidden area for refining it. Ten cupellation hearths were found during survey: one dated to the early colonial period, four did not have associated diagnostic artifacts, and five were used during the 20th century. The most intact set of features is located where the Río Cebada Cancha enters the Río San Juan, close to an occupied estancia. It consists of *huayrachina* remains located on a high point above the homestead, a small stone platform for grinding ore, and a cupellation hearth that was constructed against a large boulder. Both the *huayrachina* and cupellation hearth were excavated, and a radiocarbon sample from the former dates to the 20th century (10 $\pm$ 50 B.P.—Beta-177732; δ13C=-25.5 0/00). Interviews that we conducted with Carlos Cuiza, a retired miner who still employs such technology at his estancia, revealed that the ore processed in this kind of facility is obtained from miners who steal—or directly appropriate—high-grade ore that is still found occasionally in pockets within large workings (Van Buren and Mills 2005). The silver ore processed at this site was probably obtained from tin mines in Porco where household members were employed as miners or as *pailliris*—women who sort ore at the entrance to the mines—and who, like Mr. Cuiza, engaged in small-scale silver production as a means of diversifying their resource base.

Not all small-scale production was illicit, although competition and conflict between producers operating at different scales probably existed, as it often does today. Mining cooperatives were founded during the Great Depression when unemployed miners sought the right to work deposits left idle by the decline in tin prices (Salazar-Soler and Absi 1998). The first mining cooperative in Bolivia, Ckacchas Libres y Palliris, was organized in Potosí in 1939 (Absi 2005:23–25); *cooperativistas* are the historical descendants of *kajchas*, now both defended and controlled by their membership in collectives that are formally recognized by mining companies and the state, and subject to their rules. Today most cooperative members in Porco are engaged in hard-rock mining, but Cooperativa Veneros Porco, the oldest cooperative in the village, has rights to the alluvial deposits along Río Todos Santos, a small stream that originates in Apu Porco. Unlike other streams in the area, Todos Santos has been visibly altered by both large- and small-scale mining. Contaminated by acid rock drainage from the large workings above, the water is described as "sour" and undrinkable by local residents. The archaeological survey identified six sites related to the small-scale extraction of tin along the banks of the Todos Santos. Three of these are tunnels driven into the alluvium in order to extract tin, two are complexes for washing and sorting the tin-containing sediment, and one is a large grinding stone associated with waste generated by triturating tin ore. In addition, the remains of a 250 m long canal were found along the western side of the river, below which the sediment was scoured to bedrock. A local resident reported that this had been done in order to remove and sort tin-containing deposits hydraulically, but how exactly this was accomplished is not clear. What had been a source of water for estancia residents and their animals became an industrial worksite that is now largely abandoned as newer cooperatives such as Cooperativa Minera Porco and Cooperativa Huayna Porco have focused on hard-rock mining.

During the first half of the 20th century, then, miners, *pailliris*, and families moved constantly between the village, the mines, and their estancias, extracting and processing ore, raising tubers and llamas, delivering lunch, and caring for children. These disparate activities were undertaken by households whose members may have carried out one or all of these jobs, creating a taskscape through their engagement with each other and the environment over time. While integrated by individuals on an experiential level as a result of daily practice, this space was not regarded as seamless. The village of Porco is conceptually bounded on the northern and southern edges by two large rock outcrops (Figure 7). On the northern side, close to where the road enters Porco, is Molle Punku, a set of upright rocks through which the Yana Machi River passes, and to the south is a tall *qaqa*

against which the adobe chimney for smelting tin was built. In Quechua, *punku* means a door through which people pass as they travel, but it also connotes a portal between the normal world of humans and the underworld. *Punkus* are often, but not always, created by *qaqas*, which are unusual rock formations that evoke anxiety, even terror, because they, too, are places where the underworld and its creatures can be accessed (Cruz 2006). Both of the outcrops in Porco are associated with the deaths of youngsters who have fallen from them and, in the case of Molle Punku, the demise of a man using dynamite while working on a municipal project to canalize the river. Both outcrops were also sites of community rituals that ceased approximately 20 years ago according to one long-time resident. While the antiquity of these features is unknown, they were certainly part of

FIGURE 7. View of contemporary Porco showing rock outcrops on northern and southern edges of town. Molle Punku is visible at center left. (Photo by Mary Van Buren, 2006.)

the landscape by the early 20th century and now exist on the edge of town, and on the edge of memory as the village swells with new residents who have pushed past the old boundaries to construct their homes.

Nash (1979), Taussig (1980), Platt (1983), Absi (2005), and others have explored the ways in which Andean miners conceptually integrate lives that are lived above and below ground, in the fields and in the mines, within worlds dominated by agrarian and capitalist values. There is no consensus on this issue, but it is clear that while there is an intertwining of belief systems, a conceptual division exists, particularly with regard to the contrast between the dark, dangerous spaces inhabited by the devil El Tío, the primary deity of the mines, and life above ground which is associated with the more beneficent forces of Pachamama and Jesus.

In Porco this division, as well as the synthesis of Andean and Christian beliefs, is marked by two chapels that have been constructed on the upper reaches of the northern flank of Cerro Huayna Porco, between the mines and the village. These chapels contain the crosses Apu Porco and Tata Kajcha, which are taken into the church each year at the beginning of May during the fiesta of Chakana (also called Cruz Velacuy or Las Cruces de Mayo). There they are adorned with chains of vegetables and honored with music, dancing, drinking, and a Catholic mass before being returned to their chapels two days later (Franco 2005). The name Tata, or "Father" Kajcha evokes independent miners of the past, and according to Absi (2005:129–131) these crosses (of which there are many in Potosí) are seen as both protectors against the dangerous power of El Tío and as alter egos of the same being: virile, satanic, and able to bring both wealth and misfortune. Franco (2005) reports that some miners in Porco regard the chapels in which the crosses Apu Porco and Tata Kajcha reside as the boundary between the two lives that they live each day, one in the mountain where the devil, or Supay, dominates, and the other in the village which is overseen by the Christian god. While many cooperative miners pass these chapels on foot during their daily commute to and from the mines, today company miners are transported by bus, thus circumventing the physical instantiation of this conceptual boundary.

Concluding Remarks

Examining the long-term history of mining from the perspective of a specific socially and materially constituted place allows the way in which workers engaged the global economy through the medium of the local landscape and the distinctive nature of the labor force that emerged to be seen. As archaeologists studying mining in other regions have noted, the very nature of the social constitution of mining communities is largely the result of the materiality experienced in the mining landscape (Knapp 1999:236). We demonstrate through archaeological and historical means how at Porco both the landscapes and the social constitution of community have changed dialectically in relation to political and economic transformations. In this regard, Porco shares many elements in common with Potosí, and in some ways the two mining centers could be considered manifestations of the same dynamics of space and landscape on different scales. However, to make such a claim negates the interrelated nature of the region as a whole and the dialectics of local and regional economies. Potosí's history is not separate from that of Porco, and in many ways their communities share a common legacy. Examining the particularities of the porqueño landscape as a dynamic interlocutor within this region in the context of an emerging global economy has the potential to bring new understanding to the relationship between the local and global.

Under Inka administration, Porco was characterized by the seasonal movement of miners and pilgrims from distant provinces. Rather than forming a common labor pool, the different tasks entailed in the production of silver—extracting, sorting, grinding, and smelting ore; refining metal; storing supplies; maintaining the work force; and conducting the appropriate rituals—were carried out in spatially distinct sites, probably by different social groups, and coordinated by state authorities. Labor and worship revolved around Apu Porco, but the population, always in flux, did not form a local community. The gyratory movement of workers continued under the Spaniards into the 17th century but under a profoundly different regime. Racial and class distinctions, usually concurrent, were expressed in the creation of a European-style settlement inhabited by mine owners, whose primary residences were elsewhere, and the reuse of Inka buildings as both residences and workspaces by teams of indigenous miners. Perhaps most importantly, Spanish property law combined with individual entrepreneurship fractured the local landscape, creating openings for the extraction of resources at different scales and by distinct social groups. Competition for mineral wealth, shaped by the nature and supply of ore, global demand, and the availability of labor and technology have characterized the Porco landscape ever since.

The revitalization of mining in the 19th century, and particularly the development of industrial tin mining at the start of the 20th, provoked the most dramatic changes in the local landscape. Centralized control of mineral deposits was asserted by a multinational company that like others of the time was intent on rationalizing production and creating a disciplined, resident workforce. As Giddens (1981:121) points out, capital commodification and the possibility of its resistance by labor are often place-based phenomena, necessitating an exploration of the local in understanding the nature of far-reaching projections into economic spaces. At Porco the consequence of these events was the development of a community that was more firmly rooted in the local, agrarian landscape than ever before, and which could use these agrarian resources to protect itself, at least in part, from the demands of the industrial workplace. The emergence of mining cooperatives in the 1930s created additional flexibility in combining agrarian and industrial work, as well as increased vulnerability to the vagaries of the global market. Cooperative miners, the successors of colonial *kajchas*, have also had an increasingly important and formal voice in national politics.

This study demonstrates the intimate relationship between human activity and the innate and attributed properties of material objects, as well as the ways in which these relations have transformed both landscapes and human affairs in Porco. Very specific attributes of the landscape in conjunction with the changing political economy shaped the way history unfolded in this mining center. Perhaps most salient is the nature of the ore deposits themselves. Easily accessible high-grade silver ores associated with distinctively shaped mountains initially drew to Porco people whose interests were simultaneously economic,

political, and spiritual. Later, the existence of lower-grade ores, as well as industrial minerals such as tin and zinc, resulted in the development of new technologies and forms of labor organization. The physical properties of the mineral deposits thus transformed social relationships, but only because of changes in the social value of metals. This is what Gell (1998) denotes as secondary agency, what Robb (2004:131) refers to as "effective agency," and that which Latour (2005:63–87) simply calls the agency of objects. However, it is important to note that in this and the other cases described above, the material world clearly does not have agency in and of itself; it only becomes an agent when enmeshed in a dialectical relationship with humans. It is the relation between people and things, and not the thing itself, which has the power to effect social change.

Acknowledgments

We owe a debt of gratitude to the many people and organizations that have contributed to the research presented in this paper. First, we must thank the team members of the Proyecto Arqueológico Porco-Potosí, particularly those who assisted during the 2006–2007 field seasons: Ludwing Cayo, Delfor Ulloa, Jason Bush, Daniel Martinez, Sheiry Vargas, Rosa Villanueva, Edwin Quispe, Julian Viscarra, Luperia Portillo, Pelagia Torrez, Malena Quispe, Maribel Quispe, Janeth Ecos, Lidia Gutierrez, and Ramiro Rojas. Dimitris Stevis provided logistical, emotional, and intellectual support throughout much of this project. We are also grateful for the comments and advice of our colleagues Ana María Presta, Susan deFrance, Catherine Julien, Ann Miles, Steven Wernke, John Janusek, and Meghan Cook, as well as three anonymous reviewers. We must also thank the Anthropology Departments at Western Michigan University, Colorado State University, and Vanderbilt University. Funding was provided by the National Science Foundation and the National Endowment for the Humanities.

References

ABERCROMBIE, THOMAS
 1998 *Pathways of Memory and Power: Ethnography and History among an Andean People.* University of Wisconsin Press, Madison.

Mary Van Buren and Brendan J. M. Weaver

ABSI, PASCALE
2005 *Los Ministros del Diablo. El Trabajo y Sus Representaciones en las Minas de Potosí*. Fundación PIEB, Instituto Francés de Estudios Andinos, Institut de Recherche pour le Dévelopement en Bolivie, La Paz, Bolivia.

AGNEW, JOHN A.
1989 The Devaluation of Place in Social Science. In *The Power of Place: Bringing together Geographical and Sociological Imaginations*, John A. Agnew and James S. Duncan, editors, pp. 9–29. Unwin Hyman, Boston, MA.

ALLEN, CATHERINE J.
2002 *The Hold Life Has: Coca and Cultural Identity in an Andean Community*, 2nd edition. Smithsonian Books, Washington, DC.

ANSCHUETZ, KURT F., RICHARD H. WILSHUSEN, AND CHERIE L. SCHEICK
2001 An Archaeology of Landscapes: Perspectives and Directions. *Journal of Archaeological Research* 9(2):157–211.

ASHMORE, WENDY, AND A. BERNARD KNAPP (EDITORS)
1999 *Archaeologies of Landscape: Contemporary Perspectives*. Blackwell, Malden, MA.

BASSO, KEITH H.
1995 Wisdom Sits in Places: Notes on a Western Apache Landscape. In *Senses of Place*, Steven Feld and Keith H. Basso, editors, pp. 53–90. School of American Research Press, Santa Fe, NM.

BASTIEN, JOSEPH W.
1985 *Mountain of the Condor: Metaphor and Ritual in an Andean Ayllu*. Waveland Press, Long Grove, IL.

BERTHELOT, JEAN
1986 The Extraction of Precious Metals at the Time of the Inka. In *Anthropological History of Andean Politics*, John Murra, Nathan Wachtel, and Jacques Revel, editors, pp. 69–88. Cambridge University Press, Cambridge, UK.

BESOM, THOMAS
2009 *Of Summits and Sacrifice: An Ethnohistoric Study of Inca Religious Practices*. University of Texas Press, Austin.

BOUYSSE-CASSAGNE, THÉRESE
1975 Pertenencia Étnica, Status Económico y Lenguas en Charcas a Fines del Siglo XVI. In *Tasa de la Visita General de Francisco de Toledo*, David N. Cook, editor, pp. 312–328. Universidad Nacional Mayor de San Marcos, Lima, Peru.

BULLOCK, STANLEY C.
1915 A Trip through Bolivia. *Engineering and Mining Journal* 100(11):421–424.

CAPOCHE, LUÍS
1959 *Relación General de La Villa Imperial de Potosí: Un Capitulo Edito en la Historia del Nuevo Mundo*. Ediciones Atlas, Madrid, Spain.

CESPEDES, RICARDO, AND PATRICE LECOQ
1998 El Horizonte Medio en los Andes Meridionales de Bolivia (Potosí). In *Los Desarrollos Locales y sus Territorios: Arqueología del NOA y sur de Bolivia*, Maria Beatriz Cremonte, editor, pp. 103–129. Universidad de Jujuy, Jujuy, Argentina.

COLE, JEFFERY A.
1985 *The Potosí Mita, 1573–1700: Compulsory Indian Labor in the Andes*. Stanford University Press, Stanford, CA.

CONTRERAS, CARLOS
1987 *Mineros y Campesinos en los Andes: Mercado Laboral y Economia Campesina en la Sierra Central siglo XIX*. Instituto de Estudios Peruanos, Lima, Peru.

COSGROVE, DENIS E.
1984 *Social Formation and Symbolic Landscape*. University of Wisconsin Press, Madison.

CRUZ, PABLO
2006 Mundos Permeables y Espacios Peligrosos. Consideraciones Acerca de Punkus y Qaqas en el Paisaje Altoandino de Potosí, Bolivia. *Boletín del Museo Chileno de Arte Precolombino* 11(2):35–50.
2009 Huacas Olvidadas y Cerros Santos. Apuntes Metodológicos Sobre la Cartografía Sagrada en los Andes del Sur de Bolivia. *Estudios Atacameños* 38:55–74.

CRUZ, PABLO, AND PASCALE ABSI
2008 Cerros Ardientes y Huayras Calladas. Potosí antes y durante el Contacto. In *Mina y metalurgia en los Andes del Sur desde la época prehispánica hasta el siglo XVII*, Pablo José Cruz and Jean-Joinville Vacher, editors, pp. 91–120. Institut de Recherche pour le Dévelopement and Instituto Francés de Estudios Andinos, Sucre, Bolivia.

DEAGAN, KATHLEEN
2002 *Artifacts of the Spanish Colonies of Florida and the Caribbean, 1500–1800. Vol. 2: Personal Possessions*. Smithsonian Institution Press, Washington, DC.

DE CERTEAU, MICHEL
1984 *The Practice of Everyday Life*, Steven Rendall, translator. University of California Press, Berkeley.

DE CIEZA DE LEÓN, PEDRO
1984 *La Crónica del Perú: Primera Parte*, Manuel Ballesteros, editor. Historía 16, Madrid, Spain.

DE OCAÑA, DIEGO
1969 *Un Viaje Fascinante por la América Hispana del Siglo XVI*, Arturo Alvarez, editor. STVDIVM Ediciones, Madrid, Spain.

DEL RÍO, MERCEDES
1995 Estructuración Étnica Qharaqhara y su Desarticulación. In *Espacios, Etnias, Frontera: Atenuaciones Políticas en el Sur del Tawantinsuyu, siglos XV–XVIII*, Ana María Presta, editor, pp. 3–47. Ediciones ASUR 4, Sucre, Bolivia.

FRANCO OLMEDO, LUIS TASKI
2005 Fiesta de la Chacana o Velar Cruz en Porco. Manuscript, Mary Van Buren, Department of Anthropology, Colorado State University, Fort Collins.

GALE, VAL, AND WILLIAMS FAMILY
2001 *Daffodils Never Hear*. Val Gale, n.p. "Daffodils Never Hear" Home Page <http://at.orpheusweb.co.uk/Daffodil/porco.htm>. Accessed 28 September 2012.

GARNER, RICHARD L.
1988 Long-Term Silver Mining Trends in Spanish America: A Comparative Analysis of Peru and Mexico. *American Historical Review* 93(4):898–935.

GELL, ALFRED
1998 *Art and Agency: An Anthropological Theory*. Oxford University Press, Oxford, UK.

GIDDENS, ANTHONY
1981 *A Contemporary Critique of Historical Materialism*. University of California Press, Berkeley.

HENDERSON, G. M.
1916 Preliminary Report on the Porco Tin Mines Ltd. Agua de Castilla, Bolivia. No. 6034, Folder 5, Box 87, Thayer Lindsley Papers, American Heritage Center, University of Wyoming, Laramie.

INGOLD, TIM
1993 The Temporality of the Landscape. *World Archaeology* 25(2):152–174.
2000 *The Perception of the Environment: Essays on Livelihood, Dwelling and Skill*. Routledge, London, UK.
2011 *Being Alive: Essays on Movement, Knowledge and Description*. Routledge, London, UK.

JAIMES, JULIO LUCAS
1905 *La Villa Imperial de Potosí: Su Historia Anecdótica—Sus Tradiciones y Leyendas Fantásticas: Su Grandeza y su Opulencia Fabulosas*. Talleres Gráficos de L. J. Rosso, Buenos Aires, Argentina.

KEANE, WEBB
2003 Semiotics and the Social Analysis of Material Things. *Language and Communication* 23(2&3):409–425.

KNAPP, A. BERNARD
1999 Ideational and Industrial Landscape on Prehistoric Cyprus. In *Archaeologies of Landscape: Contemporary Perspectives*, Wendy Ashmore and A. Bernard Knapp, editors, pp. 229–252. Blackwell, Malden, MA.

LANGER, ERICK D.
1996 The Barriers to Proletarianization: Bolivian Mine Labour, 1826–1918. *International Review of Social History* 41:27–51

LAPHAM, HEATHER A.
2001 More than a "Few Blew Beads": The Glass and Stone Beads from Jamestown Rediscovery's 1994–1997 Excavations. *Journal of the Jamestown Rediscovery Center* 1. Preservation Virginia <http://www.apva.org/resource/jjrc/vol1/lapham.pdf>. Accessed 28 September 2012.

LATOUR, BRUNO
2005 *Reassembling the Social: An Introduction to Actor-Network-Theory*. Oxford University Press, Oxford, UK.

LECHTMAN, HEATHER
1996 Dirty Copper or Chosen Alloy? A View from the Americas. *Journal of Field Archaeology* 23(4):477–514.
2007 The Inka, and Andean Metallurgical Tradition. In *Variations in the Expression of Inka Power*, Richard L. Burger, Craig Morris, Ramiro Matos, editors, pp. 323–365. Dumbarton Oaks, Washington, DC.

LECHTMAN, HEATHER, AND SABINE KLEIN
1999 The Production of Copper-Arsenic Alloys (Arsenic Bronze) by Cosmelting: Modern Experiment, Ancient Practice. *Journal of Archaeological Science* 26(5):497–526.

LECOQ, PATRICE, AND RICARDO CESPEDES
1996 Nuevas Investigaciones Arqueológicas en los Andes Meridionales de Bolivia: Una Visión Prehispánica de Potosí. *Revista de Investigaciones Históricas*, pp. 183–267. Universidad Autónoma Tomás Frías, Potosí, Bolivia.
1997 Nuevos Datos Sobre la Ocupación Prehistórica en los Andes Meridionales de Bolivia. *Cuadernos* 9:111–152. Revista de la Facultad de Humanidades y Ciencias Sociales, Universidad Nacional de Jujuy, Jujuy, Argentina.

LENGYEL, STACEY N., JEFFREY L. EIGHMY, AND MARY VAN BUREN
2010 Archaeomagnetic Research in the Andean highlands. *Journal of Archaeological Science* 38(1):147–155.

MENZEL, SEWALL H.
2004 *Cobs, Pieces of Eight and Treasure Coins*. American Numismatic Society, New York, NY.

MINING AND SCIENTIFIC PRESS
1912 London. Progress at the Geevor.—Tin Mining Booming.—Development in Bolivia. *Mining and Scientific Press* 26 October:538.

MITCHEM, JEFFREY M., AND MCEWAN, BONNIE G.
1988 New Data on Early Bells from Florida. *Southeastern Archaeology* 7(1):39–49.

MITRE, ANTONIO
1981 *Las Patriarcas de la Plata: Estructura Socio-económica de la Mineria Boliviana en el Siglo XIX*. Instituto de Estudios Peruanos, Lima, Peru.

MONTES DE OCA, ISMAEL
1989 *Geografía y Recursos Naturales de Bolivia*, 2nd edition. Academica Nacional de Ciencias de Bolivia, La Paz, Bolivia.

MORPHY, HOWARD
1995 Landscape and the Reproduction of the Ancestral Past. In *The Anthropology of Landscape: Perspectives on Place and Space*, Eric Hirsch and Michael O'Hanlon, editors, pp. 184–209. Clarendon Press, Oxford, UK.

NASH, JUNE
1979 *We Eat the Mines and the Mines Eat Us: Dependency and Exploitation in Bolivian Tin Mines*. Columbia University Press, New York, NY.

PENTLAND, JOSEPH BARCLAY
1975 Informe S*obre Bolivia. Colección de la Cultura Boliviana*, Vol. 13, Jack Aitken Soux, translator. Casa de la Moneda, Potosí, Bolivia.

PLATT, TRISTAN
1983 Conciencia andina y conciencia proletaria. Qhuyaruna y ayllu en el norte de Potosí. *Revista Latinoamericana de História Económica y Social* 2:47–73.
1996 Producción, tecnología y trabajo en la Rivera de Potosí durante la República temprana. *Cuadernos de Historia Latinoamericana* 3. AHILA, Münster, Germany.
1997 *Historias Unidas, Memorias Escindidas: las Empresas Mineras de los Hermanos Ortiz y la Construcción de las Élites Nacionales. Salta y Potosí, 1800–1880*. Universidad Andina Simon Bolivar, Sucre, Bolivia.
2000 Señorío Aymara y Trabajo Minero. De la Mita al K'ajcheo en Potosí (1538–1837). In *Potosí: Plata Para Europa*, Juan Marchena, editor, pp. 189–210. Fundación Del Monte/Universidad de Sevilla, Seville, Spain.

PLATT, TRISTAN, THÉRESE BOUYSSE-CASSAGNE, OLIVIA HARRIS, AND THIERRY SAIGNES (EDITORS)
2006 *Qaraqara-Charka: Malku, Inca y Rey en la Provincia de Charcas (siglos XVXVII): Historia Antropológica de una Confederación Aymara*. IFEA/Plural Editores/FBCB/University of St. Andrews, La Paz, Bolivia.

PLATT, TRISTAN, AND PABLO QUISBERT
2007 Knowing Silence and Merging Horizons: The Case of the Great Potosí Cover-Up. In *Ways of Knowing: Anthropological Approaches to Crafting Experience and Knowledge*, Mark Harris, editor, pp. 113–138. Berghahn Books, New York, NY.

POTTER, JAMES
2004 The Creation of Person, the Creation of Place: Hunting Landscapes in the American Southwest. *American Antiquity* 69(2):322–338.

PRESTA, ANA MARÍA
1992 Juan Ortiz de Zárate: An Entrepreneur in Sixteenth Century La Plata, Charcas (Modern Bolivia). Master's thesis, Department of History, Ohio State University, Columbus.
1999 Gonzalo Pizarro y el Desarrollo de Porco. Patronazgo y Clientelismo en un Yacimiento Charqueño Inicial, 1538–1576. *VI Reunión de Historiadores de la Minería Latinoamericana*, Lima, Peru.
2000 *Encomienda, Familia y Negocios en Charcas Colonial (Bolivia): Los Encomenderos de La Plata 1550–1600*. IEP Ediciones, Lima, Peru.
2008 La Primera joya en la Corona en el Altiplano Surandino. Descubrimiento y Explotación de un Yacimiento Minero Inicial: Porco, 1538–1576. In *Mina y Metalurgia en los Andes del Sur Desde la Época Prehispánica Hasta el Siglo XVII*, Pablo José Cruz and Jean-Joinville Vacher, editors, pp. 201–229. Instituto Francés de Estudios Andinos, Sucre, Bolivia.

ROBB, JON E.
2004 The Extended Artefact and the Monumental Economy: A Methodology for Material Agency. In *Rethinking Materiality: The Engagement of Mind with the Material World*, Elizabeth DeMarrais, Chris Gosden, and Colin Renfrew, editors, pp. 131–139. McDonald Institute for Archaeological Research, Cambridge, UK.

RODRÍGUEZ OSTRIA, GUSTAVO
1989 Los mineros: Su Proceso de Formación (1825–1927). *Historia y Cultura* 15:75–118.

ROSTWOROWSKI DE DIEZ CANSECO, MARÍA
1988 *Conflicts over Coca Fields in XVIth-Century Perú*. University of Michigan Museum of Anthropology, Ann Arbor.

ROWE, JOHN
1982 Inca Policies and Institutions Related to the Cultural Unification of the Empire. In *The Inca and Aztec States, 1400–1800: Anthropology and History*, G. Collier, R. Rosaldo, and J. Wirth, editors, pp. 93–118. Academic Press, New York, NY.

SALAZAR-SOLER, CARMEN, AND PASCALE ABSI
1998 Ser Minero en Huancavelica y Potosí: una Aproximación Antropológica. *Journal de la Société des Américanistes* 84(1):121–145.

SALLNOW, MICHAEL J.
1981 Communitas Reconsidered: The Sociology of Andean Pilgrimage. *Man*, new ser., 16(2):163–182.
1987 *Pilgrims of the Andes: Regional Cults in Cusco*. Smithsonian Institution Press, Washington, DC.

SERRANO BRAVO, CARLOS
2004 Historia de la Minería Andina Boliviana (siglos XVI–XX). Manuscript, UNESCO, Potosí, Bolivia.

SINGEWALD, JOSEPH T., AND BENJAMIN L. MILLER
1917 New Developments in the Porco District, Bolivia. *Engineering and Mining Journal* 103:329–333.

SMALE, ROBERT L.
2010 *"I Sweat the Flavor of Tin." Labor Activism in Early Twentieth-Century Bolivia.* University of Pittsburgh Press, Pittsburgh, PA.

SMITH, MARVIN, AND M. E. GOOD
1982 Early Sixteenth-Century Glass Beads in the Spanish Colonial Trade. Cottonlandia Museum, Greenwood, MI.

STERN, STEVE J.
1988 Feudalism, Capitalism, and the World-System in the Perspective of Latin America and the Caribbean. *American Historical Review* 93(4):829–872.

TANDETER, ENRIQUE
1981 La Producción Como Actividad Popular: "Ladrones de Minas" en Potosí. *Nova Americana* 4:43–65.
1993 *Coercion and Market: Silver Mining in Colonial Potosí 1692–1826.* University of New Mexico Press, Albuquerque.

TAUSSIG, MICHAEL
1980 *The Devil and Commodity Fetishism in South America.* University of North Carolina Press, Chapel Hill.

URTON, GARY
1981 *At the Crossroads of the Earth and the Sky: An Andean Cosmology.* University of Texas Press, Austin.

VAN BUREN, MARY, LUDWIN CAYO, DELFOR ULLOA, ROSA VILLANUEVA, AND BRENDAN WEAVER
2006 Proyecto Arqueológico Porco-Potosí: Gestión 2006. Manuscript, Unidad Nacional de Arqueología UNAR, La Paz, Bolivia.

VAN BUREN, MARY, LUDWIN CAYO, ROSA VILLANUEVA, SHERRY VARGAS, BRENDAN WEAVER, DAN MARTINEZ, AND JASON BUSH
2007 Proyecto Arqueológico Porco-Potosí: Gestión 2007. Manuscript, Unidad Nacional de Arqueología UNAR, La Paz, Bolivia.

VAN BUREN, MARY, AND BARBARA H. MILLS
2005 *Huayrachinas* and *Tocochimbos*: Traditional Smelting Technology of the Southern Andes. *Latin American Antiquity* 16(1):3–25.

VAN BUREN, MARY, AND ANA MARÍA PRESTA
2010 The Organization of Inka Silver Production in Porco, Bolivia. In *Distant Provinces in the Inka Empire: Toward a Deeper Understanding of Inka Imperialism*, Michael A. Malpass and Sonia Alconini, editors, pp. 173–192. University of Iowa Press, Iowa City.

VAN BUREN, MARY, AND BRENDAN J. M. WEAVER
[2012] Exigir una diferencia: El uso estratégico de las cerámicas inkas provinciales en el Periodo Colonial Temprano. In *Ocupación Inka y Dinámicas Regionales en los Andes (Siglos XV–XVI)*, Claudia Rivera, editor. IFEA, La Paz, Bolivia.

WEAVER, BRENDAN J. M.
2008 Ferro Ingenio: An Archaeological and Ethnohistorical View of Labor and Empire in Colonial Porco and Potosí. Master's thesis, Department of Anthropology, Western Michigan University, Kalamazoo.

WEEKLY SUN
1912 Bolivia's Tin Resources. A Promising Flotation. *Weekly Sun* 30 November:3. Singapore.

ZULAWSKI, ANN
1987 Wages, Ore Sharing, and Peasant Agriculture: Labor in Oruro's Silver Mines, 1607–1720. *Hispanic American Historical Review* 67(3):405–430.

MARY VAN BUREN
DEPARTMENT OF ANTHROPOLOGY
COLORADO STATE UNIVERSITY
FORT COLLINS, CO 80523

BRENDAN J. M. WEAVER
DEPARTMENT OF ANTHROPOLOGY
VANDERBILT UNIVERSITY
124 GARLAND HALL
NASHVILLE, TN 37235

Ann F. Ramenofsky
C. David Vaughan
Michael N. Spilde

Seventeenth-Century Metal Production at San Marcos Pueblo, North-Central New Mexico

ABSTRACT

Histories of the early colonial period of the remote New Mexican colony (A.D. 1540–1680) are framed in terms of pueblo conversion, conflicts between church and state, and accommodation-resistance between the pueblos and the colonizers. Missing from these histories are detailed discussions of mining and metal production, even though it is widely recognized that Spaniards came north looking for metal beginning with Coronado's entrada in A.D. 1540. Accumulating archaeological evidence is beginning to change historical understanding of this neglected part of colonization history. In north-central New Mexico, San Marcos Pueblo is a microcosm of early colonial mining activity in the colony. To elucidate the San Marcos story, relevant histories, geology, archaeology, and materials are used. This broad methodological approach helps reveal the pattern of 17th-century metal production in the colony. The results are important for building knowledge about metal production in the New Mexico colony and for expanding scholarly understanding about this significant part of Spanish colonization on the far northern frontier.

Introduction

Two (often conflicting) goals drove Spanish conquest and colonization of the Americas: the conversion of Native Americans to Catholicism and the search and extraction of precious metals. Conventional histories of early colonial New Mexico (A.D. 1540–1680) are decidedly one-sided, written largely as though conversion of Native peoples and Spanish settlement were the only goals (Kessell 1987; Riley 1999). This is true even though Coronado came north in A.D. 1540 looking for the seven gold cities of Cibola (Flint 2002; Flint and Flint 2005). Coronado failed to discover any gold. After that failure, the Spanish shifted their focus to

exploration, settlement, and conversion. Themes that pepper early colonial New Mexico history include descriptions of those conversions, conflicts between church and state over the appropriation of Indian labor, and accommodation and resistance of Pueblo peoples toward the Spanish invaders. Native resistance erupted in the Pueblo Revolt of 1860 that terminated the Spanish presence in New Mexico for 12 years (Knaut 1995; Liebmann 2006). The success of the revolt is testimony to both the short-lived, multipueblo political strategy and its enmity for the Spanish.

There is no question that conversion, church-state conflict, and accommodation-resistance characterize the first 140 years of Spanish conquest in New Mexico, but does the absence of historical discussion of mining or metal production mean that this crucial component of the Spanish enterprise in the Americas simply did not exist in the colony? Was there no prospecting, assaying, or metal production in early colonial New Mexico? Although the absence of historical discussion suggests this is the case, some scholars have asserted that Spanish enslavement of Native peoples in Spanish mines was one cause of the Pueblo Revolt (Northrup 1959; Long 1964; Milford 1996). Even though this opinion accords well with Spanish practices in general (Bakewell 1971, 1984, 1988) and the fact that slaving was practiced in the colony (Hackett 1923–37; Brooks 2002), how could Native peoples be enslaved in mining if there was no mining?

What makes the question of metallurgy even more perplexing is that early Spanish observers, including conquistadors, governors, and priests, thought there was metallurgical potential in New Mexico (Hackett 1923–1937; Hammond and Rey 1927, 1953, 1966). Some documents refer to rich lodes of metallic minerals, the extraction of silver, and Spanish ownership of mines (Hammond and Rey 1940, 1953, 1966). Despite these comments, most historical or anthropological writings (Bandelier 1890–1892; Kessell 1987, 2002; Weber 1992) ignore the subject, leaving the impression that New Mexico is metal poor. Adolph Bandelier (1890–1892 [3]:195), for instance, stated emphatically, "The current notion of rich Spanish mines and of great metallic wealth which Spaniards derived from the territory are pure myths and fables."

In essence, then, the impression derived from historical descriptions of conquest and colonization of New Mexico is that, although initially the Spanish were seeking metallic minerals (Ramenofsky and Vaughan 2003), metal production was not part of the conquest effort during the early colonial period (A.D. 1540–1680). In fact, the earliest documentary evidence of metallurgy dates to the 18th century (Henricks 1999).

The lack of discussion about metallurgy is a genuine gap in historical understanding of the story of conquest of New Mexico, but its absence should not be taken as evidence that mining was of no consequence to colonists or that little effort was expended in finding and extracting metals. The opposite is the case. Metal was being produced during the early colonial period in New Mexico. History and archaeology are the two traditional evidentiary sources pertinent to writing the metallurgical story of early colonial New Mexico. Different reasons explain why neither historians nor archaeologists have considered the topic.

Historians' silence with regard to metal production is surprising, given the economic importance of metal to the Spaniards. If primary records about mining and metallurgy in New Mexico existed in some archive, it seems highly probable that historians would have mentioned their presence. Perhaps such records do exist, but additional archival problems complicate historical silence. During the Pueblo Revolt, countless documents were lost or destroyed; those that are known are thin, lacking in detail, and often contain conflicting information (Bandelier 1910; Vaughan 2006 for discussion). Although there are some purported mining claims from the pre-revolt period (Ayer 1916; Hammond and Rey 1953; Christiansen 1974), there are no known mining texts or other documents describing the nature of the mining venture or the role of Native peoples in that venture. Without primary documents, most historical discussions of mining in the early colonial New Mexico colony fall into the realm of speculation.

Lack of archaeological research and discussion on the question of metallurgy in New Mexico is explained by other factors. First, historical archaeology in the Southwest has a checkered history and, until recently, has been largely ignored by most archaeologists who study the Southwest (Majewski and Ayers 1997; Kulisheck 2005; Liebmann 2006). During the early decades of the 20th century, some mission communities, such as Awatovi, Pecos, Abo, and Gran Quivira, were excavated for building artifact chronologies (Kidder 1936; Montgomery et al. 1949; Toulouse 1949; Kidder 1958) or as part of the direct historical approach (Nelson 1914, 1916). This early interest soon gave way to the near-exclusive focus on prehistory by archaeologists who studied the Southwest. Second, because the majority of archaeologists have little training in history (Galloway 1995, 1997), they tend to read the secondary historical literature and to follow the lead of historians, accepting those documents at face value (Towner 2000; Ramenofsky and Feathers 2002). Accordingly, most archaeologists have neither undertaken historiographic analysis of available documents to determine the likelihood of metallurgy nor explored the signatures of the metallurgical process in the archaeological record. Instead, they have assumed that the absence of historical discussion of mining and metallurgy in surviving documents means the absence of metallurgy (for exceptions, Warren and Weber 1979; Vierra et al. 1997).

Because the archaeological record is independent of the documentary record (Fox 1993), it can be used to investigate independently the nature and extent of metal production in the colony. Such investigations are underway. In the last decade, archaeologists have undertaken excavation and analysis of several pre-revolt metal production sites in New Mexico, including San Marcos Pueblo (Ramenofsky 2003; Ramenofsky and Vaughan 2003), Comanche Springs (Ramenofsky 1997; Vaughan and Ramenofsky 1999; Vaughan 2006), Pa'ako Pueblo (Lycett 1998, 1999, 2000, 2001, 2002, 2003; Thomas 2002), and at the Palace of the Governors in Santa Fe (Vaughan 2006) (Figure 1). Although the archaeological record of metallurgy is a collective record, lacking the precision of the written word, accumulating physical evidence of metallurgy is unambiguous and compelling. It demonstrates that ore extraction and metal production played a role, perhaps a significant one, in the initial centuries of Spanish conquest in New Mexico.

FIGURE 1. Pre-revolt metallurgy sites in New Mexico. (Map by Ann Ramenofsky, 2006.)

One goal of this paper is to set the record straight on the question of pre-revolt metallurgy in the remote New Mexico colony by showing that metallurgy was underway by the 17th century. The spatial focus of the discussion is on one settlement, San Marcos Pueblo, located in north-central New Mexico. Although only a single place, it is significant. The San Marcos metallurgical evidence is from a recent multi-year field investigation in which the discovery of metal production was a principal objective (Pierce and Ramenofsky 2000; Ramenofsky 2001, 2003). Second, San Marcos is within 5 km of the Cerrillos Hills, an area that Governor de Vargas established as a mining district, El Real de los Cerrillos, in 1695 (Espinosa 1942; Milford 1996; Kessell et al. 1998). Third, some documentary sources have suggested that the Spanish were exploiting ore deposits in the Cerrillos Hills before the Pueblo Revolt of 1680 and that at least some preliminary assaying occurred at San Marcos (Milford 1996).

This paper is an archaeological evaluation of the historical suggestions regarding pre-revolt metallurgy, exploring the physical evidence of metallurgy at San Marcos Pueblo. It also tries to change historical understanding of the early colonial enterprise in New Mexico by demonstrating that metal production was part of initial Spanish conquest.

In what follows, historical and geological context are considered, along with the archaeology of metallurgical features, luminescence and radiocarbon assessments of age, and multiscale material analyses of the metallurgical debris. Each arm of this approach is designed to elucidate the nature of the early colonial period activities at San Marcos and to provide a framework for future studies. Synthesis across the component parts results in a preliminary picture of early metallurgy at San Marcos and in the larger New Mexico colony. The use of all available kinds of information creates a balanced historical narrative, one that favors neither Spanish nor Native viewpoints.

Finally, this paper suggests that the nature of the smelting record at San Marcos is a microcosm that reflects the larger, currently known pattern of metal production in the colony before the Pueblo Revolt. Like other pre-revolt known smelting locations, San Marcos was not a mining camp. In fact, available archaeological and historical evidence suggests there were no mining camps in New Mexico until after the Spanish Reconquista. San Marcos was a native settlement that was occupied for centuries prior to Spanish conquest (Nelson 1912–1915; Ramenofsky 2001). Native occupation continued after Spanish colonization and the establishment of a mission in 1638 (Hodge et al. 1945; Thomas 2000). Reducing ores to metals certainly occurred during this period of missionization. Smelting in this context is significant on two counts. Regardless of who directed the metallurgical activities, smelting in Indian communities provided a ready labor pool for mining and metallurgy. In addition, the scale of production was small. Following Spanish conquest, the establishment of missions, and metal production, the structure of the community may well have changed, but evidence from San Marcos suggests that smelting was an infrequent activity inserted into the daily activities of the pueblo.

Metallurgical Potential of the New Mexico Colony

Table 1 summarizes the metallurgical information for the New Mexico colony from the early colonial documentary record (Milford 1996, for a similar discussion). The 28 references in the table are limited to metal mining and exclude other potential economic resources such as salt. Although there are numerous ways to analyze and evaluate the observations in Table 1, the focus here is on a few significant contextual variables: (1) whether the observations were made by eyewitnesses, (2) whether the observers had any familiarity with mining and metallurgy, and (3) the position of the observer in the Spanish imperial hierarchy.

Important differences separate those individuals who stated that mining and smelting were worthwhile ventures from those who stated the opposite (Table 2). Of the 28 observations, 26 address directly the potential metallurgical wealth of the colony. The remaining two observations relate indirectly to mining: Don Alonso de Oñate, brother of Don Juan de Oñate (first governor of the colony), was addressing a grievance concerning an ore assay sent by his brother to Mexico City; the second indirect metallurgical reference mentions the remains of forging iron at Sandia Pueblo during the attempted *reconquista* of the colony in 1681. Of the 26 directly relevant observations, 21 (81%) stated that New Mexico had extractable metal resources. Countering these observations were five individuals (19%) who believed there were no metals of value in New Mexico.

As a group, the 21 individuals who believed that New Mexico had metallurgical potential were quite different from the 5 who held the opposite opinion. With the exception of one letter from the Viceroy of New Spain in 1601, all of these 21 individuals were eyewitnesses (Table 2) and had traveled through at least part of the colony. Six were members of either the Espejo or the Rodriguez-Chamuscado entradas; the other eight were associated with the Oñate settlement. In addition, at least six of the observers were miners. Don Juan de Oñate and Vincente de Zaldívar Mendoza both came from mining families in Zacatecas, Mexico. Oñate was a mining engineer who, following his removal as governor from New Mexico,

returned to Spain to become chief inspector of mines (Milford et al. 1998). Hernán Gallegos, notary of the Rodriguez-Chamuscado expedition, stated that all nine soldiers who joined that entrada were miners, but only two gave testimony before the viceroy (Hammond 1927:54). In 1694 Roque Madrid assessed a Cerrillos Hills lead mine that had purportedly been owned by his father before the Pueblo Revolt (Kessell et al. 1998:125).

The five individuals who described the New Mexico colony as "metal poor" were neither miners nor well informed about the colony. Two of them, Vasquez de Coronado and Juan de Ortega, were eyewitnesses. The remarks of Vasquez de Coronado must be seen in the context of his failed entrada. Although interested in discovering metal, Coronado had no familiarity with mining and was not prepared to assay samples of ore. Juan Ortega, the second eyewitness, gave testimony about the Oñate colony but had spent only three months in New Mexico (Milford 1996). His negative comment regarding metallurgical potential seems unlikely to be true, given that the other colonists who gave testimony had spent more time in the colony and were uniform in their positive assessment of the metallurgical potential of New Mexico (Table 1). The other three negative assessments of metallurgical potential came from viceroys who, from available historical documentation, had never visited the colony but who certainly had greater political clout than the explorers, governors, and settlers who had journeyed north (Table 1).

The significant question regarding the negative assessment by the viceroys is why? Why did the most powerful political figures in New Spain come out against the possibility of metallic minerals in New Mexico? At least two interpretations are possible. If gold and silver were the standards for metallurgical wealth, then the assessment of New Mexico as not worth the investment was reasonable during the 16th century. A letter from Viceroy Marquis de Montesclaros to the king (Table 1) supports this view. In that letter, the viceroy stated he had assayed ores sent by Don Juan de Oñate and that "the richest ore produce one-eighth part copper, without any trace of silver" (Hammond and Rey 1953[2]:1001). Apparently, copper was not worth economic development (Barrett 1987),

TABLE 1
OBSERVATIONS OF METALLIC MINERAL POTENTIAL OF THE NEW MEXICO COLONY

Observer	Expedition	Date	Metallurgical Potential	Source
Hernandó de Alarcón	Coronado	1540	-metal potential Near Zuni	Twitchell 1911–1912 Long 1964
Francisco Vásquez de Coronado	Coronado	1540	-metal poor	Hammond and Rey 1940:117–178; Long 1964
Pedro de Bustamente*	Rodriguez-Chumascado	1582	-copperish steel-like metal - San Marcos mentioned as adjacent to mines (Cerrillos Hills) -5 mine prospects South of Albuquerque	Bolton 1916:150; Long 1964
Hernán Gallegos**	Rodriguez-Chamuscado	1582	-copperish-like metal seen at San Marcos -visited mines in Cerrillos -other rich veins south of Albuquerque -ore returned to Mexico City and assayed	Hammond and Rey 1927: 28–29, 53–54, 57; Long 1964
Philipe de Escalante*	Rodriguez-Chamuscado	1582	-metal potential (11 mine prospects) along Rio Grande trench near Socorro	Bolton 1916:157 Long 1964; Milford 1996
Hernando Barrando*	Rodriguez-Chamuscado			
Viceroy, Count de Coruña to King		1582	no signs of gold or silver in the colony	Bolton 1916:159; Long 1964
Pérez de Luxán	Espejo	1582	-silver in southern New Mexico near Hatch, New Mexico - antimony and silver near Manzanos -rich mines near Hopi; Luxan thinks they're worthless -Cerrillos Hills: rich veins; mentions San Marcos	Bolton 1916:180,181; Long 1964
Antonio de Espejo	Espejo	1583	-rich mines west of Hopi, containing silver -rich mines in vicinity of Cerrillos Hills	Bolton 1916:187, 189; Long 1964
Castaño de Sosa	De Sosa	1591	-explored Cerrillos Hills; no silver discovered	Hammond and Rey 1966:289; Long 1964
Marcos Farfán*	Oñate exploration and settlement	1598	-Arizona: veins of silver; claims staked out and assays made	Bolton 1916:240.244; Long 1964 Milford 1996
Vincente de Zaldívar Mendoza*	Oñate exploration and settlement	1602	-explored mines in the Cerrillos Hills -built small smelters according to Diego de Zubia [see below]	Hammond and Rey 1953 [2]:815
Joseph Brondate*	Oñate exploration and settlement	1601	-metal potential in Cerrillos Hill near San Marcos	Hammond and Rey 1953 [2]:630; Long 1964
Marcelo de Espinosa*	Oñate exploration and settlement	1601	-Indians do not have metal -silver lodes in Cerrillos Hills near San Marcos -smelting at San Marcos produced metal	Hammond and Rey 1953 [2]:636–637; Long 1964
Diego de Zubia	Oñate exploration and settlement	1601	-Vincente de Saldivar, *Sargento Mayor* for Onate smelted ore at San Marcos	Hammond and Rey 1953 [2]:821,826, Long 1964; Milford 1996
Alférez Keibus de Termiño de Bañelos	Oñate exploration and settlement	1601	-mines discovered ear San Marcos; smelting by mercury and also by heat	Hammond and Rey 1953 [2]:829; Long 1964; Milford 1996

TABLE 1 (CONTINUED)
OBSERVATIONS OF METALLIC MINERAL POTENTIAL OF THE NEW MEXICO COLONY

Observer	Expedition	Date	Metallurgical Potential	Source
Juan de Ortega*	Oñate exploration and settlement	1601	-Indians did not have metal -had not heard that there were mines although Govenor Oñate believed there were	Hammond and Rey 1953 [2]:663, 667; Long 1964; Milford 1996
Don Juan de Oñate*	Oñate exploration and settlement	1599	-metal potential in colony -great wealth is possible	Hammond and Rey 1953 [1]:421–422; Long 1964; Milford 1996
Viceroy to the King		~1601	-metal potential in New Mexico	Long 1964:38–39
Viceroy, Marquis de Montesclaros, letter to the King		1605	-Onate sent ores from New Mexico to Mexico for assaying. Assay produced on 1/8 part copper and no silver -no gold or silver in the colony; Indians are so poor that they weave dog hair, not cotton	Hammond and Rey 1953 [2]:1001–1002; Long 1964; Milford 1996
Don Alonso de Oñate letter to the King***		1601	-a grievance against the report of the Viceroy regarding assaying of ore sent by Juan de Oñate. Oñate sent silver ore, not copper	Hammond and Rey 1953 [2]:581; Long 1964;
Marquis de Guadalcázar in letter to King		1620	-Mines are possible but have not been verified -Colony maintained only for benefit of Indians	Hammond and Rey 1953 [2]:1140; Long 1964; Milford 1996
Fray Gerónimo de Zárate Salmerón		1616–1626	-metal potential including copper, lead, sulfur, turquoise -no knowledgeable personnel to extract metal	Long 1964:45–46; Milford 1996
Fray Alonso de Benavides		1630	-great metal potential, especially near Socorro including both silver and gold. -no knowledgeable personnel to extract metal	Hodge et al. 1945:16–17; Milford 1996
Fray Juan de Prada		1638	-Metal potential including gold and silver -no knowledgeable personnel to extract metal	Hackett 1923–1937 [3]:109; Milford 1996
Juan Domingez de Mendoza	Governor Otermin's attempted Reconquest	1681	- evidence of iron smithing including forge in an abandoned Indian church at Sandia Pueblo	Hodge 1934:157; Simmons and Turley 1980:31
Captain Roque Madrid		1694	-Visits the abandoned and in-filled lead mine in the Cerrillos hills (known as Cerro de San Marcos) owned by his father before the Pueblo Revolt	Kessell et al. 1998 [part 1]:125
Don Diego de Vargas Letter to Viceroy		1695	-silver mines six leagues from Santa Fe	Kessell et al. 1998: 78–79,601
		1696	-Sierra Azul silver mines and vermilion containing mercury in Arizona -sent vermilion ore to Mexico City for assaying -concerned about discovering rich metal resources in the colony	Kessell et al. 1998:703

*Testimonies before the Viceroy of New Spain
**Notary of the Rodriguez-Chumascado Entrada
***Brother of Don Juan de Oñate

TABLE 2
HISTORICAL DOCUMENTS SUMMARY OF METAL POTENTIAL

	Metal Rich	Metal Poor	No Mention of Metallurgical Potential	Total
Total Observations	21	5	2	28
Eye-Witnesses	20	2		
No visit to Colony	1	3		
Miners	6	0		
Civil Authority	0	3		

even though another official stated that smelting copper could be used as coinage in a colony where there was none (Long 1964:38–39). On the other hand, Homer Milford (1996:18–25) has argued that behind the viceroyal assessments lay issues involving the political status of Oñate and whether New Mexico would become an independent colony. Metallurgical production could make New Mexico politically independent, in which case Juan de Oñate would remain *adelantado* and thus retain his governor-like, independent military and administrative control over the colony. Absence of exploitable metallic ores, on the other hand, would mean that Oñate would be removed as governor and that New Mexico would remain an impoverished borderland under the control of the viceroy.

Given the available information and the temporal distance of some 400 years, it is impossible to know the cause of the negative viceregal assessments of potential metallurgical wealth of the New Mexico colony. What is clear is that once the viceroyal stamp of "metal poor" was placed on the colony, it guided later official views for nearly 200 years.

Cerrillos Hills and San Marcos Pueblo

Despite the ambiguity regarding the metallurgical possibilities of the entire colony, the initial documentary record is clear in terms of the metallic mineral potential of the Cerrillos Hills area. Of the 28 individuals listed in Table 1 above, 9 mention the Cerrillos Hills as having potential mineral wealth, and several individuals (for example, Marcelo de Espinosa and Vincente de Zaldívar Mendoza) mention assaying Cerrillos Hills ores either in the hills or at San Marcos. When this information is combined with the establishment of Cerrillos Hills as a mining camp

after the reconquista (Espinosa 1942; Milford 1996; Kessell et al. 1998) and the comment made by Roque Madrid regarding the Cerrillos Hills lead mine owned by his father *before* the revolt (Table 1), it is reasonable to suggest that the Cerrillos Hills may have been a Spanish mining district before the Pueblo Revolt of 1680. Spanish miners defined a mining district as a named, organized, and spatially bounded mining area. If this is the case, then Cerrillos Hills is the earliest mining district in what is now the United States. Other researchers (Jones 1904; Warren 1974) have made similar assertions. It seems likely that the Cerrillos Hills were an important location for the development of mining and metallurgy in early colonial New Mexico.

The economically important minerals in the Cerrillos Hills can be divided into two groups: metallic minerals and turquoise. The Cerrillos Hills are part of a Tertiary age, orogenic system of intrusive and extrusive volcanics that extend as a chain from the San Pedro Mountains in the south through the Ortiz Mountains, terminating with the Cerrillos Hills (Figure 2). Metallic minerals of commercial value occur along this entire chain. The six Cerrillos Hills stand above the Santa Fe Plain and are the remnants of larger and resistant intrusive masses that pushed up during the Tertiary volcanic episodes (Disbrow and Stoll 1980). Metal minerals occur as veins in these Tertiary age deposits, both between lower sedimentary beds and upper intrusive and extrusive volcanics and within the volcanic units (Disbrow and Stoll 1980). The matrix of the volcanics in which the metal minerals occur are predominately monzonite with varying amounts of hornblende or augite-biotite (Disbrow and Stoll 1980).

The principal metallic minerals of the Cerrillos Hills are relatively low grade, largely sulfidic

FIGURE 2. The Cerrillos Hills area. (Map by Ann Ramenof-sky, 2003.)

ores that require roasting before the metal can be efficiently extracted (Table 3). Commercial extraction of these ores began in the late-19th century and peaked between 1910 and the late 1940s (Lingren et al. 1910; U.S. Geological Survey 1965; Disbrow and Stoll 1980). As measured in pounds, zinc was the most important metal produced during that period, followed by lead, copper, and silver.

In New Mexico, neither the gold nor the silver in the Cerrillos Hills were particularly important economically, at least prior to the advent of silver mining in 1861 and the arrival of the railroad in 1879 (Milford 1996). Gold, in

fact, is excluded from Table 3 because it was never produced in any quantity (Northrop 1959; U.S. Geological Survey 1965). Silver tended to occur with galena (silver-lead sulfide). Historically, silver extraction began with the patio process, a cold reduction technology in which salt and mercury were used to amalgamate silver with mercury, thereby separating it from other nonmetallic minerals (Probert 1997). The absence of cinnabar (mercury sulfide) deposits in New Mexico meant that mercury had to be imported. Although there are 17th-century records of such transport into New Mexico (Chavez 1973), it appears that this was not a common practice. The absence of mercury, coupled with the costs of transport, limited the use of this process throughout the colony, including its application to the silver-bearing galena of the Cerrillos Hills. Even during the industrial boom in the Cerrillos Hills, silver does not appear to have been produced in huge quantities.

Like the Cerrillos Hills, San Marcos Pueblo is frequently mentioned in the known documentary record, a fact at least partially explained by the geographic proximity of the pueblo to the mineral deposits (Vaughan 2006) (Figure 2). Six of the nine individuals who mentioned the Cerrillos Hills' metallic minerals also visited or mentioned San Marcos. Indeed, some Spanish explorers expressly linked metallurgy at San Marcos to mineral deposits in the Cerrillos Hills. For example, the notary for the 1581 Rodriguez-Chamuscado expedition, Hernán Gallegos, described assaying a "coppery-steel like ore," possibly chalcopyrite, at San Marcos that was derived from the Cerrillos Hills (Hammond and Rey 1996:86–88). This was followed by more visits to both the Cerrillos Hills and San Marcos by other expeditions (Antonio de Espejo in 1583 and Gaspar de Sosa in 1591). Twenty years after the Rodriguez-Chamuscado exploration, the Oñate colonists again collected ore from the Cerrillos Hills and assayed it at San Marcos. The assay yielded "four ounces" of metal (Hammond and Rey 1953[2]:630,641).

Even though the surviving documents provide no additional details about San Marcos and metal production, several facts make it possible to infer from both archaeology and history that the San Marceseños had knowledge of minerals and passed that knowledge on to Spanish prospectors. First, San Marceseños knew some

TABLE 3
CERRILLOS HILLS METALLIC MINERALS

Metal	Sulfide Ores	Oxide Ores	Carbonate Ores
Lead	Galena		Cerussite
Zinc	Sphalerite	Zincite	
Copper	Chalcocite	Cuprite	Azurite
	Bornite		
	Chalcopyrite		Malachite
Silver	Argentite		
Iron	Pyrite	Magnetite	

Source: Northrup 1959; Klein and Dana 1993

of the physical properties of metallic minerals. After about A.D. 1350, lead-based glaze paint designs dominated all decorated ceramics in the Rio Grande corridor. San Marcoseños were major producers of these wares, trading them beyond the confines of San Marcos (Shepared 1942, 1965; Warren 1979; Motsinger 1997). Lead was the principal flux used to melt silica in the glaze paint recipe, and lead minerals from the Cerrillos Hills were the principal source of this flux (Habicht-Mauche et al. 2000). Second, documentary evidence suggests that when the Spanish visited the pueblo seeking information about potential metal deposits, the San Marcoseños provided that information and even escorted some Spaniards to the Cerrillos ore deposits (Bandelier 1892[3]:92–93; Hammond and Rey 1927:28; Milford 1996).

Integrating and interpreting across the historical sources permits construction of a very different picture of metal extraction than that portrayed in historical textbooks. In contrast to conventional wisdom, it appears that the Spanish were exploring and testing a range of metallic minerals in New Mexico, beginning no later than A.D. 1581. The Cerrillos Hills in north-central New Mexico constituted an early mining region from which lead and possibly other metals were extracted. Because of its geographic proximity, its available pool of labor,

and Native knowledge of some of the properties of lead, San Marcos Pueblo was pulled into this metallurgical story. The task, now, is to expose the evidence and tell the story buried at the pueblo.

Contextualizing San Marcos Pueblo

Beginning in the 15th century, Native populations in New Mexico began the aggregation that resulted in the establishment of, at least, 36 extremely large pueblos that visually dominated the settlement landscape of the Rio Grande corridor as well as the Jemez Mountains and the Lower Chama valley. San Marcos is one of these pueblos and constitutes one of eight such settlements in the Galisteo Basin (Figure 3). Shortly before or during the Pueblo Revolt, Native peoples permanently abandoned most of these aggregated settlements. These large villages were spatially extensive and architecturally complex, containing single- or multistory room blocks, made of stone masonry or adobe as well as extramural features, including ramadas, kivas, plazas, and deep middens (Mera 1940; Bernardini 1998; Potter 1998; Spielmann 1998). Although physically impressive, the final spatial configuration of aggregated settlements represents the end product of hundreds of years of building, modification, abandonment, and reoccupation.

Although Native occupation of San Marcos began in the late-13th or early-14th century (Nelson 1912–1915; Reed 1954) and continued until the Pueblo Revolt, occupation appears to have been discontinuous, punctuated by periods of abandonment and reoccupation (Ramenofsky 2001). During the long occupational history, the settlement expanded to incorporate approximately 24 hectares with room count estimates greater than 2,000 (Figure 4). In 1638, Franciscans established a mission complex at San Marcos (Hodge et al. 1945; Thomas 2000), and at least one priest, Fray Manuel Tinoco, lived at the pueblo until the Pueblo Revolt of 1680. At the beginning of the Pueblo Revolt, however, the Indians killed Fray Tinoco while he was away from the pueblo (Hackett 1923–1937[3]:329).

At the time that the senior author initiated archaeological research of the pueblo, the Archaeological Conservancy had completed its acquisition of the entire property. Change in ownership made it possible to undertake

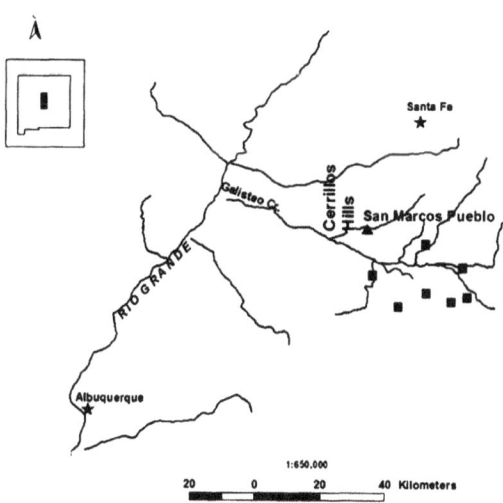

FIGURE 3. Galisteo Basin pueblos. (Map by Ann Ramenofsky, 2003.)

systematic investigation of all 24 hectares. In the initial phase, archaeologists constructed a fined-grained topographic map and undertook systematic surface collections to identify midden deposits (Figure 4). With midden locations established, intensive surface collection was undertaken to build an occupational history of Native use of the pueblo. During this phase, small pieces of metallurgical debris were recovered. The highest concentration of this debris was located east of the mission complex in one area, noted in Figure 4 as "metallurgical block." The block overlapped with parts of two room blocks as well as with Midden 4. In the second phase, the senior author undertook intensive exploration of the

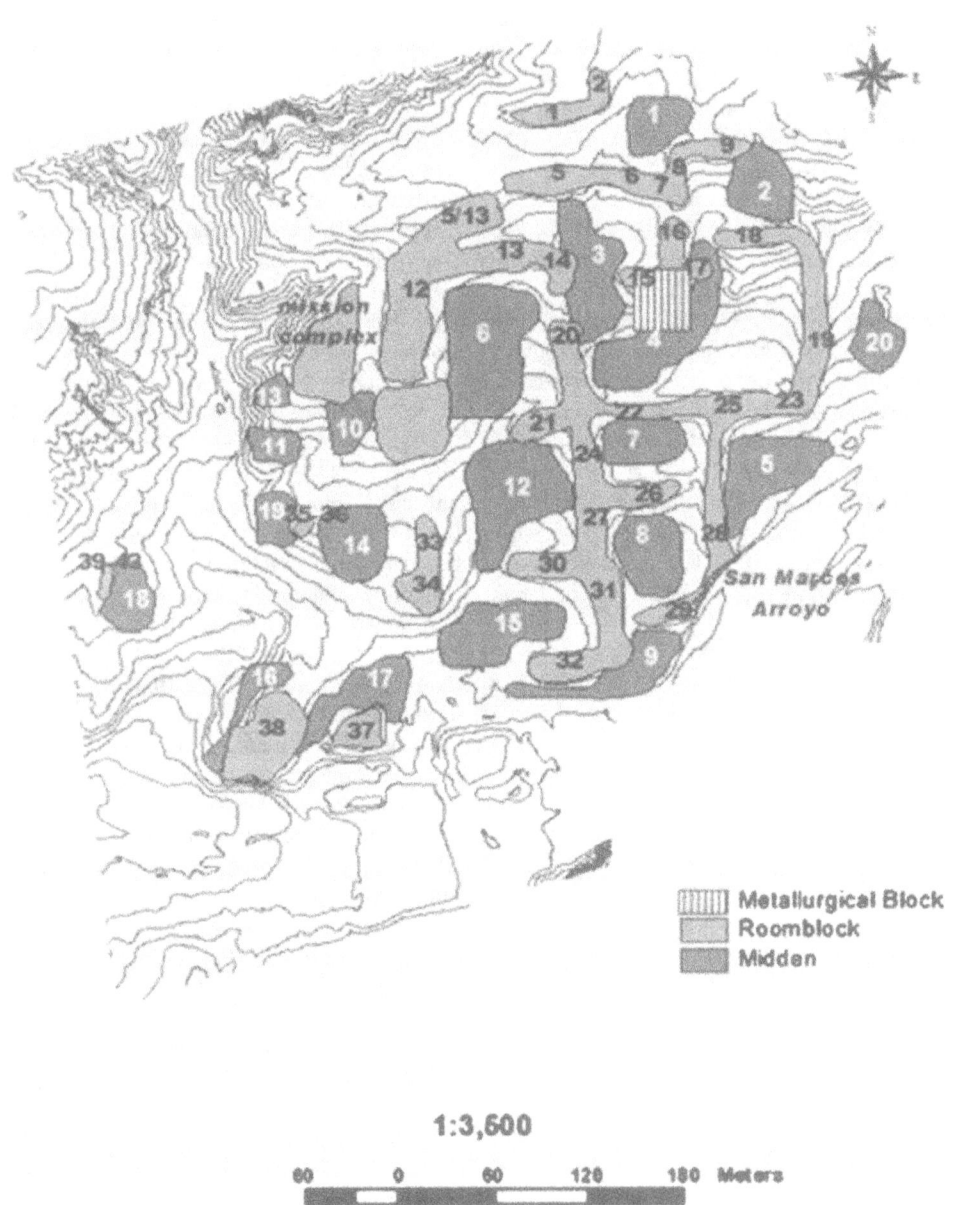

1:3,600

FIGURE 4. Topography, room blocks, midden, and metallurgical block, San Marcos Pueblo. (Drawing by Shawn Penman and Ann Ramenofsky, 2000.)

metallurgical block in order to determine the nature of metal production suggested by the recovered metallurgical debris.

Metallurgical Facilities

The production of metal through fire smelting is a complex and "messy" technology that generally includes ore cutting, crushing, sorting, and, in the case of sulfidic ores, roasting. To extract metal from ore requires burning charcoal or other fuels, adding fluxes to the charge, tapping slags during the smelt, and cleaning and repairing the furnace between smelting episodes (Tylecote 1986; Craddock 1995). Although each of these activities can result in a distinct archaeological footprint that, in turn, creates an archaeological record, the entire sequence can be vastly more difficult to document, especially where metallurgical sites are repeatedly used or the various uses of facilities change over time.

At San Marcos, the senior author used a number of discovery strategies to document several portions of the metal extraction process (Figure 5), including systematic surface collection, magnetometry, and excavation. These strategies resulted in the documentation of two parts of the metallurgical process. Feature A

was shown to be a series of formal smelter bases. Feature B may also have served as an informal smelter at one time, but that evidence was virtually destroyed by later use. In its last phase of use, Feature B became a dumping site for metallurgical debris. Given the proximity of these features to each other, as well as their overlapping age determinations, they appear to have been two parts of a larger sociotechnological system. These features were positioned on a south-facing terrace, and it is likely that this position was deliberately chosen to take advantage of local updrafts. The features were shallowly buried and were constructed in previously abandoned room sections of older adobe room blocks.

Smelter Floors (Feature A)

Feature A was a series of formal, well-constructed, and superimposed furnace floors with small pieces of vertical wall sections, still intact along parts of the feature margin (Figure 6). As is the case with adobe smelters generally (Henderson 2000), only parts of the bases and small pieces of vertical walls had survived, making it impossible to reconstruct the entire structure. The San Marcos smelters may have been shaped like vertical-sided cylinders, open basins, or enclosed structures. The degree of oxidation across the surviving basins suggests a controlled air supply, directed to the heart of the fuel and ore charge (although this oxidation could have been created in any of these configurations). In the case of the closed structure, oxygen could have been supplied by using bellows or tuyeres, rather than natural updraft.

The plan of the smelters was circular, measuring approximately 1 m in diameter. At the east margin, the structure was banked against the remnants of an adobe wall. In plan view, archaeologists identified two relatively intact upper basins that were well designed and superimposed. The more recent basin was of a slightly smaller diameter than the lower one. Inside the most recent basin, as well as below each floor, was a thick bed of fine, pinkish-red ashy sediments. The floors were composed of fine adobe, thin in cross section, and relatively free of rock fragments. By contrast, the collapsed furnace walls were composed primarily of an unsorted thick and granular adobe.

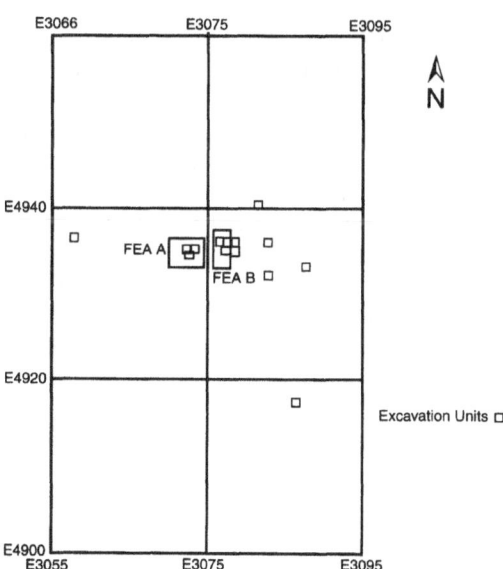

FIGURE 5. Metallurgical block with features identified. (Drawing by Ann Ramenofsky, 2003.)

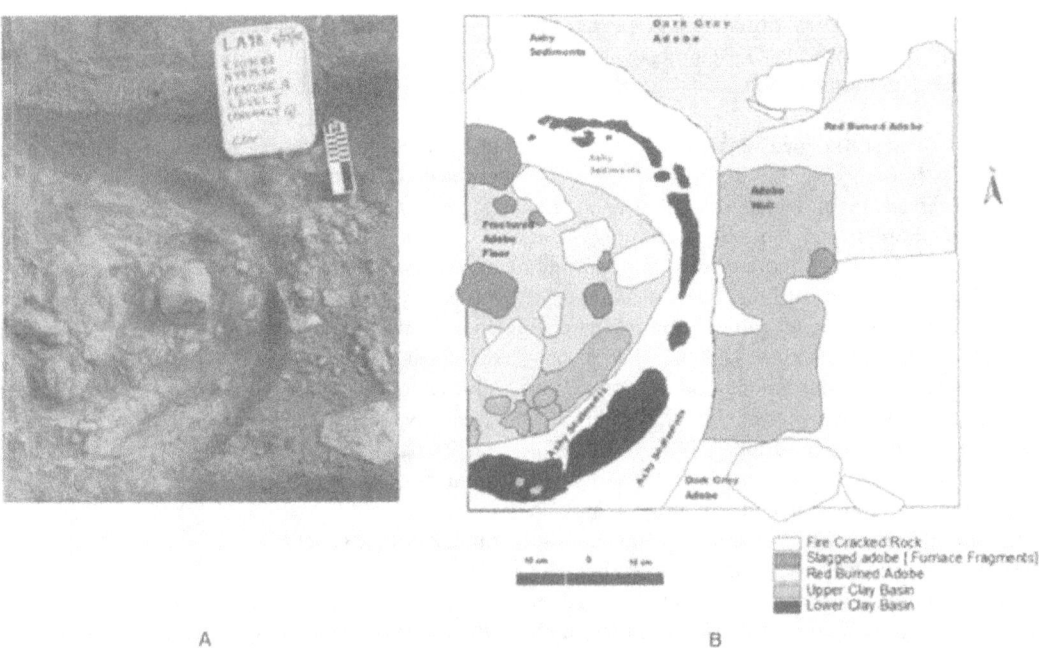

A   B

FIGURE 6. Photograph and plan map of Smelter Bases. (Photo by C. David Vaughan, 2003; drawing by Ann Ramenofsky and Shawn Penman, 2004.)

The alternating stratification of ashy sediments and fine adobe floors suggested at least three episodes of furnace construction and use at this location. The only visible part of the oldest furnace floor was a thick layer of ash. These ashy sediments were likely the remnants of the fuel used to heat the ore in the smelter. Above this ash was the oldest intact floor section, inside of which was a second level of fuel ash from a more recent smelt. This, in turn, was followed by yet another burned adobe floor containing an additional layer of ashy sediments. After each smelt, it appears that the metallurgists at San Marcos purposefully left the fuel ash from a completed smelt in place, perhaps as insulation, and then constructed a new floor composed of fine, perhaps sieved, clay sediments in (or on top of) this ash. Subsequent heating episodes altered the ashy-clay sediments into the ceramic-like sections of the fired basins. Finger impressions were faintly visible on some parts of the innermost basin.

Sediment color across the feature varied from red to grey-black, suggesting either a poorly controlled firing atmosphere or perhaps a change in the firing atmosphere throughout the life of the smelter. At the edges of the smelter, the colors were dark grey, grey-red, or light red. Toward the center of the feature, iron in the sediments became much more oxidized, and the color ranged from reddish brown to red-orange.

Only certain types of metallurgical debris were abundant across the inner basin floor (further detailed below). Categories of artifacts recovered from the smelter include pieces of burned adobe furnace walls and floor, some of which had either vitrified or become slagged during smelting. Fire-cracked rock was present only occasionally. Equally significant were the artifact types not present. There were no metal products, virtually no charcoal, and only the smallest pieces of metallurgical slag on smelter floors. The dominance of smelter remnants and the virtual absence of all other kinds of metallurgical artifacts suggest that cleaning of metal byproducts occurred after each of the smelting episodes.

Slag Pit (Feature B)

By comparison with the smelter bases, Feature B was less formal, less defined, and more difficult to interpret. Structurally, it was a shallow pit, approximately 1.5 m in diameter, ringed and filled with metallurgical debris (Figure 7), and uniformly dark gray in color. The stratigraphic position of the pit suggested that it was the most recent use of this space. The pit had been excavated into the fill and floor of a room, following abandonment of the room, and sections of the older floor were still intact outside the feature boundary. Directly north of the pit were upright slabs that appeared to part of a milling station. The slabs extended below the base of the feature and were stratigraphically at the same level as the older floor remnant.

The structure, composition, and artifact inventory of the pit suggest that it was used as a dumping site or "clean out" station during the various smelting episodes. Metallurgical debris was common and randomly distributed in the pit in unordered piles. Debris categories included droplets of corroded metal; metallurgical slag; concentrations of charcoal; and burned, vitrified, and slagged adobe. Toward the base of the pit, a few late glaze-paint sherds were recovered, including one with slag adhering to the rim edge.

The archaeometallurgical record at Feature B goes beyond the minimal historical references in elucidating the activities themselves. The furnace bases and the clean-out pit appear to be two parts of a larger metallurgical operation that was well planned and deliberate. The remains of the smelters suggest that metallurgists had a clear construction plan in mind, and the repeated use of the smelter suggests that the plan worked. The adjacent pit was the location where metallurgical debris was discarded after cooling.

Age of the Metallurgical Facility

The pervasive scholarly belief that metallurgical production was not part of the initial colonizing effort of New Mexico makes it essential to establish the age of the metallurgical features at San Marcos as precisely as possible. While a post-revolt temporal affiliation would not necessarily rule out the possibility of pre-revolt metallurgical activity at San Marcos, a pre-revolt temporal affiliation would more closely link the archaeology and history. It would also support the presence of pre-revolt metallurgical activity in the colony.

Even though no artifacts indicative of an 18th- or 19th-century temporal affiliation were discovered in the vicinity of the metallurgical

A   B

FIGURE 7. Photograph and plan drawing of metallurgical debris pit. (Photo by Ann Ramenofsky; drawing by Ann Ramenofsky and Shawn Penman, 2004.)

block, the senior author undertook a more rigorous program of ratio-scale archaeological dating, including luminescence and radiocarbon, to more precisely bracket construction and use of the facility. Both dating methods produce calendrical age estimates, but they "date" different kinds of events, and the age estimates themselves convey different kinds of temporal information. Consequently, differences between these methods are importantly to identify.

First, radiocarbon dates are death events, whereas luminescence dates are direct dates of manufacturing or use of artifacts, including ceramics or burned adobe. Second, radiocarbon dates require calibration, but luminescence dates do not. This difference is especially important for young samples because the radiocarbon calibration curve during this period is relatively flat and produces multiple intercepts. Third, the error terms around the two kinds of dates have different meanings. Radiocarbon dates are probability statements reflected in the 2σ confidence interval. The percent error term of a luminescence date is not a probability statement but is, rather, the sum of analytical error accumulated throughout the measurement processes. Precision of the age estimate increases as the size of the percent error decreases. Percent error of less than 10% is considered precise.

Luminescence dating of metallurgical debris is a relatively recent method (Gautier 2001). To control for the possibility of low precision luminescence dates, on the one hand, and the problem of young radiocarbon samples on the other, both methods were used to increase confidence in estimating metallurgical ages. Dating samples derived from both features. Convergence in age estimates between these two dating

methods, as well as within each feature, pointed to simultaneous construction and use prior to the Pueblo Revolt.

Luminescence Age

As compared to radiocarbon dating, luminescence dating is a far more complicated method (for more detail, Aitken 1985, 1989, 1990, 1998; Smith et al. 1986; Rhodes 1988; Feathers 1997, 2000). Luminescence can be measured as either heat or light (Huntley et al. 1985); for the San Marcos material, optical stimulating luminescence (OSL) was employed using an SAR Post-IR blue OSL technique (developed by Banerjee et al. 2001). Analyses were undertaken at the Luminescence Dating Laboratory of the Research Laboratory for Archaeology and History of Art at the University of Oxford (Rhodes 2003). Eleven potential dating samples were submitted, including pieces of vitrified adobe, burned adobe, and several glaze-paint rim sherds. Of these, six specimens were selected for luminescence analysis because they demonstrated acceptable OSL signal sensitivity, had acceptable growth characteristics, and had an acceptable degree of variability between aliquots (Table 4) (Figure 8). The specimens derived from both features and included two pieces of vitrified adobe, two pieces of burned adobe, and two glaze-paint rim sherds.

Luminescence ages of the six samples from both features range from A.D.1400 to 1916, but the dates have variable precision. The dates on two vitrified adobe fragments, 2081-1 (1920±110) and 2087-2 (1800±20) are not reliable. The vitrified adobe had weak luminescence signals and slow growth rates. Edward Rhodes

TABLE 4
LUMINESCENCE DATES FROM SMELTING FACILITIES, SAN MARCOS PUEBLO

FS No.	Feature	Level	Kind of Sample	Luminescence Age Age (A.D.)	Percent Error	Age
2081-1	A	3	Vitrified Adobe	1916	12.8	1920± 110
2081-2	A	3	Burned Adobe	1652	9.33	1650± 30
2081-3	A	3	Burned Adobe	1537	9.11	1540± 40
2087-1	B	2	Glaze E Rim	1528	9.00	1530± 40
2087-2	B	2	Vitrified Adobe	1802	9.39	1800± 20
2097-1	Below B	5	Indeterminate Glaze base	1406	13.7	1410± 80

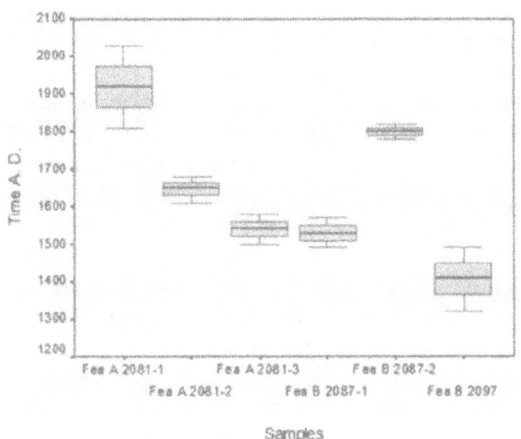

FIGURE 8. Luminescence dates from smelter and debris pit. (Drawing by Ann Ramenofsky, 2003.)

(2003) reports similar difficulties in dating vitrified adobe from smelting sites in Swaziland. One of the glaze-paint ceramic sherds (FS 2097-1), stratigraphically below the slag pit, also had a very high percent error with a luminescence age estimate of A.D. 1410±80. Although this estimate occurs prior to European conquest, the sherd came from a level below the slag pit and, despite the high error term, may be valid.

On the other hand, the cluster of three dates from both features, i.e., burned adobe 2081-2 (A.D. 1650±30), burned adobe 2081-3 (A.D. 1540±40), and one glazed-paint E sherd 2087-1 (A.D. 1530±40) have the smallest error terms and appear to reliably bracket smelter construction and use to the 16th and 17th centuries (Figure 8). Given that the error terms of the two burned adobe dates do not overlap and were derived from different parts of the furnace, they are likely describing different smelting episodes. If this is correct, then the two smelts occurred nearly 100 years apart. The earlier smelt is represented by burned adobe fragment 2081-3, with a luminescence age of (A.D. 1540±40). The later smelting date, A.D. 1650±30, (2081-2), derives from the inner basin of the furnace and likely relates to the use of that floor. The glaze-paint E sherd mingled with the metallurgical debris from Feature B (2087-1) describes the manufacturing date of that ceramic (for further discussion, Ramenofsky and Feathers 2002). The fact that the ceramic age of A.D. 1530±40 overlaps with the earlier burned adobe smelter date suggests that both ceramic and metal production were occurring at the pueblo in the mid-late 16th century.

In sum, three luminescence dates produced reliable results. The smelting dates have a range of more than 100 years. At the very least, the luminescence analyses point to metal production well before the Pueblo Revolt, perhaps as early as the mid- to late-16th century.

Radiocarbon Dating

Because no charcoal was recovered from the furnace, two radiocarbon samples from the same level but different areas of Feature B were submitted to Beta Analytic for analysis (Table 5). Only one of the dates, 189890 [A.D. 1450–1660], produced an age estimate in which the two-sigma range overlapped with the reliable luminescence dates. The second radiocarbon date, 189891 [A.D. 1300–1450], was much earlier than the reliable luminescence estimates but overlapped with the anomalous luminescence ceramic date. Although this radiocarbon estimate cannot be associated with the slag pit, the date

TABLE 5
RADIOCARBON DATES OF SMELTING FACILITIES, SAN MARCOS PUEBLO

Beta Analytic No	FS Number	Material	Size (grms)	Conventional ^{14}C Age	δ^{13}C	2σ Calibrated Age (A. D.)
189890	2093 Feature B	Wood Charcoal	24	330 ± 50	-24.2	1450–1660
189891	2087 Feature B	Wood Charcoal	< 1	570 ± 50	-23.7	1300–1450

may be referencing the earlier use of the feature area when Feature B was part of a room block. When use of the area changed from habitation to metal production, the charcoal somehow became incorporated into the later pit.

On balance, four of the eight dated samples yielded age estimates sufficiently consistent to infer that the smelter was constructed and used in the 100 or so years before the Pueblo Revolt of 1680. Three luminescence dates have good precision and suggest at least two episodes of metallurgical production. Because the standard deviation of the reliable radiocarbon date incorporates all the luminescence dates, it is not possible to use that estimate to determine when in that interval ores were being smelted or, more likely, tested. On the other hand, because the radiocarbon estimates span the luminescence range, they add further support to a pre-revolt date of the metallurgical activity. As with the discovery of archaeometallurgical features, there is agreement between the archaeological and historical records regarding the exploitation of metallic minerals at San Marcos well before A.D. 1680.

Analysis of Metallurgical Debris

By the mid-16th century, the Spanish were adapting European metallurgical knowledge to their new American setting. Much of the earliest mining in the Caribbean was placer mining of gold, but recently, excavations at La Isabela (Deagan and Cruxent 2002; Thibodeau et al. 2007) suggest that silver extraction through lead cupellation was undertaken shortly before abandonment of the town. In Mexico, smelting of silver ores began in the 1530s, and by 1550, Cerro Rico silver from Potosi, Bolivia, was being produced (Bakewell 1997). In 1560, Georgius Agricola (1912) published his massive metallurgical encyclopedia of mining and metallurgy, and that volume became the standard for metal mining and extraction well into the 19th century (Young 1970). By the mid-1560s, the patio process had been invented and had elevated significantly the scale of silver production in Mexico and Peru (Probert 1997).

Largely due to gaps in historical and archaeological knowledge of New Mexico's early metal production, this general historical knowledge of metal production within the Spanish Empire is essential background for understanding metal production in the colony. Because of these gaps, little is known about the identity of New Mexico's 17th-century metallurgists, their level of expertise, nor how they selected and prepared different types of ore. It is uncertain whether fluxes were used in reducing these ores to metal or which metals were being extracted (for an exception, Vaughan 2006). In terms of archaeology, metallurgical excavation at Pa'ako Pueblo is the only comparable project to the San Marcos investigation. At Pa'ako, archaeologists documented a large "industrial terrace," used for what appears to have been attempts at a number of different metallurgical processes, including iron forging and the successful production of copper, which also contributes important knowledge and context (Lycett 1998, 1999, 2000, 2001, 2002, 2003; Thomas 2002).

The disparity between general knowledge of Spanish metal production and archaeometallurgy in New Mexico dictates an analytical strategy for the San Marcos record that maximizes the information potential at multiple scales. The general analytic goal is to create a description from which researchers could broadly infer the metallurgical sophistication of the miners, the temperatures of the smelt, and the type of metal(s) produced. Analysis begins with a general characterization of the metallurgical assemblage and ends with electron miscroscopy of a small subsample of the entire assemblage.

Assemblage Scale Analysis

Because no metal products were recovered from the excavation or surface collection, the macroscopic examination was limited to metallurgical byproducts. Initial examination of these artifacts revealed a more or less consistent set of characteristics that were employed to create categories of smelting byproducts. The units varied according to the glassiness or graininess of the piece and included metallurgical slag, slagged or vitrified adobe, burned adobe, and incompletely reduced ore or charge.

Metallurgical slag is generally a dense, vesiculated, dark, sometimes glassy, and often magnetic solid that is produced by smelting. Because slag prevents the metal formed from reoxidizing during smelting, metallurgical slag is an essential component as well as a byproduct of producing metal (Bachmann 1982). In preindustrial metallurgical technology, slags tend to be relatively heavy and dense by volume because substantial amounts of metal remained trapped within the slag and thus are not extracted during the smelt. Metallurgical slags are generally crystalline, microscopically; however, macroscopically, they appear "glassy," a characteristic that results from the melting of silica and other nonmetallic minerals in the ore body (called gangue). The color of the glass varies, but it generally follows that the darker the glass, the more metal-rich the slag.

Slagged or vitrified adobe is typically the broken and burned or heated remnants of the furnace, including its floor and walls. Since they lack entrapped metal, these smelting byproducts tend to be lighter by volume than metallurgical slag and grainier because of the presence of aplastics or other mineral grains such as quartz. When the furnace becomes sufficiently hot or the duration of the smelt sufficiently long, silica grains in the adobe vitrify or, in extreme cases, become "frothy" or highly vesiculated. In other cases, the vitrified adobe flows and coats one or more surfaces of unvitrified adobe, giving it a glassy appearance. Slagged adobe is formed when the siliceous slag produced during the smelt adheres to the inside of the furnace, again giving the recovered fragments a glassy surface. In cross-section, either of these materials can be either vesicular or grainy.

Burned adobe, as opposed to vitrified and slagged adobe, retains its granular structure throughout. There is no evidence of either vitrification or slagging.

Finally, *incompletely smelted ore* has characteristics of both glass formation typical of metallurgical slags as well as characteristics of ore or country rock from which the metal was extracted. As a result, it has both visible glassiness and graininess.

All material from both features greater in size than 11.2 mm was sorted into one of the four categories (Table 6). Because material less than 11.2 mm was too small to reliably separate by category, it was lumped together and assigned its own category. Although some metallurgical debris was recovered from other excavation units, a total of 68 kg or .068 metric tons of material (99%) was derived from features A and B.

The abundance of items within the different categories of metallurgical debris varies across and between the features, and that variation reflects feature function. Burned adobe, followed by slagged or vitrified adobe, is the most abundant type of metallurgical debris (accounting for 80% by weight and 57% by count) of the entire assemblage. Whether measured in terms of counts or weights, most of the forms of adobe were recovered from the smelter bases (Feature A) and were related to the furnace walls. In addition, the smelter bases contained virtually no metallurgical slag or incompletely smelted ore, and this absence most likely reflects the removal of the remaining contents of the furnace after each episode of metal extraction. By contrast, 84% of all other categories of metallurgical

TABLE 6
COUNTS AND WEIGHTS OF METALLURGICAL DEBRIS FROM FEATURES, SAN MARCOS PUEBLO

	Burned Adobe		Other Metallugical Debris							
			Metallurgical Slag (A)		Slagged or Vitrified Adobe (B)		Incompletely Reduced Charge (C)		Material less than 11.2 mm (D)	
	Count	*Weight (grams)*	*Count*	*Weight (grams)*	*Count*	*Weight (grams)*	*Count*	*Weight (grams)*	*Count*	*Weight (grams)*
Feature A	3,521	35,476.73	3	2.22	572	7,587.10	1	2.97	538	302.41
Feature B	1,129	19,474.83	782	1,034.28	112	3,311.39	24	78.56	1,454	843.04
TOTAL	4,640	54,951.56	785	1,036.50	684	10,898.49	52	81.53	1,992	1,145.45

debris (metallurgical slag, incompletely smelted ore, and all small debris) was recovered from this pit. Moreover, the relatively larger quantities of small pieces of slag in the slag pit suggest that the slag was being broken up before it was discarded into the pit.

The preliminary macroscopic analysis of these materials suggests that the metallurgists at San Marcos had sufficient knowledge to achieve their goal of extracting metal. This inference is readily apparent in a comparison of slags to incompletely smelted charge. The slags are glassy, heavy, and dark, and many pieces contain flow lines indicative of a slag sufficiently fluid to allow the movement of metal droplets through the slag and down to the base of the furnace where they could be drained out. The incompletely smelted pieces are much less common, representing only a small percentage of the total assemblage. The ratio of glassy slag counts to incompletely smelted ore counts is high, 15:1. In other words, during all the hypothesized smelting operations, most of the charge was reduced to metal and byproducts, leaving only a small percentage of material incompletely reduced.

The location of the features combined with and the careful construction of the furnace, and macroscopic identification of materials points to a well-planned and well-executed smelting operation. The furnaces were used multiple times, and the actual reduction processes yielded abundant burned and vitrified adobe and a predominance of relatively clean metallurgical slag.

SEM Analysis of Metallurgical Debris

Because some metal is trapped in most metallurgical debris and is especially common in slag, a microscopic analysis was also undertaken to investigate the extraction processes involved, to identify the metals present, and to determine the operating temperatures of the smelts. This "fingerprinting" method was limited to scanning electron microscopy (SEM), conducted in the Institute of Meteoritics at University of New Mexico (UNM). The SEM laboratory at UNM contains a JEOL 5800LV SEM, equipped with secondary and backscattered electron and cathodoluminscence (CL) imaging detectors. An Oxford Analytical ultra thin-window Energy-Dispersive X-ray Spectrometer (EDS) and an

Oxford Isis 300 X-ray analyzer are attached to the microscope. The analytical software provides semi- to fully quantitative EDS analysis down to boron, along with high-resolution image acquisition, processing, and analysis.

SEM is a relatively course-grain materials approach that identifies elemental concentrations relative to each other across different areas of a thin section (Figure 9). It is a useful first approximation for characterizing the chemical composition of metallurgical debris samples. Polished thin sections were prepared for 27 specimens, comprised of items from each of the assemblage scale categories. For each thin section, multiple spectra were acquired and interpreted. These multiple analyses allow researchers to confidently describe the elemental composition of each section. Nineteen of these thin sections contain important metallurgical information (Table 7).

In terms of metal content, neither gold nor silver is present in the samples. Copper and lead occur both in glass and as pure metal, and they are present in all 19 thin sections. Had one element been far more frequent in the samples than the other, it could be inferred that one or the other was the exclusive focus of the smelts. This, however, is not the case. The frequencies of lead and copper by thin section are approximately equal, with copper glass or metal identified in 15 sections and lead glass or metal in 18.

Several inferences from the SEM metallurgical data are possible. On the one hand, some

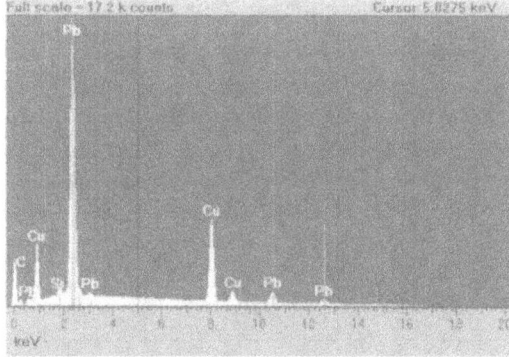

FIGURE 9. Scanning electron micrograph of one spectrum showing copper and lead metal. (Image by authors, 2004.)

TABLE 7
OCCURRENCE BY THIN SECTION OF COPPER AND LEAD

Thin Section No.	Category Type	Cu Metal	Cu glass	Pb Metal	Pb Glass	Cu and Pb Metal	Cu and Pb Glass
1	Slag			x	x	x	
2	Vitrified adobe	x		x	x		
6	Metal prill	x		x	x		
7	Slag			x	x	x	
11	Incompletely smelted ore			x	x	x	x
12	Vitified adobe	x		x		x	
13	Slag	x		x			
15	Burned adobe	x		x	x		
16	Slag				x		
17	Burned adobe	x	x		x	x	x
18	Incompletely smelted ore	x	x		x	x	
19	Slag			x			
20	Incompletely smelted ore	x		x		x	
21	Metal prill	x			x		
22	Burned adobe	x					
23	Burned adobe				x		
24	Slag		x	x			
25	Slag	x	x		x		x
26	Vitrified adobe			x	x	x	

of the data suggest that the reduction of copper was the metallurgical objective. Copper and lead co-occur in 15 thin sections, but in 13 of those cases, copper is present as metal. To obtain copper from a reduction process requires temperatures of approximately 1300° C. Lead, in contrast, melts at a relatively low temperature, approximately 327° C, and can easily volatilize (Tylecote 1986). Where both lead metal or lead glass and copper metal are consistently present, it is reasonable to suggest that copper extraction was the goal. This inference presupposes a number of other factors, including an assumption that the metallurgist(s) at San Marcos wanted to, could, and did control temperatures inside the furnace(s). If they did, then the extraction of copper may have been their primary objective and the reduction of lead minerals was an unintended consequence of copper smelting. If this inference is correct, the elemental data from 13 cross-sections suggest that extracting copper, not lead, was the purpose of 17th-century metallurgy at San Marcos.

Alternatively, it is possible that different smelts were directed toward different products:

copper in some cases, lead in others. One of the thin sections of slag contains only copper metal; three other slag samples contain only pure lead metal or glass. Although the presence of these elementally "pure" samples may have resulted from the way the pieces fractured during cooling, the purity of the specimens could just as likely reflect different smelting goals. In one or more instances, it is possible that lead extraction was the goal; in other cases, the metallurgists were extracting copper.

A third inference that could explain the analytical results has neither lead nor copper as the metallurgical objective. Rather than working to extract one or another sort of metal, the metallurgists may have been simply testing ores to determine their metallic mineral constituents. The search for silver may have been part of that testing. This inference regarding testing accords well with the absence of metal products at the site as well as with the small size of the smelting operation. If the metallurgists were testing rather than extracting a particular metal, they would have introduced unsorted ore samples containing commonly associated metallic minerals into the furnace, along with charcoal and perhaps other compounds. The furnace contents were then fired and allowed (or made) to reach temperatures high enough to potentially smelt both copper and silver. Silver is, in fact, similar to copper in both hardness and in smelting temperature and is commonly associated with ores of both lead and copper. Although the possibility of searching for silver is intriguing, this inference is difficult to make, given the absence of silver in any SEM spectra. On the other hand, that absence could be accounted for by the sampling selection for SEM analysis or the fact that silver is not present in the selected ore samples. Although testing rather than extracting fits the setting and the nature of the assemblage better than the other inferences, whether metallurgical testing included the search for silver cannot be validated by the available data.

No direct analysis of possible sources was undertaken, but several considerations point to the Cerrillos Hills as the predominate source of the ores. As described earlier, many ores in the Cerrillos Hills occur as sulfides (Table 3) (Northrop 1959), and many of the SEM spectra show the presence of sulfur in the samples, along with copper or lead. Of these, seven thin sections containing copper also appear to contain sulfur, suggesting that the ore constituents may have been chalcopyrite ($CuFeS_2$), bornite (Cu_5FeS_4), or chalcocite (Cu_2S). Similarly, sulfur co-occurrs with lead in five thin sections, suggesting that galena (PbS) from the Cerrillos Hills was the source. Finally, zinc is a common element in the Cerrillos Hills, occurring in the research samples as sphalerite (ZnS). Elemental analysis shows that zinc was common to very common in 11 thin sections.

Additionally, the use of the Cerrillos Hills ores is logical on geographical-based grounds. The Cerrillos Hills deposits are the closest source of ores containing this suite of metallic minerals. Moreover, San Marcoseños were using Cerrillos Hills lead in the production of glaze-paint ceramics (Habicht-Mauche et al. 2000) and, as noted above, may have shown Spanish explorers the Cerrillos source locations. Other sources of metallic mineral deposits, particularly the Magdalena Mountains considerably south of San Marcos, were an alternative source especially for lead (Huntley 2008), but it makes

little sense that metallurgists would mine these ores and then transport them to San Marcos when the Cerrillos sources were within walking distance of the pueblo.

In sum, the materials analysis not only strengthens the references in the historical record regarding metallurgy but also adds essential empirical weight to historical understanding. The analytical results suggest that the metallurgists at San Marcos may have been testing the Cerrillos ores for lead, copper, and possibly silver. Their metallurgical byproducts, however, show only copper and lead. In some cases, lead is associated with a copper ore and, in other cases, lead and copper occur independently. The materials evidence, as well as the geographic location supports the suggestion that the Cerrillos Hills were the likely source of those metals, adding further weight to the possibility that the Cerrillos area was considered a mining district during the 17th century.

Who and Why of the San Marcos Metallurgy

The archaeological and materials analyses raise questions about the social and economic contexts of metal production at the pueblo. Unfortunately, neither question can be answered directly from the available evidence. Metal production is a complex technology in which learning and long-term training play a significant role. In essence, technological recipes are learned and reflected in both products and residues. Consequently, as argued by Cyril Smith (1981), Heather Lechtman (1977), and more recent social theorists of archaeometallurgy (Ehrenreich 1991; Glumac 1991; Bijker et al. 1994; Ehrhardt 2005), analysis of the technology is a window into the learning networks and the metallurgists themselves.

Because metallurgy in New Mexico is a Spanish introduction, colonists or even Franciscans could have transferred the technology to Native artisans, or they could have produced the metals themselves. On both archaeological and historical grounds, it seems likely that the Spanish or mestizos were the metallurgists at San Marcos. The San Marcos operation was well planned, and the metallurgists knew what they wanted and how to obtain their goals. The slags are relatively clean with counts of incompletely smelted byproducts very low when compared to the counts of slags and burned adobe (Table 6). The metallurgists working at San Marcos were not experimenting with method; they knew how to produce metal.

In addition, the numbers of miners and metallurgists in New Spain after 1540 swelled in response to major silver strikes in Mexico (Bakewell 1971, 1984, 1997). Miners migrated north with the mining frontier (Radding 1997), and it seems highly probable that some of these miners ended up prospecting and assaying in New Mexico. In the 1630s, Pedro de Perea, commander of the Presidio of Sinaloa, brought colonists and soldiers from Sinaloa, Chihuahua, and New Mexico to develop mining and ranching in the Sonora and San Miguel valleys (Naylor and Polzer 1986). James Brooks (2002) mentions that Juan Moraga, a mestizo, was a blacksmith in Santa Fe in the 1660s. Finally, in the 16th and 17th centuries, Indian communities were relatively open so that Hispanos and mestizos could have been present during smelting operations (Hall 1984; Ebright 1994). Andrew Knaut (1995) recounts that the first Spanish infirmary in the colony was in San Felipe, not in Santa Fe. If Spanish colonists went to San Felipe for medical reasons, why not use San Marcos as a location for metal production?

The presence of the Spaniards or mestizos as metallurgists at San Marcos does not necessarily mean that Indians were excluded from metal production. In fact, selecting San Marcos as a location for occasional smelting made excellent strategic sense. The pueblo was adjacent to metal resources; San Marcoseños understood some of the properties of metallic minerals and even knew source locations; and the pueblo was large enough to provide a labor force for extraction, ore preparation, and the construction of smelting facilities.

Regarding the "why" of production, there are both general and specific answers. At the most general level, demonstration that metal production was underway at least by the 17th century aligns with the colony's empire goals. Spaniards came north looking for metal, and there is every reason to assume they continued this search through the production stage.

Answering the "why" regarding the suite of metals that were observed in the San Marcos assemblage is, of course, more difficult to answer—especially given the lack of product. Several economic possibilities are possible, including testing, perhaps for silver, rather than extraction or circulation of product. Because the colony was poor and remote from the heart of the empire, metal was a scarce resource and highly valued by colonists. If lead and copper were being produced, these products were likely immediately circulated beyond the confines of the pueblo. Lead metal could have become bullets. There are suggestions in the literature that, after conquest, the Spanish controlled lead sources for the production of bullets (Mills 2002). The presence of lead glass and metal from San Marcos could offer some support for that position. Copper, by contrast, was not highly valued by the Spanish in New Spain (Barrett 1987), but this statement does not mean that colonists did not value copper. The metal, for instance, may have been used to produce ornaments. Alfred Kidder (1932) recovered 15 copper crucifixes from Pecos Pueblo, and the Pa'ako excavations have yielded numerous small pieces of sheet copper. Alternatively, copper may have used as an internal standard of exchange.

Conclusions

To date, neither historians nor archaeologists have made metal exploration a part of the early colonial history of Spanish colonization and settlement in New Mexico. The story has focused on religious conversion, accommodation, and resistance by pueblos and Apacheans, conflict between church and state, and the initial failure of the colony as demonstrated by the Pueblo Revolt. Because of the lack of primary documents on mining and metallurgy, historians have not been able to address whether metallurgy was part of the colonial enterprise. Archaeologists have accepted historical silence on the question of metal production at face value and have not undertaken independent investigation of the material record. Over the years, the absence of any discussion regarding mining and metal production has translated as absence of metallurgy.

This background makes the discovery and archaeological documentation of 16th- and 17th-century smelting at San Marcos all the more significant. It changes historical understanding and places the topic within the purview of

Ann F. Ramenofsky, C. David Vaughan, and Michael N. Spilde

historical and archaeological scholarship. Although the scale of metallurgy at this native settlement was small and likely occasional, the physical evidence obtained is unambiguous. Metal production, including copper, lead, and possibly silver, was underway at San Marcos well before the Pueblo Revolt.

To tell this historical archaeological story required evaluating all pieces of evidence, including history, geology, archaeology, and materials. Although laborious, this kind of analysis promotes the integration of archaeology and history. The interdisciplinary methodology, for instance, provided support for some of the earliest historical comments regarding mining and metallurgy in the Cerrillos Hills and San Marcos Pueblo. Even though the archaeological smelters at San Marcos cannot be linked firmly to either the 1581 or 1601 historical descriptions of smelting at the pueblo, the archaeology and history are aligned and point to the pueblo as a smelting place. In addition, the analytical methodology provides a framework for future investigation. The reading of documents can and must not be blindly accepted or rejected; the simple collection of slag cannot be used to suggest what was being extracted. Both kinds of information must be evaluated separately before integration can emerge.

Finally, the success of this research has suggested new avenues of interdisciplinary research. The San Marcos story is a beginning, and what is not yet known is significant. It remains uncertain precisely who was involved in the smelting episodes and how many other smelting facilities were present at the pueblo and in other locations. Only the barest knowledge exists about other pre-revolt smelting locations like Pa'ako Pueblo (Lycett 1998, 1999, 2000, 2001, 2002, 2003), Comanche Springs, and the Palace of the Governors (Vaughan 2006). From San Marcos, there is no definitive information about the products. Most significant, the importance of metal production in the Spanish colonial enterprise in New Mexico or the role of Native peoples in that venture remains unclear.

To move beyond this preliminary but important description will require cooperative research venues among archaeologists, historians, and materials scientists. New archival research in Mexico and Spain may turn up information on mines, miners, and the metallurgical process. Additional archaeological research will be required on numerous fronts. New field survey and excavation directed toward the discovery of mining and metal extraction need to be undertaken. As more locations are discovered, questions of Spanish-Native interaction or technology transfer can be explored along with the consideration of how and whether there are settlement and demographic shifts in response to metal production. With enough baseline data, perhaps the question can be explored of whether Native involvement in metal extraction was a contributing factor in the Pueblo Revolt. Because archaeologists are not trained in the identification of slags or metallic minerals, they will also need materials sciences training (or work with materials scientists) to determine aspects of the process, as well as the types of metals being extracted. New beginnings, however, are always exciting, and the authors are hopeful that this preliminary effort will stimulate the emergence of such ventures.

Acknowledgments

Grants from the McCune Charitable Foundation supported this metallurgical investigation. Several individuals helped enormously with the excavation and analysis of the metallurgy, including William Baxter, Jennifer Boyd, Leslie Cohen, Connie Constan, Teresa Cordua, Jeremy Kulisheck, Candace Lewis, Courtney Porreca, Kari Schleher, Natalina Tsosie, Benjamin Wood, and Bart Wright. Shawn Penman helped greatly with the construction of maps. We thank them all. Errors of interpretation or understanding are ours alone.

References

AGRICOLA, GEORGIUS
1912 *De Re Metallica*, Herbert C. Hoover and Lou H. Hoover, translators [from first Latin edition of 1556]. Reprinted in 1950 by Dover Publications, London, England, UK.

AITKEN, MARTIN J.
1985 *Thermoluminescence Dating.* Academic Press, London, England, UK.
1989 Luminescence Dating: A Guide for Non-Specialists. *Archaeometry* 31(1):147–159.
1990 Luminescence Dating. In *Science-Based Dating in Archaeology*, Martin J. Aitken, editor, pp. 141–186. Longman Press, London, England, UK.

1998   *Introduction to Optical Dating: The Dating of Quaternary Sediments by Photon-Stimulated Luminescence.* Oxford University Press, Oxford, England, UK.

AYER, MRS. EDWARD E. (TRANSLATOR)
1916   *The Memorial of Fray Alonso de Benavides 1630,* annotated by Frederick W. Hodge and Charles F. Lummis. R. R. Donnelley, Chicago, IL.

BACHMANN, HANS-GERT
1982   *The Identification of Slags from Archaeological Sites.* Institute of Archaeology, Occasional Publication, No. 6. London, England, UK.

BAKEWELL, PETER J.
1971   *Silver Mining and Society in Colonial Mexico, Zacatecas, 1546–1700.* Cambridge University Press, Cambridge, England, UK.
1984   *Miners of the Red Mountain: Indian Labor in Potosi, 1545–1650.* University of New Mexico Press, Albuquerque.
1988   *Silver and Entrepreneurship in Seventeenth-Century Potosi.* University of New Mexico Press, Albuquerque.
1997   Technological Change in Potosi: The Silver Boom of the 1570s. In *Mines of Silver and Gold in the Americas,* Peter J. Bakewell, editor, pp. 75–95. Galliard Printers, Great Yarmouth, Norfolk, England, UK.

BANDELIER, ADOLPH F.
1890–1892   *Final Report of Investigations among the Indians of the Southwestern United States* (Parts 1–2). In Papers of the Archaeological Institute of America. American Series, Vols. 3–4. John Wilson and Son, Cambridge, MA.
1910   *Documentary History of the Rio Grande Pueblos of New Mexico.* Papers of the School of American Archaeology, No. 13. Archaeological Institute of America, [Santa Fe, NM?].

BANERJEE, D., A. S. MURRAY, L. BØTTER-JENSEN, AND A. LANG
2001   Equivalent Dose Estimation Using a Single Aliquot of Polymineral Fine Grains. *Radiation Measurements* 33(1):73–94.

BARRETT, ELINOR M.
1987   *The Mexican Colonial Copper Industry.* University of New Mexico Press, Albuquerque.

BERNARDINI, WESLEY
1998   Conflict, Migration, and the Social Environment: Interpreting Architectural Change in Early and Late Pueblo IV Aggregations. In *Migration and Reorganization: The Pueblo IV Period in the American Southwest,* Katherine A. Spielmann, editor, pp. 91–114. Anthropological Research Papers, Vol. 51. Arizona State University, Tempe.

BIJKER, WIEBE E., THOMAS P. HUGHES, AND TREVOR PINCH (EDITORS)
1994   *The Social Construction of Technological Systems: New Directions in the Sociology and History of Technology.* MIT Press, Cambridge, MA.

BOLTON, HERBERT. E.
1916   *Spanish Explorations in the Southwest 1542–1706.* Charles Scribner's Sons, New York, NY.

BROOKS, JAMES F.
2002   *Captives and Cousins: Slavery, Kinship, and Community in the Southwest Borderlands.* University of North Carolina Press, Chapel Hill.

CHAVEZ, FRAY ANGELICO
1973   *Origins of New Mexico Families in the Spanish Colonial Period: In Two Parts, the Seventeenth (1598–1693) and the Eighteenth (1693–1821) Centuries.* Calvin Horn Publishers, Albuquerque, NM.

CHRISTIANSEN, PAIGE W.
1974   *The Story of Mining in New Mexico.* New Mexico Bureau of Mines and Mineral Resources, Socorro.

CRADDOCK, PAUL T.
1995   *Early Metallurgy, Mining, and Production.* Smithsonian Institution Press, Washington, DC.

DEAGAN, KATHLEEN, AND JOSÉ M. CRUXENT
2002   *Archaeology at La Isabela: America's First European Town.* Yale University Press, New Haven, CT.

DISBROW, ALAN E., AND WALTER C. STOLL
1980   *Geology of the Cerrillos Area, Santa Fe County.* New Mexico Bulletin, No. 48. New Mexico Bureau of Mines and Mineral Resources, Socorro.

EBRIGHT, MALCOLM
1994   *Land Grants and Lawsuits in Northern New Mexico.* University of New Mexico Press, Albuquerque.

EHRENREICH, ROBERT M. (EDITOR)
1991   *Metals in Society: Theory beyond Analysis.* MASCA Research Papers in Science and Archaeology, No. 8 (Part 2). The University Museum, University of Pennsylvania, Philadelphia.

EHRHARDT, KATHLEEN L.
2005   *European Metals in Native Hands: Rethinking Technological Change 1640–1683.* University of Alabama Press, Tuscaloosa.

ESPINOSA, J. MANUEL
1942   *Crusaders of the Rio Grande: The Story of Don Diego de Vargas and the Reconquest and Refounding of New Mexico.* Institute of Jesuit History, Chicago, IL.

FEATHERS, JAMES K.
1997   Application of Luminescence Dating in American Archaeology. *Journal of Archaeological Method and Theory* 4:1–66.

2000 Luminescence Dating and Why It Deserves Wider Application. In *It's about Time: A History of Archaeological Dating in North America*, Stephen E. Nash, editor, pp. 152–167. University of Utah Press, Salt Lake City.

FLINT, RICHARD
2002 *Great Cruelties Have Been Reported: The 1544 Investigation of the Coronado Expedition.* Southern Methodist University, Dallas, TX.

FLINT, RICHARD, AND SHIRLEY CUSHING FLINT (EDITORS)
2005 *Documents of the Coronado Expedition, 1539–1542: "They were not Familiar with his Majesty nor They wish to be his Subjects."* Southern Methodist University Press, Dallas, TX.

FOX, RICHARD A.
1993 *Archaeology, History, and Custer's Last Battle.* University of Oklahoma Press, Norman.

GALLOWAY, PATRICIA
1995 *Choctaw Genesis: 1500–1700.* University of Nebraska Press, Lincoln.
1997 Conjoncture and Longue Durée: History, Anthropology, and the Hernando de Soto Expedition. In *Hernando de Soto Expedition: History, Historiography, and Discovery in the Southeast*, Patricia Galloway, editor, pp. 283–294. University of Nebraska Press, Lincoln.

GAUTIER, ANNAÏG
2001 Luminescence Dating of Archaeometallurgical Slag: Use of the SAR Technique for Determination of the Burial Dose. *Quaternary Science Reviews* 20 (5–9):973–980.

GLUMAC, PETAR (EDITOR)
1991 *Recent Trends in Archaeo-Metallurgical Research.* MASCA Research Papers in Science and Archaeology, No. 8 (Part 1). The University Museum, University of Pennsylvania, Philadelphia.

HABICHT-MAUCHE, JUDITH A., STEPHEN, T. GLENN, HOMER MILFORD, AND A. RUSSELL FLEGAL
2000 Isotopic Tracing of Prehistoric Glaze-Paint Production and Trade. *Journal of Archaeological Science* 27(8):709–713.

HACKETT, CHARLES W. (EDITOR)
1923–1937 *Historical Documents Relating to New Mexico, Nueva Viscaya, and Approaches Thereto, to 1773.* Collected by Adolph and Fanny R. Bandelier. 3 vols. Carnegie Institution of Washington, Washington, DC.

HALL, G. EMLEN
1984 *Four Leagues of Pecos: A Legal History of the Pecos Land Grant 1800–1933.* University of New Mexico Press, Albuquerque.

HAMMOND, GEORGE P.
1927 *Don Juan de Oñate and the Founding of New Mexico.* Publications in History, Historical Society of New Mexico, Vol. 2. El Palacio Press, Santa Fe, NM.

HAMMOND, GEORGE P., AND AGAPITO REY (EDITORS)
1927 *The Gallegos Route of the Rodriguez Expedition to New Mexico.* El Palacio Press, Santa Fe, NM.
1940 *Narratives of the Coronado Expedition, 1540–1542.* University of New Mexico Press, Albuquerque.
1953 *Don Juan de Oñate: Colonizer of New Mexico, 1595–1628.* 2 vols. University of New Mexico Press, Albuquerque.
1966 *The Rediscovery of New Mexico 1580–1594.* University of New Mexico Press, Albuquerque.

HENDERSON, JULIAN
2000 *The Science and Archaeology of Materials: An Investigation of Inorganic Materials.* Routledge, London, England, UK.

HENDRICKS, RICK
1999 Spanish Colonial Mining in Southern New Mexico: A Spanish to English Translation of Documents Relating to El Paso, the Organ Mountains, and Santa Rita del Cobre. *The Mining History Journal: The Sixth Annual Journal of the Mining History Association*:143–162. Sedalia, CO.

HODGE, FREDERICK W., GEORGE P. HAMMOND, AND AGAPITO REY
1945 *Fray Alonso de Benavides' Memorial of 1634.* University of New Mexico Press, Albuquerque.

HUNTLEY, DAVID J., DOROTHY I. GODFREY-SMITH, AND MICHAEL W. THEWALT
1985 Optical Dating of Sediments. *Nature* 313(10):105–107.

HUNTLEY, DEBORAH
2008 *Ancestral Zuni Glaze-Decorated Pottery: Viewing Pueblo IV Regional Organization through Ceramic Production and Exchange.* University of Arizona, Anthropological Papers, No. 72. University of Arizona Press, Tucson.

JONES, FAYETTE A.
1904 *New Mexico Mines and Minerals: Being an Epitome of the Early Mining History and Resources of New Mexico Mines*, World's Fair edition. New Mexico Printing Company, Santa Fe.

KESSELL, JOHN L.
1987 *Kiva, Cross, and Crown: The Pecos Indians and New Mexico, 1540–1840.* Southwest Parks and Monuments Association, Tucson, AZ.
2002 *Spain in the Southwest.* University of Oklahoma Press, Norman.

KESSELL, JOHN L., RICK HENDRICKS, AND MEREDITH DODGE
1995 *To the Royal Crown Restored: The Journals of Don Diego de Vargas, New Mexico 1692–94.* University of New Mexico Press, Albuquerque.

1998 *Blood on the Boulders: Journals of Don Diego de Vargas, 1694–1697.* University of New Mexico Press, Albuquerque.

KIDDER, ALFRED V.
1932 *The Artifacts of Pecos.* Yale University Press, New Haven, CT.
1936 The Glaze Paint, Culinary, and Other Wares. In *The Pottery of Pecos*, Vol. 2. Yale University Press, New Haven, CT.
1958 *Pecos New Mexico: Archaeological Notes.* Andover Professional Paper, No. 68. Phillips Academy, Washington, DC.

KLEIN, CORNELIUS
2002 *Manual of Mineralogy*, 22nd edition. John Wiley, New York, NY.

KLEIN, CORNELIUS S., AND JAMES D. DANA
1993 *Manual of Mineralogy.* John Wiley, New York, NY.

KNAUT, ANDREW
1995 *The Pueblo Revolt of 1680: Conquest and Resistance in Seventeenth-Century New Mexico.* University of Oklahoma Press, Norman.

KULISHECK, JEREMY R.
2005 The Archaeology of Pueblo Population Change on the Jemez Plateau, A.D. 1200–1700. Doctoral dissertation, Department of Archaeology, Southern Methodist University, Dallas, TX.

LECHTMAN, HEATHER
1977 Style in Technology: Some Early Thoughts. In *Material Culture: Styles, Organization, and Dynamics of Technology*, Heather Lechtman and Robert S. Merrill, editors, pp. 3–19. West Publishing Company, St. Paul, MN.

LIEBMANN, MATTHEW J.
2006 *"Burn the Churches, Break up the Bells": The Archaeology of the Pueblo Revolt Revitalization Movement in New Mexico, A.D. 1680–1696.* Doctoral dissertation, Department of Anthropology, University of Pennsylvania, Philadelphia, PA. UMI Microfilms International, Ann Arbor, MI.

LINGREN, WALDEMAR, LOUIS C. GRATON, AND CHARLES H. GORDON
1910 *The Ore Deposits of New Mexico.* U.S. Geological Survey, Professional Paper, No. 68. Washington, DC.

LONG, WILLIAM W.
1964 A History of Mining in New Mexico during the Spanish and Mexican Periods. Master's thesis, Department of History, University of New Mexico, Albuquerque.

LYCETT, MARK T.
1998 Archaeological Excavations at LA 162, Bernalillo County, New Mexico, between 21 June and 19 August, 1997, under permit SE-120. Report to New Mexico Historic Preservation Division, Santa Fe, from University of Chicago Archaeological Field Studies Program, Chicago, IL.

1999 Archaeological Excavations at LA 162, Bernalillo County, New Mexico, between 21 June and 18 August, 1998, under permit SE-134. Report to New Mexico Historic Preservation Division, Santa Fe, from University of Chicago Archaeological Field Studies Program, Chicago, IL.
2000 Archaeological Excavations at LA 162, Bernalillo County, New Mexico, between 21 June and 12 August, 1999, under permit SE-144. Report to New Mexico Historic Preservation Division, Santa Fe, from University of Chicago Archaeological Field Studies Program, Chicago, IL.
2001 Archaeological Excavations at LA 162, Bernalillo County, New Mexico, between 21 June and 17 August, 2000, under permit SE-156. Report to New Mexico Historic Preservation Division, Santa Fe, from University of Chicago Archaeological Field Studies Program, Chicago, IL.
2002 Archaeological Excavations at LA 162, Bernalillo County, New Mexico, between 18 June and 5 August, 2001. Report to New Mexico Historic Preservation Division, Santa Fe, from University of Chicago Archaeological Field Studies Program, Chicago, IL.
2003 Archaeological Excavations at LA 162, Bernalillo County, New Mexico, between June and August 2002. Report to New Mexico Historic Preservation Division, Santa Fe, from University of Chicago Archaeological Field Studies Program, Chicago, IL.

MAJEWSKI, TERESITA, AND JAMES E. AYRES
1997 Toward an Archaeology of Colonialism in the Greater Southwest. *Revista de Arqueologia Americana* 12:55–86.

MERA, HERBERT P.
1940 *Population Changes in the Rio Grande Glaze Paint Area.* Laboratory of Anthropology, Technical Series Bulletin, No. 9. Santa Fe, NM.

MILFORD, HOMER E.
1996 *Cultural Resources Survey for the Real de los Cerrillos Abandoned Mine Lands Project, Santa Fe County, New Mexico.* New Mexico Abandoned Mine Land Bureau, Report No. 1996-1. Mining and Minerals Division, Energy, Minerals and Natural Resources Department, Santa Fe, NM.

MILFORD, HOMER E., RICHARD FLINT, SHIRLEY C. FLINT, AND G. VIGIL
1998 *Nuevas Leyes de las Minas de Espana: 1625 Edición de Juan de Oñate* (New Laws of the Mines of Spain: 1625 Edition of Juan de Oñate). Facultad de Minas, Universidad de Guanajuato, Guanajuato, Mexico.

MILLS, BARBARA J.
2002 Acts of Resistance: Zuni Ceramics, Social Identity, and the Pueblo Revolt. In *Archaeologies of the Pueblo Revolt*, Robert W. Preucel, editor, pp. 85–98. University of New Mexico Press, Albuquerque.

MONTGOMERY, ROSS G., WATSON SMITH, AND JOHN O. BREW

1949 *Franciscan Awatovi: The Excavation and Conjectural Reconstruction of a Spanish Mission Establishment at a Hopi Town in Northeastern Arizona.* Reports of the Awatovi Expedition, No. 3. Papers of the Peabody Museum of American Archaeology and Ethnology, No. 36. Harvard University, Cambridge, MA.

MOTSINGER, THOMAS N.

1997 Tracking Protohistoric Glazeware Specialization in the Upper Rio Grande Valley, New Mexico. *Kiva* 63(2):101–116.

NAYLOR, THOMAS H., AND CHARLES W. POLZER (EDITORS)

1986 *The Presidio and Militia on the Northern Frontier of New Spain.* University of Arizona Press, Tucson.

NELSON, NELS C.

1912–1915 Field Notes of the Excavations at San Marcos Pueblo. Manuscript, American Museum of Natural History, New York, NY.

1914 *Pueblo Ruins of the Galisteo Basin, New Mexico.* Anthropological Papers, Vol. 15, Pt. 1. American Museum of Natural History, New York, NY.

1916 Chronology of the Tano Ruins, New Mexico. *American Anthropologist* 18(2):159–180.

NORTHROP, STUART A.

1959 *Minerals of New Mexico*, revised edition. University of New Mexico Press, Albuquerque.

PIERCE, CHRISTOPHER D., AND ANN F. RAMENOFSKY

2000 Summary of the 1999 Field Season at San Marcos Pueblo (LA 98) by the University of New Mexico, SE-272. Manuscript, New Mexico Historic Preservation Division Santa Fe.

POTTER, JAMES M.

1998 The Structure of Open Space in Late Prehistoric Settlements in the Southwest. In *Migration and Reorganization: The Pueblo IV Period in the American Southwest*, Katherine A. Spielmann, editor, pp. 137–164. Anthropological Research Papers, Vol. 51. Arizona State University, Tempe.

PROBERT, ALAN

1997 Bartolome de Medina; The Patio Process and the Sixteenth-Century Silver Crisis. In *Mines of Silver and Gold in the Americas*, Peter J. Bakewell, editor, pp. 96–130. Galliard Printers, Great Yarmouth, Norfolk, England, UK.

RADDING, CYNTHIA

1997 *Wandering Peoples: Colonialism, Ethnic Spaces, and Ecological Frontiers in Northwestern Mexico, 1700–1850.* Duke University Press, Durham, NC.

RAMENOFSKY, ANN F.

1997 Excavation Summary: LA 1490, Comanche Springs. Manuscript, New Mexico Historic Preservation Division, Santa Fe.

2001 Summary Report of the 2000 Season of Archaeological Research at San Marcos Pueblo (LA 98) (Permit SE-155, ABE-427). Report to New Mexico Historic Preservation Division, Santa Fe, from Department of Anthropology, University of New Mexico, Albuquerque.

2003 Report on an Archaeological Investigation of Metallurgy at San Marcos Pueblo (LA 98) Summer 2002. Report to New Mexico Historic Preservation Division, Santa Fe, from Department of Anthropology, University of New Mexico, Albuquerque.

RAMENOFSKY, ANN F., AND JAMES K. FEATHERS

2002 Documents, Ceramics, Tree-Rings, and Luminescence: Estimating Final Native Abandonment from the Lower Rio Chama. *Journal of Anthropological Research* 58(1):121–159.

RAMENOFSKY, ANN F., AND C. DAVID VAUGHAN

2003 Jars Full of Shiny Metal: Analyzing Barrionuevo's Visit to Yuque Yunque. In *The Coronado Expedition from the Distance of 460 Years*, Richard Flint and Shirley C. Flint, editors, pp. 116–139. University of New Mexico Press, Albuquerque.

REED, ERIC

1954 A Test Excavation at San Marcos. *El Palacio* 61(10):323–343.

RHODES, EDWARD J.

1988 Methodological Considerations in the Optical Dating of Quartz. *Quaternary Science Reviews* 7(3–4):395–400.

2003 *Luminescence Dating Report of San Marcos Pueblo.* Luminescence Dating Laboratory, OSL Dating Report, No. 146. Research Laboratory for Archaeology and the History of Art, University of Oxford, Oxford, England, UK.

RILEY, CARROLL L.

1999 *Kachina and the Cross: Indians and Spaniards in the Early Southwest.* University of Utah Press, Salt Lake City.

SHEPARD, ANNA O.

1942 *Rio Grande Glaze Paint Ware: A Study Illustrating the Place of Ceramic Technological Analysis in Archaeological Research.* Contributions to American Anthropology and History, No. 39. Carnegie Institution of Washington, Washington, DC.

1965 Rio Grande glaze Paint Pottery: A Test of Petrographic Analysis. In *Ceramics and Man*, F. A. Matson, editor, pp. 62–87. Viking Fund Publications in Anthropology, No. 41. Aldine Publishing, Chicago, IL.

SMITH, BERTHE W., MARTIN J. AITKEN, E. J. RHODES, P. D. ROBINSON, AND D. M. GELDARD

1986 Optical Dating: Methodological Aspects. *Radiation Protection Dosimetry* 17(2):229–233.

SMITH, CYRIL STANLEY

1981 *A Search for Structure.* The MIT Press, Cambridge, MA.

SPIELMANN, KATHERINE A.
1998 The Pueblo IV Period: History of Research. In *Migration and Reorganization: The Pueblo IV Period in the American Southwest*, Katherine A. Spielmann, editor, pp. 1–30. Anthropological Research Papers, Vol. 51. Arizona State University, Tempe.

THIBODEAU, A. M., D. J. KILLICK, J. RUIZ, J. T. CHESLEY, K. DEAGAN, M. J. CRUXENT, AND W. LYMAN
2007 The Strange Case of the Earliest Silver Extraction by European Colonists in the New World. *Proceedings of the National Academy of Sciences* 104(9): 3663–3666.

THOMAS, DAVID H.
2000 Excavations at Mission San Marcos, New Mexico, SE-143 and BE-022, Summer 1999. Manuscript, New Mexico Museum, New Mexico Historic Preservation Division, Santa Fe.

THOMAS, NOAH
2002 Appendix 10: Preliminary Analysis of Materials from the Seventeenth-Century Industrial Facility at LA 162, Bernalillo County, New Mexico. In Report of Archaeological Investigations at LA 162, Bernalillo County, New Mexico, between 18 June and 5 August, 2001, Mark T. Lycett, editor, pp. 230–241. Report to New Mexico Historic Preservation Division, Santa Fe, from University of Chicago Archaeological Field Studies Program, Chicago, IL.

TOULOUSE, JOSEPH H., JR.
1949 *The Mission of San Gregorio de Abo*. School of American Research Monographs, No. 13. University of New Mexico Press, Albuquerque.

TOWNER, RONALD H.
2000 Dendrochronology and Historical Records: Concordance and Conflicts in Navajo Archaeology. In *It's about Time: A History of Archaeological Dating in North America*, Stephen E. Nash, editor, pp. 168–185. University of Utah Press, Salt Lake City.

TWITCHELL, RALPH EMERSON
1911–1912 *The Leading Facts of New Mexican History*. Torch Press, Cedar Rapids, MI.

TYLECOTE, RONALD F.
1986 *The Prehistory of Metallurgy in the British Isles*. Institute of Metals, London, England, UK.

UNITED STATES GEOLOGY SURVEY
1965 *Mineral and Water Resources of New Mexico*. USGS Bulletin, No. 87. New Mexico Institute of Mining and Technology, Socorro.

VAUGHAN, C. DAVID
2006 *Taking the Measure of New Mexico's Miners, Mining, and Metallurgy*. Doctoral dissertation, Department of Anthropology, University of New Mexico, Albuquerque. UMI Microfilms International. Ann Arbor, MI.

VAUGHAN, C. DAVID, AND ANN F. RAMENOFSKY
1999 Mining Slag for Knowledge at Comanche Springs, New Mexico. Poster presented at the Oxford International Conference, Oxford, England, UK.

VIERRA, BRADLEY J., MICHAEL N. SPILDE, IBRAHIM H. GUNDILER, AND ROBERT H. WEBER
1997 Analysis of Slag Samples. In *A Presidio Community of the Rio Grande: Phase III Testing and Historical Research at San Elizario, Texas, Vol. 1*, Bradley J. Vierra, June-el Piper, and Richard Chapman, editors, pp. 491–496. Office of Contract Archaeology, University of New Mexico, Albuquerque.

WARREN, A. HELENE
1974 An Archaeological Survey of the Occidental Minerals Corporation Proposed Mining Project Area in the Cerrillos District, Santa Fe County, New Mexico, conducted for the Rocky Mountain Center on the Environment. Report to New Mexico Historic Preservation Division Santa Fe, from Santa Fe Laboratory of Anthropology, NM.

1979 The Glaze Paint Wares of the Upper Middle Rio Grande. In *Archaeological Investigations in Cochiti Reservoir, New Mexico, Vol. 4, Adaptive Changes in the Northern Rio Grande Valley*, Jan V. Biella and Richard Chapman, editors, pp. 187–216. Office of Contract Archaeology, University of New Mexico, Albuquerque.

WARREN, A. HELENE, AND ROBERT H. WEBER
1979 Indian and Spanish Mining in the Galisteo and Hagan Basins. *New Mexico Geological Society Special Publication* 8:7–11. Socorro.

WEBER, DAVID J.
1992 *The Spanish Frontier in North America*. Yale University Press, New Haven, CT.

YOUNG, OTIS E., JR.
1970 *Western Mining: An Informal Account of Precious-Metals Prospecting, Placering, Lode Mining, and Milling on the American Frontier from Spanish Times to 1893*. University of Oklahoma Press, Norman.

ANN F. RAMENOFSKY
DEPARTMENT OF ANTHROPOLOGY, MSC01-1040
UNIVERSITY OF NEW MEXICO
ALBUQUERQUE, NM 87131

C. DAVID VAUGHAN
DEPARTMENT OF ANTHROPOLOGY, MSC01-1040
UNIVERSITY OF NEW MEXICO
ALBUQUERQUE, NM 87131

MICHAEL N. SPILDE
INSTITUTE OF METEORITICS
EARTH AND PLANETARY SCIENCES
UNIVERSITY OF NEW MEXICO
ALBUQUERQUE, NM 87131

www.ingramcontent.com/pod-product-compliance
Lightning Source LLC
Chambersburg PA
CBHW080944120626

46546CB00010B/2830